PSYCHOLOGY OF GROUP INFLUENCE

(second edition)

Edited by

PAUL B. PAULUS
*The University of Texas
at Arlington*

WITHDRAWN

LAWRENCE ERLBAUM ASSOCIATES, PUBLISHERS
1989   Hillsdale, New Jersey   Hove and London

Cover illustration by Deborah Farrell Dowdle, University of Arkansas.

Lawrence Erlbaum Associates, Inc., Publishers
365 Broadway
Hillsdale, New Jersey 07642

Library of Congress Cataloging in Publication Data
Psychology of group influence / edited by Paul B. Paulus — 2nd ed.
    p. cm.
    Includes bibliographies and indexes.
    ISBN 0-8058-0445-5 (cloth)
    ISBN 0-8058-0545-1 (pbk)
    1. Small groups—Psychological aspects.   2. Influence (Psychology)
3. Identity (Psychology)   4. Spatial behavior.   5. Social
psychology.   I. Paulus, Paul B.
HM133.P79 1989
302.3'4—dc19   88-36616
                                                                    CIP

Printed in the United States of America
10   9   8   7   6   5   4   3   2   1

Contents

Preface

About 10 years ago we began our work on the first edition of **Psychology of Group Influence** (Paulus, 1980). It was felt that there was much exciting work being done in the area of groups that was not presented in a coherent format. **Psychology of Group Influence** was designed to showcase some of these new developments as well as providing a systematic overview of some of the basic issues in the area. The reception of this volume and its individual chapters has been most gratifying in terms of citation frequency and influence on research activity.

At the time of the publication of the first edition of **Psychology of Group Influence,** we felt that activity on groups was accelerating. This certainly turned out to be the case as indicated in part by the various volumes on groups that have appeared in the last 8 years (e.g., Hendrick, 1987a, 1987b; McGrath, 1984; Paulus, 1983). During this time many new developments have occurred in most of the topic areas covered in the first edition. Accordingly, six of the chapters have been revised in light of these developments. In some cases, intervening research activity had not significantly altered the status of a particular area. These chapters were not selected for revision since the versions in the first edition still serves as a reasonable overview. There have also been some interesting topic areas that have developed since the first edition. Five new chapters were selected to highlight these issues. Although the stylistic approach of the chapters varies somewhat, an attempt was made to make the volume interesting reading to a broad range of social psychologists and students. Some of the chapters focus primarily on a review and conceptual organization of the literature. Others emphasize the development of some new theoretical perspectives. Yet all of the chapters help in providing an overview of some of the major issues in the psychology of group influence. Since the breadth of the field makes it difficult to effectively represent the broad range of interesting issues, this volume focuses on issues that are fundamental to much of group behavior. It can serve as a basic text for undergraduate and graduate courses on groups. In graduate courses, you may want to supplement with readings from the first edition of **Psychology of Group Influence** or the other volumes cited earlier. These volumes contain chapters on issues such as leadership, coalition formation, and bargaining which are not covered in the present volume.

This volume is motivated by the belief that group psychology is a central and important activity for social psychology. It is anticipated that activity in this area will continue to generate interesting findings and ideas. Hopefully, this volume will serve as a useful guidepost in this process.

I am most appreciative of the efforts of the contributors and their support during the revision process. It might also be noted that without the encouragement and support of Larry Erlbaum, there would not have been a first or second edition of **Psychology of Group Influence.**

Paul B. Paulus

REFERENCES

Hendrick, C. (Ed.). (1987a). *Group processes: Review of personality and social psychology* (Vol 8). Beverly Hills, CA: Sage.

Hendrick, C. (Ed.). (1987b). *Group processes and intergroup relations: Review of personality and social psychology* (Vol 9). Beverly Hills, CA: Sage.

McGrath, J. E. (1984). *Groups: Interaction and performance.* Englewood Cliffs, NJ: Prentice-Hall.

Paulus, P. B. (Ed.). (1980). *Psychology of group influence.* Hillsdale, NJ: Lawrence Erlbaum Associates.

Paulus, P. B. (Ed.). (1983). *Basic group processes.* New York: Springer-Verlag.

To my mother Alice and my late father Paul for their influence.

1 An Overview and Evaluation of Group Influence

Paul B. Paulus
University of Texas at Arlington

SOME BACKGROUND AND PERSPECTIVES

What is the psychology of group influence? Frankly, we have been rather arbitrary in our choice of issues to reflect this topic. Any topic that examines social influence processes in groups can be seen as fitting within this category, and in this volume we have by no means exhausted the range of issues that could fit under this umbrella. However, we have tried to focus on some of the major topics and some of the exciting new developments that have not been adequately covered in prior publications.

The study of the psychology of group influence is an interesting and fundamental area of study. It deals with a whole range of intriguing questions about how individuals are influenced by the groups to which they belong or with whom they are involved, and how these groups are in turn influenced by their members. How do groups influence our performance of various tasks? How do we react to the spatial distances among group members? What happens when we become emotionally involved in groups? How do certain environmental conditions affect group behavior? How do newcomers become fullfledged members of a group? How do groups react to those who disagree with the majority view? What determines how members see themselves as part of a group? How do groups make decisions or come to a consensus about an issue? How do the different ways in which decisions are reached influence group member satisfaction? How can groups work together to remember events they have experienced? What are some of the ways in which we incorporate part of the group experience into our own identity? These are just some of the issues that are addressed in *Psychology of Group Influence*.

1

The study of psychology of group influence has a long and distinguished record in social psychology. The very first experimental study in social psychology was concerned with the influence of other presence (Triplett, 1898). Some of the classic studies in social psychology fall within the confines of group influence. Sherif's work on norms (Sherif, 1936) and intergroup conflict (Sherif & Sherif, 1953), the research by Lewin and his colleagues (e.g., Lewin, Lippet, & White, 1939), Asch's (1956) work on conformity, Schachter's (1951) studies of reactions to deviates are just a few examples. In the late 60s and early 70s the social facilitation (Chapter 2), the bystander intervention (Latane & Darley, 1970), and group polarization (Chapter 8) phenomena generated a lot of excitement and research activity. Although, there appeared to be decline in overall activity in the area of groups during the 1960s and 1970s (Steiner, 1974), there were a significant number of exciting new developments in the area of group influence in the late 1970s. Many of these were highlighted in the first edition of *Psychology of Group Influence* (Paulus, 1980).

Steiner (1974, 1983, 1986) has written a number of interesting analyses of factors related to activity level in the area of groups. He has suggested that the time-consuming nature of the research and the lack of interesting theoretical issues may have accounted for some of the reduction in interest in the past 30 years. He also suggested that interest level in groups research may reflect the extent to which societal events lead social scientists to focus on the importance of group dynamics in human affairs. Frankly, it is difficult to evaluate the *health* of research in the area of groups. It would seem to be true that the proportionate level of activity on groups has declined since the early days. However, this would seem inevitable since there were only a small number of research social psychologists and many of them happened to be investigating topics on groups. As the number of social psychologists increased, the diversity of topics addressed naturally increased. This same trend continues today, with social psychologists addressing an ever wider range of basic and applied issues. So on a relative as well as absolute basis, one would expect any standard topic to experience some attrition of research interest.

There appears to be little disagreement that research on groups in social psychology reached a low point during the heyday of dissonance, attribution, and social cognition. However, at present, the level of activity on intergroup behavior and intragroup processes is strong in both the U.S. and Western Europe. Furthermore, this activity seems to be driven by a variety of interesting ideas and theories. If one considers the activities of group scholars in the fields of management and organizational behavior, clinical psychology, health, criminal justice, environmental psychology, and families as part of the *set* of group research, the activity level today is quite impressive. Even in the more restrictive domain of experimental social psychology, there appears to be a high level of interest in groups (cf. Hendrick, 1987a, 1987b).

Research activity in social psychology is driven by theoretical ideas and empirical phenomena. Sometimes a provocative empirical finding generates a large amount of research designed to understand its underlying features and limitations (e.g., bystander intervention). At other times, a theory tends to generate a broad range of ideas and research (e.g., dissonance theory). In most cases, it is some combination of interesting findings and provocative ideas that lead to the stimulation of a high degree of research activity. In this light, it is interesting to note one difference between much of the *old* research on groups and the *new look* in groups. The old research focused primarily on empirically documenting the various features of a group phenomenon. Although the basic phenomena were often quite provocative, the research generated was often not motivated by interesting theoretical ideas. Certainly, there was a testing of hypotheses about the role of various factors in the phenomena, but the research was phenomena driven rather than theory driven. In contrast, research in the 50s through 70s in some of the more active areas of social psychology can be seen as primarily theory driven (e.g., dissonance, attribution). It seems that ideas play a stronger role in sustaining a broad range of research activity in social psychology than empirical phenomena. In this light it is of interest that much of the recent excitement in group psychology as reflected in this volume centers around ideas as well as phenomena.

I would venture, however, that the study of groups will never become the dominant activity of academic social psychologists. There are a number of factors inherent in research on groups that will limit the number of scholars who will become engrossed in this topic. Research on groups often is expensive in terms of time and subjects. In an environment where number of publications in respectable journals is taken as a primary indicant of success, the incentive value of groups research is rather low. This makes group research an unlikely choice for graduate students and young scholars unless they have a strong intrinsic interest in the subject matter. Another problem with group research is the relative paucity of provocative theoretical issues. Although there have always been some interesting theoretical issues, other topic areas seemed to generate a larger number of interesting or counterintuitive hypotheses (e.g., interpersonal attraction, attitudes, social cognition). One reason for this may be that it is easier to come up with hypotheses about processes at the level of one individual since our subjective experiences and personal introspections provide a wealth of data. Our personal intuitions and introspections may be less useful for conceptualizing processes at the group level.

Even though the level of activity may be moderate, it is likely that groups research will always be a solid part of the overall enterprise in social psychology. This may in part reflect the influence of societal forces as suggested by Steiner. However, there are many who are convinced that groups represent one of the most fundamentally unique concerns of social psychology. As noted by Berger in Steiner (1986), many subareas of social psychology (e.g., social learning and social cognition) derive much of their sustenance from other disciplines in psychology, and as these areas develop, they may become indistinguishable from their core disciplines. The study of groups, however, is an activity of social psychology not inevitably reducible to the concerns of other topic areas. In addition, most social processes occur in group contexts and a full understanding of their role in social behavior requires an examination of the issues at the level of groups. Moreover, research on groups typically involves some degree of *realistic* social activity—either as part of the procedures or of the measures employed. It is thus less subject to *artificiality* problems that beset the topic areas that use only symbolic stimuli and paper and pencil responses (cf. Markus & Zajonc, 1985). Finally, some of the most compelling concerns of our society are related to group phenomena. Intergroup and international conflict, productivity, leadership, societal unrest or social movements, the drug crisis, urban gangs, and the functioning of families are just a few examples. It would seem likely that social psychologists who are desirous of making a significant contribution to society as well as their discipline will continue to investigate group processes. In sum, although groups research does not dominate social psychology, it certainly is alive and well as one of its core areas and will likely outlast many of its competitors in staying power.

AN OVERVIEW OF PSYCHOLOGY OF GROUP INFLUENCE

The chapters in *Psychology of Group Influence* cover a broad range of topics that provide a fairly coherent picture of the field. We have included some of the basic topics in this area as well as some that have only recently developed. We have attempted to showcase the latest empirical and theoretical developments in each of these areas.

The chapters are based solidly on a number of foundations. Many cite the seminal work and ideas of early thinkers in the area such as LeBon, Lewin, and Festinger. Some of the chapters have a strong empirical base as the research on these particular topics has been ongoing for a number of years. Others deal with issues that only recently have seen increased research attention. Most of the chapters have a strong theoretical basis. Some provide theoretical integration and analyses of the wide variety of results in particular area. Others suggest new perspectives to guide future research in developing areas. The chapters focus on a broad range of psychological processes such as drive, attention, self-awareness, self-regulation, approach-avoidance, memory, information processing, and appropriation. However, the major focus of each of the chapters is to highlight group influences on these basic processes.

Basic Group Influence

The first four chapters focus on the basic dimensions and processes involved in groups—the presence of others, involvement in groups, spatial distancing among group members, influence of number of group members, and spatial arrangement. One common theme in these chapters is the approach/avoidance dilemma. We can't very well do without groups and derive many benefits from group membership, but at the same time we seem to have some fears about group involvement. Geen's chapter on social facilitation highlights the fear and avoidance element involved in observer or audience situations. Knowles analyzes in detail the approach and avoidance processes involved in spatial distancing in groups. Prentice-Dunn and Rogers' chapter on deindividuation examines the issue of seeking and avoiding loss of self-awareness in groups. Paulus and Nagar examine those factors that influence positive and negative reactions to interactions in group settings.

One of the most basic topics in group influence is that of the presence of others. This issue was the concern of the first social psychology experiment (Triplett, 1898) and has been the focus of consistent examination since that time. Geen provides a detailed review and analysis of this research with humans. He analyzes the ability of three major theoretical approaches to account for the evidence obtained—drive based theories, self theories, and attentional/information processing theories. He examines a broad range of empirical effects–arousal, task performance, attention, and inhibition of behavior. He suggests that various types of theories may be differentially applicable to two somewhat different audience contexts–ones that elicit anxiety or embarrassment and ones that do not. It is clear from Geen's review that the issue of other presence is much more complex than most of us probably anticipated. His analysis brings conceptual coherence to this area of study, however, and provides a solid basis for future research.

While other presence is certainly the most basic feature of group situations, social distance might be considered the most basic dimension of social interaction. This interesting topic has been examined mostly under the rubric of *personal space*. Early studies assumed that humans required and maintained certain minimal distance zones in various types of interactions. If these were violated, individuals would become uncomfortable and attempt to compensate in some particular manner. Knowles deals with the research on this topic and presents an affiliative conflict theory of spatial behavior. This theory has its basis in part in Lewin's field theory (Lewin, 1938) and builds on the ideas of Argyle and Dean (1965). He provides an elegant and detailed analysis of spatial behavior in groups and is able to integrate much of the literature's complexities in terms of this model. The affiliative conflict theory allows for an understanding of those conditions under which people will compensate or reciprocate in response to spatial intrusions. Knowles also develops the implications of this model for understanding spatial behavior in various group, audience, and crowd situations.

One aspect of groups that has been of interest for a long time has been the tendency of individuals to submerge their identities within the group. This type of process has been pointed to in explaining mob behavior and other extreme acts committed in group contexts. Prentice-Dunn and Rogers examine in detail the contribution deindividuation theory has made to the understanding of these and other phenomena. Deindividuation is generally viewed as a state of lowered self-awareness that can result from involvement in group activities. This state can be associated with disinhibited or antinormative behavior as well as increased levels of aggressive behavior. Prentice-Dunn and Rogers examine the history of the concept and recent theoretical and empirical developments. They combine concepts from self-awareness theory and control theory of self-regulation into a comprehensive understanding of the role of deindividuation in social behavior. Prentice-Dunn and Rogers propose that such disinhibition may derive from two different types of antecedents, which in turn affect either degree of public or private self-awareness. They evaluate various alternative viewpoints and apply deindividuation to such domains as aggression, prosocial behavior, sports, and religious experiences. In doing so, they provide a very compelling analysis of the means by which groups may have a powerful influence on the actions of their members.

Group behavior can occur in a wide range of environments. Certain features of these environments may influence the behavior of group members. Two environmental factors that have been extensively related to group processes are density and spatial factors. Paulus and Nagar outline some of the major issues that have been examined in studies of these two environmental variables. They summarize the basic findings and suggest several perspectives for integrating this literature. Interestingly, while crowding and spatial proximity may sometimes produce strongly negative reactions, at other times reactions may be quite positive. An environment-social interaction model is presented to facilitate the understanding and prediction of positive and negative group outcomes that occur under various group/environmental conditions. The implications of this model for the study of group processes in laboratory and naturalistic situations are developed.

Influence Processes in Groups

The second section of this volume focuses on various ways in which groups influence its members. Groups may have goals, norms, or traditions that require some degree of uniformity among its members. Newcomers to groups may thus be subject to a variety of techniques by the group to socialize them. Those who persist in being different may elicit strong reactions but may also influence the other group members. We may be members of a wide variety of groups and our identification with groups may have a strong impact on our self-concept and behavior.

Before one can become subject to many of the major group processes, one has to join and become accepted by the group. Moreland and Levine examine this process in some detail and provide the first comprehensive theoretical and empirical analysis of the processes by which newcomers are socialized in groups. Building on their earlier work on group socialization, they present a broad theoretical framework and organize the extensive literature within it. The major focus of the chapter is on the dual processes of assimilation and accommodation by which newcomers become full members of the group. They examine a wide variety of factors that influence these processes and the different strategies that can be employed by the newcomer and the group to facilitate them. By integrating the research on newcomers and oldtimers, they provide a broad overview of the major findings and provide a solid basis for future research on this interesting topic.

Newcomers to groups tend to be the focus of quite a bit of attention by group members. In a sense, they stick out as different from the rest of the group. In a similar vein, group members also pay close attention to members whose opinions deviate from those in the group. Most groups tend to exert some degree of pressure on individuals to conform to group norms or consensus about an issue. Levine examines different models designed to explain this process and how groups respond to those whose opinions deviate from the group. He summarizes both the classic literature on opinion deviance and more recent studies and provides a coherent summary of the basic findings and their implications. Much of the early research on this topic examined the influence of the majority on the minority. Stimulated in part by the research and ideas of Moscovici, for the past 20 years there has been increased examination of the influence of the minority on the majority. Levine reviews this interesting and provocative literature and deals with the role of various individual and group characteristics. He evaluates and critiques several theoretical perspectives in light of the empirical literature and points to a number of unresolved issues.

Both the Moreland and Levine chapter on newcomers and the Levine chapter on opinion deviance deal with the issue of being different and the implications this has for bidirectional influence processes in groups. The area of opinion deviance is more developed theoretically and provides a potentially fertile basis for understanding some aspects of the group socialization of the newcomer. Alternatively, the group socialization research suggests that deviance may yield quite different reactions in different phases of the group socialization process. Hopefully, these two topic areas will benefit by a recognition of these potential areas of commonality. Both of these chapters also continue the approach/avoidance theme. The newcomer chapter deals with the approach and avoidance tendencies of the newcomer in conjunction with the acceptance and rejection by the group. Levine's chapter contrasts the tendency toward consensus in groups with the alternative tendency toward conflict and change. So these chapters greatly broaden the dynamics of approach and avoidance in the contexts in group socialization and social influence.

A somewhat more comprehensive analysis of social influence processes in groups is the focus of the chapter by Turner and Oakes. They are concerned with the nature of the psychological group and the conditions that influence individuals to perceive themselves as part of the group. They use a new theory, known as self-categorization theory, to provide a compelling, cognitively based analysis of basic social influence processes. Self-categorization is derived in part from developments in social identity theory by Tajfel and Turner (1986). Turner and Oakes summarize the basic elements of both social identity theory and self-categorization theory and demonstrate the utility of self-categorization theory for understanding group cohesion, the effects of intergroup conflict, conformity, minority influence, and group polarization. Self-categorization theory thus provides a useful means of integrating a broad range of issues and suggests a number of interesting new directions for research.

The self-categorization theory relates nicely to some of the issues addressed in the preceding chapters. The theory has a number of implications about the conditions involved in group formation that are relevant to the discussion by Paulus and Nagar of spatial factors in group formation. For example, spatial factors may lead one to categorize oneself as a member of the proximal group. The theory also provides a basis for integrating the conformity and minority influence literature highlighted in the Levine chapter. Self-categorization theory focuses on the relationship between personal and social identity, and Turner and Oakes point out how this process can lead to feelings of distinctiveness as well as depersonalization. This analysis parallels the discussion of the seeking and avoiding of deindividuation.

Social and Cognitive Processes in Interactive Groups

The third section of this book deals with the broad issue of exchange of information or ideas in groups. It is concerned with the social influence process related to this exchange, a variety of outcomes of this process, as well as a detailed analysis of the nature of the process. The first two chapters focus mostly on these processes in decision-making groups. The first is concerned with a detailed analysis of the decision-making process and the second with effects of the rules by which this process occurs. The second two chapters deal with memory processes involved when groups share information. One of these deals with the nature of this process while the second focuses on the extent to which individuals take on the ideas exchanged as their own.

One of the important activities that occurs in groups is that of decision making. Stasser, Kerr, and Davis focus on the difficult task of representing group behavior and organizing group level data in the complex domain of decision making. They analyze the social influence processes that play a role in decision making in groups, and they propose several mathematical models to describe the processes involved in the development of consensus. These models combine individual dispositions or resources to predict group outcomes and are able to handle rather complex interactive group processes. They go beyond the simplistic unidirectional or noninteractive analyses that are the staple of much research in social psychology and discuss the various processes involved in developing group consensus and showcase the ''strength in numbers'' effect. This effect reflects the fact that the direction of influence in decision-making groups is typically in the direction of the position held by most of the members. However, their model allows both for majority and minority influence. The chapter ends with a treatment of various computer simulation models designed to reflect the nature of the group discussion process on the way to consensus. Their analyses of group decision making provides a very solid foundation for future efforts in this important area of study.

Whenever groups make decisions, there are inevitably rules about how the decision will relate the preferences of the individuals in the group. These rules may specify unanimity, majority, or plurality as a basis for coming to a group decision. Obviously, the type of decision rule will greatly affect the nature of the interaction among the group members and their feelings about the process. It is these issues that are the concern of the chapter by Miller on the social psychological effects of group decision rules. He reviews evidence that group decision rules influence the nature and quality of the group decision, the content of the group discussion, members' perception of the process, and their feelings toward one another. Although this is a relatively new area of research, there is already a fairly consistent picture available. Miller provides some conceptual coherence to this literature and points to numerous directions for future research.

The Miller and Stasser et al. chapters complement each other quite nicely. Both deal with decision-making groups and examine the influence of a variety of task features and the role of different types of influence processes. Yet while Stasser et al. look at the microprocesses of consensus development, Miller takes a step back to examine a variety of side-effects of decision-making rules. Thus, these two chapters allow us to see both the trees and the forest of group decision-making processes.

An important part of the group decision-making process is the memory of group members for the content of the discussion. Recently, there has been an increased interest in studying directly these memory processes. Clark and Stephenson deal with group collaborative remembering in face-to-face interactive groups. This is the process of negotiation and coming to an agreement about what actually happened in some mutually experienced event. They review a number of classic and current perspectives that have dealt with this process. They summarize relevant research and theories on group productivity, mock juries, individual and group recall, and transactive memory. They present their latest work on this topic and suggest directions for further empirical, theoretical, methodological, and applied efforts. The emphasis of Clark and Stephenson on the "social reality" of group memories is consistent with the emphasis by Turner and Oakes on group level concepts and analyses. The topic of group remembering certainly is an exciting and promising area of research.

When groups share information in the course of discussion, decision making, or as part of collaborative remembering, this is inevitably an active cognitive process. Wicklund deals with the intriguing issue of how acting on information or ideas affect one's sense of ownership of this information. Thus, in the case of collaborative recall, information provided by others may become or reinforce one's own memories. In any social context, however, where an individual is presented with ideas (whether these be moral principles, values, or thoughts), an individual can personally incorporate, internalize, or appropriate these. By acting on ideas presented in groups, we may come to internalize values, incorporate new beliefs, develop new skills, or falsely claim origination of ideas. Wicklund deals with these as instances of appropriation and provides a detailed conceptual analysis of this process. He analyzes the impact of activity on appropriation from a variety of perspectives—memory, attribution, and desire for control. He also deals with the influence of self-awareness and perspective taking on the appropriation process. The chapter contains a number of provocative ideas relevant to the issues of group remembering, minority influence, and group decision making. It closes with an interesting contrast of plagiarism and internalization from a societal perspective. Wicklund's chapter thus presents the other side of the coin of the group remembering process. Clark and Stephenson look at the individual contributions to the group product, whereas Wicklund looks at the group's contribution to the individual's sense of "own ideas."

LOOKING BACKWARD AND FORWARD

In the past 10 years there has been considerable progress in the area of group influence. We seem to have a better theoretical handle on many issues. Our theoretical concepts provide an increased clarity as to the important dimensions and processes involved in the basic phenomena. There are also a number of interesting new directions evident. There is an increased concern with the study of interactive groups. Group level concepts and perspectives are being developed (e.g., self-categorization and group remembering). Computer simulations are being employed to facilitate our understanding of the complexities involved in group interaction. The area of study is continually being enriched by new ideas and approaches. It is likely that significant progress will be made on a number of fronts in the next 10 years. However, it is also likely that the same issues that have intrigued scholars for many years will continue to intrigue them for years to come.

Although we have made significant strides in the area of group influence, there remain significant gaps that need to be addressed in the future. There is a need for more heuristic theoretical models to drive a broad range of interesting research questions. Some of the theoretical models have been borrowed from other domains of psychology and social psychology. This is certainly a useful technique, but it is likely that a full understanding of group phenomena will require models of somewhat different scope or focus. This point has been strongly emphasized by some of the European social psychologists (e.g., Moscovici, cf. Chapter 7; Tajfel and Turner, cf. Chapter 8). In the related disciplines of organizational and environmental psychology and family studies, somewhat broader and comprehensive interpersonal models have been developed that may be of use to group psychology (see for example affiliative conflict theory in Chapter 3).

Although greater sophistication is needed in theory development, the study of group influence is also limited by its almost exclusive focus on groups in short-term laboratory settings. Given our concern for eventual applicability, it would be useful to have group studies in a greater range of settings and paradigms. Of course, this occurs to some extent in the more applied disciplines concerned with organizations, families, and the environment. Yet many of the basic issues studied by laboratory oriented social psychologists could benefit greatly from an examination of this process in realistic group settings, with groups that spend more than one hour together, and with natural groups. This issue is developed in Chapter 4. Yet while these remain some lofty goals for group researchers to achieve, there has been much progress in developing an understanding of influence processes in groups. This volume has demonstrated the growth and maturity this field has achieved and also its even greater potential for enlightening many important issues of group dynamics in the future.

REFERENCES

Argyle, M., & Dean, J. (1965). Eye contact, distance, and affiliation. *Sociometry, 28,* 289–304.

Asch, S. E. (1956). Studies of independence and conformity: A minority of one against a unanimous majority. *Psychological Monographs: General and Applied, 70,* 1–70.

Hendrick, C. (Ed.). (1987a). *Group processes: Review of personality and social psychology* (Vol 8). Beverly Hills, CA: Sage.

Hendrick, C. (Ed.). (1987b). *Group processes and intergroup relations: Review of personality and social psychology* (Vol 9). Beverly Hills, CA: Sage.

Latane, B., & Darley, J. M. (1970). *The unresponsive bystander: Why doesn't he help?* New York: Appleton-Century-Crofts.

Lewin, K. (1938). *The conceptual representation and the measurement of psychological forces.* Durham, NC: Duke University Press.

Lewin, K., Lippet, R., & White, R. (1939). Patterns of aggressive behavior in experimentally created "social climates." *Journal of Social Psychology, 10,* 271–299.

Markus, H., & Zajonc, R. B. (1985). The cognitive perspective in social psychology. In G. Lindzey & E. Aronson (Eds.), *The handbook of social psychology* (Vol. 1, pp. 137–230). New York: Random House.

Paulus, P. B. (Ed.). (1980). *Psychology of group influence.* Hillsdale, NJ: Lawrence Erlbaum Associates.

Schachter, S. (1951). Deviation, rejection, and communication. *Journal of Abnormal and Social Psychology, 46,* 190–207.

Sherif, M. (1936). *The psychology of social norms.* New York: Harper & Row.

Sherif, M., & Sherif, C. W. (1953). *Groups in harmony and tension.* New York: Harper & Row.

Steiner, I. D. (1974). Whatever happened to the group in social psychology? *Journal of Experimental Social Psychology, 10,* 94–108.

Steiner, I. D. (1983). Whatever happened to the touted revival of the group? In H. Blumberg, A. Hare, V. Kent, & M. Davies (Eds.), *Small groups and social interaction* (Vol. 2, pp. 539–548). New York: Wiley.

Steiner, I. D. (1986). Paradigms and groups. In L. Berkowitz (Ed.), *Advances in experimental social psychology* (Vol. 19, pp. 251–289). Orlando, FL: Academic Press.

Tajfel, H., & Turner, J. C. (1986). The social identity theory of intergroup behavior. In S. Worchel & W. G. Austen (Eds.), *Psychology of intergroup relations* (2nd Ed., pp. 7–24). Chicago: Nelson-Hall.

Triplett, N. (1898). The dynamogenic factors in pacemaking and competition. *American Journal of Psychology, 9,* 507–533.

BASIC GROUP INFLUENCE

2 Alternative Conceptions of Social Facilitation

Russell G. Geen
University of Missouri

The influence of the presence of others on behavior has generally been treated as part of the broader phenomenon of social facilitation and inhibition of performance. The earliest study of social facilitation showed that performance on a motor task is enhanced by the presence of others doing the same task (Triplett, 1898). The major proportion of studies on social facilitation in the decade following Triplett's report involved a coaction paradigm similar to his. Eventually, however, the study of coaction faded to a secondary position and was supplanted by interest in the influence of passive audiences, an interest motivated to a large degree by the obvious implications of this approach for the practical problem of stage fright (Dashiell, 1935). This relative emphasis on the study of audience influence has been accompanied by the elaboration of intervening variables to explain audience effects, and much of this review is devoted to a discussion of those variables. Although in some cases the theoretical explanations that have been offered for audience influence may explain coaction effects equally well, the development of theory has been carried out primarily within the study of the former and not the latter. In this review, the primary emphasis is on studies of the effects of audiences on performance. Coaction effects are discussed where appropriate.

In discussing the influence of audiences on performance in the present context it is important to emphasize that we are concerned only with *passive* audiences. In making this narrow delineation of audience function we are assuming that audiences can have both motivational and directional effects on an individual without necessarily taking direct action toward that person. We are of course familiar with some of the influences of active audiences. They include the provision of social reinforcers, punishments, and feedback cues; the supplying of information; and the elicitation of information from the person in return. A crowd that cheers or boos a football team, a studio audience shouting answers to a quiz show contestant, and a group of reporters grilling a political candidate all exemplify active audiences that may have both motivational and directive effects on behavior. The study of audience effects such as these is potentially interesting and, in fact, constitutes a large part of what has been called social facilitation research in lower animals. Nonetheless, when audiences are discussed in terms of their social facilitation or inhibition of human performance, it is customary to consider only the effects of their passive presence. As will be made clear later in this chapter, competing theoretical explanations of the social facilitation effect[1] differ in the extent to which they consider the principal influence of passive audiences to be either motivational or directive.

HISTORY OF SOCIAL FACILITATION RESEARCH

The earliest report of the effects of a passive audience on behavior was reported in 1904 by Meumann (cited by Cottrell, 1972), who showed that performance on a simple motor task was facilitated first by the unexpected entrance of the experimenter into the room and later by the more controlled presence of a passive spectator. The first study to be reported in English was that of Moore (1917), who studied the debilitating effects of an audience on the solving of complex multiplication problems and found that audience presence interfered with performance about as much as did conditions designed to create emotional states such as fear and anger. Moore's suggestion that the effect of an audience was mediated by embarrassment prefigured modern notions of evaluation apprehension and fear of failure as critical variables in social facilitation.

In the early decades of this century several investigators took up the study of social facilitation by audiences, with mixed results. The purpose of this chapter is not to review this literature, which has been adequately summarized and interpreted in previous publications (Cottrell, 1972; Dashiell, 1935; Kelley & Thibaut, 1954). We must, however, make a note of one matter. From its inception until the mid-1960s the study of social facilitation by audiences had two characteristics. First, it revealed inhibition of performance about as often as facilitation. Second, although there was no shortage of theoretical formulations for the data, no single theoretical formulation that could account for performance increments and decrements with a single set of postulates had been developed. Probably because of these two problems, interest in the study of effects of audiences diminished throughout the 1930s. By the 1940s it was for all practical purposes extinguished. With few exceptions matters remained thus until 1965, when Zajonc published a paper that not only provided a coherent theoretical

---

[1]As is common in the literature on this subject, the term *social facilitation effect* will be used in a general sense to include both social facilitation and inhibition of performance.

analysis of social facilitation but also resolved the paradox of why the published data had supported the inference of both incremental and decremental effects. In so doing, it initiated a revival of interest in these matters that persists to the present time.

Zajonc's (1965) analysis of social facilitation rested on two assumptions. The first was that the physical presence of other people creates a state of increased arousal which functions as a drive. The second was that the tendency to make a response is a multiplicative function of the habit strength for that response and drive level, as given in the Hull-Spence equation $E = DxH$. From these premises Zajonc concluded that the presence of others facilitates performance when the task is familiar or easy but inhibits it when the task is novel or difficult. Likewise, the presence of an audience enhances performance of a well-learned response but hampers the acquisition of a new one. Applying this theoretical position to the early studies of social facilitation, Zajonc (1965) noted that the key to reconciling discrepancies in the findings was the nature of the response elicited in each study. With a task that could be characterized as relatively simple, such as pursuit-rotor tracking, audience presence should facilitate performance (Travis, 1925). When a task could be characterized as relatively difficult, such as memorization, an audience should produce performance decrements (Pessin, 1933). It should be noted that Allport (1924) anticipated this reasoning by noting a connection between the type of task used and the direction of the influence exerted by the presence of others. Writing on the coaction setting, Allport concluded that the company of coworkers appeared to facilitate ''overt'' behavioral responses like writing, but to hinder ''intellectual'' responses like learning and reasoning. Dashiell (1930) reached a similar conclusion from his studies of passive audiences, in which the presence of observers produced increased speed of responding on certain intellectual tasks, but diminished accuracy.

The dozen years that followed the appearance of Zajonc's 1965 paper yielded numerous experimental investigations of audience effects, most of which were animated by Zajonc's arguments. Some sought to test his viewpoint (e.g., Henchy & Glass, 1968), and still others challenged it with alternative explanations (e.g., Blank, Staff, & Shaver, 1976). In 1977 Geen and Gange reviewed this literature and concluded that at that time the most parsimonious theoretical explanation for the social facilitation effect was still to be found in drive theory. In the years since that review the situation has changed greatly, and today such a confident assertion of the primacy of the drive theoretical approach is not warranted. Instead, several sophisticated alternatives have found considerable support in experimental studies. The remainder of this chapter is devoted to a description of the various viewpoints currently being espoused as explanations of the social facilitation effect and the evidence that has been adduced from studies designed to test those viewpoints.

The theoretical approaches fall into three broadly defined classes. The first is the already mentioned drive theory, according to which the presence of others has a nondirective motivational effect on behavior in that socially engendered drive simply multiplies with the habit strength of correct or incorrect responses. The second is an approach that emphasizes the role of observers in magnifying the extent to which the observed person is motivated to make a favorable impression. The third general viewpoint is that the presence of others leads to facilitation or inhibition of performance through its effects on attention and information processing. This idea has only recently been proposed and as yet little direct evidence for it exists.

DRIVE THEORY

The drive theoretical approach to social facilitation rests on the assumption that the presence of others creates increased drive. The validity of the approach rests on evidence supporting this assumption. Some evidence has been sought in two ways. First, several investigators have attempted to show that the presence of others is accompanied by activation of various physiological systems. As is shown in the following section, evidence for increased psychophysiological activation is mixed and inconclusive. However, drive theorists do not as a rule equate drive with physiological activation. In Hullian theory drive is simply a construct that is useful in showing a connection between states of deprivation or strong stimulation and such response parameters as frequency, intensity, and latency. Research on the hypothesized effects of drive traditionally involves manipulation of conditions leading to differential habit strengths and levels of drive, and prediction of outcomes from an assumption of a multiplicative relationship between the two. Most studies that are reported as support for the drive theory of social facilitation are of this type. In the sections that follow both types of evidence, psychophysiological and behavioral, are summarized.

Psychophysiological Evidence

The first study to report a relationship between the presence of an audience and physiological arousal was carried out by Burtt (1921). Subjects who played the role of defendant in a mock jury trial were instructed to lie in response to some questions and to respond truthfully to others. Responses were made either to the experimenter alone or to the experimenter plus a small group of other people. The inclusion of the small group led to higher levels of both respiration and blood pressure following lies than the levels shown by subjects communicating with the experimenter only. The experiment did not include a condition in which no audience was present. In the 4 decades following this study a relatively small amount of research on audience effects was reported, leading Zajonc (1965) to assert that evidence for the social drive hypothesis was both scarce and indirect. The evidence that Zajonc cited for his approach drew heavily on studies showing a positive relationship between population density and arousal in lower animals. More recently, a similar link between audience size and arousal has been shown in humans (e.g., Aiello, Thompson, & Brodzinsky, 1983; Latane & Harkins, 1976).

The state of the psychophysiological evidence at the present time is not encouraging for proponents of the social drive hypothesis. A relative handful of studies has addressed the question, and the evidence from those studies is equivocal. The published research shows a preference among investigators for the palmar sweat (PS) measure as an indicator of audience-induced drive. Some studies have shown that the level of PS is higher in subjects who work at a complex motor task in view of a physically present audience than in those who perform alone (Martens 1969a, 1969b, 1969c). Droppleman and McNair (1971) found that PS gradually increased in subjects as they first prepared for, and then delivered, a speech into a tape recorder while being observed by an experimenter. A similar finding was reported by Karst and Most (1973) among subjects who had previously been shown to become anxious over public speaking. Geen (1976b, 1977) also showed increased PS during a session in which subjects were required to work on a difficult anagrams task while being watched by the experimenter.

Not all the evidence from studies involving palmar sweating supports the drive theory of social facilitation, however. A series of experiments by Cohen and his associates (Bargh & Cohen, 1978; Cohen, 1979, 1980; Cohen & Davis, 1973) reveals predictable audience effects on behavioral measures of social facilitation but no influence on PS measures.

In reviewing the evidence on the PS measure in social facilitation experiments, Carver and Scheier (1981a, 1981b) have argued that PS is in fact an indicator not of arousal, but of attention to, and interaction with, one's environment (Dabbs, Johnson, & Leventhal, 1968). When one's attention is directed toward the environment, his or her level of PS may increase, whereas when attention is focused inward toward the self the direction of PS may go in the other direction, i.e., there may occur a "palmar drying." The latter effect has in fact been shown in a situation involving heightened self-focusing by Paulus, Annis, and Risner (1978). Carver and Scheier explain Martens's findings of increased PS in audience settings by noting that Martens measured PS *between trials* of the subject's task, a time during which subjects' attention was usually directed away from the task and toward the immediate surroundings (Martens, 1969a).[2]

To test their hypothesis, Carver and Scheier (1981b) conducted a study (which will be described in more detail below) in which subjects were given the

---

[2]Geen (1967b, 1977) used a technique by which PS prints were obtained just after the task period. However, because the sheet on which the imprint was made had been attached to the subject's finger before the beginning of the task, it is possible that pretask PS was the major contribution to the outcome.

task of copying German prose in two 5-minute sessions. In the first session the experimenter was in the room but out of sight of the subject. Moreover, he paid no attention to the subject. In the second session, the experimenter was again present but he either ignored or carefully watched the subject as he or she worked. Measures of PS were taken at four times: before the first task (baseline), during the first task, just prior to the second task, and during the second task. The results were consistent with Carver and Scheier's viewpoint. All subjects showed decreased PS activity, relative to baseline levels, during the first task. Subjects in the audience condition (i.e., anticipating being observed by the experimenter) showed a large increase in PS just before the second task began, whereas subjects who expected to continue with an inattentive experimenter showed no change. PS levels then decline for subjects in both groups during the second task. Thus, to summarize, increased PS in the audience was found prior to the learning trial, but PS *decrease* occurred during the period of the task itself.

Some experiments have involved physiological measures other than palmar sweat, but because of the small number of these studies and the lack of replication of the results we can consider them only suggestive at best. McKinney, Gatchel, and Paulus (1983) examined the influence of audience size and individual differences in speech anxiety on arousal in a public speaking situation. Subjects were required to prepare and deliver a short speech either to the experimenter alone or to an audience of 2 or 6 people. The clearest finding from the study was that both heart rate and skin conductance increased monotonically across the period from the baseline measure, through a 5-min preparatory period, to the delivery of the speech, regardless of the size of the audience. McKinney and his colleagues found that individual differences in speech anxiety had no effect on physiological reactions, but that they did moderate the effect of audience size on self-reports of nervousness and depression. In general, subjects high in speech anxiety were more nervous and depressed in the presence of an audience of six persons than in the presence of two, whereas those low in speech anxiety showed the opposite. Differences among the relevant group means were not reported, so we do not know whether these apparent differences were both significant. It should also be noted that this experiment did not include a no audience condition. Its relevance to the social facilitation effect is therefore only indirect. Several other studies that have sought effects of audiences on heart rate have shown no evidence of such an influence (Borden, Hendrick, & Walker, 1976; Geen, 1979; Henchy & Glass, 1968), although Singerman, Borkovec, and Baron (1976) did find that giving a speech brought about a significant increase in heart rate over than shown during a preparatory period. In addition, Knight and Borden (1979), found evidence of increased heart rate and finger pulse volume in subjects awaiting a public speaking task.[3]

---

[3]Caution should be taken in interpreting HR as an indicator of general activation. Some investigators have defined HR increases as indicators of motivation and readiness to respond to cues (e.g., Fowles, 1983).

Studies in which arousal is inferred from electrodermal measures likewise provide little support for drive theory. Neither Borden et al. (1976), Geen (1979), nor Henchy and Glass (1968) found evidence that audiences create increases in skin conductance levels. However, anticipation of public speaking led to increasing conductance levels in the study by Knight and Borden (1979). Furthermore, Geen (1979) found that during the first trial of a paired-associates learning task, subjects showed a greater number of spontaneous skin conductance (SCR) responses in the presence of an observer than when alone. Why subjects should show increased phasic activity, as in the SCR, but no change in tonic conductance, is not clear. Moore and Baron (1983) have suggested that the SCR may reflect a basic motivational process associated with stress or threat, whereas skin conductance level reflects cognitive processing. Given that Geen (1979) considered the audience to be a stimulus for evaluation apprehension, in which threat should be implicit, this reasoning is consistent with the general theory underlying the study.

Some evidence consistent with the drive theoretical approach comes from studies in which arousal is defined in terms of muscle tension. Chapman (1973, 1974) observed higher levels of muscle action potential in subjects who listened to a recording in the presence of the experimenter than in subjects who listened alone. Moreover, the effect was found whether the experimenter was visible or hidden behind a screen. However, Chapman's studies are susceptible to alternative explanations on methodological grounds (see Moore & Baron, 1983) and may not, therefore, represent strong support for drive theory.

Finally, we should note that in none of the studies reviewed here has any attempt been made to demonstrate a causal link between physiological arousal and performance. A path model, for example, in which an audience-behavior relationship is mediated by arousal could be tested against an alternate path lacking such a mediating step. In fact, with one exception, the studies on social facilitation do not even report evidence of correlations between arousal and performance. In that single exception, Beam (1955) found that students facing various socially evaluative events in real life performed more poorly on a paired-associates task before the event than they did after the event had passed. Beam also showed a positive correlation between paired-associates performance and palmar sweat prior to the event.

To summarize, a clear case has not been made for a relationship between social presence and increased physiological arousal in experiments on social facilitation. This lack of convincing evidence does not invalidate an explanation of the social facilitation effect in terms of drive theory, however, because, as was noted earlier, the construct of drive is not grounded in physiological processes. Furthermore, the use of psychophysiological measures creates problems of its own because of problems associated with low correlations among measures and lack of clarity as to what psychological processes are reflected in psychophysiological ones (Fowles, 1983; Lacey, 1967). On the other hand, research on the effects of population density has shown a connection between density and physiological arousal (e.g., Evans, 1979; Paulus, McCain, & Cox, 1978), so the assumption that the presence of others induces arousal should not be abandoned entirely.

Behavioral Evidence

To understand the behavioral evidence for the drive theory of social facilitation, it is necessary to review the basic assumption behind the application of that theory. If we assume that the social setting produces drive, than we need only vary the amount of habit strength associated with responses in that setting and to predict that dominant responses will be energized at the expense of subordinate ones. Occurrence of such an energization process constitutes evidence for the drive theoretical approach.

Researchers have specified dominant and subordinate responses in experiments through one of several methods. Some studies have involved the creation of implicit response hierarchies by means of manipulation of the amount of practice allowed the subject across a number of responses. After this manipulation the relative strength of each response is measured under audience and nonaudience conditions (Cottrell, Wack, Sekerak, & Rittle, 1968; Zajonc & Sales, 1966). Other investigators have assumed that response hierarchies are reflected in varying levels of performance across variations in a task. Examples are studies showing that audiences inhibit learning of a task but facilitate performance once learning has occurred (Hunt & Hillery, 1973). Still other approaches involve the effects of audiences on emission of common (dominant) word associations (Blank, 1980; Matlin & Zajonc, 1968) or of "set" responses rather than set-breaking ones (Cohen & Davis, 1973). In each of these cases, dominant and subordinate responses are identified, and the effects of audiences on them can be specifically predicted.

One prediction that clearly follows from the drive theory of social facilitation is that observation of a person engaged in a learning task should facilitate the learning of noncompetitional material but inhibit the learning of competitional material. Although numerous studies have shown that audiences produce inhibition of performance on difficult tasks, evidence for true social *facilitation* on simpler tasks is less abundant. To a large extent this is because most experiments on the social facilitation effect are not designed to be sensitive to both facilitation and inhibition. In one study that was so designed, Cottrell, Rittle, & Wack (1967) found audience facilitation of learning of a noncompetitional paired-associates list only among subjects who had been designated as good paired-associates learners. Somewhat stronger evidence comes from a study by Geen (1983), which was designed to test two hypotheses. The first was that observation by an evaluative observer would produce drive-relevant effects on learning of both easy (i.e., highly competitional) and difficult (less competitional) lists. The second was that reducing the threat potential of the observer would weaken both effects. The latter was accomplished by instructions describing the observer

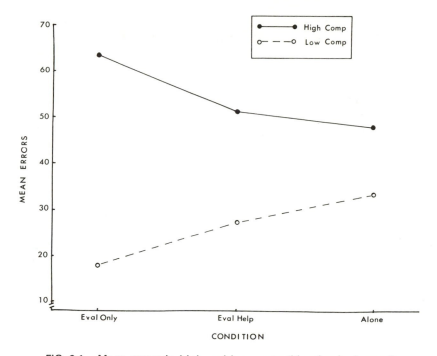

FIG. 2.1. Mean errors in high and low competitional paired-associates task as a function of evaluation treatment. Drawn from data reported by Geen (1983).

as a person who wished to observe performance so that he could later help the subject on a subsequent task. The results of the study showed that, relative to subjects who performed alone, those who learned in the presence of an evaluative observer produced fewer errors in the learning of an easy list and more errors in the learning of a difficult one. In addition, describing the observer in a relatively unthreatened way eliminated both effects (Fig. 2.1.).

Antecedents of Socially Induced Drive

Although most researchers who follow the drive theoretical approach agree with the Hull-Spence formulation in a general way, they do not all agree on the reasons that social presence creates increased drive. Four explanations have been given; we will label these, respectively, the *mere presence, evaluation apprehension, distraction/conflict,* and *social monitoring* explanations.

Mere presence.   Shortly after Zajonc published his first (1965) paper on the drive theory of social facilitation, a controversy arose over whether audiences or coactors could produce increased drive simply by being present or whether they had to represent a potential threat to the person. Zajonc (1980) has used the term "mere presence" to characterize the former viewpoint, according to which no assumptions need be made about what other people are doing or what interpretations the individual may place on their presence. This definition of the conditions for the social facilitation effect is a purely operational one. It is therefore the one most often attacked by those who seek intervening variables in the process. For that reason, evidence for the mere presence hypothesis usually consists of demonstrations that the social facilitation effect occurs even when the operation of some specified intervening variable can be ruled out. Most often, the intervening variable in question is a state of anxiety that ostensibly arises from the person's perceptions of the others as potential evaluators or competitors.

Markus (1978) has delineated the experimental conditions that must be met for a true test of the mere presence hypothesis. The tasks that are used, both simple and complex, should not elicit evaluation apprehension by themselves, i.e., they should not include criteria for "good" and "bad" performance. In addition, a true *alone* condition must be created, i.e., one in which the subject does not expect for performance to be of any interest to the experimenter and, hence, to be measured or recorded. For this reason, some routine activity should best serve as the relevant behavior.

In Markus's (1978) study, subjects were asked to remove their shoes, to put on and then remove some unfamiliar outer garments, and finally to replace their own shoes. These acts were ostensibly incidental to the real experiment, and thus presumably irrelevant to any apprehension that the experiment would otherwise elicit. While they carried out these acts, the subjects were either alone or in the presence of an experimental confederate who, in turn, either attended to or ignored the subject. Handling their own shoes constituted behavior that was assumed to be a simple task for the subjects, whereas donning and doffing unfamiliar garments was assumed to be a more complex task. Markus reported results that gave mixed support to the mere presence hypothesis. Subjects were significantly slower in handling the unfamiliar clothing when they were in the presence of either an attentive or an unattentive confederate than when they were alone. If we assume that the unattentive confederate was "merely present," this finding supports the argument that evaluation apprehension is not necessary for the social facilitation effect. However, only subjects who were observed by the confederate were significantly faster in removing and replacing their own shoes than were subjects performing alone. Thus social facilitation was found only in the condition designed to create evaluation apprehension.

More recently, Schmitt, Gilovich, Goore, and Joseph 1986) have observed that Markus's "true alone" condition may actually have contained features that elicited evaluation anxiety. Schmitt et al. (1986) therefore repeated the essential feature of Markus's (1978) study with the possibly questionable features eliminated. As part of an alleged prelude to an experiment, subjects were asked first to type their name on a computer, and then to type the name backwards with numbers interspersed among the letters. Some subjects carried out this task while alone, whereas other subjects were observed by the experimenter. Still others were in the company of a person who was both blindfolded and fitted with earphones. The latter defined the mere presence condition. Schmitt et al. (1986) found that the presence of another person, whether merely present or observing, was associated with greater speed in the simple name-typing act, but with slower performance of the more complicated typing task. This finding is consistent with Markus's data and further supports the idea that the presence of others may produce the social facilitation effect without necessarily producing evaluation apprehension.

Several other studies have also reported data that are generally favorable (Haas & Roberts, 1975; Rajecki, Ickes, Corcoran, & Lenerz, 1977; Rittle & Bernard, 1977). Sometimes, therefore, the presence of others may produce the social facilitation effect even when anxiety over performance is not involved. The two explanations for the effect need not be regarded as antagonistic, however. Each may be a better explanation than the other under some conditions but a less acceptable one under other conditions (Markus, 1978; Paulus, 1983). As is noted in greater detail in the final section of this chapter, when the conditions of a study are likely to induce strong feelings of evaluation anxiety (a test, experimental instructions stressing performance, observation by a person or persons who can convey social approval or disapproval, etc.), a theory involving evaluation apprehension may provide the explanation that best describes what is actually happening. However, in studies that do not involve high levels of induced apprehension (e.g., Schmitt et al., 1986), other explanations may be either more parsimonious or more easily inferred.

Evaluation Apprehension.   As has already been noted, the most commonly cited alternative to the mere presence hypothesis is the idea that audiences and coactors create the conditions for anxiety over evaluation of the individual's performance. An audience elicits arousal only when it is regarded as a potential evaluator and dispenser of rewards and punishments. Coactors do so only when they are regarded as competitors for available rewards. Cottrell et al. (1968) introduced this hypothesis in a study in which the presence of others was shown to energize dominant responses only when the others constituted an observing audience. The presence of blindfolded and inattentive persons had no effect on subjects' arousal levels. Following that study, several others elaborated upon it by supporting, in varying degrees, the conclusion that audiences perceived as potential evaluators elicit more arousal than those which are "merely" present (e.g., Henchy & Glass, 1968; Sasfy & Okun, 1974).

The reason an evaluating audience elicits apprehension has been the subject of some controversy. Cottrell (1972) proposed that the presence of others is a learned source of activation that acquires its arousal potential by serving as a conditioned stimulus for anticipation of positive or negative outcomes. With this argument Cottrell expanded upon the drive theory of social facilitation by introducing an incentive component. Expectation of a negative outcome resulting from audience evaluation leads to the experience of fear, anxiety, or anticipatory frustration, all of which are stimuli for increased drive. Expectation of a positive outcome activates a conditioned excitement indicative, in Hullian terminology, of a fractional anticipatory goal response. Because incentive resulting from this response energizes responses in the same way as drive, expectation of either positive or negative outcomes should produce the social facilitation effect.

The evidence from most studies on evaluation apprehension supports Cottrell's hypothesis only in part. Evaluation apprehension has been shown to be related to expectation of negative outcomes, but, with one exception (Good, 1973), to be unrelated to anticipation of positive effects (cf. Weiss & Miller, 1971).[4] For example, a series of studies by Geen and his students (Geen, 1976b, 1977, 1983) has shown that when evaluating observers are said to be interested in judging subjects' performance only so that they may later render assistance on future tasks, the level of evaluation apprehension is significantly lower than when no such qualification is stated. Assigning a helpful role to the evaluator converts the eventual outcome into something more positive than it would otherwise be.

If evaluation apprehension arises from fear of failure before the audience, it may be thought of as a state of anxiety. As such, it should be influenced by individual differences in tendencies to become anxious in evaluation situations. The more highly anxious the person customarily is in such situations, the greater should be the intensity of the anxiety state. The moderating effects of trait anxiety on state anxiety in the presence of an audience has been shown in several studies (Berkey & Hoppe, 1972; Ganzer, 1968; Geen, 1976b, 1977, 1985a; Paivio, 1965). The finding of an interaction between trait anxiety and audience conditions strengthens the argument that audience presence creates a condition of evaluation apprehension. This is an important point, because in recent years the evaluation apprehension hypothesis has been attacked on both theoretical (e.g., Glaser, 1982) and empirical (e.g., Abrams & Manstead, 1981; Bond & Titus, 1983; Manstead & Semin, 1980) grounds. Evidence of a trait-state interaction involving test anxiety, however, is difficult to explain without assuming that the state somehow has a component of evaluation anxiety in it (cf. Spielberger, 1972).

Locating the source of evaluation apprehension in the audience situation is relatively easy given what both research and common sense tells us about stage fright and performance anxiety. Identifying a cause for evaluation apprehension in the coaction setting requires a few additional assumptions. Most observers consider the effects of coactors on performance to be mediated by feelings of

---

[4]For a more extensive discussion of theorizing and early studies bearing on this issue see reviews by Geen (1980a) and Geen and Gange (1977).

competition (Cottrell, 1972; Geen, 1980a). The presence of coworkers raises the possibility of being outperformed. Being bested in competition is probably regarded by most people as a failure, so that realization of the possibility of losing in competition may serve as a cue for evaluation anxiety. Several studies have shown that coaction effects on performance are found most often in situations in which feelings of competition are either induced by instructions or inferred from general experimental procedures (see Geen & Gange, 1977, for a review). For example, Beck and Seta (1980) manipulated frequency of feedback indicative of success in a simple motor task requiring repetition of a sequence of responses. Two coacting subjects were thereby placed on various combinations of FR4 and FR7 schedules. The highest rate of responding was found when both subjects received feedback on an FR4 schedule. Beck and Seta proposed that when both subjects receive a high level of feedback, the situation produces enhanced feelings of competitiveness and a consequent elevation of drive levels.

Geen (1980a) has also cited evidence from previous studies suggesting that the coaction effect may be mediated by the presence of the experimenter. As a purveyor of rewards and punishments, the experimenter may serve as a strong cue for the feelings of competition in the coaction setting. In a study discussed at greater length below, Geen, Thomas, and Gammill (1986) found that subjects experienced greater evaluation apprehension in the coaction setting when the experimenter was present than when the coactors performed by themselves. Coactors were, in fact, no more anxious when the experimenter was out of the room than were subjects who performed the task alone.

To summarize, the evaluation apprehension hypothesis has been supported by a large number of studies published since Cottrell et al. (1968) first proposed it. As was noted earlier, conditions in social facilitation experiments often contained numerous cues for anxiety and apprehension in subjects. Given such conditions, explaining social facilitation effects in terms of anxiety may be appropriate, especially when such effects are shown to be moderated by individual differences in trait anxiety.

Distraction/Conflict. A third drive-related explanation of social facilitation has been described by Baron and his associates, who attribute the effect to attentional conflict. The position taken by Baron and his colleagues (e.g., Baron, 1986) is that the presence of others, as observers or coactors, distracts the individual from his or her task. Distraction leads to attention conflict when the attentional demands made by the others and by the task are sufficiently great and of roughly equal magnitude, and the person's capacity for attention is smaller than the combined demands. Attentional conflict, once elicited, increases drive and has consequent drive-like effects on performance. Furthermore, social comparison processes may play an important role in distraction. A person may be motivated to look to others present in the situation in order to obtain information regarding how well he or she is performing.

Baron and his colleagues have supported their argument in several studies

(Sanders, 1981). Their earliest work demonstrated that distraction by a nonsocial stimulus can elevate drive (Sanders & Baron, 1975). In a subsequent experiment, they established that a social distractor and a nonsocial one have approximately the same effects on both performance and related physiological reactions. Moore et al. (1984) conducted an investigation of reaction time in which they measured both speed of reaction to a signal and physiological reactions that occurred between the signal and a preceding stimulus that marked the beginning of a foreperiod. Heart rate typically decreases and skin conductance levels increase during the foreperiod. Moore and his colleagues found that subjects performing alone revealed these typical responses. When subjects were distracted by either an observer or by a flashing light, however, both of the physiological responses were attenuated. Moreover, the effects of the social and nonsocial distractors were virtually the same. In addition, the two had similar effects in leading to slower reaction times than were shown by subjects acting alone. Finally, an experiment on paired associates by Baron, Moore, and Sanders (1978) revealed that subjects who worked before an audience not only showed predictable social facilitation effects, but also described themselves as more distracted than those who worked alone.

In studies addressed to the role of social comparison processes in the social facilitation effect, the evidence is consistent with the distraction/conflict hypothesis, but it can also be interpreted as providing support for the evaluation apprehension explanation. In an experiment on coaction, Sanders, Baron, and Moore (1978) found the social facilitation effect among subjects who had been told that the task revealed their level of ability. This could indicate that subjects motivated to know whether they were actually manifesting ability were likely to look to the coactors for social comparisons, but it could also reveal anxiety over competition and fear of relative failure. The same alternative explanation applies to the further finding by Sanders et al. (1978) that the social facilitation effect was found among subjects told that they and the coactors were doing the same task. When the coactors did a task different from the subject's, no effect was found. We would expect feelings of competition to be highest when all persons are performing the same task. In another experiment cited as evidence for social comparison and distraction, Gastorf, Suls, and Sanders (1980) found that Type A subjects showed better performance on a simple task, and poorer performance on a complex one, in a coaction setting than when alone. No such effect was found among Type B subjects. Gastorf and his associates also showed that Type A persons were less attentive to the task than were Type Bs, a finding that would suggest the possible operation of social comparison processes. However, it may also reflect the fact that Type As express greater fear of failure than do Type Bs (Gastorf & Teevan, 1980), which would be consistent with the evaluation apprehension hypothesis.

Elsewhere it has been argued that most studies on the distraction/conflict approach to social facilitation have not been designed in such a way that alternative explanations based on evaluation apprehension could be entirely ruled out (Geen, 1981b). A subsequent study in Baron's research program did, however, control for evaluation apprehension while demonstrating distraction/conflict effects. In this ingenious experiment (Groff, Baron, & Moore, 1983), subjects were informed that their task was to observe and judge the facial expressions of a person shown on a television screen. In one condition the face shown was that of a person who was said to be evaluating the subject's performance and who was sitting well within the subject's field of vision while being televised. In this condition, therefore, subjects had no need to be distracted from the task in order to monitor the evaluator. Evaluation apprehension would presumably be strong, but distraction/conflict should be relatively weak. Subjects in a second condition were likewise observed by the evaluator, but their task was to judge the expressions of a different person on the television screen. Evaluation apprehension was therefore no greater than in the other condition, yet distraction/conflict was presumably higher.

The Groff et al. (1983) experiment is interesting for another reason. Whereas most studies of social drive infer drive from relatively complex behaviors, in this study a simple task was used. Subjects maintained muscle tension by squeezing a plastic bottle while carrying out the judging task. The squeeze response was not said to be related to the test in any way. Increased drive should energize the squeeze response, thereby decreasing its latency and increasing its intensity. The results of the study showed that the strength of the squeeze response was greater, and the latency shorter, in the high conflict than the low conflict condition. Subjects who were placed under low conflict did not differ significantly from those who performed alone. Although Groff et al. (1983) conceded that they may not have generated enough evaluation apprehension to allow an adequate test of that process, their study does conceptually separate apprehension from conflict, and represents the strongest evidence to date for the distraction/conflict theory of social facilitation.

We may summarize the literature on the distraction/conflict approach to social facilitation by noting that considerable evidence has been presented in support of the position. Often the conditions that evoke distraction and conflict can also be antecedents of evaluation apprehension, so that a clear cut distinction between the two approaches cannot be drawn. However, in at least one study (Groff et al., 1983) the two approaches appear to have been effectively compared.

Social Monitoring.   In speculating on possible reasons that the "mere presence" of others generates drive, Zajonc (1980) elaborated on his earlier position by suggesting that socially engendered drive may be the product of uncertainty. Because the presence of others always implies interaction, the person must be constantly prepared to respond to changes in the social environment. Often these changes cannot be entirely anticipated, and they therefore become stimuli for uncertainty.

Guerin and Innes (1982) have extended Zajonc's views to a process that they call *social monitoring*. Because others create uncertainty and a readiness to respond, the individual must periodically observe them in an attempt to anticipate what they may do. In general, Guerin and Innes (1982) conclude that "the more predictable the future behaviour of the other, the less attention is needed" (p. 12). The purpose of social monitoring is to reduce uncertainty regarding the possible behavior of others. The presence of others should therefore elicit less arousal when those others can be monitored than when they cannot. The ability to monitor could possibly eliminate increased arousal entirely. However, an audience will elicit arousal, even though it can be monitored, when it is paying close attention to the individual, because the individual is relatively uncertain as to what the audience may do. The greatest amount of uncertainty should be elicited by an audience that is nearby, attentive to the subject, and outside the subject's range of monitoring. Such is the case, for example, when an observer sits behind the subject (e.g., Geen, 1979). As Guerin and Innes note, the findings of such studies generally show a strong social facilitation effect. On the other hand, an inattentive audience should elicit little or no monitoring even though monitoring is possible. Experiments involving this condition show that it is not associated with the social facilitation effect (e.g., Cottrell, Wack, Sekerak, & Rittle, 1968).

Guerin (1983) conducted an experiment designed to test the social monitoring hypothesis. Subjects were given a paired associates list consisting of items with either a high or a low degree of interresponse competition. Social facilitation was expected among subjects learning the less competitional (easy) list whereas social inhibition was predicted among those learning the more difficult one. Some subjects learned the list alone. Others were attended by an associate of the experimenter who sat either behind or in front of the subject. When the associate sat in view of the subject he was either attentive or inattentive. Guerin found that these social arrangements had no effect on subjects who learned the easy list, but they did influence learning of the difficult list. As Fig. 2.2 shows, the mean number of errors was greatest in the two conditions expected to have such an effect according to the social monitoring hypothesis: the one in which the associate sat behind the subject and could not, therefore, be monitored, and that in which the associate was in view and attentive. These findings are consistent with Guerin's reasoning. They do not rule out one alternative possibility, however. It is important to recognize that even when the associate sat behind the subject, he was facing in the subject's direction and the subject undoubtedly knew this from the placement of the associate's chair. Thus, the Attentive and the Behind conditions had one feature in common: in both the subjects knew that they were being watched. Subjects who knew they were being looked at may have been more distracted from the task than those who knew they were not being watched. That distraction induces drive increase is a well-established finding in social facilitation research, as we have seen.

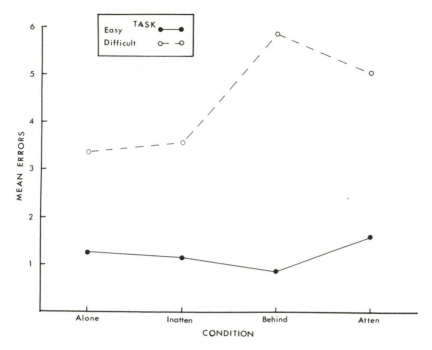

FIG. 2.2.   Mean errors in easy and difficult paired-associates task as a function of location of experimenter. Drawn from data reported by Guerin (1983).

DIRECTIVE INFLUENCES IN SOCIAL FACILITATION

A major alternative to the drive theory of social facilitation comes from the idea that the presence of others creates either explicit or implicit demands on the person to behave in some specific way. In general, the person is enjoined to present the best possible appearance to others, either by attempting to perform up to some standard or by refraining from actions that would invite social censure. Such behaviors are assumed to be dictated by norms and customs. When others are present their presence in some way enhances the prescriptive power of such standards. How this happens is what the various self-presentation approaches to social facilitation seek to explain. Whereas drive theory assigned only a motivational role to observers and coactors, the self-presentation viewpoint treats social presence as a source of behavioral direction. Several versions of this approach have been formulated.

Self-Awareness

An early alternative to the drive theory of social facilitation was proposed by Duval and Wicklund in their book *A Theory of Objective Self-Awareness* (1972) and in a subsequent review by Wicklund (1975). In the latter, self-awareness is defined as "a state in which the person takes himself to be an object" (p. 234). While the person is in this state, attention is focused inwardly upon the self. This focusing causes the person to compare the actual self, which may be engaged in some task at the time, to the idealized self, which embodies an optimal level of performance for that task. Self-awareness can be initiated by any stimulus that promotes the turning of attention inward. The most commonly used in research designed to test the theory has been a mirror; numerous studies have shown that observation of one's reflection in a mirror produces behavior that reduces the discrepancy between actual and ideal performance (Wicklund, 1975). The presence of observers or coactors may raise one's level of self-awareness in a similar way. The presence of others, by eliciting increased self-awareness and thereby prompting realization of the self-ideal discrepancy, may motivate the person to improve performance on whatever task is at hand.

This theory was criticized by Geen (1980b) primarily on the grounds that although it accounted for the social facilitation of performance by the presence of others, it did not easily explain the commonly reported findings of social inhibition. More recently, however, this criticism has been answered by Carver and Scheier (1981a, 1981b).

Their theory assumes that the task that the subject is given at the beginning of the experiment makes salient a standard for behavior on that task (i.e., a set of acts that will lead to the "correct" solution). The presence of an audience or coactors enhances self-awareness in the subject and makes him or her more cognizant of both the level of performance being manifested at the moment and the salient standard. The subject thereupon compares performance to the standard; any discrepancy between the two feeds back to the behavioral system and initiates action to match performance to the standard. If a task is relatively easy, this action has a good chance of being successful. Hence, social facilitation may occur. However, if subjects estimate their chance of actually bringing behavior into line with the standard to be poor, their response will be to stop trying and to withdraw from the situation. The result will be an inhibition of performance traceable to the presence of others. Obviously, this is more likely to happen on a difficult task than on an easy one.

Self-Presentation

Another approach to social facilitation that proposes a directional influence in social presence is based on the premise that people generally try to present the best possible appearance to others and to make a favorable impression (Schlenker, 1980). This being the case, observers or coactors may not only motivate individuals to work hard at whatever task is being carried out, but also exacerbate the person's sense of embarrassment when performance leads to failure. Failure is not likely to happen when the task is a simple or familiar one, so that the increased motivation is sufficient to produce improvement. Difficult tasks are often failed, however, at least at the outset. Embarrassment elicited by such failure may cause stress and cognitive interference of sufficient intensity to disrupt performance.

Bond (1982) conducted an experiment designed to distinguish between drive theory and the self-presentation approach described here. A paired-associates transfer task was used. In one condition the transfer list contained a few pairs from the original list along with a large number of new ones; thus a few easy items were embedded in a list consisting of predominantly difficult items. Subjects learned the transfer list either alone or in the presence of a single observer. Drive theory would presumably predict that the presence of the observer would facilitate learning of the familiar items but hinder learning of the new ones. From self-presentation theory Bond reasoned that embarrassment and cognitive interference caused by failure on the hard items would produce a general breakdown in performance so that the observer's presence would cause impairment of learning of all items, whether easy or difficult. Bond's findings supported this prediction. In addition, he ran a second condition in which a few difficult items were interspersed among many easy ones. On this task he found that the presence of the observer did not impair learning of the difficult items. However, contrary to what was predicted, the presence of the other did not facilitate learning of difficult items within an otherwise easy list. Altogether, Bond's data appear to give partial support to the self-preservation viewpoint. It should be noted, however, that Sanders (1984) has raised some questions about the assumptions underlying Bond's study.

The findings from two recently reported studies conducted in natural settings can be interpreted as support for the hypothesis that the presence of an audience creates a motive for self-presentation. In one such study Strube, Miles, and Finch (1981) examined the effect of an audience on jogging speed. Runners selected for study were men and women running in a university fieldhouse, with any given runner chosen for observation only if she or he were running alone at least 30 meters from another runner. Possible coaction effects were ruled out by this procedure. Three conditions were compared. In a *no spectator* condition an observer timed the runner unobtrusively. In an *inattentive spectator* condition the observer made brief eye contact with the runner but then pretended to be occupied by other matters. In an *attentive spectator* condition the observer gazed at the runner and attempted to maintain prolonged eye contact. Subsequent questioning established that eye contact was maintained in almost every case. The results showed that subjects who were observed by an attentive spectator increased running speed significantly more than did subjects who were not observed. Running before an inattentive spectator did not affect speed.

Similar findings have been reported by Worringham and Messick (1983). People were surreptitiously photographed by means of a hidden movie camera as they ran along two 45-yard sections of a footpath. All subjects ran the first section alone. Upon reaching a bend in the path, two-thirds of the runners encountered a confederate of the experimenter seated near the path. The confederate faced some of the subjects but was turned away from the others. Compared to a group of control subjects who did not encounter the confederate, those who came upon the confederate facing them increased their running speed over the second segment of the path significantly. Those who saw an inattentive confederate did not increase speed more than control subjects.

It must be admitted that neither of these natural experiments was designed in such a way that alternative theoretical explanations could be tested. Nevertheless, self-presentation seems the most probable explanation. In both cases, only an attentive spectator affected performance. It is possible that being attended to in this way caused subjects to be distracted from the task at hand, i.e., running, but this explanation does not account for the increase in running speed. Likewise, an attentive observer may have elicited uncertainty, the stress of which may have motivated subjects to run more rapidly. However, the simplest explanation of the findings would seem to be that runners who were observed were concerned about the impression they were making on the observers, and were motivated to present themselves in the best possible light by increasing their running speed.

In an earlier section of this review it was argued that evaluation apprehension in the presence of observers arises from anticipation of failure and subsequent anxiety. From this observation should follow the further argument that if subjects can somehow be induced to anticipate positive outcomes prior to performing before an audience, their anxiety should be reduced and, along with it, the magnitude of the social facilitation effect. On the other hand, prior failure should exacerbate, or at least not reduce, evaluation apprehension. In support of this idea, Lombardo and Catalano (1978) found that subjects who had been led to believe that they did poorly on an initial task showed a more drastic breakdown of performance on a second task than did subjects who had not been given the first task. Seta and Hassan (1980) expanded upon this finding by showing that subjects who had failed a preliminary task performed more poorly on a subsequent task while observed than while working alone whereas subjects who had enjoyed success on the first task performed no differently before an observer than did those who worked alone. In an experiment similar to that of Seta and Hassan, Geen (1979) also found that induction of failure before the task produced the typical social facilitation effect: poorer performance on a complex task by subjects who were observed by the experimenter than by subjects performing in isolation. However, Geen also found that when subjects had first succeeded on a prior task they performed better on the difficult second task while being observed than did subjects working alone.[5] This social *facilitation* of performance was found only when the first and second tasks were highly similar in nature.

---

[5]A discussion of ways in which the Geen (1979) and Seta and Hassan (1980) studies may have differed is given by Seta and Seta (1983).

This latter finding cannot be explained by drive theory. It may, however, indicate the effects of a self-presentation phenomenon. Previously successful subjects may have believed that they created a favorable impression on the experimenter and, as a consequence, may have been motivated to maintain that good impression on the second task. In spite of the difficulty of the items, they may have been so highly motivated to expend effort and to persist that they enjoyed success. To test this possibility, Geen (1981a) conducted a study designed to assess the effects of prior success and failure on persistence at an insoluble task. Prior success-failure was found to interact with the presence or absence of an observer. Subjects who had failed on a preceding task were less persistent on the insoluble second task while being observed than were subjects who had also previously failed, but who did the second task alone. However, subjects who went into the insoluble task after a success experience were more persistent when observed than when working alone. This finding supports the idea that a previous success may motivate subjects to work harder at maintaining a favorable impression than they would have worked without that experience.

Inhibition of Undesirable Behavior

An additional directive influence that social presence may have on performers is the inhibition of responses that the person considers socially undesirable. Such response withholding may influence the social facilitation effect in differing ways. In this section we consider three lines of research that converge on the notion of behavioral inhibition.

One of the earliest demonstrations of drive effects in social facilitation was reported by Matlin and Zajonc (1968), who instructed subjects to respond to verbal stimuli in a word association task. Each subject did this both alone and before an observer in counterbalanced order. The prediction from drive theory was that subjects would give more common associates when observed than when doing the task alone. Matlin and Zajonc found some support for this prediction and attributed the finding to the energization of dominant habits at the expense of subordinate ones. In a subsequent study, Blank et al. (1976) used a procedure similar to that of Matlin and Zajonc and once again found evidence that subjects gave word associations of greater overall commonality when they were observed than when they were not. However, the greatest difference between the alone and observed condition was found in regard to the number of unique and idiosyncratic associations made by the subject. Significantly fewer unique responses (i.e., responses manifested by no other subject) were given in the presence of the observer than in isolation. This finding is not easily explained in terms of drive theory. Blank and his colleagues proposed that subjects restrained themselves from making unusual responses while being observed so that they would avoid looking strange to the observer. In a subsequent study, Blank (1980) has shown that subjects suppress the expression of socially undesirable words in the presence of an observer, suggesting further a motivation to avoid behaving in ways that could invite disapproval.

Further evidence that observation leads to an inhibition of behavior thought to be socially undesirable has been reported by Berger and his associates (Berger et al. 1981; Berger, Carli, Garcia, & Brady, 1982). According to this viewpoint, the audience effect is manifested in the way information is processed and rehearsed. Processing and rehearsal of material to be learned may involve overt practice (e.g., moving one's lips while reading, counting out loud, or counting on one's fingers), or it may involve more symbolic mediation, such as mental imagery or various mnemonic devices. Berger et al. (1981) have proposed that although overt motoric mediation is frequently used in learning, symbolic mediation may not be, especially when the learning involves unfamiliar material and little time is allowed for development of symbolic codes. Learning familiar materials, on the other hand, may involve more symbolic mediation because responses can be readily symbolized at the outset of the task. The upshot of all this is that if for any reason the person is constrained not to engage in overt practice, learning unfamiliar material will be hampered whereas learning familiar material will not. The latter may, in fact, be facilitated because elimination of overt practice will force the learner to rely more on symbolic mediation.

Berger and his colleagues maintain that being observed by an audience inhibits overt motoric rehearsal because of a cultural norm that discourages such activity. Thus persons who must learn while being observed by others feel constrained not to utilize the processes that would be most effective in learning unfamiliar material, and to utilize more than before the covert processes that should facilitate learning familiar material. Because recall should vary more or less directly with the effectiveness of rehearsal and encoding, the presence of an audience should facilitate performance on familiar tasks but hinder performance on unfamiliar ones. The same prediction would follow from drive theory. Instead of postulating increased drive, however, Berger and his colleagues explain their findings in terms of conformity to a social norm made salient by the presence of observers.

In two experiments, Berger et al. (1981) found support for their hypothesis. In the first, the presence of an observing experimenter led to more suppression of overt practice and to poorer learning of six unfamiliar words than was found among subjects who performed the learning task alone. The presence of the experimenter did not facilitate learning of six familiar words, because performance was generally good in both the observed and alone conditions. This finding was attributed to a ceiling effect due to the shortness of the list to be learned. In the second experiment a list of twelve familiar words was used. Subjects who performed before an observing experimenter learned more of these words than did subjects working alone, as predicted. The presence of the experimenter again suppressed overt motoric rehearsal. In addition, use of silent rehearsal was reported more by subjects who were observed than by those learning in isolation. Finally, in neither experiment was observation by the experimenter accompanied by higher levels of self-reported anxiety, a finding at variance with the evaluation of apprehension hypothesis.

The third line of research that has linked the presence of an audience to response inhibition comes out of research by Geen on anxiety and passive avoidance (e.g., Geen, 1985b, 1986). Briefly stated, the major hypothesis of this research is that when persons are highly anxious in an evaluative situation and are also unable to leave the situation physically, they respond by withholding responses in order to avoid committing errors. If the presence of observers elicits evaluation apprehension, one reaction to the audience setting may be cautiousness and conservatism in responding, reflected in a low response rate.

In one study designed to test this idea, Geen (1985a) gave a difficult anagrams task to male subjects who had previously been classified as high or low scorers on the Sarason Test Anxiety Scale. The subject attempted to solve the anagrams while either alone or in the company of the experimenter, who, in turn, either quietly observed the subject or observed in such a way as to indicate that he was carrying on a constant evaluation of performance. On the basis of previously reported evidence (e.g., Geen, 1976b), it was expected that the latter condition would produce the highest levels of evaluation apprehension. In addition, an assessment was made of the subject's anxiety level just before the task began and again immediately after the subject had finished the task.

The major dependent measure of the study was the number of anagrams attempted by the subject, consisting of correct solutions, incorrect attempts at solutions, and partial solutions. The mean number of anagrams attempted in each condition is shown in Table 2.1. Among subjects high in test anxiety, being evaluated by the observing experimenter was associated with a low number of attempts, relative to the number in other conditions. In addition, change scores in anxiety, indicating increased anxiety during the task, were greatest among evaluated subjects that were high in test anxiety (Table 2.2). Finally, the magnitude of increase in state anxiety was correlated negatively with the number of anagrams attempted in every condition (Table 2.3). The results, taken together,

TABLE 2.1
Mean Number of Anagrams Attempted

	Test Anxiety	
Treatment	High	Low
Alone	6.60^a	6.10^{ab}
Observed	5.30^{ab}	6.30^a
Evaluated	3.80^c	6.70^a

Note. Cells bearing common subscripts are not significantly different from each other at the .05 level by a Duncan multiple range test. From Geen (1985a).

TABLE 2.2
Mean State Anxiety Change Scores

Treatment	Test Anxiety	
	High	Low
Alone	3.1	1.1
Observed	4.1	1.9
Evaluated	6.2	1.9

From Geen (1985a).

TABLE 2.3
Correlation Coefficients Relating State Anxiety Change
to Number of Anagrams Attempted

Treatment	Test Anxiety	
	High	Low
Alone	-.36	-.20
Observed	-.43	-.16
Evaluated	-.58	-.35

From Geen (1985a).

indicate that evaluative observation led to increased anxiety, which, in turn, motivated subjects to withhold responding and hence to attempt solution of only a few anagrams. This conclusion was further supported by the findings of a subsequent experiment (reported in the same paper) in which subjects were given difficult anagrams either while working alone or while being evaluated. In addition, subjects were told that guessing was permitted and that even partial incorrect solutions could provide some indication of their ability. When these additional instructions were given, no difference in number of attempts was found between the two conditions.

In a second study of response withholding, Geen, Thomas, and Gammill (1988) tested the joint effects of observation and coaction on performance. The rationale for the study lay in the hypothesis suggested by Geen (1980b) that coaction effects should be greatest when the experimenter was present at the time

TABLE 2.4
Mean Change in State Anxiety from Before
Task to After Task

Subject Condition	Locus of Experimenter	
	Present	Absent
Coaction	12.81[a]	7.57[b]
Alone	6.37[b]	5.62[b]

Note. Cells having common subscripts are not significantly different at the .05 level by a Duncan multiple range test. From Geen, Thomas, and Gammill (1988).

TABLE 2.5
Mean Number of Anagrams Attempted

| Subject Condition | Locus of Experimenter | |
	Present	Absent
Coaction	7.43^a	16.50^c
Alone	14.68^b	16.37^c

Note. Cells having common subscripts are not significantly different at the .05 level by a Duncan multiple range test. From Geen, Thomas, and Gammill (1988).

of coaction. For reasons already given elsewhere, it was expected that coacting subjects would experience more evaluation apprehension with the experimenter observing than when they performed alone. Female subjects attempted to solve the difficult anagram set either singly or in noninteracting groups of four. The female experimenter either remained in the room and monitored the subject(s) or left the room for the duration of the task. As the data reported in Tables 2.4, 2.5, and 2.6 indicate, the effect of coactors on both increase in state anxiety and number of anagrams attempted was greater when the experimenter was present and observing than when he was out of the room. Again, changes in state anxiety were negatively correlated with number of anagrams attempted.

Summary

Several hypotheses have been offered concerning a directive role played by passive audiences in social facilitation experiments. In every case, the audience is said to evoke concern over one's level of performance and to motivate the person to behave in certain ways in order to bring performance into line with some implicit standard. The audience does not do this by communicating directly to the person or by setting an example. It is assumed that behavior is controlled by some internalized norm that is made salient through processes initiated by the passive presence of others. As yet these various viewpoints are supported by only a few experimental studies. To a large extent the self-presentation approaches to social facilitation are founded on the same assumptions as the evaluation ap-

TABLE 2.6
Magnitude of Correlation Between Change in State Anxiety and Number of Anagrams Attempted

| Subject Condition | Locus of Experimenter | |
	Present	Absent
Coaction	−0.65	−0.58
Alone	−0.49	−0.36

From Geen, Thomas, and Gammill (1988).

prehension viewpoint. Both assume that a state of apprehensiveness is engendered by social encounters in which the behavior of the person is explicitly or implicitly judged. In fact, the evaluation apprehension hypothesis has been modified (e.g., Geen, 1979) in such a way as to make it conceptually quite similar to the notion of self-presentation. These matters are discussed in the final section of this chapter.

ATTENTIONAL EFFECTS OF PRESENCE OF OTHERS

A third theoretical approach to the effects of the presence of others follows from contemporary studies of information processing and attention. According to this viewpoint, the effect of audiences and coactors is mediated by a temporary condition of *stimulus overload* to which the person responds with a defensive narrowing of attention. The approach has been most extensively described in a recent review by Baron (1986; see also Moore & Baron, 1983), who has linked cognitive overload to the attentional conflict that arises from the distracting presence of others during performance of a task. Distraction and attentional conflict have already been discussed. Whereas Baron formerly considered distraction-engendered conflict to be a source of drive, he now (Baron, 1986) prefers to define it as a condition for cognitive overload. This shift in theoretical emphasis is due in part to the lack of evidence linking social presence to physiological arousal and in part to the desirability of relating distraction-conflict theory to other topics in distraction research, such as distraction and persuasion (e.g., Baron, Baron, & Miller, 1973) and distraction and stress (e.g., Cohen, Glass, & Singer, 1973).

The attentional conflict produced by distraction places demands on the person that may exceed the person's attentional capacity. It is assumed that each person has a finite amount of such capacity, and that as demands for attention increase, the less spare capacity remains for other activities such as problem solving. One result of this is increased effort to attend, which can in turn lead to a momentary increase in arousal (Kahneman, 1973). I would extend Baron's argument only by proposing that the other hypothesized effects of social presence reviewed in this paper can place demands on attentional capacity similar to those arising from attentional conflict. Both evaluation anxiety and uncertainty have been shown in various studies to have such attentional effects (e.g., Glass & Singer, 1972; Sarason, 1984; Wine, 1982).

One immediate consequence of an overtaxed attentional system is a process of selective narrowing of attention to a relatively small number of central stimuli. This reduction of the range of cue utilization has been described by several writers (Easterbrook, 1959; Geen, 1980a; Hockey, 1979; Mueller, 1976, 1979). This process represents the creation of a system of attentional priorities caused by a breakdown in parallel processing. The person must attend to a few stimuli at a time because the ability to process several alternative inputs has been momentarily disrupted (Walley & Weiden, 1973). Reduction in the range of stimuli to which the person attends has effects on the performance of simple and complex tasks similar to those hitherto attributed to increased drive (Cohen, 1978). Simple tasks require attention to a relatively small number of central cues, whereas complex tasks demand attention to a wide range of cues. If we assume that stimulus overload motivates elimination of cues over a given range regardless of whether the task is simple or complex, it should terminate attention to irrelevant distractors when the task is easy, but cause interference with important task-related stimuli when the problem is more complex. The consequence for behavior is improvement of performance on the simple task (through elimination of distractors) but impairment of performance on the complex task (because of diminished attention to central cues). The whole approach to social facilitation and inhibition through attentional mechanisms is summarized in Fig. 2.3. Only a few studies to date have examined the possible role of the presence of others in the attentional process. Bruning et al. (1968) carried out an experiment in which the experimenter was either out of sight of the subject or in full view and attending while the subject worked on a serial learning problem. Subjects in one condition were given additional information that was relevant to the material to be learned whereas other subjects were provided with additional irrelevant material which served as a potential distractor. Control subjects received no additional information. Bruning and his associates found that observation by the experimenter improved the performance of subjects who were given additional irrelevant information, compared to that of nonobserved subjects. In addition, observation hindered the performance of subjects given relevant additional information. The investigators concluded that increased drive arising from observation by the experimenter produced a narrowed range of cue utilization, so that valuable information helped less, and distracting material distracted less. The findings are also consistent with an explanation based on stimulus overload. Distraction, anxiety, or uncertainty arising from being observed may have prompted a defensive restriction of attention to a narrow range of central cues.

In an extension of the Bruning et al. (1968) study, Geen (1976a) found that the narrowing of cue utilization among observed subjects was moderated by individual differences in test anxiety. A significant cue by observation by anxiety interaction indicated that the effect found by Bruning and his colleagues, described above, was more characteristic of subjects high in test anxiety than those scoring low in that variable. This finding is not surprising, in that we would expect highly anxious subjects to find conditions of high stimulation stressful to a greater degree than the less test anxious.

An attentional approach to social facilitation and inhibition that is similar to the one just described has been suggested by Manstead and Semin (1980). This viewpoint is based on Schiffrin and Schneider's (1977) distinction between *automatic* and *controlled* processing of information. Automatic processing de-

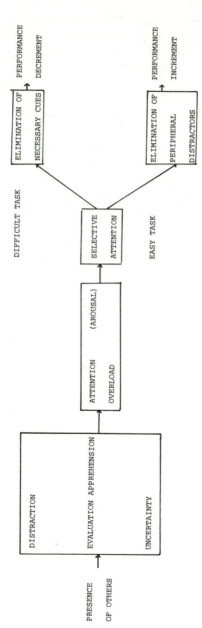

FIG. 2.3. Model of attentional explanation of social facilitation and inhibition of performance.

velops over time as the person becomes more and more familiar with the task and pays progressively less attention to task demands. Once performance has become routine, attention is no longer required. Controlled processing is required when performance has not become routinized and attention must be paid to the task demands. From this it follows that automatic processing is not limited by attentional capacity, whereas controlled processing is. Applying these ideas to social facilitation, Manstead and Semin (1980) have proposed that performance on novel or complex tasks, which require considerable controlled processing, is impaired by the presence of others because the others make competing demands for the person's attention. Performance of familiar, easy, or overlearned tasks, which are processed automatically, make no such demands. Instead, the presence of others may focus attention on these otherwise ignored behavioral sequences and may thereby bring about an improvement in performance.

CONCLUSIONS

What may we conclude about social facilitation? Drive theory, which once offered the singular advantage of parsimony, has now been shown to provide only part of the explanation for the effect. However, no other theory has as yet provided a convincing alternative account of the data. Much can be said in support of all the viewpoints that have been reviewed here, but none appears to command the high ground as drive theory did in the 1960s and 1970s. This is not to say that the drive approach has been rejected totally. It has not, and it is still invoked as an explanation for social facilitation to some extent. However, the original drive model for the phenomenon is not often encountered any longer, and a number of investigators who were once closely associated with that viewpoint now incorporate nondrive assumptions in their approaches (e.g., Baron, 1986; Geen, 1979; Paulus, 1983; Seta & Seta, 1983). The conclusion that may be best warranted by the evidence at the present time is that each approach reviewed in this chapter may explain certain features of the phenomenon without fully accounting for all of the aspects of the problem. To a certain extent this is true, yet the conclusion is not a satisfying one. An attempt should be made at suggesting some resolution of the various viewpoints, and in this final section one such attempt will be made.

In reviewing the major challenges to the drive theoretical approach, it is helpful to recall that the approach was based on two assumptions: (1) that social settings, by producing response uncertainty, performance anxiety, or attentional conflict, are the direct cause of increased drive, and (2) that the drive thus produced energizes dominant responses to a greater extent than subordinate ones. The major criticism of the first assumption comes from those who have emphasized self-presentation and self-awareness as mediators of the social facilitation effect. To these critics, the most important consequence of the audience or coaction situation is not increased drive, but the directive influence of the social setting on behaviors aimed at either making a good impression or avoiding a bad one. Criticism of the second assumption comes from those who argue that even though arousal or drive may be elicited by the social setting, the effect is not a simple response energization. As we have seen, one version of the attentional approach to social facilitation includes the premise that attentional overload is arousing and that selective attention is a means of reducing this aversive state. It is important to note that the approaches taken by Baron (1986), Geen (1976a), and Manstead and Semin (1980) account for both social facilitation of performance on simple tasks and social inhibition of performance on difficult tasks. They do so, moreover, without invoking the notion of drive as a response energizer.

By way of a general conclusion, two premises are suggested. The first is that in situations that have potential for causing a person embarrassment or loss of the esteem of others, the presence of other people produces a state of evaluation apprehension and anxiety. This state can have both cognitive and motivational effects. The cognitive effect is a state of attentional overload which, as has been noted earlier, can elicit either social facilitation and social inhibition depending on task demands (Fig. 2.3). The motivational effect is manifested in the person's desire to protect the self image by engaging in behaviors that make the person look good, or, perhaps even more important, allow him or her to avoid looking bad.

The second premise is that in the absence of evidence that the situation has the potential for causing anxiety, other explanations of the social facilitation effect may be more parsimonious or more consistent with the nature of the situation. The distraction/conflict viewpoint, as we have seen, predicts the same cognitive effects as those already noted. In addition, uncertainty can led to stress and interference with cognitive processing. Often, as has been observed elsewhere (Geen, 1981b), distinguishing the effects of evaluation apprehension from those of distraction/conflict is difficult. The point being made here is that when the conditions for increased anxiety cannot be demonstrated, distraction/conflict or uncertainty explanations may explain the observed effects equally well. A simple scheme of the two premises is given in Fig. 2.4.

Much of the literature reviewed in this chapter can be subsumed by this scheme. The older studies on evaluation apprehension (e.g., Cottrell et al., 1968; Henchy & Glass, 1968) may be regarded as cases in which other presence elicited anxiety, which in turn influenced cognitive and attentional processes in ways described earlier. More recent studies in which self-presentational and self-awareness variables have been invoked to explain the social facilitation effect (e.g., Blank et al., 1976; Berger et al., 1981) exemplify the case in which anxiety motivates behavior that is self-protective and calculated to maintain a favorable image of the self. When anxiety is not an obvious or salient feature of the situation, the presence of others may still lead to cognitive overload and its

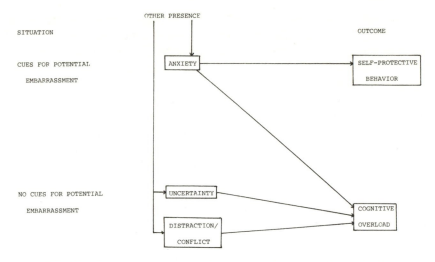

FIG. 2.4. Suggested scheme of processes in the social facilitation effect.

consequences, either by producing uncertainty (e.g., Guerin & Innes, 1982; Zajonc, 1980) or by creating distraction and conflict (Baron, 1986).

The scheme presented here has the additional advantage of articulating with research in the area of anxiety. For example, Covington (1985) has shown that anxiety reactions to failure on an examination are mediated largely by a breakdown in the person's feelings of competence and ability, which is reported as being humiliating. Sarason (1972) has also stressed that test anxiety is a state of worry that accompanies a focusing of attention on one's lack of ability. The connection between test anxiety and the social facilitation effect is one that has been noted before (Ganzer, 1968; Geen, 1976b), but the scheme presented here makes the association somewhat more explicit.

A general integrative model of social facilitation has also been proposed by Paulus (1983), whose viewpoint bears certain similarities to the one offered here. Paulus has proposed that social facilitation may be described as the result of three states that arise during performance of tasks. One such state is *arousal,* characterized as ''a psychological or emotional state of energization similar to that hypothesized in Hull-Spence theory'' (p. 104). This state may or may not include a component of physiological activation. Another state is *effort,* which reflects motivation to perform and which is manifested in speed of response, attentiveness, and amount of care expended. The third state is one of *task-irrelevant processing,* which is revealed in off-task focusing of attention. Paulus states that when a person is in a social setting that has potential for increasing negative consequences, arousal, task-irrelevant processing, and increased effort all increase. This is most likely to occur when the social setting leads the person to focus attention on himself or herself, and to become more self-aware. Being evaluated or competing with others are two social conditions that can evoke increased self-awareness. Several ideas discussed in this chapter appear in Paulus's integration.

In the case of social facilitation, effort, arousal, and task-irrelevant thinking have different effects on performance depending on the difficulty of the task. Whether social facilitation or social inhibition of performance occurs depends on the relative weights of the three states. When the task is easy or familiar, increased arousal facilitates performance by energizing dominant responses, as drive theory would predict. In addition, increased effort further facilitates performance. Because of the undemanding nature of the task, irrelevant processing has little influence on the outcome. When a difficult task is given, however, the result changes. Arousal hinders performance by energizing dominant incorrect behaviors. Task-irrelevant thinking interferes with the cognitive work necessary for performance. Only increased effort facilitates action, and it is outweighed by the other two effects. As a result, overall performance suffers.

We may take some liberties with Paulus's (1983) analysis by speculating on how his viewpoint may amplify what we have said here about criticisms of drive theory. In terms of the two assumptions of that approach noted above, Paulus (1983) would seem to suggest that arousal has its effects on social facilitation largely in ways specified by the original drive theory. Such effects are only part of the total, however, Effort enters in mainly at the level of the first assumptions. That is to say, insofar as processes other than, or in addition to, arousal are elicited by the social setting, one of these processes is maintenance of a good impression. To this end subjects will expend motivated effort. Finally, task-irrelevant processing enters at the level of the second assumption and the criticisms of it. Again insofar as effects other than response energization take place, one such effect could be off-task focusing. This in turn could cause attentional overload and the narrowing of attention discussed earlier.

ACKNOWLEDGMENT

I am grateful to Bob Baron and Tony Manstead for helpful comments on ideas expressed in an earlier draft of this chapter.

REFERENCES

Abrams, D., & Manstead, A. S. R. (1981). A test of theories of social facilitation using a musical task. *British Journal of Social Psychology, 20,* 271–278.

Aiello, J. R., Thompson, D. E., & Brodzinsky, D. M. (1983). How funny is crowding, anyway? Effects of room size, group size, and the introduction of humor. *Basic and Applied Social Psychology, 4,* 193–207.

Allport, F. H. (1924). *Social psychology*. Boston: Houghton-Mifflin.

Bargh, J. A., & Cohen, J. L. (1978). Mediating factors in the arousal-performance relationship. *Motivation and Emotion, 2,* 243–257.

Baron, R. S. (1986). Distraction/conflict theory: Progress and problems. In L. Berkowitz (Ed.), *Advances in experimental social psychology* (Vol. 19, pp. 1–40). New York: Academic Press.

Baron, R. S., Baron, P. H., & Miller, N. (1973). The relation between distraction and persuasion. *Psychological Bulletin, 80,* 310–323.

Baron, R. S., Moore, D. L., & Sanders, G. S. (1978). Distraction as a source of drive in social facilitation research. *Journal of Personality and Social Psychology, 36,* 816–824.

Beam, J. C. (1955). Serial learning and conditioning under real-life stress. *Journal of Abnormal and Social Psychology, 51,* 543–551.

Beck, H. P., & Seta, J. J. (1980). The effects of frequency of feedback on a simple coaction task. *Journal of Personality and Social Psychology, 38,* 75–80.

Berger, S., Carli, L. C., Garcia, R., & Brady, J.J. (1982). Audience effects in anticipatory learning: A comparison of drive and practice-inhibition analyses. *Journal of Personality and Social Psychology, 42,* 478–486.

Berger, S. M., Hampton, K. L., Carli, L. L., Grandmaison, P. S., Sadow, J. S., & Donath, C. H. (1981). Audience-induced inhibition of overt practice during learning. *Journal of Personality and Social Psychology, 40,* 479–491.

Berkey, A. S., & Hoppe, R. A. (1972). The combined effect of audience and anxiety on paired-associates learning. *Psychonomic Science, 29,* 351–353.

Blank, T. D. (1980). Observer and incentive effects on word association responding. *Personality and Social Psychology Bulletin, 6,* 267–272.

Blank, T. D., Staff, I., & Shaver, P. (1976). Social facilitation of word associations: Further questions. *Journal of Personality and Social Psychology, 34,* 725–733.

Bond, C. F. (1982). Social facilitation: A self-presentational view. *Journal of Personality and Social Psychology, 42,* 1042–1050.

Bond, C. F., & Titus, L. J. (1983). Social facilitation: A meta-analysis of 241 studies. *Psychological Bulletin, 94,* 264–292.

Borden, R.J., Hendrick, C., & Walker, J. W. (1976). Affective, physiological, and attitudinal consequences of audience presence. *Bulletin of the Psychonomic Society, 7,* 33–36.

Bruning, J. L., Capage, J. E., Kozuh, J. F., Young, P. F., & Young, W. E. (1968). Socially induced drive and range of cue utilization. *Journal of Personality and Social Psychology, 9,* 242–244.

Burtt, H. E. (1921). The inspiration-expiration ratio during truth and falsehood. *Journal of Experimental Psychology, 4,* 1–23.

Carver, C. S., & Scheier, M. F. (1981a). *Attention and self-regulation: A control-theory approach to human behavior*. New York: Springer-Verlag.

Carver, C. S., & Scheier, M. F. (1981b). The self-attention-induced feedback loop and social facilitation. *Journal of Experimental Social Psychology, 17,* 545–568.

Chapman, A.J. (1973). An electromyographic study of apprehension about evaluation. *Psychological Reports, 33,* 811–814.

Chapman, A. J. (1974). An electromyographic study of social facilitation: A test of the "mere presence" hypothesis. *British Journal of Psychology, 65,* 123–128.

Cohen, J. L. (1979). Social facilitation increased evaluation apprehension through permanency of record. *Motivation and Emotion, 3,* 19–33.

Cohen, J. L. (1980). Social facilitation: Audience versus evaluation apprehension effects. *Motivation and Emotion, 4,* 31–33.

Cohen, J. L., & Davis, J. H. (1973). Effects of audience status, evaluation, and time of action on performance with hidden-word problems. *Journal of Personality and Social Psychology, 27,* 74–85.

Cohen, S. (1978). Environmental load and the allocation of attention. In A. Baum & S. Valins (Eds.), *Advances in environmental research* (pp. 1–29). Hillsdale, NJ: Lawrence Erlbaum Associates.

Cohen, S., Glass, D. C., & Singer, J. E. (1973). Apartment noise, auditory discrimination, and reading ability. *Journal of Experimental Social Psychology, 9,* 407–422.

Cottrell, N. B. (1972). Social facilitation. In C. G. McClintock (Ed.), *Experimental social psychology* (pp. 185–236). New York: Holt.

Cottrell, N. B., Rittle, R. H., & Wack, D. L. (1967). The presence of an audience and list type (competitional and noncompetitional) as joint determinants of performance in paired-associates learning. *Journal of Personality, 35,* 425–434.

Cottrell, N. B., Wack, D. L., Sekerak, G. J., & Rittle, R. H. (1968). Social facilitation of dominant responses by the presence of an audience and the mere presence of others. *Journal of Personality and Social Psychology, 9,* 245–250.

Covington, M. V. (1985). Test anxiety: Causes and effects over time. In H. M. van der Ploeg, R. Schwartzer, & C. Spielberger (Eds.), *Advances in test anxiety research* (Vol. 4, pp. 55–68). Berwyn, IL: Swets North America.

Dabbs, J. M., Johnson, J. E., & Leventhal, H. (1968). Palmar sweating: A quick and simple measure. *Journal of Experimental Psychology, 78,* 347–350.

Dashiell, J. F. (1930). An experimental analysis of some group effects. *Journal of Abnormal and Social Psychology, 25,* 190–199.

Dashiell, J. F. (1935). Experimental studies of the influence of social situations on the behavior of individual human adults. In C. Murchison (Ed.), *Handbook of social psychology* (pp. 1097–1158). Worcester, MA: Clark University Press.

Droppleman, L. F., & McNair, D. M. (1971). An experimental analog of public speaking. *Journal of Consulting and Clinical Psychology, 36,* 91–96.

Duval, S., & Wicklund, R. A. (1972). *A theory of objective self-awareness.* New York: Academic Press.

Easterbrook, J. A. (1959). The effect of emotion on cue utilization and organization of behavior. *Psychological Review, 66,* 187–201.

Evans, G. W. (1979). Behavioral and physiological consequences of crowding in humans. *Journal of Applied Social Psychology, 9,* 27–46.

Fowles, D. C. (1983). Motivational effects of heart rate and electrodermal activity: Implications for research on personality and psychopathology. *Journal of Research in Personality, 17,* 48–71.

Ganzer, V. J. (1968). The effects of audience presence and test anxiety on learning and retention in a serial learning situation. *Journal of Personality and Social Psychology, 8,* 194–199.

Gastorf, J. W., Suls, J., & Sanders, G. S. (1980). Type A coronary-prone behavior pattern and social facilitation. *Journal of Personality and Social Psychology, 38,* 773–780.

Gastorf, J. W., & Teevan, R. C. (1980). Type A coronary-prone behavior pattern and fear of failure. *Motivation and Emotion, 4,* 71–76.

Geen, R. G. (1976a). Test anxiety, observation, and range of cue utilization. *British Journal of Social and Clinical Psychology, 15,* 253–259.

Geen, R. G. (1976b). The role of the social environment in the induction and reduction of anxiety. In C. D. Spielberger & I. G. Sarason (Eds.), *Stress and anxiety* (Vol. 3, pp. 105–126). Washington, DC: Hemisphere.

Geen, R. G. (1977). The effects of anticipation of positive and negative outcomes on audience anxiety. *Journal of Consulting and Clinical Psychology, 45,* 715–716.

Geen, R. G. (1979). Effects of being observed on learning following success and failure experiences. *Motivation and Emotion, 3,* 355–371.

Geen, R. G. (1980a). Test anxiety and cue utilization. In I. G. Sarason (Ed.), *Test anxiety: Theory, research, and applications* (pp. 43–61). Hillsdale, NJ: Lawrence Erlbaum Associates.

Geen, R. G. (1980b). The effects of being observed on performance. In P. Paulus (Ed.), *Psychology group of influence* (pp. 61–97). Hillsdale, NJ: Lawrence Erlbaum Associates.

Geen, R. G. (1981a). Effects of being observed on persistence at an insoluble task. *British Journal of Social Psychology, 20,* 211–216.

Geen, R. G. (1981b). Evaluation apprehension and social facilitation: A reply to Sanders. *Journal of Experimental Social Psychology, 17,* 252–256.

Geen, R. G. (1983). Evaluation apprehension and the social facilitation/inhibition of learning. *Motivation and Emotion, 7,* 203–212.

Geen, R. G. (1985a). Evaluation apprehension and response withholding in solution of anagrams. *Personality and Individual Differences, 6,* 293–298.

Geen, R. G. (1985b). Test anxiety and visual vigilance. *Journal of Personality and Social Psychology, 49,* 963–970.

Geen, R. G. (1986). *Test anxiety, persistence, and response withholding under conditions of repeated failure.* Unpublished manuscript, University of Missouri.

Geen, R. G., & Gange, J. J. (1977). Drive theory of social facilitation: Twelve years of theory and research. *Psychological Bulletin, 84,* 1267–1288.

Geen, R. G., Thomas, S. L., & Gammill, P. (1988). Effects of evaluation and coaction on state anxiety and anagram performance. *Personality and Individual Differences, 6,* 293–298.

Glaser, A. N. (1982). Drive theory of social facilitation: A critical reappraisal. *British Journal of Social Psychology, 21,* 265–282.

Glass, D. C., & Singer, J. E. (1972). *Urban stress.* New York: Academic Press.

Good, K. J. (1973). Social facilitation: Effects of performance anticipation, evaluation, and response completion on free association. *Journal of Personality and Social Psychology, 28,* 270–275.

Groff, B. D., Baron, R. S., & Moore, D. S. (1983). Distraction, attentional conflict, and drivelike behavior. *Journal of Experimental Social Psychology, 19,* 359–380.

Guerin, B. (1983). Social facilitation and social monitoring: a test of three models. *British Journal of Social Psychology, 22,* 203–214.

Guerin, B., & Innes, J. M. (1982). Social facilitation and social monitoring: A new look at Zajonc's mere presence hypothesis. *British Journal of Social Psychology, 21,* 7–18.

Haas, J., & Roberts, G. D. (1975). Effect of evaluative others upon learning and performance of a complex motor task. *Journal of Motor Behavior, 7,* 81–90.

Henchy, T., & Glass, D. C. (1968). Evaluation apprehension and the social facilitation of dominant and subordinate responses. *Journal of Personality and Social Psychology, 10,* 446–454.

Hockey, R. (1979). Stress and cognitive components of skilled performance. In V. Hamilton & D. M. Warburton (Eds.), *Human stress and cognition: An information-processing approach* (pp. 141–177). New York: Wiley.

Hunt, P. J., & Hillery, J. M. (1973). Social facilitation in a coaction setting: An examination of the effects over learning trials. *Journal of Experimental Social Psychology, 9,* 563–571.

Kahneman, D. (1973). *Attention and effort.* Englewood Cliffs, NJ: Prentice-Hall.

Karst, T. D., & Most, R. (1973). A comparison of stress measures in an experimental analogue of public speaking. *Journal of Consulting and Clinical Psychology, 41,* 342–348.

Kelley, H. H., & Thibaut, J. W. (1954). Experimental studies of group problem solving and process. In G. Lindzey (Ed.), *Handbook of social psychology* (Vol. 2, pp. 735–785). Reading, MA: Addison-Wesley.

Knight, M. L., & Borden, R. J. (1979). Autonomic and affective reactions of high and low socially anxious individuals awaiting public performance. *Psychophysiology, 16,* 209–213.

Lacey, J. I. (1967). Somatic response patterning and stress: Some revisions of activation theory. In M. Appley & R. Trumbull (Eds.), *Psychological stress* (pp. 14–37). New York: Appleton-Century-Crofts.

Latane, B., & Harkins, S. (1976). Cross-modality matches suggest anticipated stage fright a multiplicative power function of audience size and status. *Perception and Psychophysics, 20,* 482–488.

Lombardo, J. P., & Catalano, J. F. (1978). Failure and its relationship to the social facilitation effect: Evidence for a learned drive interpretation of the social facilitation effect. *Perceptual and Motor Skills, 46,* 823–829.

Manstead, A. S. R., & Semin, G. R. (1980). Social facilitation effects: Mere enhancement of dominant responses? *British Journal of Social and Clinical Psychology, 19,* 119–136.

Markus, H. (1978). The effect of mere presence on social facilitation: An unobtrusive test. *Journal of Experimental Social Psychology, 14,* 389–397.

Martens, R. (1969a). Effect of an audience on learning and performance of a complex motor skill. *Journal of Personality and Social Psychology, 12,* 252–260.

Martens, R. (1969b). Effect on performance of learning a complex motor task in the presence of spectators. *Research Quarterly, 40,* 317–323.

Martens, R. (1969c). Palmar sweating and the presence of an audience. *Journal of Experimental and Social Psychology, 5,* 371–374.

Matlin, M. W., & Zajonc, R. B. (1968). Social facilitation of word associations. *Journal of Personality and Social Psychology, 10,* 435–460.

McKinney, M. E., Gatchel, R. J., & Paulus, P. B. (1983). The effects of audience size on high and low speech-anxious subjects during an actual speaking task. *Basic and Applied Social Psychology, 4,* 73–87.

Moore, D. L., & Baron, R. S. (1983). Social facilitation: A psychophysiological analysis. In J. Cacioppo & R. Petty (Eds.), *Social psychophysiology: A sourcebook* (pp. 434–366). New York: Guilford Press.

Moore, D. L., Logel, M. L., Weerts, T. C., Sanders, G. S., & Baron, R. S. (1984). *Are audiences distracting? Behavioral and physiological data.* Unpublished manuscript, University of Iowa.

Moore, H. T. (1917). Laboratory tests of anger, fear, and sex interests. *American Journal of Psychology, 28,* 390–395.

Mueller, J. M. (1976). Anxiety and cue utilization in human learning and memory. In M. Zuckerman & C. D. Spielberger (Eds.), *Emotions and anxiety: New concepts, methods, and applications* (pp. 197–229). Hillsdale, NJ: Lawrence Erlbaum Associates.

Mueller, J. M. (1979). Anxiety and encoding processes in memory. *Personality and Social Psychology Bulletin, 5,* 288–294.

Paivio, A. (1965). Personality and audience influence. In B. Maher (Ed.), *Progress in experimental personality research* (Vol. 2, pp. 127–173). New York: Academic Press.

Paulus, P. B. (1983). Group influence on individual task performance. In P. B. Paulus (Ed.), *Basic group processes* (pp. 97–120). New York: Springer-Verlag.

Paulus, P. B., Annis, A. B., & Risner, H. T. (1978). An analysis of the mirror-induced objective self-awareness effect. *Bulletin of the Psychonomic Society, 12,* 8–10.

Paulus, P. B., McCain, G., & Cox, V. C. (1978). Death rates, psychiatric commitments, blood pressure, and perceived crowding as a function of institutional crowding. *Environmental Psychology and Nonverbal Behavior, 3,* 107–116.

Pessin, J. (1933). The comparison effects of social and mechanical stimulation on memorizing. *American Journal of Psychology, 45,* 263–270.

Rajecki, D. W., Ickes, W., Corcoran, C., & Lenerz, K. (1977). Social facilitation of human performance: Mere presence effects. *Journal of Social Psychology, 102,* 297–310.

Rittle, R. H., & Bernard, N. (1977). Enhancement of response rate by the mere physical presence of the experimenter. *Personality and Social Psychology Bulletin, 3,* 127–130.

Sanders, G. S. (1981). Driven by distraction: An integrative review of social facilitation theory and research. *Journal of Experimental Social Psychology, 17,* 227–251.

Sanders, G. S. (1984). Self-presentation and drive in social facilitation. *Journal of Experimental Social Psychology, 20,* 312–322.

Sanders, G. S., & Baron, R. S. (1975). The motivating effects of distraction on task performance. *Journal of Personality and Social Psychology, 32*, 956–963.

Sanders, G. S., Baron, R. S., & Moore, D. L. (1978). Distraction and social comparison as mediators of social facilitation effects. *Journal of Experimental Social Psychology, 14*, 291–303.

Sarason, I. G. (1972). Experimental approaches to test anxiety: Attention and the uses of information. In C. D. Spielberger (Ed.), *Anxiety: Current trends in theory and research* (Vol. 2, pp. 381–408). New York: Academic Press.

Sarason, I. G. (1984). Stress, anxiety, and cognitive interferences: Reactions to tests. *Journal of Personality and Social Psychology, 46*, 929–938.

Sasfy, J., & Okun, M. (1974). Form of evaluation and audience expertness as joint determinants of audience effects. *Journal of Experimental Social Psychology, 10*, 461–467.

Schiffrin, R. M., & Schneider, W. (1977). Controlled and automatic human information processing: II. Perceptual learning, automatic attending, and a general theory. *Psychological Review, 84*, 127–187.

Schlenker, B. R. (1980). *Impression management: The self-concept, social identity, and interpersonal relations*. Monterey, CA: Brooks-Cole.

Schmitt, B. H., Gilovich, T., Goore, N., & Joseph, L. (1986). Mere presence and social facilitation: One more time. *Journal of Experimental Social Psychology, 22*, 242–248.

Seta, J. J., & Hassan, R. K. (1980). Awareness of prior success or failure: A critical factor in task performance. *Journal of Personality and Social Psychology, 39*, 70–76.

Seta, J. J., & Seta, C. E. (1983). The impact of personal equity processes on performance in a group setting. In P. B. Paulus (Ed.), *Basic group processes* (pp. 121–147). New York: Springer-Verlag.

Singerman, K. J., Borkovec, T. D., & Baron, R. S. (1976). Failure of "misattribution therapy" manipulation with a clinically relevant target behavior. *Behavior Therapy, 7*, 306–313.

Spielberger, C. D. (1972). Conceptual and methodological issues in anxiety research. In C. D. Spielberger (Ed.), *Anxiety: Current trends in theory and research* (Vol. 2, pp. 481–493). New York: Academic Press.

Strube, M. J., Miles, M. E., & Finch, W. H. (1981). The social facilitation of a simple task: Field tests of alternative explanations. *Personality and Social Psychology Bulletin, 7*, 701–707.

Travis, L. E. (1925). The effect of small audience upon hand-eye coordination. *Journal of Abnormal and Social Psychology, 20*, 142–146.

Triplett, N. (1898). The dynamogenic factors in pacemaking and competition. *American Journal of Psychology, 9*, 507–533.

Walley, R. E., & Weiden, T. D. (1973). Lateral inhibition and cognitive masking. *Psychological Review, 80*, 284–302.

Weiss, R. F., & Miller, F. G. (1971). The drive theory of social facilitation. *Psychological Review, 78*, 44–57.

Wicklund, R. A. (1975). Objective self-awareness. In L. Berkowitz (Ed.), *Advances in experimental social psychology* (Vol. 8, pp. 233–275). New York: Academic Press.

Wine, J. D. (1982). Evaluation anxiety: A cognitive-attentional construct. In H. W. Krohne, & L. Laux (Eds.), *Achievement, stress, and anxiety* (pp. 207–219). Washington, DC: Hemisphere.

Worringham, C. J., & Messick, D. M. (1983). Social facilitation of running: An unobtrusive study. *Journal of Social Psychology, 121*, 23–29.

Zajonc, R. B. (1965). Social facilitation. *Science, 149*, 269–274.

Zajonc, R. B. (1980). Compresence. In P. Paulus (Ed.), *Psychology of group influence* (pp. 35–60). Hillsdale, NJ: Lawrence Erlbaum Associates.

Zajonc, R. B., & Sales, S. (1966). Social facilitation of dominant and subordinate responses. *Journal of Experimental Social Psychology, 2*, 160–168.

3 Spatial Behavior of Individuals and Groups

Eric S. Knowles
University of Arkansas

In a three dimensional world, distance and location are part of the warp onto which social life is woven. Human encounters cannot take place without location being part of the interaction. Spatial behavior is ever present, public, shared, and mostly innocuous. Ironically, it is exactly these same qualities that make spatial location the hidden dimension of social behavior (Hall, 1966).

Location Issues are Ever Present

Space and time are everywhere; we can't escape either. They are fundamental dimensions of human existence, dimensions that underlie our life's tapestry. They permeate and structure interpersonal encounters. Interpersonal distance and spacing are more than "mere geography" though, for they invariably engage psychological and social issues. Lewin's (1951) field theory is a geographical representation that translates personal and social life into distance, location, movement, barriers, and adjacency. Lewin (1938, 1951) used psychological distance—the feeling of closeness or remoteness from a person, feeling, or goal—as an inevitable present component of reactions to persons, places, and situations.

Location Issues are Public

Where I stand or sit or look is available to all who see me; I cannot keep it hidden. Spatial behavior is communicative. If I move toward you, or away from you, or even if I stand still, my behavior is available as a message. And, it is a message about me, about you, and about us. Whether a person's location was planned or accidental, strategic or expressive, interpreted by others as inconsequential or meaningful, it is exposed and available for any of these inferences.

Location Issues are Shared

Our public spatial behavior is also interactive. In shared space, where I locate restricts your use of space, and your use of a shared space alters my options. Location behavior in a public setting engages various group level issues, such as common fate, implicit communication, negotiation and collaboration, interactive determination. Even personal space, as it is usually studied, is a collective phenomena. When I take a step closer to you, you are necessarily a step closer to me.

Location Issues are Innocuous

The role of space and location in our social tapestry is largely unnoticed, but not unimportant. Interpersonal positions tend to be background features of most encounters, and therefore are processed rather automatically. Often, when we see a person or a group, we are only implicitly aware of their location. Their location is "transparent" in the sense that we don't focus our attention on location, or don't focus on it long. Rather, we *see through* the location to focus our attention on the person or group, their actions, or the setting (Wegner & Giuliano, 1982). However, our understanding of and judgments about the person, group, action, and setting rely on the tacit meaning and messages embodied in location.

Strategy for this Chapter

This chapter explores the *interpersonal* meanings of locations, how we use space *vis à vis.* other people. It is aimed at conceptualizing and understanding the spatial behavior of individuals and groups. The focus is on theory, on conceptualizing the processes regulating spatial behavior, rather than on reviewing the literature. In particular, this chapter attempts to account for how spacings occur, to conceptualize the processes that underlie locational selection, and to explain the varied reactions to these locations. There are recent reviews of the literatures on personal space (Aiello, 1987; Hayduk, 1983), spatial dynamics of groups (Knowles, 1980), and on individual reactions to audiences and crowds (Borden, 1980). The research summarized in these reviews provides the data, the raw scenery for this excursion.

Two theoretical goals underlie this chapter. The first goal is to clarify and promote affiliative conflict theory (Argyle & Dean, 1965; Knowles, 1980) as a robust theory of spatial behavior. The full potential of this theory is not readily apparent from Argyle and Dean's (1965) original 2-page presentation. The affiliative conflict theory is still often relegated to the status of a minor theory, predicting only homeostasis. This chapter attempts to show that it is an explicit, detailed, and widely applicable theory of spatial behavior.

A second goal of this chapter is to apply Kurt Lewin's field theory (1938, 1951) in a fairly direct and faithful way. The affiliative conflict theory can be subsumed under Lewin's general framework. Doing so, I believe, provides a greater understanding of spatial behavior and allows affiliative conflict theory to be extended beyond its limited origins.

THEORETICAL UNDERPINNINGS

Personal Space and Bounded Areas

A bounded bubble surrounding a person or group served as an early and incomplete metaphor for spatial behavior (Evans & Howard, 1973; Sommer, 1959). This misplaced conceptualization was spawned and reinforced by our phenomenology of spatial behavior as discrete and discontinuous. Animals have territories that seem clearly and absolutely bounded by markers, by movements, by flight, or by aggressive reactions (Hediger, 1950). For us, the realization that someone is too close or intrusive is usually not a gradual apprehension; it jumps into awareness at a single moment as we turn focal attention to what previously had been only implicit awareness of location.

These direct and vicarious experiences of spatial behavior as discrete events draw our attention to the boundaries rather than to the underlying processes. This phenomenology gave rise to our early theories of spatial behavior, which focused on territorial areas, on protected spaces, and on boundaries that separate public from private.

Robert Sommer (1959, 1969) introduced psychology to the concept of personal space, which he defined as ''an area with an invisible boundary surrounding a person's body, into which intruders may not come'' (p. 26). Related concepts such as a ''body buffer zone'' (Horowitz, Duff, & Stratton, 1964; Kinzel, 1970) or a ''joint interactional space'' (Goffman, 1971; Kendon, 1977) perpetuated the view that just as each of us possesses some physical volume (our bodies) that displaces air, each of us also possesses some social volume (personal or group space) that displaces others.

Metaphors drive our measurement and our measures reinforce our metaphors. Early researchers measured the discrete point on an approach line that marked the boundary of personal space. For instance, Kinzel (1970) placed subjects at the hub of an imaginary eight-spoked wheel. As he walked toward subjects along each spoke, he asked them to say ''Stop'' when they felt he was approaching too close. In a more disguised procedure, Dosey and Meisels (1969) asked subjects to ''Walk slowly toward the other person; when you reach him or her, stop and wait until I tell you to return'' (p. 94). In each case, the "stop" distance was taken as the perimeter of personal space.

This two-dimensional representation of the personal space bubble was common in laboratory measures (Hartnett, Bailey, & Gibson, 1970; Rawls, Trego, McGaffey, & Rawls, 1972) and paper and pencil measures (Duke & Nowicki, 1972; Pederson, 1973) of personal space. It was applied to groups (Knowles, 1973; Goffman, 1971; Kendon, 1977) in a direct analogy.

Figure 3.1 shows this bounded bubble view of both individual and group spatial behavior. Note the two assumptions that this conceptualization conveys. First, the spatial bubble is the property of the person or group. It is attached to them regardless of where they are and does not arise out of interaction with the environment. Second, reactions are discrete. If others are outside of your boundary, they are inconsequential; but if others step across that boundary, they are intrusive.

Field Theory

There are images other than the bubble available. Lewin's (1938, 1951) field theory provides several. Lewin (1938) conceptualized behavior as occurring in a psychological field made up of regions, locations, paths, and goals. Lewin used these geographical terms as metaphors for complex psychological and social processes. For many social scientists and for some problems, Lewin's metaphors become too remote, too esoteric, or too abstract to apply easily. However, the study of spatial behavior allows the metaphor to be applied rather directly and concretely.

FIG. 3.1.   Depictions of (a) Individual and (b) Group space as bubbles of protection with discrete boundaries.

Lewin's metaphor embodies two important assumptions that fit well with the study of spatial behavior. First, Lewin assumed that behavior is purposeful, goal-directed, and functional, even when these are outside of the actor's awareness. Spatial and nonverbal behavior is understandable only in the context of a field of goals and purposes (Patterson, 1983). Second, Lewin assumed that behavior is the joint function of the person's goals, desires, needs or plans, coupled with the environment's demands, constraints, and possibilities. The spatial behavior of individuals and groups reflects in a special way an accommodation between the entity's purposes and the situation's possibilities.

Force Fields.   Lewin (1938) represented the person situated at one location in a psychological landscape. The various personal goals, short and long-term, give definition to different regions of this life space, and mark them as attractive or unattractive. These goals, amplified by needs or tensions in the person, produce forces for movement toward some goals and away from others. The activity of personality is to negotiate among and move through the fields of forces to achieve desired goal states while avoiding undesired ones.

For Lewin (1938), a goal could be either attractive or unattractive. That is, it could set up forces to approach that goal or forces to avoid that goal. Lewin knew that the valence of the goal was a joint function of the incentive properties of the goal joined with the strength of the tension or need within the person. For instance, an attractive goal could have a high valence for a person at times when that goal was needed, and low valence when there was little tension for that goal.

Another key element of Lewin's theory was that the strength of the force between the person and a goal region is a joint function of the valence of the goal and its psychological closeness or remoteness. Psychological forces are not constant with increasing closeness to the goal; they show a systematic change, a goal-gradient over distance. As a goal moves closer to the person, the forces pushing the person toward or away from that goal get stronger.

For Lewin (1938, p. 165), psychological distance meant the number of "psychological regions" traversed by the path between the present location and the goal. As a practical matter, psychological distance often translated fairly directly into space, time, or effort.

The desire for interaction operates like a force field. Consider the goal of finding out the time of day. One possible goal region would be to ask someone what time it is. Some people you could ask have a higher incentive value for this goal than other people. They seem more likely to own a watch, know the time, or be accurate in their time keeping. The stronger is your need to know the time, the more important these incentive characteristics of the other person will be. Great effort required to make the request will dampen its likelihood.

Power fields.   Lewin described the force field as originating within and owned by the person. It was his or her subjective, psychological landscape created by personal goals, valences, and pathways. Occasionally, Lewin would remind us that some of the forces are exogenous, created by powerful others or social institutions and imposed on our life space. They enter our life space, have a valence, and force a reaction, but they are *externally* decreed. They are not dependent upon the tensions or needs of the person for the goal. These imposed forces he termed *power fields*. A child's avoidance of playing with a forbidden object results from "an inducing field of force of an adult (A). If this field of force loses its psychological existence for the child (e.g., if the adult goes away or loses his authority) the negative valence also disappears" (Lewin, 1935, pp. 98–99).

Lewin (1938) used the concept of a power field specifically to describe personal space issues: ". . . the effect of the power field of a stranger upon a child depends not only upon the character of the child, the stranger, and the situation, but also upon the physical distance between the child and the stranger" (pp. 168–169). Lewin noted that the social influence represented by this power field decays with distance and is greater when the other person is facing toward rather than facing away.

AFFILIATIVE CONFLICT THEORY OF SPATIAL BEHAVIOR

Background

Lewin's (1938, 1951) field theory is particularly adapted to the analysis of situations where goals conflict. An approach-approach conflict describes a situation where two different goal regions are both desired, establishing forces pulling a person in incompatible directions. For instance, someone who wants to study tonight so that they can do well on a test tomorrow, but also wants to go to a basketball game with their friends knows the dynamics of an approach-approach conflict.

Sometimes the same goal region is occupied by different goals with opposite valences that establish both approach and avoidance forces. This describes an approach-avoidance conflict.

Argyle and Dean (1965) applied a Lewinian-like goal-conflict theory to issues of personal space and intimacy. Argyle and Dean observed that all interactions involve an expression of some level of intimacy at verbal, paraverbal, and nonverbal levels. This expression, which is unavoidable and intrinsic to the interpersonal interaction, is both desired and feared; that is, intimacy is a psychological goal region that engages both approach and avoidance tendencies. Argyle and Dean suggested that "The approach forces include the need for feedback . . . and sheer affiliative needs" (p. 292), while "The avoidance components include the fear of being seen, the fear of revealing inner states, and the fear of seeing the rejecting responses of others . . .'' (p. 293).

Knowles (1980) expanded Argyle and Dean's approach-avoidance conflict model and applied it to the spatial behavior of individuals and groups in a variety of situations. The formal statement of Knowles' affiliative conflict theory is presented in Table 3.1. The theory and its implications are probably easier to see in the schematic presentation given in Fig. 3.2. Figure 3.2 shows approach-avoidance gradients and the resultant discomfort in two sorts of situations. The first is when our subject, the person or protagonist, is alone and does not desire interaction. The second is when our subject is in a group situation, created by desiring to be with or interact with another person. The sections below describe in detail the affiliative conflicts in these situations.

Force Fields When Alone

Consider the situation where a person is alone and someone else advances too close. This is usually referred to as a personal space invasion. In an invasion, no interaction is taking place and there is no expectation or desire for interaction. Thus, an approach gradient has a functional value of zero that does not change with interpersonal distance (see Fig. 3.2A). However, our subject does desire to avoid contact with the invader. The closer the intruder comes, the stronger becomes the person's desires to avoid or escape the encroachment, the intimacy, the vulnerability. This desire establishes an avoidance gradient, one that increases with closeness. The height of this gradient is dependent on distance and the characteristics of invader, not so much on the goals or characteristics of the subject.

A key postulate of this theory is that the amount of discomfort with the situation is related to the *discrepancy* in the strengths of approach and avoidance gradients. When the approach forces balance the avoidance forces, then an equilibrium is established. When this equilibrium is not achieved, that is, when approach desires exceed avoidance forces, or when avoidance tendencies are greater than the approach, then there are forces left over in the system to fuel the discomfort and motivate subsequent actions to reduce the discomfort.

In the invasion situation depicted in Fig. 3.2A, the approach gradient is zero. The discrepancy between the gradients is solely a product of the strength of the avoidance gradient. Since the avoidance forces increase with closeness and approach forces are absent, discomfort and the energy for action increase with closeness. The amount of discomfort is represented by the shaded area in Fig. 3.2A and produces the discomfort function in Fig. 3.2B. The closer an invader comes, the more uncomfortable a person feels. At some point, the discomfort passes the threshold created by an inertia for action and the victim acts to reduce the discomfort. In most situations, the victim turns away, moves, or uses some other means to reestablish greater distance. Many strategies are available, of

TABLE 3.1
Affiliative Conflict Theory

1. Interpersonal situations engage avoidance tendencies--desires to avoid getting too close, too intimate, too exposed, too committed--that are induced by the presence and characteristics of others.

   1a. Variations in the avoidance tendency reflect primarily differences in the characteristics of the other person.
   1b. In interpersonal situations avoidance tendencies decrease with psychological distance from the goal.
   1c. Avoidance gradients are nonlinear, decreasing more quickly at close distances and more slowly at far distances. With geographical distance avoidance gradients decrease as a square root of distance from the other person.
   1d. The intercept or intensity of the avoidance gradients vary more than the slopes.

2. Some situations, such as those in which interaction occurs or is desired, establish approach tendencies--desires to establish a relationship, become closer, know, and be known, more intimately.

   2a. The intensity and form of approach tendencies are affected primarily by the needs and goals of the person.
   2b. In interpersonal situations approach tendencies are variable in direction and often increase with psychological distance from the goal.
   2c. Approach gradients are nonlinear, changing more quickly at close distances than at far distances. The particular form of the approach gradient often follows a logarithmic or power function of distance from the other person, but the specific parameters depend on the person's needs and goals.
   2d. Both the intercept and slope of approach gradients vary depending on the needs and purposes of the person.

3. Discomfort with an interpersonal situation is a result of the discrepancy between approach and avoidance tendencies.

   3a. In a noninteraction situation, in which approach forces are absent, discomfort, arousal, and other reactions reflect only the avoidance tendencies.
   3b. In a situation in which approach forces are present, the approach and avoidance gradients cross, creating an equilibrium of greatest comfort. Movement away from this equilibrium in either direction produces greater discomfort.

4. Discomfort with a particular distance motivates adjustments to reduce the discomfort.

   4a. Discomfort can be reduced by changing the current distance back toward the equilibrium point.
   4b. Discomfort can be reduced by making compensatory changes in some other dimension of intimacy so that the total expression of intimacy moves back toward the equilibrium point.
   4c. Discomfort can be reduced by altering the approach tendency and/or the avoidance tendency so that the equilibrium point moves closer to the current distance.
   4d. Discomfort can be reduced by leaving the field.

NON~INTERACTION

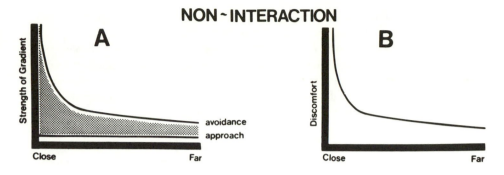

INTERACTION

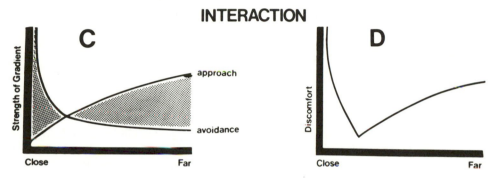

FIG. 3.2. Graphic representation of the affiliative conflict theory of approach and avoidance gradients and resultant discomfort. (See text for explanation.)

course, including warning the invader or seeking social support (Knowles & Brickner, 1981).

Force Fields in an Interaction

In an interaction, a person desires to engage another person. Even if the interaction is limited to answering a request for the time, a positively valenced goal region (e.g., answering a question) is established. Since the person has some desire for or acceptance of an interaction, an approach gradient is established.

Approach Gradients. Approach forces are a product of the goals, needs, desires, and purposes of the person. Accepting interaction as a goal creates approach forces which tend to pull the person closer to the goal object. Factors which increase the person's craving for an interaction increase the pressures to move closer (Gifford, 1982).

Because they are a product of the particular goals and purposes of the person, approach forces are quite variable in strength and form. For instance, the approach gradients for intimacy and other interpersonal goals often decreases with closeness.[1] When the goal object must be touched before any consumption can begin, then the approach forces get stronger with increasing closeness to the goal. But other sorts of goal objects "reach out in space" to bring satisfaction. When they are desired, friendship, intimacy, warmth from a fire, or music are probably more valued the more remote and inaccessible they are. The more friendship, warmth, or music one gets, the less one needs. Thus, many interpersonal goals establish approach gradients that actually decrease with closeness to the goal. Not only do different goals create different gradients forms, but the same interaction can engage several goals, serving several purposes at once.

Avoidance Gradients.   Avoidance forces are still active even though the interaction is desired. Loss of freedom, invasion of privacy, fear of rejection or hurt, fear of being seen are still negatively valenced goals and are still active in the interpersonal situation. These negative aspects are implied by the presence of the other person, and thus operate like a Lewinian power field, pretty much independently of the purpose or desirability of the interaction. If the other person is attractive (Banziger & Simmons, 1984), similar in status (Gifford, 1982), or cooperative (Mehrabian, 1968) then the avoidance forces are weaker and interactions occur at a closer distance. If the other person is intimidating (Strube & Werner, 1984), or disfigured (Rumsey, Bull & Gahagan, 1982), or dissimilar in status (Gifford, 1982) then avoidance forces are stronger and the interaction takes place at a further distance. Gifford and Gallagher (1985) suggest that some people through their defensiveness may be more susceptible to avoidance forces created by the closeness of others.

Stigma are characteristics of the other person that increase the avoidance gradient and affect spatial behavior. Rumsey, Bull, and Gahagan (1982) found that pedestrians stood further away from a person with a stigma (birthmark or a bruise under the right eye) than from a person without the stigma. Moreover, pedestrians who stood on the right side of the person (the side with the stigmatizing mark) stood farther away than pedestrians who stood on the left side. The stigmatizing mark operated on the subjects as a power field with its influence radiating away from its point of origin. Theodore White (1961, p. 197) relates that immediately after John F. Kennedy won the Democratic Party nomination for president, his advisors, aides, and family stood farther away, acknowledging spatially the increased power of his position.

Situations can impose power fields that act more generally on avoidance

---

[1]The possibility that approach gradients show positive slopes over distance contrasts with Miller's (1944, 1959) view of approach-avoidance conflicts, but not necessarily with Lewin's (1938). See Knowles (1980) for an extended discussion of this issue.

tendencies. Long (1984) observed that settings with greater inherent tension (an infirmary, a Dean's office, or dentist's waiting room) lead to greater avoidance tendencies than situations with less tension (lounges, a music room, a plaza).

The avoidance gradients in an interaction can be assumed to be very similar to the avoidance gradients in an invasion. Both are created by the presence of the other person and leave when the other person leaves. The capacity for another person to dominate a space and influence the people in it is a consistent characteristic of that person (Esser, 1970; Sossin, Esser, & Deutsch, 1978). In keeping with this analysis, I have drawn the avoidance gradients in 3.2A and 3.2C with the same slopes and intercepts.

Comfortable Interaction Distance. In an interaction situation, the two gradients intersect at an equilibrium point where the approach forces equal and balance out the avoidance forces. The discrepancy in the strengths of the two gradients determines the amount of discomfort with the distance and the amount of energy available for addressing this discomfort. This discrepancy is depicted by the shaded area in Fig. 3.2C. The discomfort with distance function for an interaction situation is depicted in Fig. 3.2D. As this curve shows, there is a distance that is most comfortable for each interaction. Movement closer than this distance increases the discomfort and movement farther away from this point increases discomfort. The discomfort produces a pressure to deal with the situation by (a) moving back toward the equilibrium point, (b) altering the underlying approach and avoidance gradients, or (c) fleeing the field.

Nonlinear Gradients. Figure 3.2 is drawn with nonlinear goal-gradients. Knowles (1978, 1980, 1983) observed in a variety of contexts that distance effects tend to fall off in a nonlinear fashion, with the largest changes at the closest distances. Logarithmic and power function transformations of geographic distance describe these relationships fairly closely and much better than a linear function.

Lundberg, Bratfisch, and Ekman (1972) advocated a "square root law of distance" for psychological reactions to world events at a distance. They noted that people judge distance very accurately, in a way that increases regularly with geographic distance. The same people, however, judge the subjective importance of events at a distance in a nonlinear fashion that decreases as the square root of distance (that is as a function of distance raised to a power of $-.5$). Knowles (1983) observed a similar square root function in several studies employing interpersonal distances. He made a strong argument for avoidance reactions decreasing as the square root of distance. The gradients in Fig. 3.2 were drawn as square root functions of distance.

Fluidity of Gradients. The affiliative conflict theory is often misrepresented as a static model, where goal gradients and equilibria are set at the initiation of an interaction and from there change slowly and only with a good deal of creaking

(Argyle & Cook, 1976). Out of this view comes the criticism that the affiliative conflict theory is homeostatic, nondynamic, and predicts only compensatory, status quo maintaining reactions (Anderson & Anderson, 1984; Capella & Greene, 1982, 1984). The criticism is inaccurate because this view of the theory is inaccurate (Hayduk, 1985). Argyle and Dean (1965), as did Lewin (1951), saw approach-avoidance dynamics in interactions as constantly changing, reacting, readjusting.

Interactions, and the goals that create and sustain them, change fluidly and easily from moment to moment. Ask a person for the time. If you receive the hour and minute in reply, the goal sponsoring the approach is satisfied and interaction ends. A return question, though, can perpetuate and deepen the interaction, raising the approach tendencies, perhaps reducing the avoidance gradient. The realization a moment later that your question is not being addressed drops the approach gradient. As subgoals are met, as interests wax and wane, as signals sent are received and returned, the approach and avoidance gradients change altering the field of forces and the point of equilibrium.

Our underlying model of spatial behavior needs to be one based on a conception of *dynamic equilibria* that are inherently unsteady, dependent upon the psychological field at the moment, and responsive to the ongoing interaction (Lewin, 1951; Hayduk, 1985). Active and changing fields of forces alter the equilibrium points and spatial preferences contingent on them.

Worchel (1986) found that rather transitory changes in the context of an interaction altered a person's approach and avoidance behavior. For instance, changes such as increased time for talking, previous isolation, altered room size and shape produced compensatory changes in subjects' interaction distance and latency of initiating a conversation. Worchel concluded that "contextual variables that should influence intimacy or the concern with interpersonal relations will also affect spatial behavior" in ways consistent with Argyle and Dean's theory (p. 252). It is clear that the subjects in Worchel's study were attentive to the immediate context and were adjusting their equilibrium points in response.

Hayduk (1985) used LISREL statistical procedures (Joreskog & Sorbom, 1981) to evaluate several different conceptual models of the processes giving rise to spatial preferences. The model that best fit his three sets of data was one that assumed a continual reassessment, where the current equilibrium was based on an adjustment of the immediately prior equilibrium for the contemporaneous situation. The model that assumed a personally or situationally consistent personal space preference was clearly inaccurate. Hayduk (1985) concluded that "Once a reference distance is set for the individual, it is the readjustments from that current preference that are dynamic. While there is stability from one observation to the next, there is continual 'fine tuning' where each 'retuning' forms part of the baseline onto which the next 'fine tuning' is overlaid" (p. 148).

When the dynamic processes of equilibrium change are better understood, we will probably find that the avoidance tendencies change more slowly than the approach tendencies. Approach gradients are force fields emanating from the needs, goals, and views of the person. Because of this subjective origin and the internal locus of control, approach tendencies are more readily and easily modified. Avoidance gradients, by virtue of their source in power fields created by the other person, are less changeable than approach gradients, less subject to momentary fluctuation.

In addition to the gradual changes described here, the phenomenal field can sometimes reorganize dramatically as the situation becomes reframed (Watzlawick, Weakland, & Fisch, 1974) or as one schema for understanding is replaced by another (Rothbart, 1981). Sussman and Rosenfeld (1982) provide an interesting example of restructuring the phenomenal field in an assessment of the spatial behavior of different nationalities. They found that, normally, Japanese sit farther apart and Venezuelans sit closer than Americans. However, both groups more closely approximate the American conversational distance when speaking English than when speaking their native language. The change in language may have changed the phenomenal field, changing the gradients of approach and avoidance.

Compensation Vs. Reciprocity

Compensation and Equilibria.   Argyle and Dean (1965) assumed that intimacy was a *joint* function of eye contact, proximity, topic intimacy, directness of orientation, smiling, and other verbal and nonverbal cues. They considered these different channels as functionally equivalent avenues to increasing or decreasing intimacy. Functional equivalence allowed one channel to compensate for deficiencies in another: "We deduce that if one of the components of intimacy is changed, one or more others will shift in the reverse direction in order to maintain the equilibrium" (p. 293).

In their original study, Argyle and Dean (1965) observed people sitting 10, 6, or 2 feet from Michael Argyle and carrying on a discussion. Eye contact was less at the closer, more intimate distances. Argyle and Dean concluded that as the intimacy of the interpersonal distance increased, the intimacy of the visual behavior decreased, as if to compensate and hold constant the sum total of intimacy. Other studies also find that physical closeness often produces compensatory changes in visual gaze, smiling, and lean (Argyle & Ingham, 1972; Coutts & Ledden, 1977). However, Aiello (1977a, 1977b; Aiello & Thompson, 1980) observed in several studies that compensation between gaze and distance characterized male subjects. The female subjects gazed most at an intermediate distance.

The compensatory changes predicted by the equilibrium corollary apply to some dimensions or communication channels more than others. For instance, changes in the confederate's distance alter the subject's visual behavior, but changes in a confederate's gaze behavior rarely affect a subject's intimacy behavior (Breed, 1972; Coutts & Schneider, 1976). Capella and Greene (1982) conclude that "the general pattern of results in adult dyads shows that persons match one another in objective speech (rate, latency, duration, and loudness), eye gaze, and verbal disclosure but that they compensate in response to excessive proximity and excessively intimate questions" (p. 91).

Unfortunately, Argyle and Dean's (1965) compensation corollary is often the only part of their theory that is discussed (e.g., Anderson & Anderson, 1982; Capella & Greene, 1982). Don't misjudge this relatively minor appendage as the central theme of their theory, though! Doing so both misunderstands their theoretical predictions and excludes much of the theoretical power.

Equilibrium Change Vs. Compensation.   The functional equivalence of the various communication channels allows compensation to occur easily. Compensation, however, is only one dynamic implied by the equilibrium model. Lewin (1951, p. 206) described the tendency for compensatory changes to be limited within the "neighborhood range" of variations, that is, for small deviations from the equilibrium. Once movement leaves the neighborhood range, the forces maintaining the equilibrium break down and the system becomes fluid. A second-order change becomes possible (Watzlawick et al., 1974) created by a radical shift in the assumptions or basic processes of the system. For instance, a step forward and a hug at the end of a personal conversation may move the intimacy out of the "local neighborhood" around an equilibrium point and signal a system change. The development of a relationship, from acquaintance to confidant, involves this sort of second-order change in the way the compensation-equilibrium dynamics operate (Altman & Taylor, 1973).

Various equilibrium changes are possible. The goals producing approach or avoidance may be redefined, so that the gradients are dramatically altered to allow a closer approach. Or the rules of correspondence between forces and behavior may be redefined. For instance, whereas previously a hug or an interpersonal distance of .25 meters would have signalled an unthinkable intrusion for our relationship, it now signifies a growing friendship.

Even within the "neighborhood range" there is a tendency for "circular causal processes" or reciprocity to operate (Lewin, 1951, p. 214), rather than homeostatic processes that produce compensation. In interpersonal situations, one person's change (greater closeness or greater distance) may alter the other person's approach or avoidance tendencies which alters the point of equilibrium, thereby creating reciprocal changes in that person's behavior.

Several theorists have wondered how reciprocal and compensatory processes occur. Most theorists realize that three things are involved—thought, feelings, and behavior—but differ on the order and importance of these influences. Some theorists employ the thought–feeling–behavior model (e.g., Capella & Greene, 1982). According to this model, the other person's behavior violates the actor's cognitive expectations. Arousal is produced in direct proportion to the discrepancy from expectations. Capella and Greene (1982) believed that reciprocity and compensation occurred automatically, solely as a result of the level of arousal. Low to moderate arousal is inherently positive and produces reciprocity; higher arousal is inherently negative and produces compensation. In Burgoon's (1978; Hale & Burgoon, 1984) version the arousal distracts at least some attention away from the conversational content and toward the relationship, producing the same outcomes but with much more cognitive processing than Capella and Greene supposed.

Kleinke's (1979, 1986) attributional explanation of reciprocity and compensation in gaze behavior placed heavy emphases on thought processes. Gaze, proposed Kleinke (1986), results in compensation "when the recipient wishes to avoid closeness with the gazing person and when the gaze is viewed as inappropriate, unmodifiable, and the product of undesirable motives" (p. 90). Reciprocity is predicted "when the recipient is motivated to seek closeness with the gazing person and when the gaze is viewed as appropriate, modifiable, and resulting from desirable intentions and motives" (p. 90).

Other theorists use a feeling–thought–behavior model. A clear example is Patterson's (1976) arousal labeling theory which was reiterated by Anderson and Anderson (1984) in their arousal-valence model. This theory suggests that changes in the other person's immediacy create arousal. At high levels of arousal, flight occurs; at low levels nothing occurs. At moderate levels of arousal (created by moderate changes in the other person's immediacy behavior), reciprocation occurs if the arousal is given a positive meaning, but compensation occurs if the arousal is given a negative meaning. The positive or negative meaning is dependent upon context and history (Anderson & Anderson, 1984; Patterson, 1982).

APPLICATIONS TO GROUPS, AUDIENCES AND CROWDS

The previous section of this chapter specified and elaborated the affiliative conflict theory as it applied to the personal space behavior of a single person alone or interacting with one other person. However, intrusions and interactions often involve more than two people. A person may find herself or himself being approached by several people rather than by just one person. A pedestrian may have to negotiate a crowded lobby past groups of people.

The affiliative conflict theory can be applied to these more complicated situations involving groups, audiences, and crowds. Although more complex, each of these situations invoke rather direct extensions of the two-person situations, extensions that reflect the overlay of several force fields at the same time. The remainder of this chapter explores through the perspective of affiliative conflict theory various forms of avoidance reactions and approach reactions to groups, audiences, queues, and crowds.

Force Fields Created by a Group or Audience

One other person creates an avoidance gradient that increases with closeness. What kind of avoidance gradient do two other people, four other people, ten other people create? The available evidence suggests the simplest sort of answer: Reactions to aggregates of others are *simple additions* of reactions to individual others.[2]

Latane (1981) proposed that the social impact of an audience increased as a function of the number of people in the audience, but that each additional person has a marginal or reduced impact. This relationship is expressed by a power function where the number of audience members is raised to some exponent which is less than 1. Various studies (Knowles, 1983; Latane & Harkins, 1976; Latane & Nida, 1980) empirically derive these exponents as between .4 and .6, with the square root function (.5) being close to the central tendency. Knowles (1983) studied judgments of how crowded an audience would make a person feel. These judgments increased regularly with the square root of the number of people, up to ten, in an audience and decreased with the square root of audience distance.

Research Paradigm for Testing Approach and Avoidance Gradients in Personal Space.   Knowles (1980) reported support for the affiliative conflict theory in Fig. 3.2 from discomfort judgments made at various distances from another person when interaction was expected and when interaction was not expected. In the "alone" situation these judgments increased as a function of distance raised to a power of $-.41$. In the "interaction" situation, discomfort started at a lower level and decreased more rapidly, as a function of distance raised to a power of $-.78$, up to a distance of approximately 2 feet. After 2 feet, discomfort with an interaction distance started to increase, this time as a function of distance raised to a power of .70.

In the Knowles (1980) study, discomfort was always judged in relation to one other person. What would be the effect on discomfort of increasing the number of other people? Knowles' revision of the affiliative conflict theory implies that the number of other people would raise the avoidance forces, since they are a product of the force field created by others, but not affect the approach forces since they are a product of the purposes and goals of the person. Comparing reactions to one and four others in the paradigm that Knowles (1980) used allows

---

[2]These additions created by multiple others are conceptually simple, but may become quite complex empirically. Since the form of the gradients is nonlinear, the addition of several gradients would accentuate the nonlinearity and appear empirically as an interaction of group size over distance. However, when the gradients over distance are described adequately or transformed to linear functions, then the additive properties become simple again. With an additive relationship, group size would increase in the intercept of the gradient but not change the slope.

a rather specific test of the expectation that groups of others would raise the avoidance gradient.

Figure 3.3 presents the discomfort-over-distance curves in alone and interaction situations for three different models. The first model, Model A, assumes that four other people would produce a higher avoidance gradient, but would leave the approach gradient unchanged. Because the avoidance tendencies operate in

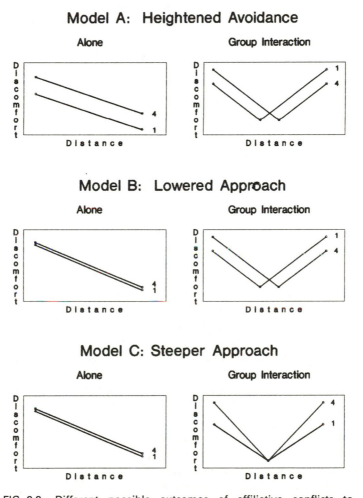

FIG. 3.3. Different possible outcomes of affiliative conflicts to groups: (a) group produces a higher avoidance gradient than one person and does not change the approach gradient, (b) group lowers the approach gradient and does not alter the avoidance gradient, and (c) group produces a steeper approach gradient and does not alter the avoidance gradient.

both the alone and the interaction condition, this model predicts that in both conditions the discomfort-over-distance functions with four people present would be elevated (i.e., have a higher intercept) from the one-person function. Without any change in the approach gradient, all the functions would remain parallel, but the optimal interaction distance to four people would be moved further away.

Model B assumes that four people would lower the approach gradient but would not alter the avoidance gradients. Because the alone condition engages no approach tendencies, discomfort from one person and four persons would be coincident in the alone condition under this model. In an interaction, the lowered approach tendency to groups would increase discomfort (i.e., the discrepancy between approach and avoidance forces) at close distances but reduce the discomfort at far distances. The net result is that the discomfort-over-distance curves would parallel Model A for an interaction, but for different causes.

Model C assumes that four people produce a steeper approach gradient and do not alter avoidance gradients. When the slope of the approach gradient varies, the discomfort-over-distance functions to groups and individuals are coincident in the alone condition, but became unparallel in the interaction situation.

The affiliative conflict theory outlined in Table 3.1 predicts the first pattern. As these models show, the comparison between the slopes in the alone condition reflect the differences in the avoidance gradient. The comparison between interaction and alone conditions reveals the properties of the approach gradient.

The following study tested these models in a role playing situation. The procedures were essentially the same as those described in Knowles (1980).

Method.   Briefly, 12 male and 12 female undergraduates received extensive individual training on how to make magnitude estimations. Experimenters took subjects individually to a large room to make judgments of how uncomfortable they would feel standing at different distances from one or four same sex people. Half of the subjects assumed that no interaction was occurring or implied; they were alone and just happened to find themselves at that distance, as might happen waiting in a hallway around school. The other half of the subjects were told to assume that an interaction was taking place and that they were talking to the other person or people as they would in the hallways around school.

Subjects moved around 12 interpersonal distances from .09 to 5.00 meters, making judgments of how much discomfort they would feel interacting or not interacting at that distance from one or four people. Subjects always faced the other person or people. Using a similar method, Gifford and O'Connor (1986) found that orientation added little to the effects of distance on perceived intimacy. The 12 distances for one person and the 12 distances for four people were randomized. Pools of same sex confederates took turns being the stimulus persons for these judgments.

After subjects completed their discomfort judgments, the experimenter asked

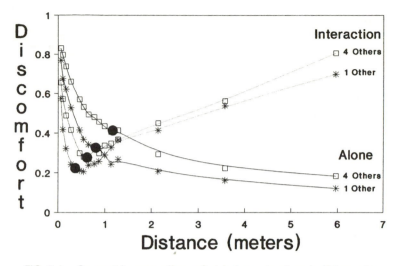

FIG. 3.4.   Geometric mean discomfort judgments at each distance to groups and individuals in interaction and alone situations. The circles indicate the point on the line corresponding to the mean stop distance.

them to indicate their stop distances from one and four others (Hayduk, 1983). That is, the experimenter asked them to walk toward one and four others and to stop at the point in the alone condition where they began to feel uncomfortable, or in an interaction condition where they felt most comfortable.

The stop distances were expected to reflect the decision criteria subjects used to determine how to respond to the experimenter's request. In the alone conditions, stop distances to one and four others were expected to occur at the same degree of subjective discomfort. In the interaction conditions, the stop distances were expected to occur at the points of minimum discomfort.

Effects of Distance.   Figure 3.4 shows the untransformed judgments of discomfort over distance. In the alone condition, the discomfort judgments decreased regularly but nonlinearly with distance. When an interaction was assumed, the discomfort judgments decreased for the first two-thirds of a meter and then increased. When distance was transformed to logarithms, these curves became much more linear, as shown in Fig. 3.5. The linearity indicates that the discomfort judgments could be fairly accurately described as logarithmic functions of distance.[3]

---

[3]In previous research (Knowles, 1980, 1983), I have found that both logarithmic functions (where distance is transformed to logarithms) and power functions (where both discomfort and distance are transformed to logarithms) accurately describe the form of the discomfort over distance. With the present data, logarithmic functions appeared to produce more linear functions than power functions. The logarithmic transformation is employed since the purpose of these transformations is to allow a simple comparison of the linear slopes of discomfort from one and four others.

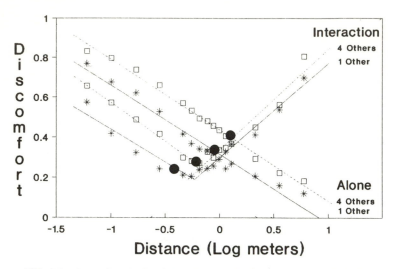

FIG. 3.5. Logarithmic fit of the distance-discomfort relationship. Distance has been transformed to a logarithmic scale. The numbers indicate the slope of the line. The circles indicate the point on the line corresponding to the mean stop distance.

Effects of Number of Others.   The discomfort judgments were greater with four than with one person. After transformation of distance to logarithms, the slopes for four persons were parallel to the lines for one person. In the "alone" condition, the lines differed in intercepts, but were very similar in slopes. In the "interaction" condition, the decreasing and increasing slopes were again fairly parallel. In the interaction situation, the decreasing and increasing lines from four others intersected at a greater distance than the intersection for one other person, but no so much further that the lines crossed to form the "W" pattern depicted in Fig. 3.3.

This pattern of results conforms most closely to the predictions from affiliative conflict theory, depicted in Fig. 3.3a, that the number of others would increase the avoidance forces without affecting the approach forces. These results imply that the effects of four others were an accumulation of the avoidance reactions to one other. The lines were additive over the logarithm of distance.

Stop Distances.   Figures 3.4 and 3.5 also present the "stop distances" plotted on the discomfort curve for each condition. In both the interaction and alone conditions, subjects indicated that they would approach closer to one person than to four. In the alone conditions, subjects approached 22 cm closer to one person than to four people. However, as can be seen in Figs. 3.4 and 3.5, these stop distances represented about the same degree of discomfort. In the interaction conditions, the stop distance from four people occurred at about the equilibrium point, but in the one person condition, the stop distance appears to be somewhat closer than the equilibrium.

Crowding Reactions to an Audience.   In another series of studies, Knowles (1983) investigated different kinds of avoidance reactions to an audience of people who were observing a person. In one study, subjects viewed slides of audiences of different sizes and apparent distances and indicated how crowded the audience made them feel. The greater number of others in the audience and their increased closeness to the subject both created feelings of greater crowding as shown in Fig. 3.6. The pattern of relationships closely paralleled the findings from the personal space study just described. As Fig. 3.7 shows, the logarithmic transformation of both axes converted the slopes of crowding judgments to straight lines. In this study and in two others, the crowding reactions were accurately described by simple power functions: Crowding = $f(N^{.5}/D^{.5})$, where N = the number of others and D = distance.

Accumulating reactions to the presence of others can occur within an audience. Griffith (1921) studied the effects of alphabetically assigned seating position within a classroom on approximately 20,000 test grades. He found a general tendency for grades from the middle of the classroom to be higher than grades from the periphery, especially early in the semester. This effect appeared

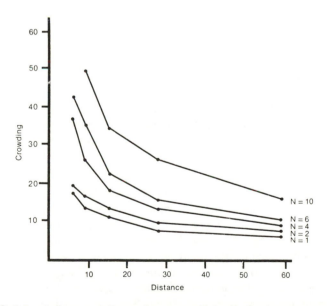

FIG. 3.6.   Judgments of crowding created by 1 to 10 others at various distances. From Knowles (1983), Figure 3. Reproduced with permission of the American Psychological Association.

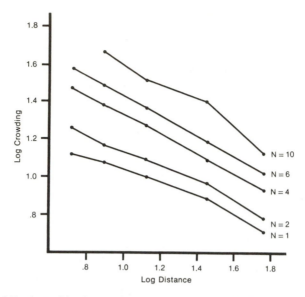

FIG. 3.7.   Logarithmic transformations of the axes in Fig. 3.6 show the power function fit of the relationship between distance, number of others, and subjective crowding. From Knowles (1983), Figure 4. Reproduced with permission of the American Psychological Association.

dependent upon a person's position within the audience. It occurred in small as well as large classes and when the students filled all or only part of the available space. Moreover, the presence of aisles or empty seats reduced the effect. Thus, Griffith's effect appeared to be a product of the proximity of near neighbors, in a way that suggested the effects of overlapping gradients of influence (Knowles, 1982). Consistent with the social facilitation literature, reactions created by the close presence of others facilitated performance on well learned material.

Summary.   These studies show generally that groups and audiences increase the avoidance gradients but not approach gradients. These findings are consistent with the proposition from affiliative conflict theory that avoidance forces are primarily a function of the characteristics of the other. More generally, they show that the simple affiliative conflict theory model developed to explain personal and dyadic spacing extends to the more complex social situations with groups and audiences. The extension occurs by overlapping the force fields of the various individuals. The idea of accumulating force fields is not novel to the affiliative conflict theory, of course. Latane's social impact theory expresses a similar idea in a more general context.

Group Formation by Establishing Approach Forces

The goal and task environment of a group may alter the strength and direction of approach forces, and thereby alter the group's use of space. Different settings and different tasks may produce different seating preferences (Broekmann & Moller, 1973). For instance, Batchelor and Goethals (1972) asked people to take chairs into and sit in a room for an individual task or for a discussion and collective decision. Not surprisingly, the requirement for a group discussion, which established approach goals within the collectivity, created much more regular seating arrangements, where side-to-side distances showed little variability and face-to-face orientation with others was maximized.

Approach forces within a group can be created quite easily. Tajfel and Turner (1979) find that simply referring to 10 people as belonging to two groups establishes a positive ingroup bias. Various field studies have demonstrated that positive attitudes and attractiveness tend to draw people together, while various negative attitudes and feelings tend to separate people (Campbell, Kruskal, & Wallace, 1966).

Ryen and Kahn (1975) studied the effects of experimentally induced ingroup and outgroup biases on how two groups spaced themselves in a common meeting area. Their study showed that the patterns of gaze and seating choice directly followed the approach and avoidance forces created by the experimenter. Cooperating individuals and groups tended to clump together and competing units tended to separate further apart than merely coacting units. Seta, Paulus, and Schkade (1976) found that these spacings were the most productive for the individuals involved. People in cooperating groups learned novel tasks at a higher level when they were close to many other members of the group; competitors' performance, however, deteriorated as they moved closer to more competitors.

In social groups such as Ryen and Kahn (1975) studied, the avoidance forces seem to be stronger and more pervasive than the approach forces. Snyder, Lassegard, and Ford (1986), for instance, found that subjects were less likely to associate themselves with a group (by wearing badges) after failure and somewhat more likely to associate after success. They concluded that group members seem motivated to avoid reflected failure rather than to approach and bask in reflected glory.

Avoidance Forces and the Protection of Group Boundaries

Groups, crowds, and other collective entities may be held together through the glue of approach tendencies. However, they have also been thought of as occupying spatial territories that act to repel nonmembers. Lyman and Scott (1967) noted that an interacting pair of people form a single unit with a boundary around the interaction and hypothesized that "every interactional territory implicitly makes the claim of boundary maintenance for the duration of the interaction" (p. 240). Kendon (1976) described this sort of facing formation (or F-formation) as one where "the participants all face inward to a small space which they cooperate together to sustain and which is not easily accessible to others who may be in the vicinity" (p. 291). These are conceptions, of course, that I think focus inappropriately on edges and spaces rather than on goals and continuities. The research looking at group boundaries, however, illustrates several important properties of affiliative-conflicts applied to these more complex entities.

Evidence from various research paradigms suggests that avoidance reactions to the individuals in a group add together to create greater avoidance gradients for groups as a whole, in ways that parallel reactions to an audience. Research on the bounded interactions of groups find that passersby actively avoid walking through a stationary interacting group (Cheyne & Efran, 1972; Knowles, 1973). The ability of a group to divert potential intruders increases with the size of the group and the status of its members (Knowles, 1973; Walker & Borden, 1976), with the physical closeness of the group members (Efran & Cheyne, 1973), and with the vigor of the group discussion (Lindskold, Albert, Baer, & Moore, 1976; Rivino, 1984). If pedestrians are forced to invade the "shared space" of the group members, they show nonverbal signs of stress and report more affective arousal (Efran & Cheyne, 1974).

Not only do groups appear strongly bounded, other research implies that the impact of an interacting group extends out into the space beyond the group. Knowles, Kreuser, Haas, Hyde, and Schuchart (1976) found that pedestrians alter their pathways to pass further from larger groups sitting on a bench. Edney and his colleagues (Edney & Jordan-Edney, 1974; Edney & Grundmann, 1979) asked groups to mark the boundary around their group space with a line of string. They found that the bounded area increased with group size but only for groups of strangers. One, two, or four friends claimed similarly sized group territories.

The space that a group uses is also protected from invasion even if it isn't occupied. For instance, pedestrians avoid walking in the use space between a window shopper and a store window (Lindskold et al., 1976) or between a photographer and a photo subject (Hosch & Himelstein, 1982).

The approach forces bonding group members together adds additional differentiation of the group from the surrounding population. Group members themselves will often protect a group's boundary and keep themselves separate from nonmembers (Fried & DeFazio, 1974). Pedestrian groups have a tendency to move the group in order to avoid an invasion of their space (Knowles, 1972), and this tendency increases with the social cohesion and with sex composition of the group (Knowles, 1972; Knowles & Brickner, 1981).

Approach Forces and the Drawing Power of Crowds and Queues

Avoidance is not the sole reaction to collections of pedestrians; passersby also can be attracted to a group of people. Milgram, Bickman, and Berkowitz (1969) demonstrated one of the ways in which a collection of people can be attractive. They had stimulus "crowds" of between 1 and 15 confederates gather on a New York sidewalk and a look up across the street at a 6th floor window. From behind that window, Milgram and his colleagues photographed the behavior of passing pedestrians. The experimental crowds induced many passersby to join the crowd and adopt its behavior. As the crowd size increased from 1 person to 15, the proportion of passersby who stopped to join in the crowd activity increased from 4% to 40%, and the proportion of passersby who directed their attention up toward the window increased from 42% to 86%. The increases with crowd size were logarithmically regular, conforming closely to Latane's (1981) social impact model. Knowles and Bassett (1976) replicated these findings with experimental crowds that gazed up into an alcove near the entrance of a university library. Their findings suggested that the distinctiveness and salience of the crowd increases its attractiveness to passersby.

Social groups can also channel preexisting approach forces. Leon Mann (1970, 1977) used confederates to create queues at bus stops in Jerusalem and Cambridge, MA, where queues almost never occurred spontaneously. Experimental queues longer than five people recruited a large proportion of new arrivals to the bus stop, effectively channelling them to join the end of the queue. In these cases, joining the queue was an instrumental response that furthered the goal of getting on a bus, but was not an end goal itself.

The queue is a particular kind of social structure, though. In terms of its approach goal (e.g., getting on the bus, purchasing a ticket), the queue is a linear system anchored at the front. When a box office puts out a "sold out" sign and closes up, the queue dissolves. When the goal object is scarce, the approach desires seem to increase with distance down the queue. Mann and Taylor (1969) interviewed queuers waiting for scarce football tickets and found with increasing distance from the ticket office, people increasingly *under*estimated, in a self-serving way, the number of people in front of them. Only when queuers were well past a point where the scarce resource would run out did they return to more realistic estimates.

The person's position in a queue is a second important anchor, a personal one (Bond, 1985; Brenner, 1973). For instance, intrusions into a queue are primarily a local phenomena reflecting this anchor. Milgram, Liberty, Toledo, and Wackenhut (1986) found that reactions to an intrusion were greatest from the person just behind the intruder, but decreased rapidly from there, in both directions. They conclude, "What is the main bonding mechanism of the queue? It resides in replicated segments. The principle focus for each person in line is the space between himself or herself and the person standing just in front. . . . The queue will hold together if each member defends the space immediately in front, which the queuer often experiences as a zone of special responsibility" (p. 689).

The differentiation of a social assembly into groups, queues, flows, and clusters establishes very complex fields of forces. Stilitz (1969) conveyed this complexity in his description of pedestrians in London Underground stations, particularly how queues waiting for tickets interacted with flows of pedestrians moving toward trains: "A queue will deflect a cross-flow if that flow is relatively light, but will give way if it is heavy. In the former case, queues often follow a "line of flow law." Thus when a queue is beginning to form, people tend to walk along a characteristic path in order to join it. This path might be a straight line or an arched but smooth curve. In either case, as the queue grows, it forms up along the line or curve in question. The natural line of flow to a queue may, however, cut across a stream of people not joining the queue. If this cross stream is heavy, the queue forms up parallel to it" (p. 827).

Nearest Neighbor Techniques for Studying Force Fields

Generalizing from the one person (personal space) or two person (interpersonal distance) case to larger aggregates involving intermingled individuals and groups involves an increase in complexity. Studies of ecological communities have developed some useful conceptual tools, called *nearest neighbor techniques,* that quantify forces of attraction and dispersion in a population (Lewis, 1978).

The nearest neighbor technique involves counting the entities (e.g., people) within a specified area and measuring the distances to their nearest neighbor or neighbors. The actual distribution of distances are then compared to a theoretical distribution based on the assumption that people were randomly distributed in space (Clark & Evans, 1954, 1955; Thompson, 1956). This comparison allows one to describe whether the entities are dispersed more evenly or are more clustered together than a random distribution. Avoidance forces would promote regular, even dispersion; whereas approach forces would heighten the clustered part of the distribution.

Burgess (1983a, 1983b; Burgess & McMurphy, 1982) has used the nearest neighbor technique to effectively study the spatial patterning within a setting. Burgess (1983a) observed spacings in a park and found that the density of the setting decreased the distance to companions, but left unaffected distances to strangers.

Burgess and McMurphy (1982) studied spacing during free play in a nursery school. With increasing age, from infant (6–18 mos) to preschoolers (30–60 mos), distances from adults increased, distances to nearest playmates decreased, and generally space use became more regular. Another study with young children found that "all ages exhibited an aggregation pattern within groups. . . .

Most groups also shared a tendency to avoid or ignore strangers'' (Burgess, 1983b, p. 165).

The affiliative conflict theory deals with forces leading to approach and avoidance of interaction. The nearest neighbor techniques provide one way of studying the consequences of these processes for the clustering and dispersal of people. Burgess' work shows the potential for using these methods to study affiliative conflicts in natural settings.

Spatial Structuring Within an Interacting Group

The studies of audiences, crowds, and nearest neighbors considered so far have not taken into account the hierarchical or functional structure within the group. They have allowed only the simplest forms of social organization, those that differentiate between group member and nonmember or between members of one entity and members of another. However, the social structures within a group should alter, channel, redirect, or at least differentiate the patterns of approach and avoidance tendencies.

Laboratory studies of reactions to crowding tend to find that when all group members are equivalent in status, males respond negatively to close, crowded conditions, whereas females tend to respond positively (Freedman, Levy, Buchanan, & Price, 1972; Ross, Layton, Erickson, & Schopler, 1973). However, this pattern breaks down when a role/status structure is introduced. Giesen and Hendrick (1977) found that a group moderator's sex rather than member sex determined these effects. With a male moderator, both male and female subjects felt more comfortable far away, but with a female moderator, subjects of both sexes felt more comfortable close. Baum and Koman (1976) found that anticipating a structured discussion led by a moderator dampened their subject's reactions to expected crowded conditions.

The approach and avoidance goals of a formal or strong leader have the power to become the goals for the group and, therefore, set its spatial agenda. Barrios and Giesen (1977) used an overheard conversation to establish the expectation that a group moderator would be hostile or friendly. Subjects then entered a room and selected where to sit for a group discussion. With a hostile moderator, subjects sat further apart from one another (1.41m) than with a friendly experimenter (1.18m). Dean, Willis, and Hewitt (1975) studied the spatial characteristics of encounters between military personnel of different rank. They found that interactions with superiors in rank occurred at greater distance if the lower rank initiated them but were unrelated to rank if the higher rank initiated them.

CONCLUSION

The previous sections reviewed the role of space and location in the dynamics of individuals and groups. The affiliative conflict theory (Argyle & Dean, 1965; Knowles, 1980) provided the specific theoretical structure for this presentation.

However, the goal-oriented, motivational approach of Lewin (1938, 1951) provided the deeper framework for understanding both the broader implications and the psychological meaningfulness of affiliative conflict theory. From this broad foundation, the revised affiliative conflict theory allows many different issues to be connected under the same theoretical umbrella.

First, the theory emphasizes the fact that moving toward others is a very different process than moving away from them. Approach forces are under the control of the person and are dependent on the wishes and goals of that person. Avoidance forces are created, like Lewinian power fields, by the characteristics of the others. Attractive, positive, weak others lead to low avoidance while unattractive, negative, potent others lead to high avoidance.

Second, the avoidance responses to and within groups and audiences are additive functions of reactions to individuals. Although I described these as "simple additions," their simplicity is masked by the nonlinear nature of the force and power fields.

Third, approach responses to groups seem not to be simple additions to responses to individuals. When a group is the object of approach, it, and not an aggregate of individuals, is the entity of concern for these goals (Wilder, 1977). Also, the social structure of a group alters attention and approach responses in ways that are not simple additions of responses to individuals.

Fourth, the affiliative conflict theory is a theory of the force fields at the moment, but the moment changes, and often it changes quite rapidly. The affiliative conflict theory is not a theory dealing with the standing features or initial conditions of an interaction. Rather it is a theory that requires a fluid, dynamic, recursive changing of the goals, forces, and fields.

Is the task finished? Is the theorizing complete? No, not at all. There are a number of unfinished, underdeveloped issues that are left to complete.

A primary weakness of this approach is its inattention to the interdependency. The goals and forces employed in the affiliative conflict theory describe only *one person*'s psychological understanding. The affiliative conflict, though, involves at least two people, the actor and the other person, each of whom responds to their own approach and avoidance fields. In most interactions, the goals, paths, equilibria points are (a) negotiated by both parties, and (b) shared in common. That most basic of questions for the study of groups, "How do we move from the individual perspective of one actor to common, shared, or intersubjective perspective of the interacting dyad or group?", applies to their spatial behavior as well (Gifford, 1982). I have dealt in this chapter with how individual fields of force overlay. A fuller theory of spatial behavior will go on to explain how individual fields integrate.

A second unfinished part of the theory concerns the nature of distance in this model and the limits of its external validity. Is this a theory of geographic location dealing with interpersonal spacing? Or is distance only a concrete metaphor for the more general feeling of a close interpersonal relationship such as would result from self-disclosure, affiliation, or a sense of community? Geographic distance does have the virtue of being concretely operational and measurable on a ratio scale. It is very unlikely that the properties of the approach and avoidance gradients illustrated in this chapter could have been identified or tested with a more abstract dimension of interpersonal closeness. But the ideas and the perspective do apply easily to other aspects of human interaction.

Let me complete this chapter with a final metaphor, one that was really my first clear metaphor for affiliative conflicts in personal space. In the fall of 1977, I was puzzling in earnest about the lack of integration between the literatures dealing with personal space invasions and interaction distance. One night I had a dream of a little child running down a beach toward a toy in the water, only to be driven back by the roar of the waves. I woke up, instantly recognizing both the scene, as Lewin's (1951) vivid description of an approach-avoidance conflict, and its meaning for my puzzle. His image still captures the essence of this chapter for me.

> a child of three years is trying to seize a toy swan from the waves on the seashore. Following the forces corresponding to the positive valence of the swan, the child will approach the swan. If, however, he comes too close to the waves, the force away from the waves may be greater than those toward the swan. In this case the child will retreat. . . . There exists . . . an equilibrium between the opposing forces at point E where their strengths are equal. . . . The children may be observed wavering around this point of equilibrium until one of the forces becomes dominant as a result of changes of circumstances or of a decision'' (p. 264).

ACKNOWLEDGMENTS

Research described in this chapter was aided by National Science Foundation Grant BNS80-16202.

REFERENCES

Aiello, J. R. (1977a). A further look at equilibrium theory: Visual interaction as a function of interpersonal distance. *Environmental Psychology and Nonverbal Behavior, 1,* 122–140.

Aiello, J. R. (1977b). Visual interaction at extended distances. *Personality and Social Psychology Bulletin, 3,* 83–86.

Aiello, J. R. (1987). Human spatial behavior. In D. Stokols & I. Altman (Eds.), *Handbook of Environmental Psychology.* New York: Wiley.

Aiello, J. R., & Thompson, D. E. (1980). When compensation fails: Mediating effects of sex and locus of control at extended interaction distances. *Basic and Applied Social Psychology, 1,* 65–82.

Altman, I., & Taylor, D. A. (1973). *Social penetration: The development of interpersonal relationships.* New York: Holt, Rinehart and Winston.

Anderson, P. A., & Anderson, J. F. (1984). The exchange of nonverbal intimacy: A critical review of dyadic models. *Journal of Nonverbal Behavior, 8,* 327–349.

Argyle, M., & Cook, M. (1976). *Gaze and mutual gaze.* Cambridge, England: Cambridge University Press.

Argyle, M., & Dean, J. (1965). Eye contact, distance, and affiliation. *Sociometry, 28,* 289–304.

Argyle, M., & Ingham, R. (1972). Gaze, mutual gaze, and proximity. *Semiotica, 6,* 32–49.

Banziger, G., & Simmons, R. (1984). Emotion, attractiveness, and interpersonal space. *Journal of Social Psychology, 124,* 255–256.

Barrios, B., & Giesen, M. (1977). Getting what you expect: Effects of expectation on intragroup attraction and interpersonal distance. *Personality and Social Psychology Bulletin, 3,* 87–90.

Batchelor, J. P., & Goethals, G. R. (1972). Spatial arrangements in freely formed groups. *Sociometry, 35,* 270–279.

Baum, A., & Koman, S. (1976). Differential response to anticipated crowding: Psychological effects of social and spatial density. *Journal of Personality and Social Psychology, 34,* 526–536.

Bond, C. F., Jr. (1985). The next-in-line effect: Encoding or retrieval deficit? *Journal of Personality and Social Psychology, 48,* 853–862.

Borden, R. J. (1980). Audience influence. In P. B. Paulus, (Ed.), *Psychology of group influence.* Hillsdale, NJ: Lawrence Erlbaum Associates.

Breed, G. (1972). The effect of intimacy: Reciprocity or retreat? *British Journal of Social and Clinical Psychology, 11,* 135–142.

Brenner, M. (1973). The next-in-line effect. *Journal of Verbal Learning and Verbal Behavior, 12,* 320–323.

Broekmann, N. C., & Moller, A. T. (1973). Preferred seating position and distance in various situations. *Journal of Counseling Psychology, 20,* 504–508.

Burgess, J. W. (1983a). Interpersonal spacing behavior between surrounding nearest neighbors reflects both familiarity and environmental density. *Ethology and Sociobiology, 4,* 11–17.

Burgess, J. W. (1983b). Developmental trends in proxemic spacing behavior between surrounding companions and strangers in casual groups. *Journal of Nonverbal Behavior, 7,* 158–169.

Burgess, J. W., & McMurphy, D. (1982). The development of proxemic spacing behavior: Children's distances to surrounding playmates and adults change between 6 months and 5 years of age. *Developmental Psychobiology, 15,* 557–567.

Burgoon, J. K. (1978). A communication model of personal space violations: Explication and an initial test. *Human Communication Research, 4,* 129–142.

Campbell, D. T., Kruskal, W. H., & Wallace, W. P. (1966). Seating aggregation as an index of attitude. *Sociometry, 29,* 1–15.

Cappella, J. N., & Greene, J. O. (1982). A discrepancy-arousal explanation of mutual influence in expressive behavior for adult and infant-adult interaction. *Communication Monographs, 49,* 89–114.

Cappella, J. N., & Greene, J. O. (1984). The effects of distance and individual differences in arousability on nonverbal involvement: A test of discrepancy-arousal theory. *Journal of Nonverbal Behavior, 8,* 259–286.

Cheyne, J. A., & Efran, M. G. (1972). The effect of spatial and interpersonal variables on the invasion of group controlled territories. *Sociometry, 35,* 477–489.

Clark, P. J., & Evans, F. C. (1954). Distance to nearest neighbor as a measure of spatial relationships in populations. *Ecology, 35,* 445–453.

Clark, P. J., & Evans, F. C. (1955). On some aspects of spatial pattern in biological populations. *Science, 121,* 397–398.

Coutts, L. M., & Ledden, M. (1977). Nonverbal compensatory reactions to changes in interpersonal proximity. *Journal of Social Psychology, 102,* 283–290.

Coutts, L. M., & Schneider, F. W. (1976). Affiliative conflict theory: An investigation of the intimacy equilibrium and compensation hypothesis. *Journal of Personality and Social Psychology, 34,* 1135–1142.

Dean, L. M., Willis, F. N., & Hewitt, J. (1975). Initial interaction distance among individuals equal and unequal in military rank. *Journal of Personality and Social Psychology, 32,* 294–299.

Dosey, M., & Meisels, M. (1969). Personal space and self-protection. *Journal of Personality and Social Psychology, 11,* 93–97.

Duke, M. P., & Nowicki, S., Jr. (1972). A new measure and social learning model for interpersonal distance. *Journal of Experimental Research in Personality, 6,* 1–16.

Edney, J. J., & Jordan-Edney, N. L. (1974). Territorial spacing on a beach. *Sociometry, 37,* 92–104.

Edney, J. J., & Grundmann, M. J. (1979). Friendship, group size and boundary size: Small group spaces. *Small Group Behavior, 10,* 124–135.

Efran, M. G., & Cheyne, J. A. (1973). Shared space: The cooperative control of spatial areas by two interacting individuals. *Canadian Journal of Behavioral Science, 5,* 201–210.

Efran, M. G., & Cheyne, J. A. (1974). Affective concomitants of the invasion of shared space: Behavioral, physiological, and verbal indicators. *Journal of Personality and Social Psychology, 29,* 219–226.

Esser, A. H. (1970). Interactional hierarchy and power structure on a psychiatric ward. In S. Hutt & C. Hutt (Eds.), *Behavioral studies in psychiatry.* New York: Pergamon.

Evans, G. W., & Howard, R. B. (1973). Personal space. *Psychological Bulletin, 80,* 334–344.

Freedman, J. L., Levy, A., Buchanan, R., & Price, J. (1972). Crowding and human aggressiveness. *Journal of Experimental Social Psychology, 8,* 528–548.

Fried, M. L., & DeFazio, V. J. (1974). Territoriality and boundary conflicts in the subway. *Psychiatry, 37,* 47–59.

Giesen, M., & Hendrick, C. (1977). Physical distance and sex in moderated groups: Neglected factors in small group interaction. *Memory and Cognition, 5,* 79–83.

Gifford, R. (1982). Projected interpersonal distance and orientation choices: Personality, sex, and social situation. *Social Psychology Quarterly, 45,* 145–152.

Gifford, R., & Gallagher, T. M. B. (1985). Sociability: Personality, social context, and physical setting. *Journal of Personality and Social Psychology, 48,* 1015–1023.

Gifford, R., & O'Connor, B. (1986). Nonverbal intimacy: Clarifying the role of seating distance and orientation. *Journal of Nonverbal Behavior, 10,* 207–214.

Goffman, E. (1971). *Relations in public.* New York: Basic Books.

Griffith, C. R. (1921). A comment upon the psychology of the audience. *Psychological Monographs, 30*(136), 36–47.

Hale, J. L., & Burgoon, J. K. (1984). Models of reactions to changes in nonverbal immediacy. *Journal of Nonverbal Behavior, 8,* 287–315.

Hall, E. T. (1966). *The hidden dimension.* Garden City, NY: Doubleday.

Hartnett, J. J., Bailey, K. G., & Gibson, F. W., Jr. (1970). Personal space as influenced by sex and type of movement. *Journal of Psychology, 76,* 139–144.

Hayduk, L. A. (1983). Personal space: Where we now stand. *Psychological Bulletin, 94,* 293–335.

Hayduk, L. A. (1985). Personal space: The conceptual measurement implication of structural equation models. *Canadian Journal of Behavioral Science, 17,* 140–149.

Hediger, H. (1950). *Wild animals in captivity.* London: Butterworth.

Horowitz, M. J., Duff, D. F., & Stratton, L. O. (1964). Body-buffer zone. *Archives of General Psychiatry, 11,* 651–656.

Hosch, H. M., & Himelstein, P. (1982). Factors influencing the violation of space between a photographer and subject. *Journal of Psychology, 111,* 277–283.

Joreskog, K. G., & Sorbom, D. (1981). *LISREL V; Analysis of linear structural relationships by the method of maximum likelihood.* Chicago: International Educational Services.

Kendon, A. (1976). The F-Formation system: The spatial organization of social encounters. *Man-Environment Systems, 6*, 291–296.

Kendon, A. (1977). *Studies in the behavior or social interaction.* New York: Humanities Press.

Kinzel, A. F. (1970). Body-buffer zone in violent prisoners. *American Journal of Psychiatry, 127*, 59–64.

Kleinke, C. L. (1979). Effects of personal evaluations. In G. J. Chelune and Associates, *Self-disclosure: Origins, patterns, and implications of openness in interpersonal relations* (pp. 57–59). San Francisco: Jossey-Bass.

Kleinke, C. L. (1986). Gaze and eye contact: A research review. *Psychological Bulletin, 100*, 78–100.

Knowles, E. S. (1972). Boundaries around social space: Dyadic responses to an invader. *Environment and Behavior, 4*, 437–445.

Knowles, E. S. (1973). Boundaries around group interaction: The effect of group size and member status on boundary permeability. *Journal of Personality and Social Psychology, 26*, 327–331.

Knowles, E. S. (1978). The gravity of crowding: Application of social physics to the effects of others. In A. Baum & Y. Epstein (Eds.), *Human responses to crowding.* Hillsdale, NJ: Lawrence Erlbaum Associates.

Knowles, E. S. (1980). An affiliative conflict theory of personal and group spatial behavior. In P. B. Paulus (Ed.), *Psychology of group influence.* Hillsdale, NJ: Lawrence Erlbaum Associates.

Knowles, E. S. (1982). A comment on the study of classroom ecology: A lament for the good old days. *Personality and Social Psychology Bulletin, 8*, 357–361.

Knowles, E. S. (1983). Social physics and the effects of others: Tests of the effects of audience size and distance on social judgments and behavior. *Journal of Personality and Social Psychology, 45*, 1263–1279.

Knowles, E. S., & Bassett, R. L. (1976). Groups and crowds as social entities: Effects of activity, size, and member similarity on nonmembers. *Journal of Personality and Social Psychology, 34*, 837–845.

Knowles, E. S., & Brickner, M. A. (1981). Social cohesion effects on spatial cohesion. *Personality and Social Psychology Bulletin, 7*, 309–313.

Knowles, E. S., Kreuser, B., Haas, S., Hyde, M., & Schuchart, G. E. (1976). Group size and the extension of social space boundaries. *Journal of Personality and Social Psychology, 33*, 647–654.

Latane, B. (1981). The psychology of social impact. *American Psychologist, 36*, 343–356.

Latane, B., & Harkins, S. (1976). Cross-modality matches suggest anticipated stage fright a multiplicative power function of audience size and status. *Perception and Psychophysics, 20*, 482–488.

Latane, B., & Nida, S. (1980). Social impact theory and group influence: A social engineering perspective. In P. B. Paulus (Ed.), *Psychology of group influence.* Hillsdale, NJ: Lawrence Erlbaum Associates.

Lewin, K. (1935). *A dynamic theory of personality.* Trans. by D. K. Adams & K. E. Zener. New York: McGraw-Hill.

Lewin, K. (1938). *The conceptual representation and the measurement of psychological forces.* Durham, NC: Duke University Press.

Lewin, K. (1951). *Field theory in social science.* New York: Harper.

Lewis, M. S. (1978). Nearest neighbor analysis of epidemiological and community variables. *Psychological Bulletin, 85*, 1302–1308.

Lindskold, S., Albert, K. P., Baer, R., & Moore, W. C. (1976). Territorial boundaries of interacting groups and passive audiences. *Sociometry, 39*, 71–76.

Long, G. T. (1984). Psychological tension and closeness to others: Stress and interpersonal distance preference. *Journal of Psychology, 117*, 143–146.

Lundberg, U., Bratfisch, O., & Ekman, G. (1972). Emotional involvement and subjective distance: A summary of investigations. *Journal of Social Psychology, 87,* 169–177.

Lyman, S. M., & Scott, M. B. (1967). Territoriality: A neglected sociological dimension. *Social Problems, 15,* 236–249.

Mann, L. (1970). Social psychology of waiting lines. *American Scientist, 58,* 390–398.

Mann, L. (1977). The effect of stimulus queues on queue-joining behavior. *Journal of Personality and Social Psychology, 35,* 437–442.

Mann, L., & Taylor, K. R. (1969). Queue counting: The effect of motives upon estimates of numbers in waiting lines. *Journal of Personality and Social Psychology, 12,* 95–103.

Mehrabian, A. (1968). Relation of attitudes to seating posture. *Journal of Personality and Social Psychology, 10,* 26–30.

Milgram, S., Bickman, L., & Berkowitz, L. (1969). Note on the drawing power of crowds of different size. *Journal of Personality and Social Psychology, 13,* 79–82.

Milgram, S., Liberty, H. J., Toledo, R., & Wackenhut, J. (1986). Response to intrusion into waiting lines. *Journal of Personality and Social Psychology, 51,* 683–689.

Miller, N. E. (1944). Experimental studies in conflict. In J. McV. Hunt (Ed.), *Personality and the behavior disorders* (Vol. 1). New York: Ronald.

Miller, N. E. (1959). Liberalization of basic S-R concepts: Extensions of conflict behavior, motivation, and social learning. In S. Koch (Ed.), *Psychology: A study of a science* (Vol. 2). New York: McGraw-Hill.

Patterson, M. L. (1976). An arousal model of interpersonal intimacy. *Psychological Review, 83,* 235–245.

Patterson, M. L. (1982). A sequential functional model of nonverbal exchange. *Psychological Review, 89,* 231–249.

Patterson, M. L. (1983). *Nonverbal behavior: A functional perspective.* New York: Springer-Verlag.

Pederson, D. M. (1973). Development of a personal space measure. *Psychological Reports, 32,* 527–535.

Rawls, J. R., Trego, R. E., McGaffey, C. N., & Rawls, D. J. (1972). Personal space as a predictor of performance under close working conditions. *Journal of Social Psychology, 86,* 261–267.

Rivino, F. M. (1984). Interactional space: Invasion as a function of the type of social interaction. *Psychological Research Bulletin, Lund University, 24*(Whole no. 4).

Ross, M., Layton, B., Erickson, B., & Schopler, J. (1973). Affect, facial regard, and reactions to crowding. *Journal of Personality and Social Psychology, 28,* 69–76.

Rothbart, M. (1981). Memory processes and social beliefs. In D. Hamilton (Ed.), *Cognitive processes in stereotyping and intergroup behavior.* Hillsdale, NJ: Lawrence Erlbaum Associates.

Rumsey, N., Bull, R., & Gahagan, D. (1982). The effect of facial disfigurement on the proxemic behavior of the general public. *Journal of Applied Social Psychology, 12,* 137–150.

Ryen, A. H., & Kahn, A. (1975). The effects of intergroup orientation on group attitudes and proxemic behavior. *Journal of Personality and Social Psychology, 31,* 302–310.

Seta, J. J., Paulus, P. B., & Schkade, J. K. (1976). Effects of group size and proximity under cooperative and competitive conditions. *Journal of Personality and Social Psychology, 34,* 47–53.

Snyder, C. R., Lassegard, M., & Ford, C. E. (1986). Distancing after group success and failure: Basking in reflected glory and cutting off reflected failure. *Journal of Personality and Social Psychology, 51,* 382–388.

Sommer, R. (1959). Studies in personal space. *Sociometry, 22,* 247–260.

Sommer, R. (1969). *Personal space: The behavioral basis of design.* Englewood Cliffs, NJ: Prentice-Hall.

Sossin, K. M., Esser, A. H., & Deutsch, R. D. (1978). Ethological studies of spatial and dominance behavior of female adolescents in residence. *Man-Environment Systems, 8,* 43–48.

Stilitz, I. B. (1969). The role of static pedestrian groups in crowded spaces. *Ergonomics, 12,* 821–839.

Strube, M. J., & Werner, C. (1984). Personal space claims as a function of interpersonal threat: The mediating role of need for control. *Journal of Nonverbal Behavior, 8,* 195–209.

Sussman, N. M., & Rosenfeld, H. M. (1982). Influence of culture, language, and sex on conversational distance. *Journal of Personality and Social Psychology, 42,* 66–74.

Tajfel, H., & Turner, J. (1979). An interpretive theory of intergroup conflict. In W. G. Austin & S. Worchel (Eds.), *The social psychology of intergroup relations.* Monterey, CA: Brooks Cole.

Thompson, H. E. (1956). Distribution of distance to Nth neighbor in a population of randomly distributed individuals. *Ecology, 37,* 391–394.

Walker, J. W., & Borden, R. J. (1976). Sex, status, and the invasion of shared space. *Representative Research in Social Psychology, 7,* 28–34.

Watzlawick, P., Weakland, J. H., & Fisch, R. (1974). *Change: Principles of problem formation and problem resolution.* New York: Norton.

Wegner, D. M., & Giuliano, T. (1982). The forms of social awareness. In W. Ickes & E. S. Knowles (Eds.), *Personality, roles and social behavior.* New York: Springer-Verlag.

White, T. H. (1961). *The making of the president, 1960.* New York: Signet Books.

Wilder, D. A. (1977). Perception of groups, size of opposition, and social influence. *Journal of Experimental Social Psychology, 13,* 253–268.

Worchel, S. (1986). The influence of contextual variables on interpersonal spacing. *Journal of Nonverbal Behavior, 10,* 230–254.

4 Deindividuation and the Self-Regulation of Behavior

Steven Prentice-Dunn
Ronald W. Rogers
University of Alabama

The conflict is ancient. As long as we have been human, we have confronted the dilemma of maintaining and individual identity versus becoming submerged in a group. Both choices are double-edged. The affirmation that we feel when basking in the glow of individual accomplishments is countered by the aching isolation of loneliness. The loosening of our hold on the ego can bring about an emotional communion of a transcendental nature, but it can also lead us to commit atrocities of horrific proportions. The alluring and alarming characteristics of each choice have contributed to a confusing mystique about human behavior, fueling countless speculations about our dualistic aspects, part *human* and yet part *anima[1]*.

It is perhaps easier to understand the need for separateness because Western cultures emphasize its importance. Directly or indirectly, all of the history of psychology has been aimed at describing the origin and development of the individual sense of self. On the other hand, very little scientific attention has been paid to the circumstances that result in the loss of self-consciousness and submergence in collective activity. We have tended to view this aspect as less than human, an atavistic reminder that we are not always in absolute control of our own behavior. Although still in its infancy, our understanding of the disinhibitory effect of crowds is beginning to take shape.

The present chapter has four primary goals. First, we review briefly the major conceptual and empirical contributions of recent theories of deindividuation. Second, we hope to remove some of the mystery and vagueness from the deindividuation phenomenon. We shall describe the system by which people regulate their own behavior and the factors that produce a breakdown in that system. Our third goal is to propose that deindividuation is not a rare occurrence that is limited to spectacular incidents of mob violence. Thus, we apply the concept to such seemingly disparate contexts as prosocial behavior, religious experiences, sports, daydreaming, drug effects, and hypnosis. Finally, the deindividuation construct is compared to contradictory actions aimed at asserting one's individuality and uniqueness.

EARLY THEORIES OF DEINDIVIDUATION

Investigators as early as LeBon (1895/1960) noted that certain group contexts insulate individuals from feelings of social responsibility and fear of reprisals for proscribed acts. Festinger, Pepitone, and Newcomb (1952) labeled these disinhibiting effects "deindividuation," essentially equating the term with anonymity. Zimbardo (1970) defined deindividuation as a process linking external conditions, internal changes, and antinormative behavior, but he concentrated on the input variables (especially anonymity) that would produce extreme violence. Zimbardo proposed a list of input conditions, inferred internal changes, and output behaviors operating in the deindividuation process. Among the antecedent variables are: anonymity, altered responsibility, group size, group activity, altered temporal perspective, arousal, sensory input overload, physical involvement in the act, noncognitive feedback, novel or unstructured situation, and altered states of consciousness. Exposure to these inputs lessens concern for social evaluation, minimizes self-evaluation and self-observation, weakens internal controls based on guilt and fear, and lowers the threshold for expressing inhibited behavior. Output behavior is characterized by absence of external stimulus control, high emotionality, impulsiveness, high intensity, perceptual distortions, amnesia, and great difficulty in termination.

Thus, Zimbardo and other earlier investigators of deindividuation tended to focus on the external conditions producing behavior harmful to others. Research testing the Zimbardo model has tended to neglect discussion of inferred subjective changes in favor of assessing the stimulus-response relationship, especially that between anonymity or altered responsibility and harm doing. Hence anonymity of the subject from the experimenter or victim and altered responsibility have been demonstrated to enhance aggression (see review by Prentice-Dunn & Rogers, 1983). The deindividuation model advanced by Zimbardo represented a considerable clarification over past formulations of the concept. It was the first extensive effort to systematize the relationship between antecedent conditions, inferred internal changes, and resultant transgressive responses. Zimbardo's lists of input variables and output behavior encouraged needed research.

Diener (1980), like Zimbardo, envisioned deindividuation as a process, but Diener lessened the emphasis of earlier researchers on anonymity in inducing disinhibited aggression. He shifted attention to group cohesiveness, collective activity, and an outward focus of attention as causes of deindividuation. According to Diener, these factors prevent people from becoming aware of themselves as individuals. This lack of self-awareness produces a disregard for personal and societal standards of appropriate conduct and produces a responsiveness to disinhibitory environmental cues.

Diener and his colleagues (see Diener, 1977, 1980, for reviews) examined the effects of several variables on socially inappropriate, but nonaggressive, behavior. They also attempted to measure the internal changes hypothesized to occur with deindividuation: lack of self-awareness, lack of conscious planning, and feelings of group unity. Diener and Kasprzyk (1978) found that focusing attention outward rather than on oneself increased feelings of group unity, decreased self-awareness, and correlated positively with disinhibited speech. Diener (1979) manipulated a battery of variables, including group activity and cohesiveness, arousal, and external focus of attention. Exposure to these conditions elicited greater disinhibition of socially inappropriate behaviors (e.g., sucking baby bottles, eating mud, making chimp noises) compared to control groups made to feel more self-aware. Individuals in the deindividuation condition reported less self-awareness, greater group cohesiveness, and more altered experience than controls.

Diener's formulation of deindividuation provided two advances over Zimbardo's model. First, Diener addressed the need for research demonstrating the construct validity of deindividuation, noting the greater appropriateness of stimulus-response explanations of disinhibited behavior unless evidence of a subjective state of deindividuation could be demonstrated. Thus, the primary research emphasis was shifted from identifying external variables initiating the deindividuation process to seeking evidence of subjective deindividuation. Diener and his colleagues found that evidence. Second, the Diener model specified a lack of self-awareness as the crucial mediator linking antecedent variables to ensuing responses. This integration of objective self-awareness theory (Wicklund, 1975) and deindividuation provided a more detailed description of the internal mechanism by which some group settings foster disinhibited behavior. Diener, however, regarded self-awareness as either focused on oneself, in general, or focused outward on the environment. Based on the work of Fenigstein, Scheier, and Buss (1975) and Buss (1980), we suggested (Prentice-Dunn & Rogers, 1983) that attention to oneself has different aspects, public and private. This distinction has crucial implications for deindividuation. As is seen shortly, deindividuation is defined as an intraindividual process in which antecedent social conditions reduce private self-awareness, thereby creating a subjective deindividuation state.

MECHANICS OF BEHAVIORAL SELF-REGULATION

We have proposed that deindividuation is produced by antecedent variables that lower private self-awareness, and thus disrupt the process of self-regulation. We now describe the disruption of self-regulation in much greater detail than we have in the past. Our first task, however, is to understand what is happening within the individual who is operating smoothly according to plan. Increasingly, psychologists have realized that the human nervous system shares many of the operating principles of computers and other machines. This information-processing approach to human behavior has been championed by Powers (e.g., 1973a, 1973b), but has received its most cogent application in the control theory of Carver and Scheier (1981). Control theory proposes that the individual can best be understood as a self-regulating system. How do people regulate their own responses? The major mechanism is the negative feedback loop (Miller, Galanter, & Pribham, 1960), summarized in the following section from the work of Carver and Scheier (1981).

Negative Feedback Loop

A common example of this governing mechanism is a thermostat. A thermostat measures the air and when it senses a discrepancy between the current temperature and the present temperature, it triggers the operation of the air conditioning unit. The air conditioner continues to operate until the discrepancy has been eliminated. Two features of the thermostat are noteworthy. First, the system is called a ''negative'' feedback loop because its purpose is to decrease or *negate* the discrepancy between the sensed air temperature and the preset standard. Second, the system is adjustable. One temperature setting an be substituted for another setting to suit individual taste; however, the basic system continues to operate in identical fashion.

Control theory proposes that humans have reference standards based on social norms, individuals ideals, or habits that are analogous to the present temperature on the thermostat. (See Fig. 4.1). In behaving, we repeatedly compare our present actions to the reference standard until the discrepancy between the two no longer exists. Consider, for example, the behavior required to rescue the victim of an accident. Action is initiated by the realization that a fellow human being is in need of help (perceptual input in Fig. 4.1). The initial comparison of an internal standard (e.g., ''Do unto others.'') to the emergency situation (comparator process) elicits the initial movement toward the victim (output function). This action has an impact on the situation (behavioral impact), which, in turn, is perceived and once again compared to the standard. Thus, as the sequence of behaviors unfolds, these acts are being checked constantly for conformity to the standard. Once the help is completed, a final check reveals that the discrepancy between present behavior and the standard has been negated, much like the thermostat's present temperature being achieved through the operation of the air conditioning.

Thus, as we regulate our own actions, we repeatedly test our present movements, thoughts, and motions against salient reference values, or standards. Just as the target room temperature may be altered, so may the standard be changed

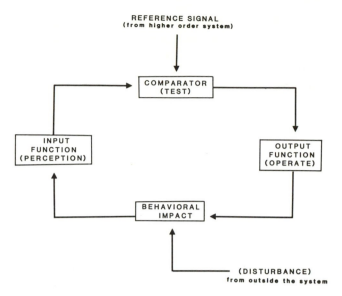

FIG. 4.1.   The functions of the negative feedback loop. From Carver and Scheier (1981).

that serves as the guide for our present conduct. In this way the negative feedback loop describes self-regulation at a variety of levels from very discrete finger movements to complex social behavior.

Hierarchy of Control Levels

Powers (1973a) has proposed that human behavior is organized on several levels each with its corresponding negative feedback loop (cf. Baumeister & Tice, 1986, Vallacher & Wegner, 1985). The lowest level of analysis consists of variations in muscle tension. Although there are several intermediate levels, most behavior of interest to social psychologists occurs at the highest levels of control: the Program level and the Principle level. Carver and Scheier (1981) described the latter as conceptual or moral principles that can be expressed in a variety of domains. Examples of standards that may be invoked at the Principle level include "Be a person of integrity" or "I am patriotic." Either of these principles may be satisfied through several strategies, or programs. The Program level, below that of Principle, consists of "if–then" decisions. For example, one method to satisfy the Principle standard of being a person of integrity is to enact the Program, "If I am asked my opinion on a topic, I will answer truthfully." Another example of a standard at the Program level that will satisfy the same principle is, "If someone helps me, I will not harm him or her."

Why does one need several levels of organization each with its accompanying type of standard? The answer lies in the nature of human activities. We don't simply *help* other people. Helping requires several steps from abstract principles to concrete steps. These diverse activities are accomplished through the existence of a hierarchy of negative feedback loops. Remember, a single feedback system consists of comparing some perceptual input to a standard and, if necessary, producing an output act that will remove the discrepancy by more closely approximate the standard. In the human hierarchy, the "output from a superordinate loop constitutes the specifications of reference values for the next lower subordinate level of loops" (Carver & Scheier, 1981, p. 129). Thus, the output from one loop resets the standard for the loop below it (see Fig. 4.1). This process is repeated all the way down the line from the Principle level to, ultimately, the Intensity level where behavior is produced in its most elementary units: changes in muscle tension.

It may be difficult to understand how the abstractions detailed in the prior discussion are translated into direct actions. Consider the following example from Carver and Scheier (1981): A man makes a pot of coffee for unexpected guests. Viewing himself as a gracious, civilized person, he knows that one strategy for achieving this goal is to provide guests with refreshments. From our previous discussion, the man's activities may be hierarchically described in Fig. 4.2.

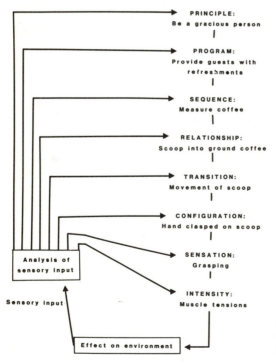

FIG. 4.2. The hierarchy of control system. From Carver and Scheier (1981).

The superordinate standard for this man at the moment is to act in a gracious manner. This standard can be seen to exist at the level of Principles or meta-scripts, in that it can be achieved in many different ways. One specific way to be gracious, when a person has guests, is to provide them with refreshments. The providing of refreshments represents a program, or script. The program character is reflected in the fact that exactly what the man gives his guests depends upon the time of day, and what there is in the pantry or liquor cabinet. . . . The coffee-making program consists of a number of discrete behaviors, some of which must be executed in a specific sequence. For example, you have to put the filter into the drip basket before you add the coffee grounds, rather than after. And you have to scoop up the grounds before you empty them into the basket. Thus there are places in this activity where sequences must be controlled. These events also imply rela-tionships—e.g., the scoop being into the ground coffee and transitions—e.g., the movement of the scoop. At lower levels of abstraction, we have configurations— e.g., the hand grasping the scoop-and sensations—e.g., the physical essence of grasping. And at the very lowest level, doing all the work, we have variations in muscle tensions. (p.132)

This example readily illustrates the several functions required to complete social behavior. In practice, the person's attention is largely directed to the Principle and Program levels because of the myriad of decisions that both entail. Sequence level activities and those below are relatively automatic.

In sum, control theory posits that individuals self-regulate by comparing their present situation to a reference value, acting to decrease the perceived discrep-ancy, and then comparing the two once again. Moreover, this negative feedback loop operates at a variety of levels of control. The self-regulating person moves with little effort through this process from one situation and one standard to others. However, under certain circumstances the system breaks down. In the absence of self-regulation at the highest levels of control, the person becomes deindividuated.

The Concept of Deindividuation

As we saw previously, deindividuation has been viewed traditionally as a triple-component S-O-R process that involves (a) the presence of situational factors present in a group, (b) internal changes involving self-awareness and altered experience, and (c) resultant disinhibited behavior (Diener, 1980; Prentice-Dunn & Rogers, 1982, 1983; Zimbardo, 1970). Recently, we proposed that the vari-ables that theoretically evoke deindividuated behavior may affect public or pri-vate aspects of self-awareness. Public self-awareness involves attention to oneself as a social object. Also concern about one's appearance and the impres-sion made in social situations fall within this domain. On the other hand, private self-awareness refers to focus on personal, covert aspects of oneself, such as perceptions, thoughts, and feelings. Thus, variables such as anonymity and responsibility diffusion reduce focus on public aspects of oneself. Conversely, manipulations involving perceptual immersion in the group and arousal reduce focus on private aspects of self-awareness by directing one's attention away from oneself.

Our differential self-awareness theory (Prentice-Dunn & Rogers, 1983) has drawn much of its substance from the theoretical foundation laid by Diener (1980) in the first edition of this book. Our theory extends Diener's work through the recognition of the public-private distinction in explaining crowd effects on people. When an individual is exposed to the antecedent variables traditionally linked to deindividuation, changes occur within the person that may disinhibit actions, but through two alternative mechanisms. First, anonymity and diffused responsibility reduce individual accountability for acts by making the individual less aware of the public aspects of himself. That is, he is less concerned with others' evaluation of him and has decreased expectations of reprisals, censure, or embarrassment for any actions. The resultant behavior may be explained in terms of expectancy-value theory: The individual is quite aware of what he is doing, he simply does not expect to suffer negative consequences for his conduct. Second, physiological arousal and group cohesiveness (i.e., perceptual immersion in the group) decrease awareness of private aspects of the self. The individual experiences an internal deindividuated state characterized by lowered private self-awareness, with concomitant altered thinking and altered emotional patterns. With a hampered capacity for self-regulation, the individual becomes more responsive to environmental cues for behavioral direction than to internal standards of appropriate conduct. The resultant behavior may range from revelrous dancing to mob violence, depending on the particular configuration of environmental cues.

Figure 4.3 summarizes the two major types of collective disinhibition delineated by differential self-awareness theory. Each category has a set of antecedent conditions that have independent effects of self-awareness and the final action. One category of behavior results from a group member's active calculations that his or her attacks on another person will not be subject to scrutiny and possible retaliation from victims and authority figures. On the other hand, uninhibited acts may result from decreased cognitive mediation of behavior. Situational cues may debilitate self-regulation of a group member's behavior when private self-awareness is reduced. It is important to recognize, therefore, that is only the upper route that produces deindividuation.

The Role of Private Self-Awareness in Deindividuation

As mentioned previously, most of the important decisions made during social interaction are made at the Principle and Program levels of control. The subordinate levels function primarily to carry out the strategies decided upon. At the

ANTECEDENT VARIABLES   COGNITIVE CHANGES   OUTPUT

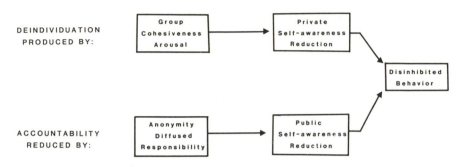

FIG. 4.3. Behavioral disinhibition predicted by differential self-awareness theory.

Principle level, for example, restraints against harming another person are maintained by internalized norms of social propriety. In order to retrieve the standards (i.e., norms, attitudes, prior actions) with which to compare present behavior, we assert that the individual must be privately self-aware. In other words attention must be directed inward to gain access to the relevant reference values. Private self-awareness is crucial to the successful operation of the negative feedback loop at the Principle and Program levels because of the several decisions that must be made.

Deindividuated persons no longer have sufficient private self-attention to work the matching-to-standard process; that is, the comparator is no longer operational at the highest levels of control (see Fig. 4.1). The affected individuals still behave, but cease to regulate their conduct at the Principle and Program levels of control. This diminished capacity for self-regulation increases the likelihood that people will engage in antinormative behaviors. Carver and Scheier (1981) noted that the lower levels of control now governing the individual's behavior have shorter time scales with more discrete and concrete standards. This is precisely why deindividuated persons are impulsive and respond with little foresight. They are inextricably wrapped up in the cues of the moment.

Once deindividuated, the higher levels of control will not influence behavior until private self-awareness becomes sufficiently present to operate the comparator at the Principle and Program levels. This increase in self-focused attention may be produced by a sudden, dramatic change in the perceptual field of the deindividuated person. We recently learned of an incident in which several middle-class youths decided to find and ridicule a derelict. Having located a homeless man sleeping on a beach, the group proceeded to verbally harass and then shove the man. This action, soon frenzied and out of control, escalated to two of the youths hitting the man with sticks. The collective violence came to an immediate halt when one blow to the victim's head resulted in an audible fracture of the skull.

Although gruesome, the above example readily illustrates the dramatic alteration of perception that may be required to return the extremely deindividuated person to normal functioning. With more moderate levels of deindividuation, a return to self-regulation occurs when the salience of stimuli evoking private self-awareness becomes greater than those cues maintaining deindividuated behavior (Prentice-Dunn & Rogers, 1983). As Diener (1980) has explained:

> If a person is being observed by others or is in a very novel situation, the deindividuation situation must be fairly strong to prevent a return to self-regulation. Similarly, if a person is mildly involved in a group and not self-aware, a decision about some extreme form of behavior (e.g., burning down a building) will probably initiate self-awareness. . . . It is likely that only a person in extremely deindividuating circumstances will not be instigated to self-regulation when faced with a choice of doing extremely antinormative behavior. (pp. 223–224)

Data supporting the role of private self-awareness in the deindividuation process are provided by prior studies. Previous researchers have investigated diverse behaviors ranging from socially inappropriate conduct (e.g., playing in mud, writing obscenities, making animal sounds, sucking baby bottles) to aggression against a victim. Persons exposed to manipulations that foster group cohesiveness report feelings of group unity, subjective lessening of individual identity, altered emotions, concentration on the moment rather than the future, and altered thinking (Diener, 1979; Prentice-Dunn & Rogers, 1980; Rogers & Prentice-Dunn, 1981). Although these studies did not explicitly measure private self-awareness, such experiences are likely the result of a lowering of private self-focus that debilitates normal processing of environmental information. The result is the creation of a subjective deindividuated state. In addition, deindividuated studies have found that accountability manipulations do not reduce private self-awareness (e.g., Diener, 1976; Zimbardo, 1970). Furthermore, manipulations concentrating specifically on lowering focus on public aspects of self-awareness have failed to yield any systematic connection with deindividuation (Diener, Dineen, & Westford, 1974; Diener, Lusk, DeFour, & Flax, 1980; Zabrack & Miller, 1972). Taken together, these lines of evidence suggest that it is only when awareness of private aspects of self is lowered that the deindividuation process is instigated.

Stronger support comes from a more direct test of differential self-awareness theory (Prentice-Dunn & Rogers, 1982). Subjects were exposed to two variables, (a) low vs. high combination of personal identification and responsibility for one's actions, and (b) low vs. high combination of group cohesiveness and arousal. Identification and responsibility were manipulated by varying information on whether or not group members were subject to scrutiny by their victims and authority figures. Group cohesiveness and arousal were manipulated through the absence or presence of cooperative games conducted while loud rock music was played.

Four findings were noteworthy. First, as predicted, exposure to the high-group cohesiveness—arousal condition reduced private self-awareness and increased aggression, when compared to the low group cohesiveness—arousal condition. Second, the study confirmed that the reduced private self-awareness created a subjective state of deindividuation consisting of two self-reported factors, Private Self-Awareness and Altered Experience. High levels of group cohesiveness arousal produced less private self-awareness and more altered experience, when compared to low levels of the variable. We had theorized that Private Self-Awareness is the crucial mediator of deindividuation with Altered Experience as a by-product. Indeed, our private self-awareness factor may be viewed as referring to the *process* of being conscious of one's thoughts and moods, whereas the altered experience component refers to the *product* of such self-directed attention (Rogers & Prentice-Dunn, 1981). Third, a path analysis demonstrated that the subjective deindividuated state mediated the effect of group cohesiveness and arousal on aggression. Finally, the personal identification-responsibility combination had no effect on either private self-awareness or the subjective deindividuated state, although low identification-responsibility did increase aggression when compared to high identification-responsibility.

Results of the above experiment have been corroborated and extended in Prentice-Dunn and Spivey (1986). An extreme deindividuation condition was developed and compared to the comparatively moderate version employed in Prentice-Dunn and Rogers (1982). The extreme condition was created by (a) prolonging exposure to the tasks used in Prentice-Dunn and Rogers (1982) from 20 to 40 minutes, and (b) the inclusion of a new activity designed to increase group cohesiveness. The latter task was a ball-and-spiral game, a physical activity that required the cooperation of the group members in order to move the ball to the designated location. Former tasks included collective solution of anagrams that formed the names of rock bands. Physiological arousal was induced throughout the activities by loud rock music (Rogers & Ketchen, 1979). In addition, repeated verbal instructions were given for subjects to focus their attention outward and not on themselves. The extreme deindividuation manipulation provoked dramatically more aggression than the moderate condition of Prentice-Dunn and Rogers (1982), as evidenced by the 21% increase in shock intensity and the 254% increase in shock duration. In addition, extremely deindividuated subjects reported decreased private self-awareness and increased altered experience relative to moderately deindividuated subjects.

In sum, research has now demonstrated the validity of the deindividuation construct. These results illustrate the potentially volatile effects of situations characterized by high degrees of group cohesiveness and physiological arousal. By focusing attention outward, such circumstances (a) shut down the self-regulation of behavior through private self-awareness reduction, and (b) enhance the likelihood that the individual's acts will be influenced by environmental stimuli (e.g., models or weapons).

We readily acknowledge the speculative nature of some of our theory. The role of self-awareness in deindividuation has been amply documented in our research and the crucial nature of self-awareness in control theory has been validated in other behavioral domains (see reviews by Carver & Scheier, 1981, 1985, 1986). Nevertheless, although it is logical to extend all of the control theory mechanisms to deindividuation, such an extension remains to be tested.

ALTERNATIVE EXPLANATIONS OF DISINHIBITED GROUP AGGRESSION

Having discussed group behavior as a function of differential self-awareness, we shall review briefly other theoretical formulations that provide explanations for deindividuation (Prentice-Dunn & Rogers, 1983). These include impression management, emergent norm, and behavioral contagion theories. Impression management theory (Lindskold & Propst, 1980; Tedeschi & Lindskold, 1976) assumes that the predominant concern for individuals in social situations is the image they project to others. This concern about others' evaluations of oneself is highly similar to Buss's (1980) concept of public self-awareness. Lindskold and Propst (1980) reviewed some of the earlier deindividuation literature, correctly concluding that the absence of evidence of an internal state left results open to alternative explanations. They proposed that the deindividuated individual exhibits transgressive behavior simply because of a decreased probability of sanctions for these acts. Hence, the impression management account is highly similar to our postulate that accountability cues lower public self-awareness. The research described in the present chapter, however, demonstrates that subjective deindividuation can indeed mediate the effects of antecedent variables on disinhibited behavior and, in addition, implicates private self-awareness reduction as the crucial instigator of the inferred internal changes. Thus, while impression management is sufficient to explain many disinhibited aggressive acts, it cannot account for deindividuated behavior.

A second explanation, emergent norm theory (Turner & Killian, 1972), posits that transgressive norms emerge from interaction among group members as they deal with ambiguous situations. Individuals in groups are subjected to crowd pressures to conform to prevalent group norms. Thus, when individuals are readily identifiable, more conformity to a disinhibitory group norm is expected (cf. Deutsch & Gerard, 1955). Emergent norm theory would predict that individuated persons would exhibit more aggression than deindividuated individuals. Mann, Newton, and Innes (1982) directly tested this hypothesis under alternatively valenced norm conditions, finding no support for such a prediction. Other deindividuation studies (e.g., Prentice-Dunn & Rogers, 1980, 1982; Rogers & Prentice-Dunn, 1981; Zimbardo, 1970) have demonstrated greater aggression among group members whose actions were not readily identifiable to one another or to authority figures. Hence, while some group disinhibition surely can be interpreted in terms of emerging group norms, the deindividuated behavior described in the present chapter is more accurately explained by differential self-awareness.

A final theory pertaining to disinhibition is behavioral contagion (Wheeler, 1966). Behavioral contagion theory holds that socially inappropriate responses are held in check because of fear of embarrassment or reprisals for such actions. This position is therefore highly similar to impression management theory's attention to public aspects of self. Should others in proximity to the individual behave in an antinormative fashion, a weakening of restraints ensues. However, deindividuated behavior has been found to occur in the absence of observation of other group members behaving transgressively.

In sum, while impression management, emergent norm, and behavioral contagion theories can account for aspects of group disinhibition that are anonymity-based, they are inadequate to explain the deindividuation process.

APPLICATIONS OF DEINDIVIDUATION

In the following section, the deindividuation construct is applied to a variety of behavioral domains. It should be noted that although much of the upcoming discussion follows from the tenets of our theory, it remains essentially speculative.

Aggression

Throughout the history of research on deindividuation, crowd violence has gained the most attention (e.g., Festinger et al., 1952; Zimbardo, 1970). The prose of LeBon (1895/1960) and Canetti (1973) richly describes the restraint-releasing forces present in mobs and the subsequent harm committed. As humans, we seem to be at once repulsed and curious about the breaking of such bonds.

In that differential self-awareness theory was initially proposed to account for collective aggression (Prentice-Dunn & Rogers, 1983), we do not dwell on the topic here. Several studies have now demonstrated that deindividuating contexts can facilitate violence in groups. Cross-cultural survey research indicates this relationship may be generalized well beyond modern Western societies. In a world-wide sample of over 200 cultures, deindividuation, measured as an observed change in consciousness due to chanting, dancing, etc., was found to be significantly related to torturing and mutilating the enemy in warfare (Watson, 1973). Most of our experiments have involved group members who were not provoked by their victims (e.g., Prentice-Dunn & Rogers, 1982; Prentice-Dunn & Spivey, 1986). However, when the future victim has been overheard insulting the group, the harm experienced by the victim has increased dramatically both in intensity and duration (Prentice-Dunn & Rogers, 1981).

Sadly, the subjects (all White) tested in one investigation of collective aggression were very sensitive to the race of their victim (Rogers & Prentice-Dunn, 1981). When groups of White participants were not insulted, they shocked Black victims less than White victims. However the reverse discrimination displayed in order to avoid the appearance of prejudice fell quickly by the wayside when the White group members were insulted. Under these circumstances, the Black victims experienced exponentially greater aggression than did White victims. Our laboratory results have been corroborated by the ingenious archival work of Mullen (1986). Analyzing 60 newspaper reports of lynching, Mullen used an algorithm called the Other-Total Ratio to predict the severity of atrocities committed by the rampaging crowd (e.g., burning, dismembering the victim). Defined in terms of the number of crowd numbers and victims, the Other-Total Ratio has been used in an impressive array of studies to explain group behavior (see review by Mullen, 1987). In the Mullen (1986) study, it was found that "as the lynchers became less self-attentive, or more deindividuated, leading to a breakdown in normal self-regulation processes, which in turn led to an increase in the transgressive behaviors represented by the composite index of atrocity" (p. 187).

Although the results of the collective aggression investigations are disturbing, there is some indication of one possible method to diffuse group violence: Deindividuated persons have been shown to follow the lead of models (Prentice-Dunn & Rogers, 1980; Spivey, 1988). Although aggressive models can facilitate similar behavior, nonaggressive models can reduce the transgressions displayed by deindividuated individuals.

Prosocial Behavior

Upon initial consideration, it seems inconceivable that the same factors that engender the horrible destruction described by Mullen (1986) can be responsible for acts that further the well-being of another person. However, as Diener (1980) has emphasized,

> deindividuation may release behaviors that many consider to be prosocial if these behaviors are inhibited by norms, by fear, or by long-term planning considerations. For example, the deindividuated person in a certain situation might be more likely

to donate a large sum of money to charity, might be more likely to risk his or her life to help another, and might be more likely to kiss friends—all behaviors that many consider mandatory. (p.232)

An extensive literature attests to the importance of a variety of situational factors that influence the occurrence of helping (See review by Latane & Nida, 1981). Studies relying on the historical, anonymity-based definition of deindividuation (e.g., Becker-Haven & Lindskold; 1978; Gergen, Gergen, & Barton, 1973; Johnson & Downing, 1979) do not aid in the present discussion, since the crucial mediator in the definition is public, not private, self-awareness. Increased private self-awareness has been shown to heighten levels of prosocial responding (e.g., Brockner, Altman, & Chalek, 1982; Gibbons & Wicklund, 1982). However, Mayer, Duval, Holtz, and Bowman (1985) noted that the relationship between self-focus and helping is complex. Apparently, increased private self-awareness, when combined with salient requests for help, is sufficient to access the needed standards at the Principle and Program levels. These standards are norms of social responsibility present in our culture and internalized by most individuals. In short, help is more likely to be forthcoming when sufficient private self-awareness is present to operate the negative feedback loop and when the request for help is sufficiently obvious to elicit a feeling of responsibility.[1]

The investigations outlined above illustrate that prosocial acts can emanate from increased self-regulation of behavior. Differential self-awareness theory predicts that the absence of self-regulation may also cause an individual to help another when the appropriate environmental cues (e.g., models, availability of aid materials, strong requests for help) are present. This proposition is being investigated currently by Spivey (1988). Subjects have been given the opportunity to help or hurt another person through the delivery of money or electric shocks. Thus on any single trial, the participants may respond by pressing one of twenty switches, ten delivering various amounts of money (prosocial responses) and ten administering differing intensities of shock (antisocial responses). Preliminary data indicate that prosocial responding can be increased through either increments or decrements of private self-awareness (i.e., individuation or deindividuation). The Spivey (1988) data suggest that the helping behavior observed is explained by two different mechanisms: that described by Mayer et al. (1985) in the case of heightened self-attention and deindividuation in the case of lowered private self-attention.

Religious Experiences

The deindividuation construct may be useful in understanding the behavior of people, especially in groups, who are involved in religious ceremonies. Sargant (1975) and Budzynski (1977) anecdotally described fervent religious activities

---

[1]Of course, as Latane and Nida (1981) explained, the costs and benefits of helping another person influence felt responsibility and the subsequent decision to actually intervene.

(e.g., revival meetings, initiation rituals) in many cultures in which the participants lose self-control and become highly suggestible. Common features of these rituals seem to be a degree of cohesiveness among the collective accompanied by dancing and chanting that may function to increase physiological arousal. When intoxicating drugs are present, they function to augment the activities by further reducing private self-attention (Hull, 1981). It seems plausible to suggest that the trance-like state often described by participants is, in fact, deindividuation as we have described it here.

Many conversion experiences may be explained by deindividuation. This is especially true of cult conversion (Hammersla, 1982). One aspect of cult conversion rituals involves the surrounding of the individual with cult members who repeatedly heap praise and concern for the welfare of the person. Called "love bombing" by some, the individual often becomes swept up in the unity of the group. Other features frequently involve marathon encounter groups and chanting or prayer. When exposed to these influences for an extended period, people often report a sudden dramatic "snapping" (Singer, 1979), after which their critical faculties become severely suppressed. It is tempting to believe that the snapping is a function of deindividuation. More specifically, it may represent the reduction of private self-awareness to such an extent that the individuals involved can no longer control their own behavior at the uppermost levels of control and therefore become highly suggestible.

Nowhere is the human dilemma of the assertion versus the dissolution of the self addressed more clearly than in the domain of religion. The satisfaction of the needs described by Maslow (1968) as self-actualization and transcendence confronts directly the "paradox of isolation and community" (Mullen & Hu, 1986, p.8). This dilemma has received contrasting answers in Western and Eastern cultures. Deindividuation has been viewed as an undesirable phenomenon in Western civilization. Both Cooley (1902) and Hoffer (1951) have equated deindividuation with the death of the psyche. Conversely, efforts to lose oneself, or attain a deindividuated state, result in the satisfaction of spiritual needs in Eastern cultures. Mullen and Hu (1986) discussed these contradictory views at length, after which they concluded, "Deindividuation seems to be an important element in the savagery of a lynch mob, just as it seems to be an important element in the path toward enlightenment. Reducing self-focused attention seems to be a necessary, but not sufficient, condition for both the very worst and the very best of human potentials" (p.10). Although such a suggestion is intriguing, it must be recognized that these two extremes differ along dimensions other than self-awareness.

Other Settings

The cognitive and behavioral changes brought about by deindividuation can occur in domains other than those previously described. Guttmann (1983) provides several excellent descriptions of deindividuation among sports spectators in ancient Rome. Although some spectator violence is calculated, the spontaneous nature of much fan behavior fueled by arousal, alcohol, external focus of attention, and group cohesiveness, is exemplified by the soccer riots that have occurred in recent times in Europe and South America (cf. Goldstein, 1983). On the other hand, most of us have at least witnessed the zany ribaldry that occurs regularly in the cities of the World Series of Super Bowl champions. It seems clear that the combination of fan identification with a team with competitive action on the field or court provides ample kindling for deindividuation (Mark, Bryant, & Lehman, 1983).

Processes similar to those described in spectators occur in athletic performance also. Cratty (1983) identified two types of thinking engaged in by athletes involved in rigorous endurance sports. First, athletes may "remain 'in contact' with their bodies and with various subsystems that produce performance." (p.149). Such associative thinking may be contrasted with dissociative strategies. Although this type of thinking may take the form of consciously engaging in diversionary thoughts, Cratty described another category in which the performer becomes spontaneous and essentially free of thoughts. It seems likely that this latter category, called "spinning out" by Carmack and Martens (1979), may be indicative of the private self-awareness reduction present in deindividuation.

It might be argued that while the deindividuation construct can explain the dissociative cognitions and spontaneity of team members, it cannot account for the same thoughts and actions in, say, a solitary distance runner. We have defined deindividuation as an intraindividual process that occurs in groups. Having demonstrated that group cohesiveness and arousal are the factors *in groups* that decrease private self-awareness, we must recognize that *individual* settings may also disrupt self-regulation through alternative means of reducing private self-focus. Should this be true, then several phenomena that do not require collective contexts may be explained by mechanisms of differential self-awareness theory.

Consider, for example, one of the most prominent theories of hypnosis (Hilgard, 1977). Viewing hypnosis as a state that differs from ordinary waking consciousness, this neodissociative interpretation combines earlier dissociative explanations with newer evidence on divided attention, brain functioning, and information processing. The hypnotized person has increased suggestibility, enhanced imagery, decreased planning for the future, and a reduction in reality testing. These characteristics are almost identical to those describing the deindividuation. It is intriguing to speculate that hypnosis may also be explained by the breakdown in negative feedback loop at the highest levels of control; in short, a sort of deindividuation outside of the confines of a group. Similarly, solitary religious experiences, alcohol effects (Hull, 1981), and even ordinary daydreaming (Fromm & Shor, 1979; Hilgard, 1979) may be related to deindividuation.

DEINDIVIDUATION: AVOIDED OR SOUGHT?

Humanistic theories in psychology have long emphasized the individual's fundamental need to maintain a separate identity from other people. Dipboye (1977) employed the term "identity seeking" to describe the actions that are instrumental to such separateness. Indeed, many thinkers (e.g., Fromm, 1965; Laing, 1960; Maslow, 1968) have equated the loss of self-awareness with mental illness. By extension, the experience of deindividuation is seen as distinctly aversive, leading to vigorous attempts to regain the lost self-awareness that makes each of us unique.

According to Snyder and Fromkin (1977, 1980) people react negatively to the perception of being highly similar or highly dissimilar to others and thus strive to maintain a moderate degree of uniqueness. Maslach and her colleagues (Maslach, 1974; Maslach, Stapp, & Stantee, 1985) used the term "individuation" to describe the individual perception of relative distinctness from other persons (Ziller, 1964). Although the public-private dimension is recognized, the individuation term employed by Maslach has centered on impression management concerns and thus is not a direct opposite of our deindividuation. Nevertheless, the assumption in the aforementioned research has been that deindividuation will lead to reassertion of one's individuality.

In contrast, the research programs of Diener (1980) and ours (Prentice-Dunn & Rogers, 1983) have amply demonstrated deindividuation to be quite the opposite experience to identity seeking. Deindividuated persons report positive affect accompanied by a reduction in self-awareness. In addition, altered thinking, altered emotional processes, and time distortion are reported.

Carver and Scheier (1981) suggested that emotions occur at relatively low levels in the hierarchy of control. Strong emotions may draw attention to lower control levels and away from the higher levels necessary for social behavior (cf. Jacobs, Prentice-Dunn, & Rogers, 1984). Should the emotion become sufficiently intense, "overall self-regulation may adjust in such a way that the level at which the emotion is being experienced temporarily becomes superordinate. . . . As attention is focused at the lower level, the person behaves single-mindedly and stereotypically in a fashion that is dictated by emotion" (p.178). Perhaps the positive emotion engendered by deindividuating circumstances provides more fuel for maintaining deindividuation. By implication, an intriguing (albeit untested) possibility exists that the experience of intense positive affect may, in fact, create deindividuation.

What then accounts for the wide gulf between the two viewpoints just discussed? We propose that the gap may be bridged by consideration of two factors, the duration of the deindividuation and the personality of the individual.

Several investigators (Diener, 1980; Dipboye, 1977; Prentice-Dunn & Spivey, 1986) have acknowledged that important differences may exist between transient and more permanent forms of deindividuation. Manipulations in most research have been of 20 min or less. Prentice-Dunn and Spivey (1986) extended the condition to 40 min, finding a dramatic increase in transgressive behavior accompanied by continued positive emotion. It seems plausible that the deindividuation produced in research studies is affectively positive because it is temporary. By providing for the expression of behavior that is normally inhibited, deindividuation can be quite rewarding (Diener, 1980). At some point, the pleasurable release from ordinary private self-awareness may become transformed into a threat to the individual and subsequently triggers identity seeking.

Aside from the time dimension, the violence of the deindividuation experience may be affected by personality variables. "One reason that deindividuation and individuation may both be sought at times is that there may be different personal needs that deindividuation and individuation serve. For example the affiliative needs may be best met in deindividuating circumstances, whereas a need for recognition and status may be best met by individuating oneself" (Diener, 1980, p.233). In addition to alternative needs being a determinant, the person's self-esteem may be related to the seeking or avoiding of deindividuation. Dipboye (1977) hypothesized that the lower the individual's self-esteem, the more likely he or she was to seek deindividuation. Suggestive evidence of this relationship has been found in a negative correlation between self-esteem and a dispositional measure of private-self-awareness (Turner, Scheier, Carver, & Ickes, 1978).

In sum, people are not consistently driven to seek or avoid deindividuation. Exposure to very powerful situations may at times render the issue meaningless. On such rare occasions, people "get in over their heads," so to speak. In the majority of cases, however, the choice and the emotional nature of the deindividuation is affected by the disposition of the person and the duration of the deindividuation experience.

CONCLUSION

Nearly 2 decades of research since Zimbardo's (1970) provocative article have provided evidence that deindividuation readily explains the complex processes that can disinhibit individual behavior in group contexts. We have applied here some of the concepts of control theory to further elucidate how the self-regulation of behavior ceases in the deindividuated person. We have speculated that the deindividuation construct describes behavior in a variety of diverse settings and that it may be very similar to disinhibition occurring outside of groups. Much experimental work remains to be done, especially in documenting the workings of the negative feedback loop and control levels in deindividuated people. Nevertheless, we hope that the present chapter has further revealed the intriguing, often paradoxical, nature of this fundamental human process.

ACKNOWLEDGMENTS

The authors gratefully acknowledge the helpful comments of Ed Diener and Brian Mullen on an earlier draft of the chapter.

Requests for reprints should be addressed to Steven Prentice-Dunn, Department of Psychology, University of Alabama, P.O. Box 870348, Tuscaloosa, AL 35487-0348.

REFERENCES

Baumeister, R. F., & Tice, D. M. (1986). Four selves, two motives, and a substitute process self-regulation model. In R. F. Baumeister (Ed.), *Public self and private self* (pp. 63–74). New York: Springer-Verlag.

Becker-Haven, J. F., Lindskold, S. (1978). Deindividuation manipulations, self-consciousness, and bystander intervention. *The Journal of Social Psychology, 105,* 113–121.

Brockner, J., Altman, S., & Chalek, H. (1982). Self-focused attention, timing, and helping behavior: A field study. *Personality and Social Psychology Bulletin, 8,* 678–684.

Budyznski, T. (1977). Turning in on the twilight zone. *Psychology Today, 11,* 38–44.

Buss, A. H. (1980). *Self-consciousness and social anxiety.* San Francisco: Freeman.

Canetti, E. (1973). *Crowds and power.* New York: Viking Press.

Carmack, M. A., & Martens, R. (1979). Motivation commitment to running, and mental states. *Journal of Sport Psychology, 1,* 25–42.

Carver, C. S., & Scheier, M. F. (1981). *Attention and self-regulation: A control-theory approach to human behavior.* New York: Springer-Verlag.

Carver, C. S., & Scheier, M. F. (1985). Aspects of self, and the control of behavior. In B. R. Schlenker (Ed.), *The self and social life* (pp. 146–174). New York: McGraw-Hill.

Carver, C. S., & Scheier, M. F. (1986). Functional and dysfunctional responses to anxiety: The interaction between expectancies and self-focused attention. In R. Schwarzer (Ed.), *Self-related cognitions in anxiety and motivation* (pp. 111–139). Hillsdale, NJ: Lawrence Erlbaum Associates.

Cooley, C. H. (1902). *Human nature and the social order.* New York: Scribner.

Cratty, B. J. (1983). *Psychology in contemporary sport* (2nd ed.). Englewood Cliffs, NJ: Prentice-Hall.

Deutsch, M., & Gerard, H. B. (1955). A study of normative and informational social influence on individual judgment. *Journal of Abnormal and Social Psychology, 51,* 629–363.

Diener, E. (1976). Effects of prior destructive behavior, anonymity, and group presence on deindividuation and aggression. *Journal of Personality and Social Psychology, 33,* 497–507.

Diener, E. (1977). Deindividuation: Causes and consequences. *Social Behavior and Personality, 5,* 143–155.

Diener, E. (1979). Deindividuation, self-awareness, and disinhibition. *Journal of Personality and Social Psychology, 37,* 1160–1171.

Diener, E. (1980). Deindividuation: The absence of self-awareness and self-regulation in group members. In P. Paulus (Ed.), *The psychology of group influence* pp. 209–242). Hillsdale, NJ: Lawrence Erlbaum Associates.

Diener, E. Dineen, J., & Westford, K. (1974). *Correlates of deindividuation in college campus crowds.* Unpublished manuscript.

Diener, E., & Kasprzyk, D. (1978). *Causal factors in disinhibition by deindividuation.* Unpublished manuscript. University of Illinois.

Diener, E., Lusk, R., DeFour, D., & Flax, R. (1980). Deindividuation: The effects of group size, density, number of observers, and group member similarity on self-consciousness. *Journal of Personality and Social Psychology, 39,* 449–459.

Dipboye, R. L. (1977). Alternative approaches to deindividuation. *Psychological Bulletin, 84,* 1057–1075.

Fenigstein, A., Scheier, M. F., & Buss, A. H. (1975). Public and private self-consciousness: Assessment and theory. *Journal of Consulting and Clinical Psychology, 43* 522–527.

Festinger, L., Pepitone, A., & Newcomb, T. (1952). Some consequences of deindividuation in a group. *Journal of Abnormal and Social Psychology, 47,* 382–389.

Fromm, E. (1965). *Escape from freedom.* New York: Holt, Rinehart, & Winston.

Fromm, E., & Shor, R. E. (1979). *Hypnosis: Developments in research and new perspectives.* New York: Aldine.

Gergen, K. J., Gergen, M. M., & Barton, W. H. (1973). Deviance in the dark. *Psychology Today, 7,* 129–130.

Gibbons, F. X., & Wicklund, R. A. (1982). Self-focused attention and helping behavior. *Journal of Personality and Social Psychology, 43,* 462–474.

Goldstein, J. H. (1983). *Sports violence.* 20New York: Springer-Verlag.

Guttmann, A. (1983). Roman sports violence. In J. H. Goldstein (Ed.), *Sports violence* (pp. 7–19). New York: Springer-Verlag.

Hammersla, J. F. (1982, August). *Cult conversions: The role of deindividuation in attitude change.* Paper presented at the meeting of the American Psychological Association, Washington, DC.

Hilgard, E. R. (1977). *Divided consciousness: Multiple controls in human thought and action.* New York: Wiley.

Hilgard, E. R. (1979). *Personality and hypnosis.* Chicago: University of Chicago Press.

Hoffer, E. (1951). *The true believer.* New York: Harper.

Hull, J. G. (1981). A self-awareness model of the causes and effects of alcohol consumption. *Journal of Abnormal Psychology, 90,* 586–600.

Jacobs, B., Prentice-Dunn, S., & Rogers, R. W. (1984). Understanding persistence: An interface of control therapy and self-efficacy theory. *Basic and Applied Social Psychology, 5* 333–347.

Johnson, R. D., & Downing, L. L. (1979). Deindividuation and valence of cues: Effects on prosocial and antisocial behavior. *Journal of Personality and Social Psychology, 37,* 1532–1538.

Laing, R. D. (1960). *The divided self.* London: Tavistock.

Latane, B., & Nida, S. (1981). Ten years of research on group size and helping. *Psychological Bulletin, 89,* 308–324.

LeBon, G. (1960). *The crowd: A study of the popular mind.* New York: Viking Press. (Original work published in 1895).

Lindskold, S., & Propst, L. R. (1980). Deindividuation, self-awareness, and impression management. In J. T. Tedeschi (Ed.), *Impression management theory and social psychological research.* New York: Academic Press.

Mann, L., Newton, J. W., & Innes, J. M. (1982). Effects of anonymity–identifiability and group norms on aggression. *Journal of Personality and Social Psychology, 42,* 260–272.

Mark, M. M., Bryant, F. B., & Lehman, D. R. (1983). Perceived injustice and sports violence. In J. H. Goldstein (Ed.), *Sports violence* (pp. 83–109). New York: Springer-Verlag.

Maslach, C. (1974). Social and personal bases of individuation. *Journal of Personality and Social Psychology, 29,* 411–425.

Maslach, C., Stapp, J., & Santee, R. T. (1985). Individuation: Conceptual analysis and assessment. *Journal of Personality and Social Psychology, 49* 729–738.

Maslow, A. H. (1968). *Toward a psychology of being.* New York: Van Nostrand Reinhold.

Mayer, F. S., Duval, S., Holtz, R., & Bowman, C. (1985). Self-focus, helping request salience, felt responsibility, and helping behavior. *Personality and Social Psychology Bulletin, 11,* 133–144.

Miller, G. A., Galanter, E., & Pribham, K. H. (1960). *Plans and the structure of behavior*. New York: Holt, Rinehart, & Winston.

Mullen, B. (1986). Atrocity as a function of lynch mob composition: A self-attention perspective. *Personality and Social Psychology Bulletin, 12,* 187–197.

Mullen, B. (1987). Self-attention theory: The effects of group composition on the individual. In B. Mullen & G. R. Goethals (Eds.), *Theories of group behavior* (pp. 125–146). New York: Springer-Verlag.

Mullen, B., & Hu, L. (1986), July). *Group composition, the self, and religious experience: East and West.* Paper presented at the British Psychological Society's International Conference on Eastern Approaches to Self and Mind, Cardiff, Wales.

Powers, W. T. (1973a). *Behavior: The control of perception*. Chicago: Aldine.

Powers, W. T. (1973b). Feedback: Beyond Behaviorism. *Science, 179,* 351–356.

Prentice-Dunn, S., & Rogers, R. W. (1980). Effects of deindividuating situational cues and aggressive models on subjective deindividuation situational cues and aggressive models on subjective deindividuation and aggression. *Journal of Personality and Social Psychology, 39* 104–113.

Prentice-Dunn, S., & Rogers, R. W. (1982). Effects of public and private self-awareness on deindividuation and aggression. *Journal of Personality and Social Psychology, 43,* 503–513.

Prentice-Dunn, S., & Rogers, R. W. (1983). Deindividuation in aggression. In R. G. Geen & E. Donnerstein (Eds.), *Aggression: Theoretical and empirical reviews: Vol. 2. Issues in research* (pp.155–177). New York: Academic Press.

Prentice-Dunn, S, & Spivey, C. B. (1966). Extreme deindividuation in the laboratory: Its magnitude and subjective components. *Personality and Social Psychology Bulletin, 12,* 206–215.

Rogers, R. W., & Ketchen, C. M. (1979). Effects of anonymity and arousal on aggression. *Journal of Psychology 102,* 13–19.

Rogers, R. W., & Prentice-Dunn, S. (1981). Deindividuation and anger-mediated interracial aggression: Unmasking regressive racism. *Journal of Personality and Social Psychology, 41,* 63–73.

Sargant, W. (1975). *The mind possessed*. New York: Penguin.

Singer, M. T. (1979). Coming out of the cults. *Psychology Today, 12,* 72–82.

Snyder, C. R., & Fromkin, H. L. (1977). Abnormality as a positive characteristic: The development and validation of a scale measuring need for uniqueness. *Journal of Abnormal Psychology, 86,* 518–527.

Snyder, C. R., & Fromkin, H. L. (1980). *Uniqueness: The human pursuit of difference*. New York: Plenum.

Spivey, C. B. (1988). *Deindividuation, modeling, and private self-consciousness: Effects on subjective deindividuation and interpersonal responding*. Unpublished doctoral dissertation. University of Alabama.

Tedeschi, J. T., & Lindskold, S. (1976). *Social psychology: Interdependence, interaction, and influence*. New York: Wiley.

Turner, R., & Killian, L. M. (1972). *Collective behavior* (2nd ed.). Englewood Cliffs, NJ: Prentice-Hall.

Turner, R. G., Scheier, M. F., Carver, C. S., & Ickes, W. (1978). Correlates of self-consciousness. *Journal of Personality Assessment, 42,* 285–289.

Vallacher, R. R., & Wegner, D. M. (1985). *A theory of action identification*. Hillsdale, NJ: Lawrence Erlbaum Associates.

Watson, R. I. (1973). Investigation into deindividuation using a cross-cultural survey technique. *Journal of Personality and Social Psychology, 25,* 342–345.

Wheeler, L. (1966). Toward a theory of behavioral contagion. *Psychological Review, 73,* 179–192.

Wicklund, R. (1975). Objective self-awareness. In L. Berkowitz (Ed.), *Advances in experimental social psychology: Vol. 8* (pp. 233–275). New York: Academic Press.

Zabrack, M., & Miller, N. (1972). Group aggression: The effects of friendship ties and anonymity.

Proceedings of the 80th Annual Convention of the American Psychological Association, 7, 211–212.

Ziller, R. C. (1964). Individuation and socialization. *Human Relations, 17,* 341–360.

Zimbardo, P. G. (1970). The human choice: Individuation, reason, and order versus deindividuation, impulse, and chaos. In W. J. Arnold & D. Levine (Eds.), *Nebraska Symposium on Motivation* (pp. 237–307). Lincoln: University of Nebraska Press.

5 Environmental Influences on Groups

Paul B. Paulus
Dinesh Nagar
University of Texas at Arlington

Environmental psychology has been an active area of concern for the past 20 years. It deals with the impact of the physical and natural environment on individual and group behavior. However, the major focus of this discipline is on demonstrating and understanding the influence of environmental variables, and not on understanding individual or group behavior. Research in the area of groups has typically focused on the nature of group processes and ignored the potential impact of features of the physical environment on such processes. This is understandable as most of these studies are done in environmentally *uninteresting* laboratory settings which are held constant across the experimental conditions. Yet in these studies some of the laboratory rooms may have one-way mirrors, and they may vary considerably in size, shape, and esthetics. Even if these features are held constant in an experiment, they might influence the generality of the results obtained. For example, mirrors and room size have been found to have a variety of effects on emotion and behavior. Mirrors may increase self-awareness and in turn influence a variety of behaviors such as aggression, conformity, and task performance (cf. Wicklund, 1980). Small rooms have been found to affect task performance, social inclinations, competitive behavior, and jury decisions relative to larger rooms (cf. Paulus, 1980).

Given the evidence that even relatively minor variations in the physical environment can have a significant impact on the effects observed in groups, it would seem important to examine this issue in regard to a wide variety of group situations. Yet there is little theoretical basis for relating the impact of environmental dimensions to such group processes as decision-making, conformity, bargaining, coalition formation, problem solving, and communication. Without some theoretical guidance, research on the influence of environmental features on group processes would seem rather haphazard and uninspired. Therefore, we focus primarily on two different traditions of research that have examined environmental factors on group processes in some detail—studies of crowding, and studies of spatial factors in social interaction. We examine their major findings and related theoretical models. An integrative model of these two research traditions is presented, and the implications of this model for other areas of research in group dynamics is developed.

CROWDING

Research on Crowding

Recently, most of the research on group dynamics in relation to environments has been done in the area of crowding. The primary concern of crowding studies has been with effects of high density conditions on group interaction and performance. Conditions of high density can come about in three distinct ways— increasing the number of people in a particular environment (increased social density), reducing the amount of space while keeping group size constant (increased spatial density), and reducing the distance between individuals (social distance). If social density is increased without commensurate increases in space, spatial density is also increased. Effects of social density independent of spatial density can be observed only when the amount of space per person is kept the same as group size increases. Each of the three dimensions of density has been shown to have an independent impact on individuals and/or groups (see Baum & Paulus, 1987; Paulus, 1980; for detailed reviews). Some of these effects are similar for the three dimensions, while others are specific to one of the dimensions. In many studies and in many real world settings, however, these dimensions are confounded and their effects not easily separable. We provide a brief overview of the major findings on crowding.

Many of the early studies of crowding were done in urban settings. These attempted to relate degree of crowding in different urban areas to various indices of pathology such as death rates, crime rates, mental hospital admissions, etc. Although some evidence exists that crowding in urban areas may be associated with relatively poor health and various forms of social disruption (e.g., Galle, Gove, & McPherson, 1972; Gove, Hughes, & Galle, 1979), the literature has been beset by inconsistencies and inferential problems. Even if consistent evidence for a relationship between urban density and some forms of pathology were observed, one could not eliminate the possibility that individuals prone to certain health problems or forms of pathology gravitate toward crowded urban areas.

Another phase of the crowding research involved experimental laboratory studies. Typically, students were exposed to various levels of density in rooms by varying room size, group size, and interpersonal distance either simultaneously or independently. In most cases students were seated and asked to engage in some social interaction or individual tasks. These studies have provided a fairly consistent pattern of results. Individual task performance is usually debilitated in highly dense conditions, although this typically involves situations in which individuals are asked to perform one complex task (Paulus, Annis, Seta, Schkade, & Matthews, 1976; Paulus & Matthews, 1980). Social interaction effects seem to be gender related, with males demonstrating social avoidance and females more intense social inclinations in highly dense situations (e.g., Ross, Layton, Erickson, & Schopler, 1973). However, gender related effects seem to occur primarily in response to variations in spatial density (Paulus, 1980).

In recent years, a number of studies have been done in naturalistic settings where crowding is realistic and resident choices are limited (avoiding the self-selection problem). For example, some of the college dormitory studies have found that simply adding one person to a two-person room increased a variety of negative emotional reactions (Baron, Mandel, Adams, & Griffen, 1976). Crowding in external areas such as hallways and lounges may also be a problem. Baum and Valins (1977) compared students living in four- to six-person suites with three bedrooms, a lounge, and a bathroom to those who shared a double-occupancy room in corridor dormitories with common bath and lounge areas for 34 students. It was found that relative to residents of the suites, corridor residents felt crowded and exhibited tendencies toward social withdrawal both inside and outside of the dormitory environment.

Prisons can also be crowded in a variety of ways. They may sometimes house considerably more inmates than the original designed capacity. This condition may make it difficult to find adequate sleeping space for all of the inmates. Two or more inmates may be assigned to live in rooms designed for one person. Dormitories may become increasingly crowded by the addition of beds and the use of double, rather than single bunks. Furthermore, overcrowded prisons may put a strain on the usage of a wide variety of prison resources such as cafeterias, recreation areas, and bathroom facilities. It is also possible that large prisons that hold many inmates may be experienced as more crowded than smaller prisons, even though both may have adequate facilities for their inmates. Large prisons would typically be associated with greater social density levels in general usage areas such as hallways and cafeterias.

Evidence suggests that each of the above features of crowded prisons may be associated with deleterious effects on inmates' feelings and health. Increased numbers of inmates in prisons or prison systems without commensurate increases in facilities have been associated with increased rates of psychiatric commitments, disciplinary infractions, suicides, and death rates among older inmates. Large prisons evidenced higher levels of psychiatric commitments and death rates among older inmates than smaller prisons (Cox, Paulus, & McCain, 1984).

As the number of inmates in a housing unit increase, feelings of crowding and illness complaint rates are increased. For example, large open dormitories which may house from 20 to 70 inmates were associated with twice as high a rate of illness complaints as single or double cells. Other studies have found that inmates in such dorms have elevated levels of blood pressure, epinephrine, and norepinephrine (D'Atri & Ostfeld, 1975; Schaeffer, Baum, Paulus, & Gaes, 1988).

In some prison studies, it was feasible to determine whether the number of people in a housing unit, the amount of space, or both were important in the observed effects of crowded housing. In general, the number of people in a unit appeared to be the most important predictor of crowding reactions. There is evidence that amount of space per person had little impact, whereas in other studies, where space reached rather low levels (e.g., 30 square feet per person or less), there were apparent negative effects (Paulus, 1988). Consistent with the college dormitory studies, having to contend with large numbers of people in one's living environment appears to be a significant source of crowding stress. Low levels of spatial density may contribute to additional crowding stress by increasing the likelihood of negative social encounters.

Theoretical Models of Crowding

Considerable evidence regarding the effects of crowding on individual and group behavior, emotion, and health has been produced. These results have inspired a broad variety of theoretical models. Some view crowding as a stressor in that it shares many characteristics commonly associated with stressful stimuli (Baum & Paulus, 1987). Others have emphasized the role of lack of control (e.g., Baron & Rodin, 1978), high levels of social stimulation (e.g., Cohen, 1978; Saegert, 1978), arousal (Evans, 1978; Paulus, 1980), and interference (Schopler & Stockdale, 1977; Stokols, 1976).

Most of the existing models are somewhat limited in scope and focus on specific aspects of dense environments. However, some integrative models have been proposed that encompass a variety of processes involved in group behavior in crowded settings. We review these models as a way of summarizing the basic issues and theoretical considerations in the crowding area that are relevant for understanding environmental influences on group behavior.

Multidensity model.   The multidensity model by Paulus (1980) was designed to summarize the major concepts and findings of the crowding area and to distinguish clearly between the distinct objective dimensions of high density situations. As seen in Fig. 5.1, social density and social distance are seen as affecting perceptions of crowding and may generate stimulus overload, interference, and social fears (or arousal). In addition, social density may lead to a scarcity of resources. Whether these experiences produce strongly negative reac-

Antecedents		Mediators	Moderators	Consequents

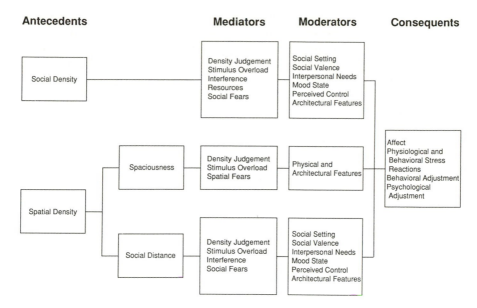

FIG. 5.1.   A multidensity model of crowding. From Paulus (1980).

tions will depend on a variety of variables that may moderate their impact. Thus, if one is in a positive or cooperative social setting, a situation where others are friends or friendly (positive valence), or the architectural features help regulate interactions (e.g., partitions or private rooms), the potential negative impact of social density and social distance may be much reduced. Similarly, if one desires interaction, is in a positive initial mood state, or feels some degree of control over one's interactions, highly dense environments should be less aversive.

Spaciousness, the amount of space available for each person in a particular area, is expected to be related to density judgments, feelings of overload, and spatial fears (e.g., claustrophobia). Physical features of the environment such as windows and high ceilings may affect the feelings of spatial crowding. It is quite evident from this model that the major effects of crowding are attributed to the social components—social density and social distance. This is consistent with evidence from a wide variety of studies (e.g., Baum & Valins, 1979; Nogami, 1976; Paulus et al., 1976). Moreover, the effect of spaciousness is expected to be moderated by a different set of factors than social density and social distance. Much evidence exists for the role of the various moderator variables, but since social and spatial density, as well as social distance, are often confounded, the precise relationship of the moderator variables to these three different density factors remains to be firmly established.

The above model was designed to deal with the broad range of effects observed in crowding studies, especially in regard to situations where the three objective aspects of crowding are manipulated or can be independently assessed. This has been the case mostly in laboratory studies and a few of the field studies. However, in most realistic crowding situations, all three of these components tend to be highly confounded, so that their differential impacts are difficult to determine. Furthermore, in these settings the nature and frequency of the interactions of the people in the crowded situation may become an important consideration. One may have to deal with a large number of unwanted and uncontrollable interactions (Baum & Valins, 1979). Consequently, Cox et al. (1984) proposed a social interaction-demand model which focuses directly on the nature of the interactions in crowded environments instead of the different types of density.

Social interaction-demand model.   The social interaction demand model incorporates many of the concepts discussed earlier. In most realistic crowding situations, the important role of the various types of density is attributed to their impact on social interactions. Increased density in terms of the number of people and their social distance is likely to interfere with desired activities (reduced access to facilities, lack of privacy, etc.), increase social stimulation or cognitive load (demands of dealing with increased interaction, noise, etc.), and increase uncertainty (unpredictability and lack of control over interactions). As seen in Fig. 5.2, each of these three components of high density conditions is predicted to be associated with somewhat distinct emotional states; interference with frustration, cognitive load with cognitive strain, and uncertainty with fear/anxiety. These emotional states are seen as responsible for the various mental, physical, and socially deleterious effects of crowded situations. The model also suggests that the verbal labels that one attaches to one's experiences in these environments

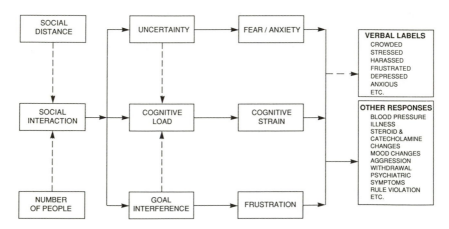

FIG. 5.2.   A social interaction-demand model of crowding. From Cox et al. (1984).

may be relatively independent from the other outcomes. That is, one's rating of the environment may be particularly sensitive to one aspect of the environment (e.g., cognitive load), while various physiological or behavioral indices may be more sensitive to others (e.g., uncertainty—Paulus, 1988).

The main contribution of this model is in its focus on the different components of social interaction in dense environments and the unique effects of these different components. It also highlights the possible independence of verbal, behavioral, and physiological outcomes of high density conditions. Other scholars have also analyzed in detail the social interaction processes involved in crowded settings (e.g., Baldassare, 1979; Epstein, 1981; Gove et al., 1979) and suggest that these processes are important in the understanding of crowding phenomena. Yet these perspectives do not specify clearly or comprehensively how specific components of the interactions in crowded settings may be responsible for certain outcomes in these situations.

Evidence for the Social Interaction-Demand Model

What evidence exists for the various proposals of the social interaction-demand model? In practice it is quite difficult to separate the unique effects of the three components of crowding. One would have to locate or manipulate situations in which at least one of the components was not operative in order to do precise tests of the model. Yet past research on crowding and the research on crowding in prisons can be accounted for nicely by this model (Cox et al., 1984; Paulus, 1988). Furthermore, the research presented in this chapter suggests the utility of the model's various distinctions.

The primary stimulus for the development of the social-interaction demand model was the research in prisons (see Paulus, 1988 for details). One major finding is that the number of residents in a particular living unit (cell, room, or dormitory), and not the amount of space, is the major factor in inmates' psychological and physiological reactions to crowded housing. This may reflect the fact that the number of individuals is more important in producing interactions with high degrees of interference, cognitive load, and uncertainty than amount of space. Large numbers of individuals in a unit are likely to be associated with problems of access to resources such as TV and showers (interference), dealing with or being exposed to many interactions (cognitive load), and coping with large numbers of unpredictable or unwanted interactions (uncertainty). At low levels of space, however, physical interference and the cognitive load of coordinating one's activities may also take its toll. Studies in college dorms (Baum & Valins, 1977) and in the laboratory (Paulus, 1980) have also demonstrated that social interaction and social density are important components of the crowding experience.

In several of the prison studies, double cells and open dorms with 30 or more inmates received similarly negative ratings relative to the positive ratings of singles. Yet only dorms yielded elevated illness complaint rates (Paulus, 1988). The dorms and double cells have similar amounts of space and doubles may involve some of the same interference and social stimulation involved in dormitory living in that one has to share one's bunk and the space around it with another person (the dorms in the studies had mostly double bunks). The major difference between doubles and dorms may be in the degree to which one is exposed to uncontrollable and unwanted interactions (uncertainty). A considerable body of literature has shown that lack of control or uncertainty in relation to a stressful stimulus is important in the extent to which health related effects are observed (Cohen, Glass, & Philips, 1979; Folkman, 1984).

A related finding is that length of time one has lived in a housing unit is not related to changes in one's evaluation of the unit along various environmental dimensions (crowding, pleasant, noisy, etc.). However, illness complaint rate declines over time in a specific housing unit, particularly in dormitories. In this light, it is of interest to note that the only verbal measure to show changes related to time in housing was perception of control over others and one's situation in the prison. Feelings of control increased over time in the dormitories. The parallel between the changes in feelings of control and illness complaint rate is consistent with the control/health relationship observed in other contexts.

These are just some of the findings that led to the development of the social interaction-demand model. Much of the research on crowding in animals and humans can be integrated by this model (cf. Cox et al., 1984; Paulus, 1988). In addition, some findings on the experience of crowding in residential environments are consistent with the model's predictions.

Crowding Experience in Residential Environments

Much of the theorizing on crowding suggests that it is important to focus on the subjective experience of crowding as distinct from the objective density conditions. For example, Stokols (1972) argued that crowding is the subjective experience of limited space. Only if such an experience occurs, should negative effects of density be observed. Other models have focused on the subjective feelings of control (e.g., Baron & Rodin, 1978), and of stimulation overload (Cohen, 1978; Saegert, 1978), as being the important factors in negative effects of high density conditions. Given the emphasis on the subjective experience of crowding, it is surprising that only a few studies have tried to examine directly the nature of this experience (e.g., Gove et al., 1979; Montana & Adamopoulos, 1984; Schultz-Gambard, Feierabend, & Hommel, 1986; Taylor, 1981).

Recently, we have examined the nature of the subjective experience of crowding that students have in their primary residences (Nagar & Paulus, 1987). We employed an extension of a survey developed by Nagar (1985) to tap the major dimensions related to crowding in residential environments by asking about the degree of spaciousness, control, privacy, noise, and relations with others in the home. The items on relations were designed to assess the broad range of positive and negative interactions that might occur in a residential environment, including interference, overstimulation, and uncertainty.

Factor analyses of these items in several samples revealed the existence of four factors—spaciousness, positive or supportive interactions, negative or disruptive interactions, and uncontrollable or unpredictable disturbances from others. In reference to the social interaction-demand model, the disruptive interactions may most closely represent the interference component, uncontrolled disturbances the uncertainty one, and spaciousness the cognitive load one.

In one study we examined the relationship of these components of crowding experience to a variety of outcome measures—sense of psychological well-being, reported physical symptoms, general affective state, and rating of the home and the neighborhood. Most of the students lived at home with their parents while the rest lived primarily in apartments, college dorms, or fraternities and sororities. The uncontrolled disturbance component was the most potent predictor of reported symptoms, with negative relations adding further predictive power. Space satisfaction and negative relations in the home both predicted well-being and affect. However, only spaciousness was a significant predictor of evaluation of one's home. These findings support the notion that different components of crowding may relate differentially to various outcomes. Consistent with the prison research (Paulus, 1988), uncontrollability was related to symptoms and spaciousness to rating of the housing.

Of course, unlike the prison and dormitory studies, students presumably had some choice in where they were living. Thus, type of residence and its density may reflect, in part, various social inclinations of its residents. Those who are reserved or shy may prefer to live at home with their parents, live alone, or at least seek out situations with a high degree of privacy (e.g., private bedrooms). To assess this possibility, we asked students to fill out various personality scales designed to tap social inclinations (shyness, sociability, sensation-seeking, and introversion/extraversion), as well as the crowding experience scale and related housing information. Only introversion/extraversion seemed to be a factor in housing selection. Those who lived at home tended to be most introverted. However, when one controls for type of housing, introversion/extraversion is not significantly related to crowding experience. This suggests that the relationships observed in the first study reflect the impact of the crowding experiences rather than a selection of certain types of environments by different types of individuals.

Individual and Cultural Differences in Sensitivity to Crowding

Obviously, not everyone will react similarly to crowded situations. Certain personal characteristics or experiences may make crowding more tolerable or may aid individuals in coping with crowded conditions. For example, it has been proposed that individuals who differ in status or power within the home may vary in their sensitivity to the effects of residential crowding (Baldassare, 1979). Children may be more prone to the effects of residential crowding since they have less control over the environment and its residents than the adults (Baldassare, 1979; Epstein, 1981; Saegert, 1982). Although some evidence for this proposition exists (Evans, 1978; Gove et al., 1979), the evidence is somewhat mixed and suggests that there may be cultural differences (Epstein, 1981). Furthermore, the presence of children may be a significant source of crowding related problems or irritation for parents (Baldassare, 1979; Gove et al., 1979). Obviously, we have much to learn about the role of status and developmental differences in the family on the experience of crowding. We would predict that if these individual characteristics are related to differences in the experience of cognitive load, uncertainty, and goal interference in a particular culture, crowding related effects will be observed.

Past experience with crowding in residential environments may influence reactivity to present conditions of crowding. If an individual has lived under crowded conditions, he or she may learn to tolerate or cope effectively with such conditions. In the prison studies, inmates who had grown up with 6 or more people in their home reacted less negatively to living in double cells or large open dorms than those who had grown up with fewer people in their homes (Paulus, 1988). Similar results were obtained in a study of crowding in mobile homes (Eoyang, 1974), while a study of tripling in college dormitories (Baron et al., 1976) found opposite results. In a similar vein, those who have lived in large cities react less negatively to crowded prison housing (Paulus, 1988) or medium size cities (Wohlwill & Kohn, 1973) than those who have lived in smaller towns.

The bulk of evidence does appear to support the idea that past crowding experience may to some extent ameliorate the impact of future crowding experiences. Because crowding varies greatly across countries and cultures, one might expect significant differences among populations from different backgrounds. It is often argued that people in crowded countries have learned to adjust to their crowded living conditions (cf. Gillis, Richard, & Hagan, 1986). Yet there have been only a small number of limited cross-cultural studies of crowding (e.g., Anderson, 1972, Draper, 1973; Schmitt, 1963). Some scholars have noted that Asians are more tolerant of noise and high density conditions than Americans (Anderson, 1972; Canter & Canter, 1971; Michelson, 1976) and are more gregarious than Westerners (Chaudhuri, 1959; Porteus, 1977). One recent study examined the hypothesis that Asians may have developed a tolerance for crowded living. Gillis et al. (1986) compared the emotional distress reported by Asian, British, and Southern European adolescents in Toronto as a function of household crowding. The Asian students evidenced less emotional reactivity to crowded housing than the other students.

While these studies provide evidence of adaptation to crowding by some cultural groups, other studies of crowded countries or urban areas suggest that such adaptation is incomplete. Neighborhood crowding has been related to increased mortality in the Netherlands and Germany (Levy & Herzog, 1974; Manton & Myers, 1977). Household crowding has been associated with increased health problems in Canada and India (Booth & Cowell, 1976; Jain, 1987). Loo and Ong (1984) examined crowding in Chinatown, San Francisco and found that Chinese residents considered crowding to be harmful, with the major perceived problems being related to environment, social conflict, health, and psychological stress. A group of residents that had grown up under the most crowded conditions (in Hong Kong) demonstrated the most negative reactions to crowding within the home but judged neighborhood crowding to be less of a problem.

There are a multitude of possible reasons for the inconsistencies among the findings on the impact of crowding history. The studies differed greatly in the nature of their populations, environmental contexts, levels of crowding, and other environmental and outcome measures. There may also be some theoretical reasons for the observed complexities. Although past exposure to crowding may increase tolerance of crowding or the ability to cope effectively with it, crowded conditions may still be evaluated in a negative fashion (Paulus, 1988; Gillis et al., 1986). Past experience with crowding may allow adjustment to moderate levels of crowding, but not to extremely high levels of density. For example, the density experienced by the Asians inside their homes and in their neighborhoods in Toronto was considerably less than that encountered by those in San Francisco. In some cultures, however, norms about family relations may effectively limit the potentially negative effects of household crowding (Levy & Herzog, 1974; Mitchell, 1971).

We are unlikely to develop a clear understanding for the basis of cross-cultural or subcultural differences until more analytically precise studies are undertaken. These studies should assess subjective evaluations, physiological and emotional reactivity, and psychological or social coping styles in response to natural and experimentally induced variations in density and different aspects of dense environments (e.g., goal interference, uncertainty, and cognitive load). Within each cultural group, precise information should be obtained on household density and past crowding history. If such studies are done across a wide range of cultures, we might be able to determine the relative importance of cultural norms and coping styles, past experience, and present density conditions.

Crowding is an ideal topic for crosscultural research. Most countries have a wide range of crowding both inside and outside of residences. We would expect that specific reactions to density might differ across cultures, but the processes hypothesized to underly the crowding process (interference, uncertainty, and cognitive load) would presumably apply to the experiences of crowding across all cultures and species (Cox et al., 1984). However, the role of moderating variables such as sexual composition of the group, group context, and degree of control may be strongly affected by cultural factors. Theoretically and methodologically sophisticated crosscultural studies will greatly aid us in developing perspectives of crowding that are not "culture bound and culture blind" (Berry, 1978).

The Role of Positive or Negative Contexts

In our prior discussion we have pointed out that some of the most important features of crowding involve the social interactions that take place in crowded settings. We have emphasized the negative aspects of these interactions and how these may yield a variety of deleterious outcomes. However, it has also been mentioned that these results are not inevitable. In positive or cooperative contexts, crowding may not be aversive and may even be a positive experience (Freedman, 1975; Seta, Paulus, & Schkade, 1976).

Freedman (1975) has proposed a density-intensity model in which crowding is viewed as an intensifier of preexisting or coincidental affective states. If the setting or group conditions elicit positive affect, increases in density should lead to increased positive affect. If negative affect is elicited, density should produce increased levels of negative affect. The fact that all-female groups may react positively to crowding while male groups react negatively has been interpreted as support for this notion. Females may enter crowded settings with positive social inclinations and feelings that are subsequently intensified in crowded settings. Males appear to be somewhat uncomfortable and competitive in social settings with strangers and this may be enhanced in dense situations. Unfortunately, most studies have not demonstrated the gender differences in orientation and affect in uncrowded settings, so the gender effects observed under crowded conditions may reflect differences in coping styles rather than intensification (Paulus, 1980). The density-intensity model does derive support from some other studies in which context was explicitly manipulated (e.g., Freedman, 1975; Freedman & Perlick, 1979; Schkade (1977). For example, Schkade (1977) found decrements in the performance of a complex task under crowded conditions when subjects anticipated failure but increments when success was expected. In a similar vein, increased group size and reduced distance hinder complex task performance in competitive settings but facilitate it in cooperative ones (Seta et al., 1976).

The importance of context is also underscored by several attributional models of crowding and spatial behavior (Patterson, 1976; Worchel & Teddlie, 1976). Worchel and Teddlie (1976) proposed that crowding leads to arousal due to spatial invasions which occur under such conditions. If in this type of situation the individual attributes the experienced arousal to spatial factors, feelings of crowding and related negative effects such as decrements in task performance will ensue. If the arousal in dense settings is attributed to other stimuli such as movies or subliminal noise, negative effects of density are reduced (Worchel & Brown, 1984; Worchel & Yohai, 1979). Patterson (1976) has similarly emphasized the importance of context. He proposes that if contextual aspects of a spatial intrusion situation are positive, the resulting arousal state is labeled in a positive way and reciprocity and enhanced intimacy may occur. However, if the arousal is labeled or appraised negatively, social avoidance or withdrawal should be evidenced. Although considerable evidence supports this type of perspective, the exact mechanisms underlying them are still the subject of serious debate (Aiello, 1987).

The moderating impact of context is nicely demonstrated by a study conducted by MacDonald and Oden (1973). They compared reactions of Peace Corps volunteers who were either living in crowded dormitory style or hotel accommodations. The couples living in unpartitioned dorms chose to live in these accommodations in order to experience the hardship they expected in their upcoming assignments. Couples in the dorms evidenced more positive affect and cooperation than those living in the hotel. The dorm residents actually regretted having to leave their accommodations. Thus, living for a short period of time in a somewhat crowded setting with a supposedly congenial group of people and with a positive attitude may be a positive experience. In fact, some research suggests that group formation in crowded situations may help ameliorate some of the negative effects of crowding.

Group Formation in Crowded Environments

Although interaction with others in a dense group situation may yield negative reactions, formation of cohesive subgroups may help buffer the crowding impact. This idea has been examined most extensively by Baum and his colleagues. Baum, Harpin, and Valins (1975) have proposed that:

Groups are social structures that have the capacity to mitigate harmful or aversive effects of high density, thereby reducing the likelihood that individual group members will experience crowding under such conditions. Group development structures the social environment, and by producing boundaries, group members are shielded from many unwanted interactions from outside the group. As a result, group members are less susceptible to the unwanted and frequently inappropriate social encounters generated in high density settings and are less likely to experience crowding. Group members are also less likely to lose control over their social experiences, as their regulation of those experiences is reinforced by the norms established by the group. Finally, the potential for interference in a setting, which is typically high in dense situations, will be less salient for group members; the structures and channels created by a group to ensure smooth and successful interaction tend to circumvent interference by identifying procedures and patterns of movement which guide the activities of the group. The resulting norms regarding social encounter and the use of space can mitigate adverse effects of high density and can reduce the probability that crowding will be experienced by group members. (pp. 186–187)

The basic idea is that group formation helps individuals regulate, control, or avoid exposure to the negative elements of crowded settings. This analysis has been extended in a later paper (Baum & Valins, 1979), but many of the proposals about the specific mechanisms involved have yet to be examined empirically. The research by Baum and his colleagues does provide some general evidence for the positive role of group formation in crowded settings. For example, residents of suites holding four to six students tend to become a fairly cohesive group (as measured by group problem solving, perceived similarity, etc.), whereas residents of corridor dorms with 17 double rooms do not appear to be very successful in forming groups in the dorm. Moreover, while corridor residents report feeling crowded, few suite residents indicated such an experience. Interestingly the group orientation differences are also evident in experimental settings in that suite residents were better able to reach agreement after group discussion than corridor residents, even when the group involved strangers. Corridor residents apparently recognized the need for more cohesive group formation and made attempts to bring friends onto their floor. When corridor residents are able to form cohesive groups on their floor, the feelings of crowding are significantly reduced (Baum et al., 1975).

When three students are assigned to live in rooms designed for two, one of the students may be left out of the activities if the other two residents form a strong relationship or coalition. In these cases, crowding related reactions are observed only with the isolates (Baum, Shapiro, Murray, & Wideman, 1979). Because residents of quadrupled rooms are less likely to be isolates (because of the possibility of pairing), quadrupled rooms do not appear to increase crowding stress relative to triples (Reddy, Baum, Fleming, & Aiello, 1981).

The work by Baum and his colleagues highlights an aspect of group process that serves to reduce the impact of crowded living conditions. Ironically, while group members are in fact the major source of crowding related problems, having a cohesive and possibly supportive relationship with some subgroup of members appears to lessen the negative impact of the other members of the group. This may partly reflect the role of social support in buffering crowding stress (Baum et al., 1979). Alternatively, the sense of control provided by being part of a cohesive residential group may limit the impact of crowding stress. Finally, the various structural, normative, and interactional features of group membership may aid the individual in regulating his or her interactions in crowded settings (Baum et al., 1975).

There is another literature that demonstrates group formation in relation to various environmental features. This research can be loosely classified as being concerned with spatial factors in social interaction. In the next section we summarize some of the results from this literature and relate it theoretically to the literature on crowding.

SPATIAL FACTORS IN SOCIAL INTERACTION

Architecture and Social Interaction

Although the various density characteristics of environments have been demonstrated to have important implications for group process, there are many other environmental features that have also been examined for their relation to group processes. One focus of some of the previous studies has been the architectural layout of residential environments. These studies have examined the influence of spatial proximity or other residential characteristics that are seen as either increasing or decreasing the potential for social interaction and development of group cohesion. The layout of a residential environment may vary in terms of spatial arrangement of the units, location of mail boxes, common stairways, and common facilities such as laundromats and pools. Any feature that increases the opportunity for social interaction should increase the degree of group development in an environment. In the classic study by Festinger, Schachter, and Back (1950) it was found that residents tended to become friends with other residents in the same building or in the same group of houses. That is, residents living near each other tended to become friends, especially if the design increased the probability of contact between them (such as those living at two ends of a common stairway). Whyte (1956) similarly found that residents of garden apartments grouped in courts tended to become friends and develop particular cultural and activity patterns that continued after many of the original residents moved. Other studies have continued to document the fact that environmental features that place individuals close together or increase their interaction with one another can increase friendship choices (see Michelson, 1976; Sommer, 1974). Osmond (1957) coined the terms sociofugal and sociopetal for environmental arrangements that encourage or discourage social interaction and group formation, respectively.

Seating: Interaction in Short-Term Settings

Another area of concern has been the impact of the arrangement of tables and chairs on social interaction patterns. When international meetings are held, the size and shape of the table sometimes become major issues. Although this would seem to be a rather subtle factor, it could have major implications for the social tenor of the meetings. Table sizes or arrangements that place participants at uncomfortably large distances from one another may inhibit the development of rapport and congeniality required for effective group interaction (Green, 1975).

Studies of seating position in group interaction have examined a variety of issues, such as the role of interpersonal distance and orientation, side-by-side and face-to-face seating, circular and rectangular arrangements, and the role of seating position in status and leadership (see Gifford, 1987; Greenberg, 1976; Patterson, 1968 for reviews). The outcomes of these studies are often contradictory, and a clarification of the role of the independent effects of interpersonal distance, orientation, and eye contact will be required to bring some semblance of order to this area of study (Greenberg, 1976). This will necessitate the use of situations in which group members are randomly assigned to seating positions and those in which group members can select and arrange their own seating (Stires, 1980). The effects of seating position appear to be very sensitive to a variety of group and individual differences (Patterson, Roth, & Schenk, 1979). For example, among strangers females react most positively to a face-to-face arrangement and males to a side-by-side one. This pattern may be reversed if the participants are friends (Fisher & Byrne, 1975). Gifford and Gallagher (1985) found that defensive or socially wary individuals are more sociable in a sociofugal situation (chairs in a row), while less defensive or trusting individuals are more sociable in sociopetal arrangements (chairs in a half-circle). These studies suggest that some people are quite comfortable and thus more sociable in sociopetal settings while others may find such settings uncomfortable and socially inhibiting.

Although considerable tentativeness is called for in discussing the effects of seating arrangements, a few general conclusions appear to be justified. Sociopetal seating arrangements (small interpersonal distance, maximization of eye contact) seem to increase the degree of interaction, communication, and friendship formation. Positions that are central (head of the table or the center of a V-shaped arrangement) are associated with the perception of leadership, tend to be selected by those who are of high status or have leadership inclinations, and may be associated with leadership behavior. The effects of seating arrangements appear to depend greatly on the phase of group interaction, the group context (friendly or cooperative versus formal or competitive), and the degree of prior acquaintanceship of the group members (Greenberg, 1976).

Yet what do these types of studies imply about the nature of group processes in environments? Some studies seem to presume a somewhat passive group of individuals that have no particular strong inclinations and are easily swayed by environmental circumstances to become more or less sociable. Alternatively, one could assume that most individuals have some desire for social contact and that the environmental features simply help channel this in one direction or another. Certainly, it seems reasonable to assume that a socially facilitative environment with much opportunity for intense social interaction would encourage development of friendships or group cohesion. Yet such a development is not inevitable. One's friends as well as one's enemies may be developed by close proximity (Ebbesen, Kjos, & Konecni, 1976; Kuper, 1953), and seating position studies have provided much evidence for the role of individual differences.

CROWDING VERSUS SOCIAL COHESION: AN ENVIRONMENT/SOCIAL INTERACTION MODEL

Although some of the literature on spatial factors in social interaction suggests that proximity to others tends to foster development of positive social relationships, most studies in the area of crowding suggest that living or working in close proximity to others can be a source of stress and lead to negative social relationships. What variables account for the discrepancies in the results of these two traditions of research? One obvious factor is that crowding studies have used levels of social interaction that exceed normative standards and are thus generally considered to be aversive. Another important factor is that most crowding studies have involved exposing people to highly dense situations in which individuals have little control over social interactions. In the spatial factor studies, residents typically can choose whether or not they will engage in the interactions with the other residents or individuals seated nearby, hence this situation is much less aversive than those encountered in crowding studies. The studies by Baum and his colleagues nicely demonstrate this duality. Residents of suites had to contend with only four to six people in their primary living environment. As each suite contained three bedrooms, a bathroom, and a lounge area, considerable control over interactions was feasible. Interactions under these conditions should lead to group development and cohesion. On the other hand, doubles residents had to share lounge and bathroom facilities with 34 residents. The high level of uncontrollable interactions under these conditions appeared to inhibit group development.

The characteristics of group members also seem to be important in determining whether crowding or social cohesion effects are observed. If the members are similar in background, race, interests, values, status etc., it appears to be more likely that friendship formation or group development will occur (e.g., Gans, 1967; Hourihan, 1984; Michelson, 1976). Similarly, research on interracial contact has found that reduced prejudice is most likely to occur when the individuals involved share similar characteristics, have a common goal, and share in cooperative relationships with one another (Stephan, 1987). As discussed earlier, crowding effects are also strongly effected by social context. Thus, it seems reasonable to argue that in situations in which the interpersonal context is positive, stress-related effects of crowding are less likely to occur and positive group relationships may be more likely to develop.

There also appear to be important individual differences in social inclinations and tolerance for crowded or sociopetal situations. For example, prison inmates who expressed a tolerance for crowding on a simulated task exhibited a lower degree of negative effects than those who expressed little tolerance (Paulus, 1988). Individuals who differ in degree of sociability, shyness, or introversion/extraversion are also likely to vary in their responsivity to environmental factors designed to encourage or discourage social interaction (e.g., Gifford & Gallagher, 1985). Socially inclined individuals may be most likely to take advantage of the socially facilitative environmental features and attempt to overcome the inhibitive ones by active attempts to increase the level of social interaction. The individual difference factor becomes particularly important when considered in relation to situations in which people can choose environments consistent with their individual characteristics. For example, those with a low tolerance for crowding may avoid crowded environments, and those who are socially inclined may seek out environments in which social contacts appear likely.

Two other factors that are important in moderating the degree of social interaction (e.g., facilitation or inhibition) observed in environments are length of time in the environment and the degree to which various psychological and/or behavioral adjustments take place. One might expect that it requires some period of time for an environment's impact on social interaction to be evident. However, the way individuals adjust to or cope in various environments may influence the outcome of this process. For example, individuals may make active attempts to overcome the socially inhibitive features of their environment by creating procedures or social structures that facilitate social interaction. Those who are uncomfortable in socially facilitative environments may spend as little time as possible there or develop techniques to minimize social interaction. Depending on the exact confluence of facilitative/inhibitory factors and moderators, one would expect socially facilitative environments to be generally characterized by positive group reactions (e.g., social cohesion, cooperation) and inhibitory environments by negative group reactions (cf. Paulus & Nagar, 1987).

We have highlighted some of the factors that appear to be important in determining the group process that is likely to occur in different environments (crowding and social avoidance versus friendship development and social cohesion). Our main points are summarized by the environment/social interaction model in Fig. 5.3. This model suggests that positive group reaction or development is most likely when the environment facilitates the probability of interaction, individuals have a high need for interaction, interaction is within an acceptable range, the context is positive, and there is some control over interactions. When these conditions are reversed (inhibitory factors), negative group reactions are likely. However, the extent to which these outcomes are observed will depend on the degree to which self-selection is possible, the length of time individuals are exposed to the environment, and the availability or feasibility of various psychological or behavioral techniques for responding to the situation.

There are a number of rather straightforward research implications of the environment/social interaction model. Techniques need to be developed to assess objectively the facilitative/inhibitory variables. Environmental psychologists should develop guidelines for specifying the degree of sociopetality/ so-

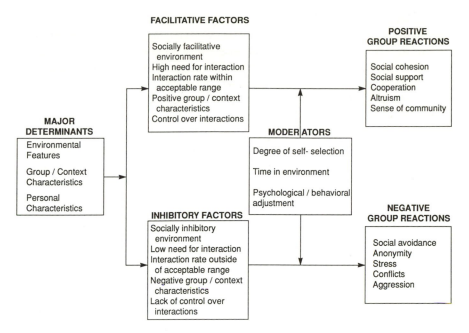

FIG. 5.3. An environment/social interaction model. (From Paulus and Nagar (1987). Reprinted with permission.

ciofugality of an environment. We need to develop measures of desire for interaction, range of acceptability of interaction rates, and degree of control over interactions. The relative importance of various group and social context characteristics (e.g., similarity, positive events) should be assessed. Once we have reasonable measures of the facilitative/inhibitive factors, we can assess more effectively the relative importance of these factors in producing positive or negative group reactions. Do all these factors contribute to group behavior in a similar additive fashion, or are certain ones more important for the development of positive or negative group interactions than others? To what extent are some of these factors able to overcome the contrary influence of the others?

Although considerable evidence exists for the role of the facilitative and inhibitory factors on group reactions, we know very little about the role of the moderators. What factors determine individual selection of particular environments or environmental arrangements? Can individuals reliably discriminate environments that differ in opportunity for social interaction and degree of control afforded over these interactions? How do individuals adjust or react over time to environments that either match or conflict with their social inclinations? These issues have been developed in some detail by Paulus and Nagar (1987) for residential environments. Yet the model is similarly applicable to any social environmental context, whether it be in the natural environment or the laboratory.

Our review has tried to shed light on the group environment process. Individuals do appear to be sensitive to various features of their environments and may select environments consistent with their background or social inclinations. Moreover, when they interact in various environments, features of these environments appear to be related to the nature of social interactions experienced and these in turn to various perceptual, affective, and health related outcomes. Those environmental features that are most strongly related to the nature of the interactions experienced are most likely to be related to crowding or cohesion effects. A comprehensive understanding of this process requires one to attend to the self-selection process, environmental features, and the nature of the social interactions.

RELEVANCE TO OTHER GROUP PROCESSES

Research on crowding and spatial factors in social interaction has provided much evidence that the environment can have a substantial impact on group processes. Some environmental contexts tend to induce a feeling of social cohesion, group development, and positive group and individual outcomes. Other environmental situations are associated with the experience of crowding, social avoidance and a variety of negative group and individual consequences. These findings have important implications for a wide variety of group phenomena. They provide empirical and theoretical bases for a broader study of the relationship of socially relevant environmental features to group processes and social interaction. Such a program of study would simultaneously enrich both the areas of environmental psychology and group dynamics. In this section we discuss the implications of environmental research and the environment/social interaction model for the influence of environmental features on other group processes such as decision-making, coalition formation, conformity, bargaining and for group interaction in various formal and informal social settings.

Laboratory Environments

In most laboratory settings, interaction is greatly limited or controlled. This is necessary to increase precision and control in evaluating the impact of various manipulations. If interaction were not controlled, the many extraneous influences would contaminate the experimental manipulations and make interpretation of the results difficult. Research participants are usually instructed to refrain from interactions not specified in the task procedures. In these laboratory settings individuals have low degrees of control over interaction or selection. Group or social context is typically fairly neutral and involves strangers with whom one may have little a priori desire for interaction. Under those conditions one might expect a reasonable degree of discomfort with socially dense or sociopetal arrangements, as well as feelings of crowding and cognitive interference or distraction. This might, in turn, be reflected in inferior processing of task information, social avoidance, and negative emotional states. One would expect inferior problem solving or decision making, reduced cooperation and increased individualism in decision making, group problem solving, bargaining, or coalition formation. Individuals may also be less conformist and more independent in socially dense environments than less dense ones because of increased antisocial tendencies. Spaciousness may have similar, but less dramatic effects. This factor may also be related to differences between all-male and all-female groups, with male groups more likely to react negatively.

However, the above outcomes are not inevitable in laboratory settings. If the context is explicitly made a positive one (e.g., cooperation is emphasized or individuals are allowed to get to know one another prior to the experiment or are already friends), these negative effects are less likely to occur (Seta et al., 1976). In fact, if the group has an initially positive social set, high density conditions and other socially facilitative environmental features may facilitate these social inclinations and lead to favorable group reactions on various group tasks or activities (Freedman & Perlick 1979). This should be particularly true if social interaction is allowed during the course of the experiment or the experience and if the group members are similar along important dimensions (e.g., age, interests, occupation) and exercise some degree of control or choice over the environmental arrangements.

The issue of control over the environment in laboratory settings is an intriguing one. In real life settings individuals may have greater control over their exposure to different environmental settings than subjects in laboratory settings. They may be able to choose rooms, seating arrangements, length of the session, and the procedures for the social interaction. However, this power may sometimes lie primarily in the leader or person in charge. In such cases, the leader may show fewer density related effects than the other participants (Rodin, Solomon, & Metcalf, 1978). Thus, to the extent that members of the group have some choice in the environmental arrangements and the interaction, the impact of environmental conditions may be lessened. Of course the nature of the group may lead to the choice of certain environmental arrangements and predispose it to certain group outcomes. Socially inclined groups should prefer socially intimate arrangements and be generally more cooperative than socially inhibited ones. Because laboratory situations are temporary, subjects may demonstrate less impact of loss of control than individuals in natural environments. Yet even in laboratory settings, variations in degree of control seem to have strong effects (Rodin et al., 1978; Sherrod, 1974).

What if subjects in experiments were allowed some degree of control over the selection of environmental conditions? This could range from freedom to arrange the physical aspects of the environment (chairs and tables) to choosing the experimental conditions (e.g., spacious vs. cramped, sociofugal vs. sociopetal, small vs. large group, cooperative vs. competitive). How would such a degree of choice and control influence the outcomes of our studies? Would different types of people end up in different conditions and produce quite different results and outcomes compared to randomly assigned subjects? Or would the simple fact of control over one's situation be the critical factor and be related to generally positive reactions to socially dense or intimate situations? Unfortunately, we have little basis for our predictions. In their desire for experimental control, researchers have avoided examining the effects of variables under conditions where self-selection, choice, or control is feasible. At the very least, it would appear important to compare findings derived from controlled experimental research to the results obtained under conditions where subjects are afforded degrees of control comparable to those in natural settings. It may very well be that some task settings will be only minimally affected while others may evidence strong effects. One might hypothesize that tasks which focus on individualistic performance of intellective tasks, effects of self-selection may not be very strong (Stires, 1980). However, on tasks that are more social in nature (e.g., group discussion) and have an affective base (e.g., judgmental tasks—Laughlin, 1980), strong effects of the degree of control or self-selection may be evident. For example, Saunders, Fisher, Hewitt, and Clayton (1985) found that responses to erotica were quite different for subjects who thought they were in fact volunteering for a study on erotica than for those who thought they were volunteering to fill out a personality scale.

Once we derive a body of knowledge about those factors that influence selection to different types of laboratory conditions, we can explicitly examine conditions under which individuals are assigned randomly to conditions incompatible with their inclinations, or allowed to choose their environments. This type of research would greatly facilitate our understanding of the combined interactive role of personality, environment, and self-selection in the basic group processes we study in laboratories. In so doing, we should significantly enhance the potential applicability of our knowledge base to natural settings.

There are indeed many real world situations to which our perspective is applicable. We have detailed its relevance for residential settings in a previous paper (Paulus & Nagar, 1987), however, it may be useful to elaborate its utility for understanding everyday social interaction situations. These situations may vary from rather informal conversation settings to more formal meetings and problem solving groups. We briefly examine several group settings from this continuum. Our treatment should not be taken as definitive in that empirical support is lacking for many of our suggestions. The main purpose of these examples is to demonstrate the heuristic value of the environmental literature for understanding group processes in realistic situations.

Informal Social Settings: Parties and Other Social Events

Much interaction takes the form of informal conversations. In fact, we often structure events to provide an intensive opportunity for such interactions (parties, retreats, conferences, reunions, etc.). These provide a chance to interact informally with friends and strangers in fairly nonthreatening situations. Although some of these events are acknowledged as being huge successes, others may be unexciting and even unpleasant. What differentiates the successful ones from unsuccessful ones? The type of people and beverages served may have an important bearing, of course. Yet some of the issues we have discussed would seem to have direct implications for understanding those factors that might facilitate or hinder informal interaction among a wide group of individuals. We briefly sketch out some hypotheses that are in line with our prior discussion and the theoretical model presented in Fig. 5.3.

For simplicity of presentation we use parties as the prototype of informal social events. It is assumed that a good party should provide an opportunity for a high number of pleasant interactions with a wide group of people. The recipe for such a party can be derived from the implications of research on crowding and spatial factors. The environment should be arranged to encourage interaction in small subgroups (prevent social density induced avoidance). Individuals should not feel constrained or limited in their interactions or in their ability to leave and enter a wide variety of small groups (do not limit control over interactions). The group context should focus on similarities among group members and avoid basing interactions on preexisting affiliations and status differences (enhance homogeneity). Attempts should be made to generate a positive atmosphere.

How can this be best accomplished? There should be a sufficient number of individuals so that one can have a wide variety of short conversations with different people. Many conversations may lose their interest level within a short period of time, and easy access and departure from conversation groups should be feasible. In parties to which distinct subgroups are invited (e.g., social cliques, students vs. faculty), tendencies toward in-group behavior may be overcome by structuring activities that encourage interaction across subgroups and those that highlight common interests or characteristics unrelated to group membership. The environmental arrangements should facilitate interaction among small groups. At parties in which participants sit in a circle around a single room, conversations may be inhibited, stilted, and uncomfortable. Arranging multiple seating and snacking places should facilitate small group formation. Chairs should be arranged in small subgroups or provided in limited numbers since they may inhibit social movement. Pleasant activities should be scheduled early to assure the development of a positive context.

Formal Social Settings: Meetings or Work Groups

Although most people look forward to parties, they often detest meetings designed for specific tasks. Academic meetings are particularly renowned for being boring and often unproductive exercises. Yet increasingly our society is run by decisions derived from meetings of selected groups of individuals. In many of the meetings the participants may know each other quite well, but the goal of the meetings is typically not social cohesion but decisions, problem solving, and task achievement. How do the environmental and group contexts influence the atmosphere of such meetings or other work situations in which social interactions occur?

There are a number of relevant variables to consider. The size of the group involved is likely to be an important factor. In fact, most meetings are explicitly designed to bring together a small subgroup to make decisions for the larger entity. If too many people are involved in the meeting, social interaction may be inhibited. Status differences may also inhibit participation of some of the members of lower status or limited experience. A critical or evaluative atmosphere may similarly prevent full participation by group members. Such an atmosphere is likely to limit full discussion of the issues and creativity (Diehl & Stroebe, 1987) and may be partly responsible for some of the disastrous decisions made in groups (Janis, 1972).

A sociopetal seating arrangement should lead to positive group reactions (communication, harmony, cohesion) if the social context is a favorable one (friends, cooperation, similarity). The participants should desire social interaction and the degree of intimacy induced by the seating arrangement should not exceed normative standards in regard to eye contact and spatial distance. Individuals who feel some control over their interactions, their specific seat, and the overall seating arrangement, should be able to tolerate fairly *close* social arrangements somewhat better than those who have no such control. Negative reactions (discomfort, conflict, minimal communication, social avoidance) should occur to the extent that the social context is a negative one (strangers, competition, heterogeneity), social interaction is not desired, degree of intimacy exceeds normative standards, and individuals have little control over the seating arrangements. Although there exists some evidence for some of these predictions (e.g., Batchelor & Goethals, 1972; Gardin, Kaplan, Firestone, & Cowan, 1973; Gifford & Gallagher, 1985), studies that systematically manipulate these factors will be required to develop a better understanding of the seating position and social interaction relationship.

Although sociopetal arrangements may have positive social consequences under certain conditions, that does not mean that the outcome of the group processes will be favorable. Group tasks that require individual assessment and critical reactions or important decisions among a range of alternatives may be accomplished best with sociofugal arrangements that inhibit socially cohesive forces and induce a sense of individuality. Thus, the impact of seating arrangements should be examined for a broad range of group tasks or goals, as well as for different phases of group interaction (Greenberg, 1976). This research should also have considerable implications for counseling situations (Gifford, 1987) and for group trainers or facilitators in organizations (Greenberg, 1976).

Crowds

One of the more intriguing issues in social psychology is the issue of crowd behavior. LeBon's (1903) influential analysis of crowd behavior stimulated scientific interest in the subject, but his notion of the ''group mind'' and the complexity of mass behavior have limited the interest of social psychologists in the study of this topic. However, there appears to be a revival of interest in the issue (e.g., Graumann & Moscovici, 1986). Furthermore, Kruse (1986) has suggested that the research findings and concepts of the crowding area may be very pertinent to an understanding of mass crowd behavior. For example, she suggests that the notions of intensification (Freedman, 1975), arousal (Evans, 1978; Paulus, 1980), constraint (Stokols, 1976), overload (Milgram, 1970), and control (Baron & Rodin, 1978) may all be useful in understanding whether crowd behavior or experiences will be positive or negative. From this perspective, the social-interaction demand model would be helpful in specifying alternative outcomes. For example, if at an athletic contest interactions among the fans occur with low degrees of uncertainty or loss of control, interference and overload, one's experience may be fairly positive. However, if there are high degrees of interference, lack of control over seating, high degrees of cognitive load due to having to manage many interactions, the experience should be a negative one. The environment/social interaction model further suggests that positive social outcomes will characterize crowds if individuals have a high need for interaction, group members are similar, the environmental or social context is a positive one, and members have control over their interactions. The types of individuals who select a particular crowd setting (e.g., soccer games in Europe), the length of exposure to the crowd, as well as direct social stimulation (contagion, leadership) by other group members are likely to have a major role in the outcomes of the crowd experience. It would appear that the crowding literature and that of spatial factors in social interaction may be fertile bases for the development of research hypotheses on crowd behavior.

SUMMARY

In this chapter we have tried to show that social interaction and group processes are inevitably intertwined in meaningful ways with the environmental contexts. This interrelationship has been explored in some detail in studies of crowding and spatial factors in social interaction. These studies have resulted in a fairly coherent picture of the environment/group interface in particular settings. Yet much remains to be known about the role of the environment in both structured and unstructured group settings. One cannot physically separate the group from its environment. Why should we do so conceptually? Furthermore, studies that examine group processes in relation to environmental features have the advantage of being of value to both the development of environmental psychology and the study of group dynamics. It does not require a large group meeting to decide on the obvious merit of such studies. However, it may be useful to have a party to which both environmental and group psychologists were invited. If this party were a social/environmental success, it might be a real boon to both disciplines.

ACKNOWLEDGMENTS

The writing of this chapter was facilitated by an Intergovernmental Personnel Agreement from the Department of Military Psychiatry, Walter Reed Army Institute of Research to the first author. Robert Gifford, Barry Ruback, and Jan Pieter van Oudenhoven made helpful comments on an earlier draft of this chapter.

REFERENCES

Aiello, J. (1987). Human spatial behavior. In D. Stokols & I. Altman (Eds.), *Handbook of environmental psychology* (Vol 1, pp. 389–504). New York: Wiley.

Anderson, E. N., Jr. (1972). Some Chinese methods of dealing with crowding. *Urban Anthropology, 1,* 141–150.

Baldassare, M. (1979). *Residential crowding in urban America.* Berkeley: University of California Press.

Baron, R. M., Mandel, D. R., Adams, C. A., and & Griffen, L. M. (1976). Effects of social density in university residential environments. *Journal of Personality and Social Psychology, 34,* 434–446.

Baron, R. M., & Rodin, J. (1978). Personal control as a mediator of crowding. In A. Baum, J. E. Singer, & S. Valins (Eds.), *Advances in environmental psychology* (Vol 1, pp. 145–190). Hillsdale, NJ: Lawrence Erlbaum Associates.

Batchelor, J. P., & Goethals, G. R. (1972). Spatial arrangements in freely formed groups. *Sociometry, 35,* 270–279.

Baum, A., Harpin, R. E., & Valins, S. (1975) The role of group phenomena in the experience of crowding. *Environment and Behavior, 7,* 185–198.

Baum, A., & Paulus, P. B. (1987). Crowding. In D. Stokols & I. Altman (Eds.), *Handbook of environmental psychology* (Vol 1, pp. 533–570). New York: Wiley.

Baum, A., Shapiro, A., Murray, D., & Wideman, M. V. (1979). Interpersonal mediation of perceived crowding and control in residential dyads and triads. *Journal of Applied Social Psychology, 9,* 491–507.

Baum, A., & Valins, S. (1977). *Architecture and social behavior: Psychological studies of social density.* Hillsdale, NJ: Lawrence Erlbaum Associates.

Baum, A., & Valins, S. (1979). Architectural mediation of residential density and control: Crowding and the regulation of social contact. In L. Berkowitz (Ed.), *Advances in experimental social psychology* (Vol 12, pp. 131–175). New York: Academic Press.

Berry, J. W. (1978). Social psychology: Comparative, societal and universal. *Canadian Psychological Review, 19,* 93–104.

Booth, A., & Cowell, J. (1976). Crowding and health. *Journal of Health and Social Behavior, 17,* 204–220.

Canter, D., & Canter, S. (1971). Close together in Tokyo. *Design and Environment, 2,* 60–63.

Chaudhuri, N. C. (1959). *A passage to England.* London: Macmillan.

Cohen, S. (1978). Environmental load and the allocation of attention. In A. Baum, J. E. Singer, & S. Valins (Eds.), *Advances in environmental psychology* (Vol 1, pp. 1–29). Hillsdale, NJ: Lawrence Erlbaum Associates.

Cohen, S., Glass, D. C., & Philips, S. (1979). Environment and health. In H. E. Freeman, S. Levine, & L. G. Reeder (Eds.), *Handbook of medical sociology* (pp. 134–149). Englewood Cliffs, NJ: Prentice-Hall.

Cox, V. C., Paulus, P. B., & McCain, G. (1984). Prison crowding research: The relevance for prison housing standards and a general approach regarding crowding phenomena. *American Psychologist, 39,* 1148–1160.

D'Atri, D. A., & Ostfeld, A.M. (1975). Crowding: Its effects on the elevation of blood pressure in a prison setting. *Preventive Medicine, 4,* 550–566.

Diehl, M., & Stroebe, W. (1987). Productivity loss in brainstorming groups: Toward a solution of a riddle. *Journal of Personality and Social Psychology, 53,* 497–509.

Draper, P. (1973). Crowding among hunter-gathers: The !Kung Bushman. *Science, 182,* 301–303.

Ebbesen, E. B., Kjos, G. L., & Konecni, V. J. (1976). Spatial ecology: Its effects on the choice of friends and enemies. *Journal of Experimental Social Psychology, 12,* 505–518.

Eoyang, C. K. (1974). Effects of group size and privacy in residential crowding. *Journal of Personality and Social Psychology, 30,* 389–392.

Epstein, Y. M. (1981). Crowding stress and human behavior. *Journal of Social Issues, 37,* 126–144.

Evans, G. W. (1978). Human spatial behavior: The arousal model. In A. Baum & Y. M. Epstein (Eds.), *Human response to crowding* (p. 283–302). Hillsdale, NJ: Lawrence Erlbaum Associates.

Festinger, L., Schachter, S., & Back, K. (1950). *Social pressures in informal groups: A study of human factors in housing.* California: Stanford University Press.

Fisher, J. D., & Byrne, D. (1975). Too close for comfort: Sex differences in response to invasions of personal space. *Journal of Personality and Social Psychology, 32,* 15–21.

Folkman, S. (1984). Personal control and stress and coping processes: A theoretical analysis. *Journal of Personality and Social Psychology, 46,* 839–852.

Freedman, J. L. (1975). *Crowding and behavior.* San Francisco: W. H. Freeman.

Freedman, J. L., & Perlick, D. (1979). Crowding, contagion, and laughter. *Journal of Experimental Social Psychology, 15,* 295–303.

Galle, O. R., Gove, W. R., & McPherson, J. M. (1972). Population density and pathology: What are the relations for man? *Science, 176,* 23–30.

Gans, H. J. (1967). *The Levittowners: Ways of life and politics in a suburban community.* New York: Pantheon Books.

Gardin, H., Kaplan, K. J., Firestone, I. J., & Cowan, G. A. (1973). Proxemic effects on cooperation, attitude and approach-avoidance in a prisoner's dilemma game. *Journal of Personality and Social Psychology, 27,* 13–18.

Gifford, R. (1987). *Environmental psychology: Principles and practice.* Newton, MA: Allyn and Bacon.

Gifford, R., & Gallagher, T. M. B. (1985). Sociability: Personality, social context, and physical setting. *Journal of Personality and Social Psychology, 48,* 1015–1023.

Gillis, A. R., Richard, M. A., & Hagan, J. (1986). Ethnic susceptibility to crowding: An empirical analysis. *Environment and Behavior, 18,* 683–706.

Gove, W. R., Hughes, M., & Galle, O. R. (1979). Overcrowding in the home: An empirical investigation of its possible pathological consequences. *American Sociological Review, 44,* 59–80.

Graumann, C. F., & Moscovici, S. (Eds.) (1986). *Changing conceptions of crowd mind and behavior.* New York: Springer-Verlag.

Green, C. S., III. (1975). The ecology of committees. *Environment and Behavior, 7,* 411–427.

Greenberg, J. (1976). The role of seating position in group interaction: A review, with application for group trainers. *Group & Organization Studies, 1,* 310–327.

Hourihan, K. (1984). Context-dependent models of residential satisfaction: An analysis of housing groups in Cork, Ireland. *Environment and Behavior, 16,* 369–393.

Jain, U. (1987). *The psychological consequences of crowding.* New Delhi: Sage.

Janis, I. L. (1972). *Victims of groupthink.* Boston: Houghton Mifflin.

Kruse, L. (1986). Conceptions of crowds and crowding. In C. F. Graumann & S. Moscovici (Eds.), *Changing conceptions of crowd mind and behavior* (p. 117–142). New York: Springer-Verlag.

Kuper, L. (1953). Blueprint for living together. In L. Kuper (Ed.), *Living in towns* (pp. 1–202). London: Cresset Press.

Laughlin, P. R. (1980). Social combination processes of cooperative problem-solving groups on verbal intellective tasks. In M. Fishbein (Ed.), *Progress in social psychology* (Vol. 1, pp. 127–155). Hillsdale, NJ: Lawrence Erlbaum Associates.

LeBon, G. (1903). *The crowd.* London: Unwin.

Levy, L., & Herzog, A. N. (1974). Effects of population density and crowding on health and social adaptation in the Netherlands. *Journal of Health and Social Behavior, 15,* 228–240.

Loo, C. M., & Ong, P. (1984). Crowding perceptions, attitudes, and consequences among the Chinese. *Environment and Behavior, 16,* 55–87.

MacDonald, W. S., & Oden, C. W., Jr. (1973). Effects of extreme crowding on the performance of five married couples during twelve weeks of intensive training. *Proceedings of 81st Annual Convention of the American Psychological Association, 8,* 209–210.

Manton, K. G., & Myers, G. C. (1977). The structure of urban mortality: A methodological study of Hanover, Germany, Part II. *International Journal of Epidemiology, 6,* 213–223.

Michelson, W. H. (1976). *Man and his urban environment: A sociological approach.* Reading, MA: Addison-Wesley.

Milgram, S. (1970). The experience of living in cities. *Science, 167,* 1461–1468.

Mitchell, R. E. (1971). Some social implications of high density housing. *American Sociological Review, 36,* 18–29.

Montana, D., & Adamopoulos, J. (1984). The perception of crowding in interpersonal situations: Affective and behavioral responses. *Environment and Behavior, 16,* 643–666.

Nagar, D. (1985). *Experiences and consequences of crowding.* Unpublished doctoral dissertation, University of Allahabad, India.

Nagar, D., & Paulus, P. B. (1987). *Residential crowding experience scale: Assessment and validation.* Unpublished manuscript. The University of Texas at Arlington.

Nogami, G. Y. (1976). Crowding: Effects of group size, room size, or density? *Journal of Applied Social Psychology, 6,* 105–125.

Osmond, H. (1957). Function as a basis of psychiatric ward design. *Mental Hospitals,* (Architectural supplements), *83,* 235–245.

Patterson, M. (1968). Spatial factors in social interactions. *Human Relations, 21,* 351–361.

Patterson, M. L. (1976). An arousal model of interpersonal intimacy. *Psychological Review, 83,* 235–245.

Patterson, M. L., Roth, C. P., & Schenk, C. (1979). Seating arrangement, activity, and sex differences in small group crowding. *Personality and Social Psychology Bulletin, 5,* 100–103.

Paulus, P. B. (1980). Crowding, In P. B. Paulus (Ed.), *Psychology of group influence* (pp. 245–289). Hillsdale, NJ: Lawrence Erlbaum Associates.

Paulus, P. B. (1988). *Prison crowding: A psychological perspective.* New York: Springer-Verlag.

Paulus, P. B., Annis, A. B., Seta, J. J., Schkade, J. K., & Matthews, R. W. (1976). Density does affect task performance. *Journal of Personality and Social Psychology, 34,* 248–253.

Paulus, P. B., & Matthews, R. W. (1980). When density affects task performance. *Personality and Social Psychology Bulletin, 6,* 119–124.

Paulus, P. B., & Nagar, D. (1987). Environmental influences on social interaction and group development. In C. Hendrick (Ed.), *Group processes and intergroup relations: Review of personality and social psychology* (Vol 9, pp. 68–90). Beverly Hills, CA: Sage.

Porteus, J. D. (1977). *Environment and behavior: Planning and everyday urban life.* Reading, MA: Addison-Wesley.

Reddy, D. M., Baum, A., Fleming, R., & Aiello, J. R. (1981). Mediation of social density by coalition formation. *Journal of Applied Social Psychology, 11,* 529–537.

Rodin, J., Solomon, S. K., & Metcalf, J. (1978). Role of control in mediating perceptions of density. *Journal of Personality and Social Psychology, 36,* 988–999.

Ross, M., Layton, B., Erickson, B., & Schopler, J. (1973). Affect, facial regard, and reactions to crowding. *Journal of Personality and Social Psychology, 28,* 69–76.

Saegert, S. (1978). High density environments: Their personal and social consequences. In A. Baum & Y. M. Epstein (Eds.), *Human response to crowding* (pp. 257–281). Hillsdale, NJ: Lawrence Erlbaum Associates.

Saegert, S. (1982). Environment and children's mental health: Residential density and low income children. In A. Baum & J. E. Singer (Eds.), *Handbook of psychology and health* Vol. 2, pp. 247–271). Hillsdale, NJ: Lawrence Erlbaum Associates.

Saunders, D. M., Fisher, W. A., Hewitt, E. C., & Clayton, J. P. (1985). A method for empirically assessing volunteer selection effects: Recruitment procedures and responses to crotica. *Journal of Personality and Social Psychology, 49,* 1703–1712.

Schaeffer, M. A., Baum, A., Paulus, P.B., & Gaes, G. G. (1988). Architecturally mediated effects of social density in prison. *Environment and Behavior, 20,* 3–19.

Schkade, J. K. (1977). *The effects of expectancy set and crowding on task performance.* Unpublished doctoral dissertation, University of Texas at Arlington.

Schmitt, R. C. (1963). Implications of density in Hong Kong. *Journal of American Institute of Planners, 32,* 210–217.

Schopler, J., & Stockdale, J. E. (1977). An interference analysis of crowding. *Environmental Psychology and Nonverbal Behavior, 1,* 81–88.

Schultz-Gambard, J., Feierabend, C., & Hommel, B. (1986, September). *Crowding and social context: Basic dimensions of experiencing crowded environments.* Paper presented at the symposium on social and environmental psychology in the European context. Lisbon.

Seta, J. J., Paulus, P. B., & Schkade, J. K. (1976). The effects of group size and proximity under cooperative and competitive conditions. *Journal of Personality and Social Psychology, 34,* 47–53.

Sherrod, D. R. (1974). Crowding, perceived control, and behavioral aftereffects. *Journal of Applied Social Psychology, 4,* 171–186.

Sommer, R. (1974). *Tight spaces: Hard architecture and how to humanize it.* Englewood Cliffs, NJ: Prentice-Hall.

Stephan, W. G. (1987). The contact hypothesis in intergroup relations. In C. Hendrick (Ed.), *Review of personality and social psychology* (Vol 9, pp. 13–40). Beverly Hills, CA: Sage.

Stires, L. (1980). Classroom seating location, student grades, and attitudes: Environment or self-selection? *Environment and Behavior, 12,* 241–254.

Stokols, D. (1972). On the distinction between density and crowding: Some implications for future research. *Psychology Review, 79,* 275–277.

Stokols, D. (1976). The experience of crowding in primary and secondary environments. *Environment and Behavior, 8,* 49–86.

Taylor, R. B. (1981). Perception of density: Individual differences? *Environment and Behavior, 13,* 3–21.

Whyte, W. H., Jr. (1956). *The organization man.* Garden City, NY: Doubleday.

Wicklund, R. A. (1980). Group contact and self-focused attention. In P. B. Paulus (Ed.), *Psychology of group influence* (pp. 189–208). Hillsdale, NJ: Lawrence Erlbaum Associates.

Wohlwill, J., & Kohn, I. (1973). The environment as experienced by the migrant: An adaptation level view. *Representative Research in Social Psychology, 4,* 135–164.

Worchel, S., & Brown, E. H. (1984). The role of plausibility in influencing environmental attributions. *Journal of Experimental Social Psychology, 20,* 86–96.

Worchel, S., & Teddlie, C. (1976). The experience of crowding: A two-factor theory. *Journal of Personality and Social Psychology, 34,* 30–40.

Worchel, S., & Yohai, S. M. L. (1979). The role of attribution in the experience of crowding. *Journal of Experimental Social Psychology, 15,* 91–104.

II

SOCIAL INFLUENCE
PROCESSES IN GROUPS

6 Newcomers and Oldtimers in Small Groups

Richard L. Moreland
John M. Levine
University of Pittsburgh

> *New things are made familiar, and familiar things are made new.*
> —Samuel Johnson

Although much research on small groups has been conducted, many interesting and important phenomena that occur in such groups remain to be explored. One such phenomenon is group socialization, or the temporal changes that occur in the relationships between a group and each of its members. We have recently developed a model of group socialization that both describes and explains these changes (Moreland & Levine, 1982). The model applies primarily (but not exclusively) to small, autonomous, and voluntary groups whose members interact regularly, are behaviorally and affectively interdependent, and share a common frame of reference.

Three basic psychological processes operate within our model: evaluation, commitment, and role transition. During *evaluation,* the group and the individual develop normative expectations for one another's behavior, monitor discrepancies between actual and expected behavior, and attempt to reduce these discrepancies. At any given time, the rewardingness of the relationship for each party depends on the degree to which the other party meets its expectations. Evaluation can involve the past, present, and future relationships between the group and the individual, as well as any alternative relationships available to either party in the past, present, or future.

Feelings of *commitment* between the group and the individual depend on the outcome of this evaluation process. Insofar as they believe that (a) their past relationship was more rewarding than other previous alternative relationships,

(b) their present relationship is more rewarding than other current alternative relationships, and (c) their future relationship will be more rewarding than other future alternative relationships, both the group and the individual become more committed to one another. As a result, they are more likely to accept one another's values, feel positive toward one another, try to meet one another's expectations, and work to build or maintain a strong relationship together.

Commitment, on the part of the group and the individual, often changes over time. If commitment rises or falls far enough, then it may reach a decision criterion for either or both parties. A decision criterion is a level of commitment that marks a fundamental change in the nature of the relationship between the group and the individual. When commitment reaches a decision criterion, the group and/or the individual attempt to produce a *role transition*. If both parties are equally committed to one another and share the same decision criterion, then the role transition proceeds smoothly. But if one party is more committed than the other, or they have different decision criteria, then the role transition becomes problematic and may not occur at all (Moreland & Levine, 1984).

Once a role transition occurs, the evaluation process begins anew, producing further changes in commitment and perhaps other role transitions. In this way, the individual can pass through five phases of group membership (investigation, socialization, maintenance, resocialization, remembrance) separated by four role transitions (entry, acceptance, divergence, exit). Figure 6.1 illustrates the typical passage of an individual through a group.

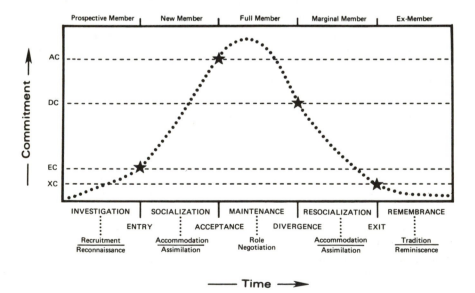

FIG. 6.1. A model of socialization in small groups. From Moreland and Levine (1982).

The relationship between a group and an individual begins with a period of *investigation*. During investigation, the group engages in recruitment, looking for people who can contribute to the achievement of group goals, while the individual engages in reconnaissance, looking for groups that can contribute to the satisfaction of personal needs. If the commitment levels of both parties rise to their respective entrance criteria (EC), then the individual undergoes the role transition of *entry* and becomes a new member.

The second phase of group membership is *socialization*. During socialization, the group attempts to change the individual so that he or she can contribute more to the achievement of group goals, while the individual attempts to change the group so that it can better satisfy his or her personal needs. Insofar as these activities are successful, the individual experiences assimilation and the group experiences accommodation. If the commitment levels of both parties rise to their respective acceptance criteria (AC), then the individual undergoes the role transition of *acceptance* and becomes a full member.

During *maintenance,* the group and the individual engage in role negotiation designed to find a specialized role for the individual that maximizes both the satisfaction of his or her personal needs and the achievement of the group's goals. If this role negotiation succeeds, then the commitment levels of both parties remain high. But if role negotiation fails and the commitment levels of both parties fall to their respective divergence criteria (DC), then the individual undergoes the role transition of *divergence* and becomes a marginal member.

The fourth phase of group membership is *resocialization*. During resocialization, the group again seeks to produce assimilation in the individual, while he or she seeks to produce accommodation in the group. If the commitment levels of both parties rise to their respective divergence criteria, then a special role transition (convergence) occurs and the individual returns to full membership. But if the commitment levels of both parties fall to their respective exit criteria (XC), then the individual undergoes the role transition of *exit* and becomes an ex-member. This second (and more common) outcome is shown in Fig. 6.1.

Finally, the relationship between the group and the individual ends with a period of *remembrance*. During remembrance, both parties engage in a retrospective evaluation of their relationship. These evaluations become part of the group's traditions and the individual's reminiscences. If they continue to influence one another's outcomes, then both parties may also engage in an ongoing evaluation of their relationship. Feelings of commitment between the group and the individual eventually stabilize at some low level.

Of the five membership phases described in our model, socialization and resocialization are especially interesting because they are so stressful for both the group and the individual. Socialization and resocialization are stressful for the same reason: The individual is a quasi-member who belongs to the group but is not fully integrated into it. This situation is inherently unstable and therefore must be resolved. The individual must either leave the group or somehow attain full membership in it. Full membership cannot be attained, however, unless both the group and the individual become sufficiently committed to one another. The more assimilation the group produces in the individual, and the more accommodation the individual produces in the group, the more likely both parties are to develop the necessary levels of commitment. Unfortunately, the individual is not always willing or able to assimilate fully into the group, nor is the group always willing or able to accommodate fully to the individual. The stress experienced during socialization and resocialization thus arises from the struggle between the group and the individual regarding how much and what type of assimilation and accommodation will occur.

The socialization and resocialization phases of group membership clearly deserve special attention from researchers who are interested in group dynamics. Many studies of resocialization have been performed, and their results have been reviewed from several perspectives (e.g., Archer, 1985; Levine, this volume; Levine & Russo, 1987). As a result, social psychologists know a great deal about the relationships between full and marginal members of small groups. Many studies of socialization have also been performed, but their results have never been adequately reviewed. As a result, social psychologists still have much to learn about the relationships between full and new members of small groups.

Our goal in this chapter is to provide a comprehensive review of theoretical and empirical work on the socialization phase of group membership. The materials for this review were generated by investigators from a variety of disciplines, including psychology, sociology, anthropology, and political science. We found papers on socialization in many kinds of groups, including businesses, churches, schools, and clubs. Although the socialization process probably varies somewhat across these different kinds of groups, we chose to search for common rather than unique phenomena. Such a strategy seemed appropriate for an initial review of a large and diverse literature.

We originally planned to organize our review around the *effects* of socialization, namely the assimilation of newcomers into a group and the accommodation of a group to its new members. However, this plan proved to be impractical for two reasons. First, assimilation has been studied far more often than accommodation, a state of affairs that characterizes research on resocialization as well (Moscovici, 1976). Second, many studies of socialization involve dependent measures (e.g., the commitment of newcomers to a group or its commitment to them) that might reflect assimilation, or accommodation, or both. Such studies are thus difficult to classify in terms of the effects of socialization. So, we chose instead to organize our review around the *causes* of socialization, focusing on those variables that seem to affect the assimilation of newcomers into a group and/or the accommodation of a group to its new members. Five general categories of variables appear to affect the socialization process. These categories are (a) the characteristics of the newcomer; (b) the newcomer's socialization tactics;

(c) the characteristics of the group; (d) the group's socialization tactics; and (e) various environmental factors.

RESEARCH ON NEWCOMERS AND OLDTIMERS

Characteristics of the Newcomer

Many studies have focused on the role of individual characteristics in the socialization process. These studies reflect the assumption that socialization proceeds more easily for some newcomers than for others. Four general categories of personal characteristics have received particular attention. These categories are (a) demographic characteristics; (b) personality traits; (c) abilities and knowledge; and (d) motivation.

Demographic characteristics. Demographic characteristics, such as age, sex, race, and status, represent relatively stable aspects of newcomers that are readily apparent to other group members. Regarding age, there is some consensus that younger newcomers are socialized more easily than older newcomers (Brett, 1980; Church, 1982; Eisenstadt, 1952; Ziller & Behringer, 1961). Ziller and Behringer, for example, studied the socialization of new children in elementary school classrooms (1st through 6th grades). Over a period of several months, various measures of each child's socialization were obtained. These measures included the friendship choices of new and old classmates, evaluative comparisons that the newcomers made between their new and old schools, and assessments by teachers of how well the newcomers were adjusting. The results revealed that younger newcomers were socialized more rapidly than older newcomers. Many factors could contribute to such age effects. Perhaps younger newcomers are more adaptable than older newcomers and thus more willing or able to undergo assimilation. Groups may also demand less assimilation from their younger members. Finally, because people often enter groups whose members are similar to them in age, younger newcomers may be more likely than older newcomers to join groups that are less well established. Accommodation is probably easier to produce in such groups.

Several studies have focused on sex differences in the socialization process, but their results have been mixed. Some researchers have found that females are socialized more easily than males (Ziller & Behringer, 1961), whereas other researchers have found that males are socialized more easily than females (Feldbaum, Christenson, & O'Neal, 1980; Newman, 1974). There is little agreement about why sex effects occur. Perhaps females are more likely than males to permit assimilation, whereas males are more likely than females to demand accommodation (Eagly, 1978; Eagly & Steffen, 1986; Eisenberg & Lennon,

1983; Hall, 1978). If so, then socialization should be easier for females in groups that demand assimilation, but easier for males in groups that permit accommodation. Sex differences in the socialization process may also depend on the sexual composition of the group. Several observers (Corsaro, 1981; Fairhurst & Snavely, 1983; Feshbach, 1969; Kanter, 1977b) have noted that socialization is more difficult when newcomers are part of a sexual minority within the group.

Only a few studies of race differences in the socialization process have been performed (Fromkin, Klimoski, & Flanagan, 1972; Ziller, Behringer, & Goodchilds, 1960), all involving the socialization of Black and White newcomers in White groups. These studies reveal no clear race differences, other than a tendency for Black newcomers to be treated more harshly than White newcomers in groups that are reluctant to admit any new members at all.

Finally, the role of a newcomer's status in the socialization process has been the focus of several studies. These studies indicate that socialization is easier for newcomers whose external social status is higher (Dodge, Schlundt, Schocken, & Delugach, 1983; Putallaz & Gottman, 1981; Zander & Cohen, 1955; Ziller & Behringer, 1961). At least two factors may contribute to these status effects. First, newcomers whose status is higher often know and use more effective socialization tactics. Putallaz and Gottman, for example, created play groups of young children and then inserted a new child into each group. These newcomers, who were classmates of the other children, had already been identified as either popular or unpopular in school. Although every newcomer was eventually accepted by his or her group, socialization was more difficult for those who were less popular. Unpopular children often behaved in ways that irritated oldtimers (e.g., by arguing or showing off), thereby delaying their acceptance.

Status effects may also occur, of course, because groups are more tolerant of higher status newcomers. Zander and Cohen (1955), for example, created small discussion groups of college students and then inserted two newcomers into each group. The oldtimers in these groups were led to believe that one of these newcomers was someone of high status, whereas the other newcomer was someone whose status was low. The newcomers themselves were unaware of their differential status and were in fact of equal status. Observations of each group's discussion, along with subsequent interviews with the newcomers, revealed that newcomers with higher status believed they were more influential, were treated better by the oldtimers, and felt more attracted to the group.

Personality traits.   Personality traits involve behavioral dispositions of newcomers that are relatively stable but not always apparent to other group members. One personality trait that seems to affect the socialization process is *adaptability,* which involves a tolerance for ambiguity (Nash & Heiss, 1967; Reichers, 1987), an openness to new ideas (Church, 1982; Morrison, 1977), and a flexibility in behavior (Eisenstadt, 1952; Mendenhall & Oddou, 1985). All of these characteristics seem to make the socialization of newcomers easier, perhaps because they facilitate assimilation. The socialization process also appears to be affected by the personality trait of *autonomy,* which involves an internal locus of control (Louis, 1980), a sense of independence and self-reliance (Klein & Ross, 1965), and an active rather than passive orientation toward the world (Eisenstadt, 1952). All of these characteristics seem to make the socialization of newcomers easier as well, perhaps because they lead to the acquisition of information that facilitates both assimilation and accommodation. Finally, a third personality trait that may affect the socialization process is *self-esteem,* which involves a general sense of personal worth and competence. Newcomers who are higher in self-esteem seem to be socialized more easily (Corsaro, 1981; Hall, 1971; Jones, 1983; Morrison, 1977), perhaps because they can better cope with the stresses that accompany both assimilation and accommodation.

There are, of course, many other personality traits that might affect the socialization process (Davis, 1968; Nicholson, 1984; Reichers, 1987; Snyder, 1979). But some observers (Morse, 1975; Van Harrison, 1978; Wanous, 1980) have suggested that socialization depends less on the personality characteristics of a newcomer than on the *match* between his or her personality and the group that he or she is joining. Socialization is presumably easier when this match is better, because less assimilation and accommodation will be required.

Abilities and knowledge.   Abilities and knowledge, like personality traits, involve aspects of newcomers that are relatively stable but not always apparent to other group members. Several studies have focused on the role of a newcomer's abilities in the socialization process. These abilities can range from the general (Davis, 1968; Mendenhall & Oddou, 1985) to the specific (Bartell, 1971; Fromkin et al., 1972; Moreland, 1985), but so long as they are relevant to the group, they tend to facilitate socialization. More competent newcomers are thus socialized more easily, perhaps because they require less assimilation and can produce more accommodation.

A newcomer's knowledge about the group can also play an important role in the socialization process. Such knowledge also ranges from the general to the specific. At the most general level, newcomers vary in their knowledge of what it is like to be a new member of any kind of group. There is some evidence (Brett, 1980; Fellin & Litwak, 1963; Van Maanen, 1984) that newcomers who have had more experience in joining small groups are socialized more easily, perhaps because they have learned more effective socialization tactics. Fellin and Litwak, for example, studied the socialization of newcomers in several suburban Detroit neighborhoods. Some of these newcomers were more experienced than others at entering and leaving small groups, because they worked at jobs in which transfers between groups were more common. Self-reports of social interaction within each neighborhood revealed that these experienced newcomers were more likely than others to be accepted by oldtimers.

At a more specific level, newcomers also vary in their knowledge of what it is like to belong to the kind of group that they are joining. Several studies have shown that socialization is easier for newcomers who have had prior experience in similar groups (Bell & Price, 1975; Carp & Wheeler, 1972; Church, 1982; Feldman, 1976a, 1976b; Hopper, 1977; Naughton, 1987; Nicholson, 1984; Pedro, 1984; Taft, 1957; Truax, Shapiro, & Wargo, 1968; Van Maanen, 1976). Hopper, for example, studied the socialization of new cadets in a Texas police academy. These cadets varied in their prior law enforcement experience, which caused them to have different views about police work as well. Cadets who were more experienced viewed police work in more realistic and less idealistic ways than did cadets who were less experienced. More experienced cadets were also more likely to complete their police training successfully. Several factors might contribute to such effects. Perhaps newcomers with prior experience in similar groups make wiser choices about which new groups to join, so that there is less need for them to undergo assimilation or to produce accommodation. Newcomers with prior experience in similar groups may also undergo a kind of *anticipatory socialization* involving assimilation prior to their actual entry into the new group. Finally, newcomers with prior experience in similar groups may develop more effective socialization tactics that they can use later in the new group.

Even more specific knowledge about a group can be obtained from the group itself. Prospective members often have personal contacts within a group who can provide information about what it is like to belong to that group. Such contacts include recruiters (Rynes, Heneman, & Schwab, 1980; Wanous, 1977, 1980), group leaders (Gauron & Rawlings, 1975; Yalom, Houts, Newell, & Rand, 1967), and friends or relatives who are (or were) group members (Decker & Cornelius, 1979; Quaglieri, 1982; Snow, Zurcher, & Ekland-Olson, 1980; Wanous, 1977). The information provided by these personal contacts, so long as it is accurate, seems to make socialization easier.

Decker and Cornelius (1979), for example , studied the socialization of new workers in several small companies. The employment records of these workers provided information about how they acquired their jobs and whether they quit within a year after being hired. The results revealed that workers who obtained their jobs through employee referrals were less likely to quit than were workers who used other means (e.g., employment agencies or newspaper advertisements). The same three factors that we mentioned earlier might contribute to this effect as well. That is, newcomers who have personal contacts within a group may be socialized more easily because they make wiser choices about which groups to join, undergo some assimilation prior to entering the group, or develop more effective socialization tactics. Sponsoring may be an important factor too. When someone induces a newcomer to join a group, both the sponsor and the newcomer may be highly motivated to complete the socialization process successfully.

Finally, the most specific knowledge about a group can be obtained by actually participating as a prospective member in its activities. Several studies (McEvoy & Cascio, 1985; Pedro, 1984; Premack & Wanous, 1985; Reilly, Brown, Blood, & Malatesta, 1981; Suszko & Breaugh, 1986; Wanous, 1977, 1980) have shown that newcomers who have obtained a "realistic preview" of the group in this way are socialized more easily. Once again, this effect may occur because newcomers who have already participated in a group's activities make wiser choices about which groups to join, undergo some assimilation prior to entering the group, or develop more efficient socialization tactics. Another factor that might be important is cognitive dissonance. Newcomers who have already participated in a group's activities may feel a need to justify their effort, both to themselves and to others. As a result, they may be more motivated to complete the socialization process successfully.

Motivation.   Motivation is a characteristic of newcomers that is both relatively unstable and not always apparent to other group members. Newcomers clearly vary in their motivation to become full group members: Some newcomers would do almost anything to gain acceptance, whereas others could leave the group with few regrets. Surprisingly, few studies have investigated the effects of motivation on the socialization process, perhaps because motivation is usually viewed as an outcome rather than a cause of socialization activities. There is widespread agreement, however, that newcomers who are more motivated to become full group members are socialized more easily (Becker & Carper, 1956; Levine & Moreland, 1985; Mortimer & Simmons, 1978; O'Reilly & Caldwell, 1981; Richardson, 1967; Schein, 1968; Taft, 1957; Trice, 1957). This effect probably occurs because newcomers who are more motivated permit more assimilation and demand less accommodation.

Newcomer Socialization Tactics

Several studies have focused on the role of special tactics used by newcomers during the socialization process. These studies reflect the assumption that some newcomers are socialized more easily than others because they have developed more effective means of dealing with the groups that they join. Four socialization tactics available to newcomers have received particular attention. These tactics are (a) conducting a better reconnaissance; (b) playing the role of a "new" member; (c) seeking patrons within the group; and (d) collaborating with other newcomers.

Conducting a better reconnaissance.   One tactic that newcomers can use to make socialization easier is to conduct a better reconnaissance of the groups that are available to them. This might seem to be a rather curious socialization tactic, since it is carried out during the investigation phase of group membership. Nevertheless, there is a good deal of evidence (Bess, 1978; Dunnette, Arvey, &

Banas, 1973; Feldman & Newcomb, 1970; Pearson, 1982; Scott, 1965; Shuval & Adler, 1980) that newcomers who conduct a better reconnaissance are indeed socialized more easily. Scott, for example, studied the socialization of pledges in college fraternities and sororities. He found that students tended to join fraternities and sororities whose members shared their own values and that pledges whose values were more similar to those of older group members were also more likely to complete the socialization process successfully.

Few researchers have studied reconnaissance, so we have little evidence about how prospective members actually obtain information about the groups that they might join. Prospective members presumably learn about such groups by participating in their activities, consulting with people who belong(ed) to those groups or are familiar with them, or inferring similarities and differences between those groups and other groups to which they themselves belong(ed). We suspect, however, that most people conduct a rather poor reconnaissance of the groups that are available to them, because after joining they exhibit so much ignorance, surprise, and disappointment as new group members (Dean, 1983; Louis, 1980b; Van Maanen, 1977; Wanous, 1980). This is perhaps understandable, given all the time and energy that a thorough reconnaissance requires.

In order to conduct a thorough reconnaissance, prospective members must somehow obtain the answers to several questions about the groups that they might join. First, prospective members must consider what they really want from each group. Some of the problems that inhibit socialization arise because newcomers are not fully aware of their own needs (Kotter, 1973; Louis, 1980b). Second, prospective members must discover what each group really has to offer them. Many groups try to impress prospective members by emphasizing the rewards rather than the costs of group membership (Wanous, 1980). Third, prospective members must discover what each group really wants from them. The requirements for attaining full membership in a group are not always communicated clearly or honestly to prospective members, and some groups may not even be fully aware of what those requirements are (cf. Rosen & Bates, 1967). Finally, prospective members must consider what they really have to offer each group. This requires a realistic assessment of personal strengths and weaknesses, an assessment that some prospective members may be unwilling or unable to perform. Once the answers to all these questions have been obtained, prospective members can assess their own commitment to the group and its commitment to them, as well as their chances of gaining entry into the group and the probable difficulty of their subsequent socialization there (cf. Feldman, 1976a; Kotter, 1973; Morse, 1975; Wanous, 1980). If prospective members still intend to join the group at this point, then they can try to make their eventual socialization easier by using a variety of strategies designed to promote acceptance. We will discuss these strategies in detail later on.

As if all of this were not difficult enough, a thorough reconnaissance would require a prospective member to investigate *every* available group. Few prospective members are probably willing to conduct such a reconnaissance. Instead, they probably carry out a cursory investigation of just one or two groups that seem potentially satisfying and postpone careful consideration of assimilation and accommodation until after the socialization process has actually begun. In this way, prospective members almost certainly make socialization more difficult for themselves and for the groups that they join.

Playing the role of a "new" member. A second tactic that newcomers can use to make socialization easier is to play the role of a "new" group member as well as possible. Several researchers have observed how newcomers actually behave in small groups and how oldtimers react to their behavior. Their results suggest that there is indeed a role that most newcomers play and that those who play it better are socialized more easily.

The role of a new group member seems to have four related aspects. First, newcomers are usually more *anxious* than oldtimers: They often appear to be nervous, wary, and excited (Buchanan, 1974; Charles, 1982; DeBont, 1962; Klein & Ross, 1965; McGrew, 1972; Van Maanen & Schein, 1979). This anxiety may reflect newcomers' ignorance and confusion about the group and its members, their concern about being accepted by oldtimers, or their distress about changing their social identity (DeBont, 1962; Mansfield, 1972; Van Maanen, 1977; Wilson, 1984; Ziller, 1964). Second, newcomers are usually more *passive* than oldtimers: They tend to be quieter and less involved in the group's activities (Becker & Strauss, 1956; Dodge et al., 1983; Feldbaum et al., 1980; McGrew, 1972; Phillips & Erickson, 1970; Putallaz & Gottman, 1981; Washburn, 1932). Third, newcomers are usually *dependent* on oldtimers: They often imitate oldtimers, ask them for advice and help, and try to ingratiate themselves in various ways (Bourne, 1967; Dalton, Thompson, & Price, 1977; Dodge et al., 1983; Feldman & Brett, 1983; Klein & Ross, 1965; Phillips, Shenker, & Revitz, 1951). Finally, newcomers are usually more *conforming* than oldtimers: They are less innovative, avoid disagreements with oldtimers, and try to adopt the group's perspective whenever possible (Bell & Price, 1975; Heiss & Nash, 1967; Insko et al., 1980, 1982; Merei, 1949; Nash & Wolfe, 1957; Putallaz & Gottman, 1981; Rose & Felton, 1955; Snyder, 1958; Walker, 1973).

A newcomer who plays this role well will clearly experience a great deal of assimilation (or at least appear to do so). Newcomers who use this tactic are thus socialized more easily because they have been altered (or seem to have been altered) to suit the group. Presumably, newcomers could also make socialization easier by behaving in ways that produce accommodation. But very little is known about how newcomers can alter a group to suit themselves, despite considerable interest in this phenomenon (e.g., Fine, 1976; Jones, 1986; Levine & Moreland, 1985; Merei, 1949; Nicholson, 1984; Schein, 1971; Van Maanen, 1978; Wanous, 1980). This lack of research is surprising, given all of the recent attention that has been devoted to efforts by marginal members to produce accommodation during the resocialization phase of group membership. Moscovici and his colleagues (Moscovici, 1976, 1985; Moscovici & Mugny, 1983; Moscovici & Nemeth, 1974), for example, have argued that the behavioral style of minority members, particularly their consistency, is a key factor in their ability to influence majority members. Whether newcomers who consistently express their needs to oldtimers might also produce accommodation is an interesting question. Perhaps marginal members, who once elicited enough commitment from the group to be accepted by it, are able to produce accommodation in more and/or different ways than are newcomers, who have not yet been fully accepted by the group.

Seeking patrons within the group.   Another tactic that newcomers can use to make socialization easier is to acquire patrons within the group. Patrons are oldtimers who help newcomers to become full group members. There are several reasons why newcomers who have patrons may be socialized more easily than those who do not. First, a patron can facilitate assimilation and accommodation by providing the newcomer or the group with the ability or motivation necessary to meet the other's expectations. Second, a patron can persuade the group to demand less assimilation or the newcomer to demand less accommodation. Third, a patron can persuade the group or the newcomer to lower its acceptance criterion. Finally, insofar as a patron serves as the primary contact between the newcomer and the group, he or she can sometimes deceive the group or the newcomer about how much assimilation or accommodation has actually occurred.

Several different kinds of patrons can be found in small groups. Some patrons are relatively uninvolved with newcomers and neither seek nor accept much responsibility for their socialization, whereas other patrons are highly involved with newcomers and care a great deal about their socialization. The lowest levels of involvement with newcomers are displayed by *models* who are chosen by newcomers as guides for their behavior (Carp & Wheeler, 1972; Charles, 1982; Dressel & Petersen, 1982; Haas, 1972, 1974; Louis, 1980b; Rosen & Bates, 1967; Schein, 1968; Shuval & Adler, 1980; Weiss, 1978; Zurcher, 1967). Dressel and Petersen, for example, studied the socialization of young men who had recently become strippers at a local night club. Interviews with these men revealed that they learned many important aspects of their new jobs, such as how to wear a G-string and dance more seductively, by watching and imitating the performances of older strippers. Newcomers usually imitate an oldtimer who is high in status (Phillips et al., 1951; Louis, Posner & Powell, 1983), but some imitation of equal-status peers also takes place (Burke & Bolf, 1986; Kram & Isabella, 1985; Louis et al., 1983). Models are often unaware of their role as behavioral guides and may behave no differently even when that role becomes apparent to them. Models may later accept credit for newcomers who are socialized successfully (and refuse blame for those who are not), but they seldom try to help newcomers directly.

Somewhat higher levels of involvement with newcomers are displayed by *trainers,* who are given the job of assimilating new members by the group. Trainers are usually oldtimers who exemplify the group's values in some way or have earned the group's trust by conforming closely to its norms themselves (Clark, 1983; Leemon, 1972). Because the group holds them responsible for the socialization process, trainers often work hard to assimilate newcomers, but they rarely take any special interest in particular persons and may deny responsibility for newcomers who later fail to be socialized successfully.

Even higher levels of involvement with newcomers are displayed by *sponsors.* Sponsors are oldtimers who bring new members into the group and thus feel responsible (or are viewed by others as responsible) for their successful socialization (Burke, 1984; Haas, 1974; McGrew, 1972; Snow et al., 1980; Trice, 1957; Zander, 1976). Sponsors include recruiters as well as friends or relatives of the newcomers. Recruiters are people who are given the job of procuring for the group the best possible newcomers. Like trainers, recruiters rarely take any special interest in particular newcomers and may deny responsibility for those who fail to be socialized successfully. Friends and relatives of newcomers, in contrast, are typically quite concerned about the socialization of the particular persons they are sponsoring, but may be indifferent or even hostile to other new group members.

Finally, the highest levels of involvement with newcomers are displayed by *mentors.* Mentors are oldtimers who develop a close, personal relationship with newcomers after they have entered the group (Burke, 1984; Cook, 1982; Feldman, 1980; Halatin, 1981; Hunt & Michael, 1983; Kanter, 1977a; Merriam, 1983; Reichers, 1987; Shapiro, Haseltine, & Rowe, 1978) and do what they can to make their socialization easier. Both mentors and their proteges can benefit from these relationships, and many proteges go on to become mentors themselves after they have become full group members (Busch, 1985; Roche, 1979).

Collaborating with other newcomers.   Whenever a group contains more than one new member, yet another tactic becomes available to newcomers. Multiple newcomers can form a peer group and collaborate with one another to make their socialization easier. This collaboration often occurs naturally, because newcomers are likely to seek one another out for solace and support (Becker, Geer, Hughes, & Strauss, 1961; Bell & Price, 1975; Mansfield, 1972; Rosen & Bates, 1967; Schein, 1968; Van Maanen, 1973, 1975). A group can also encourage collaboration among newcomers by treating them as a "group" in their own right (cf. Moreland, 1986; Rohlen, 1973). In either case, newcomers who collaborate with one another are generally socialized more easily (Eisenstadt, 1952; Feldman, 1980, 1981; Kram & Isabella, 1985; Louis et al., 1983; Posner & Powell, 1985; Shuval, 1975; Zurcher, 1967).

Kram and Isabella (1985), for example, studied the role of peer relationships in the socialization of new employees at a large manufacturing company. These employees reported being involved in three general kinds of peer relationships. "Information peers" had relatively weak relationships with one another and spent most of their time simply gossiping about the company. "Collegial peers," whose relationships with one another were stronger, gossiped as well but also discussed personal concerns, career plans, and so on. Finally, the strongest relationships were found between "special peers," who discussed topics of every sort and tried to provide emotional support for one another. All three kinds of peer relationships were regarded as helpful by the new workers, but special peers were valued most highly.

Collaboration among newcomers can make their socialization easier in at least two ways. First, newcomers often aid one another in undergoing whatever assimilation the group demands. Such aid is sometimes indirect, as when one newcomer imitates another's behavior, uses social comparison to gauge progress toward full group membership, or feels less self-conscious because there are other new people in the group. More direct forms of aid can also occur, as when one newcomer asks another for advice about how to behave or encourages other newcomers in their efforts to gain acceptance from the group. Second, newcomers who share some dissatisfaction with the group can often demand and produce accommodation (Becker, 1964; Church, 1982; Mortimer & Simmons, 1978; Phillips & Erickson, 1970; Van Maanen, 1984). When newcomers work together in this way, they become more confident that their complaints are justified and less fearful of harassment by the group (Dornbusch, 1955; Evan, 1963). As a result, they can sometimes wield considerable normative and informational influence of their own on oldtimers.

Characteristics of the Group

Several studies have focused on the role of group characteristics in the socialization process. These studies reflect the assumption that socialization proceeds more easily in some groups than in others. Five characteristics of small groups have received particular attention. These characteristics are the group's levels of (a) development; (b) performance; (c) manning; (d) "openness"; and (e) cohesiveness.

Level of development. When a group forms, the relationships among its members are often rather chaotic. There is much uncertainty (and sometimes conflict) about what the group will be like and how each member will fit in. As time passes, the group begins to develop (Tuckman, 1965). Relationships among members stabilize, and the group's structure and dynamics become more complex. The entry of a newcomer into the group can threaten this development by forcing members to alter their relationships with one another (Goodman, 1981; Kaplan & Roman, 1961; Saravay, 1978). This threat is presumably greater in more established groups, which may respond to newcomers by demanding a great deal of assimilation and permitting very little accommodation. Socialization should thus be easier in groups that are poorly developed. Several studies (Katz, 1982; Merei, 1949, 1971; Ziller & Behringer, 1961) have yielded results consistent with this hypothesis.

Katz (1982), for example, studied temporal changes in several research and development groups within a large corporation. These groups ranged in "age" from several months to several years. Over a period of about 4 months, data on the communications among the members of these groups were collected. The results revealed that the members of "younger" groups communicated more often with outsiders and were more open to their ideas, whereas the members of "older" groups were more insular and conservative. Clearly, newcomers would have found socialization to be more difficult in the older groups. An extensive discussion of how the socialization process might vary across different levels of group development can be found in Moreland and Levine (1987).

Level of performance.   Whether by chance or by design, some groups are more successful than others at performing their tasks. A group's level of performance can have a strong impact on its reactions toward newcomers. When a group is succeeding, its members are usually satisfied with the group and therefore reluctant to make many changes in it. The potential benefits associated with admitting new members may seem few in comparison to the potential risks associated with their admission. When a group is failing, however, its members are usually dissatisfied with the group and therefore eager to make some changes in it. Under these conditions, the potential risks associated with admitting new members may seem few in comparison to the potential benefits associated with their admission. This suggests that newcomers should be socialized more easily in groups whose performance is poor. The available evidence (Fromkin et al., 1972; Insko et al., 1980; Moreland, 1985; Zander, 1976; Ziller, 1962; Ziller & Behringer, 1960) indicates that this is indeed the case.

Ziller and Behringer (1960), for example, created small groups of college students and asked them to perform a dot estimation task. Afterwards, some groups were told that their performance was good, whereas other groups were told that their performance was poor. A "knowledgeable" newcomer (who had been trained at dot estimation) was then inserted into each group, whose members were asked to perform the task again. Observations of the interactions among new and old group members, along with their interpersonal evaluations, revealed that newcomers in "unsuccessful" groups had more influence on oldtimers and were evaluated more positively than were newcomers in "successful" groups. Effects such as these probably occur because groups that are failing demand less assimilation and permit more accommodation than do groups that are succeeding.

Level of manning.   Barker (1968) has argued that one of the most important characteristics of a small group is its level of manning. An undermanned group has too few members to perform all of the tasks associated with its various activities, whereas an overmanned group has more members than it needs to perform those tasks. Although a group's level of manning is clearly related to its level of performance, these two characteristics are not the same: Undermanned groups sometimes succeed, whereas overmanned groups sometimes fail. Undermanned groups are presumably more eager than overmanned groups to admit new members. Newcomers should thus be socialized more easily in a group whose level of manning is low. The results of several studies (Petty & Wicker, 1974; Wicker & Mehler, 1971) are consistent with this hypothesis.

Petty and Wicker (1974), for example, created small groups of college students and asked them to race slot cars around a track. This activity required the performance of three separate tasks. Some groups (optimally manned) contained three members, whereas other groups (undermanned) contained only two members. After racing the cars for awhile, each group was told that it had either succeeded or failed. A newcomer was then inserted into the group and allowed to practice driving the car. The oldtimers were then asked to vote on whether the newcomer should remain in the group. The results revealed that oldtimers in undermanned groups were more likely than those in optimally manned groups to accept the newcomer, regardless of whether their groups had previously succeeded or failed. Socialization in undermanned groups is probably easier because those groups demand less assimilation and permit more accommodation than do overmanned groups.

Level of "openness".   Ziller (1965) has argued that many group processes depend upon whether the group is "open" or "closed." An open group has a relatively unstable membership: Newcomers frequently enter and oldtimers frequently leave such a group. In contrast, a closed group has a relatively stable membership: Newcomers rarely enter and oldtimers rarely leave such a group. Because they have had more experience with newcomers, open groups are more likely than closed groups to develop effective socialization tactics. As a result, newcomers should be socialized more easily in open than in closed groups. The available evidence (Mendenhall & Oddou, 1985; Schild, 1962; Ziller, 1962; Ziller, Behringer, & Jansen, 1961; Zurcher, 1970) suggests that this is indeed the case.

Ziller et al. (1961), for example, created small groups of college students and asked them to perform a dot estimation task. In some (open) groups, the oldtimers were warned that a newcomer might join them later; in other (closed) groups, the oldtimers were given no such warning. After each group performed the task once, a knowledgeable newcomer was inserted and the group was asked to perform the task again. Observations of the interactions among new and old group members, along with their interpersonal evaluations, revealed that newcomers in open groups had more influence on oldtimers, were spoken to more often, and were evaluated more positively than were newcomers in closed groups.

An interesting analogy can be drawn between a group's level of openness toward newcomers and the level of knowledge that newcomers have about a group. Ziller (1965) described an open group as one that has had some experience with new members and is therefore knowledgeable about them. This sort of knowledge seems analogous to the general knowledge about small groups available to someone who has been a newcomer in many of them. But as we noted earlier, more specific forms of knowledge about a group may also be available to at least some new members. For example, some newcomers may have belonged to similar groups in the past, had personal contacts within the group, or already participated in the group's activities. Are analogous sources of knowledge about newcomers available to a group? We believe that they are and that they too might facilitate the socialization process.

Consider, for example, a group that has already had some experience with new members and hence is relatively open. At a very general level, such a group possesses valuable knowledge about the problems and opportunities associated with socialization. But more specific knowledge is also available to the group about how to socialize the particular kinds of new members that it has encountered. If a newcomer is similar to someone who entered the group in the past, especially someone who completed the socialization process successfully, then the group will be relatively open to him or her. However, the group will be relatively closed to a newcomer who is different from anyone who ever joined the group before (unless, of course, all previous newcomers were difficult or impossible to socialize). Knowledge about a newcomer acquired through prior experience with similar persons should thus make his or her socialization easier. Our analogy suggests at least three factors that might contribute to this effect. First, prior experience with similar persons may help the group to make a wiser choice about whether or not to admit the newcomer. Second, prior experience with similar persons may cause the group to undergo a kind of *anticipatory socialization* involving accommodation prior to the newcomer's actual entry. Finally, prior experience with similar persons may allow the group to develop more effective socialization tactics that it can use later with the newcomer.

Even more specific knowledge about a newcomer becomes available when he or she has personal contacts within the group. These contacts can provide valuable information about what that person would be like as a new member. This information, so long as it is accurate, should also make socialization easier. The same three factors that we just mentioned could contribute to this effect as well. That is, a newcomer who has personal contacts within a group may be socialized more easily because the group makes a wiser choice regarding his or her admission, undergoes some accommodation prior to his or her entry, or develops more effective socialization tactics. And sponsoring may again be an important factor.

When a newcomer is induced to join a group by one or more of its members, both the newcomer and his or her sponsor(s) may be highly motivated to complete the socialization process successfully.

Finally, a group is most knowledgeable about a newcomer who has actually participated as a prospective member in some of its activities. Knowledge of this sort should also make the socialization of the newcomer easier. Once again, this effect might occur because the group makes a wiser choice regarding the newcomer's admission, undergoes some accommodation prior to his or her entry, or develops more effective socialization tactics. Another factor that might be important is cognitive dissonance. If someone who participated in the group's activities as a prospective member was admitted as a newcomer but failed to become a full member, then the group would feel and perhaps look foolish. To reduce such dissonance, the group should be motivated to help the person gain acceptance.

Cohesiveness.   A cohesive group is one that is appreciated by its members because they like one another, enjoy the group's activities, endorse the group's values, and/or believe that group membership is essential for the achievement of their personal goals (Cartwright, 1968). Several studies (Feldman, 1977, 1980; Heiss, 1963; Mills, 1957; Nash & Heiss, 1967) have shown that newcomers are socialized more easily in cohesive groups. Nash and Heiss, for example, created small groups of college students (all of whom were friends) and asked them to interpret various Rorschach inkblot cards. Initially, each person was asked to fill out several personality scales and to evaluate his or her group and its members. The latter measures provide information about group cohesiveness. After working on the task for awhile, one oldtimer from each group was transferred to another group whose members were strangers to him or her. All of the groups then worked on the task again. Finally, the new and old members of each group were asked to evaluate the group and one another. The results revealed that newcomers in more cohesive groups were less anxious about their relationships with oldtimers and more confident of acceptance than were newcomers in less cohesive groups.

These effects of group cohesiveness on the socialization process are difficult to explain. Because they are satisfied with their membership, oldtimers in cohesive groups are often reluctant to make any changes in those groups. They should thus permit very little accommodation and demand a great deal of assimilation (Merei, 1949, 1971), making the socialization of new members harder. However, assimilation may be much more likely to occur in cohesive groups, making the socialization of new members easier. The same aspects of a group that cause oldtimers to appreciate it may appeal to newcomers as well, so newcomers in cohesive groups may permit more assimilation and demand less accommodation (Sheridan, 1985). And cohesive groups are known for the conformity of their members (Festinger, Schachter, & Back, 1950; Schachter, 1951), so newcomers may receive more consistent training from oldtimers in such groups.

Group Socialization Tactics

Many studies have focused on the role of special tactics used by groups during the socialization process. These studies reflect the assumption that socialization proceeds more easily in some groups because they have developed more effective means of dealing with new members. Five socialization tactics available to groups have received particular attention. These tactics are (a) conducting a better recruitment; (b) initiating newcomers; (c) encapsulating newcomers within the group; (d) encouraging oldtimers to serve as patrons for newcomers; and (e) training newcomers in a consistent manner.

Conducting a better recruitment.   One tactic that a group can use to make socialization easier is to conduct a better recruitment of its prospective members. Once again, this might seem to be a rather curious socialization tactic, since it is carried out during the investigation phase of group membership. Nevertheless, several studies have shown that socialization proceeds more easily in groups that conduct a better recruitment (Adams, 1983; Bell & Price, 1975; Feldman, 1980; Lewicki, 1981; Mulford, Klonglan, Beal, & Bohlen, 1968; Mulford, Klonglan, & Warren, 1972; Pascale, 1984; Wamsley, 1972; Wanous, 1977, 1980). Mulford and his colleagues (1968), for example, asked newly hired Civil Defense workers to describe the recruitment and socialization practices of the groups they had just joined. Objective measures of the workers' job performance were also obtained. The best workers were found in groups that were more selective in their hiring or that devoted more time and energy to training. However, training improved job performance primarily in groups that were less selective. The newcomers in more selective groups did not benefit from training, perhaps because they already possessed the skills necessary to perform their jobs well.

Research on recruitment (Arvey & Campion, 1982; Snow et al., 1980) indicates that a group can obtain information about its prospective members in a variety of ways, including (a) formal or informal discussions with prospective members; (b) observation of prospective members who participate in group activities; (c) consultation with friends, relatives, or acquaintances of prospective members; and (d) inferences about similarities and differences between prospective members and other persons familiar to the group. Groups vary, of course, in the amount of time and energy that they devote to these activities. But the fact that newcomers often surprise and disappoint oldtimers (cf. Bartell, 1971; Leemon, 1972; Wanous, 1980) suggests that the recruitment efforts of many groups could be improved.

In order to conduct a thorough recruitment, a group must somehow obtain the answers to several questions about its prospective members. These questions are analogous to those that prospective members must answer about the groups that they might join. First, the group must consider what it really wants from each prospective member. Some of the problems that inhibit socialization arise because oldtimers are not fully aware of the group's goals or disagree about them. Second, the group must discover what each prospective member really has to offer it. Many prospective members try to impress a group by emphasizing the advantages rather than the disadvantages of their admission (Wanous, 1980). Third, the group must discover what each prospective member really wants from it. Some prospective members may not be fully aware of their needs (Kotter, 1973; Louis, 1980b), and others may be unwilling or unable to communicate their needs to the group. Finally, the group must consider what it really has to offer each prospective member. This requires a realistic assessment of the group's strengths and weaknesses, an assessment that some oldtimers may find disturbing (Schuetz, 1944; Ziller, 1965). Once the answers to all these questions have been obtained, a group can assess its own commitment to each prospective member and his or her commitment to the group, as well as its chances of getting each prospective member to join and the probable difficulty of socializing that person afterwards (cf. Feldman, 1976a, 1976b; Kotter, 1973; Morse, 1975; Wanous, 1980). If the group still intends to admit a prospective member at this point, then it can try to make his or her eventual socialization easier by using a variety of strategies designed to promote acceptance. We will discuss these strategies in detail later on.

Earlier we noted how difficult it can be for a prospective member to conduct a thorough reconnaissance of every group that he or she might join. It is somewhat easier for a group to conduct a thorough recruitment of all its prospective members, because the necessary work can be divided among oldtimers. But this advantage can be lost if oldtimers fail to agree about the recruitment of prospective members or cannot work together smoothly at their various recruitment activities. By and large, we suspect that groups are not much better at recruitment than prospective members are at reconnaissance. Most groups probably carry out a cursory investigation of just a few prospective members who seem potentially acceptable and postpone careful consideration of assimilation and accommodation until after the socialization process has actually begun. Once again, such an approach almost certainly makes socialization more difficult for everyone concerned.

Initiating newcomers.   A second tactic that a group can use to make socialization easier is to initiate new members. Initiations can range from informal harassment of newcomers by oldtimers (Dornbusch, 1955; Graves, 1958; Haas,

1972, 1974; Hong & Duff, 1977; McCarl, 1976; Schein, 1964, 1968; Vaught & Smith, 1980; Van Maanen, 1973; Walker, 1973; Wanous, 1980) to formal ceremonies in which newcomers try to demonstrate their acceptability by meeting various challenges posed by oldtimers (Aronson & Mills, 1959; Clark, 1983; Feldman, 1977; Gerard & Matthewson, 1966; Haas, 1974; Kanter, 1968; Leemon, 1972: Nuwer, 1978; Rohlen, 1973; Schopler & Bateson, 1962; Trice & Beyer, 1984; Van Gennep, 1908/1960; Van Maanen & Schein, 1979; Weiss, 1967). Rohlen, for example, described an elaborate initiation process carried out by a large Japanese bank. Over a period of 3 months, new employees were forced to (a) meditate and fast together at a Zen monastery; (b) participate in basic training exercises at an Army base; (c) perform voluntary services within the local community; (d) vacation together at an isolated youth hostel; and (e) complete a rigorous 25-mile hike. The owners of the bank were convinced that these initiation activities were essential for the effective socialization of their new employees.

Many groups initiate their newcomers in some way, and harsher initiations generally seem to facilitate socialization (but see Feldman, 1977; Finer, Hautaluoma, & Bloom, 1980; Hautaluoma & Spungin, 1974). The benefits of such initiations have been attributed to several factors. First, a harsh initiation may cause newcomers to experience cognitive dissonance regarding their membership in the group (Aronson & Mills, 1959; Gerard & Matthewson, 1966). In order to reduce such dissonance, some newcomers may become more committed to the group and thus more willing to permit whatever assimilation the group demands. Second, a harsh initiation may provide the group with valuable information about its new members (Clark, 1983; Haas, 1972). Newcomers who refuse to be initiated, participate in their initiation grudgingly, or fail to be initiated successfully reveal to the group that they are potentially unwilling or unable to become full members. The group can then respond by ejecting such persons or altering its socialization tactics to deal with them more effectively. Third, a harsh initiation may discourage those newcomers whose commitment to the group is weak, causing them to leave before becoming full members (Aronson & Mills, 1959). The sooner such persons depart, the less trouble they are likely to create for the group. Finally, a harsh initiation may demonstrate to newcomers how dependent they are on oldtimers (Pascale, 1984; Schopler & Bateson, 1962). Many initiations seem designed to weaken or confuse newcomers and to remind them that they are not yet acceptable to the group. Assimilation is more likely to occur among newcomers who experience such initiations.

Although harsh initiations seem to facilitate the socialization process, some observers have suggested that socialization is easier when newcomers are treated positively rather than negatively by oldtimers (Lewicki, 1981; Nash & Heiss, 1967; Schein, 1968; Wanous, 1980). Newcomers who receive positive treatment may feel grateful to the group, causing them to permit more assimilation and demand less accommodation. However, there is little evidence as yet that this socialization tactic really works.

Encapsulating newcomers within the group.   Another tactic that a group can use to make socialization easier is to maximize the amount of time and energy that newcomers devote to the group and minimize the amount of time and energy that they devote to other relationships. Groups that use this tactic encourage newcomers to interact as often as possible with ingroup members and as seldom as possible with outgroup members. Socialization seems to proceed more easily in these groups (Bourne, 1967; Brein & David, 1971; Carey, Peterson, & Sharpe, 1974; Feldman, 1980; Galanter, 1980; Kanter, 1968; Kotter, 1973; Louis et al., 1983; Manning, 1970; Reichers, 1987; Wamsley, 1972; Zurcher, 1967). Kanter, for example, used historical records to investigate the socialization practices of Utopian communities founded in America between the Revolutionary and Civil Wars. She found that many of these communities engaged in both "renunciation" and "communion" practices. Renunciation, which involved the destruction of existing relationships between newcomers and people outside of the community, was accomplished through such tactics as physical isolation and dramatic alterations in appearance, language, or customs. Communion, which involved the creation of new relationships between newcomers and people within the community, was accomplished through such tactics as shared labor and the elimination of private property. Utopian communities that engaged in renunciation and communion practices were generally more successful than those that did not engage in these practices.

Although encapsulating newcomers within a group seems to facilitate their socialization, the reasons for this effect are unclear. Perhaps newcomers who are less involved in a group find it more confusing or are more distracted by outside relationships, so that they are less likely to undergo assimilation or produce accommodation. Outsiders may also interfere with the socialization process by encouraging newcomers to permit less assimilation, demand more accommodation, or leave the group entirely. Newcomers who are more involved in a group may also develop better socialization tactics and use them more frequently and effectively. The group can also develop better socialization tactics and use them more frequently and effectively when newcomers are more involved. In either case, both assimilation and accommodation are more likely to occur. Finally, newcomers who are more involved in a group may also be more dependent on it. This dependence should lead them to permit more assimilation and demand less accommodation.

Encouraging oldtimers to serve as patrons for newcomers.   Yet another tactic that a group can use to make socialization easier is to encourage oldtimers to help newcomers become full group members. As we noted earlier, a patron can (a) help to produce whatever assimilation or accommodation is required; (b) persuade the group to demand less assimilation or the newcomer to demand less accommodation; (c) persuade the group or the newcomer to lower its acceptance criterion; and (d) deceive the group or the newcomer about how much assimilation or accommodation has actually occurred. All of these activities are likely to facilitate the socialization process.

How can a group encourage such activities? Its methods depend on the type of patronage involved. Regarding *models,* the group should do what it can to ensure that oldtimers conform to group norms, so that newcomers are given every opportunity to observe the kind of behavior that they are expected to exhibit themselves (Pascale, 1984). Deviance among oldtimers should be hidden from newcomers whenever possible, or otherwise punished in ways that discourage newcomers from similar misbehavior. And insofar as newcomers imitate one another, those who permit too little assimilation or demand too much accommodation should also be punished quickly and publicly. *Trainers* should be selected with great care and encouraged to become personally involved with all new members. One means of ensuring such involvement might be to punish trainers for newcomers whose socialization fails and reward trainers for newcomers whose socialization succeeds. *Sponsors,* whether they be recruiters or simply friends or relatives of new members, should also be held responsible for socialization failures and successes. It might also be helpful for the group to discourage sponsorship by those oldtimers (a) whose friends or relatives seem likely to require substantial assimilation or unlikely to be assimilated successfully; (b) whose judgment about which prospective members are acceptable seems poor; or (c) who seem incapable of helping newcomers to become full group members. Finally, the group should reward oldtimers who become *mentors,* especially those who perform that role best. Because most mentor-protege relationships seem to develop spontaneously (cf. Burke, 1984; Hunt & Michael, 1983), however, the use of such rewards may not guarantee successful mentoring.

Training newcomers in a consistent manner.   A final tactic that a group can use to make socialization easier is to provide consistent training for its new members. Newcomers who receive or observe inconsistent training are likely to become confused about what the group expects of them. As a result, they may be less willing or able to undergo whatever assimilation is necessary for them to become full group members.

There are three ways in which a group can provide consistent training for its new members. First, the group should ensure that each newcomer is trained in about the same way by every oldtimer (Adler & Shuval, 1978; Feldman, 1976a, 1976b; Graen, Orris, & Johnson, 1973; Ondrack, 1975; Pascale, 1984; Rosen & Bates, 1967; Shuval, 1975). Ondrack, for example, studied the socialization of new nurses in several hospitals whose staff members varied in the homogeneity of their job-related attitudes and values. When staff members were relatively homogeneous, newcomers received consistent cues from oldtimers and thus were socialized more easily. But when staff members were relatively heterogeneous, newcomers received inconsistent cues from oldtimers and thus were socialized less easily. Second, the group should encourage each oldtimer to train every newcomer in about the same way (Dornbusch, 1955; Leemon, 1972; Rohlen, 1973; Wamsley, 1972; Zurcher, 1967). Finally, the group should try to train successive newcomers in about the same way (Becker, 1964; Jones, 1986; Mortimer & Simmons, 1978; Van Maanen, 1978; Van Maanen & Schein, 1979). This can be facilitated by having each generation of newcomers participate in the training of its successors, on the assumption that people will train others in the same ways that they were trained themselves. Another interesting way in which socialization can be made more consistent over time involves the use of "war stories" (cf. Charles, 1982; Van Maanen, 1984). These are cautionary tales about actual or apocryphal newcomers from the past whose experiences reflect important aspects of the socialization process. Each generation of newcomers hears the same war stories and thereby receives the same messages about becoming a full group member.

Environmental Factors

Finally, a few studies have focused on the role of environmental factors in the socialization process. These studies reflect the assumption that some environments are more conducive than others to successful socialization. Three environmental factors have received particular attention. These factors are (a) dangers; (b) opportunities; and (c) third parties.

Dangers. One environmental factor that seems to affect the socialization process is the presence of dangers. Socialization appears to proceed more quickly, if not more easily, in groups that perform dangerous activities or operate within dangerous environments (Haas, 1972, 1974; McCarl, 1976; Van Maanen, 1973; Vaught & Smith, 1980; Weiss, 1967). During the Second World War, for example, many observers remarked on the relative speed with which newcomers were socialized in combat versus noncombat units (cf. Stone, 1946). Such effects may occur for two reasons. First, the members of dangerous groups often need special skills to perform their activities. Anyone who lacks these skills endangers not only himself or herself, but everyone else in the group as well. Newcomers thus pose a threat to oldtimers that is best avoided by a thorough and rapid assimilation of the new members into the group. Second, groups that perform dangerous activities or operate within dangerous environments are often highly cohesive. The members of such groups like and trust one another and feel a great deal of solidarity. Anyone who is not liked or cannot be trusted disrupts that solidarity and can endanger the group by disrupting its performance. Once again, the thorough and rapid assimilation of new members into the group is the best means of avoiding this threat.

The effects of dangers on the socialization process suggest several interesting questions. For example, most of the research in this area has focused on physical dangers, but social dangers, such as conflicts with other groups, might affect socialization as well. Also, most of the dangers that have been studied threaten a whole group rather than individual members. A newcomer can escape such dangers by simply leaving the group (or not joining it), but (loyal) oldtimers cannot escape in this way because that would prevent the group from achieving its goals. Under these conditions, the group should demand a great deal of assimilation and permit very little accommodation, and the available research evidence suggests that this is indeed what happens. But are newcomers never threatened by dangers that oldtimers can escape, and are newcomers *and* oldtimers never threatened by dangers that none (or all) of them can escape? Under these conditions, the balance between assimilation and accommodation might well be altered. Finally, many researchers have studied the effects of dangers on group cohesiveness (Stein, 1976). Their results indicate that dangers can increase the cohesiveness of a group under certain conditions, namely when the group already possesses a minimal level of cohesiveness, everyone in the group feels threatened, and the dangers can be escaped if all group members work together. If assimilation and accommodation can be regarded as sources of group cohesiveness, then these same conditions might also play an important role in moderating the effects of dangers on socialization.

Opportunities.   Another environmental factor that seems to affect the socialization process is the availability of alternative relationships for either newcomers or the group. When these opportunities occur before entry, they tend to make socialization easier. Prospective members who can choose among several groups are generally more committed to the groups that they finally join than are prospective members with fewer options. O'Reilly and Caldwell (1981), for example, asked MBA students who had recently accepted a job offer to describe any other offers they had considered before reaching their final decisions. Six months later, the same students were recontacted and asked how committed they were to their new jobs and how satisfied they were with those jobs. The results revealed that both commitment and satisfaction were higher among students whose job opportunities were initially greater. As a result, these newcomers probably permitted more assimilation and demanded less accommodation, thereby facilitating their socialization. A similar effect may well occur for groups: A group that can choose among several prospective members is probably more committed to the ones it finally admits than is a group with fewer options (cf. Ross & Ellard, 1986). Socialization is thus facilitated because the group demands less assimilation and permits more accommodation.

When opportunities occur after entry, however, they can make socialization more difficult. For example, newcomers who can leave one group and enter others are socialized less easily than are newcomers who have fewer options

(Hvinden, 1984; Richardson, 1967; Rose & Warshay, 1957; Schein, 1971). The former persons are less committed to the group (cf. Moreland & Levine, 1982; Rusbult, 1980) and thus permit less assimilation and demand more accommodation. Once again, a similar effect may occur for groups: A group that can eject some new members and admit others is socialized less easily than a group with fewer options. The former group is less committed to its new members and thus demands more assimilation and permits less accommodation.

Third parties.   A final factor that seems to affect the socialization process is the presence of third parties. These are individuals or groups who have some relationship with newcomers or oldtimers and thereby influence their behavior. Third parties can have both direct and indirect effects on socialization. At the most direct level, third parties often advise the group and its new members about how the socialization process should proceed (Bell & Price, 1975; Brett, 1980; Carp & Wheeler, 1972; Feldman, 1976a, 1976b; Friebus, 1977; Pearson, 1982; Trice, 1957). Friebus, for example, asked student teachers to describe anyone who had helped them to adjust to their new jobs. He found that many people, including friends, relatives, other teachers, and even some pupils, served as "coaches" for these new teachers at one time or another. Of course, the advice of such persons can be either helpful or harmful. Helpful advice includes (a) encouraging newcomers to permit more assimilation, demand less accommodation, or lower their acceptance criteria; (b) encouraging the group to demand less assimilation, permit more accommodation, or lower its acceptance criterion; (c) providing the group or its new members with accurate information about what kind of assimilation or accommodation is needed and how it can be produced; (d) deceiving the group or its new members about how much assimilation or accommodation has already occurred; and (e) discouraging the group or its new members from ending their relationship. Harmful advice can take just the opposite forms.

At a more indirect level, third parties also generate social comparison information that the group and its new members can use to evaluate the rewardingness of their relationship together (cf. Hoffman & O'Neal, 1985; Levine & Moreland, 1987; Oldham, Kulik, Stepina, & Ambrose, 1986; Thomas, 1986). This information may be offered directly to the group or its new members, or may just be available to them. Social comparison information generated by third parties can also have positive or negative effects on the socialization process. When that information leads to upward comparisons, the relationship between the group and its new members seems less rewarding. Newcomers may decide to permit less assimilation and demand more accommodation, while the group may decide to demand more assimilation and permit less accommodation. Both parties may also decide to raise their acceptance criteria. In all of these cases, the socialization process becomes harder. But when the information leads to downward comparisons, the relationship between the group and its new members seems more rewarding. Newcomers may decide to permit more assimilation and demand less accommodation, while the group may decide to demand less assimilation and permit more accommodation. Both parties may also decide to lower their acceptance criteria. In all of these cases, the socialization process becomes easier.

Finally, at a very indirect level, third parties can affect socialization by merely maintaining their relationships with the group and its new members. The more involving those relationships are, the more time and energy they require and the harder it will be for the group and its new members to complete their socialization successfully.

As we mentioned earlier, many groups try to limit the effects of third parties on the socialization process by isolating their newcomers from the outside world (Carey et al., 1974; Clark, 1983; Galanter, 1980; Kanter, 1968). It is worth noting, however, that this tactic is most often used by groups that seem unacceptable to outsiders, who may thus feel obliged to interfere. Outsiders may actually cooperate in socialization when groups seem acceptable to them. In fact, since few groups can eliminate the effects of third parties on the socialization process, it might be wiser for them to welcome whatever cooperation those third parties are willing to offer. Some groups have tried to use this tactic as a means of facilitating the socialization of their new members. Whyte (1956), for example, reported that some corporations devote as much time and energy to the socialization of a new executive's spouse as they do to the socialization of the executive himself.

CONCLUSIONS

Our purpose in writing this chapter was to review and integrate research on newcomers and oldtimers in small groups. We began with a general model of group socialization (Moreland & Levine, 1982). According to that model, the relationship between a group and an individual is characterized by reciprocal influence and temporal change. As both parties evaluate the rewardingness of their relationship, their feelings of commitment toward one another rise or fall. Whenever those feelings grow strong or weak enough to cross their decision criteria, a role transition takes place and the relationship between the group and the individual is altered. Evaluations then begin anew, producing further changes in commitment and (perhaps) other role transitions. As a result, the individual passes through several phases of group membership.

Two of those membership phases, socialization and resocialization, are especially interesting because they can be so stressful for both the group and the individual. Socialization and resocialization are stressful because the individual is neither fully in nor fully out of the group. There are only two ways in which this awkward situation can end: The individual must either become a full member of the group or leave it entirely. The resocialization phase of group membership has received considerable attention from social psychologists, but the socialization phase has been largely overlooked. We felt that it was time to redress this imbalance.

Our review of research on newcomers and oldtimers revealed that the socialization process is quite complex and that many factors can influence its success. The available research suggests that assimilation and accommodation are affected by characteristics of the newcomer (demographics, personality traits, abilities and knowledge, motivation); the newcomer's socialization tactics (conducting a better reconnaissance, playing the role of a "new" member, seeking patrons within the group, collaborating with other newcomers); characteristics of the group (levels of development, performance, manning, "openness," cohesiveness); the group's socialization tactics (conducting a better recruitment, initiating newcomers, encapsulating newcomers within the group, encouraging oldtimers to serve as patrons for newcomers, training newcomers in a consistent manner); and various environmental factors (dangers, opportunities, third parties). For example, socialization is easier if the newcomer has higher external status, more self-esteem, and greater ability; if the group is poorly developed, failing, and undermanned; if the newcomer plays his or her role well, seeks patrons within the group, and collaborates with other newcomers; if the group encapsulates newcomers, encourages oldtimers to serve as their patrons, and trains them in a consistent manner; and if the environment is dangerous, alternative relationships are not available, and third parties encourage assimilation and accommodation.

Although many factors seem to affect the socialization process, the psychological bases for their effects are not well understood. We have interpreted most of these effects in terms of assimilation and accommodation. In our opinion, factors that facilitate socialization do so because they increase the amount of assimilation and accommodation that occurs or decrease the amount required for acceptance. Similarly, factors that inhibit socialization do so because they decrease the amount of assimilation and accommodation that occurs or increase the amount required for acceptance. Our interpretation is somewhat speculative, however, because few researchers have attempted to measure assimilation or accommodation directly. New research on the socialization process is needed—research that investigates more closely the strategies employed by newcomers and oldtimers in their struggle to reach acceptance. But such research cannot be conducted until a more sophisticated theoretical analysis of the socialization process becomes available. Our general model of group socialization seems to offer a useful framework for such an analysis.

The Socialization Process

Socialization begins when the commitment levels of the group and the individual reach their respective entry criteria and the role transition of entry occurs. Typically, the acceptance criteria of both parties are higher than their entry criteria, and neither party's level of commitment reaches its acceptance criterion immediately after entry. During socialization, the group attempts to produce assimilation in the individual and undergoes accommodation, whereas the individual attempts to produce accommodation in the group and undergoes assimilation. If socialization is successful, then the commitment levels of both parties eventually reach their respective acceptance criteria and the role transition of acceptance occurs.

Each party's motivation to produce acceptance is influenced by two factors. One factor is the perceived probability that acceptance can be achieved (expectancy), and the other factor is the anticipated rewardingness of this role transition (value). These two factors probably combine in a multiplicative fashion. A group's or an individual's expectancy of achieving acceptance is determined by that party's perceptions of (a) the difference between its own commitment level and acceptance criterion, and (b) the difference between the other party's commitment level and acceptance criterion. As the sum of these differences decreases, the perceived probability of achieving acceptance increases, because the closer the group's and the individual's commitment levels are to their respective acceptance criteria, the easier it becomes for either party to produce acceptance. The value of acceptance for the group or the individual is determined by the absolute level of that party's acceptance criterion. The higher that criterion is, the more committed the group or the individual will feel when acceptance occurs, and hence the more rewarding that role transition will be.

If the group and the individual are motivated (to the same or different degrees) to produce acceptance, then they must decide how to achieve that goal. Six general strategies are available. Three of these strategies are *self-oriented*, because the group and/or the individual change something about themselves in order to make acceptance more likely. First, each party could lower its own acceptance criterion, which would reduce the difference between its current commitment level and the level of commitment that it views as necessary for acceptance. Second, each party could alter its expectations to match the other's behavior, which would increase its satisfaction with that behavior and thereby raise its commitment level. Third, each party could alter its own behavior to match the other's expectations, which would increase the other party's satisfaction with that behavior and thereby raise its commitment level. When used by the group, these three strategies reflect different forms of accommodation. When used by the individual, they reflect different forms of assimilation.

The remaining three strategies are *other-oriented*, because the group and/or the individual change something about one another in order to make acceptance more likely. First, each party could lower the other's acceptance criterion, which would reduce the difference between that party's current commitment level and the level of commitment that it views as necessary for acceptance. Second, each party could alter the other's expectations to match its own behavior, which would increase the other party's satisfaction with that behavior and thereby raise its commitment level. Third, each party could alter the other's behavior to match its expectations, which would increase its satisfaction with that behavior and thereby raise its commitment level. When used by the group, these three strategies reflect different forms of assimilation pressure. When used by the individual, they reflect different forms of accommodation pressure.

The likelihood that the group or the individual will select a particular strategy depends on its beliefs about (a) the utility of that strategy for producing acceptance, and (b) the present and future costs of implementing the strategy. Several general factors will influence these beliefs, regardless of the particular strategy that is being considered. Regarding the perceived utility of a strategy, other-oriented strategies probably seem more effective than self-oriented strategies to the group, whereas self-oriented strategies probably seem more effective than other-oriented strategies to the individual. These beliefs reflect the general assumption that individuals are more malleable than groups (Latané, 1981). Also, both parties probably regard the utility of a strategy as inversely related to the distance between the target's current commitment level and acceptance criterion. This belief reflects the assumption that strategies are more effective when small, rather than large, changes in commitment levels and/or acceptance criteria are required. Regarding the perceived costs of implementing a strategy, the group and the individual will believe that a strategy is costly, and therefore less attractive, insofar as it has negative internal (e.g., cognitive inconsistency) and/or external (e.g., social embarrassment) consequences.

In addition to these general factors that influence decisions about all six strategies, many specific factors can affect the group's and the individual's decisions regarding particular strategies. In discussing these strategy-specific factors, we focus first on the three self-oriented strategies and then on the three other-oriented strategies.

Lower own acceptance criterion.   Both the group and the individual are likely to lower their own acceptance criteria when they are uncertain about the appropriateness of those criteria. Uncertainty may occur because an acceptance criterion has been held for only a short time and has not been applied in other relationships. In such cases, parties that lower their acceptance criteria are unlikely to believe that they have seriously compromised their standards, nor are they likely to worry that others will view them as too eager for acceptance.

Alter own expectations.   Once again, both the group and the individual are likely to alter their own expectations to match the other party's behavior when they are uncertain about the appropriateness of those expectations. Uncertainty may occur because expectations have been held for only a short time and have not been applied in other relationships. Both parties also may be uncertain about the appropriateness of their expectations when those expectations are based on "unreliable" information (e.g., hearsay about the other party's behavior). When uncertainty occurs, parties that alter their expectations are unlikely to feel that they have seriously compromised their standards, nor are they likely to worry that others will view them as too eager for acceptance.

Alter own behavior.   Both the group and the individual are likely to alter their own behavior to match the other party's expectations when they are aware of these expectations, perceive them to be reasonable, and possess the knowledge and skills necessary to fulfill them. Factors that promote an awareness of the other party's expectations include past experience with that party, knowledge of other relationships in which that party has been involved, and clear and consistent communications regarding that party's expectations. Factors that enhance the perception that the other party's expectations are reasonable include the knowledge that others have fulfilled these expectations and the belief that such fulfillment leads to acceptance. Factors that increase the knowledge and skills available for fulfilling the other party's expectations include physical and mental ability, previous experience in similar relationships, and the quantity and quality of training that the other party provides. Sometimes the group and the individual can deceive one another into believing that their expectations have been fulfilled when in fact they have not. Such deception will be avoided when it seems likely to cause future problems for their relationship.

Lower other party's acceptance criterion.   Both the group and the individual are likely to lower the other party's acceptance criterion when they feel confident that they know what that criterion is, believe that the other party is uncertain about its appropriateness, and have enough power to change it. Confidence about the other party's acceptance criterion is enhanced by knowledge about other relationships in which that party has been involved and by explicit statements that party has made about its criterion. The belief that the other party is uncertain about the appropriateness of its acceptance criterion is strengthened when that party has held its criterion for only a short time and has not applied it in other relationships. Finally, power to change the other party's acceptance criterion is increased by the control of any resources (e.g., information, money, status) that it desires.

Alter other party's expectations.   Once again, both the group and the individual are likely to alter the other party's expectations when they feel confident that they know what these expectations are, believe that the other party is uncertain about their appropriateness, and have enough power to change them. Confidence about the other party's expectations is enhanced by knowledge about other relationships in which that party has been involved and by explicit statements that party has made about its expectations. The belief that the other party is uncertain about the appropriateness of its expectations is strengthened when that party has held those expectations for only a short time, has not applied them in other relationships, and has based them on "unreliable" information. The power to change the other party's expectations is increased by the control of any resources that it desires. Finally, the efforts of each party to alter the other's expectations can be affected by the perceived reasonableness of those expectations. Expectations seem more reasonable if others have fulfilled them and if such fulfillment has led to acceptance. Both the group and the individual are less likely to alter expectations that seem reasonable to them.

Alter other party's behavior.   The group and the individual are likely to alter the other party's behavior to match their own expectations when they are aware of these expectations, perceive them to be reasonable, and have enough power to change the other party's behavior. Factors that promote an awareness of one's own expectations for another party include past experience with that party, knowledge of other relationships in which that party has been involved, and prior thought and communications about one's expectations. Factors that enhance the perception that one's own expectations are reasonable include the knowledge that others have fulfilled these expectations and the belief that such fulfillment leads to acceptance. Factors that strengthen one's power to alter the other party's behavior include not only the control of any resources that it desires, but also that other party's physical and mental ability, its previous experience in similar relationships, and the quality and quantity of training that one has provided for it. Sometimes the group and the individual can deceive themselves into believing that their expectations have been fulfilled when in fact they have not. However, such self-deception often causes future problems in their relationship.

We have focused thus far on factors that influence the group's and the individual's motivation to produce the role transition of acceptance and their selection of a particular strategy to accomplish that goal. It is important to realize, however, that neither party is limited to a single strategy. In many cases, two or more strategies can be employed. Sometimes these strategies are used simultaneously, as when the individual lowers his or her own acceptance criterion and at the same time tries to alter the group's behavior. At other times these strategies are used sequentially, as when the group first tries but fails to alter the individual's expectations and then later must alter its own behavior instead.

Of course, the use of sequential strategies is not restricted to cases in which an initial strategy fails to move the group or the individual toward acceptance. For example, after reducing the difference between an individual's acceptance criterion and commitment level by lowering that person's acceptance criterion, the group might seek to (a) increase the individual's commitment level, and/or (b) reduce the difference between its own acceptance criterion and commitment level by altering its expectations for the individual's behavior. Because of reciprocation and imitation, one party's use of a particular strategy (e.g., lowering its acceptance criterion) can also increase the likelihood that the other party will use the same strategy. The dynamic quality of the socialization process thus becomes clear: The group's and the individual's efforts to achieve acceptance at one point in time can influence both their own and one another's behavior at a later time.

Unresolved Issues

Several other issues concerning newcomers and oldtimers in small groups also deserve more attention. One such issue involves the failure of most researchers to study the *process* of socialization. Our analysis of that process revealed that the group and the individual can employ many different strategies in their struggle to reach acceptance. But no one has attempted to measure these strategies directly. Instead, most researchers have been satisfied to measure the *outcome* of socialization, namely acceptance. Acceptance has been operationalized in a variety of ways, including (a) newcomers' evaluations of the group and its evaluation of them; (b) newcomers' influence on the group and its influence on them; (c) the performance of newcomers; and (d) newcomers' desire to remain in the group and its desire to retain them. It would be better, in our opinion, to investigate *how* the group and the individual produce these and other aspects of acceptance. This can be accomplished by measuring more directly the six socialization strategies that we described earlier. It would be especially interesting and informative to discover how the use of those strategies by the group and the individual changes over time.

Another important issue involves similarities and differences in the socialization of various types of newcomers. It is possible to differentiate among *charter members,* who come together to create a new group (Brinthaupt & Levine, 1985; Brinthaupt, Levine, & Moreland, 1986); *visitors,* who only expect to remain in a group for a brief time and thus do not participate fully in its activities (Brein & David, 1971; Church, 1982; Furnham & Bochner, 1986; Mendenhall & Oddou, 1985; Walker, 1973); *transfers,* who have recently belonged to a similar or affiliated group (Bateman, Karwan, & Kazee, 1983; Brett, 1980; Edstrom & Galbraith, 1977; Eisenstadt, 1952; Feldman & Brett, 1983; Keller & Holland, 1981; Richardson, 1967; Schild, 1962; Taft, 1957); *replacements,* who take the place of former group members (Chesler, Van Steenberg, & Brueckel, 1955; Grusky, 1960, 1963); and *regular newcomers,* who are joining an ongoing group, expect to remain in it for a long time, have not belonged to similar groups in the past, and are not replacing any former group members. Very little comparative work has been done on these different types of newcomers. A better understanding of their similarities and differences might also shed light on such related phenomena as tokenism (Kanter, 1977) and group mergers (Marks & Mirvis, 1986).

Although we have focused on the relationships between newcomers and full members of small groups, newcomers can have relationships with other types of group members as well. For example, newcomers often interact with prospective members, other newcomers, marginal members, and ex-members of the groups that they join. In some groups, newcomers are encouraged to recruit prospective members. This tactic may be effective because newcomers are similar to prospective members and therefore are trusted by them. Also, newcomers may be enthusiastic recruiters because of their need to reduce any dissonance caused by unpleasant socialization experiences (cf. Levine & Valle, 1975). As we noted earlier, newcomers often collaborate with one another to make their socialization easier. Relationships between newcomers and marginal members, however, can make socialization easier or more difficult. Although most groups are unlikely to appoint marginal members as trainers, they may adopt that role anyway. When marginal members want to regain acceptance, they may try to strengthen newcomers' commitment to the group in the hope that their efforts will be taken as proof of their own commitment. But when marginal members do not want to regain acceptance, or believe that it cannot be regained, they may try to weaken newcomers' commitment to the group in the hope that their efforts will damage or even destroy the group. Finally, newcomers sometimes encounter ex-members who have strong feelings about their previous experiences in the group or about the group's current behavior. These ex-members may try to strengthen or weaken the commitment of newcomers to the group, thereby affecting the difficulty of their socialization.

Because the socialization and resocialization phases of group membership are so similar, our analysis of the socialization of new members may shed light on the resocialization of marginal members as well. Resocialization can thus be viewed as a period during which the group and the individual struggle to reach convergence by strengthening their feelings of commitment toward one another (through assimilation and accommodation) and/or lowering their divergence criteria. Many of the factors that seem to affect the socialization process may thus affect the process of resocialization too. For example, resocialization is probably easier if the marginal member has higher external status, more self-esteem, and greater ability; if the group is poorly developed, failing, and undermanned; if the individual plays the role of a "marginal" member well, seeks patrons within the group, and collaborates with other marginal members; if the group encapsulates marginal members, encourages full members to serve as patrons for them, and retrains them in a consistent manner; and if the environment is dangerous, alternative relationships are not available, and third parties encourage assimilation and accommodation.

Finally, we should mention briefly three other areas of research that may prove to be useful in understanding newcomers and oldtimers in small groups. One line of work concerns how groups of animals react to the introduction of newcomers (e.g., Bernstein, 1964; Castell, 1969; Kawai, 1960). Although the risks of generalizing from animal to human behavior are well known, studies of infrahuman social behavior can often be a rich source of hypotheses for research on human behavior. The second line of work involves the transmission of social norms across generations of subjects (Jacobs & Campbell, 1961; MacNeil & Sherif, 1976; Rose & Felton, 1955; Weick & Gilfillan, 1971; Zucker, 1977). This research has focused on the degree to which newcomers can be induced by oldtimers to accept different kinds of group norms. Finally, the third line of work deals with role transitions of various sorts (Burr, 1972; Frese, 1984; Glaser & Strauss, 1971; Louis, 1980a; Moreland & Levine, 1984; Nicholson, 1984; Schwartz, 1979; Strauss, 1968; Van Gennep, 1908/1960). Although primarily concerned with some general factors that facilitate and inhibit movement from one role to another, analyses of role transitions suggest several specific factors that might affect the socialization process.

ACKNOWLEDGMENTS

Preparation of this paper was partially supported by Grant BNS-8316107 from the National Science Foundation. We would like to thank Sam Gaertner, Chuck Miller, Paul Paulus, Wendy Wood, and Al Zander for their helpful comments on an earlier version of the paper.

REFERENCES

Adams, D. S. (1983). Selection, investigation, and four types of members in the Red Cross chapter: A typology of voluntary association members. *Journal of Voluntary Action Research, 12*, 31–45.

Adler, I., & Shuval, J. (1978). Cross pressures during socialization for medicine. *American Sociological Review, 43*, 693–704.

Archer, D. (1985). Social deviance. In G. Lindzey & E. Aronson (Eds.), *The handbook of social psychology* (Vol. 2, pp. 743–804). New York: Random House.

Aronson, E., & Mills, J. (1959). The effect of severity of initiation on liking for a group. *Journal of Abnormal and Social Psychology, 59*, 177–181.

Arvey, R. D., & Campion, J. E. (1982). The employment interview: A summary and review of recent research. *Personnel Psychology, 35*, 281–322.

Barker, R. G. (1968). *Ecological psychology.* California: Stanford University Press.

Bartell, G. D. (1971). *Group Sex: A scientist's eyewitness approach to the American way of swinging.* New York: Wyden.

Bateman, T. S., Karwan, K. R., & Kazee, T. A. (1983). Getting a fresh start: A natural quasi-experimental test of the performance effects of moving to a new job. *Journal of Applied Psychology, 68*, 517–524.

Becker, H. S. (1964). Personal changes in adult life. *Sociometry, 27*, 40–53.

Becker, H. S., & Carper, J. W. (1956). The elements of identification with an occupation. *American Sociological Review, 21*, 341–347.

Becker, H. S., Geer, B., Hughes, E. C., & Strauss, A. L. (1961). *Boys in white: Student culture in medical school.* New Brunswick, NJ: Transaction Books.

Becker, H. S., & Strauss, A. L. (1956). Careers, personality, and adult socialization. *American Journal of Sociology, 62*, 253–263.

Bell, C. G., & Price, C. M. (1975). *The first term: A study of legislative socialization.* Beverly Hills, CA: Sage.

Bernstein, I. S. (1964). The integration of rhesus monkeys introduced to a group. *Folia Primativa,* *2,* 50–63.

Bess, J. L. (1978). Anticipatory socialization of graduate students. *Research in Higher Education,* *3,* 289–317.

Bourne, P. G. (1967). Some observations of the psychosocial phenomena seen in basic training. *Psychiatry, 30,* 187–196.

Brein, M., & David, K. H. (1971). Intercultural communication and the adjustment of the sojourner. *Psychological Bulletin, 76,* 215–230.

Brett, J. M. (1980). The effect of job transfer on employees and their families. In C. L. Cooper & R. Payne (Eds.), *Current concerns in occupational stress* (pp. 99–136). Chichester, England: Wiley.

Brinthaupt, T. M., & Levine, J. M. (1985, June). *Self- and other-perceptions of charter members and newcomers in task groups.* Invited paper presented at the Sixth International Conference on Groups, Networks, and Organizations, Nags Head.

Brinthaupt, T. M., Levine, J. M., & Moreland, R. L. (1986, April). *Newcomers and charter members in small groups.* Paper presented at the meeting of the Eastern Psychological Association, New York City.

Buchanan, B. (1974). Building organizational commitment: The socialization of managers in work organizations. *Administrative Science Quarterly, 19,* 533–546.

Burke, R. J. (1984). Mentors in organizations. *Group and Organization Studies, 9,* 353–372.

Burke, R. J., & Bolf, C. (1986). Learning within organizations: Sources and content. *Psychological Reports, 59,* 1187–1196.

Burr, W. R. (1972). Role transitions: A reformulation of theory. *Journal of Marriage and the Family, 34,* 407–416.

Busch, J. W. (1985). Mentoring in graduate schools of education: Mentors' perceptions. *American Educational Research Journal, 22,* 257–265.

Carey, S. H., Peterson, R. A., & Sharpe, L. K. (1974). A study of recruitment and socialization in two deviant female occupations. *Sociological Symposium, 11,* 11–24.

Carp, R., & Wheeler, R. (1972). Sink or swim: The socialization of a federal district judge. *Journal of Public Law, 21,* 359–393.

Cartwright, D. (1968). The nature of group cohesiveness. In D. Cartwright & A. Zander (Eds.), *Group dynamics: Research and theory* (pp. 91–108). New York: Harper and Row.

Castell, R. (1969). Communication during initial contact: A comparison of squirrel and rhesus monkeys. *Folia Primativa, 11,* 206–214.

Charles, M. T. (1982). The Yellowstone Ranger: The social control and socialization of federal law enforcement officers. *Human Organization, 41,* 216–226.

Chesler, D. J., Van Steenberg, N. J., & Brueckel, J. E. (1955). Effects on morale of infantry team replacement and individual replacement systems. *Sociometry, 19,* 587–597.

Church, A. T. (1982). Sojourner adjustment. *Psychological Bulletin, 91,* 540–572.

Clark, R. P. (1983). Patterns in the lives of ETA members. *Terrorism: An International Journal, 6,* 423–454.

Cook, M. H. (1982). Mentoring: A two-way street to professional development. *Training and Development Journal, 36,* 4.

Corsaro, W. A. (1981). Friendship in the nursery school: Social organization in a peer environment. In S. R. Asher & J. M. Gottman (Eds.), *The development of children's friendships* (pp. 207–241). Cambridge, England: Cambridge University Press.

Dalton, G. W., Thompson, P. H., & Price, R. L. (1977). The four stages of professional careers: A new look at performance by professionals. *Organizational Dynamics, 6,* 19–42.

Davis, F. (1968). Professional socialization as subjective experience: The process of doctrinal conversion among student nurses. In H. S. Becker, B. Geer, D. Reisman, & R. T. Weiss (Eds.), *Institutions and the person* (pp. 235–251). Chicago: Aldine.

DeBont, W. (1962). Identity crisis and the male novice. *Review for Religion, 21*, 104–128.

Dean, R. A. (1983). Reality shock: The link between socialization and organizational commitment. *Journal of Management Development, 2*, 55–65.

Decker, P. J., & Cornelius, E. T. (1979). A note on recruiting sources and job survival rates. *Journal of Applied Psychology, 64*, 463–464.

Dodge, K. A., Schlundt, D. C., Schocken, I., & Delugach, J. D. (1983). Social competence and children's sociometric status: The role of peer group entry strategies. *Merrill-Palmer Quarterly, 29*, 309–336.

Dornbusch, S. M. (1955). The military academy as an assimilating institution. *Social Forces, 33*, 316–332.

Dressel, P. L., & Petersen, D. M. (1982). Becoming a male stripper: Recruitment, socialization, and ideological development. *Work and Occupations, 9*, 387–406.

Dunnette, M. D., Arvey, R. D., & Banas, P. A. (1973). Why do they leave? *Personnel, 50*, 25–39.

Eagly, A. H. (1978). Sex differences in influenceability. *Psychological Bulletin, 85*, 86–116.

Eagly, A. H., & Steffen, V. J. (1986). Gender and aggressive behavior: A meta-analytic review of the social psychological literature. *Psychological Bulletin, 100*, 309–330.

Edstrom, A., & Galbraith, J. R. (1977). Transfer of managers as a coordination and control strategy in multinational organizations. *Administrative Science Quarterly, 22*, 248–263.

Eisenberg, N., & Lennon, R. (1983). Sex differences in empathy and related capacities. *Psychological Bulletin, 94*, 100–131.

Eisenstadt, S. N. (1952). The process of absorption of new immigrants in Israel. *Human Relations, 5*, 223–246.

Evan, W. M. (1963). Peer group interaction and organizational socialization: A study of employee turnover. *American Sociological Review, 28*, 436–440.

Fairhurst, G. T., & Snavely, B. K. (1983). Majority and token minority group relationships: Power acquisition and communication. *Academy of Management Review, 8*, 292–300.

Feldbaum, C. L., Christenson, T. E., & O'Neal, E. C. (1980). An observational study of the assimilation of the newcomer to the preschool. *Child Development, 51*, 497–507.

Feldman, D. C. (1976a). A contingency theory of socialization. *Administrative Science Quarterly, 21*, 433–452.

Feldman, D. C. (1976b). A practical program for employee socialization. *Organizational Dynamics, 5*, 64–80.

Feldman, D. C. (1977). The role of initiation activities in socialization. *Human Relations, 30*, 977–990.

Feldman, D. C. (1980). A socialization process that helps new recruits succeed. *Personnel, 57*, 11–23.

Feldman, D. C. (1981). The multiple socialization of organization members. *Academy of Management Review, 6*, 309–318.

Feldman, D. C., & Brett, J. M. (1983). Coping with new jobs: A comparative study of new hires and job changers. *Academy of Management Journal, 26*, 258–272.

Feldman, K. A., & Newcomb, T. M. (1970). *The impact of college on students*. San Francisco: Jossey-Bass.

Fellin, P., & Litwak, E. (1963). Neighborhood cohesion under conditions of mobility. *American Sociological Review, 28*, 364–376.

Feshbach, N. D. (1969). Sex differences in children's models of aggressive responses toward outsiders. *Merrill-Palmer Quarterly, 15*, 249–258.

Festinger, L., Schachter, S., & Back, K. (1950). *Social pressures in informal groups: A study of human factors in housing*. New York: Harper and Row.

Fine, G. A. (1976, September). *The effect of a salient newcomer on a small group: A force field analysis.* Paper presented at the meeting of the American Psychological Association, Washington, D. C.

Finer, W. D., Hautaluoma, J. E., & Bloom, L. J. (1980). The effects of severity and pleasantness of initiation on attraction to a group. *Journal of Social Psychology, 111,* 301–302.

Frese, M. (1984). Transitions in jobs, occupational socialization, and strain. In V. L. Allen & E. van de Vliert (Eds.), *Role transitions: Explorations and explanations* (pp. 239–252). New York: Plenum.

Freibus, R. J. (1977). Agents of socialization involved in student teaching. *Journal of Educational Research, 70,* 263–268.

Fromkin, H. L., Klimoski, R. J., & Flanagan, M. F. (1972). Race and competence as determinants of acceptance of newcomers in success and failure work groups. *Organizational Behavior and Human Performance, 7,* 25–42.

Furnham, A., & Bochner, S. (1986). *Culture shock: Psychological reactions to unfamiliar environments.* London: Methuen.

Galanter, M. (1980). Psychological induction into the large group: Findings from a modern religious sect. *American Journal of Psychiatry, 137,* 1574–1579.

Gauron, E. F., & Rawlings, E. I. (1975). A procedure for orienting new members to group psychotherapy. *Small Group Behavior, 6,* 293–307.

Gerard, H. B., & Matthewson, G. C. (1966). The effects of severity of initiation on liking for a group: A replication. *Journal of Experimental Social Psychology, 2,* 278–287.

Glaser, B. G., & Strauss, A. L. (1971). *Status passage.* Chicago: Aldine.

Goodman, M. (1981). Group phases and induced countertransference. *Psychotherapy: Theory, research, and practice, 18,* 478–486.

Graen, G., Orris, J. B., & Johnson, T. W. (1973). Role assimilation processes in a complex organization. *Journal of Vocational Behavior, 3,* 395–420.

Graves, B. (1958). Breaking out: An apprenticeship system among pipeline construction workers. *Human Organization, 17,* 9–13.

Grusky, O. (1960). Administrative succession in formal organizations. *Social Forces, 39,* 105–115.

Grusky, O. (1963). Managerial succession and organizational effectiveness. *American Journal of Sociology, 69,* 21–31.

Haas, J. (1972). Binging: Educational control among high steel iron workers. *American Behavioral Scientist, 16,* 27–34.

Haas, J. (1974). The stages of the high steel iron worker apprentice career. *Sociological Quarterly, 15,* 93–108.

Halatin, T. J. (1981). Why be a mentor? *Supervisory Management, 26,* 36–39.

Hall, D. T. (1971). A theoretical model of career subidentity development in organizational settings. *Organizational Behavior and Human Performance, 6,* 50–76.

Hall, J. A. (1978). Gender effects in decoding nonverbal cues. *Psychological Bulletin, 85,* 845–857.

Hautaluoma, J. E., & Spungin, H. (1974). Effects of initiation severity and interest on group attitudes. *Journal of Social Psychology, 93,* 245–259.

Heiss, J. S. (1963). The dyad views the newcomer: A study of perception. *Human Relations, 16,* 241–248.

Heiss, J. S., & Nash, D. (1967). The stranger in laboratory culture revisited. *Human Organization, 26,* 47–51.

Hoffman, J. V., & O'Neal, S. F. (1985, April). *Beginning teachers and changes in self-perceived sources of influence on classroom teaching practices.* Paper presented at the meeting of the American Educational Research Association, Chicago.

Hong, L. K., & Duff, R. W. (1977). Becoming a taxi dancer: The significance of neutralization in a semi-deviant occupation. *Sociology of Work and Occupations, 4,* 327–342.

Hopper, M. (1977). Becoming a policeman: Socialization of cadets in a police academy. *Urban Life, 6,* 149–170.

Hunt, D. M., & Michael, C. (1983). Mentorship: A career training and development tool. *Academy of Management Review, 8,* 475–485.

Hvinden, B. (1984). Exits and entrances: Notes for a theory of socialization and boundary-crossing in work organizations. *Acta Sociologica, 27,* 185–198.

Insko, C. A., Gilmore, R., Moehle, D., Lipsitz, A., Drenan, S., & Thibaut, J. W. (1982). Seniority in the generational transition of laboratory groups: The effects of social familiarity and task experience. *Journal of Experimental Social Psychology, 18,* 557–580.

Insko, C. A., Thibaut, J. W., Moehle, D., Wilson, M., Diamond, W. D., Gilmore, R., Solomon, M. R., & Lipsitz, A. (1980). Social evolution and the emergence of leadership. *Journal of Personality and Social Psychology, 39,* 431–448.

Jacobs, R. C., & Campbell, D. T. (1961). The perpetuation of an arbitrary tradition through several generations of a laboratory microculture. *Journal of Abnormal and Social Psychology, 62,* 649–658.

Jones, G. R. (1983). Psychological orientation and the process of organizational socialization: An interactionist perspective. *Academy of Management Review, 8,* 464–474.

Jones, G. R. (1986). Socialization tactics, self-efficacy, and newcomers' adjustments to organizations. *Academy of Management Journal, 29,* 262–279.

Kanter, R. M. (1968). Commitment and social organization: A study of commitment mechanisms in utopian communities. *American Sociological Review, 33,* 499–517.

Kanter, R. M. (1977a). *Men and women of the organization.* New York: Basic Books.

Kanter, R. M. (1977b). Some effects of proportions on group life: Skewed sex ratios and responses to token women. *American Journal of Sociology, 82,* 965–990.

Kaplan, S. R., & Roman, M. (1961). Characteristic responses in adult therapy groups to the introduction of new members: A reflection on group processes. *International Journal of Group Psychotherapy, 11,* 372–381.

Katz, D. (1982). The effects of group longevity on project communication. *Administrative Science Quarterly, 27,* 81–104.

Kawai, M. (1960). A field experiment on the process of group formation in the Japanese monkey (Macaca Fuscata) and the releasing of the group at Ohirayama. *Primates, 2,* 181–253.

Keller, R. T., & Holland, W. E. (1981). Job change: A naturally occurring field experiment. *Human Relations, 34,* 1053–1067.

Klein, D. C., & Ross, A. (1965). Kindergarten entry: A study of role transition. In H. J. Parad (Ed.), *Crisis intervention: Selected readings* (pp. 140–149). New York: Family Service Association of America.

Kotter, J. P. (1973). The psychological contract: Managing the joining up process. *California Management Review, 15,* 91–99.

Kram, K. E., & Isabella, L. A. (1985). Mentoring alternatives: The role of peer relationships in career development. *Academy of Management Journal, 28,* 110–132.

Latane, B. (1981). The psychology of social impact. *American Psychologist, 36,* 343–356.

Leemon, T. A. (1972). *The rites of passage in a student culture.* New York: Teachers College Press.

Levine, J. M., & Moreland, R. L. (1985). Innovation and socialization in small groups. In S. Moscovici, G. Mugny, & E. Van Avermaet (Eds.), *Perspectives on minority influence* (pp. 143–169). Cambridge, England: Cambridge University Press.

Levine, J. M., & Moreland, R. L. (1987). Social comparison and outcome evaluation in small groups. In J. C. Masters & W. P. Smith (Eds.), *Social comparison, social justice, and relative deprivation: Theoretical, empirical, and policy perspectives* (pp. 105–127). Hillsdale, NJ: Lawrence Erlbaum Associates.

Levine, J. M., & Russo, E. (1987). Majority and minority influence. In C. Hendrick (Ed.), *Review of personality and social psychology* (Vol. 8). Beverly Hills, CA: Sage.

Levine, J. M., & Valle, R. S. (1975). The convert as a credible communicator. *Social Behavior and Personality, 3,* 81–90.

Lewicki, R. J. (1981). Organizational seduction: Building commitment to organizations. *Organizational Dynamics, 10,* 4–21.

Louis, M. R. (1980a). Career transitions: Varieties and commonalities. *Academy of Management Review, 5,* 329–340.

Louis, M. R. (1980b). Surprise and sense-making: What newcomers experience in entering unfamiliar organizational settings. *Administrative Science Quarterly, 25,* 226–251.

Louis, M. R., Posner, B. Z., & Powell, G. N. (1983). The availability and helpfulness of socialization practices. *Personnel Psychology, 36,* 857–866.

MacNeil, M. K., & Sherif, M. (1976). Norm change over subject generations as a function of arbitrariness of prescribed norms. *Journal of Personality and Social Psychology, 34,* 762–773.

Manning, P. (1970). Talking and becoming: A view of organizational socialization. In J. D. Douglas (Ed.), *Understanding everyday life* (pp. 239–256). Chicago: Aldine.

Mansfield, R. (1972). The initiation of graduates in industry: The resolution of identity-stress as a determinant of job satisfaction in the early months at work. *Human Relations, 25,* 77–86.

Marks, M. L., & Mirvis, P. H. (1986, October). The merger syndrome. *Psychology Today,* pp. 36–42.

McCarl, R. S. (1976). Smokejumper initiation: Ritualized communication in a modern occupation. *Journal of American Folklore, 89,* 49–63.

McEvoy, G. M., & Cascio, W. F. (1985). Strategies for reducing employee turnover: A meta-analysis. *Journal of Applied Psychology, 70,* 342–353.

McGrew, W. C. (1972). Aspects of social development in nursery school children with emphasis on introduction to the group. In N. Blurton-Jones (Ed.), *Ethological Studies of child behavior* (pp. 129–156). Cambridge, England: Cambridge University Press.

Mendenhall, M., & Oddou, G. (1985). The dimensions of expatriate acculturation: A review. *Academy of Management Review, 10,* 39–47.

Merei, F. (1949). Group leadership and institutionalization. *Human Relations, 2,* 23–39.

Merei, F. (1971). The pair and the group: Experiments in group dynamics with children. *Comparative Group Studies, 2,* 17–24.

Merriam, S. (1983). Mentors and proteges: A critical review of the literature. *Adult Education Quarterly, 33,* 161–173.

Mills, T. (1957). *Group structure and the newcomer.* Oslo: Oslo University Press.

Moreland, R. L. (1985, June). *Assimilation and accommodation in Little League baseball teams.* Invited paper presented at the Sixth International Conference on Groups, Networks, and Organizations, Nags Head.

Moreland, R. L. (1986). Social categorization and the assimilation of "new" group members. *Journal of Personality and Social Psychology, 48,* 1173–1190.

Moreland, R. L., & Levine, J. M. (1982). Group socialization: Temporal changes in individual-group relations. In L. Berkowitz (Ed.), *Advances in experimental social psychology* (Vol. 15, pp. 137–192). New York: Academic Press.

Moreland, R. L., & Levine, J. M. (1984). Role transitions in small groups. In V. L. Allen & E. van de Vliert (Eds.), *Role transitions: Explorations and explanations* (pp. 181–195). New York: Plenum.

Moreland, R. L., & Levine, J. M. (1987). Group dynamics over time: Development and socialization in small groups. In J. McGrath (Ed.), *The social psychology of time.* Beverly Hills, CA: Sage.

Morrison, R. F. (1977). Career adaptivity: The effective adaptation of managers to changing role demands. *Journal of Applied Psychology, 62,* 549–558.

Morse, J. J. (1975). Person-job congruence and individual adjustment. *Human Relations, 28,* 841–861.

Mortimer, J. T., & Simmons, R. G. (1978). Adult socialization. *Annual Review of Sociology, 4,* 421–454.

Moscovici, S. (1976). *Social influence and social change.* London: Academic Press.

Moscovici, S. (1985). Innovation and minority influence. In S. Moscovici, G. Mugny, & E. van Avermaet (Eds.), *Perspectives on minority influence* (pp. 9–51). Cambridge, England: Cambridge University Press.

Moscovici, S., & Mugny, G. (1983). Minority influence. In P. Paulus (Ed.), *Basic group processes* (pp. 41–65). New York: Springer-Verlag.

Moscovici, S., & Nemeth, C. (1974). Social influence II: Minority influence. In C. Nemeth (Ed.), *Social psychology: Classic and contemporary integrations* (pp. 217–249). Chicago: Rand McNally.

Mulford, C. L., Klonglan, G. E., Beal, G. N., & Bohlen, J. M. (1968). Selectivity, socialization, and role performance. *Sociology and Social Research, 53,* 68–77.

Mulford, C. L., Klonglan, G. E., & Warren, R. D. (1972). Socialization, communication, and role performance. *Sociological Quarterly, 13,* 74–80.

Nash, D., & Heiss, J. (1967). Sources of anxiety in laboratory strangers. *Sociological Quarterly, 8,* 215–221.

Nash, D., & Wolfe, A. W. (1957). The stranger in laboratory culture. *American Sociological Review, 22,* 400–405.

Naughton, T. J. (1987). Effect of experience on adjustment to a new job situation. *Psychological Reports, 60,* 1267–1272.

Newman, J. E. (1974). Sex differences in the organizational assimilation of beginning graduate students in psychology. *Journal of Educational Psychology, 66,* 129–138.

Nicholson, N. (1984). A theory of work role transitions. *Administrative Science Quarterly, 29,* 172–191.

Nuwer, H. (1978, October). Dead souls of hell week. *Human Behavior,* pp. 53–56.

Oldham, G.R., Kulik, C. T., Stepina, L. P., & Ambrose, M. L. (1986). Relations between situational factors and the comparative referents used by employees. *Academy of Management Journal, 29,* 599–608.

Ondrack, D. A. (1975). Socialization in professional schools: A comparative study. *Administrative Science Quarterly, 20,* 97–103.

O'Reilly, C. A., & Caldwell, D. F. (1981). The commitment and job tenure of new employees: Some evidence of postdecisional justification. *Administrative Science Quarterly, 26,* 597–616.

Pascale, R. (1984, May 28). Fitting new employees into the company culture. *Fortune,* pp. 28–43.

Pearson, J. M. (1982). The transition into a new job: Tasks, problems, and outcomes. *Personnel, 61,* 286–290.

Pedro, J. D. (1984). Induction into the workplace: The impact of internships. *Journal of Vocational Behavior, 25,* 80–95.

Petty, R. M., & Wicker, A. W. (1974). Degree of manning and degree of success of a group as determinants of members' subjective experiences and their acceptance of a new group member. *Catalog of Selected Documents in Psychology, 4,* 1–22.

Phillips, E. L., Shenker, S., & Revitz, P. (1951). The assimilation of the new child into the group. *Psychiatry, 14,* 319–325.

Phillips, G., & Erickson, E. (1970). *Interpersonal dynamics in the small group.* New York: Random House.

Posner, B. Z., & Powell, G. N. (1985). Female and male socialization experiences: An initial investigation. *Journal of Occupational Psychology, 58,* 81–85.

Premack, S. L., & Wanous, J. P. (1985). A meta-analysis of realistic job preview experiments. *Journal of Applied Psychology, 70,* 706–719.

Putallaz, M., & Gottman, J. M. (1981). An interactional model of children's entry into peer groups. *Child Development, 52,* 986–994.

Quaglieri, P. L. (1982). A note on variations in recruiting information obtained through different sources. *Journal of Occupational Psychology, 55,* 53–55.

Reichers, A. E. (1987). An interactionist perspective on newcomer socialization rates. *Academy of Management Review, 12,* 278–287.

Reilly, R. R., Brown, B., Blood, M. R., & Malatesta, C. Z. (1981). The effects of realistic previews: A study and discussion of the literature. *Personnel Psychology, 34,* 823–834.

Richardson, A. (1967). A theory and a method for the psychological study of assimilation. *International Migration Review, 2,* 3–30.

Roche, G. R. (1979). Much ado about mentors. *Harvard Business Review, 57,* 14–16, 20, 24, 26–28.

Rohlen, T. P. (1973). "Spiritual education" in a Japanese bank. *American Anthropologist, 75,* 1542–1562.

Rose, A. M., & Warshay, L. (1957). The adjustment of migrants to cities. *Social Forces, 36,* 72–76.

Rose, E., & Felton, W. (1955). Experimental histories of culture. *American Sociological Review, 20,* 383–392.

Rosen, B. C., & Bates, A. P. (1967). The structure of socialization in graduate school. *Sociological Inquiry, 37,* 71–84.

Ross, M., & Ellard, J. H. (1986). On winnowing: The impact of scarcity on allocators' evaluations of candidates for a resource. *Journal of Experimental Social Psychology, 22,* 374–388.

Rusbult, C. E. (1980). Commitment and satisfaction in romantic associations: A test of the investment model. *Journal of Experimental Social Psychology, 16,* 172–186.

Rynes, S. L., Heneman, H. G., & Schwab, D. P. (1980). Individual reactions to organizational recruiting: A review. *Personnel Psychology, 33,* 529–542.

Saravay, S. M. (1978). A psychoanalytic theory of group development. *International Journal of Group Psychotherapy, 28,* 481–507.

Schachter, S. (1951). Deviation, rejection, and communication. *Journal of Abnormal and Social Psychology, 46,* 190–207.

Schein, E. H. (1964). How to break in the college graduate. *Harvard Business Review, 42,* 93–101.

Schein, E. H. (1968). Organizational socialization and the profession of management. *Industrial Management Review, 9,* 1–15.

Schein, E. H. (1971). The individual, the organization, and the career: A conceptual scheme. *Journal of Applied Behavioral Science, 7,* 401–426.

Schild, E. O. (1962). The foreign student, as stranger, learning the norms of the host culture. *Journal of Social Issues, 18,* 41–54.

Schopler, J., & Bateson, N. (1962). A dependence interpretation of the effects of a severe initiation. *Journal of Personality, 30,* 633–649.

Schuetz, A. (1944). The stranger: An essay in social psychology. *American Journal of Sociology, 49,* 499–507.

Schwartz, W. (1979). Degradation, accreditation, and rites of passage. *Psychiatry, 42,* 138–146.

Scott, W. A. (1965). *Values and organizations.* Chicago: Rand McNally.

Shapiro, E. C., Haseltine, F. P., & Rowe, M. P. (1978). Moving up: Role models, mentors, and the patron system. *Sloan Management Review, 19,* 51–58.

Sheridan, J. E. (1985). A catastrophe model of employee withdrawal leading to low job performance, high absenteeism, and job turnover during the first year of employment. *Academy of Management Journal, 28,* 88–109.

Shuval, J. T. (1975). From "boy" to "colleague:" Processes of role transformation in professional socialization. *Social Science and Medicine, 9,* 413–420.

Shuval, J. T., & Adler, I. (1980). The role of models in professional socialization. *Social Science and Medicine, 14,* 5–14.

Snow, D. A., Zurcher, L. A., & Ekland-Olson, S. (1980). Social networks and social movements: A microstructural approach to differential recruitment. *American Sociological Review, 45,* 787–801.

Snyder, E. C. (1958). The Supreme Court as a small group. *Social Forces, 36,* 232–238.

Snyder, M. (1979). Self-monitoring processes. In L. Berkowitz (Ed.), *Advances in experimental social psychology* (Vol. 12, pp. 85–128). New York: Academic Press.

Stein, A. A. (1976). Conflict and cohesion: A review of the literature. *Journal of Conflict Resolution, 20,* 143–172.

Stone, R. C. (1946). Status and leadership in a combat fighter squadron. *American Journal of Sociology, 51,* 388–394.

Strauss, A. (1968). Some neglected properties of status passage. In H. S. Becker, B. Geer, D. Riesman, & R. S. Weiss (Eds.), *Institutions and the person* (pp. 265–271). Chicago: Aldine.

Suszko, M. K., & Breaugh, J. A. (1986). The effects of realistic job previews on applicant self-selection and employee turnover, satisfaction, and coping ability. *Journal of Management, 12,* 513–523.

Taft, R. (1957). A psychological model for the study of social assimilation. *Human Relations, 10,* 141–156.

Thomas, J. G. (1986). Sources of social information: A longitudinal analysis. *Human Relations, 39,* 855–870.

Trice, H. M. (1957). A study of the process of affiliation with Alcoholics Anonymous. *Quarterly Journal of Studies on Alcohol, 18,* 39–54.

Trice, H. M., & Beyer, J. M. (1984). Studying organizational cultures through rites and ceremonies. *Academy of Management Review, 9,* 653–669.

Truax, C. B., Shapiro, J. G., & Wargo, D. G. (1968). Effects of alternate sessions and vicarious therapy pretraining on group psychotherapy. *International Journal of Group Psychotherapy, 18,* 186–198.

Tuckman, B. W. (1965). Developmental sequence in small groups. *Psychological Bulletin, 63,* 384–399.

Van Gennep, A. (1908/1960). *The rites of passage* (M. B. Vizedom & G. L. Caffee, translators). Illinois: University of Chicago Press.

Van Harrison, R. (1978). Person-environment fit and job stress. In C. L. Cooper & R. Payne (Eds.), *Stress at work* (pp. 175–208). Chichester: Wiley.

Van Maanen, J. (1973). Observations on the making of policemen. *Human Organization, 32,* 407–418.

Van Maanen, J. (1975). Police socialization: A longitudinal examination of job attitudes in an urban police department. *Administrative Science Quarterly, 20,* 207–228.

Van Maanen, J. (1976). Breaking in: Socialization to work. In R. Dubin (Ed.), *Handbook of work, organization, and society* (pp. 67–130). Chicago: Rand McNally.

Van Maanen, J. (1977). Experiencing organization: Notes on the meaning of careers and socialization. In J. Van Maanen (Ed.), *Organizational careers: Some new perspectives* (pp. 15–48). New York: Wiley.

Van Maanen, J. (1978). People processing: Strategies of organizational socialization. *Organizational Dynamics, 7,* 19–36.

Van Maanen, J. (1984). Doing new things in old ways: The chains of socialization. (Pp. 211–246). In J. L. Bess (Ed.), *College and university organization.* New York: New York University Press.

Van Maanen, J., & Schein, E. H. (1979). Towad a theory of organizational socialization. In B. Staw (Ed.), *Research in organizational behavior* (Vol. 1, pp. 209–264). Greenwich, CT.: JAI Press.

Vaught, C., & Smith, D. L. (1980). Incorporation and mechanical solidarity in an underground coal mine. *Sociology of Work and Occupations, 7*, 159–187.

Walker, T. G. (1973). Behavior of temporary members in small groups. *Journal of Applied Psychology, 58*, 144–146.

Wamsley, G. L. (1972). Contrasting institutions of Air Force socialization: Happenstance or bellweather? *American Journal of Sociology, 78*, 399–417.

Wanous, J. P. (1977). Organizational entry: Newcomers moving from outside to inside. *Psychological Bulletin, 84*, 601–618.

Wanous, J. P. (1980). *Organizational entry: Recruitment, selection, and socialization of newcomers.* Reading, MA: Addison-Wesley.

Washburn, R. W. (1932). A scheme for grading the reactions of children in a new social situation. *Journal of Genetic Psychology, 40*, 84–99.

Weick, K. E., & Gilfillan, D. P. (1971). Fate of arbitrary traditions in a laboratory microculture. *Journal of Personality and Social Psychology, 17*, 179–191.

Weiss, H. M. (1978). Social learning of work values in organizations. *Journal of Applied Psychology, 63*, 711–718.

Weiss, M. S. (1967). Rebirth in the Airborne. *Transaction, 4*, 23–26.

Whyte, W. H. (1956). *The organization man.* New York: Simon & Schuster.

Wicker, A. W., & Mehler, A. (1971). Assimilation of new members in a large and a small church. *Journal of Applied Psychology, 55*, 151–156.

Wilson, S. R. (1984). Becoming a yogi: Resocialization and deconditioning as conversion process. *Sociological Analysis, 46*, 301–314.

Yalom, I. D., Houts, P. S., Newell, G., & Rand, K. H. (1967). Preparation of patients for group therapy. *Archives of General Psychiatry, 17*, 416–427.

Zander, A. (1976). The psychology of removing group members and recruiting new ones. *Human Relations, 29*, 969–987.

Zander, A., & Cohen, A. R. (1955). Attributed social power and group acceptance: A classroom experimental demonstration. *Journal of Abnormal and Social Psychology, 51*, 490–492.

Ziller, R. C. (1962). The newcomer's acceptance in open and closed groups. *Personnel Administration, 5*, 24–31.

Ziller, R. C. (1964). Individuation and socialization: A theory of assimilation in large organizations. *Human Relations, 17*, 341–360.

Ziller, R. C. (1965). Toward a theory of open and closed groups. *Psychological Bulletin, 64*, 164–182.

Ziller, R. C., & Behringer, R. D. (1960). Assimilation of the knowledgeable newcomer under conditions of group success or failure. *Journal of Abnormal and Social Psychology, 60*, 288–291.

Ziller, R. C., & Behringer, R. D. (1961). A longitudinal study of the assimilation of the new child into the group. *Human Relations, 14*, 121–133.

Ziller, R. C., Behringer, R. D., & Goodchilds, J. D. (1960). The minority newcomer in open and closed groups. *Journal of Psychology, 50*, 75–84.

Ziller, R. C., Behringer, R. D., & Jansen, M. J. (1961). The newcomer in open and closed groups. *Journal of Applied Psychology, 45*, 55–58.

Zucker, L. G. (1977). The role of institutionalization in cultural persistence. *American Sociological Review, 42*, 726–743.

Zurcher, L. A. (1967). The Naval Recruit Training Center: A study of role assimilation in a total institution. *Sociological Inquiry, 37*, 85–98.

Zurcher, L. A. (1970). The "friendly" poker game: A study of an ephemeral role. *Social Forces, 49*, 173–186.

7 Reaction to Opinion Deviance in Small Groups

John M. Levine
University of Pittsburgh

Disagreement is a pervasive aspect of group life. Whether group members are children deciding which game to play, executives considering a new advertising strategy, or professors discussing curriculum changes, lack of consensus is the rule rather than the exception. Regardless of its source, disagreement can have important consequences for the group. On the positive side, disagreement can stimulate creative solutions to group problems and enhance the group's ability to adapt to its environment. On the negative side, disagreement can hamper group problem solving by producing defensiveness and hostility among members and, in extreme cases, can precipitate group dissolution.

Opinion divergence in many groups is bimodal and asymmetrical. That is, only two distinct positions are represented, and fewer individuals hold one position than the other. In such cases, opinion divergence involves some form of conflict between the smaller faction (minority members, or deviates) and the larger faction (majority members). Researchers interested in this form of conflict have typically created laboratory groups containing a minority and majority and then studied the behavior of one faction or the other.[1] During the 1950s and 1960s, work on disagreement in small groups focused primarily on the responses of minority members. A large number of studies sought to determine the circumstances under which individuals who hold a minority position in a group adopt the position held by the majority (see reviews by Allen, 1965; Hollander &

---

[1]The work of Stasser, Kerr, and Davis on freely interacting groups seeking to reach a consensus (chapter 9, this volume) represents an important exception to this research strategy.

Willis, 1967; Kiesler & Kiesler, 1969). Substantially less attention was devoted to the behavior of majority members. Relevant studies focused on majority members' feelings toward minority members and efforts to elicit conformity from them; the possibility that majority members might be influenced by the minority was generally ignored (Levine, 1980; Moscovici, 1976). Since the early 1970s, social psychologists have shown increasing interest in how majority members behave in situations of bimodal and asymmetrical divergence of opinion. Stimulated by Moscovici's work on minority influence (Moscovici & Faucheux, 1972; Moscovici, Lage, & Naffrechoux, 1969), researchers have sought to clarify the circumstances under which individuals who hold a majority position in a group adopt the position held by the minority. (See Levine & Russo, 1987, for a review of research on majority and minority influence.)

The purpose of the present chapter is to examine theoretical and empirical work dealing with majority reaction to opinion deviance in small groups. Opinion deviance is defined as an opinion expressed by a minority of group members that differs from the modal opinion of a physically present or realistically simulated majority of group members. The term opinion is used broadly to encompass judgments of stimuli ranging from simple perceptual items to complex attitudinal issues.

Given the above definition, two research areas fall outside the scope of the present review. One line of work concerns reaction to behaviors or conditions that are perceived as violating codified laws or widely accepted cultural norms of a society. Such behaviors/conditions include crime and delinquency, drug abuse, homosexuality, mental illness, physical handicap, and the like. Contemporary research on these kinds of "nonopinion" deviance focuses on the labeling process by which certain individuals are designated as deviates and on the implications of this process for the subsequent cognitions and behaviors of both labelees and labelers (Archer, 1985; Herman, Zanna, & Higgins, 1986; Jones, Farina, Hastorf, Markus, Miller, & Scott, 1984). Although it is no doubt true that some types of nonopinion deviance (e.g., emitting unpleasant body odor—Levine & McBurney, 1986) are perceived as arising from underlying opinion deviance and this inferred opinion deviance influences majority reaction, the present review is restricted primarily to studies investigating reaction to overt (as opposed to inferred) opinion deviance. The second line of work excluded from the present review involves evaluation of an attitudinally dissimilar target in a dyadic situation where deviation from group consensus is not explicit (Byrne, 1971; Griffitt, 1974). It is possible to argue that because many attitudes are anchored in reference groups, people perceive that anyone who disagrees with them is deviating from the modal opinion of their reference group. If so, it might be argued that reaction to disagreement in a dyad is merely a special case of reaction to perceived attitudinal deviance from group consensus. However, because a disagreer's *deviance* is more salient when the relevant group consensus is explicit rather than implicit, it seems appropriate to treat the two situations separately.

PLAN OF THE PAPER

In the following pages, I review theoretical formulations and empirical research dealing with reaction to opinion deviance in small groups. This review is divided into three major sections. The first (theoretical perspectives) summarizes and contrasts the traditional "functionalist" position of Festinger (1950, 1954) and the more recent "genetic" position of Moscovici (1976, 1985b). In the second section (empirical investigations), early studies derived from Festinger's (1950) model are presented, followed by a discussion of more recent research. Finally, the third section (unresolved issues) presents suggestions for future research.

THEORETICAL PERSPECTIVES

Festinger's and Related Models

Festinger (1950) posited that pressure toward group uniformity arises from two sources: (a) social reality: Group members seek consensus to validate opinions not anchored in physical reality, and (b) Group locomotion: group members seek consensus in order to move toward group goals. When opinion discrepancies exist among group members, uniformity pressures (arising from one of the above sources) produce communication directed toward reducing the discrepancies. Communication can resolve opinion discrepancies in two ways: The deviate may change his or her opinion toward the modal group opinion, or the group may change its modal opinion toward the deviate's opinion. In addition, the group may redefine its boundaries by rejecting the deviate. Festinger offered several hypotheses concerning variables that affect communication toward and rejection of deviates. He suggested, for example, that both the magnitude of communication pressure and the tendency to reject opinion deviates vary positively with the degree of opinion discrepancy among group members, the relevance of the issue to group function, and the level of group cohesiveness.[2]

In 1954 Festinger published an extension and elaboration of his earlier ideas concerning the origins and consequences of pressure to uniformity. He presented several new hypotheses relevant to reaction to opinion deviance, including the suggestions that cessation of social comparison with an attitudinally dissimilar target is accompanied by hostility and is more likely when the target is perceived as different on other attributes consistent with the opinion discrepancy. In addition, Festinger recast the motive ostensibly underlying desire for opinion uniformity. In 1950, Festinger seemed to suggest that opinion uniformity is sought

---

[2]Although formal mathematical models of Festinger's (1950) theory have been developed (e.g., McWhinney, 1968; Simon & Guetzkow, 1955a, 1955b), these models have had little impact on empirical research.

because it provides a *flattering* self-appraisal. According to this view, people want uniformity because it confirms that their present opinion is correct. In 1954, Festinger argued that opinion uniformity is desired because it is essential to obtaining an *accurate* self-appraisal. According to this view, people want uniformity because it allows them to determine whether or not their present opinion is correct.[3]

Israel (1956) extended Festinger's analysis in several ways. For example, he explicitly distinguished between (a) *corroborative* evaluation, in which an individual seeks to obtain support for an opinion in which he or she is highly involved, and (b) *informative* evaluation, in which an individual seeks to evaluate the correctness of an opinion in which he or she has little confidence and emotional involvement. Israel also argued that, in contrast to Festinger's position, similar others are *not* always necessary for stable self-evaluation (e.g., a person seeking informative evaluation can sometimes learn a good deal by comparing with dissimilar others). Finally, Israel noted that expression of overt hostility toward a deviate is different from rejection of the deviate. Overt hostility is a sanction used during attempts to alter the deviate's opinion; rejection is a response that occurs when influence attempts fail and are abandoned.

Orcutt (1973) made a similar distinction between *inclusive* and *exclusive* reaction to deviance. The former reflects an attempt to alter the opinion of a deviate who is perceived as amenable to persuasion; the latter reflects an attempt to exclude from the group a deviate who is perceived as unresponsive to influence. According to Orcutt's analysis, the greater the perceived scope, stability, and value centrality of deviance, the more likely are majority members to make an internal, or personal, attribution for the deviate's behavior, which in turn leads to an exclusive rather than an inclusive reaction.

Other theorists have extended Festinger's (1950, 1954) ideas by suggesting more complex typologies of reaction to disagreement. In discussing referent power in small groups, Collins and Raven (1969) argued that people who desire to achieve uniformity with others (O) can use one or more of the following techniques: changing their opinion to make it consistent with O's opinion; attempting to change O's opinion through persuasion; cognitively distorting the disagreement by minimizing the amount or importance of the opinion discrepancy; rejecting O by perceiving O as unattractive, dissimilar, or irrelevant to the issue; and differentiating O so that O's opinion is not perceived as reflecting O's "real" qualities. Newcomb's (1953, 1959, 1961) balance model of social interaction suggests still other ways in which majority members might respond to

---

[3]Although my focus is on opinions, it should be noted that Festinger's (1954) discussion of the "unidirectional drive upward" implies that when ability is being assessed people desire flattering as well as accurate information (Gruder, 1977).

opinion deviance. These include compromise following communication and "agreeing to disagree."[4] (See Newcomb, 1953, and Burnstein, 1969, for balance interpretations of studies dealing with reaction to opinion deviance.)

The models of reaction to deviance discussed so far (with the partial exception of Israel's 1956 formulation) assume that people desire group consensus, attempt to attain consensus when it is absent, and respond negatively to individuals who impede consensus (deviates). These assumptions, although still widely held, have not gone unchallenged.

One line of attack has come from investigators interested in social comparison processes. As mentioned earlier, Israel (1956) suggested that at least two motives can underlie social comparison: desire for accurate self-appraisal (informative evaluation) and desire for flattering, or validating, self-appraisal (corroborative evaluation). Moreover, Israel hypothesized that similar others are not always sought out for social comparison. These ideas have been restated and elaborated by a number of authors in the years since 1956 (e.g., Brickman & Bulman, 1977; Goethals & Darley, 1977, 1987; Gruder, 1977; Levine, 1983; Levine & Moreland, 1987; Singer, 1981; Thornton & Arrowood, 1966; Wills, 1981). Because desire for opinion similarity is a basic premise of Festinger's and related models of reaction to deviance, the notion that similar others are *not* always preferred for opinion validation and/or evaluation poses rather serious problems for these models.

The assumption that social relations are based on the desire for opinion uniformity has also been challenged from another quarter. Several theorists have argued that individuals have a strong need to feel unique, which can only be satisfied by differentiating themselves from others (e.g., Codol, 1984; Lemaine, 1974; Lemaine, Kastersztein, & Personnaz, 1978; Snyder & Fromkin, 1980; Ziller, 1964). According to this analysis, opinion similarity is a threat to personal distinctiveness. Therefore, instead of seeking agreement with others, people who wish to feel unique desire *disagreement*.

The most far-reaching attack on the assumptions underlying traditional conceptions of reaction to deviance has been offered by Moscovici. In contrast to previous theorists who analyzed social influence in groups, Moscovici views the minority as a source as well as a target of influence and seeks to explain innovation (minority influence) as well as conformity (majority influence) (Moscovici, 1974, 1976, 1980, 1985a, 1985b; Moscovici & Faucheux, 1972; Moscovici & Mugny, 1983; Moscovici & Nemeth, 1974; Moscovici & Paicheler, 1983).

---

[4]It should be noted that Newcomb's balance formulation predicts the same relationship between opinion similarity and attraction as does Byrne's reinforcement model (Byrne, 1969, 1971; Clore & Byrne, 1974). A major difference, pointed out by Byrne (1969), is that the balance model has led to a more comprehensive typology of reactions to disagreement than has the reinforcement model.

Moscovici's and Related Models

Moscovici believes that his "genetic" model of social influence should replace the traditional "functionalist" approach. He therefore spends a good deal of time criticizing the earlier model and reinterpreting studies designed to test it. Moscovici states that the functionalist position emphasizes asymmetrical influence, in which majorities can be sources (but not targets) of influence and minorities can be targets (but not sources) of influence. The genetic position, in contrast, emphasizes symmetrical influence in which both majorities and minorities are potential sources and targets of influence. Previous investigators have underestimated the probability of minority influence, according to Moscovici, because of an incorrect assumption that deviates are easily expelled from groups and a preoccupation with "nomic" majorities (that have strongly internalized beliefs) and "anomic" minorities (that lack such beliefs).

Related to the distinction between asymmetrical and symmetrical influence is Moscovici's contention that the functionalist model emphasizes only social control, whereas the genetic model also emphasizes social change. He states that investigators working within the functionalist tradition believe that all group members must have identical values and judgmental criteria. This leads to the assumptions that deviance threatens the group and the deviate is deficient, which in turn produce pressure on the deviate to alter his or her position. The genetic position, in contrast, assumes that social change is a crucial aspect of influence, which can only be investigated by viewing minorities as influence sources and majorities as influence targets.

Concerning the psychological mechanisms that mediate influence, Moscovici asserts that the functionalist perspective focuses on dependence relations and the need to reduce uncertainty, whereas the genetic perspective focuses on conflict and behavioral style. Researchers working in the functionalist tradition assume that influence is mediated by "effect dependence," based on desire to win the approval of others, and "information dependence," based on desire to hold a correct view of reality (Jones & Gerard, 1967). In regard to information dependence, the functionalist model assumes that stimulus ambiguity produces uncertainty, which in turn leads to conformity to others' opinions. Moscovici argues that neither dependence nor uncertainty is a critical determinant of majority or minority influence. Instead, he asserts that influence is directly related to the production and resolution of conflict. According to the genetic model, disagreement produces both interpersonal and intrapersonal conflict, and the essence of influence is conflict negotiation. The magnitude of conflict in a given situation is affected by four factors: the discrepancy between the majority and minority positions, the nature of the response alternatives (categorical versus variable), individuals' commitment to their positions, and the possibility of excluding the minority.

Moscovici views behavioral style, which involves the organization, timing, and intensity of responses, as the most important determinant of both majority and minority influence. Of the several behavioral styles that he originally identified, only two have received systematic research attention in majority/minority influence situations. *Consistency,* defined as the maintenance of a position over time and modality, is assumed to enhance influence. *Rigidity,* a variant of consistency in which the influence source is perceived negatively, is assumed to reduce influence. The impact of behavioral style on influence is presumably mediated by recipients' attributions about the source's underlying dispositions (certainty and commitment in the case of consistency; inflexibility and dogmatism in the case of rigidity).[5]

Moscovici also contrasts the functionalist and genetic models in terms of the norms that underlie influence and the forms that influence can take. Regarding norms, the functionalist model considers only the objectivity norm, which involves the need to verify opinions against the criterion of objective accuracy. The genetic model considers, in addition to the objectivity norm, the preference norm, which assumes that several desirable positions can exist simultaneously, and the originality norm, which involves the desire for novelty. Regarding forms of influence, the functionalist model recognizes only conformity, which is assumed to foster individual and social development. (Innovation, when it occurs, is presumably instigated by persons who have acquired high status through prior conformity—Hollander, 1958, 1964.) In contrast, the genetic model recognizes three forms of influence: conformity (i.e., majority influence that reduces conflict); normalization (i.e., reciprocal influence that avoids conflict); and innovation (i.e., minority influence that creates conflict). According to Moscovici, conformity occurs when the majority is nomic (i.e., has strongly internalized beliefs) and the minority is anomic (i.e., does not have such beliefs), normalization occurs when there is no clear criterion for deciding among competing positions and group members are relatively uncommitted to their positions, and innovation occurs when the minority is nomic and the majority is either nomic or anomic. In the nomic minority/nomic majority case, the minority is effective because it causes a breakdown in the enforcement of majority norms and elicits majority attention to its position.

In comparing conformity and innovation, Moscovici suggests that majority and minority influence represent qualitatively different means of resolving conflict. Majorities induce a *comparison* process, whereby minority attention is focused on the social implications of the majority-minority disagreement. In order to hold a valid opinion and gain acceptance from the majority, the minority often exhibits manifest (public) change toward the majority's position. However, because the minority does not engage in active information processing about the

---

[5]Similar arguments have been made about the impact of stylistic factors in dyadic persuasion settings (e.g., Apple, Streeter, & Krauss, 1979; Erickson, Lind, Johnson, & O'Barr, 1978; Newcombe & Arnkoff, 1979).

issue in question, it is unlikely to exhibit latent (private) influence. Minorities, in contrast, induce a *validation* process, whereby majority attention is focused on the issue underlying the disagreement. This causes the majority to engage in active information processing about the issue, which in turn often produces latent change toward the minority's position. However, because the majority does not want others to view it as deviant, it is unlikely to show manifest change. According to Moscovici, then, majorities are more likely to produce compliance than conversion, whereas minorities are more likely to produce conversion than compliance.

Moscovici also deals with how minorities are perceived and evaluated by majorities. He suggests that minority members elicit ambivalent reactions from majority members. On the one hand, minorities are often disliked and rejected, because they neither confirm majority members' views of reality nor provide social approval. On the other hand, minorities are often grudgingly respected and admired for upholding their views in the face of majority opposition.

Several authors, while acknowledging the incisiveness of many of Moscovici's observations, have criticized his analysis of social influence. Some of these criticisms have focused on Moscovici's efforts to discredit functionalist interpretations of prior studies and to reinterpret these studies in his own terms. For example, Levine (1980) discussed weaknesses in Moscovici's arguments that dependence, power, and uncertainty have little impact on social influence (see also Doms, 1984; Kelvin, 1979; and Wolf, 1979, 1987). Other criticisms have centered on the adequacy of the genetic model. Levine (1980) noted problems with Moscovici's analysis of behavioral style, including his failure to distinguish clearly between consistency and rigidity. Additional problems regarding the definition and impact of behavioral style were pointed out by Maass and Clark (1984), who also raised questions about Moscovici's attributional explanation of the effectiveness of minority consistency. A different, though still critical, assessment of Moscovici's attributional analysis was recently offered by Chaiken and Stangor (1987). The strongest challenges to Moscovici's position, however, have concerned his two-process account of majority and minority influence. On the one hand, it has been suggested that a single process is responsible for both kinds of influence (e.g., Doms, 1984; Latane & Wolf, 1981; Tanford & Penrod, 1984; Wolf, 1987). On the other hand, it has been suggested that multiple cognitive processes may underlie both majority and minority influence (Chaiken & Stangor, 1987). These and related issues concerning the adequacy of the genetic model are discussed in later sections.

Moscovici's formulation has also been elaborated and extended by theorists who are sympathetic to the basic thrust of his arguments. In seeking to clarify the differences between majority and minority influence, Nemeth (1985, 1986, 1987) suggested that disagreement from majorities and minorities has different effects on attention, thought, and problem solving. She asserted that majorities produce a narrow focus on the position that they advocate, whereas minorities produce a broader focus on new information and alternative positions. (Note that this idea differs from Moscovici's contention that minorities produce more thinking about their own position than do majorities.) The different attentional focus produced by majorities and minorities presumably occurs because individuals exposed to majorities are more likely to feel stress, assume that the influence source is correct, and resolve the disagreement-induced conflict quickly. According to Nemeth, majority and minority influence have different consequences for thinking and problem solving. Minorities tend to produce issue-relevant, divergent thinking, which leads to creative problem solutions. Majorities tend to produce message-relevant, convergent thinking, which leads to uncreative solutions.

Maass, West, and Cialdini (1987) also focused on the cognitive and motivational processes underlying conversion and the characteristics of minorities that trigger these processes. They argued that, compared to majorities, consistent minorities are more likely to focus attention on the stimulus under consideration and to produce nondefensive and divergent thinking about the stimulus. In regard to why minorities have these effects, Maass et al. suggested three possible explanations. First, because a minority is typically more distinctive, or salient, than a majority, a minority will draw more attention to its message. Second, because a minority is typically perceived as less credible than a majority, a minority will elicit more cognitive processing of its message (cf. Nemeth, 1986). This enhanced processing may be due, at least in part, to the relatively low stress that minorities elicit. Finally, because a minority is subjected to more social pressure than is a majority, a consistent minority is more likely to be seen as courageous and committed to its position, which in turn will increase its persuasiveness.

A rather different, and more ambitious, effort to extend Moscovici's formulation seeks to explain innovation in large institutional contexts. Mugny and his colleagues have proposed a "psychosociological" theory of minority influence that emphasizes the importance of social categories and ideology (Mugny, 1982, 1984b; Papastamou, 1984; Papastamou & Mugny, 1985). Mugny distinguished three social entities linked by three relationships. The *power* dictates norms and rules within an institution or society, the *population* submits to the power's domination and accepts (to a greater or lesser degree) the power's ideology, and the *minority* actively challenges the power. The power and the population are linked by *domination,* the power and the minority are linked by *antagonism,* and the minority and the population are linked by *influence.* Thus, the power seeks to maintain its domination over the population while weakening or destroying the minority, and the minority implacably opposes the power while trying to influence the population to adopt its position.

Mugny argued that minority influence is dependent on the population's representation, or image, of the minority. In order to win the population, the minority must be perceived as consistent and unyielding vis-à-vis the power, but as willing to negotiate with the population. Mugny therefore suggested that behavioral style (consistency/inconsistency) defines the antagonistic relationship between the minority and the power, whereas negotiation style (flexibility/rigidity) defines the influence relationship between the minority and the population. A rigid negotiating style, which refuses to make any concessions to the population, is unsuccessful because the population will perceive the minority's consistency as dogmatism. This perception, in turn, makes it likely that the population will attribute the minority's position to some stable, idiosyncratic characteristic ("naturalization") and will view the minority as an outgroup. These negative perceptions of the minority are encouraged by the power as part of its efforts to maintain domination.

EMPIRICAL INVESTIGATIONS

The review of empirical research on reaction to opinion deviance is divided into two sections. The first (early studies) deals with investigations conducted during the 1950s to test Festinger's ideas about social pressure in groups. These studies are examined together and in some detail because they derive from a single theoretical formulation and often have been leveled and sharpened in subsequent reviews. The second section (later studies) deals with more recent research. Because these later studies do not share a common theoretical foundation (i.e., some are based loosely on Festinger's model, some are derived from Moscovici's position, and still others are based on ad hoc hypotheses), they are organized in terms of the major independent variable(s) under investigation: extremity and content of the deviate's position; consistency of the deviate's position; deviate's interference with group locomotion; and group context of deviance. Where appropriate, data obtained in these studies are related to relevant theoretical positions.

Early Studies

In an initial investigation, Festinger, Schachter, and Back (1950) interviewed residents of married-student housing developments regarding their attitudes toward a tenants' organization. Data from one housing project (Westgate) indicated that the greater the cohesiveness of the living unit (defined as the percentage of ingroup sociometric choices), the smaller the percentage of individuals who deviated from modal group opinion regarding the tenants' organization. In addition, deviates in Westgate received fewer sociometric choices than did conformers, suggesting that deviation may have led to rejection. However, because of the correlational nature of the data, it is also possible that initial rejection caused individuals to deviate, or some third variable produced the relationship between deviation and rejection.

In a subsequent laboratory study, Festinger and Thibaut (1951) investigated how extremity of a potential recipient's position, pressure toward uniformity, and possibility of subgroup formation affected communication and opinion change in small groups. Subjects sent notes to one another regarding opinion issues; instructions were used to manipulate pressure toward uniformity and ostensible homogeneity/heterogeneity of group members (which was assumed to influence the perceived ease of subgroup formation). Results indicated that communication varied directly with the extremity of the recipient's position and communication to extremists was greater in the high than in the medium and low pressure to uniformity conditions. In the homogeneous condition (where subgroup formation was unlikely), amount of communication to extremists did not change significantly over time in any of the three pressure conditions. In contrast, in the heterogeneous condition (where subgroup formation was likely), communication to extremists decreased over time in the medium- and low-pressure conditions but not in the high-pressure condition. Finally, data indicated that higher pressure toward uniformity and lower possibility of group division produced more opinion change among group members.

In a related study (Gerard, 1953), subjects communicated about which of two issues was more important, as well as the correct position on each issue. Gerard's results concerning the impact of extremity of a potential recipient's position, pressure toward uniformity, and possibility of subgroup formation were generally in accord with those of Festinger and Thibaut (1951). In addition, Gerard found that subjects classified as majority and minority members (on the basis of the issue that they considered more important) behaved differently during the experimental session. Majority members tried harder to influence minority members to change their opinion on the issue they had chosen than vice versa; minority members tried harder to influence one another than did majority members.

Although informative about communication processes in small groups, neither Festinger and Thibaut's (1951) nor Gerard's (1953) study provided a direct test of majority reaction to deviance from group consensus. Since deviance was not manipulated in either study, the number of "deviates" varied unsystematically within and between groups. That is, because deviation was defined in terms of discrepancy from each subject's position rather than discrepancy from group consensus, the number of deviates perceived by each subject could vary widely, depending on the subject's own position. Fortunately, several additional studies derived from Festinger's (1950) model do not have this problem.

In one such experiment (Festinger, Gerard, Hymovitch, Kelly, & Raven, 1952), subjects in small groups were led to believe that they held either a majority or a minority position on an attitudinal issue. Majority subjects were told that several group members agreed exactly with their position, that 1 or 2 members disagreed slightly, and that 1 member disagreed substantially. Minority subjects were told that no other group members agreed exactly with their position, that 1 or 2 members disagreed slightly, and that several members disagreed substantially. Subjects then ostensibly communicated with other group members using notes. Results revealed that majority subjects exhibited less opinion change than did minority subjects. In addition, majority subjects communicated most to "extreme" deviates and least to other conformers. Interestingly, manipulations of group cohesiveness, expertise of group members, and existence of a correct answer had relatively little effect on majority subjects' communication.

A related study was conducted by Hochbaum (1954). In this experiment, subjects were initially led to believe that, compared to other group members, they had either high or low ability in judging clinical case histories. Then, subjects expressed an opinion on an additional case and learned either that all group members but one agreed with their opinion (majority subjects) or that all group members disagreed with their opinion (minority subjects). They then used notes to communicate about the case. Although relatively few majority subjects changed position (compared to minority subjects), more change occurred among low-ability than among high–ability majority subjects. In addition, majority subjects tried harder to influence other group members than did minority subjects.

In perhaps the most influential (and, according to Berkowitz, 1971, most misrepresented) study of majority reaction to opinion deviance, Schachter (1951) assigned subjects to either high or low cohesive groups in which members discussed an opinion topic that was either relevant or irrelevant to the group's purpose. Each group contained 5 to 7 naive subjects and three confederates (mode, slider, deviate). The mode agreed with the modal group position throughout the discussion. The slider started as an extreme deviate, but gradually came to agree with the modal position. The deviate maintained an extremely unpopular opinion throughout the discussion.

During the face-to-face discussion, the deviate received more overall communication than the slider, who in turn received more than the mode. Communication to the mode remained uniform over time, communication to the slider decreased, and communication to the deviate tended to increase steadily in all conditions except high-cohesive-relevant, where a final decrease occurred. This decrease was exhibited primarily by subjects who rejected the deviate on a post-experimental sociometric measure, and strong rejectors began decreasing their communication to the deviate earlier than did mild rejectors. Although these results generally support the hypothesis that communication is used to achieve group uniformity, Schachter also found that the greatest total communication to the deviate occurred in the low-cohesive-irrelevant condition, where, according to Festinger's (1950) theory, pressure to uniformity should be lowest (Mills, 1962).

Following the discussion, subjects filled out a sociometric questionnaire and nominated group members to committee positions varying in attractiveness. In general, the deviate was rejected more than the slider and mode, who were liked about equally. Sociometric responses were influenced by group cohesiveness (more deviate rejection in the high than in the low cohesive condition), but not by issue relevance. In contrast, committee nominations were influenced by issue relevance (more deviate rejection in the high than in the low relevance condition), but not by group cohesiveness.

Emerson (1954) conducted a partial replication of Schachter's (1951) study, using high school rather than college students and omitting the relevance manipulation. Although Emerson's sociometric rating and committee nomination data generally paralleled Schachter's findings, Emerson obtained less overall rejection of the deviate. Moreover, Emerson found that communication to the deviate consistently rose over time with no final decline in any condition. (No data on communication to the slider or mode were presented.) Emerson argued that because his subjects were younger than Schachter's and hence less confident in their opinion, they may have sought to achieve group uniformity by changing their own position rather than by rejecting the deviate. Consistent with this interpretation, Emerson found that more subjects changed toward the deviate's position in his study than in Schachter's experiment.

The final experiment discussed in this section was designed to investigate how majority members react to a deviate who threatens group goal attainment (Schachter et al., 1954). Subjects were schoolboys in several European countries who participated in group competition involving the construction of model airplanes. Instructions were used to manipulate valence of the group goal and probability of goal attainment. During discussion of which plane to build, a confederate deviated from group consensus and thereby retarded group locomotion. In the countries in which subjects accurately perceived the experimental manipulations, the deviate was underchosen, compared to other group members, as both a work partner and club president. Although rejection of the deviate as a work partner was generally greater in the low probability than in the high probability condition, the valence manipulation did not affect this measure. Moreover, neither probability nor valence strongly influenced choice of the deviate as club president or intensity of communication directed toward the deviate.

What can be concluded regarding the level of empirical support for Festinger's (1950, 1954) analysis of pressure to uniformity in groups? Based on the studies reviewed above, it appears that Festinger's model has been only partially confirmed. The cumulative evidence indicates that, compared to conformers, deviates receive increased communication and decreased liking. In contrast, support is weaker for the impact of variables that presumably influence the intensity of majority members' reactions to minority members (e.g., group cohesiveness, issue relevance). This may be due, at least in part, to the manner in which these variables were operationalized. Cohesiveness, for example, was manipulated by varying subjects' perception of their similarity to one another (Festinger et al., 1952) or their interest in the group activity (Schachter, 1951).

Although some evidence exists for the effectiveness of these manipulations (Back, 1951), other techniques for influencing cohesiveness (e.g., varying interdependence among group members) may be superior (Cartwright, 1968). Perhaps by using stronger manipulations of cohesiveness and relevance in laboratory groups or by capitalizing on higher levels of these variables in natural groups, greater support might be obtained for Festinger's model. As will become clear in the following section, research based on Festinger's ideas did not cease in the middle 1950's, when he and his colleagues turned to other questions. Moreover, recent studies provide support for certain aspects of Festinger's formulation.

Later Studies

Extremity and Content of the Deviate's Position

On the basis of Festinger's and related theories as well as Moscovici's formulation, it would be expected that the extremity of a deviate's position would affect majority members' reaction to the deviate. The functionalist position predicts that extreme deviates will receive more communication and less liking than will moderate deviates. The genetic position predicts that the relationship between deviate extremity and majority opinion change will vary depending on the ease with which the deviate can be rejected (Moscovici, 1985b). Neither the functionalist nor the genetic model assigns an important role to the content of the deviate's position, although Moscovici (1985b) has suggested that behavioral style conveys information about the deviate's position on an issue (explicit content) as well as his or her psychological state (implicit content).

Sampson and Brandon (1964) varied the extremity of a deviate's position by having a confederate either present herself as racially bigoted (role deviate) or liberal (role conformant) and then either disagree (opinion deviate) or agree (opinion conformant) with group consensus regarding treatment for a Black juvenile delinquent. Results indicated that the opinion deviate, as compared to the opinion conformant, received more overall communication, more expressions of hostility, more requests for information, and fewer expressions of solidarity. In contrast, the role deviate, as compared to the role conformant, received less overall communication, fewer expressions of hostility, and less information. Finally, subjects saw themselves as less similar to the role deviate than to the role conformant and liked the role deviate less than the role conformant. These findings suggest, consistent with Orcutt's (1973) analysis, that the opinion deviate was perceived as more amenable to persuasion than was the role deviate and hence elicited an inclusive rather than an exclusive reaction from majority members.

In a study designed to test derivations from Helson's adaptation-level theory, Hensley and Duval (1976) investigated majority members' reactions to several degrees of deviate extremity. Subjects, in groups of 10, were led to believe that 7

individuals agreed and 2 disagreed with their opinion regarding a juvenile delinquency case. The two minority responders (who agreed with one another) exhibited one of five levels of disagreement with the majority. Results suggested that
as the minority's position became more extreme, majority members (a) perceived
more opinion similarity within both the majority and minority subgroups, (b)
became more attracted to other majority members and less attracted to minority
members, (c) perceived majority members as more correct and minority members as less correct, (d) communicated less to other majority members and more
to minority members, and (e) wrote less hostile messages to other majority
members and more hostile messages to minority members. It is important to
note, however, that trend analyses revealed significant quadratic components in
several of the above relationships, indicating that majority members' reactions
do not always vary as a simple linear function of the extremity of the deviate's
position.

A nonlinear relationship between deviate extremity and majority response has
also been revealed in another study. Levine and Ranelli (1978) led subjects, in
simulated four-person groups, to believe that 2 group members consistently
agreed with their initial opinion on an attitudinal issue and that the third member
(target) (a) agreed with modal group opinion, (b) deviated by a moderate amount
(i.e., 3 points on a 9-point scale), giving a neutral "neither agree nor disagree"
response, or (c) deviated by an extreme amount (i.e., 6 points). Results indicated
that subjects evaluated the modal target more favorably than both the moderate
and extreme deviates, who did not differ significantly from one another. Although the moderate and extreme deviates were liked about equally, the moderate deviate was perceived as less confident in her position and was less able to
influence subjects' opinion than was the extreme deviate. In addition, subjects
directed less communication to the moderate than to the extreme deviate.

Levine and Ranelli (1978) speculated that the relatively intense dislike elicited
by the moderate deviate was due to the "fence straddling" content of her
position. In order to obtain additional information concerning this factor, Levine
and Ruback (1980) assessed majority members' reactions to a neutral deviate
espousing one of three rationales for her position: ambivalence (balanced approach and avoidance tendencies toward the opposing response options); ignorance (insufficient information to make a decision); or indifference (lack of
concern about the issue). Subjects' evaluations of the three deviates differed
significantly (the ambivalent deviate was liked more than the ignorant deviate,
who in turn was like more than the indifferent deviate). These results indicate
that the content, as well as the extremity, of a deviate's position can affect
majority members' responses (cf. Batchelor & Tesser, 1971; Burnstein, 1982).

The importance of position content has also been revealed in other studies. In
an experiment by Brown (1970), groups of subjects who held a moderate position regarding treatment for a delinquent were confronted by a confederate, who,
after initially agreeing with modal group opinion, moved to either an extremely

nurturant or an extremely punitive position. Although the two deviates adopted positions equidistant from modal group opinion, the punitive deviate was liked less and was less influential than the nurturant deviate. Paicheler (1976) had a confederate consistently deviate from group consensus by espousing either an extremely profeminist (progressive) or antifeminist (reactionary) attitude. Results indicated that the profeminist deviate produced substantial movement toward his position, whereas the antifeminist deviate produced bipolarization (i.e., some subjects moved toward the deviate's position and some moved away). Additional analyses (Paicheler, 1977) revealed that (a) the antifeminist deviate was more effective with subjects who initially held his position than with those who opposed it, and (b) the profeminist deviate was more effective with subjects who initially opposed his position than with those who held it (see Mugny, 1979; Paicheler, 1979b). In a later study, Paicheler (1979a) found evidence that the impact of profeminist and antifeminist deviates was also influenced by the sex of the deviate and the sex composition of the majority (homogeneous, heterogeneous). Finally, data obtained by Maass, Clark, and Haberkorn (1982) indicated that both the content of the deviate's position and the deviate's perceived self-interest in this position can affect majority members' opinion change (cf. Nemeth & Wachtler, 1973).

In concluding this section, it is important to mention research designed to test Mugny's psychosociological theory of minority influence. Although, as discussed earlier, Mugny is explicitly interested in how *rigidity* affects minority influence, his studies actually appear to assess the impact of *extremity*. Most of Mugny's experiments used a paradigm in which subjects who believed that industry was only partially responsible for pollution read a statement that placed total blame on industry. According to Mugny, this statement represented a minority position in relation to power. The rigidity/flexibility of the minority was operationalized in terms of the sanctions recommended for industrial polluters (e.g., "rigid": shutdown of manufacturing; "flexible": monetary fines). After reading the statements, subjects expressed their views about the causes of pollution on both direct items (that were explicitly presented in the statement) and indirect items (that were implied in the statement). Mugny's studies provided suggestive evidence that moderate (flexible) minorities produce more direct influence than do extreme (rigid) minorities; that the influence of extreme minorities increases if subjects are prevented from attributing the minority's position to idiosyncratic personal characteristics and if subjects view themselves as members of the same social category as the minority; and that moderate minorities produce similar levels of direct and indirect influence, whereas extreme minorities produce more indirect influence (see reviews by Mugny, 1982, 1984b; Papastamou, 1984; Papastamou & Mugny, 1985). Although intriguing, these findings must be accepted cautiously. The most complete review of this research (Mugny, 1982) revealed that results often failed to replicate from study to study and complex *a posteriori* interpretations were needed to make sense of the data.

Summary. Data presented in this section indicate that both the extremity and content of the deviate's position can importantly affect majority reaction. Results generally show that extreme deviates are evaluated less favorably than are moderate deviates. Evidence regarding how deviate extremity affects opinion change is less clear. Data indicate that the impact of extremity on opinion change is affected by the content of the deviate's position (Levine & Ruback, 1980) and the type of change (direct vs. indirect) that is assessed (Mugny, 1982). Moreover, the location of the deviate's position relative to the midpoint of the response scale (Maass & Clark, 1984; Nemeth & Endicott, 1976) and the ease of rejecting the deviate (Moscovici, 1985b) may play a role. In addition to moderating the effect of deviate extremity, the content of the deviate's position is important in its own right. Latane and Wolf (1981) argued that "opinion conversion takes place only when the minority position is inherently and demonstrably more correct than that of the majority" (p. 452). Evidence indicates that content affects majority reaction when extremity is held constant (Brown, 1970; Paicheler, 1976), and the operation of this variable is influenced by such factors as the deviate's perceived self-interest (Maass et al., 1982).

Consistency of the Deviate's Position

In addition to the extremity and content of the deviate's position, the consistency with which this position is maintained over time and modality is also likely to affect majority reaction. From the functionalist perspective, one could argue that majority members' motives to achieve social reality and group locomotion are thwarted more by a consistent than by an inconsistent deviate. If so, majority members would be expected to direct more communication toward a consistent than an inconsistent deviate and, if the communication fails to elicit conformity, to feel more hostility toward the consistent deviate. From the genetic perspective, Moscovici (1976) argued that behavioral style is "the only variable with explanatory power" (p. 110) when an individual or a subgroup influences a group and that minority consistency is a necessary (though not a sufficient) condition for this type of influence to occur. Moscovici and Nemeth (1974) suggested that majority members perceive a consistent minority as highly confident in the validity of its position. This perception causes majority members to assume that the minority's position may be correct and their own position may be incorrect. In the case of an inconsistent minority, majority members presumably do not perceive the minority as confident and hence do not assume that its position may be correct. (Note that this argument suggests, in contradiction to Moscovici's general position, that consistent minorities are influential because they produce informational dependence on the part of majority members.)

A number of studies have been conducted to assess the impact of consistency on minority influence. Some evidence indicates that consistent minorities exert more influence (and elicit higher confidence ratings) than do inconsistent minorities. Other evidence, however, suggests that the relationship between consistency and influence is more complex than originally supposed. Because the empirical support for these generalizations has been presented elsewhere (Levine, 1980; Maass & Clark, 1984; Moscovici, 1985b), I will discuss general themes rather than present an exhaustive review of individual experiments.[6]

Unambiguous issues.   Much of the research investigating the impact of minority consistency has dealt with unambiguous perceptual issues. In an early test of the consistency hypothesis, Moscovici et al. (1969) had 6-person groups make color judgments of blue slides that differed in brightness. In one condition 2 confederates deviated from group consensus by giving nonveridical (i.e., "green") responses on 100% of the slides. Results showed that subjects in this consistent minority condition gave more "green" responses than did control subjects who responded privately to the slides. In an inconsistent minority condition, where the two confederates gave "green" responses on 67% of the slides, subjects gave very few "green" responses. When later judging the color of ambiguous blue-green discs, subjects in the consistent minority condition labeled more discs "green" than did subjects in the control condition. These results suggest that the consistent minority altered subjects' perceptual code as well as their overt responses. In addition, subjects showed a greater change in perceptual code when they had *not* been overtly influenced by the consistent minority than when they had. As might be expected, the inconsistent minority did not affect subjects' perceptual code (Moscovici, 1976). Finally, consistent minority members were perceived as relatively incompetent, confident, and "neutral" in attractiveness.

Moscovici and Lage (1976) reported an expanded version of the Moscovici et al. (1969) study. In addition to the conditions described above, Moscovici and Lage included a consistent 1-person minority condition, in which a single confederate gave "green" responses on all slides, and two majority conditions. In the unanimous majority condition, a single subject was confronted by 3 confederates who gave "green" responses on all slides. In the nonunanimous majority condition, 2 subjects were confronted by 4 confederates who consistently gave "green" responses. Results indicated that compared to the consistent 2-person

---

[6]Although Tanford and Penrod (1984) sought to clarify the relationship between minority consistency and minority influence, their definition of consistency was flawed. Rather than distinguishing between repetitive responses (i.e., identical responses on all trials), patterned responses (i.e., variable responses that are correlated with variable stimulus properties), and systematic response shifts (i.e., unidirectional response change along an attitudinal continuum), Tanford and Penrod chose to lump all three types together under the heading of "consistent." They reserved the term "inconsistent" for random or unsystematic responses. Unfortunately, this approach obscures important differences in how repetitive responses and systematic response shifts affect minority influence on perceptual and attitudinal issues.

minority: the consistent 1-person minority did not elicit a substantial number of "green" responses; the nonunanimous majority was approximately equally influential; and the unanimous majority was much more influential. Regarding changes in subjects' perceptual code, *only* the consistent 2-person minority altered subjects' threshold for classifying ambiguous blue-green discs. Regarding subjects' perceptions and evaluations of minority members, confederates in all three minority conditions were perceived as relatively incompetent; confederates in the consistent 2-person minority condition were viewed as relatively confident; and confederates in the consistent 1-person and inconsistent 2-person minority conditions were relatively disliked.

Several additional experiments have been conducted to clarify how consistency affects minority influence on perceptual issues. Nemeth, Swedlund, and Kanki (1974) compared the impact of 2-person minorities emitting one of three response patterns on blue slides: repetitive (e.g., "green" on all slides); correlated (e.g., "green" on bright slides and "green-blue" on dim slides); and random ("green" and "green-blue" on both bright and dim slides). Results indicated that minority influence in the correlated condition was higher than in the random condition and as high as in the repetitive condition. In a subsequent study, Nemeth, Wachtler, and Endicott (1977) had 1, 2, 3, or 4 confederates consistently deviate from modal group opinion by giving "blue-green" responses to blue slides. These investigators found that as minority size increased, minority members' perceived competence and likeability increased and their perceived confidence decreased. Moreover, all four minority conditions elicited a relatively large number of "blue-green" responses (compared to a control condition), and the amount of movement toward the minority's position was positively correlated with subjects' combined judgments of the minority's competence and confidence. Finally, using an Asch-type line estimation task, Doms (1984; Doms & Van Avermaet, 1985) investigated whether the impact of a consistent minority is affected by the amount of social support available to the majority (cf. Allen, 1975). Doms' research suggests that the more social support (i.e., agreement) majority members receive, the more resistant they are to minority influence.

Ambiguous issues.   In addition to studies using unambiguous perceptual stimuli that allow only one correct answer, other experiments investigating deviate consistency have employed stimuli that, at least in principle, permit more than one acceptable response. Moscovici and Faucheux (1972) reported research in which groups of experimental subjects observed a confederate use a consistent, though arbitrary, criterion in categorizing stimuli (visual patterns or words). Compared to control groups containing only naive subjects, experimental groups were more likely to employ the confederate's criterion when responding to the stimuli (see also Nemeth & Wachtler, 1973). Recently, Nemeth and colleagues have investigated the influence of consistent minorities and majorities on problems that permit solutions varying in originality (Nemeth, 1986; Nemeth

& Kwan, 1985, 1987; Nemeth & Wachtler, 1983). Their results suggest that minorities elicit more creative solutions than do majorities.

Deviate consistency has also been investigated using "ambiguous" stimuli of another kind—attitudinal issues. Research suggests that the impact of consistency on minority influence is affected by a number of variables. These include: the extremity and content of the deviate's position (see previous section); the deviate's general confidence (expressed, for example, by choosing the head chair at a discussion table) (Nemeth & Wachtler, 1974); the number of cognitive categories that majority members use to describe the deviate (Ricateau, cited in Moscovici, 1976); the size of the minority and majority (Latane & Wolf, 1981; Snortum, Klein, & Sherman, 1976; Tanford & Penrod, 1983, 1984; Wolf & Latane, 1983, 1985); and the level of group cohesiveness (Wolf, 1979, 1985).

Several experiments using attitudinal stimuli operationalized deviate inconsistency as directional response shift (i.e., movement toward or away from the majority position). Levine and colleagues conducted a series of studies investigating how majority members react to the direction and distance of deviate movement (e.g., Levine & Ranelli, 1978; Levine, Saxe, & Harris, 1976; Levine, Sroka, & Snyder, 1977). In these experiments subjects, in simulated groups of 4, voted several times regarding appropriate treatment for a juvenile delinquent. In most conditions subjects were led to believe that two group members consistently agreed with their initial position; the responses of the third member (target) varied across conditions. Between votes subjects sent notes to the target and received prewritten notes restating the target's previous vote. Following the last vote, subjects rated the target on several scales.

Levine et al. (1976) investigated majority members' reactions to a target who consistently agreed with modal group opinion, consistently disagreed, gradually moved from disagreement to agreement, or gradually moved from agreement to disagreement. Target attractiveness in the four conditions was rank-ordered: consistent agreement > disagreement-agreement > agreement-disagreement > consistent disagreement. Regarding target influence, subjects shifted toward the target's terminal position (and away from modal group opinion) in the agreement-disagreement, but not in the consistent disagreement, condition. These findings, which were replicated by Levine et al. (1977), indicate that deviate consistency was *not* a necessary condition for deviate influence in this situation. Finally, subjects directed most communication to the consistent disagreer, an intermediate amount to the disagreer-agreer and agreer-disagreer, and least to the consistent agreer.

In the disagreement-agreement and agreement-disagreement conditions of the previous study, the target moved from one end of the response continuum to the other. Levine and Ranelli (1978), in addition to investigating majority reaction to the three stable targets described earlier, used a 2 × 3 design to assess reaction to targets who shifted a short distance toward or away from modal group opinion and who manifested high, medium, or low net agreement with the majority position. They found that targets who moved toward modal opinion were liked better than targets who moved away and that targets who manifested high net agreement were liked better than those who manifested medium or low agreement. Regarding target influence, subjects moved toward the target's terminal position in both the medium- and low-agreement conditions, indicating again that deviate consistency was not essential for deviate influence. Finally, subjects generally directed more communication to targets moving toward rather than away from modal opinion, perhaps because the former targets were seen as more amenable to persuasion.

Although, as the above studies show, consistency is not a necessary condition for minority influence on attitudinal issues, it is no doubt true that majority members' attributions about a deviate can affect his or her persuasiveness and attractiveness (Moscovici & Nemeth, 1974; Mugny, 1982; Papastamou, 1986).[7] At least three interrelated factors seem likely to affect the attributions made to a shifting attitudinal deviate.

One factor is the deviate's overt response pattern, which was manipulated in several studies mentioned above. Levine and associates (1976, 1977) and Levine and Ranelli (1978) found systematic relationships between a deviate's direction of movement and attributed motives. In all three studies deviates who moved toward modal group opinion were perceived as desiring group approval and as influenced by majority members' votes and subject's notes; deviates who moved away from modal group opinion were viewed as wanting to demonstrate assertiveness and independence.

The social pressures ostensibly acting on a shifting attitudinal deviate can also affect how he or she is perceived and responded to (cf. Morris & Miller, 1975; Wilder, 1978). Levine et al. (1977) found that two targets responding identically vis-à-vis the subject's position were perceived differently depending on other group members' response positions. For example, a target who shifted from agreement to disagreement with the subject was seen as more confident in his position and as more assertive when other group members agreed with the subject (and thereby provided an inhibiting cause for the target's movement) than when other group members disagreed with the subject (and thereby provided a facilitating cause for the target's movement). Moreover, the former target was evaluated more favorably and was more influential than the latter target. It seems likely that majority members' reactions to shifting deviates in other studies (e.g., Kiesler & Pallak, 1975; Nemeth & Brilmayer, 1987) were also mediated by the perceived social pressures acting on the deviates.

A third factor that probably affects majority members' attributions about a

---

[7]Allen and Wilder (1978) obtained evidence suggesting that such attributions also influence the *perceived* persuasiveness of consistent and inconsistent targets.

shifting deviate is the deviate's expressed reason for changing his or her position. Although this variable has not been directly investigated, relevant studies have been conducted in other contexts. As mentioned previously, Levine and Ruback (1980) found that majority members' evaluations of a consistent deviate were affected by the reason that she gave for her position. In a study on response to majority pressure, Ruback and Levine (1978) led subjects to believe that 3 group members disagreed with their opinion regarding a delinquent. A fourth member (target) either moved from disagreement to agreement or from agreement to disagreement with the subject's position and expressed one of several reasons for her opinion shift. Results indicated that both the target's direction of movement and alleged reason for shifting position affected subjects' conformity to majority pressure and liking for the target.[8]

Attributions and the impact of consistent minorities.   Recall that Moscovici and Nemeth (1974) argued that the confidence attributed to a consistent deviate is a critical determinant of his or her ability to influence majority members. Although several studies have found that consistent deviates are indeed perceived as relatively confident (e.g., Maass et al., 1982; Moscovici & Lage, 1976; Nemeth & Wachtler, 1974), there are reasons to be cautious in inferring that attributed confidence *causes* influence. First, other research indicates that a deviate's perceived confidence is not always strongly associated with his or her ability to exert influence (e.g., Nemeth et al., 1977; Richardson & Cialdini, cited by Maass & Clark, 1984). Second, even in studies where deviate confidence is correlated with deviate influence, it is possible that influence was mediated by other factors and subjects simply used confidence as an after-the-fact explanation for their opinion change. Finally, evidence obtained in dyadic persuasion settings suggests that a source's perceived confidence and ability to influence others are not related in a simple linear fashion (London, 1973).[9]

To test directly the impact of perceived deviate confidence, Ruback and Levine (1979) conducted two studies in which subjects, in groups of 4, observed a target either consistently disagree with modal group opinion regarding a delinquent (Study 1) or gradually move from agreement to disagreement (Study 2). In both studies, subjects received notes from the target expressing one of several patterns of confidence in his position (e.g., in Study 1 the target expressed

---

[8]Interesting research on reaction to gain and loss of social support was recently conducted by Kerr, MacCoun, Hansen, and Hymes (1987). Although these investigators failed to obtain evidence in several conditions that movement toward a decision alternative encourages further similar movement (a "momentum effect"), they did not include a condition in which initial group unanimity was broken by a target who gradually shifted to a deviate position. It was this condition that produced a momentum effect in the studies conducted by Levine and associates.

[9]Data indicate that *actual* confidence can increase an individual's ability to influence others in a face-to-face group seeking to reach a joint decision (Spitzer & Davis, 1978).

consistently high, consistently low, increasing, or decreasing confidence). Ruback and Levine found that although subjects in both studies accurately perceived the target's level of confidence, in neither study did perceived confidence significantly affect subjects' evaluation of the target or movement toward his position.

In addition to questions concerning the causal relationship between perceived deviate confidence and deviate influence, more general criticisms of Moscovici's attributional analysis have been offered. Maass and Clark (1984) argued that Moscovici's position is flawed because it cannot account for the results of certain studies and because it departs in important ways from Kelley's (1967, 1972) attribution theory. In order to redress these problems, Maass and Clark presented a more stringent application of Kelley's ideas to minority influence, employing the attributional principles of covariation, augmenting, and discounting. In a recent discussion of the minority influence literature, Chaiken and Stangor (1987) criticized both Moscovici and Nemeth (1974) and Maass and Clark (1984) for their emphasis on attributions regarding the minority's underlying dispositions (e.g., confidence). Chaiken and Stangor suggested that attention should be given instead to attributions regarding the validity of the minority's message (cf. Eagly & Chaiken, 1984). They also sounded a note of caution regarding the utility of any attributional model as a complete explanation of minority influence, arguing that such models are relevant primarily when majority members are motivated to maximize the validity of their opinions.

Majority/minority influence and compliance/conversion.   As discussed earlier, Moscovici (1980, 1985a, 1985b) suggested that majority and minority influence represent qualitatively different means of resolving conflict. According to this analysis, consistent majorities induce a comparison process and elicit compliance (manifest change) but not conversion (latent change). In contrast, consistent minorities induce a validation process and elicit conversion but not compliance. A number of experiments have assessed the impact of majority and minority influence on compliance and conversion. The bulk of available evidence suggests that, congruent with Moscovici's hypothesis, minorities have their primary impact at the latent level (Maass & Clark, 1984.[10]Data that majorities have their primary impact at the manifest level are not as strong (Allen, 1965; Kiesler & Kiesler, 1969; Maass & Clark, 1984; Mackie, 1987). Moreover, few studies have assessed the attentional and cognitive effects of majority and minority disagreement, and the results of these studies provide mixed support for

---

[10]The weakest evidence for this generalization involves work using the chromatic afterimage technique to determine if individuals exposed to minority pressure actually *see* blue slides as green (Doms & Van Avermaet, 1980; Moscovici & Doms, 1982; Moscovici & Personnaz, 1980, 1986; Personnaz, 1981; Personnaz & Guillon, 1985; Sorrentino, King, & Leo, 1980). See also Maass and Clark (1986), Mugny (1984a), and Wolf (1985).

Moscovici's hypotheses (e.g,. Maass & Clark, 1983; Mackie, 1987; Nemeth, 1986; Personnaz & Guillon, 1985).

Since Moscovici first posited that majority and minority influence represent qualitatively different processes, several alternative explanations of these two forms of influence have been offered. Because a detailed discussion of these formulations is beyond the scope of this chapter (see Levine & Russo, 1987), I present only a brief summary of their major points.

Latane and Wolf (1981; Wolf & Latane, 1983, 1985) and Tanford and Penrod (1984) have argued that a single process is responsible for both majority and minority influence and that these two forms of influence differ in quantitative rather than qualitative terms. Both theoretical formulations explain influence primarily in terms of the relative number of group members holding majority and minority opinions. (Mullen's, 1983, self-attention model, although not applied to minority influence, is also consistent with a single-process interpretation.) Given their ability to account for substantial variance in previous studies, Latane and Wolf's and Tanford and Penrod's models must be taken seriously. Nevertheless, because they fail to specify the psychological processes underlying majority and minority influence, their adequacy as explanatory models is open to question. Moreover, these models do not deal explicitly with the suggestion, discussed earlier, that majorities and minorities have different effects on compliance and conversion.

In contrast to the models just discussed, other single-process explanations of majority and minority influence do posit underlying psychological mechanisms. Wolf (1979, 1987) argued that both majority and minority influence are mediated by dependence. Whereas majorities often elicit both normative and informational dependence, minorities derive whatever strength they have from informational dependence alone. Although plausible, these suggestions do not really constitute a single-process explanation of majority and minority influence, because somewhat different mechanisms are assumed to operate in the two cases. A related proposal was made by Doms (1984; Doms & Van Avermaet, 1985), who also suggested that informational dependence may mediate both majority and minority influence. In addition, Doms asserted that social support is a crucial determinant of the impact of minorities as well as majorities. Doms' research indicates that majorities and minorities operating under identical social support conditions produce similar levels of public influence. By failing to deal with private influence, however, Doms' analysis only partially addresses the question of whether majority and minority influence are mediated by a single process.

In addition to the single-process explanations discussed above, dual-process and multiple-process explanations have also been offered to explain majority and minority influence. Two dual-process explanations were presented earlier in the section describing Moscovici's genetic model (Maass et al., 1987; Nemeth, 1985, 1986, 1987). Recently, Chaiken and Stangor (1987) suggested that multi-

ple cognitive processes (e.g., heuristic processing, attributional reasoning, mes-
sage- and issue-relevant thinking) may underlie both majority and minority influence. These authors asserted that the motives that operate in majority and
minority settings constrain the cognitive processes that produce influence in
these settings. Chaiken and Stangor hypothesized that qualitative differences in
influence processes are likely when different motives operate in the two settings,
whereas quantitative differences are likely when the same or similar motives
operate (see also Mackie, 1987).

Summary.   Substantial empirical and theoretical attention has been devoted
to clarifying how majority reaction to deviance is affected by the consistency of
the deviate's position. This work indicates that the impact of consistency is much
more complex than initially assumed.

When an unambiguous perceptual stimulus is used and the minority espouses
an extreme position, a 2-person minority exhibiting interindividual and intraindividual response consistency seems essential for minority influence (Moscovici
& Lage, 1976). However, response consistency need not involve simple repetition in order to be effective (Nemeth et al., 1974), a single consistent deviant can
be influential if he or she adopts a "moderate" position (Nemeth et al., 1977),
and the amount of social support available to the majority can affect deviate
influence (Doms, 1984).

On ambiguous stimuli, such as attitudinal issues, a number of factors can
affect the impact of deviate consistency on influence. These include the extremity and content of the deviate's position, the deviate's general confidence
(Nemeth & Wachtler, 1974), the number of cognitive categories used to describe
the deviate (Ricateau, cited in Moscovici, 1976), the size of the minority and
majority (e.g., Latane & Wolf, 1981; Tanford & Penrod, 1984), and the level of
group cohesiveness (Wolf, 1979, 1985). Moreover, in contrast to unambiguous
perceptual stimuli, on attitudinal issues deviate consistency is not a critical
determinant of deviate influence. In fact, evidence indicates that a conformer-
turned-deviate is much more influential than a consistent deviate (Levine et al.,
1976, 1977). Factors likely to affect attributions about a shifting attitudinal
deviate (and thereby other kinds of reactions to him or her) include (a) the
deviate's direction of movement vis-à-vis modal group opinion (Levine &
Ranelli, 1978; Levine et al., 1976), (b) the social pressures ostensibly acting on
the deviate (Kiesler & Pallak, 1975; Levine et al., 1977), and (c) the deviate's
expressed reason for espousing his or her position (Ruback & Levine, 1978).

Finally, there is controversy regarding Moscovici's attributional analysis of
minority influence and his comparison/validation model of compliance and conversion. On the basis of Maass and Clark's (1984) and Chaiken and Stangor's
(1987) criticisms, it is clear that Moscovici's attributional analysis suffers from a
number of weaknesses. Similarly, his comparison/validation model, in its cur-

rent form, is not adequate to account for the full range of manifest and latent changes produced by majorities and minorities (Chaiken & Stangor, 1987; Maass et al., 1987; Mackie, 1987; Nemeth, 1986).

Deviate's Interference with Group Locomotion

In the studies reviewed in the last two sections, majority members' reactions to deviance presumably were influenced in large part by their desire to validate or evaluate the correctness of their opinions. Recall that in addition to desire for opinion validation (social reality), Festinger (1950) posited that desire for group locomotion also produces pressure to uniformity in small groups. A number of studies have investigated how majority members respond to a deviate's interference with group locomotion toward valued goals (e.g., Schachter et al., 1954). These studies have operationalized deviance as either opinion disagreement or overt disruption of group performance (e.g., failure to follow instructions). Although the latter operational definition does not conform to my original definition of opinion deviance, studies investigating reaction to disruption of group performance are reviewed here because they clarify the impact of certain variables (e.g., status) that are likely to affect reaction to opinion deviance.

Degree of interference.   In a study by Berkowitz and Howard (1959), small groups of subjects making judgments about a labor-management dispute were led to believe that one member disagreed with modal group opinion. Subjects who believed that prizes would be awarded on the basis of group performance (high interdependence) communicated more to the deviate and were less desirous of future interaction with him than were subjects who believed that prizes would be awarded on the basis of individual performance (low interdependence). Thus, a deviate who interfered with group goal attainment received more pressure to change and more eventual rejection than a deviate who did not interfere.

Wiggins, Dill, and Schwartz (1965) assessed majority members' reaction to a deviate who cheated on a reading comprehension test, thereby reducing the probability that the group would win a monetary prize. The deviate's penalty (and therefore his interference with group goal attainment) was high, medium, or low. Results indicated that the greater the deviate's interference, the less he was liked.

Singer, Radloff, and Wark (1963) placed subjects into competing teams to discuss human relations problems. A confederate on each team either disrupted team performance (heretic) or deserted to join the competing team (renegade). Subjects were more negative toward the renegade than toward the heretic, presumably because the renegade was seen as more threatening to team success. These findings are consistent with other data suggesting that ingroup members who adopt outgroup positions are strongly disliked (Iwao, 1963; Smith, Williams, & Willis, 1967).

In a study examining how threat to group survival affects reaction to deviance, Lauderdale (1976) had a confederate deviate from the modal opinion of a small group discussing treatment for a delinquent. Halfway through the experimental session a high-status authority either did or did not threaten the future existence of the group. Although the authority in the threat condition did not clarify the basis for his comment, subjects probably assumed that he was dissatisfied with the discussion and the deviate was at fault. Consistent with this line of reasoning, the deviate was evaluated more negatively in the threat than in the no-threat condition.[11]

Miller and colleagues investigated the impact of group decision rules (majority, unanimity, dictatorship) on reaction to attitudinal deviance. Because such rules influence whether a deviate can impose his or her opinion on the group, they affect the deviate's ability to interfere with attainment of group consensus. Results of two experiments revealed that deviates were rejected more when the decision rule allowed them to produce group decisions unfavorable to the majority than when the rule did not allow this outcome (Miller & Anderson, 1979; Miller, Jackson, Mueller, & Schersching, 1987).

In a recent study, Earle (1986) found evidence that the type of issue under consideration can influence how majority members react to an attitudinal deviate's interference with group goal attainment. In this study, subjects in small groups were given either an individual or group goal to evaluate either an informational or value issue. In all conditions, a confederate deviated from modal group opinion on the issue. Earle's data indicated that when the informational issue was involved, the deviate was rejected more in the group goal than in the individual goal condition. In contrast, when the value issue was involved, type of goal did not affect deviate rejection.

Finally, it is important to mention research indicating that, in addition to the deviate's degree of interference with group goal attainment, his or her perceived responsibility for this interference can also influence majority reaction. Jones and deCharms (1957) and Burnstein and Worchel (1962) led subjects to believe that a deviate who impeded group performance either was or was not responsible for his behavior. (In the latter condition, the deviate was presented as having low intelligence or defective hearing.) Both experiments revealed that the responsible deviate was rejected more than the nonresponsible deviate.

Deviate status.   A substantial amount of attention has been devoted to how deviate status affects majority reaction to interference with group locomotion. Early work was done by Hollander (1958, 1964), who posited that an individual

---

[11]In a later experiment, Lauderdale, Parker, Smith-Cunnien, and Inverarity (1984) examined the effect of external threat on the *creation* of deviance. They found that, even when no opinion deviate was present, the lowest-ranked group member was rejected more in threat than in no-threat conditions. This rejection was exhibited most strongly by high-status group members.

who conforms to group norms and demonstrates competence gains status, or "idiosyncrasy credit," which in turn allows the individual to deviate from group norms. In a study designed to test these ideas, Hollander (1960) found that past conformity to procedural norms increased the influence of a task-competent confederate when he began violating these norms. Although Hollander's idiosyncrasy credit hypothesis is widely accepted, newer studies designed to test it have yielded equivocal results (Bray, Johnson, & Chilstrom, 1982; Ridgeway & Jacobson, 1977; Wahrman & Pugh, 1972, 1974).

Ridgeway (1978) recently proposed an alternative to Hollander's hypothesis about the relationship between conformity and status. She argued that task-oriented groups award status on the basis of a member's perceived contribution to task accomplishment and generally prefer group-motivated to self-motivated contributions. In order for a member's contribution to be accepted, others must pay attention to it and evaluate it as valuable. Attention is greater if the member has high external status characteristics (e.g., high ability), exhibits substantial nonconformity, and uses a dramatic behavioral style. Evaluation occurs on two dimensions: competence and motivation. If a member's contribution is legitimate (i.e., conforms to his or her expected performance), then the member's motive will not be assessed, and the contribution will be evaluated solely in terms of its perceived competence. In contrast, if a member's contribution exceeds what is legitimate, then his or her motive will be assessed. Ridgeway's model suggests a number of interesting hypotheses about the relationship between conformity and status in small groups. Although empirical support for the model is still somewhat limited (e.g., Ridgeway, 1981, 1982), it provides a needed elaboration and extension of Hollander's formulation. In addition, Ridgeway (1984) has used aspects of her model to clarify more general issues concerning the relative merits of dominance and performance theories of status (e.g., Berger & Zelditch, 1983; Lee & Ofshe, 1981; Mohr, 1986; Nemeth, 1983; Ofshe & Lee, 1983; Tuzlak & Moore, 1984).

Other studies suggest that a deviate's status and degree of interference with group locomotion interact in determining majority members' reactions. Wiggins et al. (1965), in addition to manipulating the deviate's degree of interference with group goal attainment, also manipulated the deviate's status by varying his alleged task competence (middle, high). Results indicated that the high-status deviate received (a) more negative evaluation than the middle-status deviate for major interference with goal attainment, and (b) less negative evaluation than the middle-status deviate for medium and low interference. Similar findings were obtained by Alvarez (1968). These results suggest that high status frees an individual to deviate on relatively trivial matters, but imposes additional constraints on matter of importance to the group.

In the studies just reviewed, deviance was unambiguously "bad," involving overt disruption of group performance. It seems likely that "good" deviance that helps the group (i.e., innovation) might be tolerated, and even demanded, from high-status individuals (cf. Coser, 1962; Hollander, 1958, 1964; Homans,

1974). Data relevant to this hypothesis were obtained by Suchner and Jackson (1976). In this experiment, subjects were led to believe that a group leader either did or did not take other members' advice in reaching a decision that was binding on the group and either did or did not make a successful decision. Suchner and Jackson found that among successful leaders those who deviated from group members' advice received *more* approval than those who conformed, whereas among unsuccessful leaders those who deviated received *less* approval than those who conformed.

Giordano (1983) recently presented an attributional analysis of the treatment accorded to high-status deviates. She argued that a deviate receives negative sanctions only if the deviate's behavior is observed by others, perceived as intentional, and attributed to a personal disposition (cf. Orcutt, 1973). Because these conditions are less likely to be fulfilled for high-status than for low-status deviates, high-status deviates are often protected from sanctions. However, if these conditions *are* fulfilled for high-status deviates (e.g., because they are under close scrutiny from other group members), then such deviates receive strong sanctions. Moreover, the high expectations often held for high-status members put them at substantial risk for punishment if they fail to meet these expectations (Hollander & Willis, 1967; Wahrman, 1970a, 1970b).

Summary.   The research reviewed in this section indicates that a deviate's interference with group locomotion toward valued goals is an important determinant of majority members' reactions. In general, the greater the deviate's interference and the greater the deviate's perceived responsibility for this interference, the less the deviate is liked (e.g., Jones & deCharms, 1957; Miller & Anderson, 1979; Wiggins et al., 1965). The impact of deviate status is less clearcut. Research designed to test Hollander's idiosyncrasy credit notion has yielded a rather confusing melange of results (e.g., Bray et al., 1982; Hollander, 1960; Wahrman & Pugh, 1972, 1974). In an extension of Hollander's position, Ridgeway (1978) has suggested that nonconformity affects status attainment by attracting attention to the deviate's task contribution and influencing perception of the deviate's motivation and competence. Studies suggest that high-status deviates are severely punished for major interference with group goal attainment, only mildly punished for minor interference, and highly rewarded for facilitation of goal attainment (e.g., Suchner & Jackson, 1976; Wiggins et al., 1965). In addition, several authors have suggested that among individuals who interfere with goal attainment, high status persons are often less likely than low-status persons to be defined as deviates and harshly punished (e.g., Giordano, 1983; Hollander & Willis, 1967; Wahrman, 1970a, 1970b).

Group Context of Deviance

So far our attention has been focused on how a deviate's overt behavior and attributed characteristics affect majority members' responses. This emphasis, although unavoidable in light of the large number of studies employing deviate behavior as an independent variable, is nevertheless one-sided, for it neglects the group context in which the deviate responds. In this regard, Allen (1985) has argued that social interaction can be construed at different levels (infragroup, intragroup, intergroup) and minority influence may be mediated by a different mechanism at each level. In order to understand how majority members define and respond to deviance, we must broaden our perspective by examining the impact of group norms, social influence among majority members, the role of group socialization, and majority members' personality characteristics.

Group norms can have powerful effects on how majority members react to deviance. Some groups have norms that demand the suppression of deviant thought and behavior (e.g., Janis, 1972; Roethlisberger & Dickson, 1939), whereas others have norms that permit and even encourage dissent (e.g., Coser, 1962; Deconchy, 1985; Dentler & Erickson, 1959). Norms permitting/ encouraging deviance may arise from several sources, including group members' desire to (a) uphold a value system that guarantees freedom of expression, (b) develop creative solutions to group problems, and (c) demarcate the boundaries of tolerable behavior within the group.

To assess the impact of an experimenter-imposed norm encouraging innovation, Moscovici and Lage (1978) manipulated the strength of the originality norm in a situation where two confederates consistently gave "green" responses to blue slides. Data indicated that subjects' tendency to give original (i.e., nonblue) responses to the slides increased as the strength of the originality norm increased. Moreover, minority members generally were liked better in the originality conditions than in another condition emphasizing the objectivity norm. In a related study reported by Moscovici (1976), a minority gave "green" responses on two-thirds of the trials and "blue" responses on remaining trials. Results revealed that subjects gave more "green" responses when the originality, rather than the objectivity, norm was dominant, suggesting that even an inconsistent minority can be influential in a situation demanding innovation.

Besides specifying how ingroup deviates should be treated and explicitly encouraging or discouraging innovation, norms can influence reaction to deviance in other ways as well. For example, norms regarding behavior toward ingroup vs. outgroup members may at least partially explain social categorization effects in minority influence (e.g., Aebischer, Hewstone, & Henderson, 1984; Maass et al., 1982; Mugny, Kaiser, Papastamou, & Perez, 1984; Perez & Mugny, 1987). Moreover, the normative context *outside* the group ("zeitgeist") may influence reaction to deviance within the group (e.g., Maass et al., 1982; Paicheler, 1976, 1977, 1979a).

In addition to explicit group norms, social influence among majority members can also affect reaction to deviance. As mentioned earlier, Doms (1984; Doms & Van Avermaet, 1985) has found that majority members who have social support are less amenable to minority influence than are majority members who do not have support. Evidence also suggests that deviate rejection is stronger among majority members who witness others react negatively toward the deviate than among majority members who do not have this experience. Wheeler and Caggiula (1966) created simulated 3-person groups in which subjects were led to believe that one member agreed and the second disagreed with their opinion on several topics. During an opinion-exchange session, subjects either did or did not hear the agreer verbally attack the disagreer for his views. Results indicated that subjects expressed more verbal aggression toward the disagreer in the attack than in the no-attack condition. Similar findings were obtained by Dedrick (1978) and Ruback and Levine (1979).

Because most of the research on reaction to deviance has employed short-term laboratory groups, little attention has been given to how majority responses are influenced by changes in the deviate's membership status (e.g., prospective member, new member, full member). In analyzing reaction to deviance in natural groups, Levine and Moreland (1985) discussed how an individual's stage of group membership (investigation, socialization, maintenance, resocialization, remembrance) affects his or her ability to produce innovation in the group. They suggested, for example, that during investigation (when the group looks for people who can contribute to the attainment of group goals and the individual looks for groups that can contribute to the satisfaction of personal needs), the ability of a prospective member to change the group is affected by several variables. These include the prospective member's perceived skills and commitment to the group, as well as the group's need for new members (cf. Arnold & Greenberg, 1980).

Very little research has been conducted on the relationship between majority members' personality characteristics and reactions to deviance. Arrowood and Amoroso (1965) found that a group member who deviated from modal opinion regarding a delinquent was liked less by first-born than by later-born majority members. Streufert (1966) asked subjects of different cognitive complexity levels to evaluate an opinion deviate in hypothetical situations varying in intimacy (a composite of spatial closeness and length of interaction). Although interaction intimacy did not affect how the least complex subjects evaluated the deviate, for subjects in higher complexity groups attraction to the deviate varied inversely with the intimacy of the hypothesized interaction. In contrast to the relatively clear-cut findings obtained in the foregoing studies, equivocal results have been found regarding the impact of majority members' affiliation motivation (Berkowitz & Howard, 1959) and dogmatism (Brown, 1970).

Summary. The research reported in this section suggests that group norms, social influence among majority members, the deviate's membership status, and majority members' personality characteristics can all affect reaction to opinion deviance. Although several scholars (e.g., Coser, 1962; Deconchy, 1985) have discussed the role of group norms in determining reaction to deviance, few investigators have conducted laboratory experiments to investigate this process (e.g., Moscovici & Lage, 1978). Moreover, little research has been done on such questions as how the normative context outside the group affects reaction to deviance within the group (e.g., Maass et al., 1982; Paicheler, 1976). In regard to social influence among majority members, relevant research suggests that such influence can occur at more than one level. Not only do majority members influence one another's susceptibility to persuasion by minority members (e.g., Doms, 1984), but they also affect one another's perception of and behavior toward these individuals (e.g., Wheeler & Caggiula, 1966). Recent theorizing about temporal changes in individual-group relations suggests that an individual's stage of group membership can importantly affect his or her ability to produce innovation in a group (Levine & Moreland, 1985). Finally, there is some evidence that individual difference factors, such as birth order and cognitive complexity, can affect reaction to opinion deviance (e.g., Arrowood & Amoroso, 1965; Streufert, 1966).

UNRESOLVED ISSUES

Although, as the previous review indicates, a substantial amount of theoretical and empirical work has been done on reaction to opinion deviance in small groups, much remains to be learned. The lacunae in our knowledge are due in large part to investigators' heavy reliance on ad hoc laboratory groups, which differ from natural groups in several important ways. For example, most laboratory groups exist for only an hour or two, whereas many natural groups exist for months, years, and even decades. This means that research conducted in laboratory settings typically provides little information about long-term temporal changes that occur between majority and minority members in natural groups (Levine & Moreland, 1985). Moreover, in most laboratory groups interaction between majority and minority members is severely restricted: The experimenter controls the responses of one faction (e.g., the minority), and members of the other faction (e.g., the majority) are not allowed to interact freely with members of either their own or the competing faction (Levine & Russo, 1987). Because such constraints are absent in most natural groups, research conducted in laboratory settings may provide a highly oversimplified picture of majority members' responses to deviates.

In this section I discuss three issues that must be addressed if investigators are to make real progress in understanding reaction to opinion deviance in natural groups. In presenting these issues, I offer a number of hypotheses that warrant empirical attention.

Majority Members' Motives

In attempting to predict reaction to deviance in a particular group setting, it is essential to understand the motives that underlie majority members' behavior (cf. Chaiken & Stangor, 1987). Some of these are *personal* motives, which reflect concern about one's own welfare. Examples include the desire to validate or evaluate one's opinions, avoid unpleasant social interactions, and gain the respect of ingroup and/or outgroup members. Others are *group* motives, which reflect concern about the welfare of the group as a whole. Examples include the desire that the group have high productivity, recruit and retain outstanding members, and continue to exist as a distinct entity. In considering how these personal and group motives affect reaction to opinion deviance, it is necessary to recognize three factors.

First, each majority member's behavior at a given point in time may be influenced by multiple motives, which vary in strength. In some cases, satisfaction of one motive has no bearing on satisfaction of other motives. In other cases, satisfaction of one motive facilitates or inhibits satisfaction of other motives. To predict the valence and intensity of a majority member's reaction to a deviate, then, one must know (a) the strength of each motive that the deviate's behavior affects, (b) the direct impact of the deviate's behavior on satisfaction of each motive, and (c) when satisfaction of one motive facilitates or inhibits satisfaction of other motives, the indirect impact of the deviate's behavior on satisfaction of each motive.

Second, each majority member's motives may vary over time. For example, an initial preoccupation with evaluating one's opinions may be supplanted by a desire that the group recruit outstanding members, which in turn may be displaced by the wish to avoid unpleasant social interactions. Such changes in a majority member's motives may produce changes in how he or she reacts to a deviate who maintains the same position over time, because the deviate's impact on goal attainment will vary depending on the majority member's dominant motive(s). In addition, a majority member may sometimes encounter different deviates at different points in time. When this occurs, the impact of a particular motive on the majority member's reaction to a deviate may depend, at least in part, on the majority member's previous experience with other deviates who facilitated or inhibited satisfaction of the same or a different motive.

Finally, different majority members may have different motives or different rank orders of the same motives. In the latter case, they may also have different perceptions of the deviate's impact on shared motives. In these situations, a given behavior by a deviate will have different implications for different majority members. In low-cohesive groups, where majority members do not think it is important to attain consensus, they may engage in little or no discussion concerning their perceptions of the deviate's behavior. In contrast, in high-cohesive groups, where majority members strongly desire consensus, they may engage in substantial discussion regarding the deviate's impact on personal and group goal attainment. Social influence, involving such processes as leadership, bargaining, coalition formation, and group polarization, may occur. One outcome of this influence may be the discovery that certain majority members are themselves deviates by virtue of their nonmodal interpretation of the deviate's behavior. In some cases these newly discovered deviates may cause more concern to other majority members than does the original deviate.

Assessment of the Deviate's Impact on Goal Attainment

So far, we have implicitly assumed that individual majority members have little difficulty ascertaining how much a deviate facilitates or inhibits the satisfaction of a personal or group motive. Although this assumption may be correct in some situations, assessment of the deviate's impact often may be problematical and hence require a substantial amount of cognitive activity. In determining how a deviate affects goal attainment, majority members may make inferences about the person based on his or her past, present, and probable future behaviors, as well as the situational factors that influence these behaviors.

When majority members have previously interacted with a person who is currently dissenting from group consensus, their recollection of the deviate's past behavior may substantially affect their interpretation of his or her present behavior. In such cases, majority members' knowledge of the deviate's former opinions, prior contributions to personal and group goal attainment, and typical style of expression may influence their assessment of the motive(s) underlying the deviate's current opinion and the probable correctness of this opinion. For example, a deviate who has rarely dissented in the past may be perceived as more concerned about group welfare and more likely to be correct than a deviate who has frequently dissented.

In deciding how a deviate's present behavior affects the achievement of their goals, majority members may seek clues about such factors as the deviate's desire to espouse a nonmodal position, confidence in this position, and motivation to strengthen or weaken the group. For example, deviance probably is seen as less intentional, and hence less likely to persist, when the deviate ostensibly is not aware of the majority position (e.g., when he or she responds first in the group) than when the deviate is aware (e.g., when he or she responds last). In addition, a deviate is probably perceived as more confident in his or her position, and hence more likely to be correct, when resisting strong rather than weak majority pressure. Finally, a deviate may be seen as less concerned about group welfare, and hence more threatening to group goal attainment, when expressing his or her disagreement to outsiders, rather than (or in addition to) insiders.

Majority members' estimates of how a deviate's future behavior will affect goal attainment may be influenced by three types of uncertainty. That is, majority members may be unsure (a) how the deviate will behave in the future, (b) what their own personal and group motives will be in the future, and (c) whether the deviate will continue to be a group member in the future. The more experience majority members have had with the deviate, the more consistent the deviate's behavior has been in the past, and the more the situational constraints acting on the deviate are likely to remain constant, the more confident majority members are likely to be that the deviate's future behavior will resemble his or her present behavior. Similarly, the more the situational constraints acting on majority members are expected to remain constant, the more confident majority members probably will be that their future motives will resemble their present motives. Finally, the less sure majority members are that the deviate will remain in the group, the less concerned they are likely to be about his or her future impact on goal attainment.

It is important to note that, rather than seeking to determine the deviate's *true* impact on goal attainment, majority members may sometimes be motivated to believe that the deviate has a more positive or negative impact than his or her behavior warrants. This reaction is likely when majority members desire to avoid the behavioral obligations demanded by the perception that the deviate either hindered or helped goal attainment. For example, majority members may feel that a deviate who persistently thwarts satisfaction of their motives should be asked to leave the group, but find it difficult to communicate this harsh request to the deviate. In such cases majority members may seek to interpret the deviate's behavior as irrelevant to the attainment of personal and group goals. To accomplish this, majority members may decide that they misunderstood the deviate's position, that the deviate did not really mean what he or she said, that the deviate will soon outgrow his or her peculiar ideas, that the issue was interpreted differently by the deviate and majority members, that the topic is unimportant, and so on.

Overt and Covert Reactions to Deviance

Assuming that majority members perceive that the deviate's behavior has implications for personal and/or group goals, they may try to reach agreement on the type, intensity, and timing of their overt responses. Efforts to attain consensus about treatment for the deviate are probably most likely when the majority is cohesive and has the time to make a joint decision. To the extent that majority members attempt to achieve consensus, social influence of the sort described earlier may occur. Conflict among majority members regarding appropriate treatment for the deviate may arise from several sources, including choice of the most effective way to alter the deviate's position (e.g., persuasive communication vs. threats) and selection of a group agent to deal with the deviate. The latter type of conflict is likely to occur when an *enforcer* role does not exist in the group or is unoccupied and too few or too many majority members wish to occupy this role. If majority members are unmotivated or unable to reach consensus about appropriate behavior toward the deviate, then they will respond to him or her as individuals. In such cases, the deviate may receive highly inconsistent information about the appropriateness of his or her conduct.

In addition to overt behavior directed toward the deviate, majority members may also have covert reactions (e.g., changes in affect or cognition regarding the deviate, the discussion topic, or other majority members). Some of these responses may occur prior to overt behavior and influence the expression of this behavior. In addition, covert responses may arise during and after the overt behavior and may be either consistent or inconsistent with it (cf. Nail, 1986). If inconsistent (e.g., guilt about treating the deviate harshly), these covert responses may produce subsequent overt behavior that differs markedly from the overt behavior expressed initially (cf. Moscovici & Neve, 1971).

Previous research on reaction to opinion deviance has generally failed to study ongoing behavioral exchanges between majority and minority members. Such exchanges may be particularly important when two or more minority members provide social support for one another. One interesting feature of these interactions is their potential for producing escalations in majority-minority hostility. For example, the minority's first public statement of its position may elicit a mild rebuke from the majority, which may produce increased extremity on the part of the minority, which in turn may stimulate a harsher majority response, and so on. Negative majority/minority relations may be exacerbated by structural changes that each faction makes in order to increase its competitive position (e.g., centralizing authority, purging "unreliable elements"). Over time such changes may push the factions so far apart that verbal disagreement gives way to physical violence.

Conclusion

The hypotheses presented in this section by no means exhaust the interesting research questions concerning reaction to opinion deviance in small groups (see also Chaiken & Stangor, 1987; Levine & Russo, 1987, and Maass, West, & Cialdini, 1987). Nevertheless, these hypotheses should be sufficient to suggest the value of studying reaction to deviance in groups that have a past and a future and that allow majority and minority members to interact in a relatively unconstrained manner. It is hoped that, in addition to conducting fine-grained analyses of the cognitive processes of individual majority and minority members, investigators will devote increased attention to the interpersonal and intergroup aspects of majority-minority relations. Systematic research on the social processes that occur within and between majorities and minorities would greatly enrich our understanding of reaction to opinion deviance.

ACKNOWLEDGMENTS

Preparation of this chapter was supported by Grant OERI-G-86-0005 from the Office of Educational Research and Improvement, Department of Education, to the Center for the Study of Learning, Learning Research and Development

Center, University of Pittsburgh, and by Grant BNS-8316107 from the National Science Foundation. Thanks are extended to Marie Cini, Paul Paulus, Eileen Russo, and Sharon Wolf for helpful comments on an earlier draft of the chapter.

REFERENCES

Aebischer, V., Hewstone, M., & Henderson, M. (1984). Minority influence and musical preference: Innovation by conversion not coercion. *European Journal of Social Psychology, 14*, 23–33.

Allen, V. L. (1965). Situational factors in conformity. In L. Berkowitz (Ed.), *Advances in experimental social psychology* (Vol. 2, pp. 133–175). New York: Academic Press.

Allen, V. L. (1975). Social support for nonconformity. In L. Berkowitz (Ed.), *Advances in experimental social psychology* (Vol. 8, pp, 1–43). New York: Academic Press.

Allen, V. L. (1985). Infra-group, intra-group, and inter-group: Construing levels of organization in social influence. In S. Moscovici, G. Mugny, & E. Van Avermaet (Eds.), *Perspectives on minority influence* (pp. 217–238). Cambridge, England: Cambridge University Press.

Allen, V. L., & Wilder, D. A. (1978). Perceived persuasiveness as a function of response style: Multi-issue consistency over time. *European Journal of Social Psychology, 8*, 289–296.

Alvarez, R. (1968). Informal reactions to deviance in simulated work organizations: A laboratory experiment. *American Sociological Review, 33*, 895–912.

Apple, W., Streeter, L. A., & Krauss, R. M. (1979). Effects of pitch and speech rate on personal attributions. *Journal of Personality and Social Psychology, 37*, 715–727.

Archer, D. (1985). Social deviance. In G. Lindzey & E. Aronson (Eds.), *Handbook of social psychology* (Vol. 2, 3rd ed., pp. 743–804). New York: Random House.

Arnold, D. W., & Greenberg, C. I. (1980). Deviate rejection within differentially manned groups. *Social Psychology Quarterly, 43*, 419–424.

Arrowood, A. J., & Amoroso, D. M. (1965). Social comparison and ordinal position. *Journal of Personality and Social Psychology, 2*, 101–104.

Back, K. W. (1951). Influence through social communication. *Journal of Abnormal and Social Psychology, 46*, 9–23.

Batchelor, T. R., & Tesser, A. (1971). Attitude base as a moderator of the attitude similarity-attraction relationship. *Journal of Personality and Social Psychology, 19*, 229–236.

Berger, J., & Zelditch, M., Jr. (1983). Artifacts and challenges: A comment on Lee and Ofshe. *Social Psychology Quarterly, 46*, 59–62.

Berkowitz, L. (1971). Reporting an experiment: A case study in leveling, sharpening, and assimilation. *Journal of Experimental Social Psychology, 7*, 237–243.

Berkowitz, L., & Howard, R. C. (1959). Reactions to opinion deviates as affected by affiliation need (n) and group member interdependence. *Sociometry, 22*, 81–91.

Bray, R. M., Johnson, D., & Chilstrom, J. T., Jr. (1982). Social influence by group members with minority opinions: A comparison of Hollander and Moscovici. *Journal of Personality and Social Psychology, 43*, 78–88.

Brickman, P., & Bulman, R. J. (1977). Pleasure and pain in social comparison. In J. M. Suls & R. L. Miller (Eds.), *Social comparison processes: Theoretical and empirical perspectives* (pp. 149–186). Washington, DC: Hemisphere.

Brown, R. D. (1970). Emotional expression, interpersonal attraction, and rejection of a deviate (Doctoral dissertation, Washington University, 1970). *Dissertation Abstracts International, 31*, 3635-A. (University Microfilms No. 70-26,849).

Burnstein, E. (1969). Cognitive factors in behavioral interdependence. In J. Mills (Ed.), *Experimental social psychology* (pp. 309–340). London: Macmillan.

Burnstein, E. (1982). Persuasion as argument processing. In H. Brandstatter, J. H. Davis, & G. Stocker-Kreichgauer (Eds.), *Group decision making* (pp. 103–124). London: Academic Press.

Burnstein, E., & Worchel, P. (1962). Arbitrariness of frustration and its consequences for aggression in a social situation. *Journal of Personality, 30,* 528–541.

Byrne, D. (1969). Attitudes and attraction. In L. Berkowitz (Ed.), *Advances in experimental social psychology* (Vol. 4, pp. 35–89). New York: Academic Press.

Byrne, D. (1971). *The attraction paradigm.* New York: Academic Press.

Cartwright, D. (1968). The nature of group cohesiveness. In D. Cartwright & A. Zander (Eds.), *Group dynamics: Research and theory* (3rd ed., pp. 91–109). New York: Harper and Row.

Chaiken, S., & Stangor, S. (1987). Attitudes and attitude change. *Annual review of psychology, 38,* 575–630.

Clore, G. L., & Byrne, D. (1974). A reinforcement-affect model of attraction. In T. L. Huston (Ed.), *Foundations of interpersonal attraction* (pp. 143–170). New York: Academic Press.

Codol, J. P. (1984). Social differentiation and non-differentiation. In H. Tajfel (Ed.), *The social dimension: European developments in social psychology* (Vol. 1, pp. 314–337). Cambridge, England: Cambridge University Press.

Collins, B. E., & Raven, B. H. (1969). Group structure: Attraction, coalitions, communication, and power. In G. Lindzey & E. Aronson (Eds.), *The handbook of social psychology* (Vol. 4, 2nd ed., pp. 102–204). Reading, MA: Addison-Wesley.

Coser, L. A. (1962). Some functions of deviant behavior and normative flexibility. *American Journal of Sociology, 68,* 172–181.

Deconchy, J. (1985). The paradox of "orthodox minorities": When orthodoxy infallibly fails. In S. Moscovici, G. Mugny, & E. Van Avermaet (Eds.), *Perspectives on minority influence* (pp. 187–200). Cambridge, England: Cambridge University Press.

Dedrick, D. K. (1978). Deviance and sanctioning within small groups. *Social Psychology, 41,* 94–105.

Dentler, R. A., & Erikson, K. T. (1959). The functions of deviance in groups. *Social Problems, 7,* 98–107.

Doms, M. (1984). The minority influence effect: An alternative approach. In W. Doise & S. Moscovici (Eds.), *Current issues in European social psychology* (Vol. 1, pp. 1–33). Cambridge, England: Cambridge University Press.

Doms, M., & Van Avermaet, E. (1980). Majority influence, minority influence and conversion behavior: A replication. *Journal of Experimental Social Psychology, 16,* 283–292.

Doms, M., & Van Avermaet, E. (1985). Social support and minority influence: The innovation effect reconsidered. In S. Moscovici, G. Mugny, & E. Van Avermaet (Eds.), *Perspectives on minority influence* (pp. 53–74). Cambridge, England: Cambridge University Press.

Eagly, A. H., & Chaiken, S. (1984). Cognitive theories of persuasion. In L. Berkowitz (Ed.), *Advances in experimental social psychology* (Vol. 17, pp. 267–359). Orlando, FL: Academic Press.

Earle, W. B. (1986). The social context of social comparison: Reality versus reassurance. *Personality and Social Psychology Bulletin, 12,* 159–168.

Emerson, R. M. (1954). Deviation and rejection: An experimental replication. *American Sociological Review, 19,* 688–693.

Erickson, B., Lind, E. A., Johnson, B. C., & O'Barr, W. M. (1978). Speech style and impression formation in a court setting: The effects of "powerful" and "powerless" speech. *Journal of Experimental Social Psychology, 14,* 266–279.

Festinger, L. (1950). Informal social communication. *Psychological Review, 57,* 271–282.

Festinger, L. (1954). A theory of social comparison processes. *Human Relations, 7,* 117–140.

Festinger, L., Gerard, H. B., Hymovitch, B., Kelley, H. H., & Raven, B. H. (1952). The influence process in the presence of extreme deviates. *Human Relations, 5,* 327–346.

Festinger, L., Schachter, S., & Back, K. (1950). *Social pressures in informal groups*. New York: Harper.

Festinger, L., & Thibaut, J. (1951). Interpersonal communication in small groups. *Journal of Abnormal and Social Psychology, 46*, 92–99.

Gerard, H. B. (1953). The effect of different dimensions of disagreement on the communication process in small groups. *Human Relations, 6*, 249–271.

Giordano, P. C. (1983). Sanctioning the high-status deviant: An attributional analysis. *Social Psychology Quarterly, 46*, 329–342.

Goethals, G. R., & Darley, J. M. (1977). Social comparison theory: An attributional approach. In J. M. Suls & R. L. Miller (Eds.), *Social comparison processes: Theoretical and empirical perspectives* (pp. 259–278). Washington, DC: Hemisphere.

Goethals, G. R., & Darley, J. M. (1987). Social comparison theory: Self-evaluation and group life. In B. Mullen & G. R. Goethals (Eds.), *Theories of group behavior* (pp. 21–47). New York: Springer-Verlag.

Griffitt, W. (1974). Attitude similarity and attraction. In T. L. Huston (Ed.), *Foundations of interpersonal attraction* (pp. 285–308). New York: Academic Press.

Gruder, C. L. (1977). Choice of comparison persons in evaluating oneself. In J. M. Suls & R. L. Miller (Eds.), *Social comparison processes: Theoretical and empirical perspectives* (pp. 21–41). Washington, DC: Hemisphere.

Hensley, V., & Duval, S. (1976). Some perceptual determinants of perceived similarity, liking, and correctness. *Journal of Personality and Social Psychology, 34*, 159–168.

Herman, C. P., Zanna, M. P., & Higgins, E. T. (Eds.). (1986). *Physical appearance, stigma, and social behavior: The Ontario Symposium, Vol. 3*. Hillsdale, NJ: Lawrence Erlbaum Associates.

Hochbaum, G. M. (1954). The relation between group members' self-confidence and their reactions to group pressures to uniformity. *American Sociological Review, 19*, 678–687.

Hollander, E. P. (1958). Conformity, status, and idiosyncrasy credit. *Psychological Review, 65*, 117–127.

Hollander, E. P. (1960). Competence and conformity in the acceptance of influence. *Journal of Abnormal and Social Psychology, 61*, 365–369.

Hollander, E. P. (1964). *Leaders, groups, and influence*. New York: Oxford.

Hollander, E. P., & Willis, R. H. (1967). Some current issues in the psychology of conformity and nonconformity. *Psychological Bulletin, 68*, 62–76.

Homans, G. C. (1974). *Social behavior: Its elementary forms* (rev. ed.). New York: Harcourt.

Israel, J. (1956). *Self-evaluation and rejection in groups: Three experimental studies and a conceptual outline*. Uppsala: Almqvist & Wiksell.

Iwao, S. (1963). Internal versus external criticism of group standards. *Sociometry, 26*, 410–421.

Janis, I. L. (1972). *Victims of groupthink: A psychological study of foreign-policy decisions and fiascoes*. Boston: Houghton Mifflin.

Jones, E. E., & deCharms, R. (1957). Changes in social perception as a function of the personal relevance of behavior. *Sociometry, 20*, 75–85.

Jones, E. E., Farina, A., Hastorf, A. H., Markus, H., Miller, D. T., & Scott, R. A. (1984). *Social stigma: The psychology of marked relationships*. New York: Freeman.

Jones, E. E., & Gerard, H. B. (1967). *Foundations of social psychology*. New York: Wiley.

Kelley, H. H. (1967). Attribution theory in social psychology. In D. Levine (Ed.), *Nebraska Symposium on Motivation* (Vol. 15, pp. 192–238). Lincoln: University of Nebraska Press.

Kelley, H. H. (1972). Attribution in social interaction. In E. E. Jones, D. E. Kanouse, H. H. Kelley, R. E. Nisbett, S. Valins, & B. Weiner (Eds.), *Attribution: Perceiving the causes of behavior* (pp. 1–26). Morristown, NJ: General Learning Press.

Kelvin, P. (1979). Book review of Moscovici (1976). *European Journal of Social Psychology, 9*, 441–446.

Kerr, N. L., MacCoun, R. J., Hansen, C. H., & Hymes, J. A. (1987). Gaining and losing social support: Momentum in decision-making groups. *Journal of Experimental Social Psychology, 23,* 119–145.

Kiesler, C. A., & Kiesler, S. B. (1969). *Conformity.* Reading, MA: Addison-Wesley.

Kiesler, C. A., & Pallak, M. S. (1975). Minority influence: The effect of majority reactionaries and defectors, and minority and majority compromisers, upon majority opinion and attraction. *European Journal of Social Psychology, 5,* 237–256.

Latane, B., & Wolf, S. (1981). The social impact of majorities and minorities. *Psychological Review, 88,* 438–453.

Lauderdale, P. (1976). Deviance and moral boundaries. *American Sociological Review, 41,* 660–676.

Lauderdale, P., Parker, J., Smith-Cunnien, P., & Inverarity, J. (1984). External threat and the definition of deviance. *Journal of Personality and Social Psychology, 46,* 1058–1068.

Lee, M. T., & Ofshe, R. (1981). The impact of behavioral style and status characteristics on social influence: A test of two competing theories. *Social Psychology Quarterly, 44,* 73–82.

Lemaine, G. (1974). Social differentiation and social originality. *European Journal of Social Psychology, 4,* 17–52.

Lemaine, G., Kastersztein, J., & Personnaz, B. (1978). Social differentiation. In H. Tajfel (Ed.), *Differentiation between social groups: Studies in the social psychology of intergroup relations* (pp. 269–300). London: Academic Press.

Levine, J. M. (1980). Reaction to opinion deviance in small groups. In P. B. Paulus (Ed.), *Psychology of group influence* (pp. 375–429). Hillsdale, NJ: Lawrence Erlbaum Associates.

Levine, J. M. (1983). Social comparison and education. In J. M. Levine & M. C. Wang (Eds.), *Teacher and student perceptions: Implications for learning* (pp. 29–55). Hillsdale, NJ: Lawrence Erlbaum Associates.

Levine, J. M., & McBurney, D. H. (1986). The role of olfaction in social perception and behavior. In C. P. Herman, M. P. Zanna, & E. T. Higgins (Eds.), *Physical appearance, stigma, and social behavior: The Ontario Symposium* (Vol. 3, pp. 179–217). Hillsdale, NJ: Lawrence Erlbaum Associates.

Levine, J. M., & Moreland, R. L. (1985). Innovation and socialization in small groups. In S. Moscovici, G. Mugny, & E. Van Avermaet (Eds.), *Perspectives on minority influence* (pp. 143–169). Cambridge, England: Cambridge University Press.

Levine, J. M., & Moreland, R. L. (1987). Social comparison and outcome evaluation in group contexts. In J. C. Masters & W. P. Smith (Eds.), *Social comparison, social justice, and relative deprivation: Theoretical, empirical, and policy perspectives* (pp. 105–127). Hillsdale, NJ: Lawrence Erlbaum Associates.

Levine, J. M., & Ranelli, C. J. (1978). Majority reaction to shifting and stable attitudinal deviates. *European Journal of Social Psychology, 8,* 55–70.

Levine, J. M., & Ruback, R. B. (1980). Reaction to opinion deviance: Impact of a fence straddler's rationale on majority evaluation. *Social Psychology Quarterly, 43,* 73–81.

Levine, J. M., & Russo, E. M. (1987). Majority and minority influence. In C. Hendrick (Ed.), *Group processes: Review of personality and social psychology* (Vol. 8, pp. 13–54). Newbury Park, CA: Sage.

Levine, J. M., Saxe, L., & Harris, H. J. (1976). Reaction to attitudinal deviance: Impact of deviate's direction and distance of movement. *Sociometry, 39,* 97–107.

Levine, J. M., Sroka, K. R., & Snyder, H. N. (1977). Group support and reaction to stable and shifting agreement/disagreement. *Sociometry, 40,* 214–224.

London, H. (1973). *Psychology of the persuader.* Morristown, NJ: General Learning Press.

Maass, A., & Clark, R. D., III. (1983). Internalization versus compliance: Differential processes underlying minority influence and conformity. *European Journal of Social Psychology, 13,* 197–215.

Maass, A., & Clark, R. D., III. (1984). Hidden impact of minorities: Fifteen years of minority influence research. *Psychological Bulletin, 95*, 428–450.

Maass, A., & Clark, R. D., III. (1986). Conversion theory and simultaneous majority/minority influence: Can reactance offer an alternative explanation? *European Journal of Social Psychology, 16*, 305–309.

Maass, A., Clark, R. D., III., & Haberkorn, G. (1982). The efffects of differential ascribed category membership and norms on minority influence. *European Journal of Social Psychology, 12*, 89–104.

Maass, A., West, S. G., & Cialdini, R. B. (1987). Minority influence and conversion. In C. Hendrick (Ed.), *Group processes: Review of personality and social psychology* (Vol. 8, pp. 55–79). Newbury Park, CA: Sage.

Mackie, D. M. (1987). Systematic and nonsystematic processing of majority and minority persuasive communications. *Journal of Personality and Social Psychology, 53*, 41–52.

McWhinney, W. H. (1968). Synthesizing a social interaction model. *Sociometry, 31*, 229–244.

Miller, C. E., & Anderson, P. D. (1979). Group decision rules and the rejection of deviates. *Social Psychology Quarterly, 42*, 354–363.

Miller, C. E., Jackson, P., Mueller, J., & Schersching, C. (1987). Some social psychological effects of group decision rules. *Journal of Personality and Social Psychology, 52*, 325–332.

Mills, T. M. (1962). A sleeper variable in small groups research: The experimenter. *Pacific Sociological Review, 5*, 21–28.

Mohr, P. B. (1986). Demeanor, status cue or performance? *Social Psychology Quarterly, 49*, 228–236.

Morris, W. N., & Miller, R. S. (1975). Impressions of dissenters and conformers: An attributional analysis. *Sociometry, 38*, 327–339.

Moscovici, S. (1974). Social influence I: Conformity and social control. In C. Nemeth (Ed.), *Social psychology: Classic and contemporary integrations* (pp. 179–216). Chicago: Rand-McNally.

Moscovici, S. (1976). *Social influence and social change*. New York: Academic Press.

Moscovici, S. (1980). Toward a theory of conversion behavior. In L. Berkowitz (Ed.), *Advances in experimental social psychology*, (Vol. 13, pp. 209–239). New York: Academic Press.

Moscovici, S. (1985a). Innovation and minority influence. In S. Moscovici, G. Mugny, & E. Van Avermaet (Eds.), *Perspectives on minority influence* (pp. 9–51). Cambridge, England: Cambridge University Press.

Moscovici, S. (1985b). Social influence and conformity. In G. Lindzey & E. Aronson (Eds.), *The handbook of social psychology* (Vol. 2, 3rd ed., pp. 347–412). New York: Random House.

Moscovici, S., & Doms, M. (1982). Compliance and conversion in a situation of sensory deprivation. *Basic and Applied Social Psychology, 3*, 81–94.

Moscovici, S., & Faucheux, C. (1972). Social influence, conformity bias, and the study of active minorities. In L. Berkowitz (Ed.), *Advances in experimental social psychology* (Vol. 6, pp. 149–202). New York: Academic Press.

Moscovici, S., & Lage, E. (1976). Studies in social influence III: Majority versus minority influence in a group. *European Journal of Social Psychology, 6*, 149–174.

Moscovici, S., & Lage, E. (1978). Studies in social influence IV: Minority influence in a context of original judgments. *European Journal of Social Psychology, 8*, 349–365.

Moscovici, S., Lage, E., & Naffrechoux, M. (1969). Influence of a consistent minority on the responses of a majority in a color perception task. *Sociometry, 32*, 365–380.

Moscovici, S., & Mugny, G. (1983). Minority influence. In P. B. Paulus (Ed.), *Basic group processes* (pp. 41–64). New York: Springer-Verlag.

Moscovici, S., & Nemeth, C. (1974). Social influence II: Minority influence. In C. Nemeth (Ed.), *Social psychology: Classic and contemporary integrations* (pp. 217–249). Chicago: Rand-McNally.

Moscovici, S., & Neve, P. (1971). Studies in social influence: I. Those absent are in the right:

Convergence and polarization of answers in the course of a social interaction. *European Journal of Social Psychology, 1,* 201–214.

Moscovici, S., & Paicheler, G. (1983). Minority or majority influences: Social change, compliance, and conversion. In H. H. Blumberg, A. P. Hare, V. Kent, & M. Davies (Eds.), *Small groups and social interaction* (Vol. 1, pp. 215–224). New York: Wiley.

Moscovici, S., & Personnaz, B. (1980). Studies in social influence V. Minority influence and conversion behavior in a perceptual task. *Journal of Experimental Social Psychology, 16,* 270–282.

Moscovici, S., & Personnaz, B. (1986). Studies on latent influence by the spectrometer method I: The impact of psychologization in the case of conversion by a minority or a majority. *European Journal of Social Psychology, 16,* 345–360.

Mugny, G. (1979). A rejoinder to Paicheler: The influence of reactionary minorities. *European Journal of Social Psychology, 9,* 223–225.

Mugny, G. (1982). *The power of minorities.* New York: Academic Press.

Mugny, G. (1984a). Compliance, conversion, and the Asch paradigm. *European Journal of Social Psychology, 14,* 353–368.

Mugny, G. (1984b). The influence of minorities: Ten years later. In H. Tajfel (Ed.), *The social dimension: European developments in social psychology* (Vol. 2, pp. 498–517). Cambridge: Cambridge University Press.

Mugny, G., Kaiser, C., Papastamou, S., & Perez, J. A. (1984). Intergroup relations, identification, and social influence. *British Journal of Social Psychology, 23,* 317–322.

Mullen, B. (1983). Operationalizing the effect of the group on the individual: A self-attention perspective. *Journal of Experimental Social Psychology, 19,* 295–322.

Nail, P.R. (1986). Toward an integration of some models and theories of social response. *Psychological Bulletin, 100,* 190–206.

Nemeth, C. (1983). Reflections on the dialogue between status and style: Influence processes of social control and social change. *Social Psychology Quarterly, 46,* 70–74.

Nemeth, C. (1985). Dissent, group processes, and creativity: The contribution of minority influence. In E. Lawler (Ed.), *Advances in group processes* (pp. 57–75). Greenwich, CT: JAI Press.

Nemeth, C. (1986). Differential contributions of majority and minority influence. *Psychological Review, 93,* 23–32.

Nemeth, C. (1987). Influence processes, problem solving and creativity. In M. P. Zanna, J. M. Olson, & C. P. Herman (Eds.), *Social influence: The Ontario Symposium* (Vol. 5, pp. 237–246). Hillsdale, NJ: Lawrence Erlbaum Associates.

Nemeth, C., & Brilmayer, A. G. (1987). Negotiation versus influence. *European Journal of Social Psychology, 17,* 45–56.

Nemeth, C., & Endicott, J. (1976). The midpoint as an anchor: Another look at discrepancy of position and attitude change. *Sociometry, 39,* 11–18.

Nemeth, C., & Kwan, J. L. (1985). Originality of word associations as a function of majority vs. minority influence. *Social Psychology Quarterly, 48,* 277–282.

Nemeth, C., & Kwan, J. (1987). Minority influence, divergent thinking, and detection of covects solutions. *Journal of Applied Social Psychology, 17,* 788–799.

Nemeth, C., Swedlund, M., & Kanki, B. (1974). Patterning of the minority's responses and their influence on the majority. *European Journal of Social Psychology, 4,* 53–64.

Nemeth, C., & Wachtler, J. (1973). Consistency and modification of judgment. *Journal of Experimental Social Psychology, 9,* 65–79.

Nemeth, C., & Wachtler, J. (1974). Creating the perceptions of consistency and confidence: A necessary condition for minority influence. *Sociometry, 37,* 529–540.

Nemeth, C., & Wachtler, J. (1983). Creative problem solving as a result of majority vs. minority influence. *European Journal of Social Psychology, 13,* 45–55.

Nemeth, C., Wachtler, J., & Endicott, J. (1977). Increasing the size of the minority: Some gains and some losses. *European Journal of Social Psychology, 7*, 15–27.

Newcomb, T. M. (1953). An approach to the study of communicative acts. *Psychological Review, 60*, 393–404.

Newcomb, T. M. (1959). Individual systems of orientation. In S. Koch (Ed.), *Psychology: A study of a science* (Vol. 3, pp. 384–422). New York: McGraw-Hill.

Newcomb, T. M. (1961). *The acquaintance processes.* New York: Holt, Rinehart, and Winston.

Newcombe, N., & Arnkoff, D. B. (1979). Effects of speech style and sex of speaker on person perception. *Journal of Personality and Social Psychology, 37*, 1293–1303.

Ofshe, R., & Lee, M. T. (1983). "What are we to make of all this?" Reply to Berger and Zelditch. *Social Psychology Quarterly, 46*, 63–65.

Orcutt, J. D. (1973). Societal reaction and the response to deviation in small groups. *Social Forces, 52*, 259–267.

Paicheler, G. (1976). Norms and attitude change I: Polarization and styles of behaviour. *European Journal of Social Psychology, 6*, 405–427.

Paicheler, G. (1977). Norms and attitude change II: The phenomenon of bipolarization. *European Journal of Social Psychology, 7*, 5–14.

Paicheler, G. (1979a). Polarization of attitudes in homogeneous and heterogeneous groups. *European Journal of Social Psychology, 9*, 85–96.

Paicheler, G. (1979b). On the comparability of experimental results. *European Journal of Social Psychology, 9*, 227–228.

Papastamou, S. (1984). Strategies of minority and majority influence. In W. Doise & S. Moscovici (Eds.), *Current issues in European social psychology* (Vol. 1, pp. 33–83). Cambridge, England: Cambridge University Press.

Papastamou, S. (1986). Psychologization and processes of minority and majority influence. *European Journal of Social Psychology, 16*, 165–180.

Papastamou, S., & Mugny, G. (1985). Rigidity and minority influence: The influence of the social in social influence. In S. Moscovici, G. Mugny, & E. Van Avermaet (Eds.), *Perspectives on minority influence* (pp. 113–136). Cambridge, England: Cambridge University Press.

Perez, J. A., & Mugny, G. (1987). Paradoxical effects of categorization in minority influence: When being an outgroup is an advantage. *European Journal of Social Psychology, 17*, 157–169.

Personnaz, B. (1981). Study in social influence using the spectrometer method: Dynamics of the phenomena of conversion and covertness in perceptual responses. *European Journal of Social Psychology, 11*, 431–438.

Personnaz, B., & Guillon, M. (1985). Conflict and conversion. In S. Moscovici, G. Mugny, & E. Van Avermaet (Eds.), *Perspectives on minority influence.* Cambridge, England: Cambridge University Press.

Ridgeway, C. L. (1978). Conformity, group-oriented motivation, and status attainment in small groups. *Social Psychology, 41*, 175–188.

Ridgeway, C. L. (1981). Nonconformity, competence, and influence in groups: A test of two theories. *American Sociological Review, 46*, 333–347.

Ridgeway, C. L. (1982). Status in groups: The importance of motivation. *American Sociological Review, 47*, 76–88.

Ridgeway, C. L. (1984). Dominance, performance, and status in groups: A theoretical analysis. In E. J. Lawler (Ed.), *Advances in group processes* (Vol. 1, pp. 59–93). Greenwich, CT: JAI Press.

Ridgeway, C. L., & Jacobson, C. K. (1977). Sources of status and influence in all female and mixed sexed groups. *The Sociological Quarterly, 18*, 413–425.

Roethlisberger, F. J., & Dickson, W. J. (1939). *Management and the worker.* Cambridge, MA: Harvard University Press.

Ruback, R. B., & Levine, J. M. (1978, March). *Reaction to gain and loss of social support: Impact of supporter's motives.* Paper presented at the meeting of the Eastern Psychological Association, Washington, DC.

Ruback, R. B., & Levine, J. M. (1979, April). *Reaction to opinion deviance: Impact of others' tolerance of deviate and deviate's expressed confidence.* Paper presented at the meeting of the Eastern Psychological Association, Philadelphia.

Sampson, E. E., & Brandon, A. C. (1964). The effects of role and opinion deviation on small group behavior. *Sociometry, 27,* 261–281.

Schachter, S. (1951). Deviation, rejection, and communication. *Journal of Abnormal and Social Psychology, 46,* 190–207.

Schachter, S., Nuttin, J., DeMonchaux, C., Maucorps, P., Osmer, D., Duijker, H., Rommetveit, R., & Israel, J. (1954). Cross-cultural experiments on threat and rejection. *Human Relations, 7,* 403–439.

Simon, H. A., & Guetzkow, H. (1955a). A model of short- and long-run mechanisms involved in pressures toward uniformity in groups. *Psychological Review, 62,* 56–68.

Simon, H. A., & Guetzkow, H. (1955b). Mechanisms involved in group pressures on deviate-members. *The British Journal of Statistical Psychology, 8,* 93–101.

Singer, E. (1981). Reference groups and social evaluations. In M. Rosenberg & R. H. Turner (Eds.), *Social psychology: Sociological perspectives* (pp. 66–93). New York: Basic Books.

Singer, J. E., Radloff, L. S., & Wark, D. M. (1963). Renegades, heretics, and changes in sentiment. *Sociometry, 26,* 178–189.

Smith, C. R., Williams, L., & Willis, R. H. (1967). Race, sex, and belief as determinants of friendship acceptance. *Journal of Personality and Social Psychology, 5,* 127–137.

Snortum, J. R., Klein, J. S., & Sherman, W. A. (1976). The impact of an aggressive juror in six- and twelve-member juries. *Criminal Justice and Behavior, 3,* 255–262.

Snyder, C. R., & Fromkin, H. L. (1980). *Uniqueness: The human pursuit of difference.* New York: Plenum.

Sorrentino, R. M., King, G., & Leo, G. (1980). The influence of the minority on perception: A note on a possible alternative interpretation. *Journal of Experimental Social Psychology, 16,* 293–301.

Spitzer, C. E., & Davis, J. H. (1978). Mutual social influence in dynamic groups. *Social Psychology, 41,* 24–33.

Streufert, S. (1966). Conceptual structure, communicator importance, and interpersonal attitudes toward conforming and deviant group members. *Journal of Personality and Social Psychology, 4,* 100–103.

Suchner, R. W., & Jackson, D. (1976). Responsibility and status: A causal or only a spurious relationship? *Sociometry, 39,* 243–256.

Tanford, S., & Penrod, S. (1983). Computer modeling of influence in the jury: The role of the consistent juror. *Social Psychology Quarterly, 46,* 200–212.

Tanford, S., & Penrod, S. (1984). Social influence model: A formal integration of research on majority and minority influence processes. *Psychological Bulletin, 95,* 189–225.

Thornton, D. A., & Arrowood, A. J. (1966). Self-evaluation, self-enhancement, and the locus of social comparison. *Journal of Experimental Social Psychology,* Supplement 1, 40–48.

Tuzlak, A., & Moore, J. C. Jr. (1984). Status, demeanor, and influence: An empirical reassessment. *Social Psychology Quarterly, 47,* 178–183.

Wahrman, R. (1970a). High status, deviance and sanctions. *Sociometry, 33,* 485–504.

Wahrman, R. (1970b). Status, deviance, and sanctions. *Pacific Sociological Review, 13,* 229–240.

Wahrman, R., & Pugh, M. D. (1972). Competence and conformity: Another look at Hollander's study. *Sociometry, 35,* 376–386.

Wahrman, R., & Pugh, M. D. (1974). Sex, nonconformity and influence. *Sociometry, 37,* 137–147.

Wheeler, L., & Caggiula, A. R. (1966). The contagion of aggression. *Journal of Experimental Social Psychology, 2,* 1–10.

Wiggins, J. A., Dill, F., & Schwartz, R. D. (1965). On "status liability." *Sociometry, 28,* 197–209.

Wilder, D. A. (1978). Perceiving persons as a group: Effects on atttributions of causality and beliefs. *Social Psychology, 41,* 13–23.

Wills, T. A. (1981). Downward comparison principles in social psychology. *Psychological Bulletin, 90,* 245–271.

Wolf, S. (1979). Behavioral style and group cohesiveness as sources of minority influence. *European Journal of Social Psychology, 9,* 381–395.

Wolf, S. (1985). Manifest and latent influence of majorities and minorities. *Journal of Personality and Social Psychology, 48,* 899–908.

Wolf, S. (1987). Majority and minority influence: A social impact analysis. In M. P. Zanna, J. M. Olson, & C. P. Herman (Eds.), *Social influence: The Ontario Symposium* (Vol. 5, pp. 207–235). Hillsdale, NJ: Lawrence Erlbaum Associates.

Wolf, S., & Latane, B. (1983). Majority and minority influence on restaurant preferences. *Journal of Personality and Social Psychology, 45,* 282–292.

Wolf, S., & Latane, B. (1985). Conformity, innovation and the psychosocial law. In S. Moscovici, G. Mugny, & E. Van Avermaet (Eds.), *Perspectives on minority influence* (pp. 201–215). Cambridge, England: Cambridge University Press.

Ziller, R. C. (1964). Individuation and socialization. *Human Relations, 17,* 341–360.

8 Self-Categorization Theory and Social Influence

John C. Turner
Penelope J. Oakes
Macquarie University

INTRODUCTION

This paper presents a new theory of group processes and illustrates its application to the related problems of social influence and group polarization. The theory is addressed to the nature of the psychological group and the individual-group relationship. What exactly is a psychological group, what are the essential psychological conditions for individuals to perceive themselves, feel and act as a group? This issue has been the central theme in the work of ourselves and colleagues for nearly 10 years. The current version of the theory developed by one of us over this time is termed *self-categorization theory* (SCT; Turner, 1982, 1984, 1985; Turner, Hogg, Oakes, Reicher & Wetherell, 1987).

We shall summarize the origins of the theory in the tradition of research on social identity theory (Tajfel & Turner, 1986) that began with the social categorization studies of Henri Tajfel and his colleagues, outline the main ideas, illustrate the usefulness of the analysis by applying it to social influence, show how it provides a unified explanation of social conformity and group polarization, and discuss some of the important and distinctive directions for research that it points to.

SELF-CATEGORIZATION THEORY AND SOCIAL IDENTITY: SOCIAL CHANGE, SOCIAL CATEGORIZATION AND THE INTERPERSONAL-INTERGROUP CONTINUUM

The origins of SCT lie in research, problems, and concepts associated with social identity theory (see Tajfel & Turner, 1986, for a statement of the theory and Brown, 1986; Hogg & Abrams, 1988, and Taylor & Moghaddam, 1987, for recent overviews). Social identity theory hypothesizes that individuals seek a positively valued distinctiveness for their own groups compared to other groups to achieve a positive social identity. Tajfel (1972) defined social identity as "the individual's knowledge that he (she) belongs to certain social groups together with some emotional and value significance to him (her) of the group membership" (p. 31). The theory provides an explanation of basic processes in intergroup competition (Turner, 1975) and the forms and strategies of intergroup behavior and social conflict in stratified societies (Tajfel, 1978, 1982). The initial insight that led to the development of SCT was the result of the convergence of three aspects of social identity research in the late 1970s: (1) the problem of the psychological group in the context of social change, (2) the implications of the social categorization studies for psychological group formation, and (3) the concept of an "interpersonal-intergroup continuum" of social behavior.

Social Interdependence and Social Change

The problem of the (psychological) group arose directly from a key prediction of social identity theory that social conflict between subordinate, low status and dominant, high status groups would tend to take place to the degree that the relevant social groups perceived cognitive alternatives to the status quo and that low status group members maintained their identification with their ingroup membership. If the latter condition were not fulfilled, it was assumed that people would tend to cope with the unsatisfactory social identity conferred by membership of a low status group by seeking to move into and identify with the higher status outgroup—either in reality or psychologically. An individual mobility strategy would substitute for social change in the relations between groups.

The question became: when would low status groups be expected to keep the loyalty of their members? When would we expect the development of sufficiently strong subjective bonds of attachment between individuals and their groups to ensure that even under conditions of negative social identity and unfavorable intergroup comparisons people would continue to define themselves in terms of such memberships and seek a collective solution to their subordination?

The traditional approximation to the concept of ingroup identification is the notion of "group cohesiveness", the degree to which members are attracted to the group, the individual members and its activities (there are other definitions, but this has been the most popular). When one looks at the explanation of cohesiveness one finds that it is assumed to be an expression of the degree of "social interdependence" (Jones, 1985) between people. The dominant theory of the group in social psychology—an implicit consensus developing from both the Lewinian "need-satisfaction" and "reinforcement-learning" traditions since the 1950s is that individuals become a psychological group to the degree that they are interdependent for the mutual satisfaction of their needs (or, in reinforcement terminology, for the achievement of rewards/positive outcomes).

The basic ideas are:

1. people are characterized by a variety of individual motives (needs, drives, desires, values, goals);

2. they associate with appropriate others in order to satisfy these needs directly or indirectly;

3. people associated with need-satisfaction (i.e., "rewards") become attractive, valued, liked in themselves;

4. over time, mutual attraction or group cohesiveness develops between people whose association mediates, has mediated or is expected to mediate the mutual satisfaction of needs; and

5. a cohesive group is a genuine psychological group with power to influence and transform the behavior and attitudes of members.

Lott and Lott (1965), for example, define group cohesiveness as that group property inferred from the number and strength of mutual positive attitudes among members and argue that "attraction will follow if one individual either directly provides another with reward or need-satisfaction, is perceived as potentially able to do so, or is otherwise associated with such a state of affairs" (p. 287). They assume like Bonner (1959, p. 66) that some degree of mutual attraction between members is a precondition of psychological group formation.

The problem with this theory quickly became obvious: It seems to preclude the cohesiveness and group belongingness of low status group members by definition. Its central prediction is that groups which satisfy individuals' needs, provide rewards and positive outcomes (such as positive social identity), which succeed in their tasks, reach their goals and win in intergroup conflict, should be more cohesive than those which are associated with deprivation, costs, failure, defeat, and other negative outcomes. Indeed, there is no basis for cohesiveness among groups which do not provide the good things of life for their members—a negative social identity, low social status, should naturally tend to induce movement out of the subordinate group.

Where was there room in this theory for the subordinate and oppressed groups of society, those which were derogated, deprived, and discriminated against?

Where were the groups with little history of success, which no one would choose to join on the basis of the rewards they provided, but whose movement into collective social and political action social identity theory was specifically concerned with? There seemed no room: This was a psychology of the rewarding group, not the deprived, suffering group. The picture provided by the interdependence theory is plausible in certain places at certain times, but there seemed little doubt also that social change could and did take place and at the instigation of oppressed, subordinate groups marked by intense collective identification. Despite the theory, we had no doubt of the phenomenon.

When one looked at the experimental studies, one found, surprisingly, only equivocal support for the central prediction of the interdependence theory. In some studies success, victory, positive outcomes, did increase group cohesiveness more than did failure, defeat, negative outcomes, but in other studies (e.g., Kennedy & Stephan, 1977) as much or even more cohesiveness was found in groups that mediated costs for members. It is possible to some degree to reconcile these disconfirmations with the reinforcement explanation of intragroup attraction (see Lott & Lott, 1965), but more recently we have confirmed that people can become more attracted to group memberships associated with failure and defeat than with success and victory, even where the members attribute the negative outcomes internally to the group rather than seeking to shift the blame elsewhere (Turner, Hogg, Oakes & Smith, 1984).

It seems that despite the almost unquestioning acceptance of the social interdependence theory it may well be inadequate. This at least was our conclusion (Turner, 1981). The fact that there are clear historical and experimental instances of strong group belongingness and collective action on the part of deprived, losing, or subordinate groups suggested that an alternative conceptualization of the psychological group was needed. A theory was needed that made low status ingroup identification possible.

Social Categorization, Intergroup Discrimination and Group Formation

At the same time that a prediction from social identity theory called into question the social interdependence perspective there was also available an empirical example of the alternative processes by which groups might form—the studies conducted in the social categorization paradigm of Tajfel and his colleagues (Tajfel, Flament, Billig & Bundy, 1971).

In this paradigm, the experimental procedures are designed to manipulate social categorization per se, the classification of subjects into distinct groups (or, from the subjects' perspective, the perception of belonging to one group as opposed to another) in isolation from all the variables that normally give group membership its social and psychological significance. The usual determinants of intragroup cohesion and intergroup attitudes are deliberately eliminated. Subjects are divided into groups on an openly random basis (e.g., Turner, Sachdev, & Hogg, 1983) or ostensibly on the basis of some trivial, ad hoc criterion (in fact in all cases subjects are actually assigned to groups randomly). There is no social interaction within or between category members. Group membership is anonymous: Each subject knows which group they belong to personally but not the affiliations of others. There are no shared goals nor any kind of link between individual needs and self-interest and acting as a group member. The group classification is supposedly simply for administrative convenience. Subjects are required to make decisions about distributing small monetary sums any way they choose between pairs of anonymous recipients (other than themselves) identified only by personal code numbers and group memberships.

Tajfel's original expectation (1978, pp. 10–11) was that subjects would be fair or cooperative or distribute the sums haphazardly. The situation had been made completely minimal precisely to function as a baseline condition in which nothing would happen and against which the effects of additional variables on intergroup relations could be measured. In fact, however, from the initial studies of Tajfel et al. (1971) onwards the highly reliable and robust finding has been that subjects tend to some significant degree to discriminate in favor of ingroup and against outgroup members (Brewer, 1979; Turner, 1975, 1981, 1983). There is now a large number of studies confirming that the social categorization of subjects into distinct groups is alone sufficient for discriminatory intergroup behavior.

Two processes have been suggested to account for these results: the cognitive process of *categorization* (Tajfel, 1969), in which classifying stimuli (including people) leads to the perceptual accentuation of intraclass similarities and interclass differences and correlated differentiations on evaluative and behavioral dimensions (Doise, 1978; Doise & Sinclair, 1973), and the *social identity/ intergroup comparison* process, in which people seek positive distinctiveness for their group (Tajfel, 1972; Turner, 1975). The two processes are discussed and integrated in Turner (1981). Alternative explanations for these data have been proposed, but so far in our judgment they are either not plausible or do not stand up empirically.

Subsequent studies have indicated that social categorization not only produces intergroup discrimination but a whole variety of effects characteristic of psychological group formation (Turner, 1981). Imposing social categorizations upon people not only leads to discriminatory intergroup behavior but also intragroup cohesion in the form of more positive attitudes towards and more reported liking of ingroup than outgroup members, ethnocentric biases in perception, evaluation and memory (e.g., Howard & Rothbart, 1978) and an altruistic orientation towards ingroup members (Turner, 1978). It is difficult to avoid the conclusion that social categorization leads to psychological group formation: The subjects demonstrate collective behavior in the form of shared responses systematically related to their own and others' group memberships, mutual attraction between ingroup members and ethnocentric attitudes and biases (see also, Moreland, 1985).

The data imply that some genuine process of identification with group membership takes place (Turner, 1975, 1978). It follows that interpersonal interdependence and attraction are not necessary conditions for group formation, as the very conditions of these experiments are designed to eliminate such factors as alternative explanations of the results. Although social categorization leads to intragroup cohesion, this is plainly an effect rather than a cause of group formation. In addition, it seems unlikely that such cohesion represents *interpersonal* attraction, as the subjects have no idea of the specific persons in their group and have no reason to suppose that, individually, they are any more likeable than outgroup members. They seem to like the people in their group just because they are ingroup members rather than like the ingroup because of the specific individuals who are members.

Research in the social categorization paradigm, therefore, seems to demonstrate both that attraction and interdependence between specific individuals are not necessary conditions for group formation and that simply imposing a shared group membership upon people can be sufficient to generate attraction between them. It provides a simple but compelling example of collective behavior in the absence of social interdependence and interpersonal contact.

The crucial *theoretical* variable in these studies is not in fact (the) social categorization per se (of subjects by the experimenter). Turner (1975) pointed out early on that this was a misconception: The essential variable is *social identification, the acceptance and internalization of the externally imposed social categorization by subjects to define the self.* It is the subjects' definition of themselves in terms of the imposed social categories that seems to be sufficient for group formation. It became possible to think of the social group as a collection of individuals who shared a social categorization of themselves and acted on this basis.

The Interpersonal–Intergroup Continuum of Social Behavior

Tajfel (1978) distinguished between "acting in terms of self" and "acting in terms of group". He developed this distinction into the idea of an "interpersonal–intergroup continuum" to describe a fundamental dimension of social interaction between people. At the "purely" interpersonal extreme of this dimension was "any social encounter between two or more people in which all the interaction that takes place is determined by the personal relationships between the individuals and by their respective individual characteristics. The "intergroup" extreme is that in which all of the behavior of two or more individuals towards each other is determined by their membership of different social groups or categories" (p. 41).

The interpersonal–intergroup continuum played a causal role in relation to the processes described by social identity theory. It was assumed that as behavior became more intergroup, social perception became more social categorical and social identity processes came into operation. Thus the continuum helped to make clear the boundary conditions of social identity theory. It was not assumed that social identity concerns were active in all situations at all times. On the contrary, it was a theory of *intergroup* relations, likely to be predictive only in situations where individuals were acting in terms of their group memberships and the relations between them. The continuum also helped to crystallize the objections of social identity researchers to individualistic theories of social conflict, which developed analyses of interpersonal or even intrapersonal processes and then extrapolated them uncritically to intergroup relations (see Brown & Turner, 1981; Sherif, 1967).

What, however, if the causal relationship between social identity processes and intergroup behavior were to be reversed? If we make a distinction between personal and social identity and assume that self-perception varies along a continuum defined by these two forms of self-definition, then it becomes possible to see shift along this identity continuum as *determining* whether social behavior is interpersonal or intergroup.

Turner (1982) argued for such a theoretical step, pointing out that there was much evidence that self-concepts were complex, multi-faceted and differentiated cognitive structures and that self-perception varied with the specific situation. There was evidence too that under certain conditions people tend to define and see themselves more in terms of their social than personal identity, i.e., more as interchangeable exemplars of their shared social category memberships than as unique persons defined by individual differences from others. For example, people tend to perceive themselves and others more in terms of their nationality when interacting or in conflict with foreigners than when interacting with compatriots (Bochner & Perks, 1971; Bruner & Perlmutter, 1957; Doise, Dechamps & Meyer, 1978).

Moreover, once one thought of social identifications as social categorizations that defined the self, then the usual cognitive effects of social categorization (stereotyping) could be understood to produce a *depersonalization* of self-perception in which the shared characteristics of the ingroup as a social category were subjectively attributed to one's individual self. Dion, Earn and Yee (1978) have found that where individual subjects fail on a task and can attribute that failure to the prejudice of outgroup members, they tend to stereotype *themselves* more strongly in terms of the corresponding ingroup category. For example, Jews who could excuse their failure by categorizing the other players as "Gentiles" identified more strongly with the Jewish stereotype in their self-descriptions than subjects who were aware of other players only as individuals. This self-stereotyping/depersonalization process seemed to provide a tentative psychological mechanism by which the qualitative transformation of individuals into a psychological group might be understood.

The basic insight which led to SCT was that shift along the interpersonal–intergroup continuum is the *effect* of self-perception becoming more social categorical under certain conditions: *group behavior is simply individuals acting in terms of a shared social identity.* Unlike in Tajfel's original definition of social identity as aspects of the self-concept derived from and based on group memberships, it was now defined directly as the (sum total of the) social categorization(s) of the self and seen as the causal basis of group processes.

Several basic theoretical issues remained to be answered before a possible new approach to the study of group processes could be considered viable. What exactly are personal and social identity? How are they to be conceptualized? How are they different, how dependent on each other, under what conditions and why does self-perception shift along the personal-social identity continuum? How does social identity produce its effects? SCT evolved as an attempt to provide systematic, predictive, and empirically testable answers.

SELF-CATEGORIZATION THEORY: THE RELATIONSHIP BETWEEN PERSONAL AND SOCIAL IDENTITY

SCT is a theory of the basic processes underlying psychological group formation. It explains group formation as a transition from personal to social identity. There is no need to state the theory formally, since this has been done elsewhere (Turner, 1985; Turner et al., 1987). The aim here is to outline the main ideas, convey the essence of the analysis and clarify some key points about the interrelationship of personal and social identity (how they may be interdependent and yet in functional conflict in any given comparative situation) and the role of categorization in producing social identity between people without denying their personal differences.

The main ideas of the theory are as follows. Personal and social identity are assumed to be components of the self-concept, cognitive representations of self. Specifically, they are self-categorizations, cognitive groupings of the self as identical (similar, equivalent, interchangeable) to some class of stimuli in contrast to some other class of stimuli. Personal and social identity differ in that they represent different levels of abstraction of self-categorization. Personal identity comprises personal self-categorizations based on intrapersonal similarities and interpersonal differences, which define how the individual as a unique person compares with relevant others on dimensions of individual differences (e.g., one's personality). Social identity comprises social categorizations of the self (ingroup-outgroup categorizations) based on social similarities and differences between people that define one as a member of certain social categories in contrast to others (e.g., American, Jewish, female, Catholic, or just *us* versus *them*). Social identity represents a more inclusive, superordinate level of abstraction than personal identity in the categorization of self.

The level of abstraction of a self-category in this context has nothing to do with its being more or less theoretical or concretely real. It refers to the degree of inclusiveness (Rosch, 1978) of the categories used to describe the self (in the sense that the category "tree" includes the category "oak" but not vice versa). Social groups contain individual persons, individual persons do not contain social groups, and thus social categorical perception is more inclusive than person perception and in this sense more abstract.

In principle, an endless variety of specific self-categories—interrelated in all possible ways—can and do exist at particular levels. Which of these self-categories at which level predominates subjectively at any time (i.e., becomes salient in self-perception) is a function of a person × situation interaction and is a central issue addressed by SCT (Oakes, 1987). It is also evident that self-categories may be more or less abstract than personal and social identity. There are self-categories based on intrapersonal differentiations (one's *real* self, ego-alien impulses, etc.), differentiations between classes of social groups (the West, NATO, etc.) and species (humanity). We assume that in general in social interaction three levels of abstraction of self-categories tend to be particularly important: the interpersonal (self as individual person), intergroup (self as social category) and interspecies (self as a human being). These are defined not by specific attributes but by the level at which people are being compared and categorized: All cultures probably have a definite idea of what it means to be human but it may well be very different.

How are these levels of self-categorization interrelated? To answer this question we must look at the determinants and effects of categorizing. SCT hypothesizes that categorizing follows the principle of *meta-contrast:* that a subset of stimuli is more likely to be categorized as a single entity to the degree that differences within that subset are less than the differences between that subset and other stimuli within the comparative context. So, for example, we call a certain group of things "chairs" because, the principle states, the differences between chairs are less than the differences between chairs and tables. Categories form so as to ensure that the differences between them are larger than the differences within them.

The *meta-contrast ratio*—the average perceived intercategory difference over the average perceived intracategory difference—provides a simple quantitative measure of the degree to which any subset of stimuli within a given frame of reference will tend to be categorized as a perceptual unit (or, in the case of people, of the degree to which a collection of individuals will be perceived as a social group). Table 8.1 provides some simple examples of when one would and when one would not categorize a collection of people as a group by this criterion.

The meta-contrast principle as described provides only a partial explanation of categorization, since it is stated purely as a comparative principle. It indicates the nature of the comparative relations between stimuli which lead them to be represented by a category. It is also important to take into account the *social meaning*

TABLE 8.1
Categorization and Meta-Contrast

Case 1: Where a Social Categorization into A versus B Would not be applied

A/B category membership:	A	B	A	...	B	A	B
Individuals' positions:	-3	-2	-1	...	+1	+2	+3
Alternative X/Y categorization:	X	X	X	...	Y	Y	Y

MCR of A/B categorization = average absolute difference between each A and each B (2.67) divided by average absolute difference between each A with each A and each B with each B (3.33) = 2.67/3.33 = 0.8. MCR of X/Y categorization = average absolute difference between Xs and Ys divided by average absolute difference within Xs and Ys = 4/1.33 = 3.01.
Individuals would be categorized into Xs and Ys, not As and Bs.

Case 2: Where the A/B Social Categorization Would be Applied

A/B category membership:	A	A	A	...	B	B	B
Individuals' positions:	-3	-2	-1	...	+1	+2	+3
Alternative X/Y categorization:	X	Y	Y	...	Y	X	X

MCR of A/B categorization = average A/B intergroup difference divided by average A/B intragroup difference = 4/1.33 = 3.01.
MCR of X/Y categorization = average X/Y intergroup difference divided by average X/Y intragroup difference = 2.89/3 = 0.96.
Individuals would be categorized into As and Bs, not Xs and Ys.

Case 3a: Where the A/B Social Categorization Might be Applied Depending on its Relative Accessibility

A/B category membership:	A	A	B	...	A	B	B
Individuals' positions:	-3	-2	-1	...	+1	+2	+3
Alternative X/Y categorization:	X	Y	Y	...	Y	X	X

MCR of A/B categorization = 3.11/2.67 = 1.17.
MCR of X/Y categorization = 2.89/3 = 0.96.

If all categories were equally accessible, individuals would be categorized into As and Bs rather than Xs and Ys. An alternative outcome could arise if the Y category was more accessible than the others. There could then be a tendency to categorize the situation in terms of being a Y or not, ignoring the intragroup differences within the Xs. The MCR of the Y category + intergroup differences between Ys and others divided by Y intragroup differences = 2.89/2 = 1.45.*

Case 3b: Where the A/B Social Categorization Might be Applied Depending on the Extent of the Comparative Context

A/B category membership:			A	A	A	B	B	B		
Individuals' positions:			-2	-1	0	+1	+2	+3		
Alternative X/Y categorization	Y	Y	X	X	X	X	X	x	Y	Y
Y positions:	-4	-3							+4	+5

MCR of A/B categorization in restricted context (from -2 to +3) = 3/1.33 = 2.26.
MCR of X/Y category in extended context (from -4 to +5) = 4/3.29 = 1.22.
If the context were such that only As and Bs were compared, then the A/B categorization could become salient and As and Bs seen as different. But if the As and Bs were being implicitly compared in terms of a wider social context, they might be categorized as Xs in contrast to Ys and perceived as similar to each other.*

Notes. 1. MCR = meta-contrast ratio: the average absolute intercategory difference divided by the average absolute intracategory difference between category members.
2. All things being equal, the higher the MCR the more likely is a categorization to become salient, but the MCR varies with the context of comparison (frame of reference) and interacts with the relative accessibility of categorizations.
* These examples raise the issue of whether one compares intercategory differences with the differences within both categories or just one focal category, e.g., does one categorize into "chairs" and "tables" or just see "chairs" against a background? It seems likely that we do both, depending on the situation.

of differences between people in terms of the *normative and behavioral content* of their actions (Oakes, 1987) and the relative accessibility of particular categorizations (the perceptual readiness of observers to use them; Bruner, 1957). We shall return to these issues presently.

Thus SCT proposes explicitly that categories form on the basis of comparison (differences being comparative relations and meta-contrast being the perception of differences between differences). This is why categorization is a relative, dynamic process, varying in content and level of abstraction with the comparative context. For example, it follows that people who are categorized and perceived as different in one context can be recategorized and perceived as similar in another context *without any actual change in their own positions*. There is nothing odd about this—it is the way that categorizing works. It is the reason why assimilation and contrast phenomena, reflecting the categorization of entities as similar to or different from each other, vary with the frame of reference, the comparative standard provided (Haslam, 1987; Sherif & Hovland, 1961). Athenians and Spartans may see themselves as poles apart (contrast) when comparing themselves solely within the Greek world, but discover a common identity (assimilation) in face of the Persian invader.

If categorization depends on comparison, the reverse is also true. The comparison of stimuli requires that they be similar (Festinger, 1954), share related attributes (Goethals & Darley, 1977), that they be in some way *comparable*, i.e., sufficiently alike such that it is meaningful to compare them. Comparison, therefore, depends on some prior process of categorization which has defined the different stimuli to be compared as equivalent at a more inclusive level. Paradoxically, comparing the differences between things always implies a higher level identity in terms of which it is meaningful to do so. Thus apples and oranges are compared as fruit, red and green as colors, but how do we compare physicists and farmers, cabbages and kings? Only by seeking for some common category within which they can be placed. The comparison process takes place in terms of the dimensions that define the higher order identity (colors are compared in terms of intensity, brightness, richness, and so on). Less abstract categories are based on comparisons within more abstract categories: A category forms from the comparison of stimuli compared in terms of a higher order identity and the resulting category forms the basis of more finely grained comparisons which can lead to more finely grained categories and so on.

It follows that personal identity depends on social identity. Personal self-categories are based on interpersonal differences which reflect intragroup comparisons, i.e., comparisons between people in terms of some shared social identity. The social categorization of others as identical to self defines the frame of reference within which intragroup comparisons produce personal identity (or one aspect of it on one dimension). Here is one sense in which personal identity is positively dependent on social identity: Personal distinctiveness is sought and measured in terms of the shared values that define social category memberships

(Codol, 1975). Similarly, social identity reflects inter- and intragroup comparisons in terms of the attributes that define some higher order identity such as being human. Social identity can be said to depend on *individual* differences in the sense that it arises from and varies with the contrast between the intergroup and interpersonal differences of individuals.

Nevertheless, there is a conflicting, competitive relationship between different levels of categorization as representations of the same stimulus situation. There tends to be an inverse relationship between self-perception as a unique individual and as an ingroup category.

The meta-contrast principle states that social categorizations of self and others become more salient as intergroup differences increase and intragroup/ interpersonal differences decrease. Personal self-categorizations gain in salience as intergroup differences decrease and intragroup/interpersonal differences increase. There is, therefore, a negative relationship across situations between the tendency to categorize at the ingroup–outgroup and at the personal self–other levels.

This inverse relationship follows from the effects of categorizing too. Tajfel (1969) hypothesizes that when a classification is superimposed on a stimulus dimension so that there is a systematic correlation between class membership and stimulus values, there will be a tendency to accentuate perceptually the similarities within classes and differences between classes on that dimension (e.g., McGarty & Penny, 1988). Thus, where an intergroup categorization is salient, perceived intergroup differences are enhanced and intragroup/interpersonal differences are reduced. Where an interpersonal categorization is salient, perceived intragroup/interpersonal differences are enhanced and intrapersonal differences reduced. The effect of categorization at one level is to enhance the associated meta-contrast and reduce the meta-contrasts which are the basis of salient categorization at other levels (and alternative categorizations at the same level). There is an inevitable and continual conflict between different levels of categorization to represent social relations between self and others.

The personal-social identity dimension of self-perception varies along the outcomes of this conflict: At one extreme, self-perception is in terms of minimum intrapersonal differences and maximum interpersonal differences and, at the other, minimum intragroup differences and maximum intergroup differences. As the social categorization of self and others increases in salience one is more likely to perceive them in terms of the shared stereotypes that define their social category memberships (shared social identity) and less likely to define self and others in terms of their personal differences and individuality.

Rosch (1978) employs the concept of the "basic level" to mean the level of abstraction that we habitually use for some classification of objects (e.g., chair rather than furniture or hard chair, typically an intermediate level of categorization) because it maximizes the similarities within categories without becoming too inclusive. One way to think of the personal-social identity continuum is that there are in a sense two basic levels in the cognitive representation of self and others. These two levels are alternative, antagonistic ways of describing social relations that are in constant competition with each other. They both increase and decrease in applicability, in strength, from situation to situation. What we see at any moment, the outcome of the conflict between them, represents a varying compromise, shifting with the relative strength of the two levels according to the relevant meta-contrasts of intergroup, intragroup, and intrapersonal differences (and the relative accessibility of the relevant categorizations). In truth, however, the essential point of the analysis is to indicate that any notion of one or two "basic", relatively stable levels of abstraction in the categorization of self and others is misconceived. The idea of a given level is useful to indicate a theoretical extreme, but in reality there is a perceptual continuum that never fully embodies any one level but arises from a dynamic, fluid process of conflict and compromise. Human beings are both individual persons and social groups, but how much they are both varies. We see them as both, but represented in a single unique configuration at any given instant.

SCT hypothesizes that self-identity shifts along this continuum and that shifts towards social identity represent the *depersonalization* of self-perception and individual behavior. Depersonalization is the tendency to perceive increased identity between self and ingroup members and difference from outgroup members, to perceive oneself more as the identical representative of a social category and less as an unique personality defined by one's personal differences from other ingroup members.

This is the essence of categorization—to produce (social) identity from (personal) differences—applied to self-perception. It is a cognitive grouping process that transforms differences into similarities. More accurately, categorization produces (interclass) differences as well as (intraclass) similarities—we need some psychologically neutral term such as perhaps *distances* to indicate the nature of precognized stimulus relations. There are distances between people, but are they differences or similarities? (Recall that the same people can be seen as either similar or different depending on how they are categorized.) Whether we perceive the same relations as differences or similarities is a key determinant of how we feel and act towards others, producing a qualitatively different social orientation towards people. Social categorization, like categorization in general, does not deny differences between people. On the contrary, it recognizes them as basic and inevitable. Yet even variability is variable, there are differences between differences: Arising from such meta-contrasts, categorization subjectively transforms differences into similarities (or distances into differences and similarities). Contrary to the normal viewpoint, which sees categorization as *based* on intraclass similarities, psychological identity is seen here as a *product* of the categorization process (based on meta-contrast).

To summarize: SCT hypothesizes that (1) the level of inclusiveness at which and the degree to which one categorizes self and others as similar or different varies with the social context within which comparison takes place, (2) the salience of shared social identity leads to the depersonalization of self-perception, and (3) depersonalization produces group behavior. A full statement of the theory requires a systematic statement of the antecedents and effects of depersonalization. We shall note these briefly and then discuss one issue, social influence, in more depth.

The antecedents of depersonalization are conditions that lead to the formation and salience of shared ingroup categories. These are that some ingroup–outgroup categorization is both highly accessible (is ready for use) and its specifications fit (comparatively and normatively) the stimulus data. We talk of the *salience* of a category to the degree that it is already in some sense available to the perceiver (is more or less accessible). If we are confronted with a grouping of people for which no appropriate categorization exists/is available, but the relevant meta-contrast is high, then we *form* a new one. So a new ingroup category emerges in a specific comparative situation to the extent that relevant differences between ourselves and others are greater than between ourselves.

Determinants of relative accessibility include learned expectations of what tends to go with what in the environment, the person's current motives, goals, and values and the degree to which some ingroup–outgroup categorization is highly valued and important for self-definition. Fit is defined by a high meta-contrast in terms of the social categorization (comparative fit) consistent with the stereotypical content of the categories (normative fit). For example, if a relevant ingroup category is already available (e.g., men/women), then it becomes salient (cognitively active) to the degree both that it is accessible (perhaps we are feminists or chauvinists and are strongly motivated to think in terms of men and women) and fits comparatively (perhaps there are men and women arguing with each other so that expressed attitudes differ more between than within the sexes) and normatively (perhaps the men are taking an antifeminist and the women a profeminist stand).

Oakes (1987) summarizes evidence congruent with these notions. Oakes and Turner (1987) conducted two studies to test the importance of fit. Experiment 1 manipulated the comparative fit between sex categories and the observed behavior of male and female confederates. Eighty 16–17-year-old school pupils of both sexes were assigned to four conditions to watch a tape and slide presentation of a 6-person discussion group. The stimulus group discussed whether two fictional persons should get married and differed between the four conditions. In the *deviance* conditions, one person disagreed with the other five members of the stimulus group (who agreed among themselves); in the *conflict* conditions, three people disagreed with the three others (the members of each subgroup agreeing among themselves). The other variable (superimposed to produce a 2 × 2 factorial design) was the sex composition of the group: one man and five women (solo conditions) versus three men and three women (collective conditions).

The crucial point about the design was that in the solo deviance and collective conflict conditions there was a correlation between the sex categorization and the expressed attitudes of the stimulus group: One man disagreed with five women or three men disagreed with three women. There was no such correlation in the solo conflict and collective deviance conditions, where two women and a man argued with three women or one man argued with two men and three women respectively. In the former conditions the sex categorization *fits* the observed data—the perceived differences within the sexes are less than the perceived differences between the sexes. In the uncorrelated conditions it does not fit—the differences within the sexes are as large as the differences between the sexes. SCT hypothesizes that subjects will categorize confederates into males and females more in the former than the latter conditions. Subjects rated one target male person who was held constant across all four stimulus group conditions. As predicted, subjects attributed the target person's attitudes to his being a typical man and sex-stereotyped him as a male and less as a female significantly more in the correlated than uncorrelated conditions. In sum, comparative fit made the target's social identity as a man salient.

Experiment 2 manipulated comparative and normative fit orthogonally. Ninety Science students were assigned to six conditions in a 3×2 experimental design. They watched a tape and slide presentation of three Arts and three Science students discussing attitudes to university life. In the *consensus* conditions there was complete agreement in the stimulus group. In the *conflict* conditions the three Arts students took one view and the three Science students took an opposite view. In the *deviance* conditions one Arts student disagreed with the other five students (who agreed among themselves). The argument was about whether university was important for social life or academic work. The subjects' stereotypes are that Arts students are pro-social life and Science students pro-academic work. In the *consistent* conditions the target stimulus individual—one Arts student who was held constant across the three agreement conditions (she was part of the Arts subgroup or the deviant depending on condition)—took the stereotypical Arts line of favoring social life over work. In the *inconsistent* conditions she took the stereotypical Science line of favoring academic work over social life. Subjects rated the target individual and the stimulus group as a whole on a variety of measures.

The different patterns of agreement manipulate the comparative fit between the Arts/Science social categorization and the observed behavior of the stimulus group. The consistent/inconsistent variable manipulated its normative fit with the content of people's attitudes. The results provided comprehensive support for the predictions derived from SCT, the most important being that the Arts/Science categorization would be most salient under conditions of both comparative and normative fit, i.e., in the consistent conflict conditions where three Arts students disagree in a stereotypical direction with three Science students.

Main findings were that the target person's attitudes were explained more in terms of her Arts social category membership (''she is an Arts student'') in the consistent conflict condition, her personality in the inconsistent deviance condition and externally in the consensus conditions. Interestingly, attribution to social category membership in the consistent conflict condition functioned as much as an internal attribution to the individual (rather than to external social pressure) as did personality. Correspondingly, she was categorized as more similar to the other Arts students and different from the Science students and expected to like the former more and the Science students less in the consistent conflict conditions. Again, the salience of a social categorization leads to explanations of people's conduct in terms of their social identity and a perceptual accentuation of that identity.

There is suggestive evidence that the salience of an ingroup–outgroup categorization does lead to the social stereotyping of the *self* (e.g., Dion, Earn & Yee, 1978). Hogg and Turner (1987a) have obtained some direct evidence that the salience of a shared social identity increases self-definition and self-stereotyping in terms of the relevant social category and produces group behavior. Seventy male and 60 female university students were assigned to intrasex or intersex conditions. In the former, one individual discussed an issue with one person of the same sex. In the latter, two males discussed an issue with two females. These subjects were not watching a stimulus group but actively and spontaneously participating in discussion. Nevertheless the issues had been carefully selected and the discussions ingeniously stage-managed to ensure that there was disagreement about the issue within and between the sexes in the intra- and intersex conditions respectively. Because there are differences of opinion within the sexes in the intrasex condition but between and not within the sexes in the intersex condition, the sex-categorization should be more salient in the latter condition.

It was found that both males and females categorized themselves as more typical of their own sex and stereotyped themselves more from before to after social interaction in terms of the traits they ascribed to their own sex in that situation in the intersex than intrasex conditions. Interestingly, the evaluative implications of self-stereotyping varied between the sexes: Males attributed both more positive and negative traits to themselves, whereas females were more ethnocentric, attributing more positive but less negative traits to themselves where sex was salient. The salience of social identity also lowered females' self-esteem and lead them to dislike and discriminate against males but raised self-esteem in males and increased their liking of and fairness to females.

Ullah (1987) tested the SCT hypothesis that self-definition in terms of a shared social category membership is associated with psychological group formation in a study of second-generation Irish youths living in England. Respondents choosing *Irish* as a self-definition showed more group formation than those choosing "half English, half Irish", who in turn showed more than those choosing English. Group formation was expressed in attraction to the Irish people and distinctive Irish culture, participation in traditional Irish cultural activities, perceived difference from English people and a negative orientation to being English.

To show how depersonalization (self-perception and action in terms of a shared social identity) can provide a systematic and unifying explanation of the major group phenomena is a large and time-consuming task, as these embody often massive amounts of research data with their own theoretical traditions and issues. We have therefore restricted our focus to three fundamental areas: group formation and cohesiveness, social cooperation and competition, and social influence. It must suffice to state that SCT explains group cohesion as an effect of the mutually perceived similarity between self and ingroup others produced by the formation and salience of shared social category memberships. Social cohesion is seen fundamentally to be a product of identity rather than vice versa (e.g., Turner et al., 1983; see Hogg, 1987). Similarly, it is assumed that social cooperation (in, for example, mixed-motive games) is a product of the transformation of individuals into a psychological group, a *we-group*, as this transforms competitive personal self-interests into collective self-interest defined by shared self-identity. Support for this analysis is provided by a series of studies on social dilemmas conducted by Brewer and Kramer showing that the salience of a superordinate social identification can raise the level of cooperation (Brewer & Kramer, 1986; Kramer & Brewer, 1984, 1986).

To illustrate the usefulness of SCT in more detail we now turn to social influence and group polarization.

SELF-CATEGORIZATION AND SOCIAL INFLUENCE

The dominant theory of social influence in social psychology is the two-process model of informational and normative influence. In this model the process of *true* influence, i.e., private acceptance, is seen as "informational" (Deutsch & Gerard, 1955; Festinger, 1950, 1954; Jones & Gerard, 1967; Sherif, 1936). It is assumed that the objective ambiguity of the stimulus world gives rise to subjective uncertainty, producing informational dependence on similar and/or expert others to reduce uncertainty, and that others are persuasive to the degree that their responses are perceived to provide evidence about reality.

This general formulation has a number of problems (Turner & Oakes, 1986). It has been criticized by Moscovici (1976) for being incapable of predicting and explaining minority influence. It has also had difficulty explaining group polarization. The formulation developed in the conformity area, but even here it has been found wanting (Moscovici, 1976; Turner, 1982, 1985).

If we take the classic conformity paradigms of Asch (1952, 1956) and Sherif (1936), we find that the traditional formulation is in fact contradicted by their results. The Asch paradigm shows that informational influence does not depend

on an ambiguous reality or the impossibility of physical reality (direct perceptual) testing. Uncertainty is produced directly by disagreement with others, by
social conflict, not by the objective ambiguity of the stimulus situation. Despite
Festinger's (1950, 1954) contention that social reality testing (consensual validation, social comparison, informational influence) only comes into play to the
degree that objective, nonsocial, physical means of appraisal are unavailable,
there is incontestable evidence from subjects' postexperimental reports that in
face of a perceptually unambiguous reality they became uncertain, doubting the
validity of their judgments and even vision, when confronted by the disagreement of a unanimous group (whether or not they conformed behaviorally).

To be more precise, however, only certain kinds of social conflict or disagreement produce uncertainty. We hypothesize, following Asch (1952), that subjective uncertainty (the opposite of what Festinger calls ''subjective validity'') only
arises from disagreement with people *with whom one expects to agree*. The naive
subject expects to agree with the unanimous majority in the Asch paradigm
because she or he has categorized the others as identical to self in relevant
respects (e.g., having normal vision, being naive subjects under the same task
instructions, operating from the same visual perspective) and assumes that they
are looking at the same invariant stimulus. If people are similar as perceivers
(they look at things from the perspective of the same goals, values, sensory
apparatus, etc.) and face the same stimulus situation, then they *should and ought*
to agree—this is a natural and rational expectation. If in general it is true, as
widely accepted, that behavior is a function of a person × situation interaction,
then identical people in the same setting should behave similarly (i.e., agree, be
consensual, display uniformity). Thus disagreement in such a context is puzzling. It implies a definite cognitive inconsistency and conflict, something that
needs explaining. One possible and potentially plausible explanation for the
inconsistency is that the error is located in oneself, that it is oneself that is in the
wrong, that is perhaps suffering from some personal defect, some subjective,
idiosyncratic bias. This is especially so where by virtue of the experimental
situation the usual possibilities have been deliberately ruled out (finding differences between perceivers, clarifying the stimulus, persuading others to change
their views) and the unanimity of the others implies strongly that the discrepancy
is caused by the deviance of one person. One does not have to conclude that this
is so, only entertain the possibility, to diminish one's initial confidence in the
validity of one's response. In others words, subjective uncertainty about the
validity of one's response is a rational attempt in this situation to make sense of
an otherwise incomprehensible cognitive conflict.

It is, therefore, disagreement with reference group others that creates uncertainty. Conversely, it is agreement and not *information* in some abstract asocial
sense that produces subjective validity (see Moscovici, 1976).

This analysis holds up in Sherif's autokinetic study. Here, too, subjects take
for granted that they are similar perceivers confronting an objectively invariant

stimulus situation. They assume that the point of light is really moving on each trial and that they are seeing the same thing. If this were not so, what would be the point of their trying to reach an agreement? If uncertainty were produced by objective ambiguity *out there,* then all perception must be uncertain and no response is more or less valid than another; it would be disagreement that is the valid representation of reality and agreement that would be inevitably arbitrary (Moscovici, 1976). To test this idea Sperling (cited in Asch, 1952) revealed to subjects in the autokinetic study that the moving point of light was actually an optical illusion (that there was no reason, therefore, to think that they were seeing the same thing, since the phenomenon was totally subjective). He found that this information, when accepted, eliminated the normal tendency to converge. Similarly, Alexander, Zucker and Brody (1970) informed subjects that the autokinetic phenomenon was purely subjective and again found a reduction in interpersonal convergence. A second study reduced the usual expectations of agreement between subjects by introducing slight procedural differences between the perceivers and again reduced convergence.

The dominant theory hypothesizes that stimulus ambiguity produces subjective uncertainty and informational dependence on others and that the latter is the basis of influence and leads to the formation of social norms and group structure. We find, however, that group formation is a precondition of influence. The social categorization of others as identical to self, as an appropriate reference group for social comparison, produces shared expectations of agreement. It is the disconfirmation of these expectations that creates subjective uncertainty and openness to influence. In Festinger's (and the dominant) theory we turn to social comparison with similar others to resolve uncertainty; but in fact it is social comparison with similar others that also creates uncertainty. One can add too that what resolves uncertainty is not a matter of information per se but *valid* information, perceived validity being socially determined by its relationship to norms and values. People do not persuade us just because they have information, but only if that information is *socially* accepted as evidence about reality. Information is never self-validating.

The central idea of the self-categorization analysis of social influence is that agreement with identical others in relevant respects in a given situation creates subjective validity. This differs from the dominant analysis in terms of (1) the source of uncertainty, (2) when we turn to similar others (not as a substitute for physical reality testing, when reality is objectively ambiguous, but when reality is assumed to be publicly invariant and one is unsure of how similar others would respond, and (3) the role of similar others (the informational value of their responses not being a matter of information per se but information about the validity of one's behavior, determined by the degree to which it is shared by ingroup members and can be attributed to external reality).

The theory rests upon two assumptions that need to be made explicit: (1) that we only expect to agree with similar others/ingroup members (similar in respects relevant to the judgment at hand), and (2) that the shared responses of ingroup others are attributed externally and hence tend to be perceived as objectively demanded, required, appropriate, correct, and so on. Thus, influence is a function of disagreement with ingroup others whose responses are distinctive, consistent, and consensual and so are seen to reflect the nature of the relevant stimulus entity (Kelley, 1967). To the degree that the responses of others are from an identical perspective to one's own, distinctive, consistent and consensual in the context of the same stimulus situation, they will tend to be perceived as valid, informative of the objective world and will be highly persuasive.

There are five hypotheses that help to summarize this theory in the context of conformity research (all united by the same basic assumption that agreement with similar others subjectively validates our responses as veridical reflections of the external world):

1. That subjective validity (Festinger, 1950; Kelley, 1967), one's confidence in the objective validity of one's opinions, attitudes, beliefs, etc., is a direct function of the extent to which similar people (in relevant respects) in the same stimulus situation are perceived, expected or believed to agree with one's own response.

2. That, conversely, subjective uncertainty is a direct function of the extent to which similar others are not perceived, expected or believed to respond similarly to oneself in the same stimulus situation.

The question arises of why should stimulus ambiguity as well as intragroup disagreement not produce subjective uncertainty? Surely a lack of objective structure in the stimulus world also creates uncertainty? The essential point is the need to distinguish between the individual *percept* (what the person sees) and the issue of the validity, of the correctness, of that percept. "Subjective uncertainty" refers to the validity rather than the perceptual content of sensory data. It differs, therefore, from what can be called "perceptual ambiguity." A person may be certain of what they see but uncertain of whether what they see is correct, or, alternatively, certain that they are correct in seeing a stimulus as perceptually ambiguous. In one sense a person can never doubt what they see—it is directly given experience—what they can doubt is the correspondence between what they know they see and the objective world.

Thus perceptual ambiguity can give rise to subjective uncertainty, but only insofar as the person does not perceive, believe or expect that like-minded others will also see a perceptually ambiguous stimulus, not because they are the same thing. In most instances in the research literature what is meant by "stimulus ambiguity" is in fact a setting where subjects believe that there is an objectively valid, unambiguously correct answer, but do not expect an immediate consensus.

3. That uncertainty-reduction may be accomplished.by: (a) the attribution of

the disagreement to perceived relevant differences between self and others, and/or (b) the attribution of the disagreement to perceived relevant differences in the stimulus situation, and/or (c) mutual social influence to produce agreement.

4. That the magnitude of the mutual pressures for uniformity between people is a multiplicative product of (a) the degree of relevant similarity mutually perceived between them, (b) the degree to which the shared stimulus situation is perceived to be similar, (c) the extent of perceived, expected or believed disagreement about that stimulus situation (subjective uncertainty), and (d) the importance of subjective validity to the group.

5. That the direction of effective influence within the group is a function of the relative persuasiveness of the members, which is based on the degree to which their response is perceived as prototypical of the initial distribution of responses of the group as a whole, i.e., the degree of relative consensual support for a member.

The last hypothesis does not imply that influence is always from the majority to the minority, that dominant norms cannot be challenged. On the contrary, it is intended to make clear that consensual validation is compatible with *individual* differences in influence, leadership, and innovation. Individuals differ in the degree to which they represent the ingroup norm (we shall demonstrate this later), a minority can create doubt and uncertainty in the majority by disagreeing (hypothesis 2). However, it is assumed that, all things being equal, a single dissenting individual perceived as having little consensual support is likely to have his or her opinion attributed to personality and/or other personal idiosyncratic factors rather than to reality and hence will have little influence (Allen, 1975). The issue is not majority or minority but the degree to which any subgroup of one or more can create uncertainty in others and project their own views as ingroup normative and reflective of reality.

There is much evidence within the minority influence tradition congruent with this hypothesis. A consistent, consensual minority of two is more influential than a consistent minority of one (Moscovici & Lage, 1976). To be influential, minorities must avoid being characterized in terms of individual psychology (Mugny, 1982; Mugny & Papastamou, 1980), personalized as individual deviants, categorized as outgroup members (Maass, Clark & Haberkorn, 1982; Mugny & Papastamou, 1982; see also Wolf, 1979, for the importance of shared group membership) and not seen as in conflict with ingroup norms or superordinate values (Maass et al., 1982; Paicheler, 1976).

Points to note are that Festinger's (1950, 1954) hypothesis of the physical reality continuum and the distinction between physical and social reality testing—that social reality testing, consensual validation, is sought only where objective, nonsocial, physical means of appraisal are unavailable—is rejected. It is assumed that perception of all reality, physical or otherwise, is socially validated through direct or indirect ingroup normative processes. One does not resort to social comparison as second best, as a substitute for direct individual perception: individual perception and consensual validation are mutual preconditions and functionally interdependent.

The distinction between normative and informational influence is also rejected. What is perceived as evidence about reality, as having informational value, is a function of the shared ingroup norm, of the degree to which some response is attributed externally to an entity. Ingroup norms are assumed to be subjectively prescriptive, productive of the feeling that one ought to see, think, or act in a certain way, because they provide information that particular responses are objectively valid and appropriate. The informational value/validity of a response and the degree to which it is ingroup normative/consensual are hypothesized to be subjectively equivalent. There is, however, a temporal dimension to private acceptance. It is not seen as an automatic, blind process that takes place without thought or cognitive activity. Individuals will sometimes go along with the ingroup assuming that it must be correct before they have had time to work out exactly how or why, presuming that this is only a matter of time. The readiness to commit oneself behaviorally before full internalization has taken place should not be confused with compliance. Outgroups produce compliance, i.e., it is people with whom one does not expect to agree, whom one cannot be influenced by, that must resort to coercion, force and power to change behavior.

Most conformity generalizations can be happily and distinctively reinterpreted within this framework (see Turner et al., 1987). So, too, can minority influence. The evidence can be summarized as showing that minority "conversion"—as Moscovici (1980) and Mugny (1984) term the private influence of a minority—depends on the minority being a distinctive, consistent, consensual subgroup, neither "individualized", "psychologized", nor categorized as outgroup members, presenting a coherent, alternative norm that is congruent with existing norms and superordinate values. We would argue that the minority viewpoint must be consensual in terms of both comparative and normative fit with the ingroup category.

Hogg and Turner (1987b, Experiments 3 and 4) summarize two studies attempting to demonstrate directly the role of self-categorization in a modified Asch conformity paradigm (see also Abrams, Wetherell, Cochrane, Hogg & Turner, 1988). In Experiment 3 subjects in each session are assigned to seven private booths and make anonymous individual judgments about the degree of social approval that is associated with a series of personality traits. The popular response for each trait, the one subjects are most likely to give, has been previously ascertained. Before judging a trait a subject hears the responses of the other six persons in the session. Each subject believes that they are responding last, but in fact the feedback from the other subjects is faked and all subjects are responding last. The six fake responses on each trial are designed so that they always fall into two implicit subgroups of approval or disapproval on the 9-point rating scale, e.g., the responses might be 3, 4, and 5 and 7, 8, and 9, where 9 is extreme disapproval. One of the fake responses is always the popular one that the subject might be expected to give in isolation.

In the uncategorized conditions neither subjects nor the fake others are categorized into groups: the subgroupings on each trial remain implicit. In the categorized conditions, subjects and "others" are categorized explicitly into two groups and the social categorization always correlates with the response subgroupings: Ingroup members always give the three responses that include the popular response. This "correct" response is always the ingroup response closest to the outgroup, e.g., if the outgroup responses are 1, 2, and 3, then the correct response might be 5 and the remaining ingroup responses 6 and 7.

The measure of conformity is the degree to which subjects shift on average away from the correct response and the outgroup in the direction of the other ingroup members. There are no informational or other differences between conditions apart from the categorization variable. In fact it is not obvious why normative or informational influence processes should operate at all in this paradigm. Subjects are anonymous, the others are not unanimous but disagree and social support is available for any one of six responses. Subjects are not particularly uncertain and are free to endorse the correct response provided by an implicit or explicit ingroup member. Nevertheless, subjects shift significantly more toward the ingroup norm in the categorized than uncategorized conditions. Furthermore, it makes no difference whether subjects are categorized into groups explicitly randomly or on the basis of previously similar judgments.

In Experiment 4 the main finding was that the direction in which subjects shift was indeed determined by which side they categorized themselves as belonging to. For example, suppose the subgroupings on a trial were 3, 4, and 5 and 7, 8, and 9, with 5 as the correct response (assumed to be the subject's own), then it was predicted that the subject would identify with the approval group and shift away from 5 towards approval. If in other conditions on the same trial the responses were shifted as a whole towards approval so that the correct response now belonged to the disapproval group—e.g., 1, 2, and 3 versus 5, 6, and 9— then it was predicted that the subject would identify with the disapproval group and shift away from 5 towards disapproval. This is exactly what was found. Shifting all six responses in one direction and holding all else constant would nevertheless produce a shift in the opposite direction, since what determined shift was the side of the intergroup boundary that subjects found themselves on. In this study the implicit groupings were so powerful that explicit social categorizations had no additional effect.

In sum, it is assumed that social influence processes are made possible by the social categorization of self as similar to some class of people in contrast to others and the consequent minimization of personal differences perceived between self and ingroup others. This idea that shared social identity is the basis of shared expectations of agreement and mutual influence processes leads to several distinctive predictions about influence simply in terms of the social contextual basis of shared identity. We shall illustrate its distinctive heuristic value with respect to group polarization. We have made the point that agreement is not merely comparative and normative but also a variable—not only can one specify quantitatively the degree of unity within a group but one can also specify the degree to which individuals differ in representing the group as a whole, in being relatively consensual (hypothesis 5). Experts, extremists, leaders are conceptualized as relatively more prototypical of the ingroup norm than are others. This provides a novel explanation of group polarization.

AN EXPLANATION OF GROUP POLARIZATION

This section suggests an explanation of group polarization that unifies it with social conformity and shows how it is a special case of normal intragroup influence. Group polarization is the tendency of group discussion or some related manipulation to extremitize the average of group members' responses on some dimension from pre- to postdiscussion in the direction of the prevailing tendency. Thus, after discussing feminism, a group of moderately *pro* feminists would tend to become, on average, more pro than they had been initially. The standard group polarization experiment comprises three stages: a pretest in which group members' initial individual views are measured (producing a pretest group mean), a group discussion to consensus (producing a unanimous group consensus), and a posttest in which members' individual views are re-recorded (producing the posttest group mean). The usual finding where polarization has taken place is that the consensus and posttest mean tend to be more extreme than the pretest mean but in the same direction (i.e., towards the pole of the scale that is closer to the pretest mean). It is this polarizing shift from pretest to posttest mean (and consensus) that poses the explanatory problem.

What is now called "group polarization" is what used to be termed the "risky shift." Moscovici, Zavalloni, Doise and colleagues in Paris, Fraser, Gouge and Billig (1971) in Bristol and Myers and Lamm (see Myers, 1982) made an important advance by reconceptualizing the data as an expression of a more general group process of polarization (Moscovici & Zavalloni, 1969). This was important for two reasons. First, it made clear that the tendency of group interaction to produce "collective extremitization" (Doise, 1971) has nothing whatsoever to do with *risk* as such, i.e., it is content-general. Polarization can occur under appropriate conditions on any response dimension (in decision-making, gambling, jury decisions, attitudinal, perceptual, judgmental ratings, and so on).

Second, it recognizes explicitly as a fundamental aspect of the phenomenon that the direction and magnitude of extremitizing shift is predicted by the pretest trend on an item, i.e., there is a reliable positive correlation between the sample pretest mean for an item and the size of shift on that item (Teger & Pruitt, 1967). Groups that are moderately pro on an item become more pro; those that are anti become even more anti. This is why we are dealing with a *polarization* of the prevailing or dominant tendency rather than just an *extremitization* of the group mean (implying a shift in any direction). Fraser et al. (1971) have reported data to suggest that the pretest mean/shift relationship is found at the level of the specific group (a correlation across groups within an item) as well as at the sample level (across items pooling groups within items). Polarizing shifts tend to be negligible and unreliable where there is no initially dominant tendency.

Why is group polarization interesting? Why is it of interest to SCT? There are several good reasons. First, it contradicts the traditional informational influence model of conformity derived from the findings of Allport, Sherif, and Asch—the idea that social norms form through a process of interpersonal averaging or convergence. Second, it contradicts this theory in a particular way. The interpersonal averaging theory is individualistic (Turner & Oakes, 1986). It implies that social influence is simply a "change in individuals induced by individuals" (Kiesler & Kiesler, 1969, p. 26), i.e., that nothing qualitatively different emerges from group interaction and that the group norm is nothing more than the sum or (in this case) average of the individual properties of members. Thus group polarization raises the classic issue of the individual-group relationship (is group psychology reducible to the psychology of the individual or is there something special, distinctive, irreducible about group psychology?) in a particularly vivid and striking way. It plainly seems to show that something special does happen in the group, that groups somehow produce emergent normative tendencies which are not reducible to an aggregation of individuals' responses as they exist in isolation. The problem of the metatheory of group psychology is posed in a concrete scientific form, as a quantitatively precise, rigorously defined issue against which alternative metatheories of the group can be tested and compared.

Because SCT sets out to provide an alternative to the traditional analysis of group processes and claims in particular to provide an interactionist (Turner & Oakes, 1986) rather than individualistic explanation of social influence, the phenomenon provides an opportunity to demonstrate that such a stance is as capable of producing an exact, testable and scientifically precise account as is traditional theory. If group behavior is to be explained as a change in the level of abstraction of self-categorization, how is this general notion to be applied to group polarization? Our aim is to show how the central hypothesis of SCT can be translated into concrete research hypotheses.

Group polarization is the greater challenge in this respect, not only because it contradicts normalization as interpersonal averaging but also because after 25 or so years attempts to explain it in terms of variants of the dual-process model have, in our judgment, failed. This is by no means everybody's judgment and so it behoves us to be precise on this point. We do not suggest that social comparison (Baron & Roper, 1976; Sanders & Baron, 1977) and persuasive arguments (Burnstein, 1982; Burnstein & Vinokur, 1977) theories (the theories currently popular in North America, less so in Europe) have not found evidence for some part of their analyses. In fact, we accept (1) the social comparison hypothesis that polarization represents a movement to more extreme positions because such positions are more valued than moderate ones and that intragroup comparison plays a part in this process, and (2) the informational influence/persuasive arguments notion that shift is mediated by the exchange of arguments perceived as novel and persuasive. What we do not accept is that either theory has yet produced a *genuinely heuristic and predictive* explanation of *why* polarization occurs, when it occurs, under what conditions either polarization or convergence on the mean occur (specified in advance rather than inferred from its occurrence) and how social value and informational processes are to be integrated. The accounts proffered are largely circular. For example, one becomes extreme by conforming to social values more extreme than the pretest or one adopts a more extreme position because there are more novel and persuasive arguments favoring that than more moderate positions. If we take Burnstein and Vinokur's persuasive arguments theory, for instance, one can accept the data, but still feel that the theory tells us what happens but not why it happens.

Now let us provide the SCT explanation. It is hypothesized that both convergence on the pretest mean and group polarization represent conformity to the normative position of the group. "Normative" is not meant in the dual-process sense of "normative influence." We are making a relatively traditional assertion that people tend to conform to the consensual position of the group, the position perceived as representing the shared views of group members. However, we assume that the consensual position is *not* defined by the mean position (although it may coincide). We define it instead as the most *prototypical* position, the position that best represents the group as a whole. All ingroup positions are more or less prototypical of the group as a whole and are aspects of the ingroup consensus. We assume, nevertheless, that some positions are more representative than others and that the one that best summarizes what the group has in common (the prototype) is the (most) normative position (for reasons given in the previous section).

The relative prototypicality of ingroup members is defined and quantified by means of the meta-contrast principle. The more an individual differs from outgroup members and the less he or she differs from ingroup members the better he or she typifies the ingroup. So for example, in a Communist party, members must differ in politics from members of more conservative, capitalist parties, but they must not be so *ultra-left* that they begin to differ significantly from other Communists. More formally, for any dimension of comparison the mean perceived difference between a given ingroup member (the target) and outgroup members divided by the mean perceived difference between the target and other ingroup members provides an index of their representativeness of the ingroup (in this comparative context). The person with the highest prototypicality ratio (the ingroup member whose average difference from outgroup members divided by his or her average difference from ingroup members produces the highest number) holds the most consensual/normative position (see hypothesis 5).

The most prototypical position (which we shall summarize sometimes as the prototype) is not necessarily the mean pretest position of ingroup members. Sometimes the prototype and the mean will coincide, sometimes the prototype will be less extreme and sometimes more extreme than the mean. These three cases are illustrated in Table 8.2. Cases 1a and 1b illustrate situations where the ingroup prototype coincides with the pretest mean, case 2 illustrates a prototype

TABLE 8.2
Relations Between the Ingroup Prototype and the Pretest Mean

Case 1a: Convergence

group membership:	O	O	I	I	I	I	I	O	O
Individuals:	W	X	A	B	C	D	E	Y	Z
scale positions:	-4	-3	-2	-1	0	+1	+2	+3	+4
MCRs:	–	–	1.4	2	2.33	2	1.4	–	–

Note. Ingroup pretest mean = 0, ingroup prototype = 0 (at C) = convergence.

Case 1b: Convergence

group membership:	O	O	O	I	I	I	I	I	O
Individuals:	W	X	Y	A	B	C	D	E	Z
scale positions:	-4	-3	-2	-1	0	+1	+2	+3	+4
MCRs:	–	–	–	1.1	1.86	2.5	2.43	1.9	–

Note. Ingroup pretest mean = +1, ingroup prototype = +1 (at C) = convergence.

Case 2: Polarization

group membership:	O	O	O	O	O	I	I	I	I(x2)
Individuals:	V	W	X	Y	Z	A	B	C	D and E
scale positions:	-4	-3	-2	-1	0	+1	+2	+3	+4
MCRs:	–	–	–	–	–	1.3	2.7	4	4

Note. Ingroup pretest mean = +2.8, ingroup prototype is between +3 and +4 (between C and D and E) = polarization.

Case 3: Depolarization

group membership:	O	O	O	I	I(x3)	O	O	O	O
Individuals:	T	U	V	A	BCD	W	X	Y	Z
scale positions:	-4	-3	-2	-1	0	+1	+2	+3	+4
MCRs:	–	–	–	2.86	8.2	–	–	–	–

Note. Ingroup pretest mean = -0.25, ingroup prototype = 0 (at B, C, and D) = depolarization.

Notes. 1. I = ingroup member, O = outgroup member.
2. MCRs = meta-contrast ratios. Unlike in Table 8.1, these MCRs apply to individual group members and can be called prototypicality ratios. They are the average absolute difference from outgroup members of an ingroup member divided by his or her average absolute difference from ingroup members. All things being equal, the higher the prototypicality ratio of an ingroup member, the more representative is that person of the ingroup as a whole.

that is more extreme than the mean, and case 3 a prototype that is less extreme than the mean. In all cases the frame of reference is operationalized as the range of positions on some issue held by the ingroup and outgroup members in the situation and the ingroup prototype is defined as above.

It is hypothesized that whether social conformity (in the sense of convergence on the mean), group polarization or depolarization (the group moving in the opposite direction to the mean) occurs depends on whether the prototype is perceived as coinciding with or more or less extreme than the pretest mean. It is assumed that the underlying process is the same—conformity to the prototype—and that what varies is only the perceived position of the norm relative to the pretest mean.

The "problem" of polarization is really the problem of traditional theory, which reduces norm formation to a process of interpersonal averaging (the exchange/pooling of individual information). It has long been evident that polarization could easily be explained as conformity if it could be shown how ingroup norms could sometimes be more extreme than the mean (e.g., Singleton, 1979). This demonstration can be made by means of the meta-contrast principle and is the explanatory heart of the present analysis. It is the relationship between the distribution of ingroup responses and the comparative context (the social frame of reference) within which the ingroup defines itself that determines the degree to which the ingroup prototype coincides with or differs from the ingroup mean.

To explain: The relative prototypicality of ingroup members, like ingroup-outgroup categorization itself, must vary with the comparative context, since it is defined by the contrast between intergroup and intragroup differences. As the comparative context changes, so does the relative prototypicality of ingroup members. For example, in the following instance where ingroup members (I) occupy the middle ground on an issue in comparison with others (outgroup members: O)—

group m'ship:	O	O	O	I	I	I	O	O	O
Individuals:	A	B	C	D	E	F	G	H	I
scale positions:	−4	−3	−2	−1	0	+1	+2	+3	+4

it is evident that ingroup member E is the most prototypical of the ingroup and that D and F are equally prototypical. If we shift the comparative context to the right of the scale (displacing the ingroup to the left) as follows—

group m'ship:	I	I	I	O	O	O	O	O	O
Individuals:	D	E	F	G	H	I	J	K	L
scale positions:	−1	0	+1	+2	+3	+4	+5	+6	+7

we find that D has now gained substantially in relative prototypicality over F (prototypicality ratios are D = 5.5/1.5 = 3.67, F = 3.5/1.5 = 2.33) and more extreme positions have become more normative than moderate positions. In fact, the extremist D now begins to approximate the mean ingroup position of E in relative prototypicality (D = 3.67 versus E = 4.5/1 = 4.5) compared to the middle ground example (where D = 2 and E = 3).

Conversely, if we shift the frame of reference to the left (and displace the ingroup to the right)—

group m'ship:	O	O	O	O	O	O	I	I	I
Individuals:	U	V	W	X	Y	Z	D	E	F
scale positions:	−7	−6	−5	−4	−3	−2	−1	0	+1

we find that what was the moderate position of F at +1 has now become an extremist and more prototypical ingroup position. As a concrete example of these kinds of shifts, imagine a social democratic party wedded to welfare capitalism. Where such a political party compares its policies to those of the extreme Right and the extreme Left and sees itself as occupying the middle ground, it will tend to see itself as *centrist* or *moderate* defining itself in terms of the views of its average member. Now suppose that it enters into a political alliance with a right-wing conservative party and that this alliance is so successful that it becomes the new political frame of reference. In this instance, its most prototypical member will no longer be at its exact center, but will tend to be on the left of the party. In comparison with the conservative party the social democrats will tend to see and define themselves as left-wing (but not too left-wing). Similarly, if it enters into an alliance and compares itself with a left-wing socialist party, it will tend to see itself as more right-wing in consequence.

The *absolute* positions of ingroup members have not changed in the earlier examples, but their positions relative to others in the frame of reference have changed and it is these comparative relations that have led to shifts in the perceived relative prototypicality and hence normativeness of ingroup members (the same obviously applies to outgroup members). It can be shown that the pretest mean of any ingroup will tend to be most prototypical of that group compared to others to the degree that the mean is at the middle of the reference dimension defined by the comparative context. This will also be true where the comparative context is defined solely by ingroup positions, i.e., where ingroup members do not make intergroup comparisons but focus only on intragroup/interpersonal differences. In this situation the ingroup mean and scale midpoint will tend to be the same by definition.

However, as ingroup responses tend to shift (whether by a change in the group or the social context is theoretically immaterial) toward the extreme of any comparative context (the other extreme being defined by outgroup comparisons), then more extreme responses will tend to gain in relative prototypicality over more moderate ones (as their average intergroup differences increase and average intragroup differences decrease relative to those of moderates) and it becomes more likely that the most prototypical response will be more extreme than the mean in the same direction. As ingroup responses move to an extreme, it becomes more likely that extremists will start to bunch up at the scale endpoint (assuming that there are limits to how extreme one can become) and so such members will decrease their mean intragroup differences as well as increase their mean intergroup differences. Examples of two possible patterns of polarized prototypes are shown in Table 8.3.

The obvious question arises at this point of where in ordinary group polarization research is (are) the outgroup(s) that we have used to define and manipulate the comparative context? Our answer is very simple: we think that they are there, but hidden. They are implicit in the response scale employed to measure subjects' attitudes. The response scale is a symbolic representation of the shared frame of reference that is subjectively salient in the experimental situation. It is a relative ordering of the different responses of different people that can be made and are known to be made to an issue. For example, an ''attitudes to Charles de Gaulle'' scale (Moscovici & Zavalloni, 1969) does not describe different aspects of de Gaulle—rather it orders the different responses of people from pro to anti

TABLE 8.3
Two Patterns of Polarized Ingroup Prototypes

Case 1:   A Symmetrical Distribution of Ingroup Responses

group membership:	O	I	I	I	I	O	O
Individuals:	X	A	B	C	D	Y	Z
scale positions:	-3	-2	-1	0	+1	+2	+3
MCRs:	-	1.67	2.26	2	1.17	-	-

Note. A symmetrical distribution of ingroup responses around the pretest mean (-0.5) produces a more extreme prototype of B at -1 (MCR = 2.26), since no individual actually holds the mean position of -0.5.

Case 2:   An Asymmetrical Distribution of Ingroup Responses

group membership:	O	O	O	I	O	I	I (x2)
Individuals:	W	X	Y	A	Z	B	C and D
scale positions:	-3	-2	-1	0	+1	+2	+3
MCRs:	-	-	-	0.66	-	2.44	3.19

Note. C and D are more prototypical than B despite the latter holding the mean ingroup position of +2 (MCR of C and D = 3.19). This example illustrates how as the ingroup's views approach one pole so the relative prototopicality of more extreme positions is enhanced by an increase in their intragroup similarities as well as their intergroup differences.

Notes.   1. I = ingroup member, O = outgroup member.
2. MCRs + meta-contrast ratios. Unlike in Table 8.1, these MCRs apply to individual group members and can be called prototypicality ratios. They are the average absolute difference from outgroup members of an ingroup member divided by his or her average absolute difference from ingroup members. All things being equal, the higher the prototypicality ratio of an ingroup member, the more representative is that person of the ingroup as a whole.

to the same social object: it is a dimension of social comparison, not a stimulus dimension. The reason that we can meaningfully employ such a scale (or attitudes to abortion, the environment, etc.) and the reason it has the possible values it does is because we know that there are in reality people who are pro and people who are anti. The same is just as true in some more ad hoc decision. When we decide on a scale to be more or less risky or in a jury to conclude guilty or innocent, be harsh or lenient, we are aware that other people might and do make different decisions—if this were not so, there would be no need for a decision, no need for the whole or part of the scale. The scale as employed is implicitly a reflection of social reality: the outgroup, those who take a different/opposed view, does not disappear from reality and our awareness of reality simply because it is not physically present in the laboratory.

When we respond on a scale in an ordinary polarization study and indicate what we think, we are also indicating what we do not think. We are identifying ourselves with others who take the same stand, saying who we are and who we are not. Who we are not, the outgroup, are people who in this situation respond differently from ourselves. This means that it is possible to use the ingroup's responses on a relevant scale as a more or less direct operationalization of the intra- and intergroup differences perceived by subjects in the situation. One can calculate the relative prototypicality of ingroup members directly from their scale responses. The simplifying assumptions can be made that approximately equal numbers of people are perceived to endorse different scale values and that any value not endorsed by an ingroup member is perceived as an outgroup response. This in fact is how the examples in Table 8.2 were derived.

At this point it should become clear why the analysis of the conditions under which the group prototype differs from or coincides with the mean exactly parallels the major empirical finding embodied in the definition of group polarization that it is the prevailing tendency of the group which best predicts the direction and magnitude of extremitization. The pretest mean will directly tend to predict the direction and magnitude of the difference between the prototype and mean, since it encapsulates the relationship between the ingroup and the social frame of reference.

Wetherell (1987) summarizes much of the evidence for the SCT analysis. Studies (Hogg, Turner & Davidson, 1988; McGarty, Turner, Hogg, Davidson & Wetherell, in preparation; Wetherell, Turner & Hogg, 1985) show that, as predicted, there is a significant positive correlation between the pretest mean and the direction and degree of polarization of the ingroup prototype, i.e., the ingroup prototype does tend to be more extreme than the pretest mean in the same direction. There is also some correlational evidence (McGarty et al., in preparation) that both the degree to which on average the ingroup prototype differs from the pretest mean across items and the degree to which groups actually shift towards their prototypes within an item predict the extent of polarization across items.

Experimental data show that the same information is more persuasive coming from ingroup/similar others than outgroup/different others, that the salience of ingroup–outgroup membership (based on for example intergroup competition) does lead subjects to perceive the ingroup norm as more extreme than the pretest mean and that group members must perceive their initial tendency as a shared group norm rather than as an aggregate of individual tendencies for group polarization to occur (Mackie, 1986; Mackie & Cooper, 1984; Wetherell et al., 1985). Also relevant is a study by Doise (1969) in which students at a Parisian school of architecture became more polarized in their opinions about themselves when confronted by the presumed opinions of a rival school.

SCT makes the distinctive hypothesis not only that explicit intergroup comparison enhances polarization but that the *direction of polarization on an item can be reversed* by changing the comparative context. Hogg et al. (1988) have confirmed that subjects perceive the ingroup norm as riskier than the pretest mean when confronted by a more cautious outgroup but as more cautious than the pretest mean when confronted by a riskier outgroup.

It is important to recall that shift to the prototypical norm is not "normative" influence in the old sense any more than it is "informational" in the old sense. Elsewhere we have referred to the process as one of referent informational influence. People shift towards persuasive arguments, but what is persuasive is not simply a matter of information that can be abstracted from the social context but of the social validation of material through its participation in an ingroup consensus. Arguments have informational validity and extreme positions are socially valued to the degree that they represent the shared responses of the ingroup as a whole, which in turn is a matter of social comparison and self-categorization relative to a specific context. This analysis, therefore, brings together social value and informational processes as dynamic, relational and not reified explanatory principles.

It also indicates the inadequacy of the individualistic interpretation of group polarization and influence. The failure of the traditional approach to explain polarization is because we have conceptualized influence as an interpersonal process in which people sought in exchanging information to minimize their personal differences (leading to convergence on the mean), but in reality polarization arises because *people seek to conform to what defines their social group as a whole in contrast to other groups*. There is a change in the level of inclusiveness in the categorization of self and others. People are defining themselves in terms of higher order ingroup categories and conforming to the response which best expresses their collective view at this level. As we have demonstrated, the prototype is not reducible to the sum or aggregate of members' individual properties, it is an *emergent property,* a distinctive normative tendency that arises from the definition of social categories as comparative *wholes.* The group (and the group norm) is more than the sum of its parts.

This analysis is not just applicable to group polarization. It is important to note that we are suggesting that much normal conformity (such as in the Sherif paradigm) which up to now has been interpreted as interpersonal averaging is conformity to the prototype under conditions where ingroup positions coincide with or are at the middle of the frame of reference. It is possible that under certain conditions the minimization of personal differences does take place (in Moscovici's, 1985, sense of "normalization"), but we suspect that much of what has passed for interpersonal averaging is conformity to the prototype.

The explanation hypothesized is not just a mathematical formula. Numerical and other operational assumptions may vary. What is important is the psychological analysis. Polarization is conformity to norms in the context of intergroup relations (Doise, 1969), since norms are expressive of group identity and vary with the social context within which that identity is defined. Conformity is not interpersonal averaging but movement to the position that represents the ingroup category as a whole. The shared norm is the precondition as well as the effect of mutual influence. What is called interpersonal convergence may come about only under conditions where the context is defined by interpersonal differences and where the objective is not a correct response but the avoidance of interpersonal conflict (Moscovici, 1985).

SOME DISTINCTIVE IMPLICATIONS AND DIRECTIONS FOR RESEARCH

SCT has a large number of distinctive implications for understanding group processes. Those to be briefly mentioned are already producing innovative directions for empirical research.

1. SCT provides an analysis of psychological group formation that is empirically quite different from the widely held social interdependence theory. It proposes that group formation is basically a social-cognitive and not a reinforcement process. It rejects the idea that the mutual satisfaction of individuals' needs (and its concomitants) is the underlying causal process. We do not dispute that individuals have needs, that they seek to satisfy them in group relations and that groups do sometimes mediate rewards for members, but we argue that the essential psychological process in group formation is shared self-categorization and that this can take place prior to or despite a lack of positive outcomes.

Research on this issue (Hogg & Turner, 1985a, 1985b; Rabbie & Horwitz, 1969; Turner, 1981; Turner et al., 1983, 1984; van Knippenberg, 1986) establishes, we suggest, three relationships between group formation/cohesiveness and social relationships associated with positive/negative outcomes: (a) social relationships associated with positive outcomes are sufficient under certain conditions for group formation (the traditional relationship), (b) social relationships associated with negative outcomes are also sufficient under certain conditions for group formation (e.g., Turner et al., 1983), and (c) social relationships associated with positive outcomes are not necessary for group formation (e.g., the social categorization studies). The social interdependence theory is really only happy with the first of these relationships; it is not, without special pleading, compatible with the second two. SCT, however, can easily explain all three. One naturally tends to identify with positive others, since one tends to define self as positive (and within the theory a positive other is someone prototypical of a valued self-category). Much evidence shows that people assume they are similar to positive others. Shared negative experiences, just like shared positive ones and other forms of common fate, provide a basis for meta-contrast and ingroup–outgroup categorization (Campbell, 1958). Shared rewards are not necessary for group formation precisely since cognitive boundaries defining the self and not need satisfaction is the basic process.

There is a mass of data supportive of SCT in relation to group formation—to do with the effects of similarities and differences, common fate, proximity, shared goals, etc.—but interestingly much of the same data is claimed as support for the reinforcement idea. Alternative predictions can be made (Turner et al., 1987, pp. 64–65) and research needs to be addressed to their examination. For example, it should be possible to manipulate the degree to which others are categorized as similar to self by varying the comparative context whilst holding constant any independently defined rewards they might provide.

2. SCT sees group formation as a distinctive, adaptive and explanatory psychological (as well as social) process. This contrasts with the interdependence theory, in which it has come to be seen basically as an epiphenomenon of positive interpersonal relationships which adds little theoretically to the explanation of social behavior. The dominant theory provides explanations of interpersonal attraction, cooperation and influence in terms of patterns of interpersonal dependence and the group emerges as an outcome of (or as the same thing as) such relationships to the degree that they have become reciprocally stabilized. The group is not a distinctive psychological process; there is no qualitative transformation of such relationships mediated by membership in a shared social unit. In SCT, however, the group is seen as being a distinct psychological process of self-categorization and depersonalization which transforms interpersonal into intragroup relations. The group, the shared social categorization of others as identical to self, is seen as playing a causal role, as being the causal precondition for processes of social attraction, cooperation and influence. There is evidence that psychological group formation can be seen as determining and making possible, and not simply reflecting, cohesion (Hogg, 1987; Turner, 1982, 1984), cooperation (Brewer & Kramer, 1986; Kramer & Brewer, 1984, 1986) and influence (e.g., Abrams et al., 1988; Hogg & Turner, 1987b; Reicher,

1984; van Knippenberg & Wilke, in press; Wagner & Zick, 1987; Wetherell, 1987).

3. An important aspect of the idea of the group as a psychologically real process is that it is an *emergent* process. Groups are psychologically—and not merely socially—more than or at least different from the sum of their individual parts. Interpersonal relations are qualitatively different from intragroup relations and group phenomena are not reducible to intra- and interpersonal processes. Others have said this before. What is different about SCT is that it has shown how individual psychological processes can give rise to emergent, superordinate group phenomena by means of a systematic, causal theory, without making any metaphysical assumptions about collective psychology. The analysis of group polarization, for example, demonstrates in a way that is systematic, conceptually and quantitatively precise and empirically predictive and testable that social norms are emergent properties of the group as whole. The norm, the prototype, cannot be derived directly from the individual properties of members; it is a higher order, category property reflecting relations within and between social category memberships in relation to a social context. The key part of this analysis showing how the relative prototypicality of category members varies systematically with comparative relations and context is directly generalizable to other areas.

4. SCT proposes an anti-individualistic model of the group. It is an attempt to explain why individuals are not individualistic (i.e., do not always act in terms of their personal selves). Implicit in much social psychology is the idea that the group is a submergence, loss, denial, or even coercion of the individual self (as in de-individuation, diffusion of responsibility, conformity as submission to group pressure). A central message of SCT is that the group is an authentic expression of self. Here, however, a paradox emerges.

The categorization process is invariably theorized to lead to the perception of classified stimuli *as more alike (or more different) than they really are*. Thus, applied to social stereotyping, for example, it is assumed that social categorization, the cognitive basis of stereotyping (Tajfel, 1969), leads us to perceive outgroup members as more similar to each other and different from us than they are in reality—as a result of the usual accentuation effects. Social stereotyping is assumed to represent a form of cognitive prejudice, a tendency to oversimplify and overgeneralize the similarities and differences between people related to their group memberships. Because SCT explains group formation in terms of the social categorization and stereotyping of the self, does this mean that psychological group formation represents a prejudice against the self, an oversimplification and overgeneralization of features of the self? Such an implication—that the group is based on a cognitive distortion of the real self—is highly individualistic and stands in contradiction to our intended argument that the group authentically embodies the self.

In seeking to resolve this paradox we have been led to the view that the traditional interpretation of categorization effects is questionable and that group formation is *cognitively rational and veridical*. In the current climate of social psychology these are heretical opinions and we shall do no more here than briefly sketch our arguments to indicate the direction in which our research is going. First, SCT holds that categorizations form and become salient insofar as they *fit* stimulus input. They become salient as functionally adaptive, appropriate, fitting representations of social reality (Oakes & Turner, 1987). It is assumed along with Bruner (1957) that categorization operates in such a way as to provide veridical representations of stimulus relations. This is not contradicted in general terms by the influence of the perceptual readiness of the organism (the accessibility of categories relevant to needs, values and expectations). Bruner assumed that fit and accessibility worked together rather than in conflict. Self-categorizations, then, reflect veridical differences between self and others.

Second, all categorizations are comparative. Personal identity, too, embodies a categorization process and is comparative. It is not that individuals are real and absolute and cognized groups are only categories. The cognized individual person is psychologically just as much a category as is the group. When one talks of an individual holding some opinion and places him or her on an attitude scale, this is a categorical/comparative judgment in which the individual (a person category) is placed relative to others (and the differences within persons reduced and between persons enhanced) just as when one identifies the group norm. The prototypical attributes that define individuals also vary with the frame of comparative reference and so on. So, theoretically speaking, it makes just as much sense to think of the individual views of group members, personal identity, as a cognitive distortion of the real similarities that exist within the group as to think of social identity as a distortion of real individual differences. The level of identity has changed but the processes have not. One level is not by definition less real than another.

Third, self-categorization takes place at different and varying levels of abstraction. Human beings are both unique individuals and social groups and in particular situations act as either in varying and relative degree. The shift in the level of abstraction of social perception takes place to reflect accurately and appropriately this behavioral flexibility of individuals. The shift from personal to social identity, then, and vice versa is in the nature of a perceptual achievement, something that enables us to deal with the social meaning of action in a richer, more subtle and complex way rather than an oversimplification of social relations. We categorize people at the level of abstraction that fits (that maximizes meta-contrast), but we understand that in other situations other levels may be more appropriate. If we speak of furniture rather than chair in some situation where this is appropriate in terms of our purposes and as the most economical mode of grouping objects, does this imply that we have somehow cognitively distorted the reality of the chair, that its identity with other furniture has been overgeneralized? No, it does not and the same applies to the perception of people more in terms of a shared social identity than as on occasion in terms of a personal identity.

Last, it is crucial to understand that all perception, all cognition and attitudinal judgment, is relative to a context, i.e., it varies with the standard against which the stimulus is compared. The social judgment literature makes it clear that, psychologically speaking, there is no such thing as absolute judgment (Eiser & Stroebe, 1972); there is no such thing as an absolute stimulus property, if by stimulus we mean the cognitively appraised entity. When we categorize someone as ingroup or outgroup, there is a judgmental assimilation (enhanced similarity to ingroup properties) or contrast (enhanced difference from ingroup properties) of the individual as perception shifts to a social categorical level (Haslam, 1987). This does not imply distortion since the shift to the social categorical level reflects the comparative context as a whole. There would be a distortion of reality if assimilation and contrast effects took place without a corresponding change in reality, but research suggests that this does not happen. Shifts in the level of abstraction of categorization reflect the metacontrasts that exist in the stimulus situation as a whole. The mistake that is made is to think that categorization reflects the stimulus as if it existed as an absolute entity isolated from the comparative context and the state of the perceiver, but in fact categorization represents the stimulus both in relation to others and in relation to self. It describes the stimulus in relation to the comparative situation as a whole. What we find is that, even if the stimulus does not appear to change in some isolated absolute sense, changes in categorization always reflect some change in the comparative situation as a whole (Haslam, 1987; Oakes, 1987; Oakes & Turner, 1987).

It is not being suggested that self-categorization is subjective and purely arbitrary. On the contrary we have suggested that it acts to represent reality. The point is that self and identity are relational, comparative, dynamic processes; they are variable outcomes of active cognition, not reified, static, absolute givens. It is time to abandon notions of a "spontaneous" self-concept—self-perception always varies meaningfully with the social situation. The self is not a fixed mental structure inside the head, as if a kind of personality trait. Self-categorization functions adaptively and dynamically to represent the individual in a set of social relations in specific social contexts. It is part of the *process* of relating to the social environment.

The suggestion that psychological group formation is cognitively rational and veridical should not be misunderstood to legitimize the many wrong things that people do and believe as group members in relation to other groups. There is no doubt, for example, that many stereotypes are wrong. We believe, however, that false stereotypes, racism, bigotry etc., are fundamentally socially determined, not the result of a maladaptive, dysfunctional psychological process.

CONCLUSION

This paper has presented a new theory of group processes, summarizing its origins, main ideas and some of the derivations and implications that we and colleagues are currently pursuing. In concluding, three caveats are in order. First, we take it for granted that a social psychological analysis of the social group is only a limited and, depending on the question one is trying to answer, not necessarily the most important part of the story. A complete picture of human group behavior must include contributions from all relevant sciences from biology to history.

Second, the theory is intended as an argument against an individualistic approach to the group. It explains how individual psychological processes can produce something more than just individuals. We assume that the relevant processes cannot be conceived to operate outside of the social context and social activity (Tajfel, 1979). We have not had time to pursue the latter point. It must suffice to say that in theorizing about the cognitive basis of group formation we assume that cognition is a social as well as a psychological process (including social influence and ideology) and that even psychologically it always exists in functional interaction with social activity (Turner & Oakes, 1986). A similar point can be made about the intimate relation between social values/affect/motivation and cognition.

Third, the theory should not be understood as an argument for the primacy of the group over the individual. It is called self-categorization theory (and not social identity theory) because it deals with the interrelation of personal and social, individual and group, and asserts the interdependence of individuality and shared, collective identity. The theory proposes that the group is a distinctive psychological process, but in so doing it reminds us that group functioning is part of the psychology of the person—that individual and group must be reintegrated psychologically before there can be an adequate analysis of either. Group formation is an emergent process that does not merely redescribe but substantively changes and therefore helps to explain the psychology of the individual.

ACKNOWLEDGMENTS

We are grateful to Willem Doise, Michael Hogg, Paul Paulus and Ad van Knippenberg for commenting on an earlier draft of this chapter.

REFERENCES

Abrams, D., Wetherell, M. S., Cochrane, S., Hogg, M. A., & Turner, J. C. (1988). *Knowing what to think by knowing who you are: Self-categorization and the nature of norm formation, conformity and group polarization.* University of Dundee, Scotland.

Alexander, C. N., Zucker, L. G., & Brody, C. L. (1970). Experimental expectations and auto-kinetic experiences: Consistency theories and judgmental convergence. *Sociometry, 33,* 108–122.

Allen, V. L. (1975). Social support for nonconformity. In L. Berkowitz (Ed.), *Advances in experimental social psychology,* (Vol. 8, pp. 2–43). New York: Academic Pres.

Asch, S. E. (1952). *Social psychology.* Englewood Cliffs, NJ: Prentice-Hall.

Asch, S. E. (1956). Studies of independence and conformity: A minority of one against a unanimous majority. *Psychological Monographs: General and Applied, 70,* 1–70. Whole No. 416.

Baron, R. S., & Roper, G. (1976). Reaffirmation of social comparison views of choice shifts: Averaging and extremitization in an autokinetic situation. *Journal of Personality and Social Psychology, 35,* 521–530.

Bochner, S., & Perks, R. (1971). National role evocation as a function of cross-national interaction. *Journal of Cross-Cultural Psychology, 2,* 157–164.

Bonner, H. (1959). *Group dynamics: Principles and applications.* New York: Ronald Press.

Brewer, M. B. (1979). Ingroup bias in the minimal intergroup situation: a cognitive-motivational analysis. *Psychological Bulletin, 86,* 307–324.

Brewer, M. B., & Kramer, R. M. (1986). Choice behavior in social dilemmas: Effects of social identity, group size and decision framing. *Journal of Personality and Social Psychology, 50,* 543–549.

Brown, R. (1986). *Social psychology* (2nd ed.). New York: The Free Press.

Brown, R. J., & Turner, J. C. (1981). Interpersonal and intergroup behavior. In J. C. Turner & H. Giles (Eds.), *Intergroup behavior.* Oxford: Basil Blackwell and Chicago: University of Chicago Press.

Bruner, J. S. (1957). On perceptual readiness. *Psychological Review, 64,* 123–151.

Bruner, J. S., & Perlmutter, H. V. (1957). Compatriot and foreigner: A study of impression formation in three countries. *Journal of Abnormal and Social Psychology, 55,* 353–360.

Burnstein, E. (1982). Persuasion as argument processing. In H. Brandstatter, J. H. Davis, & G. Stocker-Kreichgauer (Eds.), *Group decision-making.* London: Academic Press.

Burnstein, E., & Vinokur, A. (1977). Persuasive argumentation and social comparison as determinants of attitude polarization. *Journal of Experimental Social Psychology, 13,* 315–332.

Campbell, D. T. (1958). Common fate, similarity and other indices of the status of aggregates of persons as social entities. *Behavioral Science, 3,* 14–25.

Codol, J.-P. (1975). On the so-called "superior conformity of the self" behavior: Twenty experimental investigations. *European Journal of Social Psychology, 5,* 457–501.

Deutsch, M., & Gerard, H. B. (1955). A study of normative and informational social influences upon individual judgment. *Journal of Abnormal and Social Psychology, 51,* 629–636.

Dion, K. L., Earn, B. N., & Yee, P. H. N. (1978). The experience of being a victim of prejudice: An experimental approach. *International Journal of Psychology, 13,* 197–294.

Doise, W. (1969). Intergroup relations and polarization of individual and collective judgments. *Journal of Personality and Social Psychology, 12,* 136–143.

Doise, W. (1971). An apparent exception to the extremitization of collective judgments. *European Journal of Social Psychology, 1,* 511–518.

Doise, W. (1978). *Groups and individuals: Explanation in social psychology.* Cambridge, England: Cambridge University Press.

Doise, W., Dechamps, J.-C., & Meyer, G. (1978). The accentuation of intra-category similarities. In H. Tajfel (Ed.), *Differentiation between social groups.* London: Academic Press.

Doise, W., & Sinclair, A. (1973). The categorization process in intergroup relations. *European Journal of Social Psychology, 3,* 145–157.

Eiser, J. R., & Stroebe, W. (1972). *Categorization and social judgment.* London: Academic Press.

Festinger, L. (1950). Informal social communication. *Psychological Review, 57,* 271–82.

Festinger, L. (1954). A theory of social comparison processes. *Human Relations, 7,* 117–40.

Fraser, C., Gouge, C., & Billig, M. (1971). Risky shifts, cautious shifts and group polarization. *European Journal of Social Psychology, 1,* 7–29.

Goethals, G. R., & Darley, J. M. (1977). Social comparison theory: An attributional approach. In J. M. Suls & R. L. Miller (Eds.), *Social comparison processes.* Washington: Hemisphere.

Haslam, S. A. (1987, May). *Self-categorization and social stereotyping.* Paper presented to 16th Annual Meeting of Australian Social Psychologists, Canberra.

Hogg, M. A. (1987). Social identity and group cohesiveness. In J. C. Turner et al., *Rediscovering the social group: A self-categorization theory.* Oxford/New York: Basil Blackwell.

Hogg, M. A., & Abrams, D. (1988). *Social identifications: A social psychology of intergroup relations and group processes.* London: Methuen.

Hogg, M. A., & Turner, J. C. (1985a). Interpersonal attraction, social identification and psychological group formation. *European Journal of Social Psychology, 15,* 51–66.

Hogg, M. A., & Turner, J. C. (1985b). When liking begets solidarity: An experiment on the role of interpersonal attraction in psychological group formation. *British Journal of Social Psychology, 24,* 267–281.

Hogg, M. A., & Turner, J. C. (1987a). Intergroup behavior, self-stereotyping and the salience of social categories. *British Journal of Social Psychology, 26,* 325–340.

Hogg, M. A., & Turner, J. C. (1987b). Social identity and conformity: A theory of referent informational influence. In W. Doise & S. Moscovici (Eds.), *Current issues in European social psychology,* (Vol. 2, 139–182). Cambridge, England: Cambridge University Press.

Hogg, M. A., Turner, J. C., & Davidson, B. (1988). *Polarized norms and social frames of reference: A test of the self-categorization theory of group polarization.* University of Melbourne and Macquarie University.

Howard, J., & Rothbart, M. (1978). Social categorization and memory for ingroup and outgroup behavior. *Journal of Personality and Social Psychology, 38,* 301–310.

Jones, E. E. (1985). Major developments in social psychology during the past five decades. In G. Lindzey & E. Aronson (Eds.), *The handbook of social psychology* (Vol. 1, 3rd ed.). New York: Random House.

Jones, E. E., & Gerard, H. B. (1967). *Foundations of social psychology.* New York: Wiley.

Kelley, H. H. (1967). Attribution theory in social psychology. In D. Levine (ed.), *Nebraska Symposium on Motivation* (Vol. 15, 192–238). Lincoln: University of Nebraska Press.

Kennedy, J., & Stephan, W. (1977). The effects of cooperation and competition on ingroup-outgroup bias. *Journal of Applied Social Psychology, 7,* 115–130.

Kiesler, C. A., & Kiesler, S. B. (1969). *Conformity.* Reading, MA: Addison-Wesley.

Kramer, R. M., & Brewer, M. B. (1984). Effects of group identity on resource use in a simulated commons dilemma. *Journal of Personality and Social Psychology, 46,* 1044–1057.

Kramer, R. M., & Brewer, M. B. (1986). Social group identity and the emergence of cooperation in resource conservation dilemmas. In H. Wilke, D. Messick, & C. Rutte (Eds.), *Psychology of decisions and conflict. Vol. 3. Experimental social dilemmas.* Frankfurt: Verlag Peter Lang.

Lott, A. J., & Lott, B. E. (1965). Group cohesiveness as interpersonal attraction: A review of relationships with antecedent and consequent variables. *Psychological Bulletin, 64,* 259–309.

Maass, A., Clark, R. D. III, & Haberkorn, G. (1982). The effects of differential ascribed category membership and norms on minority influence. *European Journal of Social Psychology, 12,* 89–104.

Mackie, D. (1986). Social identification effects in group polarization. *Journal of Personality and Social Psychology, 50,* 720–728.

Mackie, D., & Cooper, J. (1984). Attitude polarization: The effects of group membership. *Journal of Personality and Social Psychology, 46,* 575–585.

McGarty, C., & Penny, R. E. C. (1988). Categorization, accentuation and social judgment. *British Journal of Social Psychology, 27,* 147–157.

McGarty, C., Turner, J. C., Hogg, M. A., Davidson, B., & Wetherell, M. S. (in preparation). *Group polarization as conformity to the prototypical group member.* Macquarie University.

Moreland, R. L. (1985). Social categorization and the assimilation of "new" group members. *Journal of Personality and Social Psychology, 48,* 1173–1190.

Moscovici, S. (1976). *Social influence and social change.* London: Academic Press.

Moscovici, S. (1980). Towards a theory of conversion behavior. In L. Berkowitz (Ed.), *Advances in Experimental Social Psychology,* (Vol. 13, 209–239). New York: Academic Press.

Moscovici, S. (1985). Social influence and conformity. In G. Lindzey & E. Aronson (Eds.), *The handbook of social psychology.* (Vol. 2, 3rd ed.). New York: Random House.

Moscovici, S., & Lage, E. (1976). Studies in social influence: III. Majority and minority influence in a group. *European Journal of Social Psychology, 6,* 149–174.

Moscovici, S., & Zavalloni, M. (1969). The group as a polarizer of attitudes. *Journal of Personality and Social Psychology, 12,* 125–135.

Mugny, G. (1982). *The power of minorities.* London: Academic Press.

Mugny, G. (1984). The influence of minorities: Ten years later. In H. Tajfel (Ed.), *The social dimension: European developments in social psychology.* Cambridge, England: Cambridge University Press and Paris: Editions de la Maison des Science de l'Homme, Vol. 2.

Mugny, G., & Papastamou, S. (1980). When rigidity does not fail: Individualization and psychologization as resistances to the diffusion of minority innovations. *European Journal of Social Psychology, 10,* 43–62.

Mugny, G., & Papastamou, S. (1982). Minority influence and psycho-social identity. *European Journal of Social Psychology, 12,* 379–394.

Myers, D. G. (1982). Polarizing effects of social interaction. In H. Brandstatter, J. H. Davis, & G. Stocker-Kreichgauer (Eds.), *Group decision-making.* London: Academic Press.

Oakes, P. J. (1987). The salience of social categories. In J. C. Turner et al., *Rediscovering the social group: A self-categorization theory.* Oxford/New York: Basil Blackwell.

Oakes, P. J., & Turner, J. C. (1987). *Perceiving people as group members: A functional approach.* Macquarie University, Australia.

Paicheler, G. (1976). Norms and attitude change: I. Polarization and styles of behavior. *European Journal of Social Psychology, 6,* 405–427.

Rabbie, J. M., & Horwitz, M. (1969). Arousal of ingroup-outgroup bias by a chance win or loss. *Journal of Personality and Social Psychology, 13,* 269–277.

Reicher, S. D. (1984). The St. Pauls riot: An explanation of the limits of crowd action in terms a social identity model. *European Journal of Social Psychology, 14,* 1–21.

Rosch, E. (1978). Principles of categorization. In E. Rosch & B. B. Lloyd (Eds.), *Cognition and categorization.* (pp. 27–48). Hillsdale, NJ: Lawrence Erlbaum Associates.

Sanders, G. S., & Baron, R. S. (1977). Is social comparison irrelevant for producing choice shifts? *Journal of Experimental Social Psychology, 13,* 303–314.

Sherif, M. (1936). *The psychology of social norms.* New York: Harper and Brothers (Harper Torchbook edition, 1966).

Sherif, M. (1967). *Group conflict and cooperation: Their social psychology.* London: Routledge, Kegan Paul.

Sherif, M., & Hovland, C. I. (1961). *Social judgment: Assimilation and contrast effects in communication and attitude change.* New Haven, CT: Yale University Press.

Singleton, R. Jr. (1979). Another look at the conformity explanation of group-induced shifts in choice. *Human Relations, 32,* 37–56.

Tajfel, H. (1969). Cognitive aspects of prejudice. *Journal of Social Issues, 25,* 79–97.

Tajfel, H. (1972). La categorisation sociale. In S. Moscovici (Ed.), *Introduction a la psychologie sociale.* (pp. 272–302). Paris: Larousse. (English MS).

Tajfel, H. (1978). *Differentiation between social groups: Studies in the social psychology of intergroup relations.* London: Academic Press.

Tajfel, H. (1979). Individuals and groups in social psychology. *British Journal of Social Psychology, 18,* 183–190.

Tajfel, H. (1982). *Social identity and intergroup relations.* Cambridge, England: Cambridge University Press and Paris: Editions de la Maison des Sciences de l'Homme.

Tajfel, H., Flament, C., Billig, M. G., & Bundy, R. F. (1971). Social categorization and intergroup behavior. *European Journal of Social Psychology, 1,* 149–177.

Tajfel, H., & Turner, J. C. (1986). The social identity theory of intergroup behavior. In S. Worchel & W. G. Austin (Eds.), *Psychology of intergroup relations* (2nd ed., pp. 7–24), Chicago: Nelson-Hall.

Taylor, D., & Moghaddam, F. M. (1987). *Theories of intergroup relations.* New York: Praeger.

Teger, A. I., & Pruitt, D. G. (1967). Components of risk-taking. *Journal of Experimental Social Psychology, 3,* 189–205.

Turner, J. C. (1975). Social comparison and social identity: Some prospects for intergroup behavior. *European Journal of Social Psychology, 5,* 5–34.

Turner, J. C. (1978). Social categorization and social discrimination in the minimal group paradigm. In H. Tajfel (Ed.), *Differentiation between social groups.* London: Academic Press.

Turner, J. C. (1981). The experimental social psychology of intergroup behavior. In J. C. Turner & H. Giles (Eds.), *Intergroup behavior.* Oxford: Basil Blackwell and Chicago: University of Chicago Press.

Turner, J. C. (1982). Towards a cognitive redefinition of the social group. In H. Tajfel (Ed.), *Social identity and intergroup relations.* Cambridge: Cambridge University Press and Paris: Editions de la Maison des Sciences de l'Homme, 15–40.

Turner, J. C. (1983). Some comments on . . . "the measurement of social orientations in the minimal group paradigm". *European Journal of Social Psychology, 13,* 351–367.

Turner, J. C. (1984). Social identification and psychological group formation. In H. Tajfel (Ed.), *The social dimension: European developments in social psychology.* Cambridge: Cambridge University Press and Paris: Editions de la Maison des Sciences de l'Homme, Vol. 2.

Turner, J. C. (1985). Social categorization and the self-concept: a social cognitive theory of group behavior. In E. J. Lawler (Ed.), *Advances in group processes* (Vol. 2, pp. 77–122). Greenwich, Connecticut: JAI Press.

Turner, J. C., Hogg, M. A., Oakes, P. J., Reicher, S. D., & Wetherell, M. S. (1987). *Rediscovering the social group: A self-categorization theory.* Oxford and New York: Basil Blackwell.

Turner, J. C., Hogg, M. A., Oakes, P. J., & Smith, P. M. (1984). Failure and defeat as determinants of group cohesiveness. *British Journal of Social Psychology, 23,* 97–111.

Turner, J. C., & Oakes, P. J. (1986). The significance of the social identity concept for social psychology with reference to individualism, interactionism and social influence. *British Journal of Social Psychology, 25,* 237–252.

Turner, J. C., Sachdev, I., & Hogg, M. A. (1983). Social categorization, interpersonal attraction and group formation. *British Journal of Social Psychology, 22,* 227–239.

Ullah, P. (1987). Self-definition and psychological group formation in an ethnic minority. *British Journal of Social Psychology, 26,* 17–23.

van Knippenberg, A. (1986). *Group-serving attribution bias as a function of intra- and intergroup relations.* Paper presented to 21st International Congress of Applied Psychology, Jerusalem, July.

van Knippenberg, A., & Wilke, H. (in press). Social categorization and attitude change. *European Journal of Social Psychology.*

Wagner, U., & Zick, A. (1987, May). *In us I do believe—persuasibility and the switching on of social identity.* Paper presented to 7th General Meeting of the European Association of Experimental Social Psychology, Varna, Bulgaria.

Wetherell, M. S. (1987). Social identity and group polarization. In J. C. Turner et al., *Rediscovering the social group: A self-categorization theory.* Oxford/New York: Basil Blackwell.

Wetherell, M. S., Turner, J. C., & Hogg, M. A. (1985). *A referent informational influence explanation of group polarization.* University of St. Andrews, Scotland, and Macquarie University, Australia.

Wolf, S. (1979). Behavioral style and group cohesiveness as sources of minority influence. *European Journal of Social Psychology, 9,* 381–395.

III SOCIAL AND COGNITIVE PROCESSES IN INTERACTIVE GROUPS

9 Influence Processes and Consensus Models in Decision-Making Groups

Garold Stasser
Miami University

Norbert L. Kerr
Michigan State University

James H. Davis
University of Illinois

INTRODUCTION

The study of interacting groups has enjoyed plenty and suffered famine through-out the history of social psychology. As Steiner (1986) notes, group dynamics was a vigorous area of scholarship during the 1950s, but its popularity waned in the 1960s, and it has seemingly not recovered. Social psychologists' interests have shifted from interacting groups to individual behavior in social contexts. In fact, the bulk of small group research over the last 20 years has focused primarily on a few topical areas such as group polarization (Myers & Lamm, 1976) and jury decision making (Stasser, Kerr, & Bray, 1982). Steiner (1986, 1983, 1974) has examined the possible reasons for the precarious status of group research in social psychology, and we do not attempt to add to his scholarly analyses. However, we heartily agree with Steiner's (1986) admonition that our neglect of group research and theory may be a detriment to social psychology as a whole:

> It seems reasonable to expect that what happens at the group level cannot contradict what we accurately understand to happen at the individual level, and that what happens at the individual level cannot contradict what we accurately understand to happen at the group level. Increased understanding of either level may augment or correct our understanding of the other. In 1985 the group is the neglected member of this partnership; it urgently needs attention. (p. 284)

We continue to believe, as we expressed in the first edition of this chapter (Stasser, Kerr, & Davis, 1980), that one of the challenges of small group research is finding useful ways of representing group behavior and convenient ways of organizing group level data. Ideally, these representations should facilitate our thinking about how group members' behavior is related to the outcomes of group interaction. Our 1980 chapter presented three models of group decision making: Davis' (1973) social decision scheme (SDS) theory; Kerr's (1981) social transition scheme model (STS); and Stasser and Davis' (1981) social interaction sequence (SIS) model. We felt that these models, each in its own way, provided ways of thinking about social influence in decision-making groups, of organizing empirical results, and of guiding future research. In spite of the scarcity of group research in general, it is gratifying to us that there has been a substantial amount of empirical and conceptual activity related to these models over the last 8 years. For example, Laughlin and his colleagues (e.g., Laughlin, 1980; Laughlin & Futoran, 1985; and Laughlin & Ellis, 1986) have applied both the SDS and STS models to groups working on intellectual tasks. There have also been extensions and elaborations of these models. For example, Kirchler and Davis (1986) extended the SDS model to accomodate status differences among members within a group. Stasser and Davis' (1981) have also presented a more refined version of the SIS model than the one contained in our earlier chapter.

The SIS model in its most general form is a computer simulation model; it, unlike SDS and STS, cannot be succinctly expressed in mathematical form. In recent years, computer simulation of group decision making has received considerable attention. Coincident with the development of SIS, Penrod and Hastie (1980) published their DICE computer model of jury decision making. This model was extended to the JUS model in Hastie, Penrod, and Pennington (1983). More recently, Stasser (in press) formulated the DISCUSS model which simulates group decision making by simulating the discussion process. In light of this progress, we have included a section on computer simulation models. In this section, we discuss briefly the approach of computer simulation, explore the similarities and differences among the SIS, DICE, JUS, and DISCUSS simulation models, and review some illustrative applications.

Although this chapter reviews a variety of models, they can all be thought of as social combination (Laughlin, 1980) or social transformation (Shifflet, 1979) models; that is, each model in its own way operates on individual dispositions (e.g., preferences, opinions, etc.) or resources (e.g., knowledge, arguments, etc.) to obtain predicted group outcomes. One distinctive feature of these models is that they predict the likelihood of each possible group decision. Because they are decision-making models, it is not surprising that they all also use group members' preferences, in one way or another, as an important unit of analysis. On the one hand, they use members' preferences as a way of tracking movement from initial disagreement to final consensus. On the other hand, several of the models make explicit use of the notion that the configuration of preferences within a group at any point in time may succinctly summarize the social influence forces operating in the group at that time. For example, one expects that a jury with 10 guilty against 2 not-guilty advocates differs from one that is split 6–6. Not only would their deliberations probably produce different proportions of guilty and not-guilty arguments, but jury members would also likely experience quite different social pressures.

Our primary objective in this chapter is to illustrate the utility of mathematical and computer models for portraying and investigating social-psychological conceptions of group process. The models that we present are distinctly social-psychological because they recognize that groups are composed of acting and reacting individuals and, at the same time, they view individuals as mutually influencing one another. Many have extolled the virtues of models for understanding social interaction (Abelson, 1968; Shultz & Sullivan, 1972; Starbuck, 1983), noting their value for articulating theory, organizing data, synthesizing ideas about individual behavior into working theories of group behavior, and so forth. We hope that our examples illustrate some of these virtues.

A second objective is to review some of the insights and understanding that have accumulated through the development and application of these models. We are particularly interested in understanding better how social influence operates in decision-making groups. In reviewing what we know or think we know, we also hope to highlight gaps in our understanding, identify interesting unanswered questions, and, perhaps, pique the interest of others in filling some of these gaps and answering some of these questions.

GROUP DECISION MAKING AND SOCIAL INFLUENCE: STRENGTH IN NUMBERS

Decision-making groups possess distinctive features which guide and constrain the dynamics of the group process. One essential feature is that some level of agreement or consensus is required to define a group choice. This required degree of consensus is termed the group's *decision rule*. The familiar unanimity rule used by most juries is a good example. Decision rules may be explicit and formal (e.g., the voting rule specified in an organization's bylaws) or implicit and informal (e.g., a chairperson's intuitive assessment that sufficient agreement exists in a meeting to consider the matter at hand settled). In this chapter, we are concerned with understanding the process by which a group moves from initial disagreement (i.e., failure to satisfy its decision rule) to agreement (i.e., satisfaction of the operative decision rule). Thus, we are interested in understanding the nature of the mutual social influence processes through which groups reach consensus.

Viewed in this light, a decision-making group is a task group. While group interaction in such contexts may also serve personal and interpersonal needs, it is primarily a means to a shared goal—reaching a group decision. Typically, the group's ultimate goal is to reach the best possible decision, but its members' immediate task is to forge a consensus by changing either their own or other members' opinions and preferences. Furthermore, members' opinions are generally publicly expressed positions. In most decision-making groups, one's privately held position is immediately less important than the position that one will publicly endorse, either overtly or by silent assent. Although public endorsements may often agree with privately held opinions, they need not always agree. The fact that people sometimes endorse positions that are contrary to their privately held beliefs is interesting in its own right. However, because we are interested in how groups reach consensus, we are primarily concerned with publicly expressed preferences and opinions.

Exploring the nature of social influence in decision-making groups can begin with a fairly simple notion—the distribution of group members' preferences across the decision alternatives. For example, consider a jury whose task is to choose between the verdict alternatives of guilty and not guilty in a criminal trial. Traditionally, a jury contains 12 persons and operates under a unanimity decision rule. We can denote the number of people in a jury preferring each decision alternative with the ordered pair (r_G, r_{NG}); thus, for example, (8, 4) would indicate that 8 jurors favor a guilty verdict and 4 jurors favor a not guilty verdict. The question we pose is: Can such a simple piece of information about the group tell us much about whether, how, and when jurors will change their preferences? Or to put the question another way: Why is the distribution of preferences within a group a useful unit of analysis for modeling social influence in decision-making groups?

Intuition suggests one prediction based on this simple piece of information— larger factions are more likely to gain converts than smaller factions. That is, in many decision-making groups, there is probably *strength in numbers*. Beyond intuition, there is also much theory and research that would lead to the same prediction (Stasser et al., 1982). A common means of social influence in groups is mutual persuasion (Burnstein & Vinokur, 1977); group members present arguments that support their own and refute others' preferences. Larger factions should have an advantage in such persuasion processes because, all other things being equal, their pool of available arguments should be larger and their access to speaking time should be greater (at least in groups like juries where every member has an equal right to participate). Indeed, research confirms that the relative size of a jury faction and its share of communication are positively related (Hawkins, 1962). Therefore, we expect larger factions to exert greater *informational influence* (Deutsch & Gerard, 1955) than smaller factions.

But the social power of larger factions is due to more than an advantage in debate (e.g., Kerr, MacCoun, Hansen, & Hymes, 1987). We also know from personal experience that group members not only have the power to persuade, they can also administer social rewards (e.g., praise, high status) or punishments (e.g., derogation, rejection from the group). Classic research (e.g., Schachter, 1951) has demonstrated that recalcitrant deviates are often punished (e.g., assigned to low-status jobs, excluded from conversation). Further, the opportunity to administer reward/punishments and the salience of such reward/punishments is likely to vary directly with faction size. For example, even in settings where there is no opportunity for persuasive argumentation, yielding tends to increase with the size of opposing factions (e.g., Asch, 1956; see also Latane & Nida, 1980). Thus, compared to smaller factions, we would also expect larger factions to exert greater *normative influence* (Deutsch & Gerard, 1955), that is, to have greater power to entice or coerce conformity to its expectations.

Festinger's (1954) social comparison theory suggests yet another source of larger factions' power. Festinger suggested that in contexts where there is no objective or logical basis to evaluate our abilities and opinions (and likewise, preferences), we use others as a basis for evaluation. When everyone agrees, there is little question of the validity of one's opinion, but when there is disagreement in the group, members' evaluations of their positions are likely to be unstable. Festinger further suggested that such instability produces pressures to obtain uniformity of opinions within a group either by changing others' positions (e.g., through persuasion), derogating the opinions of those who disagree, or, in the face of continued disagreement, excluding the deviants from the group. Thus, Festinger's theory not only anticipates a search for information (mutual informational influence) and a search for social support (with attendant mutual normative influence), but also suggests that group members will try to move from disagreement to agreement even when they are not required to satisfy some decision rule.

Festinger (1950) also suggested that uniformity in opinion is generally functional for *group locomotion*, movement toward group goals. As noted earlier, in decision-making groups, achieving agreement is not just functional for reaching group goals, it is itself a goal. Group members may change their public position not because they have been persuaded, have conformed in response to social reinforcement, or are trying to adopt a socially sanctioned position, but simply to contribute to group locomotion. Such movement is like what Cialdini (e.g., Cialdini et al., 1976) has termed "elastic shifts," strategic changes in position designed to meet immediate situational pressures. This would be encouraged if lack of progress toward consensus were costly. For example, jurors often lose their regular income while serving on a jury, and prolonged jury deliberations can entail considerable opportunity costs. Such costs may not only motivate personal flexibility or acquiescence, but may also underlie the use of normative influence; the frustration and expense of stalemate can make those who deviate and block consensus rather unpopular (see Levine, Chapter 7 in this volume). All other things being equal, larger factions should also gain power from this desire for group locomotion. Larger factions are closer to satisfying the decision rule than smaller factions and, thus, reaching agreement on more popular alternatives will generally be faster and simpler. There is also evidence that even before any group deliberation has occurred, group members believe that the larger a faction is, the more likely that the group will adopt its position (e.g., Kerr & Watts, 1982; Kerr et al., 1987). Thus, changing one's position toward a relatively small faction may be viewed as opposing the probable course of group locomotion.

In summary, knowing the distribution of members' preferences may summarize a great deal about the process and product of group decision making. We have speculated that fundamental influences processes such as persuasion, normative pressures, and striving for uniformity are related to faction sizes within a group. If this is so, knowing how members distribute their support across the decision alternatives should tell us much about what a group is likely to decide. As a result the consensus models that we consider use faction size in one way or another in their representations of group process. Moreover, for many types of groups and decision tasks, these models successfully make use of formulations that embody *strength-in-numbers* notions.

Strength-in-numbers, however, is undoubtedly too simplistic to account for all of the complexities of social influence in decision-making groups. Indeed, the exceptions may be as interesting as the rule. For example, some factions may be disproportionately influential because of the position they support. Those who favor acquittal in a jury tend to be more influential than those who favor conviction (MacCoun & Kerr, 1988; Stasser et al., 1982). Group members who support the correct solution to certain problems are generally more influential than their incorrect cohorts (Laughlin, 1980; Laughlin & Ellis, 1986).

Moreover, there are surely many characteristics of individual members that mediate influence of their factions. It is often desirable to consider the impact of members' confidence, status, talkativeness, expertise, and the like, on their influence within the group. Although not denying that there is generally strength-in-numbers, we wish also to consider how individual differences among group members may shift the distributions of social power and, thereby, alter the outcome of a group's deliberation. Incorporating relevant individual differences into models of group behavior is a worthwhile and challenging endeavor, and we speak to this concern at several points.

Finally, strength-in-numbers, while a heuristically useful notion, is too vague to yield precise descriptions of group process and predictions of group decisions. Similarly, we want to address the possibility that there are many distinctly and interestingly different varieties of group process that can be characterized generally as strength-in-numbers. In sum, we need more precise ways of describing and representing how members' preferences are combined or transformed to yield a group decision.

THE SOCIAL COMBINATION OF DISPARATE
OPINIONS AND MUTUAL INFLUENCE: SOCIAL
DECISION SCHEMES

There are a number of important social settings in which the flow of interpersonal influence is largely one-way (often many-to-one), and indeed much social conformity research has focused on such instances. However, a freely interacting task-oriented group immediately suggests exchange and mutuality of influence among individuals as well as among factions of various sizes. Members' disparate preferences for action or conflicting proposals for task completion must be resolved through concession, compromise, yielding, or the like in order to achieve the consensus that establishes the group solution or decision. Our aim here is to develop a theoretical account of the process whereby this occurs. We first present a very general model or approach that admits easily of special case models. It is the special case models that actually embody the substantive theory relevant to particular situations.

Initial development of the social decision scheme model (Davis, 1973) had its origin in group problem-solving models (e.g. Lorge & Solomon, 1955; Restle & Davis, 1962). The emphasis was on input-output relations in which the model predicted group outcomes, given individual member input and assumptions about the intervening social interaction. The relatively simple word problems first considered in this work were intellectually stimulating but rarely socially provocative; these simple problems later gave way to more complex tasks (attitudinal judgments, adjudication of criminal cases, poltical policy issues, etc.) as research emphases moved from problem solving to decision making.

The basic social decision scheme model is described in the immediately following section, a discussion that also notes some of the ways individual and group decision processes particularly depend on the decision problem at issue. (A more general discussion of the representation of group consensus as a combinatorial process is given in Davis, 1982.) Then, some theoretical elaborations to accommodate individual differences are outlined.

Social Decision Schemes

One conceptual problem relevant to interaction at the group level is that a great many events happen simultaneously or in close temporal proximity to each other. A good example is a small group of people attempting to arrive at a common position on a controversial social issue. In such instances members may hold disparate views, and their positions may be in flux. We need then some conceptual means of summarizing this complex system of interpersonal accommodations, yet one that remains relevant to the *group level*. The notion we use for accomplishing this summary is the social decision scheme—a consequence of the situational and personal norms as well as of members' values and attitudes peculiar to that task, situation, and so on. Basically, for every possible way group members can array themselves vis-à-vis the task or issue confronting the group, the social decision scheme predicts a group outcome.

To obtain such a summary of group process, we must be able to specify a set of mutually exclusive and exhaustive preference alternatives for groups and individuals; this set may be denoted as $A_1, A_2, \ldots, A_n$. For example, a political caucus may be required to choose one of 3 candidates to support; in which case $n = 3$, and the 3 candidates constitute the task-defined set of mutually exclusive preference alternatives for caucus members as well as the possible decision outcomes for the group. For other tasks the set of alternatives may be ordered so that in some sense $A_1 < A_2 < \ldots < A_n$. For example a group may choose to advocate a course of action from a set of alternatives that are spaced along a risk dimension, or a budget committee may be required to allocate a particular amount of money for a project from a set of feasible allocations.

Given a task-defined set of n alternatives, the goal is to predict or specify the probability P_i that a group will choose the alternative A_i. Thus we usually speak about the probability distribution over the possible outcomes $\mathbf{P} = (P_1, P_2, \ldots, P_n)$. As suggested by our earlier discussion, an important consideration in arriving at the likelihood that a group of r members will adopt a given alternative, A_i, is the number of advocates that A_i has at the *onset* of the group's interaction. Therefore we can characterize a group by the initial distribution of members' preferences over the task-defined alternatives—$(r_1, r_2, \ldots, r_n)$, where r_i is the number of advocates of A_i, and $r_1 + r_2 + \ldots + r_n = r$. For example, given a political caucus of 6 people ($r = 6$) having to choose one of 2 candidates ($n = 2$) to support, the following distinguishable distributions (r_1, r_2) may occur: (0, 6); (1, 5); (2, 4); (3, 3); (4, 2); (5, 1); and (6, 0). In general, there are $m = \binom{n + r - 1}{r}$ ways that r persons can array themselves over the n alternatives. Thus in the foregoing case, where $n = 2$ and $r = 6$, $m = \binom{6 + 2 - 1}{6} = [7!/(6!\ 1!)] = 7$. Several examples of the m ways r people can array themselves over n alternatives are given in Table 9.1. Obviously, m quickly becomes very large as the number of alternatives or group members increases (e.g., if $r = 4$, $n = 4$, then $m = 35$; if $r = 4$, $n = 5$, then $m = 56$; $r = 8$, $n = 5$, then $m = 792$, and so on). Even modest experiments can quickly become unfeasibly expensive in subjects, and single-occasion or lone group field studies cannot easily address questions depending on such subject-expensive arrays.

It is important to note that the distinguishable distribution $(r_1, r_2, \ldots, r_n)$ of the group may change with time and/or circumstance [e.g., a group having a (3, 3) distribution may change to a (4, 2) distribution if a member changes preference]; however, for now we are concerned only with the initial distinguishable distribution. That is, for the present, we consider only how the factions are arrayed over the alternatives at the onset of group interaction. Moreover, the concept of a distinguishable distribution implies that alternatives are distinguishable whereas members are not distinguishable. Less formally we might say that

TABLE 9.1
Examples of the Possible Arrays of Opinions or Response
Alternative Preferences Logically Possible in Groups of
Size r and n Response Alternatives

r = 4, n = 2		r = 4, n = 3			r = 2, n = 4				r = 6, n = 2	
A_1	A_2	A_1	A_2	A_3	A_1	A_2	A_3	A_4	A_1	A_2
4	0	4	0	0	2	0	0	0	6	0
3	1	0	4	0	0	2	0	0	5	1
2	2	0	0	4	0	0	2	0	4	2
1	3	3	1	0	0	0	0	2	3	3
0	4	3	0	1	1	1	0	0	2	4
		1	3	0	1	0	1	0	1	5
		0	3	1	1	0	0	1	0	6
		1	0	3	0	1	1	0		
		0	1	3	0	1	0	1		
		2	2	0	0	0	1	1		
		2	0	2						
		0	2	2						
		2	1	1						
		1	2	1						
		1	1	2						

the distinguishable distribution emphasizes the number of supporters for each alternative while ignoring the characteristics of the members who are providing that support. Obviously this approach deemphasizes individual differences in status, power, ability, and so on. We see later that this restriction can be relaxed to address specific kinds of individual differences directly.

At this point the role of a social decision scheme can be stated more precisely. For every possible distinguishable distribution that may occur at the onset of the group's interaction, the social decision scheme specifies the probability that the group will choose each of the task-defined alternatives. As stated earlier, m such distinguishable distributions can occur and the decision scheme must account for all m distributions. Ultimately we are interested in predicting the probability that each alternative will be chosen, given a number of groups of size r interacting in similar circumstances. For example, what is the probability that 6-person juries will acquit (A_1), convict (A_2), or be hung (A_3), given a particular set of evidence, a specified time to deliberate, the same definition of reasonable doubt, and so on? Answering such a question requires that we either know or can estimate how many of the groups array themselves according to each of the m distinguishable distributions.

In general, the m distinguishable distributions ($r_1, r_2, \ldots , r_n$) are not equally likely to occur. We shall use π_i to denote the probability that the ith distinguishable distribution will occur. At least two possibilities exist for estimating the probability, π_i. First, π_i may be estimated directly in many experiments by counting the relative frequency of each distinguishable distribution. This possiblity requires that the preferred position of each group member be clearly stated at the onset of discussion or elicited privately by the experimenter prior to discussion. However, such pretesting or direct observation of members' pre-discussion preferences is often not possible, and π_i must therefore be estimated indirectly. To obtain indirect estimates, an independent sample of the population of individuals from which groups are composed can be queried regarding their preferences for the decision alternatives. The responses to this survey can then be used to estimate the probabilities $p_1, p_2, \ldots, p_n$, that *individuals* will privately select or prefer each of the alternatives, $A_1, A_2, \ldots, A_n$. If groups are randomly composed from this population, we may then use the probability estimates, $p_1, p_2, \ldots, p_n$, to obtain an indirect estimate of π_i, the probability that the ith distinguishable distribution will occur at the onset of discussion. The indirect estimate $\hat{\pi}_i$ is given by the general term of the multinomial expansion,

$$\hat{\pi}_i = (r_1, r_2, ^r \ldots, r_n) p_1{}^{r_1} p_2{}^{r_2} \ldots p_n{}^{r_n} \tag{1}$$

For example, suppose that 60% of an independent random sample of individuals favored A_1, given a two-alternative task (i.e., $n = 2$). Then $p_1 = 0.6$ and $p_2 = 0.4$. Given this information, the estimated probability $\hat{\pi}_4$ of the 4th distinguishable distribution (1, 3) for $r = 4$ and $n = 2$ in Table 9.1 is given by $\hat{\pi}_4 = (_1{}^4{}_3)$ $(0.6)^1 (0.4)^3 = [4!/(1! \ 3!)] \ (0.6) \ (0.064) = 0.154$. In a similar manner, the probabilities of the other possible distinguishable distributions can be computed yielding a row vector of probabilities $\hat{\pi} = (\hat{\pi}_1, \hat{\pi}_2, \ldots, \hat{\pi}_5) = (.130, .346, .346, .154, .026)$. These probabilities tell us, among other things, that the most likely outcomes when sampling 4 individuals from a population having 60% favoring A_1 are the distinguishable distributions (3, 1) and (2,2). Obtaining 4 who agree on A_2 at the onset of discussion [i.e., (0,4)] is very unlikely but possible (given $\hat{\pi}_5 = .026$).

Of course, the interesting prychological questions begin after we have estimated the likelihood of each distinguishable distribution either by direct observation of members' prediscussion preferences or by indirect estimation using an independent sample and equation (1). In other words, given the state of opinion in the group at the onset, we next consider a means of summarizing the mutual accommodation process that leads to consensus. And, as implied earlier, that summary function is served by the social decision scheme. Examples of familiar social decision schemes are sometimes labeled as "majority rules" or "mutual compromise," both of which are vague for our purposes. What about the occurrence of nonmajorities? Where shall the compromise decision be located between two or more contending parties? Even though we might not be able to specify the group response with certainty, given a particular state of the group, we would at least like to state explicitly the probability of an alternative being chosen.

Thus we define the probability d_{ij} of the group choosing the jth response alternative A_j, given the ith distinguishable distribution. In order to account for all possibilities, a decision scheme must specify the probability, d_{ij}, for each of the n alternatives given each of the m distinguishable distributions. Thus, for example, when $n = 2$ and $r = 4$ as depicted on the left-hand side of Table 9.1, we must specify $(5)(2) = 10$ [i.e., m times n] probabilities to define a particular decision scheme. The probabilities that define a particular social decision scheme are often arranged in a $m \times n$ stochastic matrix $\mathbf{D}$ where each row is associated with a particular distinguishable distribution and each column with one of the decision alternatives. Various examples of social decision scheme matrices for the simple cases when $r = 6$, $n = 2$, and when $r = 4$, $n = 3$ are given in Table 9.2, along with verbal descriptions of the social resolution process they are intended to model. Note that in writing out the matrix $\mathbf{D}$, more conceptual detail is required than is available from the phrases such as majority rules. For one thing, a majority may not exist. That is, several possible group states contain no majority—e.g., (2, 1, 1) for $r = 4$, $n = 3$—yet such groups may reach a consensus. A subscheme is thus required to implement the majority rules plan, specifying the probability with which each possible outcome will occur. Thus, in the top of Table 9.2, note that for the 6-person groups considering two alternatives a simple majority rule will yield a decision in all but one of the seven possible opinion states of members. When equally split ($r_1 = 3$, $r_2 = 3$), some subscheme is required; equiprobability (which is rather like tossing a fair coin in this case) is one possibility, but there are many others also possessing intuitive appeal.

We noted at the outset that the probability distribution of group decisions across the n alternatives is an outcome of theoretical concern. If we denote the probability of a group chosing decision alternative j as P_j, then it is possible to write

$$P_j = \Sigma_i \, \pi_i \, d_{ij} \qquad (2)$$

where the summation is across all possible distinguishable distributions, π_i is the probability of the ith distinguishable distribution, and d_{ij} is the entry in the decision scheme matrix that gives the probability of decision j for groups having the ith distinguishable distribution. For example, suppose that we applied a "Majority/Equiprobability" decision scheme (as illustrated in Table 9.2) to the simple case when $r = 4$ and $n = 2$ (as given in Table 9.1). Moreover, let us use the estimated probabilities, $\hat{\pi}_i$, computed earlier using equation (1) when $p_1 = 0.6$ (and $p_2 = 0.4$): $\hat{\pi} = (.130, .346, .346, .154, .026)$. Armed with this information regarding the likelihood of each distinguishable distribution and the knowledge (or assumption) that a Majority/Equiprobability scheme is applicable, we can compute the probability, P_1, that a randomly sample group will choose A_1 using equation (2): $P_1 = (.130)(1.0) + (.346)(1.0) + (.346)(.50) + (.154)(0.0) + (.026)(0.0) = .65$. The probability of A_2 being chosen by a group in this case can be computed similarly and yields $P_2 = .35$.

It is customary, and convenient for less simple cases, to express the probability distribution of group decisions $\mathbf{P} = (P_1, P_2, \ldots, P_n)$ as the matrix product of the vector π and the decision scheme matrix $\mathbf{D}$:

TABLE 9.2
Examples of Social Decision Scheme Matrices with Descriptive Labels Summarizing the Apparent Social Interaction Responsible for Establishing Consensus

r_1, r_2	Proportionality[a]		Majority/ Equiprob[b]		Majority/A_1[d]	
	A_1	A_2	A_1	A_2	A_1	A_2
(6, 0)	1.00	0.00	1.00	0.00	1.00	0.00
(5, 1)	0.83	0.17	1.00	0.00	1.00	0.00
(4, 2)	0.67	0.33	1.00	0.00	1.00	0.00
(3, 3)	0.50	0.50	0.50	0.50	1.00	0.00
(2, 4)	0.33	0.67	0.00	1.00	0.00	1.00
(1, 5)	0.17	0.83	0.00	1.00	0.00	1.00
(0, 6)	0.00	1.00	0.00	1.00	0.00	1.00

r_1, r_2, r_3	Proportionality[a]			Averaging[c]			Majority/A_1[d]		
	A_1	A_2	A_3	A_1	A_2	A_3	A_1	A_2	A_3
(4, 0, 0)	1.00	0.00	0.00	1.00	0.00	0.00	1.00	0.00	0.00
(0, 4, 0)	0.00	1.00	0.00	0.00	1.00	0.00	0.00	1.00	0.00
(0, 0, 4)	0.00	0.00	1.00	0.00	0.00	1.00	0.00	0.00	1.00
(3, 1, 0)	0.75	0.25	0.00	1.00	0.00	0.00	1.00	0.00	0.00
(3, 0, 1)	0.75	0.00	0.25	0.50	0.50	0.00	1.00	0.00	0.00
(1, 3, 0)	0.25	0.75	0.00	0.00	1.00	0.00	0.00	1.00	0.00
(1, 0, 3)	0.25	0.00	0.75	0.00	0.50	0.50	0.00	0.00	1.00
(0, 3, 1)	0.00	0.75	0.25	0.00	1.00	0.00	0.00	1.00	0.00
(1, 0, 3)	0.25	0.00	0.75	0.00	0.50	0.50	0.00	0.00	1.00
(0, 1, 3)	0.00	0.25	0.75	0.00	0.00	1.00	0.00	0.00	1.00
(2, 2, 0)	0.50	0.50	0.00	0.50	0.50	0.00	1.00	0.00	0.00
(2, 0, 2)	0.50	0.00	0.50	0.00	1.00	0.00	1.00	0.00	0.00
(0, 2, 2)	0.00	0.50	0.50	0.00	0.50	0.50	1.00	0.00	0.00
(2, 1, 1)	0.50	0.25	0.25	0.00	1.00	0.00	1.00	0.00	0.00
(1, 2, 1)	0.25	0.50	0.25	0.00	1.00	0.00	1.00	0.00	0.00
(1, 1, 2)	0.25	0.25	0.50	0.00	1.00	0.00	1.00	0.00	0.00

Note. For the upper set of matrices $r = 6$, $n = 2$; for the lower set $r = 4$, $n = 3$.

[a]These cases illustrate a strict proportionality scheme for which the probability that an alternative will be chosen is the proportion of members advocating it [i.e., $P(A_i) = r_i/r$]. Note that many variations of a proportionality scheme are possible. For example, it may be that alternative A_1 is inherently more attractive, in which case proportions associated with A_i would have a disproportionately larger weight than proportions associated with the other alternatives.

[b]Majority; equiprobability otherwise. Even for this relatively simple case a majority scheme is not adequate for all possibilities; we must introduce a subscheme (vix., equiprobability) for the (3, 3) instance. It is interesting to note that for $r = 6$, $n = 2$ an "averaging" scheme (see the following) would have produced an identical matrix to the one obtained using a "majority-equiprobability" scheme. The equivalence of these two schemes does not hold for more than two alternatives. It is often the case that conceptually different schemes make identical predictions if r or n are small but make quite different predictions as r and/or n becomes large.

[c]Strict arithmetic averaging. This scheme makes "sense" only if the alternatives can be ordered in some way. Given a plausible ordering, the averaging scheme captures a "compromise" process. (Averages falling exactly between two adjacent alternatives were treated by assigning equiprobability to each alternative.) Note that many variations on an averaging theme may exist. For example, alternatives may be given differential weights to reflect differences in inherent attractiveness.

[d]If a simple majority exists it determines the outcome: otherwise A_1 is chosen.

$$P = \pi D \qquad (3)$$

which, in the simple example used above, expands to

$$P = (.130, .346, .346, .154, .026) \begin{vmatrix} 1.0 & 0.0 \\ 1.0 & 0.0 \\ 0.5 & 0.5 \\ 0.0 & 1.0 \\ 0.0 & 1.0 \end{vmatrix} = (.65 \ .35).$$

Of course other choices of **D** may yield quite different predicted distributions of group decisions. For example, the decision environment, prevailing social norms, or inherent demands of the task may result in a decision process whereby A_1 is chosen by a group only if all members prefer A_1 initially; any dissent results in the group choosing A_2. Such a process would be represented by a different pattern of probabilities in the decision scheme matrix **D** [viz., (1.0, 0.0) in the first row and (0.0, 1.0) in the remaining rows]. And, for this process **P** = (.13, .87). Thus, **D** not only represents theoretical notions about the decision process but also yields predicted probabilities of group decisions. To this point we have considered only a few possiblities for **D**, but the form of the **D** matrix is sufficiently flexible to accommodate a variety of ideas about decision and influence processes.

An example from conformity research, using the classic experimental setup popularized by Asch (1956), will help to further illustrate how ideas about social influence can be represented in social decision scheme notation. In that situation a subject was requested to select one of three responses—one of which was correct, one a moderate error, and the third an extreme error. Recall that the typical subject, responding after a majority of 7 "others" (persons ostensibly similar to oneself but actually confederates of the experimenter), tended to make an error if the majority did so about one-third of the time, although an error is very rare for subjects responding alone. Recall too that one early result suggested that a majority of 3 was sufficient to produce the "conformity effect." Although the original Asch studies used three response alternatives one of which was correct, one a moderate error, and the third an extreme error, we will consider a simplified version in which A_1 is the correct response and A_2 an incorrect response. The social decision scheme matrix might be represented as in the left-hand side of Table 9.3. Owing to the choice of an obviously easy task, a subject can easily recognize a correct alternative and would expect that others would agree; that is, one would expect that the probability of (8, 0) would be close to 1.00 in the real world. (In fact, about 0.975 of independent samples of individuals typically judge correctly on this task.) The contrived occurrence of a (1,7) split, with the naive subject in the minority, resulted in a consensus (i.e., "yielding by the subject") about one-third of the time. That is typically d_{82} is about 0.33, a surprising result in view of the almost 100% choice of A_1 by a

TABLE 9.3
Social Decision Scheme Matrices Illustrating Standard Conformity
Situations from the Group Perspective

Probability of Distribution	Response Distribution	General Case Correct A_1	General Case Incorrect A_2	Proportionality Correct A_1	Proportionality Incorrect A_2
$\pi 1$	$(8, 0)^a$	d_{11}	d_{12}	1.00	0.00
$\pi 2$	$(7, 1)$	d_{21}	d_{22}	0.87	0.13
$\pi 3$	$(6, 2)$	d_{31}	d_{32}	0.75	0.25
$\pi 4$	$(5, 3)$	d_{41}	d_{42}	0.62	0.38
$\pi 5$	$(4, 4)$	d_{51}	d_{52}	0.50	0.50
$\pi 6$	$(3, 5)$	d_{61}	d_{62}	0.38	0.62
$\pi 7$	$(2, 6)_b$	d_{71}	d_{72}	0.25	0.75
$\pi 8$	$(1, 7)^b$	d_{81}	d_{82}	0.13	0.87
$\pi 9$	$(0, 8)$	d_{91}	d_{92}	0.00	1.00

[a]For the Asch setting (8, 0) would be the most likely case it freely interacting groups are composed of naive subjects.
[b]The experimentally contrived case of (1, 7) would be highly improbable, given a group of naive subjects.

random sample of naive individuals. Indeed it was just such counterintuitive findings that fostered interest in the experimental results. However, the subject must surely have experienced some surprise that the probability of the (1, 7) distribution was not near zero, as one might expect from past experience, but actually occurred by experimental contrivance rather frequently over trials. From the point of view of "informational social influence" (Deutsch & Gerard, 1955), the relative frequency of (1, 7) that the subject experienced was in sharp contrast to that expected (8, 0) in such a situation.

Of course the focus of this chapter is on the freely interacting group rather than on the single many-to-one context exemplified by the experimental setup of Asch, in which discussion was discouraged and no collective task response was required. Thus we are interested in other distributions of opinion, preferences, and so forth, within a group besides the (1,7), (1,3), and (1, 2) instances that have been frequently studied in conformity research. Another advantage of viewing social decision schemes as the resolution of conflict or disparities in outlook is that the overall picture given by the social decision scheme matrix, **D**, provides for *mutuality* of influence. Individual members and subgroups, such as majority-minority factions, are for some group tasks less easily characterized by certain yield-not yield dichotomies than by the probabilities d_{ij}. Moreover, the flexibility of representation provided by **D** allows such probabilities to change with task, population, rewards, and a number of other social realities.

The notion that minorities do not always or inevitably yield to majorities has received considerable elaboration through the work of Moscovici and his colleagues (e.g., Moscovici, 1980; Moscovici & Faucheux, 1972; Moscovici & Nemeth, 1974). Many of the general situational factors that control or affect the nature of conformity in the traditional Asch many-to-one situation have been summarized by Allen (1965, 1975); Mugny (1980) and Nemeth (1986) have extended and summarized recent research on minority influence.

The social decision scheme model aims not only to accommodate these important conceptions of majority and minority, but to incorporate within a single theoretical structure the influence exerted by factions of any size, including the important case of equal subgroups. Moreover the possibility of mutual influence must be recognized in most group consensus environments.

For example, imagine that a lone dissenter almost always yields (that is, with probability near 1.00) in a two-alternative response system. This accounts for only a small set of the distinguishable distributions. Clearly a more comprehensive conceptual system is needed for the many possible ways that r persons can distribute themselves over n alternatives. Another intuitively attractive influence principle, testable by social decision scheme theory for the situations in which it is relevant, might be that influence is constant from member to member. But the direction of influence is not established with *certainty* by the "weight of numbers" or by the relative sizes of competing subgroups, but rather with some probability. Thus we might specify a "proportionality" principle such as that given in the right-hand portion of Table 9.3. Observe that such an influence principle is defined for all nine of the distinguishable distributions. The idea can be easily extended to $n = 3$ alternatives, but this would require 45 rows in the matrix **D**, when $r = 8$. (We have already illustrated the proportionality principle when $r = 4$ and $n = 3$ in the lower-left-hand portion of Table 9.2.) From this point of view the research question can be economically stated in terms of the parameters $[d_{ij}]$ that make up the entries of the matrix **D**; an important programmatic question might be to uncover through empirical investigation reasonable estimates for d_{ij}, given a particular social context, task, population, and the like.

From whatever source estimates of the $[d_{ij}]$ parameter values may be derived (e.g., conventional wisdom, custom, some social influence theory, etc.), straightforward tests are possible. For example, the matrices in Table 9.2 might each be a rendition of different theories about interpersonal influence processes involved in achieving consensus. Considering the bottom three matrices in Table 9.2 ($r = 4$, $n = 3$), the different implications of the theories are evident if we imagine that every one of the 15 distinguishable distributions is as likely as every other and calculate the final group probability distribution for each matrix in turn. In other words, suppose that $\pi_1 = 1/15 = 0.0667$ for all i, and we compute, using equation 3, the probability of each decision (P_1, P_2, P_3) for each of the three **D** matrices in the bottom half of Table 2. These computations yield predictions of (0.333, 0.333, 0.333) for the $\mathbf{D}_{Pr}$ matrix constructed on a proportionality principle; (0.200, 0.667, 0.200) for the $\mathbf{D}_{Av}$ matrix constructed on an averaging principle; and (0.600, 0.300, 0.100) for the $\mathbf{D}_{Maj/A1}$ matrix constructed on a "majority otherwise A_1" principle (indicating that A_1 is an obvious choice if, and only if, a majority does not prefer another alternative). The latter case is not unlike the Asch (1956) situation in which an obviously correct alternative is chosen unless a (critical) majority of three influences the lone dissenter to yield.

Thus, ideas about social influence can be given an explicit form, permitting easily testable point predictions. For example, given the foregoing illustration, the proportionality principle predicts that the alternatives A_1, A_2, A_3 are equally likely to be chosen by a group, whereas the averaging and "majority otherwise A_1" principles predict quite different patterns of outcomes. Each set of predictions can be examined for goodness-of-fit to observed data, thereby competitively contrasting the notions embodied in the various decision scheme matrices. Such a procedure is characteristic of research taking a *model-testing* approach: A priori models of social influence and compromise are postulated and subsequently evaluated in terms of observed data.

Complementary to the foregoing model-testing approach, one can adopt a *model-fitting* strategy (see Kerr, Stasser, & Davis, 1979, for an elaboration). Rather than postulating various forms of the social decision scheme matrix D the researcher can obtain an estimated matrix D that best describes the transition from distinguishable distributions to final group decision. That is, having observed π (or estimated π using equation 2) and the relative frequency distribution P of group decisions over the alternatives, we can derive an estimate of D that best satisfies the equation $P = \pi D$. There are various procedures for estimating D; see Laughlin, Kerr, Davis, Halff, and Marciniak (1975) and Kerr, Atkin, Stasser, Meek, Holt, Meek, and Davis (1976) for illustrative examples of the model-fitting approach. Once the decision scheme matrix D is estimated, we may describe the social process it seems to represent.

To this point, much of the discussion implies response alternatives that are discrete, unordered choices, although characteristics such as correctness, popularity and so on might sometimes be identified with one or another of them. In such cases we would not expect compromise as suggested by the general averaging principle (used in the aforementioned example) to be operative or even possible. However, in cases in which the set of alternatives may be ordered, or even reflect an underlying continuum, the possibility of compromise arises; the choice an alternative located between those favored by disparate factions offers a mutual outcome not available in the earlier examples.

Compromise and Mutual Accommodation. In fact, social influence situations in which the group response lies between extremes advocated by the members is perhaps encountered as often as the "either/or" setup that disallows compromise. For example, the group polarization research typically requires the group to choose from a set of alternatives ordered on an attitudinal or risk dimension (see, Myers & Lamm, 1976 for examples). The possibility of compromise is especially attractive as a purposeful plan for settling disputes and may arise as a consequence of other social norms engaged in the situation. The use of social decision scheme theory to address such compromise is illustrated in a study of Davis, Cohen, Hornik, and Rissman (1973). Two-person groups debated and ultimately reached a decision on a social issue (percentage of university control that should be invested in undergraduates or percentage of the national budget that should be spent on pollution control). The dyad members played the role of representatives of a political party from different districts who had come together to form the county committee and "hammer out" the party's position for the county. Three different group compositions were studied by different pairings of members who had been summarily obligated to different constituencies. That is, some members were responsible for reporting to constituencies characterized by one distribution of preferences over the response alternatives, whereas others were to report to constituents who had a different distribution. The shape of the constituent distributions varied such that the extent of disagreement between the two members could be altered. Davis et al. (1973) tested several different versions of compromise models (e.g., each pair moves through equal distances regardless of where their positions might lie along the set of alternatives). Moreover, they extended these ideas to models that included members' personal preferences as well as the positions representing their constituencies' sentiments—a variation that did not as a rule lead to significant improvements in predictions. In general they found that "equi-distance compromise" models yielded quite accurate predictions.

A point that concerns us here is the illustration of special case compromise models within the general context of social decision scheme theory. We illustrate the ideas using only two forms of the compromise model, one requiring equal movement of each member and the other assuming unequal movement by the pair. The two matrices given in Table 9.4 are the social decision scheme matrices **D** for the equi-distance compromise model (left-hand side) that gave accurate

TABLE 9.4
Social Decision Scheme Matrices Illustrating Two Different Versions
of Compromise in Dyads on a Four-Alternative Task in Which
Alternatives Reflect an Underlying Continuum

	Equi-Distance Compromise				Unequal Compromise			
	A_1	A_2	A_3	A_4	A_1	A_2	A_3	A_4
(2,0,0,0)	1.00	0.00	0.00	0.00	1.00	0.00	0.00	0.00
(0,2,0,0)	0.00	1.00	0.00	0.00	0.00	1.00	0.00	0.00
(0,0,2,0)	0.00	0.00	1.00	0.00	0.00	0.00	1.00	0.00
(0,0,0,2)	0.00	0.00	0.00	1.00	0.00	0.00	0.00	1.00
(1,1,0,0)	0.50	0.50	0.00	0.00	0.10	0.90	0.00	0.00
(1,0,1,0)	0.00	1.00	0.00	0.00	0.00	0.10	0.90	0.00
(1,0,0,1)	0.00	0.50	0.50	0.00	0.00	0.10	0.90	0.00
(0,1,1,0)	0.00	0.50	0.50	0.00	0.00	0.10	0.90	0.00
(0,1,0,1)	0.00	0.00	1.00	0.00	0.00	0.00	0.10	0.90
(0,0,1,1)	0.00	0.00	0.50	0.50	0.00	0.00	0.10	0.90

predictions in the Davis et al. (1973) experiment and a model (right-hand side) that might arise if those alternatives with the larger index number possessed some persuasive appeal in their own right. In other words the bias represented in the right-hand matrix might reflect increased influence for members who advocated higher-numbered alternatives. The difference in decision outcomes is evident if we again assume that the probability of each of the distinguishable distributions is constant, $\pi_i = 0.10$. The resulting distributions of group decisions predicted by the two models, respectively, are (0.15, 0.35, 0.35, 0.15) and (0.11, 0.23, 0.47, 0.19). A variety of other compromise processes may be defined and easily represented in terms of social decision scheme matrices. Moreover, the compromise notions developed above can be extended to groups larger than dyads.

Individual Differences

The term "individual differences" has a long and useful history in psychology, but because people can vary in so many ways, it is necessary to specify what differences are relevant to any particular application. Obviously, individual differences in intellective abilities, social tendencies, and emotional reactivity are among those that have special implications for group discussion, consensus, and performance. In one sense, the probabilistic character of the general social decision scheme model recognizes individual variability along with that from other sources; individuals and groups choose a decision alternative only with some probability. However, it would be useful to have a means for dealing more explicitly with individual differences—especially those immediately relevant to the goal of reaching a consensus in a particular decision environment. To this end, we outline below two approaches to incorporating individual differences within the group decision model described earlier.

Sampling from Different Populations. It is familiar from cultural anthropology and cross-cultural psychology, that some populations of individuals systematically react differently to the same stimuli or environmental challenges. People in different social categories within a culture may also react differently. For example, Nagao and Davis (1980) summarized results from several independent studies using the same mock trial and experimental conditions and observed that females were consistently more likely than males to favor conviction of a defendant accused of rape. Given the content of the case, such findings were not startling, but demonstrated clearly the value of recognizing individual differences to improve understanding of the consensus process and increase accuracy in predicting verdict outcomes.

Indeed, the sometimes controversial "Scientific Jury Selection" techniques (Schulman, Shaver, Colman, Emrick, & Christie, 1973; and Kairys, Schulman, & Harring, 1975) are predicated upon the notion of identifying populations or subpopulations of potential jurors that are differently disposed in verdict preferences, given the same trial experience. Demographic characteristics such as age, sex, education, religion, membership organizations, and the like may be associated with general behavioral tendencies relevant to a case at trial—e.g., members of organizations advocating a ''return to law and order'' are thought to favor convicting accused thieves, muggers, and the like more often than nonmembers. If one side possesses the requisite information (through surveys or access to experienced community leaders), there is the possibility of obtaining a disproportionate number of favorably disposed jurors through a strategic use of challenges at voir dire.

What are some likely effects of such a strategy, given that jury membership is in fact manipulated successfully as implied above? The prospect of empirically addressing this question in practice seems remote, even if the many legal and ethical constraints on such research could be overcome. Such a dilemma permits an illustration of an additional advantage of explicit models—simulating outcomes under reasonable assumptions about parameter values that have been suggested by, but cannot be estimated directly from, empirical research (cf. Davis & Kerr, 1986).

Imagine there exist two mutually exclusive and exhaustive populations from which the membership of small task-oriented groups may be drawn, but Population X and Population Y are sampled with different probabilities, u and (1–u) respectively. To continue with the jury example, the probability of a juror (later) being a guilty-sayer is $p_G = uP(G|X) + (1-u)(G|Y)$, where $P(G|X)$ probability of a guilty vote given Population X membership, and in general $P(G|X) \neq P(G|Y)$. If the inequality is large and the difference in sampling rates substantial, p_G can be greatly affected. The potential, long-run effect on a jury has been explored in a ''thought experiment'' by Tindale and Nagao (1986). They first calculated the verdict consequences of sampling from three differently disposed populations (strong, weak, or no guilt bias), as might be involved in a change of venue; see Fig. 9.1. Next they predicted verdict distributions assuming that ''scientific jury selection'' procedures resulted in successfully sampling from two distinct clusters (differently disposed subpopulations), and some possible

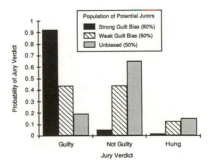

FIG. 9.1. Predicted jury verdict consequences as a result of change in venue. Reproduced by permission. From Tindale and Nagao (1986), *Organizational Behavior and Human Decision Processes, 37*, 409–425.

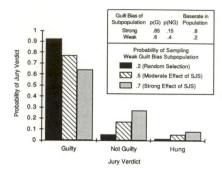

FIG. 9.2. Predicted jury verdict consequences when the use of SJS allows differential sampling from two identifiable clusters within the population. Reproduced by permission. From Tindale and Nagao (1986), *Organizational Behavior and Human Decision Processes, 37*, 409–425.

outcomes are presented in Fig. 9.2. Finally, Tindale and Nagao assumed both a change of venue and differential sampling as described here, and these results are given in Fig. 9.3.

These simulations are important because they illustrate how relatively small and plausible individual differences might produce substantial effects at the group level. For our purposes, they demonstrate how individual differences may be accommodated theoretically. Obviously, such composition phenomena are quite general, and in no sense limited to the jury.

Contributing Differently to Consensus. The preceding discussion admits individual differences only in terms of input differences in group composition. That is, members of different identifiable populations are presumed to differ in their likelihood of preferring one alternative over another. Of course, it is possible that members may differ in ways that affect the group's interaction. Members may be more or less influencial by virtue of their social status, gregariousness, or task-relevant competence. Or, in other cases, it may be that some members are more influencial because they occupy identifiable roles (e.g., president or supervisor). When there are characteristics of members that may plausibly affect their impact on a group's decision, it is potentially useful in applying social decision scheme models to be able to distinguish one group member from another.

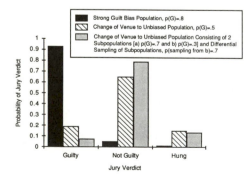

FIG. 9.3. Predicted jury verdict consequences resulting from the use of SJS to both change venue and differentially sample jurors. Reproduced by permission. From Tindale and Nagao (1986), *Organizational Behavior and Human Decision Processes, 37*, 409–425.

In all applications considered to this point, decision alternatives, but *not* persons, were treated as distinguishable. Treating persons as distinguishable increases the number of possible distinguishable distributions, *m*, that must be represented in the model. For example, we considered earlier the simple case of a 4-person group deciding between two alternatives; that is, $r = 4$ and $n = 2$. If we treat the members as indistinguishable, there are $m = \binom{n + r - 1}{r} = \binom{2 + 4 - 1}{4} = 5$ possible distinguishable distributions; the five possibilities are given on the left-hand side of Table 9.1. However, if we treat the members as distinguishable, then it is insufficient, for example, to represent all groups with one-person minority favoring A_1 as $(1, 3)$. When we say that members are distinguishable, we are saying that it is important to specify which of the four members is in the 1-person minority. Therefore, the $(1, 3)$ case when members are treated as indistinguishable, expands to four possibilities when the four members are distinguishable. As Kirchler and Davis (1986) noted, if *both* members and decision alternatives are distinguishable, the number of possible distinguishable distributions is given by $m = n^r$. Thus, in our example of $r = 4$ and $n = 2$, the number of possible arrays of opinion when members occupy identifiable roles within the group is $m = 2^4 = 16$ (as opposed to 5 when members are treated as indistinguishable). [Note that, in general, $n^r > \binom{n + r - 1}{r}$, and for many cases the inequality is very large. However, in many applications, we may reduce the number of possibilities by not viewing each person as distinct from all others; rather, we may need to be concerned only with categories of people (e.g., Republicans vs. Democrats or males vs. females).]

In many task-oriented groups, a role or status structure develops with time, whereas, in other contexts, roles or statuses may be assigned at the outset or imported from outside the group. In any case, individual differences are at the heart of the social structure. Chair, secretary, and treasurer are familiar titles reflecting particular interaction roles, but tasks or situations can give rise to variously defined roles, some of which may pertain to the performance of a given task (e.g., positions on an athletic team) while others may be more socially oriented (such as "most talkative or dominant member"). Kirchler and Davis (1986) extended the social decision scheme model to accommodate such role designations. They established differing levels of member status within 3-person groups. These groups completed three tasks—one intellective task that had a correct answer and two judgmental tasks that had no correct answer. Models that attributed more influence to higher status members (i.e., "power-wins" models) successfully accounted for decisions on the judgmental tasks when status differences were large within a group. When members were of equal status, "majority-wins" characterized the decision processes for judgmental tasks. In contrast, when solving the intellective task, members' relative statuses seemed not to affect their influence; having the right answer was more important in that correct members, regardless of their status, were generally able to prevail.

Thus, Kirchler and Davis (1968) demonstrated that decision processes are affected not only by task type (intellective vs. judgmental) but also by the status composition of the group. Moreover, they illustrated how the social decision scheme model can be extended to accommodate individual differences.

Summary and Prospects

In this section, we have considered a means of formulating theoretical notions about the establishment of group consensus in a formally explicit way. We have taken the view that the often disparate preferences or opinions in a small task-oriented group are combined or compromised to yield predictable patterns of group decisions. Such a process is typically what we mean by mutual interpersonal influence—a group-level phenomenon accompanied by many complex social events occurring simultaneously or in close temporal and spatial proximity. Social decision scheme theory offers a way to represent such events economically and explicitly, and at the same time admits easily of special case models for particular decision environments. It is the special case model of course that carries the theoretical content; the general social decision scheme notion is only an approach to theoretical analysis.

Several extensions of the general social decision scheme model are intuitively attractive. One of these elaborations addresses individual differences and group composition, and two such approaches to this general problem were outlined earlier. Other elaborations are obviously necessary, especially those addressing the task format that in turn affects the social process. For example, consider a decision environment in which the individual member proposed a preference *order* (a set of alternatives ranked according to desirability) during interaction in contrast to the more commonly studied single preference. Ono and Davis (1987) have proposed a version of such a model, but this work is not discussed here, because empirical tests are still in progress (see also Crott, Zuber, & Schermer, 1986, for similar work). Another theoretical problem posed by response format is suggested by the task to choose an amount of something that may fall anywhere along a continuum. Damage awards, allocations, financial settlements, etc. can take, in principle, any value within an interval defined by the task, custom, or practical constraint. The discrete choice models considered heretofore have not yet a counterpart in the continuous variable case.

THE SOCIAL TRANSITION SCHEME (STS) MODEL

The social transition scheme (STS) model is an extension of the social decision scheme approach. A simple example illustrates the nature of this extension. Suppose a 5-person group must choose from among three decision alternatives. Furthermore, suppose that the initial distinguishable distribution of the group is (3, 1, 1). The standard SDS logic would specify a decision scheme which would predict the likelihood of the group choosing each alternative; for example, if a majority primary scheme were hypothesized, the SDS model would predict that the group would ultimately choose the first response alternative, A_1. The **D** matrix summarizes the likelihood of such initial-split to final-decision transitions. By contrast, the STS model does not focus on the group's final decision, but rather upon the successive changes in group members' positions during interaction. In other words, the STS model either estimates or predicts (depending upon one's research strategy) the likelihood of transitions from one distinguishable distribution of group members' opinion to another. In our hypothetical example, an application of the model would result in an estimation or prediction of the likelihood of shifting from the "group state" (3, 1, 1) to (3, 2, 0), (4, 0, 1), (2, 1, 2), etc. Formally, the STS representation of the process is summarized by an $m \times m$ transition matrix, **T**, the i-th row of which specifies the probabilities of transition from the i-th distinguishable distribution to each of the $j = 1, 2, \ldots, m$ distinguishable distributions. In the earlier example, $r = 5$ and $n = 3$; therefore, **T** is $m \times m = 21 \times 21$.

Because a discussion of *process* implies behavior changes across time, it is important to specify how the passage of time will be represented in a process model. There are at least two potentially useful ways to break up group behavior across time defining two classes of STS models. The first class, the STS *shift* models, takes each transition from one "group state" to another in the interval of time during which the sequential process is observed. For a shift model, a group has either satisfied a decision rule (e.g., unanimity) or will shift with certainty to a new "group state"; no allowance is made for indefinite stalemate. A somewhat more complex class of STS models is the STS *rate* models. Here, the end of some fixed time interval (a "polling" interval)[1] defines the moment at which the group state is determined. Although they are related, the shift and rate models give somewhat different representations of the group decision-making process. Shift models are concerned only with the path that the process takes, while rate models are concerned with both the path the group takes and how quickly it is moving.

The examples in Table 9.5 of **T** matrices for rate and shift models may help illustrate how these models represent process. Both matrices represent a kind of "proportionality" process. For example, in both instances (3, 1) groups move to (4, 0) three times as often as they move to (2, 2). Likewise, within each matrix (2, 2) groups are equally likely to move to (3, 1) and (1, 3). Furthermore, both matrices suggest a "unanimity" decision rule' when groups reach the unanimity states (4, 0) or (0, 4), they remain there (and presumably reach a decision).

However, the shift matrix represents what will happen on the k-th shift (re-

---

TABLE 9.5
Examples of T Matrices for STS Shift and Rate Models Where
the Number of Alternatives is 2 and Group Size is 4

Distribution Before	STS SHIFT MODEL[a]				
	Distribution After the kth Shift				
the kth Shift	(4,0)	(3,1)	(2,2)	(1,3)	(0,4)
(4,0)	1.00				
(3,1)	0.75	0.00	0.25		
(2,2)		0.50	0.00	0.50	
(1,3)			0.25	0.00	0.75
(0,4)					1.00

Distribution on	STS RATE MODEL[a]				
	Distribution on Poll k + 1				
Poll k	(4,0)	(3,1)	(2,2)	(1,3)	(0,4)
(4,0)	1.00				
(3,1)	0.09	0.88	0.03		
(2,2)		0.02	0.96	0.02	
(1,3)			0.03	0.88	0.09
(0,4)					1.00

[a] Zero entries are left blank except for those occurring on the main diagonal of
the shift matrix.

gardless of how much time has elapsed since the k-1 shift), while the rate matrix represents what will happen during the time between the polls k and $k + 1$. Thus, in the rate matrix, groups may remain in the same state with a high probability particularly if the time interval between polls is relatively short, while, in the shift matrix, groups by definition cannot remain in the same state [except for the "absorbing states" (4, 0) and (0, 4)]. If we can assume that the probabilities in these matrices remain the same throughout the group's interaction (i.e., the probabilities are stationary) and that the probabilities are unaffected by where the group has been previous to its current state, then both shift and rate models can be used to predict the final group decision as well as the path the group took in reaching a decision.

For example, the shift matrix in Table 9.5 would predict that a (2, 2) group would move to (1, 3) with a probability of .5. If the group did shift to (1, 3), it would return to (2, 2) with a probability of .25 or reach a unanimous decision with a probability of .75 on the subsequent shift. In this manner, the shift model can predict the likelihood that a group will follow various paths through the states to reach one of the unanimous states. In a similar manner, the rate matrix would predict that a (2, 2) group would shift to (1, 3) on the next poll with a probability of 0.02. If this shift to (1, 3) occurred, the group would return to the (2,2) state with a probability of 0.03, stay in the (1,3) state with a probability of 0.88, or reach a unanimous decision with a probability of 0.09 on the subsequent poll. Thus, the rate model would predict not only the likelihood of the group taking various paths but also how much time (i.e., how many polls), on average, it would take the group to move through these paths.

Like the SDS model, the STS model may employ either a *model-fitting* or a *model-testing* strategy. Recall that under a model-fitting strategy, one would attempt to estimate the best-fitting social transition scheme from one set of data and either cross-validate on another sample or examine the plausibility of the estimate vis-à-vis other evidence. With this strategy, the objectives of the model are primarily descriptive; a descriptive summary of the decision-making process can be produced within the framework of the STS model. The relative frequencies, t_{ij}, of observed transitions in an established T matrix is the model's formal representation of this process. The pattern of the entries in such T matrices under various conditions can be examined to answer questions about the decision-making process of interest.

In the model-testing approach one compares the goodness-of-fit for several social transition schemes which are plausible, a priori, and/or span the range of reasonable model alternatives. The emphasis of the model is primarily predictive when this strategy is employed. The investigator constructs a T matrix whose entries are constrained by theoretical assumptions about the nature of the group decision-making process. To the extent that the model can accurately predict the observed transition (and hence, final product) data, those theoretical assumptions receive support. Studies by Davis, Stasser, Spitzer, and Holt (1976) and Godwin and Restle (1974) illustrate these two strategies.

Exploring Key Assumptions

The utility of the STS model depends, in part, on whether certain assumptions are valid. A number of the earliest applications of the model were devoted to exploring such assumptions. For example, an important assumption is that one can obtain the data necessary to apply the model without seriously altering the group process. There are at least two viable data collection techniques: (a) asking group members at regular intervals to indicate their currently most favored position (e.g., Stasser & Davis, 1976), or (b) continuously monitoring group members' preferences by having them signal (e.g., to a computer) any change in preference (e.g., Kerr, 1981). The former technique is more obtrusive and, thus, potentially more reactive. Kerr (1982) compared mock juries in which jurors were privately polled once every minute by the experimenter with juries who were not polled during deliberation. Periodic polling did not affect jury conviction rates or member perceptions of deliberation. There were some hints that polled groups were less likely to hang and could reach decisions faster, but none of these effects was significant. So it seems possible to follow member preferences continuously without seriously disrupting the group.

The complexity of the STS model may be reduced drastically in those cases where it is possible to satisfy two assumptions—stationarity and path independence. Stationarity implies that the process does not change over time; that is, the likelihood of a particular transition is constant throughout the group's interaction. Path independence means that the likelihood of shifting into a particular "group state" (i.e., distinguishable distribution) is independent of all previous states of the group except the current one. The investigation of the issues of stationarity and path independence represents more than preliminary steps in the construction of parsimonious models. These issues address fundamental questions about the nature of small group interaction: viz., how does the nature of the interaction change over time and how does the history of the group alter its future course? Using a mock jury task, Kerr (1981) obtained evidence that group decision making was both path dependent and nonstationary. The path dependence resembled a "momentum" effect—once someone shifted in one direction, further shifts in that direction were more likely than if no such initial shift had occurred. For example, the probability of a group member switching from a Guilty to a Not Guilty position (rather than the other way around) was .70 in groups that were evenly split [i.e., where $(r_G, r_{NG}) = (3, 3)$] at the start of deliberation. But this probability was higher (viz., .90) if the current even split in the group had been preceded by a defection to the Not Guilty side [i.e., a shift from (4, 2) to (3, 3)]. Subsequent research (Kerr et al., 1987) suggests that members of decision-making groups don't just jump on the bandwagon when they see another member switch positions. Rather, the momentum effect observed by Kerr (1981) seems to reflect group members reacting similarly (but not simultaneously) to arguments voiced during deliberation. The nonstationarity observed by Kerr (1981) reflected greater strength in numbers near the end of deliberation than near the beginning. For example, the probability of a minority member joining the majority when the jury was split (2, 4) was .73 during the first half of deliberation, but the same shift had a probability of .96 during the last half.

Interestingly, the path dependence and nonstationarity effects were fairly weak; one could predict the pattern of shifts-in-position almost as well with a simple model that incorrectly ignored these effects as one could with a much more complicated model which did not. Thus, where a group moves next as it travels down the road to agreement may depend most heavily on where it is right now, and not very heavily upon the route by which it got here or upon how long it has been traveling.

Exploring Task, Member, and Group Factors

One useful way of applying the STS model is to examine in a group decision-making context variables previously studied in less complex social influence contexts (e.g., attitude change, conformity). For example, many studies of conformity and attitude change have asked: Are males or females more influenceable? Consistent with the overall pattern in this previous research (e.g., Eagly, 1978), Kerr (1981) found that the transition schemes for all-male and all-female mock juries were statistically indistinguishable.

There is also considerable evidence from the attitude change literature (e.g.,

Sherif & Hovland, 1961) that those who take more extreme positions are less easily influenced than those taking less extreme positions. This suggests that, all other things being equal, group factions taking extreme positions should be less likely to experience defections than less extreme factions. Kerr (1983) examined group distributions in which factions of equal size differed only in their extremity. For example, in a 4-person group with a (2, 2, 0, 0, 0, 0) distribution across ordered alternatives, an extremity hypothesis predicts that transitions into the first alternative are more likely than transitions into the second alternative. The extremity hypothesis was confirmed.

Some early conformity research (Asch, 1956) suggested that as the size of a group of confederates making an incorrect judgment increased, the probability of conformity by an isolated subject also increased up to a point and then tended to level off. Other work (e.g., Gerard, Wilhelmy, & Conolley, 1968) suggested that conformity may increase steadily with majority size. Using the STS model, Kerr and MacCoun (1985) were able to examine this issue in decision-making groups. They found that a group member who was a minority-of-one was relatively less likely to shift towards the majority (rather than draw a convert from the majority) when the majority consisted of 2 persons than when it had 5 or 11 persons. There was little difference between the latter two conditions, but this was not necessarily because larger majority factions were not more powerful. It was because even with only 5 persons in the majority, almost all shifts (viz. 96%) were towards rather than away from the majority.

The power of the majority, at least for certain tasks, was nicely demonstrated in a model-testing STS application by Goodwin and Restle (1974). Groups of 3 to 6 members attempted to reach consensus on which of four multidimensional stimulus arrays another (bogus) group had chosen as "most outstanding." Rather than fit observed transition data using the STS model, Goodwin and Restle tested the goodness-of-fit of several plausible theoretical processes that might underlie such transitions. For example, a *random model* that predicted that group members randomly changed their opinions until group consensus was reached could be confidently rejected. They also tested a *dyadic model* which assumed that each member at a different position than one's own exerts the same degree of attraction as every other such member. The dyadic model was also frequently refuted by their data. Larger subgroups seemed to have more "drawing power" than smaller subgroups.

This finding led Godwin and Restle to examine two subgroup models. The first assumed that each subgroup (i.e., faction) of a fixed size had a unique *attractiveness*, which determined the probability of another member joining that position. This model was found to be significantly less accurate than a more complex one in which the attractiveness of a subgroup depended not only upon the size of the subgroup, but also upon the overall size of the group. The estimates of the attractiveness parameters for this fourth model suggested that subgroups with all but one group member were extremely attractive, and all subgroups with at least a majority were also very much more attractive than the submajority subgroups. For example, consider the results for Godwin and Restle's 6-person groups. Denoting the attractiveness of a faction with i persons as β_i and setting $\beta_1 = 1.0$, they obtained the following estimates: $\hat{\beta}_2 = 2.48$, $\hat{\beta}_3 = 8.33$, $\hat{\beta}_4 = 46.0$, and $\hat{\beta}_5 = 189.1$. Clearly, the attractiveness (or drawing power) of a subgroup increased very rapidly as the size of the subgroup reached and surpassed a majority.

A related question is whether pluralities also have unusual (i.e., disproportionate) drawing power in group discussion. To explore this question, Kerr (1983) estimated and contrasted some key elements of estimated T matrices for groups seeking consensus on social issues with ordered alternatives (e.g., strongly agree to strongly disagree with an attitudinal statement). For example, if a plurality's drawing power in group discussion is proportional to its size, the person in the middle of a group with a (2, 1, 1) split should be twice as likely to shift toward the larger faction on his or her left as to shift toward the smaller faction on the right. However, the actual observed probability of the former type of shift was .93, significantly higher than the .67 value suggested by a simple proportionality model.

Godwin and Restle's (1974) and Kerr's (1982) studies also illustrate how application of the STS model can inform us about the nature of the social influence processes occurring in decision-making groups. If there is even a rough proportionality between the size of a faction and the number of persuasive arguments it will generate, we would expect the drawing power of a faction to be roughly proportional to its size. In terms of the Godwin and Restle models, this implies that $\beta_i = i \beta_1$. But, as we noted earlier for the 6-person groups, $\hat{\beta}_i$ far exceeds $i \beta_1$; e.g., $\hat{\beta}_6 = 189.1 \gg 6 \beta_1 = 6$. Such data for judgmental decision tasks seem more simply explained in terms of some sort of normative social influence process. For example, members of very small minorities may recognize the low probability of prevailing and the high costs of continuing to hold out, and yield to the majority.

Although the STS model is fairly new, there have been several other interesting applications. These include:

(a) contrasts of different-sized groups (12- and 6-person juries are characterized by similar transition schemes, which differ in interesting ways from 3-person juries; Kerr & MacCoun, 1985);

(b) contrasts of groups with and without discussion time limits (the estimated T matrices for mock juries with and without time limits are not distinguishable; Kerr, 1981);

(c) contrasts of factions separated by small vs. large distances (defections from majority factions toward a minority faction are more likely when there is more room for compromise between them; Kerr, 1983);

and (d) contrasts between social issues of high and low importance (Kerr, 1983, observed somewhat faster movement for low importance issues, but no other clear process differences).

Thus, the STS model has demonstrated that one can describe, analyze, and predict groups' movement down the road to agreement by utilizing the momentary distribution of member preferences in the group as the primary unit of analyses. This basic approach can also be the basis for more elaborate predictive models. For example, others have extended the basic idea of examining transition probabilities to explore a variety of group processes which take place across time or across trials (e.g., group induction of a rule or concept, Laughlin & McGlynn, 1986; the development of cooperation in iterated social dilemmas, Komorita, 1987). Additionally, several computer models that are discussed in the next section elaborate on the basic idea of an STS rate model; they are models of group movement that incorporate individual difference variables such as confidence and influenceability.

SOCIAL TRANSITIONS AND MEMBER CHANGE: SIS, DICE, AND DISCUSS MODELS

SDS and STS models represent group movement and decision making at the level of the group. The decision scheme matrix D in SDS theory describes the relationship between the distribution of sentiment among members at the onset of discussion and the group's final decision. The transition matrix T in STS notation describes the movement of groups from one configuration of opinion to another. These models emphasize the idea that the distribution of opinions within a group at one point in time forecasts what is likely to occur at a later time. This forecast depends on social processes that generate systematic and predictable patterns of change during the group's interaction.

SDS and STS share several features that make them very attractive and useful: they accomodate different theories and types of social influence; their basic structure is amenable to concise mathematical expression; and, considering the complexity of group interaction, their application requires relatively little data. In sum, such models provide general and flexible frameworks for examining and thinking about group decision processes. There are times, however, when research questions and goals require closer examination of what is happening within the group. A theme of this chapter is that decision schemes and social transitions reflect groups members' mutual and reciprocal influence. But, because decision schemes and social transitions are group level expressions, they are necessarily somewhat removed from what individual members are doing from moment to moment.

In this section, we discuss a set of models that focus more directly on what is happening at the level of members' interactions. Stasser and Davis' (1981) social interaction sequence (SIS) model follows very closely the conceptual and notational traditions of the SDS and STS models. A similar, but independently developed, model is Penrod and Hastie's (1980) DICE model. Among other similarities, the SIS and DICE models both operate on the assumption that the likelihood that members will change their opinions depends on the distribution of support within a group—a theme that continues from the SDS and STS traditions. The DISCUSS model (Stasser, in press) breaks from this tradition in some respects. It represents group discussion and decision as information sampling and integration, building on points of view expressed in Burnstein and Vinokur (1977), Kaplan (1977), and Anderson and Graesser (1976).

Besides their focus on individual member behavior, the SIS, DICE and DISCUSS models share other features. Most notably, they are computer simulation models. Unlike the SDS and STS models, they cannot be stated as closed mathematical expressions. Rather they attempt to capture the dynamics of group influence in computer programs. These programs: (a) maintain records of each member's opinion state (e.g., Juror A currently favors *guilty* but has some doubt); (b) compute probablilities of critical events occurring given the present conditions within a group (e.g., likelihood of Juror A switching to *not-guilty* given that he is unsure and 8 of his fellow jurors favor not-guilty); and (c) using these probabilities, identify which of the possible events happen. This last step of converting probabilities to occurrences is accomplished using a Monte Carlo technique. To illustrate the Monte Carlo strategy, consider the following juncture in the simulation of a group's interaction. Member X of a 9-person committee currently supports the motion before the group but is wavering. The remaining eight members are split four to four. Further suppose that the theoretical relations being modeled suggest that Member X has a .1 chance of switching to the opposition and a .9 of staying on the next vote. A Monte Carlo procedure determines whether she switches or stays by sampling a random number from a uniform distribution of numbers ranging 0 to 1. If the number sampled is less than .1, X switches; otherwise, she stays.

In a typical simulation of group process, the steps of computing probabilities, determining what *actually* happens given these probabilities, and updating members' records to reflect changes are repeated for each member for each of many time periods. Moreover, a simulation ordinarily runs many groups under identical circumstances in a manner analogous to running many replications in an empirical study. (Obviously, computer simulation can require considerable computing capacity and time. This requirement was not a trivial consideration in the past, but is of little concern today. The computing demands of programs like those used for the SIS, DICE, and DISCUSS models are within the capabilities of the current generation of desk-top, personal computers.)

One advantage of computer simulation is that a model can accommodate complex relationships. In fact, the complexity of a simulation model is often limited only by the ingenuity of the researcher and the skills of the programmer. Complexity can grow in two ways. First, a program can keep a continually updated record of many variables pertaining to the socio-psychological states of individual members (e.g., preference, recall of facts, certainty of opinion, persuability, talkativeness, etc.) and to the group's social/task climate (e.g., faction sizes, time pressures or limits, explicit or implicit decision rules, etc.). Second, a program can accommodate numerous sequential dependencies among events. For example, a model can specify the effect of Member X switching her vote on the probabilities that other members will switch on the next vote or the effect of no member switching over a series of votes on the likelihood that discussion will end in a stalemate.

Permitting a degree of complexity in a model is necessary when one tries to decompose group movement into the sequential actions and reactions of individual group members. As Abelson (1968) states, "Computer simulation in principle permits bridges to be built between islands of theoretical analysis that otherwise might remain unrelated, namely, the psychology of individuals and the behavior of large groups" (p. 288). In sum, computer models can translate ideas about what group members do into predictions about what groups end up doing.

Admitting that some complexity is necessary is not to be taken as an endorsement of unduly complex models. The goals of parsimony and plausibility are as relevant to the development of computer models as to other forms of theoretical expression. For a model to be theoretically and practically useful, it must maintain some simplicity by focusing on some processes to the exclusion of others. At the same time, the model should be plausible and consistent with existing theoretical and empirical evidence. The compromise between sufficient and excessive complexity and the attempt to blend theoretical and empirical evidence is accomplished in slightly different ways by the SIS, DICE, and DISCUSS models.

SIS Model

The SIS model represents members in terms of their preference among the decision alternatives and their level of certainty. For example, given a two-alternative task (e.g., guilty vs. not-guilty in a jury trial or pass vs. defeat a motion in a committee), the SIS model classifies members in one of four states at a given point in time depending on preference (A_1 or A_2) and certainty (certain or uncertain). Group interaction is recorded as members' movement into and out of these preference/certainty states.

Changes of preference and certainty are thought to follow orderly patterns. In part, these patterns are due to a presumed dependence between level of certainty and changes of preference. In the model, individuals who are certain of their preference will not change their minds. For them to actively consider adopting a new preference, their confidence in their present position must be eroded. Moreover, the model assumes that individuals who change their preference are, at least momentarily, uncertain. These assertions about the dependence between certainty and opinion change imply that members may change in one of two ways at any point in time: They may become certain or uncertain of their current preference *or*, if currently uncertain, they may change their preference.

At the core of the SIS model is the notion of an *influence function*, a formal expression that specifies the relationship between the probability of change (be it a change of certainty level or preference) and the current distribution of opinion within the group. To express the idea of an influence function more formally using the notation of the SDS and STS models, let r_1 and r_2 denote the number of members preferring each of two decision alternatives, A_1 and A_2, respectively. Then the distinguishable distribution or group state is expressed as (r_1, r_2). As r_1, the number of advocates for A_1, increases (and, thus, r_2 decreases) further changes in favor of A_1 should be facilitated. That is, increasing r_1 should increase the probabilities of changes in favor of A_1 including: an uncertain A_1-advocate becoming certain, an uncertain A_2-advocate switching to A_1, and a certain A_2-advocate becoming uncertain (and, thus, becoming a candidate for switching to A_1 during subsequent interaction). Of course, increasing r_2, the number of A_2 advocates, should have the obverse effects.

In the end, the SIS model requires that one be more exact about the form of the relationship between faction sizes and probabilities of members' changing certainty level or preference. Many possibilities for the exact form of the influence function are suggested by the social influence literature (cf. Latane & Nida, 1980; Godwin & Restle, 1974; Penrod & Hastie, 1980; and Stasser & Davis, 1976). Stasser and Davis (1981) used functions based on the idea that a faction's ability to induce change favoring its position is related to its proportional size. This proportionality idea implies, for example, that a faction of 3 in a 12-person group and a faction of 2 in a 6-person group have the same influence potential, other things being equal. Using the data from several mock jury studies, Stasser and Davis (1981) examined the behavior of the SIS model using both linear and nonlinear (viz., cubic and quadratic) functions of proportional faction size to account for movement of members' among preference and certainty states. They found that linear functions predicted movements from certainty to uncertainty (and vice versa) whereas changes of preference were best predicted by a positively accelerating (quadratic) function of proportional size. This accelerating influence function for preference changes predicts that a faction's ability to persuade the uncertain members of the opposition increases rapidly as the faction grows beyond a mere majority. Note that this result for preference changes is consistent with the findings of Godwin and Restle (1974) which were discussed earlier.

Stasser and Davis (1981) supposed that purely informational influence during discussion would tend to generate linear influence functions whereas accelerating functions suggest normative pressures in addition to informational influence.

Thus, they concluded from this application of the SIS model to mock jury data that members' revisions of certainty are primarily responsive to the informational content of discussion whereas changes of preference, when members are uncertain, are affected by both normative and informational influences. They further noted that this conclusion converges nicely with the idea in the social influence literature that *public* change is more susceptible to normative pressures than is *private* change (cf. Allen, 1965). In a decision-making group, a member's waxing and waning of certainty are not necessarily apparent to others whereas a change of opinion, as evidenced by formal votes or informal expressions of preference, is public.

The influence functions summarize the theoretical notions about social influence that underlie a particular instantiation of the SIS model. As Stasser and Davis (1981) illustrated in their examination of several plausible forms for the influence functions, various theories of social influence can be competitively evaluated in terms of their ability to account for the results of existing group decision data. However, the ability to account for existing data is only a part of the value of a working computer model. It can also be used to evaluate the effects of changing basic parameters of decision environments. The SIS model receives as input the distribution of opinions and certainty in the population from which groups are composed, group size, number of decision alternatives, assigned decision rule (e.g., simple majority, two-thirds majority, unanimity), and maximum discussion time. In addition to predicting the distribution of group decisions (or the likelihood of particular decisions), the SIS computer model outputs the distribution of members preferences and their level of certainty as they leave the group and the amount of time that the group took to reach a decision. Thus, armed with a set of influence functions that seem to capture the social influence dynamics, one can explore the probable effects of changing the values of input variables (e.g., group size, decision rule, etc.) on the likelihood of particular group decisions, and on member's postdecisional preferences and certainty. For example, Stasser and Davis (1981) examined the predicted effects of group size and assigned decision rule and found that the model predicted higher postdecisional certainty for members of larger groups deliberating under unanimity rules.

DICE Model

Penrod and Hastie's (1980) DICE model was developed primarily as a model of jury decision making but, as the authors noted, the underlying theoretical analysis could apply to other kinds of groups. In fact, the model could apply to any two-alternative decision task. Hastie et al. (1983) extended DICE to obtain the JUS model which permits multiple ordered decision alternatives (e.g., first degree murder, second degree murder, ... , reckless manslaughter). In many ways, the DICE and SIS models are similar. For example, at the heart of the DICE model is the idea that the likelihood of a juror switching a vote from guilty to not-guilty (or vice versa) increases as the size of the opposing faction increases. Moreover, the DICE model accepts as input the distribution of opinions in the population from which juries are composed, jury size, and decision rule.

There are two differences between the models that are noteworthy. First, the DICE model does not distinguish uncertain from certain members, but does include a *persuasion resistance* (PR) parameter that serves a related function. In composing a simulated jury, the DICE model assigns jurors an initial PR value (either randomly to simulate naturally occurring individual differences or systematically to reflect known or hypothesized differences among subpopulations of jurors). Jurors with higher PR values are less likely to change than ones with low PR values. The PR parameter plays another role in that it is incremented when a juror switches sides to accommodate the empirical evidence that jurors rarely change their vote and then subsequently revert to their original position.

A second difference concerns the ways in which the DICE and SIS models end discussion. Both models stop discussion if enough members agree to satisfy an assigned decision rule. But, in the absence of a sufficient consensus, the SIS model stops discussion after a maximum allowed discussion time has been exceeded, whereas the DICE model identifies a "critical time (TL) beyond which jurors are unwilling to continue deliberation unless it appears that there is a strong possibility of reaching a verdict" (Penrod & Hastie, 1980, p. 143). When the TL has elapsed the program checks to see if anyone has changed their vote within the past few ballots. If so, the critical time is renewed and deliberation continues; if not, the jury is considered deadlocked (i.e., "hung").

In sum, DICE and SIS were built to mimic similar patterns of influence in decision-making groups. At the core of each model is a routine that simulates the effects of discussion on members' opinions. As Hastie et al. (1983) noted, however, these models do not mimic the actual behavior of discussion but instead they try to capture the results of discussion. That is, there are no parts of the computer programs that represent members recalling information, formulating arguments, speaking, or integrating the contents of discussion into their assessments of the decision alternatives. But both models presume, based on strong empirical evidence, that these actions of discussion will generate predictable changes during the course of discussion.

Penrod and Hastie (1980) and Hastie et al. (1983) demonstrated how DICE and its progeny JUS can account for available deliberation results. Just as importantly, these models also provide convenient ways of conceptualizing the related processes of jury selection, balloting, deliberating and rendering a verdict (see, for example, the presentation of the JUS model in Hastie et al., 1983). Moreover, the models provide a means of projecting beyond the available evidence. For example, Hastie et al. (1983) examined the predicted effects of changing jury size (from 12 to 6) and found that simulated 6-person juries were more likely than the actual 12-person juries to choose extreme verdicts (i.e., first-degree murder or not guilty as opposed to intermediate verdicts of second-degree murder or manslaughter). Tanford and Penrod (1983) simulated the effects of a resolute minority on the outcomes of deliberation for 6- and 12-person groups using varying decision rules (e.g., simple majority, two-thirds majority, or unanimity). Among other things, their simulations suggested that 6-person juries are more affected by a resolute minority than 12-person juries. Somewhat surprisingly decision rule did not seem to affect the degree of minority impact.

DISCUSS Model

Whereas SIS, DICE, and JUS model the moment-to-moment *results* of discussion, DISCUSS models discussion processes—turn-taking in speaking, recalling and presenting information, and revaluating preferences. Its development was motivated by empirical work examining the flow of information through discussion (Stasser & Titus, 1985, 1987).

DISCUSS (Stasser, in press) is a computer simulation model that is based on an information processing view of group decision making. Group members are represented as information integrators and are presumed to develop a ledger of supporting and opposing information for each alternative. Their preferences are determined by the information that they currently recall. From this perspective, discussion serves to fill in the ledger of information by reminding members of information that they have momentarily forgotten or by giving them information that they never had. As members receive new or are reminded of old information, they reevaluate their preferences. A group decision is reached when a sufficient number of members agree to satisfy the operative decision rule. In sum, the model starts with the information that members are given before discussion and ends with a predicted group decision.

Input to the DISCUSS model includes group size, the number of decision alternatives, and the number of items of information available about each alternative. Items of information are identified as supporting or opposing decision alternatives. Items can also be assigned different weights to reflect differences in importance or extremity. Group members are distinguished by the informational items that they receive before discussion. Moreover, simulated group members can themselves weight differently the items when forming or reevaluating their preferences. Thus, members can disagree initially because they have been given or recall different information or because they weight the information differently.

The DISCUSS program simulates group formation and discussion by these basic steps:

Prediscussion Recall—For each member, DISCUSS computes a probability of item recall (which depends in part on how much information each member receives) and then determines, using a Monte Carlo procedure, the items actually recalled out of the total set received.
Prediscussion Preference—Given the items recalled and their weights, DISCUSS

computes each member's initial preference. The present version of DISCUSS uses an averaging algorithm for integrating information to form preferences.

Discussion—For each discussion period, DISCUSS samples the discussant and the item discussed from the discussant's memory. The model can simulate either equal or unequal rates of participation among members. An ADVOCACY version of the model makes items supporting a member's current preference more likely to be sampled than opposing items. A NONADVOCACY version represents members as impartial fact-finders in that their current preference does not bias their contributions.

Preference Update—DISCUSS adds the discussed item to the members' memories and recomputes their preferences. A NONORM version of DISCUSS assumes that discussion serves only to exchange information but that members may continue to weight information differently. A NORM version assumes that discussion not only informs but also serves to reduce disagreement about the importance or evaluative extremity of information; that is, in the NORM version, any discrepancies in members' weighting of an item is reduced when an item is discussed.

Decision—If a sufficient number of members agree, DISCUSS terminates discussion and records the decision. Otherwise, DISCUSS continues to the next discussion period. (DISCUSS also ends discussion if no new information is contributed over a predetermined number of discussion periods.)

Although DISCUSS is predominantly an information sampling and integration model, it does include various ways for social processes to intrude on information processing. ADVOCACY versions permit current preferences to bias the informational content of discussion. NORM versions assume that members resolve, at least in part, their differences regarding the relative importance and evaluative extremity of information when it is discussed. In these versions, discussion is not viewed as purely rational or asocial information processing.

Unlike the other models that we have considered, DISCUSS has not yet been extensively tested with empirical data. This lack of tests is due in part to its being relatively new. Moreover, DISCUSS requires a different type of database. Models in the SDS tradition (SDS, STS, and SIS) and the DICE/JUS models use initial preference distributions as input to the group's interaction whereas DISCUSS starts with the way in which information is distributed among group members before discussion. There are few data sets where the explicit information distribution is available.

An exception is a study by Stasser and Titus (1985), who manipulated what decision-relevant information each member had before discussion. In some conditions of their experiment, they distributed information before discussion so that members individually had information that was biased against the best alternative, but each group collectively could identify this best choice by pooling members' information. Although there was this potential for pooling, few groups identified the best choice when the members received such biased sets of information before discussion. Stasser (in press) demonstrated that this failure could be accounted for by the information sampling and integration dynamics as represented in DISCUSS. Indeed, a NONADVOCACY/NORM version of the model postdicted very well the decisions of Stasser and Titus' (1985) groups. The model's success in this case suggests that the failure of their groups to discover the choice favored by their collective knowledge need not be attributed to defective information processing as in "groupthink" (Janis, 1972) or to conformity pressures negating informational influence. The NONADVOCACY/NORM version of DISCUSS represents members as unbiased fact-finders whose only fault is their poor memory. The social pressures in NORM pertain to resolving any differences among members in the weighting or importance attached to information after it is mentioned. Therefore, these social pressures are treated as secondary to information exchange in this model. However, one might still wonder if the social pressures as represented in NORM were critical to simulating the failure of Stasser and Titus' (1985) groups to effectively pool information. In this regard, it is interesting to note that the NONADVOCACY/NONORM simulated groups were actually less likely to discover the best option under the conditions that Stasser and Titus (1985) considered. What these simulations highlight is that group discussions, even when represented as members' unbiasedly sampling what they know, do not necessarily compensate for uneven distributions of information among members.

DISCUSS, being primarily a model of discussion process, can explore the effects of varying discussion dynamics on group level summaries such as social decision and transition schemes. The DISCUSS program provides as an option SDS and STS summaries of simulation results. For example, one might wonder whether a "cold" information processing account of discussion (as in the NONADVOCACY/NONORM version) produces different patterns of movement than a "warm" processing version (as in ADVOCACY/NORM). Table 9.6 presents the SDS and STS summaries for 100 ADVOCACY/NORM and 100 NONADVOCACY/NONORM simulated groups. In all cases, 4-person simulated groups were deciding between two alternatives which had equal amounts of supporting information. In the simulations, members received an unbiased subset of the total information before discussion; these subsets were distributed among members so that each group collectively had the total set of information.

The results demonstrate that advocacy discussions with resolution of members' weighting differences (i.e., ADVOCACY/NORM) generates a strength-in-numbers pattern in the STS matrix and a strong majority social decision scheme. The strength-in-numbers effects are evidenced in the transitions of (3, 1) and (1, 3) groups who were more likely to move to the unanimous (4, 0) or (0, 4) states than to the split (2, 2) state. In contrast, cold information processing as represented in the NONADVOCACY/NONORM model reversed the strength-in-numbers effect. In this case, (3, 1) and (1, 3) groups were more likely to return to (2, 2) than go to unanimous agreement. As a result, many of these groups did not reach decisions giving rise to the high proportion of *hung* groups in the SDS summary. However, when NONADVOCACY/NONORM groups did reach de-

TABLE 9.6
SDS and STS Summaries of the Simulation of
NONADVOCACY/NONORM and ADVOCACY/NORM Decision-Making Groups

NONADVOCACY/NONORM Simulation Results

	STS T Matrix						SDS D Matrix			
	$k+1$						Decision			
	(0,4)	(1,3)	(2,2)	(3,1)	(4,0)		A	B	Hung	N
(0,4)	1.00					(0,4)		1.00		5
(1,3)	0.05	0.78	0.16	0.01		(1,3)	0.04	0.48	0.48	23
k (2,2)		0.10	0.79	0.11		(2,2)	0.31	0.19	0.50	36
(3,1)		0.02	0.13	0.80	0.05	(3,1)	0.46	0.19	0.35	26
(4,0)				0.50	0.50	(4,0)	0.70		0.30	10

ADVOCACY/NORM Simulation Results

	STS T Matrix						SDS D Matrix			
	$k+1$						Decision			
	(0,4)	(1,3)	(2,2)	(3,1)	(4,0)		A	B	Hung	N
(0,4)	--	--	--	--	--	(0,4)	--	--	--	0
(1,3)	0.21	0.61	0.15	0.03	0.01	(1,3)	0.15	0.85	0.00	27
k (2,2)	0.02	0.14	0.68	0.15	0.02	(2,2)	0.50	0.40	0.10	40
(3,1)		0.02	0.11	0.70	0.17	(3,1)	0.82	0.18	0.00	22
(4,0)					1.00	(4,0)	1.00			11

cisions, initial majorities were much more likely to prevail than were initial minorities. An interesting footnote is the fact that DISCUSS permits a brief discussion even when groups are initially in agreement. As evident in the last line of the STS matrix, this brief discussion was sufficient to create disagreement in one half (5) of the 10 NONADVOCACY/NONORM groups who started in a (4, 0) state. Moreover, the SDS matrix reveals that 3 of these groups never recovered their initial agreement. In sum, nonadvocacy information exchange does not generate patterns of movement that are typical of decision-making groups. But including advocacy and normative resolution of members' differential weighting of information produces patterns more suggestive of strength-in-numbers social influence.

Our wonders, however, if even the ADVOCACY/NORM version of DISCUSS is sufficiently *warm* to account for a wide-range of decision-making data. The strength-in-numbers patterns generated by this model (see Table 9.6) are not particularly strong. The model with its rather mild versions of normative and conformity pressures may be able to account for decision making when tasks or situations encourage decisions based on information but may give an inadequate account when decision making is driven by normative concerns. For example, Hastie et al. (1983) identified two dominant modes of deliberation in their juries: verdict-driven and evidence-driven. Their verdict-driven style is characterized by frequent polling and frequent statements of preference whereas the evidence-driven style postpones polling and expressions of preference until the evidence has been reviewed. The present versions of DISCUSS may be more appropriate for evidence-driven, than for verdict-driven, deliberations. Similarly, Kaplan and Miller (1987) argued that some tasks are amenable to resolution by argument because there is an abundance of relevant facts to consider (argument-rich tasks) whereas other decisions are more matters of judgment or social value and lack relevant factual arguments (argument-poor tasks). Again, we suspect that the DISCUSS model is better suited for modeling decisions for argument-rich than argument-poor tasks.

One advantage of computer modeling is that it forces one to be very explicit about how social processes are represented. Being explicit makes the strengths and limitations of a model more apparent. The DISCUSS model is clearly, first and foremost, an informational influence model and as such provides a useful way of modeling information flow during group discussion. However, we suspect that it may not provide enough opportunity for other kinds of social influence to operate. Of course, another advantage of modeling is that the recognition of deficiencies sometimes suggests remedies. For example, Hartwick, Sheppard, and Davis (1982) reviewed evidence that speakers may bias their arguments (or recall of facts) to fit the perceived sentiments of the audience, and they suggested that speakers in a group may likewise slant their recall in light of the prevailing sentiment in the groups. Thus, normative influence may intrude much more actively at the point of information recall than any of the present versions of DISCUSS admit. The ADVOCACY versions permit recall to be biased by the speaker's preference but not by his or her perception of others' preferences. However, because the model keeps a continually updated record of everyone's preference, it could very easily adjust recall probabilities to reflect not only the speaker's but also others' preferences. Furthermore, the present versions of DISCUSS do not consider uniformity pressures. That is, in the model, all opinion change emanates from discussed information, not from any concerns about moving the group toward consensus. It seems possible in principle to add a consensus-seeking component to the model and, thereby, make it applicable to a wider range of tasks and situations.

GROUP INFLUENCE AND CONSENSUS MODELS:
A REPRISE

We have reviewed a series of group decision-making models that address how member preferences and dispositions are transformed or combined to yield a collective decision. The SDS model provides the most general representation by expressing the group process as a probabilistic rule applied to initial member preferences. STS extends the SDS approach to examine movement from one alignment of member preferences to another during the course of interaction.

Finally, the several computer models considered (SIS, DICE, JUS, and DIS-CUSS) further decompose the movement of groups into a series of discussion events. Thus, the models can be thought of as progressing from the general group level representation, spanning the entire interaction as provided by SDS, to the more specific representation of group members' behavior occuring over brief periods of time as in the DISCUSS model.

A particularly attractive feature of these models is that they share units of analysis—most notably, the distribution of members' preferences (i.e., the distinguishable distribution in SDS terminology) and the decision rule. As a result, they are upwardly commensurable. For example, a **T** matrix in an STS model can in principle generate a **D** matrix in SDS. Moreover, as Stasser and Davis (1981) illustrated, a particular choice of influence functions in the SIS model leads to comparable STS rate and shift models with the aid of a few simplifying assumptions. And, as illustrated earlier, the DISCUSS model can generate both **T** and **D** matrices. The advantage of such commensurability goes well beyond having shared notation and terminology and includes the potential for integrating the empirical findings and theoretical developments associated with each model. In sum, these models offer many different ways of representing group influence and decision making, but, at the same time, permit one to move from one representation or level of analysis to another.

We have reviewed applications of the models and, in doing so, raised many substantive issues. Earlier, we suggested that there often may be strength in numbers in decision-making groups due to four different social influence processes: normative influence, informational influence, social comparison, and group locomotion. The fact that strength in numbers often characterizes social influence in decision-making groups is hardly a controversial or surprising result. Moreover, it should be evident that characterizing social influence as strength-in-numbers is not sufficiently precise, by itself, to yield useful predictive and descriptive models of group decision making. On the one hand, there are many qualitatively different modes of influence that give rise to patterns of opinion change and convergence that can be generally described as strength-in-numbers. On the other hand, there are decision tasks and environments that seem to generate quite different kinds of group interaction.

For example, Laughlin (1980; Laughlin & Ellis, 1986) suggested that various kinds of decision tasks can be viewed as falling at different points along a continuum from judgmental to intellective tasks. Intellective tasks are ones for which one alternative can be demonstrated to be the correct answer (according to a commonly accepted system of inference or body of culturally shared knowledge). Typical examples of intellective tasks are mathematical problems or items on a vocabulary test. In contrast, judgmental tasks are ones that have no demonstrably correct answer. In fact, if a task is purely judgmental, there would be few, if any, logical or factual bases for defending a particular preference. Examples of tasks that are highly judgmental include guessing which of a random sequence of events will occur next or choosing the most aesthetically pleasing picture from a set of abstract paintings. Frequently studied group-decision tasks such as mock jury cases probably fall somewhere in the midrange of the continuum. For instance, a jury case typically provides evidence and lines of argument supporting one decision over another. Yet, the available evidence and arguments are rarely sufficiently compelling to identify a demonstrably correct verdict.

Laughlin and Ellis (1986) reviewed studies that used SDS and STS analyses and suggested that strength-in-numbers processes such as "majority rules" seem to characterize interaction when groups are considering tasks that lack demonstrably correct answers. When groups attempt to solve intellective tasks, their decision process is more aptly described as "truth-wins" or "truth-supported wins." That is, if a correct answer is easily demonstrated or obvious when proposed, a correct minority (even a minority of one) can prevail (i.e., truth-wins). In the event that a correct answer is more difficult to demonstrate, a "truth-supported wins" process seems to emerge; a single correct member may not be able to persuade the group but a correct minority of two usually can. Thus, for intellective tasks, it seems that informational influence favors the correct faction which may or may not be the largest faction.

Laughlin and Ellis (1986) also identified a class of tasks that are not only judgmental but also engender relatively little personal commitment to particular alternatives. For these tasks, any alternative that is favored by at least one group member is as likely to win as any other supported alternative. That is, an *equiprobability* decision scheme seems to apply; it is as though groups resolve their differences by flipping a coin, and faction size seems to matter little. Of course, we doubt that groups actually resort to flipping a coin (or some similar random process) to resolve their differences. It is more likely that nuances of personality (e.g., dominance) or interaction (i.e., facial expressions) become more important as tasks become extremely subjective. Or it may be that the group recognizes that there is virtually no basis for resolving the issue by debate and thus converges on the first position that is advocated (if that position is at least minimally acceptable to most of the members). At any rate, it seems that for many kinds of tasks social influence processes do not necessarily favor larger factions.

In addition to task types, we suspect that there are various modes or types of social influence that may provide important exceptions and qualifications to the strength-in-numbers character of group decision process. Probably the best known and most inclusive taxonomy of social influence processes is French and Raven's (1959) bases of social power. Several of these correspond closely to social influence processes we have already considered; normative influence corresponds to reward/coercive power, whereas informational influence and, to some degree, social comparison represent varieties of informational power. French and Raven also distinguished a number of social influence processes which, like reward/coercive power, are socially dependent (i.e., depend on characteristics of the influencing agent), but, unlike reward/coercive power, do not require surveillance of the influencing agent. We sometimes change our opinions or behaviors because someone has expert power (i.e., has special expertise, like a physician in medical matters), referent power (i.e., is someone with whom we identify or wish to emulate, like an admired celebrity), or legitimate power (i.e., is someone who has the legitimate right to dictate our behavior, like someone of higher rank in a military setting). It seems very likely that these social influence processes also arise in decision-making groups. All other things being equal, we would expect the preferences of group members who are recognized as more knowledgeable on the decision task, serve as important referents for other group members, and occupy positions of authority (e.g., group leader) to attract greater support. We have suggested several ways that member attributes can be accommodated in social-combination models.

For example, Kirchler and Davis (1986) manipulated perceptions of group members' task ability (akin to expertise) in an application of the social decision scheme model. They found that a "power wins" decision scheme which incorporated differences in members' apparent ability accounted for decisions at judgmental tasks better than the simple majority wins scheme (which treated group members as indistinguishable). For an intellective task, ability differences were less important; a "truth-wins" model provided the best overall fit. Thus, Kirchler and Davis' data suggest that expert power is more important for judgmental tasks than for intellective tasks. In much the same way, social combination models could be used to explore such individual difference and group structure factors as member attractiveness, in/outgroup membership, and formal status in the group (e.g., leader).

A more recent taxonomy of social influence processes has been suggested by Cialdini (1984). Again, many of Cialdini's psychological principles underlying effective social influence attempts correspond to social influence processes we have already discussed (e.g., Cialdini's "liking" principle corresponds to French and Raven's notion of referent power; his "authority" principle includes elements of expert and legitimate power), but some are novel. For example, Cialdini suggests that concessions toward an opponent engage a norm of reciprocity; one feels obligated to reciprocate such concessions. This notion makes clear predictions about the sequencing of shifts between opposing factions in decision-making groups, predictions which have not but could be explored using more process-oriented social-combination models (e.g., STS and SIS). A related question is whether and when concessions on one decision task lead to reciprocated concessions from others on subsequent decision tasks; although there is much anecdotal evidence for such "log rolling," it has not been the subject of systematic social psychological study.

Our emphasis on traditional avenues of social influence has lead us to emphasize two mechanisms of influence: information exchange (argumentation) and expressions of preference (whether formal as in voting or informal as in evaluative statements made during the course of discussion). There is a wealth of other kinds of interactional data that one could incorporate into models of influence. For example, one could consider not only what is said during discussion but how it is said. Word choice and syntax as well as attendant nonverbal behaviors (gestures, posture, eye movements, and the like) may affect the persuasiveness of arguments and the impact of normative appeals. Important technical advances in data acquisition (e.g., video recording) and major conceptual developments in analyzing interaction data (e.g., block models, Arabie, Boorman, & Levitt, 1978; sequential periodicities, Gottman & Bakeman, 1979; modes of verbal expression, Stiles, 1978; and relational data, Iacobucci & Wasserman, 1987) hold considerable promise for the direct study of interaction. (See Dabbs & Ruback, 1987, for a summary and review.)

Unfortunately, advantages offered by most techniques for interaction research have been largely confined to the investigation of dyads; applications to larger groups continue to be fairly intractable. It is also evident that a substantial gap still remains between the tallying of conversational nuances, speaker sequences, discussion climate, etc., and the necessary theoretical notions that actually connect these components of interaction with the group product or decision. However, it is equally evident that important beginnings have been made on developing both necessary conceptual equipment and the means for gathering such data.

Finally, we note that our focus on the processes leading to the group decision has overlooked group influence that extends beyond the point of the decision. We mentioned briefly that the SIS model can in theory address members' postdecisional certainty, and thus perhaps commitment to the group's decision (Stasser & Davis, 1981), and the DISCUSS model can conceivably model postdiscussion recall of discussed information. But, in fact, there has been little systematic effort to model influence beyond the group's actual interaction. The influence processes that remain operative after the group disbands may differ from those that seem to drive the emergence of a consensus during the groups interaction.

For example, Moscovici (1980) and his colleagues (e.g., Mugny, 1980; Nemeth, 1986) have argued that there is a qualitative difference between social influence by majorities and minorities. They have suggested that minority influence depends strongly on the style with which minority members defend their position and is usually not apparent in public compliance but is manifest in altered majority thinking and ultimately in private opinion change. Therefore, the strength-in-numbers quality that often characterizes the movement of groups to consensus may be less descriptive of the impact of group interaction on private opinions that members carry away from the group. Although the models as we have presented them take the group decision as the datum to be predicted, this endpoint is certainly not dictated by the social combination perspective that they embody. One could take private opinions assessed some time after a group discussion has ended or a group decision has been reached as the output of interest rather than the group decision per se.

Certainly, extensions of social combination models to incorporate other aspects of interaction such as nuances of verbal and nonverbal expression and to address postdecisional influence require more than cosmetic changes. However, we mention these possibilities not only because such changes may enhance the models but also because these additional aspects of group influence may be most fruitly understood when put in the context of the decision-making group's primary and immediate task—the task of fashioning a consensus of members' publicly expressed preferences. Thus, for example, it seems that a model of the group's postdecisional influence on members should be predicated on an adequate model of how the decision is fashioned in the first place. Similarly, it seems unlikely that one can fully understand the impact of conversational styles and nonverbal punctuations, as manifested in decision-making groups, while ignoring the influence of discussion content and overt statements of preferences.

ACKNOWLEDGMENTS

This chapter was completed while James Davis was a Fellow at the Center for Advanced Study of Behavioral Sciences. National Science Foundation grants to Garold Stasser (BNS-8505707) and James Davis (BNS-8700864) supported work on this chapter.

REFERENCES

Abelson, R.P. (1968). Simulation and social behavior. In C. Lindzey & E. Aronson (Eds.). *Handbook of social psychology* (Vol. 2, pp. 274–356). Reading, MA: Addison-Wesley.

Allen, V. L. (1965). Situational factors in conformity. In L. Berkowitz (Ed.), *Advances in experimental social psychology* (Vol. 2). New York: Academic Press.

Allen, V.L. (1975). Social support for nonconformity. In L. Berkowitz (Ed.), *Advances in experimental social psychology* (Vol. 8). New York: Academic Press.

Anderson, N. H., & Graesser, C. (1976). An information integration analysis of attitude change in group discussion. *Journal of Personality and Social Psychology, 34,* 210–222.

Arabie, P., Boorman, S. A., & Levitt, P. R. (1978). Constructing block-models: How and why. *Journal of Mathematical Psychology, 17,* 21–63.

Asch, S. E. (1956). Studies of independence and submission to group pressure: I. On minority of one against a unanimous majority. *Psychological Monographs, 70* (9 Whole No. 417).

Burnstein, E., & Vinokur, A. (1977). Persuasive argumentation and social comparison as determinants of attitude polarization. *Journal of Experimental Social Psychology, 13,* 315–332.

Cialdini, R. B. (1984). *Influence: How and why people agree to things.* New York: William Morrow.

Cialdini, R. B., Levy, A., Herman, C. P., Kozlowski, L. T., & Petty, R.E. (1976). Elastic shifts of opinion: Determinants of direction and durability. *Journal of Personality and Social Psychology, 34,* 663–772.

Crott, H. W., Zuber, J. A., & Schermer, T. (1986). Social decision schemes and choice shift: An analysis of group decisions among bets. *Journal of Experimental Social Psychology, 22,* 1–21.

Dabbs, J. M., & Ruback, R. B. (1987). Dimensions of group process: Amount and structure of vocal interaction. In L. Berkowitz (Ed.), *Advances in experimental social psychology* (Vol. 21). New York: Academic Press.

Davis, J. H. (1973). Group decision and social interaction: A theory of social decision schemes. *Psychological Review, 80,* 97–125.

Davis, J. H. (1982). Social interaction as a combinatorial process in group decision. In H. Brandstatter, J. H. Davis, & G. Stocker-Kreichgauer (Eds.), *Group decision making.* London: Academic Press.

Davis, J. H., Cohen, J. L., Hornik, J. A., & Rissman, A. K. (1973). Dyadic decision as a function of the frequency distributions describing the preferences of members' constituencies. *Journal of Personality and Social Psychology, 26,* 178–195.

Davis, J. H., & Kerr, N. L. (1986). Thought experiments and the problem of sparse data in small group performance research. In P. S. Goodman (Ed.), *Designing effective work groups.* San Francisco: Jossey-Bass.

Davis, J. H., Stasser, G., Spitzer, S. E., & Holt, R. W. (1976). Changes in group members' decision preferences during discussion: An illustration with mock juries. *Journal of Personality and Social Psychology, 34,* 1177–1187.

Deutsch, M., & Gerard, H. B. (1955). A study of normative and informational social influences upon individual judgment. *Journal of Abnormal and Social Psychology, 51,* 629–633.

Eagly, A. H. (1978). Sex differences in influenceability. *Psychological Bulletin, 85,* 85–116.

Festinger, L. (1950). Informal social communication. *Psychological Review, 57,* 271–282.

Festinger, L. (1954). A theory of social comparison processes. *Human Relations, 1,* 117–140.

French, J. R. P., Jr., & Raven, B. H. (1959). The bases of social power. In D. Cartwright (Ed.), *Studies in social power.* Ann Arbor: University of Michigan Press.

Gerard, H. G., Wilhelmy, R. A., & Conolley, E. S. (1968). Conformity and group size. *Journal of Personality and Social Psychology, 8,* 79–82.

Godwin, W. F., & Restle, F. (1974). The road to agreement: Subgroup pressures in small group consensus processes. *Journal of Personality and Social Psychology, 30,* 500–509.

Gottman, J. M., & Bakeman, R. (1979). The sequential analysis of observational data. In M. E. Lamb, S. J. Soumi, & G. R. Stephenson (Eds.), *Social interaction analysis: Methodological issues.* Madison: University of Wisconsin Press.

Hartwick, J., Sheppard, B. H., & Davis, J. H. (1982). Group remembering: Research and implications. In R. A. Guzzo (Ed.), *Improving group decision making in organizations.* New York: Academic Press.

Hastie, R., Penrod, S. D., & Pennington, N. (1983). *Inside the jury.* Cambridge, MA: Harvard University Press.

Hawkins, C. (1962). Interaction rates of jurors aligned in factions. *American Sociological Review, 27,* 689–691.

Iacobucci, D., & Wasserman, S. (1987). Dyadic social interactions. *Psychological Bulletin, 293–* 306.

Janis, I. L. (1972). *Victims of groupthink.* Boston: Houghton Mifflin.

Kairys, D., Schulman, J., & Harring, S. (Eds.). (1975). *The jury system: New methods for reducing prejudice.* Cambridge, MA: National Jury Project and National Lawyers Guild.

Kaplan, M. F. (1977). Discussion polarization effects in a modified jury paradigm: Informational influences. *Sociometry, 40,* 261–271.

Kaplan, M. F., & Miller, C. E. (1987). Group decision making and normative versus informational influence effects of type of issue and assigned decision rule. *Journal of Personality and Social Psychology, 53,* 306–313.

Kerr, N. L. (1981). Social transition schemes: Charting the group's road to agreement. *Journal of Personality and Social Psychology, 41,* 684–702.

Kerr, N. L. (1982). Social transition schemes: Model, method, and applications. In H. Brandstatter, J. H. Davis, & G. Stocker-Kreichgauer (Eds.), *Group decision making*. Orlando/London: Academic Press.

Kerr, N. L. (1983, June). *Studies of the group decision making process*. Paper presented at the Third International Conference on Group Processes, Nags Head, NC.

Kerr, N. L., Atkin, R. S., Stasser, G., Meek, D., Holt, R. W., & Davis, J. H. (1976). Guilt beyond a reasonable doubt: Effects of concept definition and assigned decision rule on judgments of mock jurors. *Journal of Personality and Social Psychology, 34,* 282–294.

Kerr, N. L., & MacCoun, R. J. (1985). The effects of jury size and polling method on the process and product of jury deliberation. *Journal of Personality and Social Psychology, 48,* 349–363.

Kerr, N. L., MacCoun, R. J., Hansen, C. H., & Hymes, J. A. (1987). Gaining and losing social support: Momentum in decision-making groups. *Journal of Experimental Social Psychology, 23,* 119–145.

Kerr, N. L., Stasser, G., & Davis, J. H. (1979). Model-testing, model-fitting, and social decision schemes. *Organizational Behavior and Human Performance, 23,* 339–410.

Kerr, N. L., & Watts, B. L. (1982). After division, before decision: Group faction size and predeliberation thinking. *Social Psychology Quarterly, 45,* 198–205.

Kirchler, E., & Davis, J. D. (1986). The influence of member status differences and task type on group consensus and member position change. *Journal of Personality and Social Psychology, 51,* 83–91.

Komorita, S. S. (1987). Cooperative choice in decomposed social dilemmas. *Personality and Social Psychology Bulletin, 13,* 53–63.

Latane, B., & Nida, S. (1980). Social impact theory and group influence: A social engineering perspective. In P. B. Paulus (Ed.). *Psychology of group influence* (pp. 3–34). Hillsdale, NJ: Lawrence Erlbaum Associates.

Laughlin, P. R. (1980). Social combination processes of cooperative problem-solving groups on verbal intellective tasks. In M. Fishbein (Ed.), *Progress in social psychology* (Vol. 1). Hillsdale, NJ: Lawrence Erlbaum Associates.

Laughlin, P. R., & Ellis, A. L. (1986). Demonstrability and social combination processes on mathematical intellective tasks. *Journal of Experimental Social Psychology, 22,* 177–189.

Laughlin, P. R., & Futoran, G. C. (1985). Collective induction: Social combination and sequential transition. *Journal of Personality and Social Psychology, 48,* 608–613.

Laughlin, P. R., Kerr, N. L., Davis, J. H., Halff, H. M., & Marciniak, K. A. (1975). Group size, member ability, and social decision schemes on an intellective task. *Journal of Personality and Social Psychology, 31,* 522–535.

Laughlin, P. R., & McGlynn, R. P. (1986). Collective induction: Mutual group and individual influence by exchange of hypotheses and evidence. *Journal of Experimental Social Psychology, 22,* 567–589.

Lorge, I., & Solomon, H. (1955). Two models of group behavior in the solution of Eureka-type problems. *Psychometrika, 20,* 139–148.

MacCoun, R. J., & Kerr, N. L. (1988). Asymmetric influence in mock jury deliberations: Jurors bias for leniency. *Journal of Personality and Social Psychology, 54,* 21–33.

Moscovici, S. (1980). Toward a theory of conversion behavior. In L. Berkowitz (Ed.), *Advances in experimental social psychology* (Vol. 13). New York: Academic Press.

Moscovici, S., & Faucheux, C. (1972). Social influence, conformity bias, and the study of active minorities. In L. Berkowitz (Ed.), *Advances in experimental social psychology* (Vol. 6). New York: Academic Press.

Moscovici, S., & Nemeth, C. (1974). Social influence: II Minority influence. In C. Nemeth (Ed.), *Social psychology: Classic and contemporary integrations*. Chicago: Rand-McNally.

Mugny, G. (1982). *The Power of Minorities*. London: Academic Press.

Myers, D. C., & Lamm, H. (1976). The group polarization phenomenon. *Psychological Bulletin*, *83*, 602–627.

Nagao, D. H., & Davis, J. H. (1980). Some implications of temporal drift in social parameters. *Journal of Experimental Social Psychology*, *16*, 479–496.

Nemeth, C. J. (1986). Differential contributions of majority and minority influence. *Psychological Review*, *93*, 23–32.

Ono, K. & Davis, J. H. (1987). *Small group decision making, preference orders, and strategic position change*. Mimeograph, University of Illinois, Champaign, Illinois.

Penrod, S., & Hastie, R. (1980). A computer simulation of jury decision making. *Psychological Review*, *87*, 133–159.

Restle, F., & Davis, J. H. (1962). Success and speed of problem solving by individuals and groups. *Psychological Review*, *69*, 520–536.

Schulman, J., Shaver, P., Colman, R., Emrick, B., & Christie, R. (1973, May). Recipe for a jury. *Psychology Today*, pp. 34–44; 77; 79–84.

Schachter, S. (1951). Deviation, rejection, and communication. *Journal of Abnormal and Social Psychology*, *46*, 190–207.

Schultz, R. L., & Sullivan, E. M. (1972). Developments in simulation in social and administrative science. In G. Guetzkow, P. Kotler, & R. L. Schultz (Eds.), *Simulation in social and administrative science: Overviews and case-examples*. Englewood Cliffs, NJ: Prentice-Hall.

Sherif, M., & Hovland, C. I. (1961). *Social judgment: Assimilation and contrast effects in communication and attitude*. New Haven, CT: Yale University Press.

Shiflett, S. C. (1979). Toward a general model of small group productivity. *Psychological Bulletin*, *86*, 67–79.

Starbuck, W. H. (1983). Computer simulation of human behavior. *Behavioral Science*, *28*, 154–165.

Stasser, G. (in press). Computer simulation as a research tool: The DISCUSS model of group decision making. *Journal of Experimental Social Psychology*.

Stasser, G., & Davis, J. H. (1976). Opinion change during group discussion. *Personality and Social Psychology Bulletin*, *3*, 252–256.

Stasser, G., & Davis, J. H. (1981). Group decision making and social influence: A social interaction sequence model. *Psychological Review*, *88*, 523–551.

Stasser, G., Kerr, N. L., & Bray, R. M. (1982). The social psychology of jury deliberation: Structure, process, and product. In N. L. Kerr & R. M. Bray (Eds.), *The psychology of the courtroom*. New York: Academic Press.

Stasser, G., Kerr, N. L., & Davis, J. H. (1980). Influence processes in decision-making groups: A modeling approach. In P. B. Paulus (Ed.), *Psychology of group influence*. Hillsdale, NJ: Lawrence Erlbaum Associates.

Stasser, G., & Titus, W. (1985). Pooling of unshared information in group decision making: Biased information sampling during group discussion. *Journal of Personality and Social Psychology*, *48*, 1476–1478.

Stasser, G., & Titus, W. (1987). Effects of information load and percentage shared information on the dissemination of unshared information during discussion. *Journal of Personality and Social Psychology*, *53*, 81–93.

Steiner, I. D. (1974). Whatever happened to the group in social psychology? *Journal of Experimental Social Psychology*, *10*, 94–108.

Steiner, I. D. (1983). Whatever happened to the touted revival of the group? In H., Blumberg, A. Hare, V. Kent, & M. Davies (Eds.), *Small groups and social interaction* (Vol. 2). New York: Wiley.

Steiner, I. D. (1986). Paradigms and groups. In L. Berkowitz (Ed.), *Advances in experimental social Psychology* (Vol. 19). Orlando/London: Academic Press.

Stiles, W. B. (1978). Verbal response modes and dimensions of interpersonal roles: A method of discourse analysis. *Journal of Personality and Social Psychology, 36,* 693–703.

Tanford, S., & Penrod, S. (1983). Computer modeling of influence in the jury: The role of the consistent juror. *Social Psychology Quarterly, 46,* 200–212.

Tindale, R. S., & Nagao, D. H. (1986). An assessment of the potential of "Scientific Jury Selection": A "Thought Experiment" approach. *Organizational Behavior and Human Performance, 37,* 409–425.

10

The Social Psychological Effects of Group Decision Rules

Charles E. Miller
Northern Illinois University

In any group, organization, or society, individuals are constantly interacting with one another in order to arrive at decisions. Examples are almost endless: A city council passes an ordinance; a family decides whether to vacation in the mountains or at the seashore; a jury returns a verdict; the stockholders of a corporation elect a chairperson of the board. All of these situations have several characteristics in common. A collection of two or more individuals must choose one alternative from among two or more alternatives. The individuals involved ordinarily have preferences among the alternatives, and these preferences often differ. One person would like the group to choose one alternative, whereas another person would like the group to choose a different alternative. A problem thus exists as to how the preferences of the different individuals are to be combined or aggregated to produce a group decision.

Groups, organizations, and societies make use of numerous mechanisms for resolving this problem of collective choice and reaching a decision. Among these mechanisms are convention or custom, electoral processes, bargaining and negotiation, interpersonal persuasion, religious codes, economic market institutions, and dictatorial decree. Many of these mechanisms amount to, or are reducible to, group decision rules. A *group decision rule* may be defined as a rule that specifies, for any given set of individual preferences regarding some set of alternatives, what the group preference or decision is regarding the alternatives (cf. Arrow, 1963). Plurality vote, majority vote, and unanimity rule are examples of commonly employed group decision rules.

My purpose in this chapter is to review much of what we presently know about the social psychological consequences of using different kinds of group decision rules. Throughout the chapter I focus on small groups such as committees or clubs, rather than on large collectivities such as entire towns or nations. Most of us are so accustomed to participating in small groups and to routinely making group decisions that we often seem unaware of the potential impact of the rules whereby the decisions are made. We recognize, of course, that group decision rules may affect the group decision itself—that is, that the use of different decision rules may lead to the making of different decisions. For example, one of the reasons that some universities require a two-thirds majority, rather than a simple majority, vote for the awarding of academic tenure is to create a conservative bias with respect to the decision. It is felt that it is better to err by denying tenure than to err by granting tenure.

We are probably much less aware, however, that group decision rules may have effects other than on the group decision itself. In particular, group decision rules may have effects that are social psychological in nature—effects on how people behave, think, and feel. In this chapter, we shall see that the factors affected by group decision rules range from the content of group discussion to the group members' perceptions of the decision-making process, and even to the members' feelings toward one another. We shall further see that the effects of group decision rules may extend to interactions with other group and decision task factors.

Owing perhaps to the nonobvious nature of some of these effects, group decision rules have not been the focus of much experimental study. There is presently no readily identifiable, clearly circumscribed literature on the social psychological effects of group decision rules. Rather, there are a few studies scattered here and there in other literatures. I find, in fact, that the entire body of research dealing with the social psychological effects of group decision rules consists of little more than a couple of dozen studies. Yet many of these effects are interesting and important enough to deserve greater attention. It is my hope that this chapter, by pulling together and summarizing much of what is currently known about such effects, might stimulate more interest in this somewhat neglected area of research.

RELATED LITERATURES

Even though the literature dealing directly with the social psychological effects of group decision rules is small, there are several literatures that are tangentially related to such effects. First, there is a fairly extensive literature consisting of axiomatic or mathematical treatments of group decision rules (Arrow, 1963; Black, 1958; Brams, 1975; Farquharson, 1969; Fishburn, 1973). This literature, however, is entirely formal in nature and not empirical. Second, there is the growing literature on procedural justice, stemming from the work of Thibaut and Walker (1975). But this literature, although it is sometimes suggestive for our purposes, has not generally been concerned with group decision rules as they are defined here (cf. Folger, Rosenfield, & Robinson, 1983; Pearson, 1982). Third, there is the literature on social decision schemes (Davis, 1973). This literature, though, is concerned with the decision rules that are implicitly or informally adopted by groups. Our concern here is with the decision rules that groups formally use—that is, the rules that are explicitly adopted or recognized as the rules for aggregating preferences in a group. Finally, there are the literatures on organizational change (Kotter & Schlesinger, 1981) and managerial decision making (Locke & Schweiger, 1979). These literatures, however, deal primarily with the extent to which group members have an opportunity to participate in decision making. Neither is concerned specifically with group decision rules.

None of these literatures, then, deals directly with the social psychological effects of group decision rules. Hence they are not considered in this chapter.

TWO IMPORTANT CHARACTERISTICS OF GROUP DECISION RULES

Group decision rules may differ from one another in terms of many characteristics. Some of these characteristics are of more importance than others with regard to the social psychological effects that the decision rules may have. In our review, we shall see that two characteristics seem to be especially important.

First, as Hastie, Penrod, and Pennington (1983) have pointed out, decision rules may differ as to their *strictness*. The strictness of a rule refers to the extent to which group members must express similar preferences in order for the group to reach a decision. Some rules require a great deal of agreement, and others do not. Unanimity rule, for example, is a strict rule because it requires that all group members agree on a particular alternative in order for a decision to occur. Majority rule is less strict, because reaching a decision under it necessitates agreement among fewer members. Rule by dictatorship is less strict still, because with it the group decision is determined entirely by the preferences of a particular group member, regardless of whether others agree with that member.

A second way that decision rules may differ is in terms of the *distribution of power* among group members. Some rules treat group members equally with respect to their formal influence on the group decision—or what the procedural justice literature refers to as outcome control (Thibaut & Walker, 1978)—and others do not. At one extreme, an authoritarian rule such as dictatorship concentrates decision-making power in the hands of a single member of the group. At the other extreme, an egalitarian rule such as simple majority rule accords every group member an equal say with respect to the group decision. Somewhere in between lies a rule such as weighted majority rule, which gives different group members different numbers of votes, and hence different amounts of power over the group decision.

These two characteristics of decision rules—their strictness and the way in which they distribute power—are not entirely unrelated. Authoritarian rules are generally not very strict, because they allot power to one or only a few group members, and therefore do not require agreement among most members for a decision to be attained. Egalitarian rules tend to be stricter, because giving more group members a say in the decision tends to mean that more members must reach agreement in order to make the decision. Still, the strictness of a decision rule and the way in which the rule distributes power are not the same thing. For example, majority and unanimity rule are both egalitarian rules, but they differ in strictness.

Although the strictness of decision rules and the distribution of power they provide both appear to produce important social psychological effects, we know more about the effects of the former than the latter. Many of the studies reviewed here provide a comparison of decision rules that differ in terms of strictness. Most of these studies were an outgrowth of rulings by the U.S. Supreme Court on the constitutionality of less-than-unanimous jury verdicts (*Apodaca, Cooper, and Madden v. Oregon*, 1972;*Johnson v. Louisiana*, 1972).Typically, these studies have involved mock juries and have compared simple majority rule or some other version of majority rule, such as two-thirds majority rule, with unanimity rule.

Relatively few studies have compared rules that differ in terms of how they distribute power. For example, only a few studies have contrasted egalitarian decision rules, such as majority rule, with more authoritarian rules, such as dictatorship or a veto requirement (e.g., Birnberg & Pondy, 1971; Holloman & Hendrick, 1972; Miller & Anderson, 1979; Miller, Jackson, Mueller, & Schersching, 1987).

THE RESEARCH ON GROUP DECISION RULES

Let us begin our review by considering the most obvious of the possible effects of group decision rules—effects on the group decision itself. This, more than any other factor, has been the focus of studies comparing different decision rules.

Effects on Group Decision Outcomes

Evidence regarding the effects of the decision rule on decision outcomes is somewhat mixed, yet there do appear to be several general trends.

Failure to Reach Decisions.   Perhaps the most frequently reported finding is that the use of unanimity rule, as compared to versions of majority rule, more often results in failure to reach a decision. Research reporting this effect includes studies that have involved simulated jury decision making (Bray, 1974; Buckhout, Weg, Reilly, & Frohboese, 1977; Foss, 1981; Hastie et al., 1983; Kerr et al., 1976; Nemeth, 1977; Saks, 1977) as well as studies that have not employed the jury paradigm (Bower, 1965a, 1965b; Birnberg & Pondy, 1971; Halfpenny & Taylor, 1973). This finding that groups are less likely to reach decisions under unanimity rule is not surprising inasmuch as unanimity represents a stricter decision requirement, and the stricter the decision requirement, the more difficult it should be to attain a decision.

Nevertheless, the difference between majority and unanimity rules in the frequency of no-decision outcomes, while consistent and typically significant, is rather small. Moreover, the simulated jury studies also show that use of the different rules has little or no effect on whether a verdict of guilty or not guilty is reached (Davis et al., 1975; Friedman & Shaver, cited in Hastie et al., 1983; Grofman, 1976; Hans, 1978; Nemeth, 1977). There has been some tendency to conclude from this that the group decision rule has little effect on group decisions. Before accepting this conclusion, however, it is important to note that in most jury studies groups have been faced with making a decision between only two alternatives, This fact may account, at least in part, for the failure of these studies to find consistent decision rule differences (Miller, 1985). Juries in which a majority or two-thirds majority of the members favor a particular verdict would not seem too likely to make a decision in favor of the *opposite* verdict, if they were required to reach unanimity. The general tendency for mock jury decisions under unanimity rule to go in the direction favored by the majority is very strong.[1]

Multiple Alternatives and Compromise Decisions. There are many situations in which the group must choose, not between just two alternatives, as in the adjudication of guilt, but among a large number of alternatives. An important difference between choosing between two alternatives and more than two is that in the latter case compromise becomes a possibility. When compromise alternatives are available, majority and unanimity rule are more likely to produce different outcomes. Unanimity rule, because it requires that the preferences of all group members be taken into account, is more likely to result in compromise decisions than are various versions of majority rule. This is shown by the findings of several studies.

For example, Harnett (1967) compared decision making under majority and unanimity rule in three-person groups. The study tested the effects of these rules on the predictive accuracy of a level of aspiration (LOA) solution versus a simple majority solution. The LOA solution was defined as follows: Each individual group member is considered to have some ranking of the alternatives from most to least preferred, and also to have some LOA with respect to this ranking. An

---

[1]There is a minor exception to this. Perhaps because instructions to jurors usually provide that guilt must be established beyond reasonable doubt, there is a tendency toward leniency in jury decision making. Juries that initially split 6-6, or 7-5 in favor of a guilty verdict, may sometimes decide in favor of not guilty (Kerr et al., 1976; Kerr & MacCoun, 1985).

individual's LOA is the worst-ranked alternative with which he or she would still be satisfied; the individual would be dissatisfied with the choice of any alternative below his or her LOA. The LOA solution is whichever alternative meets or exceeds the aspiration levels of the most members. The level of aspiration choice is thus a kind of compromise.

In Harnett's (1967) study, the task for each group was to decide what type of multiple-choice exam, out of three specified, they would prefer to take. Each subject was to be paid according to his or her performance on the exam. Different individuals had different preferences for the exams, and groups were composed so that the level of aspiration solution always differed from the simple majority solution. The following two situations were created:

		Situation 1 Individual			Situation 2 Individual		
		I	II	III	I	II	III
	1	X	X	$\underline{Y}$	X	$\underline{Y}$	Z
Rank	2	$\underline{Y}$	$\underline{Y}$	$\underline{X}$	$\underline{Y}$	$\underline{X}$	$\underline{X}$
	3	$\underline{Z}$	$\underline{Z}$	Z	$\underline{Z}$	Z	Y

$\underline{}$ = level of aspiration

Majority solution	X	X
Level of aspiration solution	Y	Y

It was hypothesized that the nature of the situation and the type of decision rule imposed would influence relative support for the solutions. In Situation 1, a strong tendency toward a majority solution was expected because the majority solution was readily identifiable and obtainable—one of the alternatives was the first preference of two of the group members. In Situation 2, on the other hand, there was no *obvious* majority solution, and therefore a greater tendency toward the level of aspiration alternative was expected.

It was also hypothesized that the assigned decision rule would affect the alternative chosen, with compromise being more necessary in reaching a unanimous decision than in reaching a majority decision. Under unanimity rule, members should be disposed to search for an alternative that satisfies as many members as possible, and hence should be more likely to adopt the LOA solution. Under majority rule, members should be more likely to settle on the majority solution.

Harnett found some support for both hypotheses: When there was an obvious majority solution, groups tended to choose it; but when no obvious majority solution existed, there was a strong tendency to choose the LOA solution. More importantly for our concerns, there was also a tendency for groups to choose the LOA compromise under unanimity rule, and the majority solution under majority rule.

When decision situations involve a number of alternatives, the alternatives may sometimes be ordered with respect to one another, or may even reflect some sort of underlying continuum. For instance, the research on group polarization (Lamm & Myers, 1978, Myers & Lamm, 1976) has focused on situations in which groups must choose among alternatives that are ordered on an attitudinal or risk dimension. Studies involving choices among alternatives lying along a continuum have also shown that the use of majority and unanimity decision rules may result in different decisions—again, because of the greater use of compromise under unanimity rule.

For example, in a study using three-person groups, Miller (1985) assigned monetary payoffs to each of several alternatives lying on a continuum so that the members of each group held a fairly typical pattern of preferences: Two of the members held preferences that were somewhat similar, that is, preferred alternatives close together on the continuum. The third held a position that was extreme relative to the other two, that is, preferred an alternative distant from the alternatives preferred by the others.

Miller found that for this pattern of preferences majority and unanimity rule led to different outcomes. Majority rule resulted in the two group members with relatively similar preferences deciding on an alternative that was close to, and usually somewhere in between, their positions. The use of unanimity rule resulted in decisions that were closer to the position of the extreme member than were the decisions under majority rule. Under unanimity rule, the less extreme members were forced to compromise and to take into account the preference of the extreme member.

This effect of decision rule was stronger when group members had complete information about one another's preferences or payoffs than when they lacked such information. With no information about preferences, there was little difference between the decisions made under majority rule and those made under unanimity. Fuller information about preferences apparently makes it easier for group members to identify solutions that represent potential compromises, and may also make the need for such compromises more evident.

Miller's (1985) study involved distributions of member preferences that were skewed.[2] The skewness of preference distributions may be critical to the likelihood of majority and unanimity decision rules leading to different decisions. The use of majority rule allows the preferences of relatively extreme members to be disregarded, whereas the use of unanimity rule requires that they be taken into consideration. In skewed distributions, preferences tend to be extreme in one direction only, thus influencing the decision in that direction under unanimity rule, as compared to majority rule.

The importance of skewness is suggested by the results of a recent study by Kaplan and Miller (1987). This study compared the effects of majority and unanimity decision rules on the decisions of 6-person mock juries regarding the

---

[2]In skewed distributions, the preferences of most of the group members are bunched together on the continuum, with those of one or a few of the members tailing off in one direction from the others.

award of either compensatory damages (compensation for medical expenses, lost wages) or exemplary damages (punitive damages intended to act as a deterrent). No difference was found between the rules for compensatory awards, but unanimity rule resulted in higher exemplary awards than did majority rule. However, the within-jury preferences regarding compensatory awards were not generally skewed, whereas those regarding exemplary awards were skewed in the direction of higher awards. In the case of exemplary awards, therefore, the results suggest greater influence on the decision by extreme members under unanimity rule.

Two other studies involving the award of damages in liability cases found no differences between decisions made according to unanimity rule and those made according to variants of majority rule. In a study involving 12-person mock juries and comparing 3/4ths majority and unanimity decision rules, Broeder (1958) found no difference in the amount of damages awarded. Bray and Stuckman-Johnson (1977) similarly obtained no difference results. One possible reason for the failure of these studies to find differences between majority and unanimity decisions is that the within-group preference distributions may not have been skewed. Another possible reason, given the Miller (1985) findings, is that the members might have lacked sufficient information regarding one another's preferences. This latter possibility seems less likely, however, because there were no restrictions on members exchanging preference information.

Some group decision situations involve not just a choice between two alternatives, or among a number of alternatives, including those that are ordered with respect to one another or that lie along a continuum, but rather a choice as to how some divisible reward is to be distributed among the group members. A study by Birnberg and Pondy (1971) suggests that in these situations, too, unanimity rule leads to compromise solutions more frequently than does majority rule.

The Birnberg–Pondy study examined decision making in three-person groups, each of which had to choose among three alternative distributions of points for the group members: An Equal-Split alternative gave each member 1 point. An All-to-Two alternative gave two of the members 2 points and the third nothing. And an All-to-One alternative gave one member 5 points and the other two nothing. Groups made decisions under one of three decision rules: Majority rule, unanimity rule, and a veto rule. The majority and unanimity rules were defined as usual. Under the veto rule, one person had a blocking veto—i.e., had two votes, compared to one vote for each of the other members, with a majority required. Each group made a series of decisions among the alternatives, with the 2- and 5-point payoffs rotated so that, across decisions, all members had equal opportunity to obtain them. Each group made one-third of its decisions under each decision rule.

Groups reached widely different decisions under the different decision rules. The results are shown in Table 10.1. As might be expected, the frequency of "no decision" outcomes was highest under unanimity rule, for which the requirement of agreement was most strict. When a decision *was* reached, there was a tenden-

TABLE 10.1
Proportion of Decisions Favoring Each Alternative Under Each
Group Decision Rule

| Decision Rule | Proportion of Decisions Favoring | | | |
	Equal-Split	All-to-Two	All-to-One	No Decision
Majority	.046	.653	.223	.078
Unanimity	.375	.074	.000	.551
Veto	.297	.518	.065	.120

Note. Adapted from Birnberg and Pondy (1971).

cy under unanimity rule to choose the alternative giving each member an equal share—a kind of compromise. Under the majority and veto rules, there was a tendency to choose the alternative giving two of the members two points and the other member nothing.

Quality of Decisions.   Besides demonstrating the occurrence of compromise under unanimity rule, Birnberg and Pondy addressed another important issue regarding the possible differential effects of group decision rules on group outcomes—that of the quality or adequacy of the outcomes. They attempted to determine whether one of the rules in their study was better than the others in that it led to superior decisions. They compared the rules in terms of the total points earned by the group members, considering a decision rule as being better if it resulted in a larger total payoff.

Majority rule resulted in the largest mean group payoff, followed by veto rule, and then unanimity rule. As Birnberg and Pondy point out, the poor performance of unanimity rule with respect to total payoff raises questions about group procedures that lay heavy stress on consensus formation. It appears that unanimity must be purchased by roughly equal individual sharing, and this may result in inferior aggregate performance.

A study by Holloman and Hendrick (1972), however, suggests that the compromise required by unanimity rule may result in superior performance when performance is measured in other ways. This study compared the adequacy of decisions made according to majority vote with those made according to a consensus procedure. Subjects watched the beginning of the film *Twelve Angry Men*, depicting the deliberations of a jury in a murder trial. They saw the initial vote of the jury, which was 11 to 1 in favor of a guilty verdict. The film was then stopped, and subjects were told that during the remainder of the film the jurors switched their votes one-by-one to not guilty. Each subject was asked to predict the order in which the jurors would change their votes from guilty to not guilty. Subsequently, subjects had to reach group decisions about the sequence of juror vote changes.

Holloman and Hendrick found that consensus decisions were significantly more accurate than decisions made by majority rule, and both were more accurate than decisions representing the average position of group members or decisions representing the position of randomly selected members. They suggest that the difference between rules is due to the fact fact that a consensus requirement forces group members to recognize, deal with, and compromise on their differences of opinion, rather than simply to ignore or deny them.

A study by Bower (1965a, 1965b) also found unanimity rule superior to majority rule. Each three-person group in this study had to select the best of 125 "investment alternatives" that differed with respect to the attributes of sales, profitability, and risk. Quality of the alternatives was defined by a complex function of the attributes that was unknown to the group members. Each member was, however, given information about the quality of ten alternatives outside the set of 125 alternatives that also differed in terms of the three attributes. Each group member's information partially overlapped that of the other two members. Half the groups made decisions under majority rule, and half under unanimity rule. The group closest to the best alternative received a prize of $30. Under a cooperative condition, the prize was divided evenly among members of the winning group. Under a competitive condition, the prize was divided $19/$10/$1 according to the closeness of the members' initial preferences to the group's final selection.

Bower found that in the cooperative condition groups made better decisions under unanimity than under majority rule. In the competitive condition groups performed better under majority rule than under unanimity, but only because of the relatively high frequency of no decision outcomes under unanimity. Considering data only from those groups that reached decisions, competitive groups also performed better under unanimity rule than under majority rule. Bower argued that unanimity rule proved superior because, being the stricter decision rule, it heightened pressures on group members to exchange information and search more intensively for better solutions. Thus, while unanimity made decision making more difficult, it also enhanced its effectiveness.

Summary.   The findings of a number of studies show that the group decision rule, in conjunction with the distribution of member preferences and the information that members have about each other's preferences, may affect the nature of the decision that a group makes. The stricter the decision rule, the more likely it is that the group will be unable to arrive at a decision. For example, the use of unanimity rule, as compared to majority rule, is more likely to lead to the group failing to reach a decision. If a decision *is* reached, stricter rules such as unanimity are more likely to result in some sort of compromise, provided the members have enough information about each other's positions to make such a compromise possible or its need apparent. In instances in which the preference distribution of group members is skewed, unanimity rule is more likely to result in a decision that takes account of the preferences of relatively extreme members, rather than ignoring them altogether. In instances in which some reward must be divided among group members, unanimity rule is more likely than majority rule to lead to equal reward divisions. There is also some evidence that the compromises required by unanimity rule may be more adequate or of higher quality than decisions made by majority rule.

Effects on Preferences of Individual Members

Not only do group decision rules differentially affect the group decision, they also differentially affect changes in the preferences of individual members of the group. In unanimous rule groups, as compared to groups using variants of majority rule, substantial preference shifts occur during the decision-making process (Hastie et al., 1983; Kaplan & Miller, 1987; Miller, 1985; Miller & Braasch, 1988). These shifts are in the direction of greater agreement among the preferences of group members. That is, there is a greater increase in agreement among group members' preferences from pre- to postdecision under unanimity rule than under majority rule.

This convergence effect (Sherif, 1936) would not be surprising if it occurred only with respect to the publicly stated preferences of the members, but it occurs with respect to their *privately* held opinions as well (Kaplan & Miller, 1987; Miller & Braasch, 1988). For example, Miller and Braasch (1988) found a greater pre- to postdecision increase in the similarity of the privately expressed preference rankings of group members under unanimity rule than under majority rule.

Not only do members' preferences tend to converge more under unanimity rule than under majority rule, they also tend to approximate more closely the eventual group decision. Thus, Miller and Braasch (1988) also found that group members' private postdecision individual preferences agreed more closely with the eventual group decision under unanimity rule than under majority rule. This approximation to the group decision was similarly demonstrated in a study by Tjosvold and Field (1983), in which subjects made individual and group decisions on the rank order of importance of the 15 items that persons might use for returning to the mother ship in the "Lost on the Moon" problem (Hall, 1971). They found that there was a stronger correspondence between individuals' postdecision preference rankings and their group's eventual rankings under a consensus procedure than under majority rule.

The greater convergence of member preferences under unanimity rule may occur for two reasons: (a) Extreme or minority members may change more toward the majority, and (b) majority members may change more toward the extreme or minority members. With respect to the change of minority members toward the majority, group members are usually more likely to defect from small factions than from large ones, and the more strict the decision requirement, the more this is true. Thus, those members with less popular preferences are less likely to maintain their initial positions or "holdout" (Hastie et al., 1983) under unanimous rule than under majority decision rules. Hastie et al. suggest that this is probably because, under unanimous rule, members with initial preferences that are unpopular cannot maintain those positions without deadlocking the decision process.

With respect to the change of majority members toward the minority, the already discussed findings of the studies by Birnberg and Pondy (1971), Harnett (1967), Kaplan and Miller (1987), and Miller (1985) are relevant. These findings indicate that under unanimity rule, as compared to variations of majority rule, less extreme members are forced to compromise and take into account the preferences of more extreme members. Whereas under majority rule the majority members can remain intransigent and ignore minority members, under unanimity they must move their positions toward those of the more extreme members, if they wish to attain a group decision. This appears to lead to greater changes, not just in majority members' publicly expressed opinions, as might be expected, but also to greater changes in their privately held preferences (Kaplan & Miller, 1987; Miller & Braasch, 1988). Perhaps the public expression of an opinion contrary to one's private position creates dissonance that leads to a change in the private position (Festinger & Carlsmith, 1959).

Summary.   The stricter the decision rule, the more likely the preferences of individual members are to change in the direction of greater agreement during the decision-making process, and the less likely members are to dissent from the final decision. These changes occur with respect to both publicly expressed and privately held preferences, and for both majority and minority members.

Effects on Satisfaction with the Group Decision

Besides affecting the outcomes of group decision making and the preferences of individual members, decision rules may affect the degree to which members are satisfied with the group decision. The findings of several studies suggest that group members are more satisfied, on the average, with decisions made under unanimity rule than with decisions made under various other rules. For example, Kerr et al. (1976) found that unanimity rule jurors were more satisfied with verdicts than were majority rule jurors, and Nemeth (1977) found that unanimity rule jurors believed in the correctness of their verdicts with greater confidence than did majority rule jurors. Both of these studies were concerned with jury verdicts regarding guilty versus not guilty. Extending this, the previously discussed studies by Kaplan and Miller (1987) and Miller and Braasch (1988), which involved decisions among multiple alternatives, also found that group members were more satisfied with decisions reached by unanimity rule than by majority rule.

The higher average levels of satisfaction with decisions under unanimity rule, as compared to decisions under majority rule, appear to be due to the fact that individual group members tend to agree more with the final decision under unanimity rule. Findings of a number of studies indicate that the satisfaction of any individual member with the eventual group decision depends on the extent to which the member agrees with the decision. For example, the Hastie et al. (1983) study found that holdout jurors—those who did not agree with the verdict of the jury—had less confidence in the verdict than did members of majority factions—who agreed with the verdict. Similarly, the Miller and Braasch (1988) study found a strong correlation (.60) between individual agreement with the group decision and individual satisfaction with the decision. And further studies by Miller and Anderson (1979) and Miller et al. (1987) also indicate that satisfaction with the group decision is determined mostly by whether one agrees with the decision. For example, the latter study found that 70% of the variance in ratings of satisfaction with the group decision was accounted for by agreement with the decision.

Exceptions to the finding that the use of unanimity rule leads to greater satisfaction with outcomes than does majority rule are found in the work of Castore (1978; Castore & Murnighan, 1978) and Green and Taber (1980). But interestingly, these exceptions are also exceptions to the typical finding that unanimity rule leads to greater agreement with the final group decision.

Castore's research compared satisfaction with and commitment to group decisions made by benevolent dictatorship (the dictator favored the majority), majority rule with formal voting, discussion to majority consensus, and unanimity. As usual, Castore found that individuals in the majority faction were more satisfied with and committed to decisions than were those in minority factions. He found, however, that the overall agreement of members with the group decisions was comparable, regardless of the procedure used to reach the decisions. He further found that satisfaction with and commitment to group decisions were greater when the decisions were made by majority procedures rather than by unanimity or dictatorial procedures.

Green and Taber (1980) compared the effects of three group decision making procedures: Nominal voting, majority rule, and consensus. Each group decision task required a group to try to rank order 10 items—for example, ten occupations according to their trustworthiness. With the nominal vote procedure, the group decision was determined by summing the rankings given by the individual group members. With majority rule, members decided by majority vote which of the items should be assigned to any given rank. With consensus, the ranks assigned by the group had to be agreed to by all the members; if any member disagreed, discussion continued until all agreed.

Green and Taber found that the group decision rule did not affect how satisfied members were with the final group decision. However, they also found that the decision rules did not differentially affect the extent to which an individual's final preferences agreed with the group decision. Nor did the decision rules affect the extent to which group members changed their initial positions toward the group's eventual position.

Taken together, the Castore (1978) and Green and Taber (1980) results suggest that unanimity rule does not always lead to more agreement with group outcomes than do majority procedures. More to the present point, the results raise a question as to whether, if agreement with group outcomes is controlled, satisfaction with the outcomes actually differs under unanimity and majority rules.

Summary.   On the average, unanimity rule leads to more satisfaction with the group decision than does majority rule. This appears to be because average satisfaction with the group decision is determined largely by the extent to which group members agree with the decision, and group members tend to agree more with the decision under stricter rules such as unanimity rule than under more lenient rules such as majority rule. In instances where unanimity rule does not result in any more agreement with the group decision than does majority rule, group members are, on the average, no more satisfied with the decision.

Effects on Group Discussion

Besides affecting the group decision and individual preferences and satisfaction with the group decision, decision rules also affect the nature of group discussion.

Time Spent in Discussion.   It appears that discussion time increases with the strictness of the decision rule, although evidence regarding this point is not entirely consistent. Mock jury studies by Davis et al. (1975), Foss (1981), Kerr et al. (1976), and Saks (1977) all found that juries using unanimity rule took longer to reach a verdict than did juries using variations of majority rule. In addition, the Davis et al. (1975) and Kerr et al. (1976) studies found that unanimity juries took more polls to reach a verdict than did two-thirds majority juries. Harnett (1967) and Miller (1985) obtained similar results in studies that involved repeated rounds of voting to reach decisions; more rounds of voting were needed to reach decisions under unanimity rule than under majority rule.

All of these findings are consistent with the greater difficulty of satisfying the requirement of unanimity as opposed to some less stringent requirement. In spite of the several studies showing that the group decision rule affects discussion time, however, a few studies have reported no significant effects or mixed results: Friedman and Shaver (cited in Hastie et al., 1983) and Kaplan and Miller (1987) found that decision rule—in each case a variant of majority rule versus unanimity rule—had no significant effect on deliberation time. Nemeth (1977) compared unanimous and two-thirds majority rules in mock juries and also found that total deliberation time showed no decision rule effects, although there was a difference in "functional" deliberation time—defined as the point at which arguments for one verdict outweighed those for the other verdict to such an extent that reversal of the group decision was essentially precluded. Unanimous rule juries required longer functional deliberation time. Finally, Tjosvold and Field (1983) compared the effects of consensus and majority decision-making procedures on decision time and found that the effects of procedure depended on the social climate. In a cooperative social climate, in which subjects were instructed to work together for mutual benefit and not try to outdo others, majority voting took longer than attainment of consensus. In a competitive social climate, in which subjects were told to try to win and show that their own ideas were superior to others, attaining consensus required more time than reaching a majority decision.

Content of Discussion.   Evidence regarding the possible effects of group decision rules on the content of group discussion is sparse and mixed. On the one hand, Saks (1977) reported that the group decision rule had no effect on deliberation content, and Hastie et al. (1983) found no effects of decision rule on the amount of questions asked, suggestions offered, or demands to take specific actions or adopt particular verdict positions.

On the other hand, Hastie et al. (1983) did find differences in the deliberation styles of juries under majority and unanimity decision rules. In unanimous juries the deliberations were "integrative" and "evidence-driven," concentrating on putting together a picture or story of what happened. In nonunanimous juries the deliberations were "discounting" and "verdict-driven," focusing on evaluating the credibility of witnesses and deciding whether certain testimony could be dismissed.

The results of Kaplan and Miller (1987) also point to the effects of decision rule on discussion content. This study, already mentioned earlier, examined the effects of majority and unanimity decision rules on discussion content in mock juries awarding either compensatory or exemplary damages. Kaplan and Miller regarded compensatory and exemplary awards as intellective and judgmental issues, respectively (see Laughlin, 1980, and Laughlin & Ellis, 1986, on the intellective-judgmental distinction). Awarding compensatory damages involves an attempt to discover a *true* or *correct* answer by making accurate estimates of compensible losses, such as medical costs. Awarding exemplary damages involves no demonstrably correct answer, but is more concerned with achieving consensus about what is moral, valued, proper, or preferred.

Kaplan and Miller hypothesized that the type of issue should affect the mode of influence—informational or normative (Deutsch & Gerard, 1955)—that group members attempt to use during discussion. Informational influence, based on factual information or information as evidence about reality, should predominate when the concern is with achieving a correct answer, i.e., when the issue is intellective. Normative influence, involving the assertion of preference and appeals to norms, should predominate when the concern is with achieving consensus, i.e., when the issue is judgmental.

Kaplan and Miller further hypothesized that the group decision rule would moderate the effect of issue type on the attempted mode of influence. Unanimity rule, which typically involves more prolonged discussion and greater difficulty in reaching decisions than does majority rule, should increase the use of the influence mode that would normally predominate for a given type of issue. For an intellective issue, unanimity rule should result in greater use of informational influence, whereas for a judgmental issue, unanimity rule should lead to greater use of normative influence.

The results of the study are shown in Fig. 10.1, which indicates the mean frequency with which group discussions included statements categorized as representing either normative or informational influence attempts. As can be seen, Kaplan and Miller found support for both of their hypotheses. In discussions regarding compensatory awards (the intellective issue) informational influence attempts were more frequent than attempts at normative influence, whereas in discussions of exemplary awards (the judgmental issue) normative influence attempts were more frequent than attempts at informational influence. Moreover, this pattern of results was stronger under unanimity rule than under majority rule.

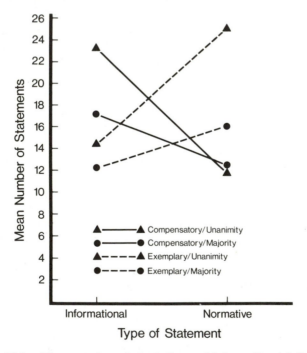

FIG. 10.1. Mean number of normative and informational influence statements as a function of type of issue and group decision rule. From Kaplan and Miller (1987).

Participation in Discussion. In addition to affecting the length and content of group discussion, decision rules may also affect the rate at which various members participate in the discussion. For example, Hastie et al. (1983) found that for members of small factions (one or two persons), the probability of participating in group discussion was much greater under unanimity rule than under 8/12ths or 10/12ths majority rule. For large factions, the tendency was reversed, with higher probabilities of participation for members of large factions under the majority rules than under unanimity. Similarly, Hans (1978) found that minority faction members participated more in discussion under unanimity rule than under 5/6ths majority rule. Thus, under unanimity rule majority faction members dominate discussion to a lesser extent than they do under majority rules.

Hastie et al. suggest several possible explanations for the interaction effect of faction size and decision rule on participation probabilities. As one possibility, they note that the atmosphere in many of their majority rule juries seemed quite adversarial, in contrast to a more deliberate, ponderous atmosphere that prevailed in many of the unanimity rule juries. They suggest that under majority rule large factions adopt a more forceful and "bullying" persuasive style because their members realize that when their goal is to achieve a faction size of only eight or ten members, they need not be worried about leaving a few opposition members untouched, or even feeling defensive.

As another possibility, Hastie et al. suggest that members of minority factions may have perceived that their probability of affecting the outcome, either by reversing the majority preference or by deadlocking the jury, was less as the decision requirement declined from unanimity to an 8 of 12 majority. Hence, they may have made fewer attempts at persuasion under the less strict decision rules.

Both these explanations of Hastie et al. essentially assume that participation in group discussion takes the form of attempts to persuade others to change their position. An alternative possibility is that in some instances group members may be attempting, not to persuade others with whom they disagree, but to provide social support for others with whom they do agree, to persuade them to maintain their positions. For example, minority members may feel more pressure to change their positions under unanimity rule than under variations of majority rule, and their relatively greater participation in discussion under unanimity rule may be a way of helping each other resist this greater felt pressure. Consistent with this possibility, Hans (1978) found not only that minority faction members participated more in group discussion under unanimity rule than under 5/6ths majority rule, but that this was due to *within-faction* discussion rather than *between-faction* persuasion attempts. That is, minority members participated at a higher rate under unanimity rule because they spent more time talking to one another, not because they spent more time trying to persuade the majority members to change their position.

Summary. Group decision rules affect the duration and content of group discussion and the extent to which various members participate. With regard to duration of group discussion, the stricter the decision rule, the more extensive discussion tends to be. Unanimous decisions take longer to reach and require more discussion than do majority decisions. Regarding the effects of decision rules on discussion content, the evidence is somewhat mixed, but a recent study by Kaplan and Miller (1987) suggests that content is affected by the interaction of decision rule with type of issue. Intellective issues normally call forth more attempts at informational influence, whereas judgmental issues usually lead to a predominance of normative influence attempts. A stricter decision rule, such as unanimity, leads to more influence attempts of the kind that normally predominate for a given type of issue. Finally, with regard to participation in group discussion, the stricter the decision rule, the more likely deviates or members of minority factions are to participate, and the less likely members of majority factions are to participate.

Effects on Perceptions of Group Discussion

Group members' feelings about and recall of the group discussion may vary as a function of the group decision rule. With regard to feelings about the group discussion, studies comparing unanimity rule and various versions of majority rule have found, on the one hand, that under unanimity rule members perceive the discussion as more uncomfortable and difficult and as involving more negative socio-emotional behavior (Green & Taber, 1980; Hastie et al., 1983; Kaplan & Miller, 1987; Nemeth, 1977). On the other hand, such studies have also found that under unanimity rule group members perceive the discussion as more adequate—as more serious, thorough, and satisfying (Hastie et al., 1983; Kaplan & Miller, 1987; Nemeth, 1977)—and feel that they have influenced others more, learned more, and were more understood and listened to (Green & Taber, 1980; Miller & Braasch, 1988).

It seems likely that group decision making is seen as more difficult and uncomfortable under unanimity rule than under majority rules because under unanimity rule some group members typically *must* change their positions (or at least their publicly expressed positions) if the group is to reach a decision, whereas under majority rules this is not necessarily the case. But even though unanimity rule typically requires difficult and unsettling change, it also typically leads to greater final consensus among group members. The higher ratings of satisfaction with discussion and other measures of perceived adequacy of the decision process (cf. Hastie et al., 1983) may be reflective of this higher degree of consensus. The importance of consensus in generating feelings of confidence and cohesiveness is well-known from work on conformity (cf. Janis, 1973).

Because decision rules differentially affect the feelings members have about group discussion, it seems possible they might also affect members' recall of the discussion. So far as I have been able to determine, however, only two studies have examined this possibility, and they produced mixed results. Saks (1977) found that majority rule jurors recalled more arguments raised during deliberation than did unanimous rule jurors. In contrast to this, Hastie et al. (1983) found that individual postdeliberation memory was unrelated to decision rule. Further research on this issue would be useful, and any consistent finding that decision rule affects the recall of group discussion would be of considerable importance.

Summary. The stricter the decision rule, the more members perceive the group discussion as being uncomfortable, difficult, and conflictful, but also as being more thorough and adequate. The possible effects of decision rules on recall of group discussion are uncertain and need further study.

Effects on Perceived Fairness of the Group Decision Rule

The literature on procedural justice might be thought to provide information about group members' judgments of the fairness of group decision rules. However, this literature has generally not examined the perceived fairness of group decision rules per se. Rather, most procedural justice research has dealt with procedures for resolving disputes between two parties, and has examined how those parties evaluate the dispute resolution procedure, depending on the extent to which the procedure affords control over the outcome (i.e., decision) or over the process (i.e., development and selection of information used to resolve the dispute) (Brett, 1986; Thibaut & Walker, 1978).

Only a few studies have explicitly examined the perceived fairness of decision rules. The findings of the previously discussed study by Kaplan and Miller (1987) suggest that, on the average, unanimity rule is seen as fairer than majority rule (although the strength of this effect is greater when the issue is judgmental than when the issue is intellective). One reason why unanimity rule might be perceived as fairer than majority rule is that, as we have already seen, it tends to result in larger changes in the preferences of group members, bringing about higher average levels of agreement and satisfaction with the eventual group decision. The Kaplan and Miller study did not specifically consider perceived fairness as a function of group members' satisfaction or agreement with the group decision. However, examination of the mean levels of satisfaction with the decision in the different experimental conditions of the study shows that they roughly parallel the mean levels of perceived fairness of the decision rule (see Table 1 of the study). Moreover, the recent Miller et al. (1987) study deliberately manipulated agreement with the group decision and found that such agreement accounted for about 10% of the variance in perceived fairness of the group decision rule.

The Miller et al. (1987) study and the earlier Miller and Anderson (1979) study show that perceived fairness of the group decision rule also depends on whether the resulting decision is representative of the preferences of group members. If it is representative, the rule tends to be seen as relatively fair; if it is not representative, the rule tends to be seen as relatively unfair. Miller et al. found that about 22% of the variance in perceived fairness of the decision rule could be attributed to the representativeness of the group decision. Representativeness is related to the decision rule that a group uses because some rules—for example, rules that are stricter or that distribute power more equally among group members—are more apt than others to result in representative outcomes.

Miller et al. (1987) note that in their study group members seem not to have regarded dictatorship as particularly unfair unless it led to an unrepresentative decision. One implication of this is that group members' judgments of the fairness of a decision rule might change as they obtain experience in making decisions under that rule. For example, a dictatorship might be seen as acceptable and fair as long as the dictator makes decisions that are representative of the group members' preferences. That is, a benevolent dictatorship may not be seen as a dictatorship, or at least may not be regarded as unfair. Only over the course of a number of decisions, when the dictator actually begins to exercise authority by making unrepresentative decisions, may the procedure be seen as unfair. Perhaps only then do the group members come to understand that all the power in the group is held by a single member.

Summary.   The perceived fairness of a group decision rule depends on the extent to which decisions made under the rule are representative of the preferences of all the group members. The more representative the decisions, the fairer the rule is perceived to be. The extent to which a group member perceives the decision rule to be fair also depends somewhat on whether decisions made according to the rule agree with the preferences of the member. The more agreeable the decisions, the more the rule is perceived as fair. Some group decision rules are more likely than others to result in representative and agreeable decisions.

Effects on Group Members' Feelings Toward One Another

Effects of group decision rules on the feelings of group members toward one another have received little attention, perhaps because these effects are even less obvious than other effects of decision rules. Only studies by Miller and Anderson (1979) and Miller et al. (1987) have had these effects as a principal focus, although some other work has had them as a peripheral concern.

Hastie et al. (1983) found that jurors under all decision rules had more favorable impressions (e.g., of persuasiveness and open-mindedness) of others with whom they agreed than of others with whom they disagreed. This finding is, of course, consistent with a large body of social psychological research (Byrne, 1971). But Hastie et al. also found an effect for decision rule, with jurors having more positive impressions of others in unanimous rule juries than majority rule juries. Similarly, Miller and Braasch (1988) found that under unanimity rule, as compared to majority rule, group members felt they had worked better together and were more willing to work together again. Because both Hastie et al. and Miller also found that unanimity rule resulted in greater eventual agreement among group members than did majority rule, it is probable that the effect of decision rule on liking was due largely to the effect of rule on agreement.

There is evidence that some individuals are aware, or anticipate, that unanimity rule is likely to produce greater agreement and more positive feelings of group members toward one another than is majority rule. Gero (1985) asked Masters of Business Administration and Masters of Social Work students—representing professions that are highly involved with group decision making in their organizational practices—to compare consensus and majority methods of decision making, using semantic differential scales. She found that students of both professions expected consensus to result in greater friendliness, cooperation, and agreement than the majority method.

The Miller and Anderson (1979) and Miller et al. (1987) studies concentrated specifically on liking among group members, and in particular liking among members of groups in which there was a single deviate. Like the Hastie et al. study, these studies found an effect for agreement, with members liking others whose preferences agreed with their own more than others whose preferences disagreed. However, these studies also found that the group decision rule had an indirect effect on liking because the rule determined whether or not a decision could be made that went against the majority of the group members and favored the deviate (i.e., whether an unrepresentative decision could be made). For example, both studies had one condition involving a deviate who was a dictator and who made a decision that opposed the majority. Both studies also had a condition involving unanimity rule in which the deviate thwarted the will of the majority and caused an unrepresentative decision by preventing the occurrence of unanimity. Results showed that in these dictatorship and unanimity conditions members tended to be especially rejecting of the deviate—moreso than when the deviate was not able to cause an unrepresentative decision. Miller et al. (1987) suggest that this strong rejection of the deviate, based on an unrepresentative decision, was linked to the perceived unfairness of the decision rule. When the decision was unrepresentative, the decision rule was seen as unfair, and the deviate was blamed for implementing or taking advantage of the unfair rule.

Summary.   Group decision rules may affect liking among group members because they tend to affect the extent to which the group decision agrees with the preferences of the members. The use of stricter decision rules usually results in decisions that are more representative of members' preferences than are decisions that result from the use of more lenient rules. In instances in which the decision rule leads to an unrepresentative decision, any group member who is regarded by the majority as responsible for the decision tends to be strongly rejected by the majority.

Effects on Perceptions of Others Outside the Group

So far we have concentrated on the effects of group decision rules on the outcomes of decisions and on the feelings, thoughts, and behaviors of group members. However, group decision rules may also affect the perceptions of persons outside the group. This is shown strikingly by the recent work of Allison and Messick (1985) on the *group attribution error*. This error consists of the tendency to assume that group decisions reflect the opinions of group members. This assumption can be erroneous because group decisions are affected not only by the members' opinions, but also by the decision rule that is used to aggregate their opinions.

One of a series of experiments reported by Allison and Messick (1985) illustrates the group attribution error. In this experiment, subjects read a brief vignette that described a recent recall election in Montana. Subjects were told (a) that either 43 or 57% of the voters voted in favor of recall; (b) that either 35, 50, or 65% of the voters had to vote in favor of the recall for it to be successful; and (c) that the recall vote therefore either succeeded or failed, as appropriate. Subjects were then asked to indicate the attitude of the typical Montana citizen toward recall—in particular, how strongly they thought the typical citizen favored the recall.

The attitude attributions of subjects were found to depend not only on the percentage of voters in favor of the recall, but also on the success or failure of the recall. For a given percentage of voters favoring recall (e.g., 57%), subjects tended to see the typical voter as more in favor of recall if the recall succeeded than if it failed. Thus, there is a tendency for outside observers to infer a correspondence between a group's decisions and its members' attitudes and to overlook the impact that the group decision rule may have in producing the decisions.

This basic effect has since been replicated in other studies (Allison & Messick, 1987; Mackie & Allison, 1987). Allison and Messick (1987) argue that people use a group's decision as a heuristic to infer the attitudes of group members. This heuristic is normally useful, as most groups typically employ decision rules that produce representative decisions. In cases where they do not, however, observers still have some tendency to believe that representativeness is present.

Worth, Allison, and Messick (1987) have just recently shown that not only outside observers, but even the actual participants in a group decision making process may commit the group attribution error with regard to the group's decisions. Apparently, even the members of decision-making groups are often unaware of the influence of the group decision rule on the final group decision. That is, given identical preference distributions for the choice of a particular alternative within a group, members will believe that the group desires that alternative more under a decision rule that results in choice of the alternative than under one that does not.

Summary. Both outside observers and the members of decision-making groups sometimes commit the group attribution error. They tend to infer the attitudes of group members from the decision of the group, disregarding the effects of the group decision rule on the decision. Thus, the fact that some decision rules are less strict or less egalitarian than others, and may thus result in less representative decisions, is ignored. The group decision is to some extent regarded as being representative of the members' preferences even when it is not.

SUMMARY AND SUGGESTIONS FOR FUTURE RESEARCH

Groups adopt a variety of procedures for the purpose of making decisions. Once a group consists of more than a few members, these procedures usually include a group decision rule as a necessary means of resolving the inevitable conflicts of interest among group members. As we have seen in this chapter, group decision rules produce a variety of social psychological effects:

First of all, the group decision rule affects the nature of the group decision itself. Stricter decision rules, such as unanimity rule, are more likely to result in the group failing to reach a decision. If a decision is reached, stricter rules are more likely to lead to some sort of compromise that takes into account the preferences of minority members. There is some evidence that these compromise decisions may be more adequate or of higher quality than decisions made under more lenient rules.

Second, the group decision rule affects both the publicly expressed and privately held preferences of individual members of the group. The stricter the decision rule, the more likely members are to change their preferences in the direction of greater agreement with one another, and the less likely they are to dissent from the final group decision.

A third effect of the group decision rule is on satisfaction with the group decision. Satisfaction with the group decision is determined mostly by agreement with the decision, and because stricter decision rules tend to result in greater agreement with the decision, they also tend to result in greater satisfaction with the decision.

Fourth, the group decision rule affects the duration and content of, and participation in, group discussion. The stricter the decision rule, the more extensive the discussion and the longer it takes to reach a decision. Discussion of intellective issues typically leads to more attempts at informational influence, whereas discussion of judgmental issues usually results in more normative influence attempts. The stricter the decision rule, the greater the tendency to use the kind of influence attempts that normally predominate for the given type of issue. Additionally, the stricter the decision rule, the more likely members of a minority faction are—and the less likely members of the majority faction are—to participate in the group discussion.

A fifth factor affected by the group decision rule is the members' perceptions of group discussion. The stricter the decision rule, the more the discussion is perceived as being uncomfortable, difficult, and filled with conflict, but the more it is also perceived as being thorough and adequate.

Sixth, group decision rules differ in terms of how fair group members perceive them to be. A member's perception of the fairness of a rule depends on both the extent to which decisions made under the rule are representative of the preferences of all group members, and the extent to which the decisions agree with the preferences of that particular member. The more representative and agreeable the decisions, the greater the perceived fairness. Stricter and more egalitarian decision rules tend to result in more representative and agreeable decisions.

Seventh, the group decision rule affects liking among group members. The liking of one member for another depends largely on how much their positions agree. One will like the other more, the greater the agreement. Liking between members also depends on the extent to which one sees the other as responsible for making a group decision that is unrepresentative. The greater the responsibility for an unrepresentative decision, the more the other is rejected. Again, stricter group decision rules tend to result in more agreement among members, and stricter and more egalitarian rules are less likely to lead to unrepresentative decisions.

Finally, the group decision rule is implicated in the group attribution error, in which persons tend to assume that the decision of a group is representative of the preferences of the members. This assumption may be mistaken because the group decision is determined not only by member preferences, but also by the group decision rule. Lenient or less egalitarian decision rules sometimes lead to decisions that are unrepresentative, in which case the group attribution error may occur.

Clearly, the social psychological effects produced by group decision rules are interesting and important enough to justify their receiving greater attention than has yet been the case. So far research on these effects has been scarce, and until now there has been no generally recognized literature concerning the social psychology of group decision rules.

Future research efforts might fruitfully take several directions. One possibility is to try to identify which aspects of group decision rules are most important in terms of their social psychological effects. In this chapter, I have suggested two characteristics of decision rules—strictness and the distribution of power—which seem particularly important. Further research is likely to reveal others. The mathematical or axiomatic work on decision rules might prove a useful source of clues as to the nature of additional characteristics of importance. In several instances, this work identifies properties of decision rules that appear to have social psychological implications or relevance (see, for example, Arrow's, 1963, conditions of nonimposition and nondictatorship).

Another important need is for research on a wider variety of decision rules. Most of the research to date has compared various versions of majority rule and unanimity rule. Other rules of interest have largely been ignored. This is unfortunate for at least two reasons: First, many rules other than majority and unanimity are in frequent use in a variety of everyday situations. For example, dictatorial rule, in which formal power is held by a single person, is quite common in settings such as the workplace. Studies involving a greater variety of decision rules would thus offer increased generalizability to real-world settings—i.e., would provide improved ecological validity.

Second, other decision rules might provide stronger manipulations of the important characteristics of rules than do majority and unanimity rule. For example, most comparisons of decision rules have involved majority and unanimity rule, even though both of these rules are egalitarian and both are relatively strict—at least in comparison to other rules, such as dictatorship. Studies comparing more authoritarian and more lenient decision rules with majority rule or unanimity rule might lead to the discovery of effects other than those reviewed here, or might demonstrate that some of the reviewed effects are stronger than they would appear to be, based only on contrasts between majority and unanimity rule (contrasts which amount to weak manipulations).

Besides studying more decision rules, we need to consider how the social psychological effects of rules are influenced by norms governing their use. Some cultures have very strong norms favoring the use of consensus procedures, such as unanimity rule. For example, the Nez Perce Indians traditionally require unanimous agreement to decide matters before the council of chiefs (McLuhan, 1971). Similarly, Quaker meetings may require a "sense of the meeting," i.e., a consensus, in order to reach a decision. Other cultures or subcultures may have norms that prescribe the use of rules that concentrate authority in the hands of a few, as with dictatorial or oligarchical rules. For example, in some cultures interpersonal disputes are commonly settled by appeal to a priest or religious authority. Findings about the social psychological effects of group decision rules may be affected by such cultural norms regarding the appropriateness of the rules.

Even within a particular culture, norms may make the use of a given group decision rule suitable in one situation but not in another. In our own culture, for example, some type of majority rule is typically deemed appropriate in the conduct of elections, whereas relatively dictatorial decision-making processes are often seen as reasonable in the business world. This suggests that the decision setting or type of task may influence the social psychological effects of decision rules.

One means of exploring the development of norms regarding the use of group decision rules—and another possible direction for future research—would be to study what conditions affect the kinds of rules that typically emerge from, or are adopted by, decision-making groups. That is, instead of *assigning* a decision rule to a group, one might place groups in various decision-making situations and see what type of decision rule the members normally decide to adopt. The sorts of decision rules that emerge would presumably be affected by factors such as the type of decision to be made, the size of the group, the group's status hierarchy, time constraints, performance demands, costs, and so on.

Some of the factors that influence the emergence of a group decision rule are probably embedded in a circular chain of causal relationships, or in reciprocal causal relationships (cf. Cartwright & Zander, 1968), with the group decision rule itself. For example, the status hierarchy of a group may influence the kind of decision rule that is adopted by the group. Groups composed of members with relatively equal status may adopt relatively egalitarian decision rules, whereas groups whose members differ sharply in status may use more autocratic rules. However, the kind of decision rule that a group employs may, in turn, affect the group's status hierarchy. It may be harder to maintain status distinctions under egalitarian rules, and more difficult to prevent these distinctions from occurring under authoritarian rules. At present, we can only speculate about such relationships of reciprocal causality.

Still another direction for future research is to move away from one-shot or single-decision studies and to begin examining sequences of decisions in ongoing groups. Few decision-making groups in the real world meet to make one and only one decision. Instead, group members are likely to interact repeatedly and to reach decisions on multiple issues. As Miller et al. (1987) have suggested, group members may only come to understand the exact nature of different decision rules through repeated experience with the rules. For example, a rule that at first appears fair might be seen as unfair only after it becomes evident that the rule can result in various highly undesirable outcomes. Looking at sequences of group decisions would thus improve the generalizability of research.

Finally, not only may the same group make many decisions over a period of time, and not only may different groups employ different decision rules, but the same group may employ different decision rules at different times for making different decisions. For example, the same departmental faculty who use a two-thirds majority rule for tenure or promotion may use a majority rule for other decisions. Virtually nothing is known about the complex problem of groups using more than one group decision rule. What are the effects or implications of using a particular decision rule in one instance and another rule in a different instance? This question and the many others raised in this chapter await further research.

ACKNOWLEDGMENTS

I wish to thank Scott Allison, Marty Kaplan, Sam Komorita, Dick Moreland, and Paul Paulus for their helpful comments on an earlier draft of this chapter.

REFERENCES

Allison, S. T., & Messick, D. M. (1985). The group attribution error. *Journal of Experimental Social Psychology, 21,* 563–579.

Allison, S. T., & Messick, D. M. (1987). From individual inputs to group outputs, and back again: Group processes and inferences about group members. In C. Hendrick (Ed.), *Review of personality and social psychology* (Vol. 8). Beverly Hills, CA: Sage.

Apodaca, Cooper, and Madden v. Oregon. 92 S. Ct. 1628 (1972).

Arrow, K. J. (1963). *Social choice and individual values* (2nd ed.). New Haven, CT: Yale University Press.

Birnberg, J., & Pondy, L. (1971). An experimental study of three voting rules. In B. Lieberman (Ed.), *Social choice* (pp. 225–242.). New York: Gordon and Breach.

Black, D. (1958). *The theory of committees and elections.* Cambridge, England: Cambridge University Press.

Bower, J. L. (1965a). Group decision making: A report of an experimental study. *Behavioral Science, 10,* 277–289.

Bower, J. L. (1965b). The role of conflict in economic decision making groups. *Quarterly Journal of Economics, 70,* 253–277.

Brams, S. J. (1975). *Game theory and politics.* New York: Free Press.

Bray, R. M. (1974). *Decision rules, attitude similarity, and jury decision making.* Unpublished doctoral dissertation, University of Illinois.

Bray, R. M., & Stuckman-Johnson, C. (1977). *Effects of juror population, assigned decision rule, and insurance option on decisions of simulated juries.* Paper presented at the meeting of the American Psychological Association, San Francisco.

Brett, J. M. (1986). Commentary on procedural justice papers. In R. J. Lewicki, B. H. Sheppard, & M. H. Bazerman (Eds.), *Research on negotiation in organizations* (Vol. 1, pp. 81–92). Greenwich, CT: JAI Press.

Broeder, D. W. (1958). The University of Chicago jury project. *Nebraska Law Review, 38,* 744–761.

Buckhout, R., Weg, S., Reilly, F., & Frohboese, R. (1977). Jury verdicts: Comparison of 6- vs. 12-person juries and unanimous vs. majority decision rule in a murder trial. *Bulletin of the Psychonomic Society, 10,* 175–178.

Byrne, D. (1971). *The attraction paradigm.* New York: Academic Press.

Cartwright, D., & Zander, A. (Eds.). (1968). *Group dynamics: Research and theory.* New York: Harper & Row.

Castore, C. H. (1978). Decision making and decision implementation in groups and organizations. In B. T. King, F. Fiedler, & S. Streufert (Eds.), *Managerial control and organizational democracy* (pp. 267–275). Washington, DC: V. H. Winston.

Castore, C. H., & Murnighan, J. K. (1978). Determinants of support for group decisions. *Organizational Behavior and Human Performance, 22,* 75–92.

Davis, J. H. (1973). Group decision and social interaction: A theory of social decision schemes. *Psychological Review, 80,* 97–125.

Davis, J. H., Kerr, N. L., Atkin, R. S., Holt, R., & Meek, D. (1975). The decision processes of 6- and 12-person mock juries assigned unanimous and two-thirds majority rules. *Journal of Personality and Social Psychology, 32,* 1–14.

Deutsch, M., & Gerard, H. (1955). A study of normative and informational social influences on individual judgment. *Journal of Abnormal and Social Psychology, 51,* 629–636.

Farquharson, R. (1969). *Theory of voting.* New Haven, CT: Yale University Press.

Festinger, L., & Carlsmith, J. M. (1959). Cognitive consequences of forced compliance. *Journal of Abnormal and Social Psychology, 58,* 203–210.

Fishburn, P. (1973). *The theory of social choice.* Princeton, NJ: Princeton University Press.

Folger, R., Rosenfield, D., & Robinson, T. (1983). Relative deprivation and procedural justifications. *Journal of Personality and Social Psychology, 45,* 268–273.

Foss, R. D. (1981). Structural effects in simulated jury decision making. *Journal of Personality and Social Psychology, 40,* 1055–1062.

Gero, A. (1985). Conflict avoidance in consensual decision processes. *Small Group Behavior, 16,* 487–499.

Green, S. G., & Taber, T. D. (1980). The effects of three social decision schemes on group process. *Organizational Behavior and Human Performance, 25,* 97–106.

Grofman, B. (1976). Not necessarily twelve and not necessarily unanimous: Evaluating the impact of Williams v. Florida and Johnson v. Louisiana. In G. Bermant, C. Nemeth, & N. Vidmar (Eds.), *Psychology and the law* (pp. 149–168). Lexington, MA: D.C. Heath.

Halfpenny, P., & Taylor, M. (1973). An experimental study of individual and collective decision-making. *British Journal of Political Science, 3,* 425–444.

Hall, J. (1971, November). Decisions, decisions, decisions. *Psychology Today,* 51–54, 86, 88.

Hans, V. P. (1978). *The effects of the unanimity requirement on group decision processes in simulated juries.* Unpublished doctoral dissertation, University of Toronto.

Harnett, D. L. (1967). A level of aspiration model for group decision making. *Journal of Personality and Social Psychology, 5,* 58–66.

Hastie, R., Penrod, S., & Pennington, N. (1983). *Inside the jury.* Cambridge, MA: Harvard University Press.

Holloman, C. R., & Hendrick, H. W. (1972). Adequacy of group decisions as a function of the decision-making process. *Academy of Management Journal, 15,* 175–184.

Janis, I. (1973). *Victims of groupthink.* Boston: Houghton Mifflin.

Johnson v. Louisiana. 92 S. Ct. 1935 (1972).

Kaplan, M. F., & Miller, C. E. (1987). Group decision making and normative vs. informational influence: Effects of type of issue and assigned decision rule. *Journal of Personality and Social Psychology, 53,* 306–313.

Kerr, N. L., Atkin, R., Stasser, G., Meek, D., Holt, R., & Davis, J. (1976). Guilt beyond a reasonable doubt: Effects of concept definition and assigned decision rule on the judgments of mock jurors. *Journal of Personality and Social Psychology, 34,* 282–294.

Kerr, N. L., & MacCoun, R. J. (1985). The effects of jury size and polling method on the process and product of jury deliberation. *Journal of Personality and Social Psychology, 48,* 349–363.

Kotter, J. P., & Schlesinger, L. A. (1981). Choosing strategies for change. *Harvard Business Review, 57*(2), 106–114.

Lamm, H., & Myers, D. G. (1978). Group-induced polarization of attitudes and behavior. In L. Berkowitz (Ed.), *Advances in experimental social psychology* (Vol. 11, pp. 145–195). New York: Academic Press.

Laughlin, P. R. (1980). Social combination processes of cooperative, problem-solving groups on verbal intellective tasks. In M. Fishbein (Ed.), *Progress in social psychology* (Vol. 1, pp. 127–155). Hillsdale, NJ: Lawrence Erlbaum Associates.

Laughlin, P. R., & Ellis, A. L. (1986). Demonstrability and social combination processes on mathematical intellective tasks. *Journal of Experimental Social Psychology, 22,* 177–189.

Locke, E. A., & Schweiger, D. M. (1979). Participation in decision making: One more look. In B. M. Staw (Ed.), *Research in organizational behavior* (Vol. 1, pp. 265–340). Greenwich, CT: JAI Press.

Mackie, D. M., & Allison, S. T. (1987). Group attribution errors and the illusion of group attitude change. *Journal of Experimental Social Psychology, 23,* 460–480.

McCluhan, T. C. (1971). *Touch the earth.* New York: Outerbridge & Dienstfrey.

Miller, C. E. (1985). Group decision making under majority and unanimity decision rules. *Social Psychology Quarterly, 48,* 51–61.

Miller, C. E., & Anderson, P. D. (1979). Group decision rules and the rejection of deviates. *Sociometry, 42,* 354–363.

Miller, C. E., & Braasch, G. (1988). *Effects of assigned decision rule and issue importance on group decisions and reactions of group members.* Unpublished manuscript, Northern Illinois University.

Miller, C. E., Jackson, P., Mueller, J., & Scherching, C. (1987). Some social psychological effects of group decision rules. *Journal of Personality and Social Psychology, 52,* 325–332.

Myers, D. G., & Lamm, H. (1976). The group polarization phenomenon. *Psychological Bulletin, 83,* 602–627.

Nemeth, C. (1977). Interactions between jurors as a function of majority vs. unanimity decision rules. *Journal of Applied Social Psychology, 7,* 38–56.

Pearson, J. (1982). An evaluation of alternatives to court adjudication. *The Justice System Journal, 7,* 420–444.

Saks, M. J. (1977). *Jury verdicts.* Lexington, MA: Heath.

Sherif, M. (1936). *The psychology of social norms.* New York: Harper.

Thibaut, J., & Walker, L. (1975). *Procedural justice: A psychological analysis.* Hillsdale, NJ: Lawrence Erlbaum Associates.

Thibaut, J., & Walker, L. (1978). A theory of procedure. *California Law Review, 66,* 541–566.

Tjosvold, D., & Field, R. H. G. (1983). Effects of social context on consensus and majority vote decision making. *Academy of Management Journal, 26,* 500–506.

Worth, L. T., Allison, S. T., & Messick, D. M. (1987). Impact of a group's decision on perceptions of one's own and others' attitudes. *Journal of Personality and Social Psychology, 53,* 673–682.

11 Group Remembering

Noel K. Clark
Geoffrey M. Stephenson
University of Kent

INTRODUCTION

The psychological literature has traditionally treated the subject of human memory in general, and remembering in particular, in terms of individual cognitive processes which allow us to function appropriately in both individual and social settings. The psychological study of remembering is, however, becoming more realistic, more applied, and, therefore, more social.

The *social* basis and functions of memory has long been recognized by sociologists and philosophers. Halbwachs' (1950) treatise *La Memoire Collective* has been translated (Halbwachs, 1980) from the French, and English readers can now better appreciate his brilliant development of the Durkheimian notion of time—and memory—as a social construct. Memories, Halbwachs suggests, fade as we lose contact with the groups that sustained them. For example, why do professors forget a group of students whose members and their activities were so vivid in the past? Unlike students, for whom their group may have lasting significance, "there exists no durable group to which the professor continues to belong, about which he may have occasion to think, and within whose viewpoint he could resituate himself to remember the past." (Halbwachs, 1980, p. 27).

In a similar vein, Wittgenstein (1953) extended Mills' (1940) views of the social nature and functions of language and its relation to social action. Wittgenstein argued that we do not remember primarily in order to represent our experiences to ourselves, but to promote particular kinds of social order and action through the medium of social interaction. This constructionist theme provides the underpinning for some recent social psychological studies of the social construction of social behavior and communication generally (e.g., Gergen, 1982; Shotter, 1984), and collective remembering in particular (Shotter, 1987).

Frederick Bartlett (1923, 1932) was the first experimental psychologist to emphasize the importance of social and group processes in memory. As we shall see, Bartlett's (1932) studies of remembering highlighted the fundamental importance of social factors in memory, although that aspect of his work has subsequently been generally neglected. It is only recently, with the development of interest in the everyday contexts in which individuals recall events (Hunter, 1979; Neisser, 1982; Wells & Loftus, 1984), that the social context has begun to impinge seriously on psychological research into human remembering.

This chapter is concerned with the phenomenon of face-to-face group or collaborative remembering, and we use Shaw's (1976) definition of a group, emphasizing the dynamic nature of group processes within social interactions, throughout the chapter:

> . . . two or more persons who are interacting with one another in such a manner that each person influences and is influenced by each other person. (p. 11)

Group remembering has distinctive properties. For example, anticipating experimental results by several decades, Halbwachs referred to the *confidence* that such collective remembering engenders in group members. He argued that we often share our recollections with those of other people who have shared the same (or a similar) experience. This allows us to *compare* our impressions of an experience, and gain several, possibly divergent, viewpoints on it. According to Halbwachs, the outcome of such comparisons is revealed in the confidence with which our impressions are held. If our recollections coincide with those of others, our confidence in them is likely to *increase*; if they do not coincide, our confidence may be undermined. There is, of course, an alternative social psychological consequence of detecting discrepancies between our own recollections and those of others—cognitive dissonance (e.g., Aronson, 1969; Brehm & Cohen, 1962; Festinger, 1957)—an issue that is dealt with in detail elsewhere (Clark & Stephenson, 1988).

Group remembering powerfully constrains group decision making and it is surprising that its role has been rarely studied by psychologists. Group remembering is also itself a decision-making process and is often an important component in the performance of task-oriented groups. It is not hard to think of examples. Juries are a case in point, where decisions are, more often than not, made on the basis of jurors' recall (or nonrecall) of the facts and arguments in a case. Interestingly, jury remembering has not featured prominently in research on jury decision making (for an exception see Hartwick, Sheppard, & Davis, 1982).

Personnel selection interview panels are another example of both group remembering as a vital component of decision making. In order to reject the *unappointable* and accept the *appointable* candidates, panel members need to remember the responses given during interviews by all candidates, even though the interviews may take place over 2 or 3 days. Members of such panels are often grateful to the one member whose clarity of recall refreshes their own, and calls to their minds the existence of some candidates whose existence would otherwise have been completely forgotten.

In addition to its intrinsic importance in decision making, group remembering is also a *technique* for the exploration of issues in individual remembering. Bartlett (1932) introduced the technique of *serial reproduction*—in which material to be remembered is passed on verbally from one to another—in order to study those social factors that he claimed permeate individual remembering. Group remembering takes serial reproduction one step further, using a technique of *collaborative reproduction*, in which two or more individuals agree on a statement about events that they all witnessed. Let us now examine the process of such collaborative remembering in some detail.

THEORETICAL BACKGROUND

Memory is Social

Remembering has generally been investigated at an intrinsically individualistic level. That is, research has focused on explanations of individual cognitive processes involved in retrieving information from memory stores. Unfortunately, a purely individual level of explanation fails to take account of the social origins of remembering, nor does it address the possible influence of the social contexts within which cognition and recall take place on the content of what is remembered, or the social purposes that often determine why we recall particular events, interactions, or discourses.

Edwards and Middleton (1986, 1987) argue that there are two senses in which human memory is social. First, we possess memories for both social events and social relationships that we have directly experienced. Theoretically, such personal memories are stored separately from more general knowledge in *episodic* rather than *semantic* memory storage (Tulving, 1972, 1983). Second, many of our memories are derived from *symbolic* communication with others during social interactions. That is, much of both our social and nonsocial knowledge is a consequence of *social communication* rather than direct experience. For example, most of us will (hopefully) not have had direct experience of being interrogated as a criminal suspect by the police, but many will possess a *script* for such an event, probably derived from fictional/factual media reports. Similarly, most people know that holding a lighted match too close to a can of petrol is likely to have an explosive result, although very few of us will have learned this fact through direct experience or observation—we have received the information symbolically (most probably linguistically) from others. Moreover, we are able to abstract scriptal knowledge (Schank & Abelson, 1977) from our own idiosyncratic social experiences, representing a transfer of information from our episodic to semantic stores.

Issues related to Edwards and Middleton's first sense of the social nature of memory—the *contents* of memory—do not concern us. It is their second sense of the social nature of memory that is relevant here—that memories "are largely derived from symbolic communications". Although social communication may take many forms (for example, newspaper articles, television and radio programes, mime, letters and books, as well as face-to-face and telephone interactions), the rest of this chapter focuses on one type of social communication in particular: face-to-face social interaction between members of a group. Particular attention will be paid to the effects of small-group interaction and negotiation on collaborative remembering.

Although Bartlett (1932) acknowledged that remembering is essentially an *intrapersonal* phenomenon, he argued that many aspects of remembering are directly determined by social factors during both comprehension and recall processes. These social factors relate to the effects of both the social context generally, and *intragroup* processes particularly, which are at play during original learning and subsequent remembering during social interactions.

With respect to the social context of remembering, Bartlett considered this to be far more than a simple frame or backdrop against which cognition and behavior takes place. He argued strongly that social context is a necessary *condition* for social action, rather than as background for such action. In particular, he viewed group membership per se as a moderating factor for both thought and behavior, regardless of the presence or absence of other group members at the time of encoding or recall.

Moreover, Bartlett argued that cognitive representation and comprehension, as well as remembering, were influenced by social group membership. He reasoned that social groups fulfill particular social and psychological needs for their members, and groups are organized and cohere as a result of the transformation of the psychosocial tendencies of their members into a group bias towards dealing with everyday circumstances in particular ways. He argued that once such biases are established, they provide individual group members with a "direct stimuli" to guide their comprehension of current experience in two ways: first, by providing a cognitive framework (i.e., schematic and scriptal knowledge) for the construction and understanding of an experience, and second, by providing an affective/emotional setting for that experience. Moreover, he asserted that group membership has most influence on individual remembering when a person remembers *for* the group, that is when they act as an agent or representative of the group in either an intra- or intergroup situation.

Bartlett's view was, then, that cognition is essentially a social activity, rather than an activity of individuals that occurs for purely intra- or interpersonal reasons. However, we have yet to consider *why* it is that he considered remembering to be such an important aspect of social life. Bartlett makes two important points about the reasons for remembering, and the nature of what is remembered in social contexts. Regarding the former, he commented that we discuss our own experiences with other people in order to compare, evaluate, or criticize our *impression* with theirs—to make social comparisons between the contents of our memory stores with those of others. However, this comparison process is not, of necessity, an attempt to achieve a more *accurate* account of what is being recalled. He viewed remembering as a process directed towards achieving social aims. Remembering in everyday life is, therefore, often a mixture of "factual" recall, and our own (group) interpretations and interpolations of the meaning of those facts. Moreover, Bartlett (1932) argued that it is the latter rather than the former that is the driving force for remembering, that is, the "facts" of a recalled experience are determined by our interpretation of those events— ". . . *there is ordinarily no direct and laborious effort to secure accuracy*" (p. 96).

Bartlett's conclusion that a major function of remembering is "value or criticise, or compare our impressions" with those of others, is essentially social psychological in its emphasis on the importance of social comparison processes. However, Bartlett's constructivist theory was opposed to the associationist psychological orientation of the time, and has only recently been appreciated for its contribution to our understanding of remembering (Neisser, 1978, 1982). Moreover, social psychological research has, until recently, paid little attention to remembering. It is for these reasons that some aspects of Bartlett's theory, in particular those related to social aspects of remembering, have yet to receive adequate empirical investigation.

Group Remembering and Social Cognition

Social psychological research has investigated several areas of social cognition closely related to remembering, for example, attitudes, beliefs and opinions. All of these rely, more or less, on subject's being able to recall past experiences in order that statements of attitudes and opinion can be made.

Bartlett's view that remembering is often concerned with social comparisons rather than veridical recall, is similar to that expressed by Festinger in his work on social comparison (1950, 1954), although the focus of attention is different. Festinger offered a theoretical account of why people compare their own opinions and abilities with those of others. He argued that we undertake social comparisons as a consequence of a drive to evaluate our abilities, beliefs, and opinions, in order to reduce our uncertainty about the world in which we live. Many abilities (and some opinions and beliefs) may be readily evaluated through nonsocial, *objective*, comparisons. For example, my ability to drive a racing car may be evaluated by comparing my lap times with those of other drivers. Note that such objective evaluations are made in relation to other people who might be expected to also possess the *relevant* ability—racing car drivers—rather than, for example, truck drivers or airline pilots.

No such objective comparisons are, however, available to evaluate most opinions and beliefs (e.g., my belief that I am a kind person). Festinger hypothesised that in such circumstances self-evaluation is again achieved by comparisons between one's self and other people. However, as no objective comparison is available, the need to self-evaluate becomes a force acting upon us to interact with others. In order to evaluate our opinions and beliefs we therefore compare those opinions and beliefs with *relevant* others, that is those whose similarity to us is salient in some way. Festinger's conclusion, therefore, was that the need to self-evaluate results in our seeking out, and joining social groups whose attitudes and beliefs (as a group) reflect our own. Within such a context, social comparisons effectively reduce the uncertainty of our social world.

Interestingly, Piaget (1928) offers a relevant account of how children learn to treat their thought processes as objects suitable for examination, requiring verification and justification through comparisons with the thought processes of others, through participation in social interactions:

> It must be the shock of our thought coming into contact with that of others, which produces doubt and the desire to prove . . . The social need to share the thought of others and to communicate our own with success is at the root of our need for verification. . . . (p. 204)

Rogoff and Mistry (1985) recently reviewed the few studies that have examined the development of mnemonic skills as a social/cultural, rather than a purely individualistic, phenomenon. They concluded that children develop memory skills as a consequence of, and in order to participate more fully in, the cultural/social situations they experience. The skills are acquired during practical activities and interactions with other people. Edwards and Middleton (1988) illustrated this phenomenon in their observational study of children (aged between 2 and 6 years) *learning* to remember through interactions with their mothers while they looked through collections of family photographs. They found that the photographs provided the impetus for conversations and remembering about not only the content of the pictures themselves, but also about their context and other recalled or inferred situations for which photographs were not available. Edwards and Middleton (1988) argue that the mothers used the photographs to demonstrate informal principles of remembering, such as ". . . the criteria for memorability, the use of other people as a mnemonic resource, and the role of contextual inference and argument in constructing a jointly sensible version of the past" (p. 3).

It is relatively rare, however, for an objective record, which can be referred back to and checked against recall, to be kept of what was said or done during social interactions and events. The only record that an interaction actually took place is, more often than not, in the memories of participants and observers (exceptions include legal proceedings where a written transcript of all that occurred is made). Such a situation is very similar to that described by Festinger in relation the evaluation of opinions and beliefs. The only way in which people can evaluate the accuracy of their recall of what was said during an interaction is by comparing their recall with that of other people who were present during the interaction.

People do not, however, compare themselves with a random assortment of other people. Both Bartlett and Festinger emphasise that comparisons are more likely to take place between people who belong to the same social group (for example, family (Edwards & Middleton, 1988), work, or political groups). Comparisons and evaluations of recall *and* opinions and abilities therefore take place within the context of relevant social group membership(s). One important consequence of group membership for individual members (according to both Bartlett and Festinger) is the resolution of uncertainty about the social world when objective comparisons are impossible.

Social comparison processes within a group may not, however, always result in the positive consequences Festinger (1954) described, either for the group as a whole or for individual members. Irving Janis (1972) described a series of problems that may occur when groups (particularly those with social or political power) become isolated from the influence of other social groups—*groupthink*, which he defined as "a mode of thinking that people engage in when they are deeply involved in a cohesive in-group, when the members' strivings for unanimity override their motivation to realistically appraise alternative courses of action" (p. 9). Moreover, many of the symptoms of groupthink described by Janis (1972) appear to reflect one extreme of the social comparison process:

1. an illusion of invunerability, shared by most or all the members . . . ;
2. collective efforts to rationalize in order to discount warnings . . . ;
3. an unquestioned belief in the group's inherent morality . . . ;
4. stereotyped views of enemy leaders as too evil . . . or as too weak or stupid . . . ;
5. direct pressure on any member who expresses strong arguments against any of the group's stereotypes . . . ;
6. self-censorship of deviations from the apparent group concensus;
7. a shared illusion of unanimity . . . ;
8. the emergence of self-appointed mind guards—members who protect the group from adverse information . . . (p. 197–198)

Janis (1972) also identified six major defects in a social group's ability to make decisions as a consequence of groupthink:

First, the group's discussions are limited to only a few alternative courses of action . . . ;

Second, the group fails to reexamine the course of action initially preferred by the majority of members . . . ;

Third, the members neglect courses of action initially evaluated as unsatisfactory . . . ;

Fourth, members make little or no attempt to obtain information from experts . . . ;

Fifth, selective bias is shown in the way the group reacts to factual information . . . ;

Sixth, the members spend little time deliberating about how the chosen policy may be hindered . . . ; Consequently, they fail to work out contingency plans. (p. 10)

More recently, Janis (1982) has added a seventh defect to this list—incomplete survey of objectives. It is likely, given that decision making often relies on information stored in group member memories, that several of the symptoms of groupthink may influence, and be influenced by, collaborative remembering. This notion is considered later in discussions of our own work.

Collaborative Remembering in Everyday Life

Collaborative remembering, the negotiation and agreement of a joint account of some past mutual experience with others, is a regular aspect of daily social interaction for many people. Whenever two or more people discuss shared experiences they negotiate an account of what happened—collaborative remembering takes place. For example, if several friends discuss the occurrences at a party they all attended the night before, they are participating in a collaborative remembering exercise. They are, of course doing far more than simply collaboratively remembering; there is a social context within which remembering takes place which, gives an overall meaning to why they are remembering. Moreover, within this social context each of the participants may possess different motivations and expectations for remembering (as they may also have had for attending) the party. Such a diversity of motives may result in several different accounts or interpretations of what was said and done being discussed.

This example illustrates the case where collaborative remembering may serve an almost purely social interactional purpose—it gives these people something to talk about. The participants' motivation to reach an agreed account of these events is probably very low, any differences between individual participants in what they recall may be readily attributed to differences in their levels of intoxication at the party, and the consequences of failing to agree an account are probably equally low.

Probably most collaborative remembering takes place in informal situations such as the one above, where there are few if any consequences contingent on reaching an agreed account. There are some social situations, however, where there is at least an expectation of, if not direct social pressure on, participants to agree a joint account of a prior event. Moreover, there may also be a requirement that the joint account be as accurate as possible, because decisions will be made on the assumption that it is accurate. Such social situations tend to be more formalized and problem focused than the one just illustrated. One example is the deliberations and decision making of trial juries in criminal cases. If a jury reaches a unanimous verdict the jurors must, during their deliberations, have agreed to a joint account of the evidence that was presented to them, and negotiated the weight to be assigned to each piece of evidence. An inaccurate or very selective joint account of the evidence, or failure to agree on the evidence, may result in the acquittal of a guilty person or the conviction of an innocent one.

Evidence based on the collaborative recall of several individuals may also be presented as testimony in a court. In his study of oral traditions, Vansina (1973) described preparations for, and procedure during, a group testimony among the Kuba people. Witnesses to an event discuss and agree their testimony together before the public presentation. An appointed spokesman then presents the joint testimony. Vansina notes that,

> The fact that such a testimony is the concern of a group gives it a special character of its own. All those present must be in agreement about all the facts related, and nothing can be related that has not been agreed to unanimously. The testimony then acquires the character of an official statement, and at the same time it is a "minimum" statement, for some of the members of the group may know fuller details about some of the facts which are included in the account. (p. 28)

Collaborative testimony is also accepted, in some circumstance, as evidence in English Courts of Law provided that one condition is met: that it is made clear that it is a collaborative account (Heaton-Armstrong, 1987). Collaboration is most frequently seen in evidence presented by the police, with one officer giving evidence on behalf of him or herself and other officers involved in the case. Sometimes the officers will sign a joint account of an incident. The police, however, still appear to believe that individual, rather than collaborative testimony has more "impact," or appears more "truthful," on the court. It is not unusual for several police officers to give almost identical testimony in court, with each claiming that they wrote up their account of the events in question individually. Official sanction for collaborative testimony was given by the Court of Appeal in 1953 (All England Law Reports), following a case where two police officers claimed, while giving testimony, that they had not collaborated when preparing their evidence, even though their notebooks were virtually identical. During the judgment the following comment was made:

This court has observed that police officers nearly always deny that they have collaborated in the making of notes, and we cannot help wondering why they are the only class of society who do not collaborate in such a manner. It seems to us that nothing could be more natural or proper, when two people have been present at an interview with a third person, than that they should afterwards make sure that they have a correct version of what was said. Collaboration would appear to be a better explanation of almost identical notes than the possession of a superhuman memory. (*R. vs. Bass*, p. 1067)

The issue of testimony based on collaborative recall has been the subject of some controversy in the experimental literature, with Alper, Buckhout, Chern, Harwood, and Slomovitz (1974) claiming that collaborative testimony introduces error, and Warnick and Sanders (1980) and Hollin and Clifford (1983) producing evidence to the contrary. Our own studies on this topic are described next.

COLLABORATIVE REMEMBERING: EMPIRICAL STUDIES

Given the possible distorting effects of social interaction on the contents of individual recall (as described by Bartlett) it is interesting to note that relatively little psychological research has explored the effects of group interaction and collaborative recall on the accuracy and completeness of what is recalled, in terms of both quantity and quality. The majority of research has examined group versus individual productivity in recall in terms of the *quantity* of accurate recall produced, and has focused on the first, (rather than the second) level of Davis's (1980) intragroup processes framework, examining the nature of *group* responses following group interaction, rather than *individual* members responses following group interaction.

Group Productivity

Studies of group productivity have generally investigated situations where group products are readily quantifiable in terms of the numbers of a physical product, or ideas, or correct solutions to problems, and so on (cf. Steiner, 1972). The stimulus material in these studies is often relatively artificial and unstructured (e.g., nonsense words and word lists). The use of structured discourse (e.g., stories or social interactions) as stimulus material is remarkably rare.

Studies comparing collaborative and individual recall have found that groups invariably recall a greater *quantity* of the stimulus material regardless of whether subjects initially recalled individually and then as a group member (e.g., Dashiell, 1935; Yuker, 1955), or in independent sets of groups and individuals (e.g., Hoppe, 1962; Lorge & Solomon, 1962; Perlmutter, 1953; Perlmutter & de

Montmollin, 1952; Ryak, 1965). Moreover, group recall has been found to be quantitatively superior to the recall of the best individual group member (Yuker, 1955).

Other studies have compared group recall performance with that of the most productive individuals in *nominal* groups (i.e., fictitious groups created by randomly combining the products of several subjects who had recalled individually). The performance of real groups has been found to be generally inferior to that of nominal groups, suggesting that group recall involves something more than group member's simply pooling and combining their own individual remembrances (Lorge & Solomon, 1962; Perlmutter & de Montmollin, 1952; Ryack, 1965). The superior reproductive recall of groups has been attributed to the fact that they possess greater resources—there is a greater probability that one member of the group will recall a fact than there is of one person recalling that fact alone. Hartwick et al. (1982) commented that the consistency with which groups are found to be quantitatively superior to individuals in recall accuracy is "quite remarkable." Even in circumstances where individual performance is known to be generally poor (e.g., in immediate recall experiments where subjects receive stimulus information together as a group), group performance is frequently found to be superior.

A number of models have described the relationship between individual and group productivity (e.g., Lorge & Solomon, 1955; Taylor, 1954; Thomas & Fink, 1961). Generally, each model makes a number of assumptions about this relationship. For example, Taylor's (1954) model assumes that a group will recall all the items that at least one of its members recalls individually. Lorge and Solomon (1955) expanded on this in their model and defined two key assumptions about the group processes that take place: (a) When at least one group member knows the correct answer they will communicate it to the group; and (b) groups will always recognize such a communication as the correct answer. These assumptions have been described as the "truth wins" model of group problem solving (Davis, 1969, 1973; Steiner, 1966).

The most frequently tested model of group performance is that of Lorge and Solomon (1955). Several studies have found that group recall performance was at a lower level than that predicted by this model from the performance of individuals (cf. Steiner, 1972). This finding has, however, been found to depend on the complexity of the stimulus material to be recalled. Results consistent with the predictions of the model have been reported in studies employing nonsense syllables as stimulus material (Hoppe 1962; Perlmutter & de Montmollin, 1952; Ryack, 1965). However, the model consistently overpredicts the quantity of group recall when the stimulus material is meaningful words or 3-digit numbers (Lorge & Solomon, 1962; Morrissett, Crannell, & Switzer, 1964).

In studies where subjects recalled individually and then as a group member (e.g., Dashiell, 1935; Perlmutter, 1953; Yuker, 1955), comparisons between group recall and that of individual group members revealed that some individuals produced recall which was more accurate than that of their respective groups. This suggests that groups, for whatever reason, do not maximize their potential "recall resources," and Lorge and Solomon's model, which assumes no group process loss, therefore overpredicts group performance. In all of these studies the stimulus material was more complex than that presented in the studies mentioned earlier: stores (Perlmutter, 1953; Yuker, 1955) and classroom incidents (Dashiell, 1935). Such findings have been used to support the view that one major consequence of group rather than individual working is lowered productivity or "social loafing" (Latane, Williams, & Harkins, 1979).

Hartwick et al. (1982) offer three possible explanations for such findings, two of which focus on the pooling of individual contributions in groups, and the third on group decision making. The first explanation contrasted the fact that in these studies individual recall subjects received stimulus material *alone*, while those in group conditions generally received stimulus material *together*, as a group. In all cases immediate recall of the material was required. Group presentation combined with immediate recall was already noted as having a deleterious effect on individual performance. In comparison to those recalling individually, each group member may possess fewer available items for pooling together, therefore, when individual and group products are compared, individual recall is likely to overpredict group performance.

The second explanation, originating from Steiner's work (1972), was that Lorge and Solomon's model defined a level of *potential* rather than actual productivity. That is, the models assume that all group members will perform perfectly, which may often not be the case. The final explanation, originating from Thomas and Fink's (1961) work, relates to group decision making. They point out that Lorge and Solomon's model assumes rationality—that group members will willingly adopt a group member's response or solution when its correctness can be demonstrated. Although the correctness of a response may be readily demonstrated with some problems (e.g., mathematical problems), it is far more difficult to demonstrate the correctness of what is recalled about, for example, a social interaction. Thomas and Fink (1961) suggest that Lorge and Solomon's "truth wins" model may be an inaccurate description of what occurs during collaborative recall. They argue that it is more likely that groups use alternative rules, for example, deciding on what to include in protocols by taking a vote and applying a "majority wins" model (e.g., Hays & Bush, 1954).

To summarize, group recall has consistently been reported as quantitatively superior to individual recall. However, models of group recall productivity based on individual performance appear to be most predictive when the material to be recalled is very simplistic and artificial (e.g., nonsense words). When material is more complex and realistic (e.g., a story), the models overpredict group performance. These conclusions are, however, based on a small number of studies. They must be considered as tentative, rather than final, until more research has been conducted into a variety of aspects of group recall.

Individual and Collaborative Recall as Repeated Measure

Several studies, as noted earlier, have examined group recall accuracy when group recall followed individual recall (e.g., Dashiell, 1935; Yuker, 1955). The effects of collaborative recall on subsequent individual recall have also been investigated, and individual recall has generally been found to be enhanced by prior group recall. For example, subjects who first recalled individually and then collaboratively, improved their performance in a subsequent individual recall test (Bekhterev & de Lange, 1924; Yuker, 1955). Moreover, Yuker (1955) and Crannell, Switzer, and Morrissett (1965) all found that individual recall became less variable when it followed collaborative recall.

One consequence of collaboration therefore appears to be that group members remain influenced by group responses after they have completed the group task, and incorporate such responses into their subsequent individual accounts. Unfortunately, interpretation of these findings is confounded by the fact that no study employed a control group that recalled individually in all recall tests—the increased accuracy of postcollaborative individual recall may be a consequence of the longer time period between encoding and recall. As Hartwick et al. (1982) noted, some support for this notion is provided by results from "mere presence" experiments (e.g., Deffenbacher, Platt, & Williams, 1974; Geen, 1971; Pessin, 1933).

In a recent study by Stephenson, Abrams, Wagner, and Wade (1986), subjects watched a videotaped police interrogation, and then answered a series of cued-recall questions about the interaction, either individually and then as a member of a dyad (I-D condition), or initially as a dyad member, and then individually (D-I condition). These two conditions (I-D and D-I) were, therefore, independent of each other. They found that the accuracy of dyadic cued-recall— that is, the number of correctly answered questions—was consistently superior to that of individuals. Moreover, the superiority of dyadic recall was not influenced by whether individual recall preceded or followed dyadic recall.

Stephenson, Abrams, Wagner, and Wade (1986) also compared the *testimonial validity* of individual and dyadic recall. The concept of testimonial validity was introduced by Stephenson, Brandstatter, and Wagner (1983), and extended by Stephenson (1984), to describe the relationship between accuracy and confidence in factual responses given by individual witnesses in legal contexts. A witness whose evidence possesses *high* testimonial validity is able to clearly discriminate between his or her accurate and inaccurate responses in terms of their confidence in each response: They will be highly confident in the accuracy of correct responses and very unsure of the accuracy of incorrect responses. A court would be wise to rely on the evidence of such a witness. However, if a witness cannot discriminate in such a way between accurate and inaccurate responses, in the worst case responding with high confidence to inaccurate answers and with uncertainty to accurate answers, their evidence will have *low* testimonial validity. A court would be ill advised if it relied on such evidence.

Stephenson, Abrams, Wagner, and Wade found that subjects who had recalled individually and then in a dyad (I-D condition) produced group responses that were more testimonially valid than were their counterparts who recalled in a dyad first and then individually (D-I condition). Although initial individual recall appears to facilitate subjects' discrimination between correct and incorrect answers during subsequent dyadic recall, initial dyadic recall interferes with subjects' ability to make such discriminations during subsequent individual recall. Given their finding that dyads consistently produced more accurate recall than individuals, the most effective (and, in psycholegal terms, reliable) combination of individual and dyadic remembering is individual followed by dyadic, resulting in greater accuracy than individual recall, without any loss in the testimonial validity of responses.

Stephenson, Abrams, Wagner, and Wade (1986) also tested three models of group recall productivity against actual recall: *Average Individual performance, Truth Wins,* and *Confidence Wins.* They found that groups consistently failed to maximize the potential of individual group members, and that *Confidence Wins* (i.e., subjective rather than objective truth) was the most adequate predictor of group performance. They concluded that group recall influences later remembering by reducing the testimonial validity of subsequent individual recall. However, prior individual recall has no significant effect on the correctness or testimonial validity of subsequent group recall.

Mock Jury Studies

A substantial amount of research has been conducted on various aspects of mock jury decision making (see Hastie, Penrod, & Pennington, 1983, for a review). However, most research has explored the group processes leading up to the jury reaching a verdict. In consequence very few studies have investigated the possible effects of collaborative recall by jurors during their deliberations on the decision-making process.

Davis (1980) described two aspects of the group processes commonly observed in mock jury studies. The first involves jurors spending their time in a more or less haphazard search for the crucial item of evidence which will prove absolutely the accused's innocence or guilt. Jurors assert which particular item of evidence this is, and this then forms the basis for their subsequent discussions. The second aspect relates to the observation that mock juries often develop clear intragroup attitudes towards the weight to be given to particular items of evidence during their deliberations. This may lead to jurors being able to recall information related to one side of a case more easily than that related to the other side, and hence bias their verdict. When jurors then discuss (i.e., collaboratively remember and evaluate) the evidence in a case, such individual recall biases are likely to result in a collaborative account which reflects those biases.

The consequences of biased individual attitudes on group decision making (particularly in *ad hoc* small groups) are well documented in the social psychological literature on group polarization (e.g., Pruitt, 1971; Stoner, 1968; Wallach, Kogan, & Bem, 1962). It is likely that collaborative remembering, as an antecedent to polarized decision making, will reflect a similar polarization, with recall being more extremely biased than that of individual group members.

Two studies that examined the influence of attitudes on collaborative, rather than individual, remembering in mock juries are Sheppard (1980) and Hartwick et al. (1982). Sheppard (1980) manipulated the composition of four-person mock juries such that each consisted of three people with similar attitudes towards particularly relevant issues, while the fourth had been identified as neutral on these issues. Sheppard reported that subjects' attitudes strongly influenced their collaborative recall of the evidence presented in the case—in fact, their collaborative recall was more biased than that of the most biased individual in the group. This suggests that errors and biases in individual recall are not necessarily counterbalanced by those of other members during collaborative recall. Indeed it appears that a process somewhat akin to groupthink (Janis, 1972) was taking place within these groups.

Hartwick et al. (1982) presented mock jurors with evidence in the form of a videotaped trial. Twenty minutes later the jurors were assigned to either individual or four-person group recall conditions, asked to produce a free recall account and complete a recognition test about the trial. Groups had to produce a single agreed account and agree on all responses to the recognition test. As expected, groups consistently outperformed individuals in terms of the greater quantity of reproductive recall produced and more accurate recognition performance. In the recognition test, groups tended to be overinclusive, identifying far more items as coming from the original than actually did appear. There are two possible interpretations of this finding: It may be a consequence of groups being too conscientious, and therefore being overinclusive to avoid *missing* any of the original items; or that no real group process occurred during the recognition task, leading to groups simply *recognizing* all items that individual group members claimed had appeared.

Various models of group reproductive recall productivity were also tested by Hartwick et al.: *truth wins, simple majority wins, truth supported wins*, and *individual performance*. They found that a refinement of the *truth wins* model—*truth-supported wins*—was the most predictive of actual reproductive recall, suggesting that groups will recall an item when a minimum of two group members recall the item accurately.

Free recall protocols were examined for errors. In terms of *confusional errors* —the inclusion of items that directly contradicted the original—they found no difference between individuals and groups in the number included. In terms of "intrusional" errors, however, Hartwick et al. found that group protocols contained fewer intrusional errors that did those of individuals. Intrusional errors are more generally known as either *reconstructive* (Bartlett, 1932), *implicational* (Stephenson, 1984), or *inferential* errors. Such errors are a consequence of schematic information processing and the selection of recalled information to accommodate the specific social need that initiated remembering (in this case, to justify a mock jury judgment) (Spiro, 1980). They are consistent with what actually occurred, and may often be used to fill in gaps in the recall of a particular event in order to maintain the account's coherence (and often its plausibility). Reconstructive errors, therefore, add normal properties or plausible detail, particularize generalities, or specify normal conditions, components, or consequences of events/utterances that appeared in the original. There are two possible explanations for Hartwick et al.'s finding. First, it may be that the greater access to accurate detail by groups reduces group members need to rely on their inferrences, or second, part of the process of collaborative remembering involves the selecting out of reconstructive from reproductive material.

Hartwick et al. found little evidence to support Sheppard's (1980) conclusion that biased individual attitudes lead to even more biased collaborative remembering. This suggests that when jurors are randomly assigned to groups, rather than on the basis of their attitudes, biased individual attitudes are unlikely to have a substantial effect on group recall.

RECENT DEVELOPMENTS

A Hypothetical Framework for Collaborative Remembering

Recently, Edwards, and Middleton (1986, 1987) have proposed an interesting analytic framework for understanding the processes that take place during collaborative recall, consisting of three hierarchically associated discourse functions: framing and orientation, correspondence functions, and affective criteria.

> *Framing and orientation*: describing how the criteria for collaborative remembering originate, and how people individually relate to these criteria once they are established.
>
> *Correspondence functions*: consisting of a semantic function describing how joint experiences are collaboratively "put into words," and a continuity function describing how information collaboratively recalled is sequenced.
>
> *Validation function*: describing how a collaborative concensus is achieved by a group regarding what to include in a joint recall.

Unfortunately, the framework described by Edwards and Middleton is extremely complex, and they have yet to provide a detailed account of how the concepts they describe might be operationalised in an experimental situation. Moreover, they have still to produce empirical evidence in support of their model.

The Notion of Transactive Memory

A novel conception of collaborative remembering has recently been proposed by Wegner (1986; Wegner, Giuliano, & Hertel, 1985): *transactive* memory systems. Wegner defined these as the combination of the memory systems of a set of interacting individuals with any communication within that set of individuals. In other words, transactive memory consists of the contents of the memory stores of particular individuals *plus* the contents of any social interaction that they participate in together. The main concerns of transactive memory research, according to Wegner, are very similar to those described earlier for collaborative remembering research: the analysis, description, and prediction of collaborative behavior generally, and remembering in particular, in terms of how groups organize remembering, process information, and generate group "products".

Wegner's (1986) account is important as it focuses attention on an aspect of the social nature of human memory that has not been systematically discussed in any other individual or collaborative remembering research—that we often use other people's memories as a resource for our own. Wegner begins his account by pointing out that it is not unusual for people to rely on external memory stores:

> Remembering an upcoming engagement, for example, is not something people have to do forever, so they rely on placing reminders in conspicuous places or following their calendars. . . . External storage is not only used as an "aid" in this way, however; often it is the central storage area for large bodies of information that cannot be retrieved elsewhere. The scrawlings one makes in a diary or daily log, for example, typically become the only record of many of the day's mundane activities. (p. 4–5)

He then extends the notion of external memory stores, arguing that such stores may either be inanimate (e.g., a book), or animate, that is, human. As with inanimate external stores, we often rely on another person's (e.g., family, friends, other students, work associates) memory store when we believe that they possess a particular piece or type of information. However, in contrast to inanimate stores, which we can usually access directly (e.g., by reading a book), access to animate stores is mediated through interpersonal communication. Moreover, the transfer of information from one person to another is frequently a dynamic interdependent process, with all parties to the interaction participating as both potential providers and receivers of information. The potential for an individual to enhance their own limited memory system through such transactive memory systems is high, as such systems are far larger and more complex than any participating individuals' own systems.

Wegner emphasizes the importance of other people as external memory stores in everyday life, arguing that collaborative recall generally takes place among groups that have been established for some time (i.e., a "transactive network" has developed). The importance of the ongoing nature of transactive memory networks lies, for example, in the need for different members to develop expertise in a variety of knowledge domains, so that they then become (either explicitly or implicitly) responsible for the provision of particular types of information to the rest of the transactive system (cf. Wegner et al., 1985).

Giuliano and Wegner (1985) provided some evidence for this by demonstrating that the transactive memory processes between members of intimate couples operate to ensure that one or other of the pair are responsible for particular types of information at all times.

Although Wegner's (1986) theory introduces a novel conceptual framework for future research, there is very little empirical evidence currently available to support his view, particularly in relation to his claim that transactive memory systems are ubiquitous in everyday life.

COMPLETENESS, QUALITY, STRUCTURE AND ERRORS IN COLLABORATIVE REMEMBERING; A RESEARCH PROGRAMME

This chapter has examined a variety of aspects of collaborative remembering. Given the vast quantity of individual remembering research, a surprisingly small number of studies have explored collaborative recall. The majority of studies that we have reviewed have investigated differences in the production of reproductive recall between individual and collaborative remembering. Collaboration has generally been found to result in increases in the quantity of reproductive recall in comparison with individual recall. However, models of group recall based on individual performance often overpredict actual group productivity, a finding generally accounted for by "process loss" explanations—groups fail to adopt appropriate recall and decision strategies and therefore do not fully utilize all the resources available from individual group members.

Several issues of theoretical importance have yet to be addressed in any detail. For example, investigations of the effects of collaborative recall on the *quality, completeness,* and *structure* of what is recalled have rarely been undertaken. Moreover, few studies have compared individual and collaborative free recall of complex discourse types such as social interactions (although some have examined recognition or cued recall, for example, Stephenson, Abrams, Wagner, and Wade (1986)). Moreover, comparisons have rarely been made between remembering by different sizes of groups (for example, dyads and four-person groups) and that of individuals within the same study. Finally, little attention has been given to possible variations between individual and groups in the types of errors made during recall. In this section, research by the authors is described, which addresses some of the issues.

RECALL OF INTERROGATIONS BY GROUPS OF POLICE AND STUDENTS

Several recent experiments have examined cued and/or free recall of social interactions by both individuals and groups. Three sets of material have been employed: an audio recording of the fictional police interrogation of a woman who alleged she had been raped (Clark, 1987; Clark, Stephenson, & Rutter, 1986; Stephenson, Clark, & Wade, 1986); a visual (slide) presentation of a transcript of that interrogation (Clark, 1987; Clark, Stephenson, & Kniveton, 1987, 1988); and a video recording (Stephenson, Abrams, Wagner, & Wade, 1986; Stephenson & Wagner, in press) of a real police interrogation of a woman who alleged she had been raped. In all the experiments the recordings were played to groups of students or serving police officers, following which subjects were distracted for several minutes and then randomly assigned to either individual, dyadic, or four-person group conditions. They were normally asked to freely recall the interrogation, and to answer specific factual questions about it (cued recall). The excerpts from the interrogations lasted approximately 5 minutes (both audio and video), and the slide presentation of the transcript was presented at a similar rate.

Observers of real police interrogations (e.g., other police officers, solicitors, social workers, and relatives) are sometimes called upon to testify in court about what occurred during police interrogations, in much the same way as our subjects were required to do. Moreover, our police subjects had experience of conducting and witnessing real interrogations during their work, and were familiar with the constraints of such a situation. In an attempt to address some of those issues neglected in previous work, we summarize some of our findings and conclusions from these experiments in terms of the completeness, quality, and structure of what was recalled by individuals and groups.

As we have seen, only a relatively small number of studies have compared individual and collaborative remembering, and the majority of these have only examined the quantity of accurate recall produced. Very few studies indeed have addressed the issue in terms (a) of the *quality* as well as the quantity of what was recalled, and (b) of the types of errors and other material that appear in recall protocols. Moreover, as Spiro (1980) noted, most studies have employed simplistic, artificial materials, rather than complex and realistic social discourses, as their stimulus. Extrapolation from the findings of such experiments to collaborative remembering of social interactions and other everyday discourses may be problematic.

In order to precisely quantify the semantic content of individual and group free recall of the social interaction employed as stimulus material in our studies, Clark et al. (1986) modified a method of protocol analysis originally designed by Kintsch and van Dijk to analyze story recall—macropropositional analysis (Kintsch & van Dijk, 1978; van Dijk & Kintsch, 1983). Such an analysis involves: (a) parsing the verbal content of the original interaction into its constituent propositions (i.e., idea units), for the interrogation this amounted to 321 separate propositions, and from this developing an hierarchical macropropositional model of the interaction; (b) parsing each recall protocol into its constituent propositions; and (c) comparing the content of protocols with the original, and classifying each recall proposition as either an accurate reproduction or otherwise.

The contents of protocols were classified into several (independent) categories: reproductive recall, correct speaker identifications, reconstructive errors, confusional errors, and metastatements. Metastatement is a category of recall that has not been examined in any earlier studies of collaborative recall. Clark (1987) defined metastatements as items:

> . . . which make comment on (i) the content or organization of a discourse, (ii) expressions of the subject's own attitudes/opinions towards a discourse, or (iii) the attribution of intentions/motives to characters in a discourse that are not explicit in the discourse. (p. 129)

Using this type of protocol analysis we discovered that collaboration had a number of effects on both free and cued recall (Clark et al., 1986; Clark, Stephenson, & Kniveton, 1987, 1988; Stephenson, Clark, & Wade, 1986).

Reproductive Recall: Quantity and Completeness

Stephenson, Clark, and Wade (1986) found that collaborative free recall protocols contained, on average, a larger amount of accurate reproductive recall, and correct identifications of speakers, than did individual protocols. Groups also answered a greater numbers of cued recall items correctly than did individuals. Moreover, Four-person groups produced more reproductive free and cued recall and were more confident than dyads (see Fig. 11.1). However, comparison of the quantity of group reproductive recall with the prediction of models of group productivity (e.g., Lorge & Solomon, 1962) revealed that, as might be expected, group performance was far lower than might have been expected from individual performance.

The correct cued recall answers of dyads were more testimonially valid (i.e., they were reported with greater confidence) than those of individuals, and the

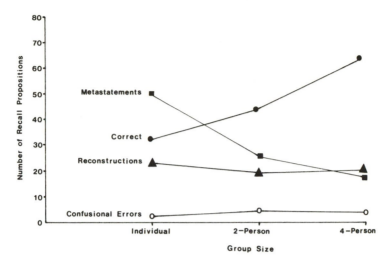

FIG. 11.1. Classification of free recall propositions according to group size. From Stephenson, Clark, and Wade (1986).

answers of four-person groups were more valid than those of dyads. Unfortunately, the incorrect answers of dyads were more testimonially invalid than those of individuals, and the answers of four-person groups were more invalid than those of dyads (Fig. 11.2). Although groups were more confident than individuals in their responses generally, individuals discriminate more clearly than groups between their confidence for correct and incorrect answers.

These findings were replicated by Clark et al. (1988) in their study of police and student individual, dyadic, and four-person group remembering. Collaborative recall again resulted (overall) in increases in accurate cued recall, reproductive free recall, and correct identification of speakers. Moreover, the correct cued recall answers of police and student dyads were again more testimonially valid than those of subjects in their respective individual conditions, and those of four-person groups were more valid than those of dyads, whilst the incorrect answers of dyads were more testimonially invalid than those of individuals, and those of four-person groups were more invalid than dyads. Other comparisons between police and student samples revealed that while police who recalled individually less reproductive free recall than did individual students, police dyads and four-person groups produced substantially more reproductive recall than their student counterparts.

As noted earlier, a few studies have compared the quantity of group reproductive free recall with that nominal groups (fictitious groups created by combining the recall of subjects who recalled individually). Preliminary comparisons between real and nominal group reproductive recall productivity from these two

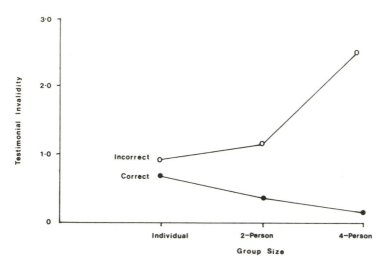

FIG. 11.2. The effect of group size on the testimonial invalidity of correct and incorrect cued recall responses. From Stephenson, Clark, and Wade (1986).

experiments revealed that nominal groups generally outperformed real groups in terms of quantity of recall. However, in terms of quality, real groups (and particularly four-person groups) recalled items that never appeared in nominal group protocols.

A further analysis of the data from these two experiments investigated what we called the gist of the interrogation within each recall condition (Clark et al., 1987). Bartlett (1932) noted that the accurately recalled parts of a discourse are not a random selection of facts from that discourse. Individuals tend to recall information in clusters rather than as individual items (Buschke, 1977; Buschke & Schaier, 1979; Tulving, 1968), and Bartlett argued that such clusters of information in free recall reflect the gist of that discourse. As such, the generation of the gist of a discourse is a consequence of comprehension and remembering processes. Gist has generally been very loosely, sometimes almost intuitively, defined. For example, Sanford and Garrod (1981) refer to dictionary definitions such as ''real ground or point, substance or pith of a matter,'' before settling for an operational definition of the gist as a summary of the main points in a discourse. Substantively, Sanford and Garrod (1981) identify three types of information that appear in the gist of a particular discourse: Main ideas are more likely to appear than their dependent ideas; main goals are more likely to appear than subgoals; and main actions in stereotyped situation are more likely to appear than details of actual actions.

In our experiments we adopted the following operational definition of a gist:

all information that was accurately recalled by 50% or more or individuals or groups within a particular recall condition. We were, therefore, asking the questions ''what information is consistently recalled, and are there differences between individual and group remembering in either the quantity or quality of this information?'' All items of information recalled by half or more of the individuals or groups within a recall condition (i.e. the gists) were identified, and compared with each other in terms of both the quantity and the quality of what was recalled, by examining the extent to which individuals, dyads, and four-person groups reproduced a common core of information.

We found that the gist of the interrogation generally increased in size in accordance with group size., For student subjects, only 3% of the original discourse appeared in the individual gist, 8% in the dyadic, and 11% in the four-person gist. A similar pattern was revealed for police subjects: 8% of the original appeared in the individual, 16% in the dyadic, and 18% in the four-person gist. In other words, individual recall was far more *idiosyncratic* and inconsistent than group recall, reflecting a strong tendency for groups to converge on a standardized version of the relevant features of the interrogation. The differences between dyadic and four-person gists, however, were far smaller than those between individual and dyadic gists for both police and student subjects. This suggests that being in a group per se has a greater effect than group size on the consistency of remembering across individuals and groups.

Moreover, we found that the four-person gist contained virtually all the items in the dyadic gist, which in turn contained virtually all the items in the individual gist, within each set of subjects. In other words, the individual gist was generally a subset of the information contained in the dyadic gist, which was itself a subset of the information in the four-person gist. Collaborative remembering, therefore, both contains and *extends* the content of individual remembering, and leads to a greater *consistency* in what is accurately recalled between groups than exists between individuals, with consistency increasing as group size increases.

When student and police gists were compared, police gists were found to be substantially larger than their respective student gists in each recall condition. Moreover, police gists contained virtually all the information in their respective student gists (i.e., the content of the student individual gist was a subset of the content of the police individual gist, and so on). Police subjects were, therefore, more consistent than students within each recall condition. Moreover, the contents of student gists were subsets of the contents of their respective police gists. Police gists, therefore, subsumed and extended the contents of student gists. This finding is probably a consequence of the fact that, in comparison with the student subjects, police subjects are likely, by the nature of their profession, to be far more familiar with both the type of social interaction to be recalled (i.e. they have greater scriptal knowledge about this type of social event), and (as a subject group) which constitutes the important and relevant facts from the interrogation that must be reported during recall.

Reproductive Recall: Quality and Structure

In this section we take the first steps towards describing some of the *qualitative* and *structural* (or organizational) similarities and differences between the contents of individual and collaborative free recall protocols. The first issue that must be addressed is a general one: How might we most appropriately characterise the quality of an individual or group's remembering? That is, how do we decide on which elements of the original should appear in a recall protocol of high quality and be missing from one of low quality? This is a far easier question to ask than to answer. It could be argued that the quality of recalled information is a purely subjective judgment—to paraphrase an old proverb—"one person's relevance is another person's irrelevance." However, one important feature of Kintsch and van Dijk's (1978; van Dijk & Kintsch, 1983) method of discourse analysis, which we employed here in a modified form, is that it allows for the generation of probabilistic models of individual remembering, and predictions from such models may be tested against actual recall. Two general models were tested: *micro-* propositional—based on a bottom-up processing model of the interaction, and *macro-* propositional—based on a top-down processing model.

Free recall by individuals and groups was compared with these models of recall. Clark et al. (1986), in their study of recall of a dramatized audio recording of an interrogation, found that the models predicted both individual and collaborative reproductive recall to a significant degree, with the macro model being consistently more predictive than the micro of both individual and group recall. There was, however, a consistent decline from individual to dyad to four-person group in the predictive powers of the models. The micro model accounted for 17% of the recall variance in the individual, 12% in the dyadic, and 10% in the four-person condition, while the macro model accounted for 25% of recall variance in the individual and dyadic, and 16.3% in the four-person condition.

These findings were replicated and extended in a subsequent study (Clark et al., 1988), where student and police subjects recalled the written script of the same interrogation. Once again, the models predicted recall significantly over all conditions, and the macro model was, as in Clark et al. (1986), far more predictive of both individual and collaborative recall than the micro. Interestingly, there was no decline in the predictive powers of either model from individual to collaborative recall. There were, in fact, sometimes *increases* in the power of the models from individual to group. In the student conditions, the micro model accounted for 6% of the recall variance in the individual, 5% in the dyadic, and 4% in the four person condition, while the macro model accounted for 25% in the individual, 29% in the dyadic, and 27% in the four-person condition. There was a similar pattern in the police conditions, with the micro model accounting for 5% of the recall variance in the individual and dyadic, and 7% in the four-person condition, while the macro model accounted for 23% in the individual and dyadic, and 25% in the four-person condition. There was, therefore, very little difference in the predictive powers of the models between recall by either student or police subjects.

The general *decrease* in the predictive power of the micro, and *increase* in the power of the macro models between these two experiments may be a consequence of the change in the medium of presentation—from a dramatized audio recording to a slide presentation of the script. Subjects who heard the audio recording only had one chance to attend to particular items of information—when they were spoken by an actor. In such circumstances recall tends to reflect the influence of both bottom-up and top-down cognitive processes. In contrast, those who read the script could (within restricted time limits) reread what they considered to be important utterances. Recall in these circumstances is likely to be far more strongly influenced by top-down, rather than bottom-up processes.

Finally, comparisons between the gists of the interrogation generated by the macropropositional models and those derived from recall protocols (see above) revealed that both individual and collaborative gists were predicted with a high degree of accuracy for both student and police subjects. In other words, the vast majority of the items predicted by the models as being the most likely to be recalled, were, in fact, recalled most consistently with both individual and group conditions, and by both student and police subjects.

Several important conclusions may be drawn from these findings. First, both individual and collaborative recall are predicted most adequately by constructivist (i.e., top-down) rather than associationist (i.e. bottom-up) models of individual cognitive processes. This suggests that groups are as dependent as individuals on the preexisting cognitive scripts and schemas of individual group members in reaching agreed accounts of complex social interactions. Second, models of recall based on individual cognitive processes are also predictive (sometimes to a lesser degree) of collaborative recall. From a cognitive viewpoint collaborative recall might therefore be characterised as individual recall "writ large." Third, the macro models of recall were equally predictive of consistent recall by both individual and groups. Fourth, none of the micro or macro models of recall tested accounted for more than 30% of the recall variance—over 70% of the variance was always unaccounted for. The current, mechanistic, cognitive models of discourse comprehension and recall can, therefore, only provide a partial explanation of either individual or collaborative recall.

It cannot be claimed, however, that the propositional models used in these studies are anything but tentative descriptions of the semantic and pragmatic content of a particular interaction. Despite their tentative nature they were remarkably predictive of accurate recall of a very complex social interaction by both individuals and groups. A general macropropositional model of social interactions which takes into account all the semantic and pragmatic content of an interaction, has currently only been described abstractly (van Dijk & Kintsch, 1983) and awaits an adequate methodology to operationalize it.

Reconstructive Errors, Confusional Errors and Metastatements

Reconstructive errors, the inclusion of material in recall protocols that was consistent with, but did not appear in the original, was influenced by collaborative remembering. Clark et al. (1986) found that collaboration per se led, on average, to a smaller number of reconstructive errors being included in protocols by student subjects, although there was no difference in the numbers included by dyads and four-person groups (Fig. 11.1). Clark et al. (1988) replicated this finding with respect to their student subjects. For police subjects, however, collaboration per se had the reverse effect, with police individuals introducing *fewer* reconstructions into their protocols than did groups.

Overall, the number of confusional errors (i.e., those that directly contradicted the original) included in protocols was very low, accounting for between one and two percent of all items recalled. Moreover, the average number of confusional errors did not vary between recall conditions for student subjects in either of these studies (Fig. 11.1). Clark et al. (1988), however, found that police four-person groups included significantly fewer confusional errors than did individuals or dyads. In comparison to student subjects, police subjects included more confusional (individual and dyadic conditions) and reconstructive errors (all conditions) in their recall protocols.

Clark et al. (1986) found that the inclusion of metastatements (i.e., items commenting on the content of the interaction or attributing motives to characters that were not explicit in the original) was also influenced by collaboration. On average dyadic protocols contained fewer metastatements than did individual protocols, and four-person protocols contained fewer than the dyadic (Fig. 11.1). These findings were replicated by Clark et al. (1988) for both police and student subjects. Interestingly, although student groups on average included between 30 and 65% of the number of metastatements included by individuals, the decrease for police groups was far more dramatic, with groups including only between 13 and 18% of the number included by individuals.

There is a suggestion (Clark et al., 1987; Stephenson, Clark, & Kniveton, 1988) that some of these interesting differences in the effect of collaboration on police subjects (e.g., greater completeness and more reconstructive errors) may have been due to the tendency of police dyads and four-person groups to employ a *script* recall strategy than was the case with police individuals or student subjects generally, who were more inclined to report the interrogation in *story* form. According to Clark et al. (1987) reporting recall as a script (i.e., recalling in the form of a dramatic dialogue in direct speech) restricts the type of material that can be included—for example, metastatements can only be included as asides from the main text of the recall. In contrast, reporting recall as a story (i.e., recalling in the form of a story with little reportage of direct speech) places no limitation on the inclusion of metastatements as part of the main text of the protocol). Moreover, when subjects recall in direct speech, there is likely to be a greater need to fill in gaps in their recall with reconstructive errors in order to make the utterances they report well rounded. There is no similar need when subjects recall as a story, as they may simply avoid reporting anything that they are doubtful about. Recalling as a story, however, imposes different requirements on what is recalled, but these are related to the need to establish an overall coherence to what is recalled rather than coherence within each utterance recalled.

Long-Term Effects of Groups on Individuals

Stephenson, Abrams, Wagner, and Wade (1986) demonstrated that individuals' completeness of, and testimonial validity in, cued-recall responses was improved by subsequent dyadic performance. However, dyads were, overall, more confident than individuals in their responses, regardless of their correctness. A subsequent experiment explored the basis of this "misplaced" confidence effect (Stephenson & Wagner, in press) and found it to be a consequence of subjects having to reach agreement on answers to each question. The most susceptible subjects were those who had completed a free recall individually, and then had to agree on cued recall responses in a dyad. They were more likely to attribute greater responsibility for (or influence on) group decisions to their partner, suggesting that diffusion of responsibility may underlie the effect. Subjects who completed a collaborative free recall before completing the cued recall individually, were *less* likely than those who had free recalled individually to be over confident in wrong answers.

Interim Conclusions from the Research Program

Several tentative general conclusions about the relationship between individual and collaborative remembering of social interactions may be drawn from the research program described earlier. The program is still in progress, and we hope to be able to provide further supporting empirical evidence for these conclusions in the near future.

Accuracy:
1. The *quantity* of both reproductive free, and accurate cued, recall increases from individual to group, and also as group size increases;
2. There is greater *consistency* in accurate free recall between dyads than there is between individuals, and between four-person groups than dyads;
3. Dyadic reproductive free recall, on average, both *contains* and *extends* the contents of individual recall. In a similar way four-person recall contains and extends the contents of dyadic recall.

Errors:
4. Collaboration may lead to a reduction in the number of reconstructive errors included in free recall;
5. There is little difference between individual and collaborative free recall in the number of confusional errors made, although it is possible that collaboration may sometimes reduce their incidence;

Metastatements (opinions and evaluations):
6. Dyadic recall leads to a reduction in the number of metastatements included in free recall in comparison to individual recall. Four-person recall leads to a further decrease in their incidence.

Confidence (cued recall):
7. Confidence in responses increases as group size increases, for both correct and incorrect answers. Groups, therefore, generally discriminate less effectively between correct and incorrect answers than do individuals;
8. Discussion during collaborative free recall decreases the level of overconfidence in incorrect answers in subsequent individual and dyadic cued recall.

THE FUTURE OF COLLABORATIVE REMEMBERING RESEARCH

How should research on collaborative remembering proceed? The final part of this chapter briefly outlines a number of important theoretical, empirical, applied, and methodological issues relating to collaborative remembering that have received little, if any, research attention to date.

Theoretical Issues

Research on group remembering has generally been problem oriented, focusing on one aspect of the phenomenon—group versus individual productivity—measured in terms of the *quantity* of accurate recall produced. Although theoretical models of group recall productivity have been developed (e.g., Lorge & Solomon, 1955), they are of limited scope. A theory of group remembering in general, and face-to-face collaborative remembering in particular, has still to be articulated. Such a theory must take into account a formidable number of factors and potential variables to have any explanatory value, the most important of which are the relationship between individual and group remembering, and the social origins, nature and functions of remembering.

The Relationship Between Individual and Group Remembering

The greatest challenge to a general theory of group remembering is that it must account for both individual and group remembering within a single theoretical framework. It would be misguided and irrational to develop a theory of group remembering that did not consider individual remembering as both a starting point and an integral element within the theory. Such a theory would, therefore, be best described as a *general theory of remembering,* as it must be able to describe the origins, processes and products of both individual and group remembering, and the relationship between them. A general theory must, however, go further and account for and *predict,* many (if not all) of the following:

1. both the quantity and *quality* of accurate individual and group remembering;
2. the confidence with which individual and groups report their remembrances, and the relationship between confidence and accuracy;
3. the different types of errors made by individuals and groups;
4. the variety of comments and evaluations reported by individuals and groups regarding their remembrances.

Although some attempts to fulfill these four basic requirements have now been made (e.g., Clark et al. 1986), a general theory of remembering is unlikely to be developed in the near future. This is despite the fact that experimental studies of human memory have a history spanning over a century. There are several reasons for this state of affairs. The most important here is a consequence of the fact that research on the cognitive processes involved in human information processing, comprehension, and remembering has adopted an extreme reductionist, associationistic approach that pays little, if any regard to either the purposes for, or contexts within which humans actually use their cognitive systems in everyday life. Such research has, more often than not, focused on extremely transient memories—those evoked during attention and working memory processes—at the expense of extensive research on aspects of everyday memory processes and usage. Fortunately, this state of affairs is gradually changing (e.g., Cohen, 1986; Neisser, 1982).

The Social Origins, Nature and Functions of Group Remembering

An integral part of any general theory of individual and group remembering ;must be a consideration of the essentially social nature of all remembering. Moreover, the social nature of remembering should be considered as having explanatory value at several levels of analysis. At the cognitive level this might be in terms of the social origins, functions, and processes involved in active schematic and script based information processing, comprehension and recall (e.g., Bartlett, 1932). At the social interactional level several different types of explanation could be made. For example, in terms of social aspects of collaborative remembering, or social functions of remembering in everyday life, or the social content of information that is acquired, stored and retrieved.

Researchers have yet to address many of these issues in any systematic way, although there has been some recent theoretical discussion of the social origins and functions of memory (e.g., Edwards & Middleton, 1986, 1988; Wegner, 1986), and of memory as a social construct (e.g., Shotter, 1987). There is, however, a crying need for social psychologists to take up the challenge posed by Bartlett's (1932) conception that remembering is an essentially social activity, and develop a truly social psychological theory of individual and group remembering.

Empirical Issues

This section outlines several key issues of more immediate, empirical importance to research on group remembering. In relation to research investigating the *products* of group recall, there are several urgent requirements. These include investigations of individual and group remembering:

1. over a number of different types of social interaction in a variety of organizational/social contexts;
2. when individuals and groups possess different motives for processing, understanding and recalling what took place during a social interaction;
3. when the recall of participants in groups is compared with that of observers;
4 when a greater variety of group sizes are employed

Moreover, although many studies have examined the effect of serial reproduction (Bartlett, 1932) on individual recall, no study has yet examined the effect of *collaborative* serial reproduction on group recall (where the recall protocol of one group is given to another as stimulus material, and the second group's recall protocol is then given to another, and so on).

There is also the need for far more detailed analyses of the group processes and discussion that take place during purposive collaborative remembering. Although some studies have already begun research in this direction (e.g., Stephenson & Wagner, in press), research in this area is again hampered by the lack of adequate methodological techniques (see following).

Applied Issues

Remembering is a social activity, and social activities normally take place in the world of everyday experience, rather than the experimental laboratory. Moreover, there is at least one important aspect of everyday remembering which, for ethical and moral reasons, is extremely difficult to introduce in laboratory studies—*consequentiality*. What we remember (or forget) in everyday life can have long-term positive or negative consequences for ourselves and others (for example, forgetting the details of an important theory during an examination may result in failure, leading to reduced job prospects and living standards). The influence of consequentiality on remembering, can only be adequately assessed in real life situations.

It is imperative, then, that investigations of individual and group remembering should display both a sound theoretical underpinning, and an applied orientation. Moreover, as social psychologists may on occasions be asked to provide advice, guidance or make comment on social psychological aspects of issues and events occurring in the world, it is important that our understanding of group remembering is not based purely on abstract experimental findings. Some research has already begun to address applied problems within experimental settings, in relation to jury remembering (e.g., Hartwick et al. 1982) and collaborative testimony (e.g., Stephenson, Clark, & Wade, 1986). However, it should not be beyond the purview of social psychologists to investigate, for example, areas of real-life decision making where it might be advantageous (or otherwise) to participate in collaborative remembering exercises before particular decisions are made. Unfortunately, we are still not in a position to make any such recommendations with any degree of certainty.

Methodological Issues

Many of the requirements described earlier for a general theory of individual and group remembering are extremely difficult to investigate due to limitations imposed by currently available research methodologies and techniques. The most crucial current methodological problems relate to the need for models of how individuals and groups represent and comprehend social interactions (and discourse processes generally) that can be adequately operationalized (i.e., methodological tools developed) and tested on a variety of everyday types of discourse. Some small moves have been made in this direction in the field of artificial intelligence, with the development of computer programs that can *comprehend* very simple stories (e.g., Schank & Abelson, 1977), and with Kintsch and van Dijk's (1978) model of story comprehension. Unfortunately, the computer program that can parse even relatively short stories and related recall protocols into their constituent propositions (however they may be defined) is still science fiction rather than fact. If such a program did exist, it would greatly reduce the time that is currently required to laboriously parse material by hand, and therefore increase the number, variety and complexity of the discourses that could be investigated.

Finally, it appears that collaborative remembering research will make progress to the extent that joint efforts are made by social and cognitive psychologists, along with psycholinguists, to develop models of individual and collaborative remembering which take into account both the social and cognitive psychological processes in the social contexts within which remembering occurs.

REFERENCES

Alper, A., Buckhout, R., Chern, S., Harwood, R., & Slomovitz, M. (1974). *Eyewitness identification: Accuracy of individual versus composite recollections of a crime.* Report no CR-10, Centre for Responsive Psychology, Brooklyn College, CUNY.

Aronson, E. (1969). The theory of cognitive dissonance: A current perspective. In L. Berkowitz (Ed.), *Advances in experimental social psychology* (Vol. 4, pp. 2–35). New York: Wiley.

Bartlett, F. C. (1923). *Psychology and primitive culture.* Cambridge, England: Cambridge University Press.

Bartlett, F. C. (1932). *Remembering: A study in experimental and social psychology.* Cambridge, England: Cambridge University Press.

Bekhterev, W., & de Lange, M. (1924). *Die ergbnisse des experiments auf dem geiete der kolletiven reflexologie.* Reported in Hartwick et al. (1982).

Brehm, J. W., & Cohen, A. R. (Eds.). (1962). *Explorations in cognitive dissonance.* New York: Wiley.

Buschke, H. (1977). Two-dimensional recall: Immediate identification of clusters in episodic and semantic memory. *Journal of Verbal Learning and Verbal Behavior, 16,* 201–215.

Buschke, H., & Schaier, A. H. (1979). Memory units, ideas, and propositions in semantic remembering. *Journal of Verbal Learning and Verbal Behavior, 18,* 549–563.

Clark, N. K. (1987). *The analysis and prediction of individual and group remembering.* Unpublished doctoral thesis, University of Kent at Canterbury.

Clark, N. K., & Stephenson, G. M. (1988). Social comparisons and memory: The social psychology of collaborative remembering. In M. Hewstone & W. Stroebe (Eds.), *The European review of social psychology* (Vol. 1). Chichester: Wiley.

Clark, N. K., Stephenson, G. M., & Kniveton, B. H. (1987, April). *Getting the gist: Individual and collaborative recall by police officers and students.* Paper presented at the Annual Conference of the British Psychological Society, Sussex University, Brighton.

Clark, N. K., Stephenson, G. M., & Kniveton, B. H. (1988). *Meetings make evidence II: A study of individual and collaborative remembering by police officers and students.* Manuscript in preparation. University of Kent at Canterbury.

Clark, N. K., Stephenson, G. M., & Rutter, D. R. (1986). Memory for a complex social discourse: The analysis and prediction of individual and group remembering. *Journal of Memory and Language, 25,* 295–313.

Cohen, G. (1986). Everyday memory. In G. Cohen, M. W. Eysenck, & M. E. Le Voi (Eds.), *Memory: A cognitive approach* (pp. 13–56). Milton Keynes: Open University Press.

Crannel, C. W., Switzer, S. A., & Morrissett, J. O. (1965). Individual performance in cooperative and independent groups. *Journal of General Psychology, 73,* 231–236.

Dashiell, J. F. (1935). Experimental studies of the influence of social situations on the behavior of individual human adults. In C. Murchison (Ed.), *Handbook of social psychology* (pp. 1097–1158). Worcester, MA: Clark University Press.

Davis, J. H. (1969). *Group performance.* Reading, MA: Addison-Wesley.

Davis, J. H. (1973). Group decision and social interaction: A theory of social decision schemes. *Psychological Review, 80,* 97–125.

Davis, J. H. (1980). Group decision and procedural justice. In M. Fishbein (Ed.), *Progress in social psychology.* Hillsdale NJ: Lawrence Erlbaum Associates.

Deffenbacher, K. A., Platt, G. J., & Williams, M. A. (1974). Differential recall as a function of socially induced arousal and retention interval. *Journal of Experimental Psychology, 103,* 809–811.

Edwards, D., & Middleton, D. (1986). Joint remembering: Constructing an account of shared experience through conversational discourse. *Discourse Processes, 9,* 423–459.

Edwards, D., & Middleton, D. (1987). Conversation and remembering: Bartlett revisited. *Applied Cognitive Psychology, 1,* 77–92.

Edwards, D., & Middleton, D. (1988). Conversational remembering and family relationships: How children learn to remember. *Journal of Social and Personal Relationships, 5,* 3–26.

Festinger, L. (1950). Informal social communication. *Psychological Review, 57,* 271–282.

Festinger, L. (1954). A theory of social comparison processes. *Human Relations, 40,* 427–448.

Festinger, L. (1957). *A theory of cognitive dissonance.* California: Stanford University Press.

Geen, R. G. (1971). Social facilitation of long-term recall. *Psychonomic Science, 24,* 89–90.

Gergen, K. J. (1982). *Towards transformation in social knowledge.* New York: Springer-Verlag.

Giuliano, T., & Wegner, D. M. (1985). The operation of transactive memory in intimate couples. Unpublished research data reported in Wegner (1986).

Halbwachs, M. (1950). *La memoire collective.* Paris: Presses Universitaires de France.

Halbwachs, M. (1980). *The collective memory.* Trans. F. J. Ditter, Jr., & V. Y. Ditter. New York: Harper Row.

Hartwick, J., Sheppard, B. L., & Davis, J. H. (1982). Group remembering: Research and implications. In R. A. Guzzo (Ed.), *Improving decision making in organizations* (pp. 41–72). London: Academic Press.

Hastie, R., Penrod, S. D., & Pennington, N. (1983). *Inside the jury.* Cambridge, MA: Harvard University Press.

Hays, D. G., & Bush, R. R. (1954). A study in group action. *American Sociological Review, 19,* 693–701.

Heaton-Armstrong, A. (1987). Police officers' notebooks: Recent developments. *Criminal law review,* 470–472.

Hollin, C. R., & Clifford, B. R. (1983). Eyewitness testimony: The effects of discussion on recall accuracy and agreement. *Journal of Applied Social Psychology, 13,* 234–244.

Hoppe, R. A. (1962). Memorizing by individuals and groups: A test of the pooling-of-ability model. *Journal of Abnormal and Social Psychology, 65,* 64–67.

Hunter, I. M. L. (1979). Memory in everyday life. In M. M. Gruneberg & P. E. Morris (Eds.), *Applied problems in memory* (pp. 1–24). London: Academic press.

Janis, I. L. (1972). *Victims of groupthink.* Boston: Houghton Mifflin.

Janis, I. L. (1982). *Groupthink.* Second edition. Boston: Houghton Mifflin.

Kintsch, W., & van Dijk, T. A. (1978). Towards a model of text comprehension and production. *Psychological Review, 85,* 363–394.

Latane, B., Williams, K., & Harkins, S. (1979). 'Many hands make light the work': The causes and consequences of social loafing. *Journal of Personality and Social Psychology, 37,* 822–832.

Lorge, I., & Solomon, H. (1955). Two models of group behavior in the solution of eureka-type problems. *Psychometrika, 20,* 139–148.

Lorge, I., & Solomon, H. (1962). Group and individual behavior in free recall verbal learning. In J. H. Criswell, H. Solomon, & P. Sappes (Eds.), *Mathematical models in small group process.* California: Stanford University Press.

Mills, C. W. (1940). Situated actions and vocabularies of motive. *American Sociological Review, 5,* 904–913.

Morrissett, J. O., Crannell, C. W., & Switzer, S. A. (1964). Group performance under various conditions of work load and information redundancy. *Journal of General Psychology, 71,* 337–347.

Neisser, U. (1978). Memory: What are the important questions? In M. M. Gruneberg, P. E. Morris, & R. N. Sykes (Eds.), *Practical aspects of memory* (pp. 3–24). London: Academic Press.

Neisser, U. (Ed.). (1982). *Memory observed: Remembering in natural contexts.* San Francisco: W. H. Freeman.

Perlmutter, H. V. (1953). Group memory of meaningful material. *Journal of Psychology, 35,* 361–370.

Perlmuter, H. V., & de Montmollin, G. (1952). Group learning of nonsense syllables. *Journal of Abnormal and Social Psychology, 47,* 762–769.

Pessin, J. (1933). The comparative effects of social and mechanical simulation on memorizing. *American Journal of Psychology, 45,* 263–270.

Piaget, J. (1928). *Judgement and reasoning in the child.* New York: Harcourt Brace.

Pruitt, D. G. (1971). Choice shifts in group discussions: An introductory review. *Journal of Personality and Social Psychology, 20,* 339–360.

R. v. Bass. (1953). *All England Law Reports.* V. 1, 1064–1068.

Rogoff, B., & Mistry, J. (1985). Memory development in cultural context.. In M. Pressley & C. Brainerd (Eds.), *Cognitive learning and memory development in children.* New York: Springer-Verlag.

Ryak, B. L. (1965). A comparison of individual and group learning of nonsense syllables. *Journal of Personality and Social Psychology, 2,* 296–299.

Sanford, A. J., & Garrod, S. C. (1981). *Understanding written language.* Chichester: Wiley.

Schank, R. C., & Abelson, R. P. (1977). *Scripts, plans, goals and understanding: An inquiry into human knowledge structures.* Hillsdale, NJ: Lawrence Erlbaum Associates.

Shaw,M. E. (1976). *Group dynamics.* New York: McGraw-Hill.

Sheppard, B. H. (1980). *Opinions and remembering revisited.* Unpublished doctoral dissertation, University of Illinois. Reported in Hartwick et al. (1982).

Shotter, J. (1984). *Social accountability and selfhood.* Oxford: Blackwell.

Shotter, J. (1987). Remembering and forgetting as social institutions. *Quarterly Newsletter of the Laboratory of Comparative Human Cognition, 9,* 11–19.

Spiro, R. J. (1980). Accommodative reconstruction in prose recall. *Journal of Verbal Learning and Verbal Behavior, 19,* 84–95.

Steiner, I. D. (1966). Models for inferring relationships between group size and potential group productivity. *Behavioral Science, 11,* 273–283.

Steiner, I. D. (1972). *Group process and productivity.* New York: Academic Press.

Stephenson, G. M. (1984). Accuracy and confidence in testimony: A critical review and some fresh evidence. In D. J. Muller, D. E. Blackman, & A. J. Chapman (Eds.), *Psychology and law: Topics from an international conference* (pp. 229–250). Chichester: Wiley.

Stephenson, G. M., Abrams, D., Wagner, W., & Wade, G. (1986). Partners in Recall: Collaborative order in the recall of a police interrogation. *British Journal of Social Psychology, 25,* 341–343.

Stephenson, G. M., Brandstatter, H., & Wagner, W. (1983). An experimental study of social performance and delay on the testimonial validity of story recall. *European Journal of Social Psychology, 13,*175–191.

Stephenson, G. M., Clark, N. K., & Kniveton, B. H. (1988). Collaborative testimony by police officers: A psycho-legal issue. In H. Wegener, F. Losel, & J. Haisch (Eds.), *Criminal behavior and the justice system: Psychological perspectives.* Berlin: Springer Verlag.

Stephenson, G. M., Clark, N. K., & Wade, G. S. (1986). Meetings make evidence: An experimental study of collaborative and individual recall of a simulated police interrogation. *Journal of Personality and Social Psychology, 50,* 1113–1122.

Stephenson, G. M., & Wagner, W. (in press). Group remembering: Prophylactic or faciliative of misplaced confidence in dyadic recall decisions? *Applied Cognitive Psychology.*

Stoner, J. A. F. (1968). Risky and cautious shifts in group decisions: The influence of widely held values. *Journal of Experimental Social Psychology, 4,* 442–459.

Taylor, D. W. (1954, June). Problem solving by groups. *Proceedings of the Fourteenth International Congress of Psychology,* Montreal.

Thomas, E. J., & Fink, C. F. (1961). Models of group problem solving. *Journal of Abnormal and Social Psychology, 63,* 53–63.

Tulving, E. (1968). Theoretical issues in free recall. In T. R. Dixon & D. L. Norton (Eds.) *Verbal behavior and general behavior theory*. Englewood Cliffs, NJ: Prentice-Hall.

Tulving, E. (1972). Episodic and semantic memory. In E. Tulving & W. Donaldson (Eds.), *Organization of memory*. New York: Academic Press.

Tulving, E. (1983). Elements of episodic memory. London: Oxford University Press.

van Dijk, T. A., & Kintsch, W. (1983). *Strategies of discourse comprehension*. London: Academic Press.

Vansina, J. (1973). *Oral tradition: A study in historical methodology*. Harmondsworth: Penguin.

Wallach, M. A., Kogan, N., & Bem, D. J. (1962). Group influence on individual risk taking. *Journal of Abnormal and Social Psychology, 65*, 75–86.

Warnick, D. H., & Sanders, G. S. (1980). The effect of group discussion on eyewitness accuracy. *Journal of Applied Social Psychology, 10*, 249–259.

Wegner, D. M. (1986). Transactive memory. In B. Mullen & G. Goethals (Eds.), *Theories of group behavior*. New York: Springer-Verlag.

Wegner, D. M., Giuliano, T., & Hertel, P. (1985). Cognitive interdependence in close relationships. In W. J. Ickes (Ed.), *Compatible and incompatible relationships*. New York: Springer-Verlag.

Wells, G. L., & Loftus, E. R. (Eds.). (1984). *Eyewitness testimony*. Cambridge, England: Cambridge University Press.

Wittgenstein, L. (1953). *Philosophical investigations*. Oxford: Blackwell & Mott.

Yuker, H. E. (1955). Group atmosphere and memory. *Journal of Abnormal and Social Psychology, 51*, 17–23.

12 The Appropriation of Ideas

Robert A. Wicklund
Universität Bielefeld

Among the inventions, creations, values, and moralities coined by humans, many such concepts or ideas lend themselves to being acted upon. The purpose of this chapter is that of explicating a hypothesis which, very abstractly stated, says that *acting on* an idea results in the *appropriation* of that idea, thus the "lifting" of that idea for oneself. What are "acting on an idea" and "appropriation of an idea"?

The background of idea-implementation is generally the group, which functions as a *source* of the idea in question. Thus the group, no matter whether the family (developmental psychology), the peer group, or the work-group provides the ideas—in the form of moral principles, values, or creative thoughts—which the person can then implement and eventually appropriate. What are the signs of appropriation in these various kinds of group contexts? The following four illustrations indicate the direction of this chapter: The group serves as a source for an idea, the person acts on the idea, and appropriation then takes place, as evidenced in the illustrations by *internalization* of a moral principle or value, by having *incorporated* a new belief and coming to behave consistent with that belief, by developing a *creative repertoire,* or by claiming to be the *author* of the idea in question.

Following these illustrations the chapter delves into the issue of appropriation and analyzes the process largely in terms of Gestalt principles. Two experiments are discussed, two alternative approaches to appropriation are sketched out, and finally, the course of appropriation—in terms of the battle between individual and group—is discussed within a developmental psychology perspective.

Four Illustrations

Certain approaches to the internalization of moral principles have hinted at an activity-appropriation connection. A detailed overview of the process of internalization by Krathwohl, Bloom, and Masia (1975) makes explicit reference to the child's actions (as well as emotional reactions) in the internalization of moral principles. The activity-internalization connection is also represented in Deci and Ryan (1985), who reject the position that internalization of values might proceed by passive routes. From an alternative theoretical perspective, internalization of specific, object-related moralities is coordinated to action via the vehicle of cognitive dissonance, according to the analysis and experimental paradigm of Aronson and Carlsmith (1963; see also Freedman, 1965; Pepitone, McCauley, & Hammond, 1967; and Turner & Wright, 1965).

As a second case in point, activity has been regarded as a prerequisite for the stability and long-term behavioral relevance of belief systems (Abelson, 1986). Thus the forming or altering of a belief (Brehm & Cohen, 1962; King & Janis, 1956), the longer-term congruency between belief and behaviors (Fazio, 1986; Fazio & Zanna, 1978; Zanna & Fazio, 1982) as well as the internal consistency of a belief-relevant message (Cohen, 1961; Zajonc, 1960) have been regarded as outcomes of belief-relevant actions. Third, there is also some theoretical and empirical hint that arriving at a creative style, or creative work, is the outcome of activities that are directed at the idea basic to the work, such as improvising on others' ideas (Gardner, 1973). Fourth, a small experimental literature indicates that actively working to formulate ideas within a group context results in individuals' overestimating their "ownership" of the resultant ideas (Ross & Sicoly, 1979; Stephenson & Wicklund, 1983). As will be shown below, these third and fourth points can readily be brought into connection with "unintended" plagiarism.

This cursory look at a sample of literature says nothing about the theoretical processes that might underlie an activity-appropriation connection, nor does such a brief overview clarify the scope of the problem area to be discussed here. For these tasks we need to deal first with some definitional issues, which will then expand themselves into theoretical issues—namely, (1) What is the scope of the term *idea* in this chapter? (2) What is the nature of the *activities* that can be brought to bear on these ideas? (3) Most centrally, through what psychological process does *appropriation* of the idea result from activity?

THE IDEA: THE RAW MATERIAL FOR APPROPRIATION

It is not our purpose here to delve into the linguistic aspects of the differences between "ideas," "concepts," "explanations" and so forth.[1] Rather, the

---

[1]The reader is referred to Martin (1982), for a treatise on "The natural history of ideas" in the sense of a person's coming to know when he "knows" and "represents" an idea.

important connotations of *idea* for the appropriation context can best be spelled out in terms of the following two characteristics.

Communicability.   An important aspect of the idea is its social character. No matter whether a moral notion, a creative literary or musical idea, a theory, or a belief or value, the appropriation process necessarily assumes that the idea can be "lifted," and verbally communicated, from one person to another. More concretely: A clear example of an idea is a moral rule, which stipulates classes of behaviors. Similarly, values and beliefs also carry behavioral implications. At the same time, a behavior-relevant idea does not necessarily have to imply an explicit code of ethics or recipe for acting. A literary passage or a musical theme,—i.e., a specific instance of an idea—can also be communicated and can serve as a basis for acting. One reads a literary passage to others, or one sings a famous musical theme. As will become more important below, the literary passage and musical theme can also serve as starting points for one's innovations or improvisations.

Operationalizability.   An idea does not tell a person concretely what to do. Rather, the idea has more the status of a concept, which people can operationalize in their own behaviors. The idea can be abstract, such as the 10 Commandments, a constitutional principle, or a moral ideal, but it can also be less abstract—i.e., someone else's operationalization—such as a piece of prose or music. No matter what level of abstraction, the important point is that the behaviors to be enacted are not contained precisely in the idea. In the case of behaving on the basis of a moral or constitutional principle the person must function as a theoretician or constitutional lawyer and derive a specific behavioral instance (an operationalization) from the idea. When acting on a creative work, the individual again has a wide latitude for the operationalization; one can attempt to copy the creative work (and thereby introduce subtle variations), interpret it, transpose it, explain it, or refute it. In short, the crucial aspect of the ideas that we are concerned with here is their operationalizability.

ACTING ON THE IDEA

The literature that we consider offers a broad spectrum of actions that qualify as individual operationalizations of an idea. Highly graphic in this respect is the free improvisation of the subjects of King and Janis (1956), where the free role-playing of an attitude position was required. Or in Gardner's (1973) characterization of the acquisition of creative styles, the pertinent action entails the endless copying, and gradually modifying, of already existing creative works. In the language of Bandura (1977), the end result of observing an instance of a moral principle is said to be the development of a moral repertoire that results from the imitation of diverse models for morality. Or in the case of idea-generating groups (Diener, 1979; Mehlhorn & Mehlhorn, 1979; Ross & Sicoly, 1979; Stephenson & Wicklund, 1983), participants act on the basis of others' contributions— altering, mixing, or copying ideas that are alive in the group setting.

One certainly cannot say that the end result of such activity is independent of the "natural" assimilability of the idea, or of the extent of constraint on the person to take action. The important point, however, is a simple one: The person's concrete actions constitute an instance, or *operationalization*, of the idea. It is useful theoretically to view this operationalization concept from the standpoint of two variables; each of them defines the extent to which a person's action constitutes an operationalization:

Activity-Passivity.   At one pole of this continuum would be the mere think- ing about an idea. One hears a piece of music, listens to a speech about the latest psychological model, or watches someone behave in line with the Golden Rule. One could label this pole the "receiver" end (Cohen, 1961; Zajonc, 1960), the "controlled" end (cf. Rotter, 1966), or simply the "passive" end. The critical aspect of passivity is that the person exerts no influence on the idea; he neither implements it nor transforms it. A step toward being more active is the verbal level. Here, even if one simply copies a family member or peer, one is using the idea in the sense of communicating it. To be sure, it can be shown readily that a mere "set" or readiness to communicate has powerful effects on how the con- tents of the communication are structured cognitively (Cohen, 1961; Zajonc, 1960). Still more active would be the translation of the idea into something concrete, which often takes place via overt motor behaviors. For instance, a moral idea is applied to an action, or a creative idea serves as the basis of one's art project.

This dimension of passive-to-active has a direct counterpart in the theoretical work of Lewin (1926) and in subsequent empirical work by Mahler (1933), whereby the lowest "reality" level consisted of wishful thinking, and then, moving through the levels of project-directed thinking, and verbal behavior, the "highest" level was reached, this corresponding to overt behavior.

Extent of Deviation of One's Operationalization from the Original Opera- tionalization.   An idea qua idea contains no explicit directions for the person's operationalization, thus any implementation of an idea is necessarily an opera- tionalization. However, one's own actions can be based on others' existing operationalizations and it thus makes sense to ask how far the "new" opera- tionalization deviates from the original one. If a would-be composer simply xeroxes a passage from a well-known composer, the deviation from the original operationalization is zero. Or if honesty means that a man does not cheat in paying income tax, and the child, likewise does not cheat on his income tax, then the child's concrete use of *honesty* has not departed from that of the model. On the other hand, if the child transforms the original operationalization into not cheating on spelling tests, or admitting to a hypocrisy, we would definitely speak of the child as having exhibited his own operationalization.

In short, these two components together—the degree of *activity* within the operationalization, plus the extent to which the operationalization departs from those shown by models—set the stage for appropriation of the idea that is operationalized.

APPROPRIATION: THE PSYCHOLOGICAL OUTCOME OF ACTING ON THE IDEA

When one improvises a speech, transposes a melody, or translates a piece of prose, there is a sense in which the product—the operationalization—is detached from the original idea and belongs to one's self. This removal from the original source, or distancing from the source, and association of the product with one's self, should be strongest at the highest level of activity. At the extreme passive end of the continuum, whereby the person does nothing more than to memorize the idea in its given, abstract semantic form, there will not be such a removal of the idea from its original source. But the foregoing is more description than explanation. To what extent can we bring psychological theory to bear on the problem?

Gestalt Psychology.   The "stimulus underway," i.e., the moving stimulus, plays a special role in Gestalt theorizing. Such moving or accelerating stimuli, (including the "Ego," Koffka, 1935, p. 285) come to dominate the perceptual field, pushing the more static elements into the background (Kahneman, 1973, p. 78). Using attribution of causality as an index of salience, McArthur and Post (1977) have demonstrated that a moving person (perhaps a person in a rocking chair) comes to the foreground of the stimulus field constituted by a perceived group. Thus the active object, or person, is accorded more causality. James (1910) has made a similar point, in hypothesizing that the more central, or visible components of the self are those that "move," such as emotions, a hypothesis that has not been lost on modern self theory (cf. Scheier, 1976; Scheier & Carver, 1977).

But what else? Movement is said to bring the object or person into the foreground of perception, and thereby result in a greater ascription of causality to that object or person. But there is still more, and this second point is critical for the present analysis. Kahneman (1973) asserts:

When a subject is told that he will see a flash of light and hear a tone at about the same time, and that he is to attend especially to one of them, the perception of

> simultaneity is biased. The stimulus that is attended to is perceived as occurring relatively sooner than the other. (pp. 79–80, 137)

Thus the perceptual reasoning leads us not just to salience per se, but also to perceived causality, and even more intriguing, to perceived primacy. This raises the possibility that salience, causality, and primacy are bound up with one another in the individual's perceptual processes, and that the tendency for an event to be perceived as occurring earlier is associated with the tendency to see that event as causal.

This implication is reified in a recent theoretical proposal by Abelson (1986), who discusses beliefs from the standpoint of their psychological "ownership" by individuals. Abelson observes that a behavioral orientation toward a belief results in, or is associated with, an increased stability of that same belief, a point documentable in the Fazio and Zanna (1978) research tradition, among others. But he pushes his point further, in suggesting that a stability-increasing, *proprietary* orientation toward a belief can result from a variety of circumstances. Among these circumstances is "attributing longevity to a belief" (Abelson, 1986, p. 232). There is no empirical work on this suggestion, but the hypothesis, according to Abelson, is that when people are requested to project their beliefs "backward in time," the result will be a greater stability.

If Abelson is right, then the sense of one's own primacy with respect to an idea is not simply something to be manipulated, but rather, is a psychological accompaniment of one's subjective ownership of the idea. Thus the sense of being earlier, or being first, should be part and parcel of appropriation of an idea, and thus one of the outcomes of idea-directed activity.

The Dual Outcomes of Activity: Primacy-Causality and Reliability

Let's return to the case of the person who actively improvises a moral principle, a belief, or a creative solution to a problem. The person is a moving, active agent, and in the Gestalt language, the person's causal nature, or causal agent self, should then move to the foreground of the stimulus field. This much follows from Kahneman's (1973) observations and from the reasoning and findings of McArthur and Post (1977). This sense of being causal, or of being the sole representative of an idea, should be regarded as an end point along a continuum. To the extent that someone has actively operationalized an idea, there will be a tendency to project one's contact with the idea, or representation of the idea backward in time. Accordingly, each time one operationalizes the idea, one moves subjectively closer to being a unique representative, or source, of the idea. Thus with the term *primacy/causality* we mean nothing more than a continuum:

1. At the one end of the continuum, whereby one has had only passive contact with the idea, the idea will appear new, and one will not feel any *origin* quality in regard to the idea.[2]

2. At the other end of the continuum, the person will have projected his representation of the idea backward in time, and will in the extreme case come to think of himself as the origin of the idea, to the exclusion of other sources.

Further, the fact of having transformed the idea to the operational level will mean that the person will become a more reliable representative of the idea—in communicating the idea as well as in behaving with respect to the idea. Only when the idea is transformed into one's own work does it acquire a high degree of internal organization and consistency (as demonstrated by Cohen, 1961, and Zajonc, 1960), and only when the idea is transformed into one's own work does it offer a stable basis for future behaviors (cf. Zanna & Fazio, 1982). Accordingly, the stability or reliability of idea-based (i.e., belief-based, moral-based, value-based) behavior, that is so desired by psychologists, will ensue to the extent that the person has undertaken an active operationalization of the idea.

These dual effects of activity—primacy/causality and reliability—are subsumed here under the rubric *appropriation* of ideas. The subsuming is viewed as a psychological necessity, in that the operationalization of an idea should, for the above-given reasons, carry both effects.

A LOOK AT APPROPRIATION IN CONCRETE INSTANCES

The existing empirical literature does not capture the idea-activity-appropriation concept in its entirety, but there are some hints that a chain of psychological events similar to those just described does take place. One finds these hints on two fronts: the increment in the person's reliability vis à vis ideas, and certain primacy/causality effects.

The Reliability Connection

Representing, or talking about, an idea can have direct ramifications for the form that the idea then takes. The person who operationalizes an idea, as in communicating it, will come to give it a personal meaning, in the sense of imparting to it

---

[2]While the *origin/pawn* terminology of deCharms (1968, p. 273) would appear to have something to do with the activity dimension that is so central here, his conception will not be discussed at length. The primary reason is that deCharms' notions do not have any direct implications for the person's appropriation of ideas that are acted upon. On the other hand, it may well be that ideas that are acted on through an "origin"-orientation, rather than a "pawn"-orientation, ultimately have greater ramifications for appropriation. If this is the case, then deCharms' approach to these problems would fit under the control-theory approach to claiming of ideas for oneself (see pp. 410–411).

greater internal stability, and in the sense of imparting greater integration to the idea via the communication. This notion finds a theoretical counterpart as early as 1947, with Allport and Postman's analysis of rumor transmission. The successive passing on of a rumor was said to be accompanied by a gradually increasing internal organization in the rumor—or in the language of Allport and Postman, sharpening, leveling, and assimilation.

Somewhat later, a dissertation by Zajonc (1960) introduced the notion of *cognitive tuning*, whereby the critical psychological dimension was the subject's "transmitter" or "receiver"-orientation to a written description of a job applicant. Those who expected to communicate the target description wrote their own versions of the communication in a style that was radically different from that of the receiver-set subjects: They showed more differentiation, complexity, unity, and organization in their own formulation. In short, as active representatives of the idea (the characterization of a job applicant), they produced a more reliable, or internally consistent communication. A very similar finding was then reported by Cohen (1961), in which the set-to-communicate resulted in subjects' eliminating contradictory material from the message.

Operationalizing an idea also results in the person's becoming a more faithful representative of the idea. This general notion has found an empirical reality in a number of research programs, one of the earliest and clearest being the study of King and Janis (1956). Subjects in one condition were given the difficult task of improvising, impromtu, a talk on the role of college students in the military. In another group the students simply read from a script, and another group received only a passive exposure to the communication. The outcome of these treatments was very clear: Those who had the difficult improvising task showed much more opinion change than did the other two groups. In accounting for these effects King and Janis (1956) were able to dismiss an "increased attention to the message" explanation, as well as a comprehension explanation. This left them, interestingly, with an account that was closely bound up with the improvisatory character of the talk:

> It seems plausible that there is a lowering of psychological resistance whenever a person regards the persuasive arguments emanating from others as his "own" ideas. . . . . the individual's belief that he is making a decision on his own initiative may increase the influence of an indirect suggestion. (p. 183)

The idea is that a certain "ownership" is basic to the person's becoming a more reliable representative of an idea. Abelson's (1986) "proprietary orientation" reflects this line of thought exactly 30 years later, but in the meanwhile, a great deal of research has accumulated to support the conclusion:

Notable among this research is a series of experiments by Fazio and Zanna (see Fazio, 1986; Zanna & Fazio, 1982). The person's behaving on the basis of the attitude (including repeatedly expressing the attitude) results in a more consistent link between the attitude and behavior.

Although there is only scant empirical documentation, segments of the arena of moral development view the *active* dealing with moral issues as promoting greater internalization—hence stability. Such developmental proposals are found in Aronson & Carlsmith (1963), Deci and Ryan (1985), and Krathwohl et al. (1975).

Quite independent of the theoretical starting point, there is good agreement in the literature that a process like idea-appropriation takes place, using the criterion of the person's representing or manifesting the idea reliably. All of the above cited hypotheses and empirical work point clearly to the conclusion that representing the idea actively leads to a kind of ownership, in the sense of becoming an internally consistent, reliable representative of the idea. Thus the stability-reliability side of the appropriation process seems clear. But what does the more cognitive side look like—the question of primacy/causality?

The Primacy/Causality Connection

"Method 635" (Mehlhorn & Mehlhorn, 1979) is a group-based idea-production technique, whereby each member of a group of six people is confronted with a standard set of problems and is asked to generate written solutions. The written solutions are then exchanged among the group members and each person has the opportunity to rework, develop, and improvise on the others' ideas. An important motivating feature of the Method 635, according to Mehlhorn and Mehlhorn, is the recognition that people invest more energy in the realization of their *own* ideas than in the realization of somebody else's ideas. Accordingly, the author of the sum of the improvisations is called the "group," and then, in the view of Mehlhorn and Mehlhorn, each individual is also thereby an author. While Mehlhorn and Mehlhorn report no measures of "ownership" or claim to ideas that objectively belong to others, one might surmise on the basis of their observations that all of the reworking, developing, and improvising on others' ideas leads to an idea-appropriation—an exaggeration of one's own relative contribution. This hypothesis finds more definite empirical support in a certain body of social psychological literature:

When the members of a group have worked toward a common end and subsequently are asked to indicate who contributed what, there is of course room for claiming something that is not "objectively" one's own. Ross and Sicoly (1979) introduce this problem with the example of coauthors fighting over first place on the article, and proceed to illustrate a certain bias effect by means of several interesting field studies. In one study subjects were assembled in dyads; each participant was given different portions of a case study about "Paula," then the group was asked to discuss various solutions to Paula's problems, taking into account the information that they had just read. The discussion was tape-recorded. Three to 4 days later the participants were invited back. Subjects were requested to write down as much as they could recall of the group's discussion.

They also estimated who had contributed which ideas to the discussion. The results—described as "egocentric bias"—were straightforward and striking: In 95% of the dyads each subject claimed the majority of the recalled statements as his own. This effect was reduced somewhat, but not eliminated, when the group product was first evaluated by the experimenter as a failure.

A subsequent study, using a similar paradigm, was conducted by Stephenson and Wicklund (1983). Students in groups of three were given the following instructions:

> What I'd like for you to do as a group is to come up with approximately 15 consequences that might result if this particular situation were to occur. (p. 68)

The situation was simply:

> Imagine that the height of everyone in the world were suddenly reduced to 12 inches. What would be some consequences that might result if this were to happen? (p. 68)

The group then proceeded to brainstorm, and once the group had generated 11 ideas, the experimenter, who was listening in, interrupted the discussion. The subjects were separated from each other and asked to write down all of the solutions that the group had generated, and further, to "cross out" all of the solutions for which the subject himself was not responsible. The results showed that the average subject claimed approximately one idea too many. This over-claiming was based directly on the content that was generated by the other subjects, in that the overclaiming index consisted of the number of times that two (or all three) subjects layed claim to the same idea.

While the extent of participants' activity was not explicitly varied in these group studies, there is the very clear suggestion that the opportunity for discussion and active building on one another's ideas was responsible for these cognitive appropriation effects. One further study should also be mentioned, where again, the subject's overt activity—in this case the implementation of a suggestion—appears to result in the lifting of another's idea.

Maier (1931) confronted subjects with a difficult cognitive task, entailing tying the ends of two cords together. The cords were suspended such that the subject was unable to reach one cord while holding the other. After uncovering several of the more obvious solutions to the problem, most subjects were hard put to find a further, and final solution. Once the subjects had been given 10 minutes to arrive at the final solution, the experimenter walked past one of the cords and set it in motion, and typically, subjects picked up on this cue and improvised on his "suggestion" sufficiently to get the two cords tied together. When they were subsequently questioned regarding how they had arrived at the solution, only one subject (of those who used the suggestion) reported that the critical idea had been offered by the experimenter's behavior. Thus again, a person's activity, based on an idea, appears to lead to the exaggeration of one's own primacy/causality and simultaneously to pushing other possible authors or sources into the background.

Although the above work consistently indicates that activity is associated with bringing oneself into the forefront as representative of the idea, none of the studies actually varies the extent of activity, thus no conclusions about our central hypothesis are possible. The following two studies thus provide an extension of this work, in that they vary the amount of idea-directed activity. Subjects' primacy/causality with respect to the idea is the dependent measure.

ACTING ON THE IDEA: TRANSLATING THE IDEA INTO ONE'S OWN LANGUAGE[3]

The primacy/causality aspects of the appropriation concept were explored here. Following either passive exposure to a list of medical suggestions, or else an active translation of those same concepts, subjects indicated how many of those concepts they had already known, and also how long they had known them.

Thus appropriation, as reflected in primacy/causality, should simply take the form of subjects' putting their own knowledge *before* that of any given, objective information source. To the extent that the translating (active) subjects are inclined to claim to have known more ideas previously, and to have known them longer—relative to the passive exposure group—there would be some evidence for the activity-idea-appropriation connection.

The subjects were 56 patient-care personnel from a hospital in Bielefeld, Germany; almost all of these were registered nurses. The subjects were run in large groups, and the study was introduced as an information-gathering exercise, whose purpose was to gather feedback on certain proposals for the modern handling of patients. The subjects found that they would be reading a text on the "humanization of patient care," and that they would subsequently respond to a number of questions pertinent to the text.

In the Passive condition, the first page of the form stated that the subject would find a text about patient-care on the second page. It was also noted that the text had already been translated from English into German. Finally the subject was requested to fill out the questions on the third page.

In the Translate condition, the directions were highly similar to those of the Passive condition, except that the instructions also introduced a request:

---

[3]"Acting on Ideas: Appropriation to One's Self." Wicklund, R. A., Reuter, T., & Schiffmann, R. (1988).

> We are attempting to formulate the text so that it is as comprehensible as possible; therefore, we are asking you to help us achieve this goal, through translating the passages that are printed in English. Please write your translations on the blank page.

The text itself contained 13 critical ideas dealing with advanced patient care and with how such concepts should be taught. The Passive group simply read the text; the Translate group translated them, per instructions.

The first appropriation measure asked subjects to mark the ideas in the text that they had already known, while the second item asked, within a forced-alternative format, how long they had known the ideas ("few weeks," "few months," "1 year," "2 years," "longer"). In addition, all subjects were asked to summarize the central ideas of the text, and to indicate on a scale the extent to which the text pleased them.

The passive- vs. translate-manipulation did not affect subjects' perception of the *total number* of critical ideas in the text. Nor was there a difference between conditions in how much subjects were pleased by the text. Interestingly, the Translate group tended to be less pleased by the text, thus there is no hint of any sort of forced compliance-liking phenomenon (cf. Brehm & Cohen, 1962; Festinger & Carlsmith, 1959; Wicklund & Brehm, 1976). The two main dependent measures showed the following: (1) The average number of ideas that the Passive group claimed to have known previously was 3.4, whereas the Translate group claimed to have known 4.9, the difference being significant. (2) The length of the time that the ideas had been known followed the same pattern. The mean for the Passive group corresponded exactly to 1 year, while that for the Translate group was 1 year and 11 months—the difference again being reliable.

Although the results are congruent with the hypothesis, one might object that the change of language (English to German) is necessary in order to obtain the effects. That is, in translating "education" to "Ausbildung," the subjects would be more prone to claim to recognize the concept, simply because the term has a higher recognition value when printed in their own language. On the other hand, it should also be remembered that the Passive group received the entire text in their native language, thus the individual terms should have been just as familiar for them. Nonetheless, to see if comparable effects might be obtainable in a qualitatively different paradigm, the following experiment was undertaken.

ACTING ON THE IDEA: SUMMARIZING PSYCHOLOGICAL CONCEPTS[4]

This second experiment is similar to the first one, except that the activity is defined through summarizing the relevant ideas, rather than through translating

---

[4]"Acting on Ideas: Appropriation to One's Self." Wicklund, R. A., Reuter, T., & Schiffmann, R. (1988).

them. The subjects were 52 psychology students, either in the first, second, or third semester of their studies. They were run in groups, in three parallel sessions, each session with a different experimenter.

The study was introduced as an investigation of memory. Subjects began by filling out questions asking for biographical information and also questions about their studies in psychology. Then they read a one-page text on the construction of theory that contained five critical psychological concepts (*Stigmatisierung, Klassifikation, Effektivität, pragmatisch,* and *affrigmatisch*). Following that, they were asked either to write a very brief fantasy-story based on a set of 8 terms that did not appear in the text (Passive condition), or else, with the help of 13 concepts taken from the list, they were asked to write a summary of the text (Active condition).

Finally, to be certain that the critical 5 concepts were salient for all subjects, subjects in both conditions were asked to write a short definition of each concept. Thus, just as Experiment I, there was some guarantee that the total number of critical concepts was not perceived differentially as a function of the activity manipulation.

The dual dependent variable of appropriation of the first experiment was condensed into one: The critical concepts were listed on the left of the page, and the subjects were asked to indicate how long they had known the concepts. The answering categories were "before my studies," "during the first semester" and "during the second semester." They could also indicate that they had not known them previously. The data analysis simply examined the number of concepts that the subject claimed to have known "before my studies."

Of the 5 concepts, the average number that subjects claimed to have known beforehand was approximately 3. There was, congruent with the hypothesis, a decided tendency for subjects in the Passive condition to have claimed fewer concepts than subjects in the Active condition, and the effect held for all three sessions (i.e., all three experimenters). The overall difference between conditions was reliable.

The control (passive) conditions in the two experiments provided baselines with respect to subjects' claimed prior knowledge of the concepts, and (in the first experiment) of the length of time the concepts had been in their repertoires. The effect of translating, and of summarizing, was to bring subjects to overestimate the extent of their knowledge repertoires prior to the informative source, i.e., the texts. Thus, in this sense, activity appears to bring the individual to neglect the source of ideas. This general effect is underlined by the finding, in the first study, that the translating subjects greatly increased their estimates of the length of time that they had already had the ideas. Moreover, the results do not seem to be mediated by differential liking for the text or by misperception of the total number of ideas in the text (Experiment I).

It should also be emphasized that the results do not indicate that subjects were claiming to have invented, or thought up anything. Rather, the effect of the activity was to project subjects' holding of the ideas backwards in time (i.e., *primacy*).[5] Theoretically, if subjects were then to work actively on the ideas in another context, where the ideas would be presented by still another source, they would again project their knowledge of the ideas to a point *prior* to that source. By this reasoning, continued working on the idea in manifold contexts should bring the *primacy/causality*, as well as reliability, to a point at which the person begins to function subjectively as author, or sole representative of the idea. This is the condition that is seen as an ideal by internalization and creativity theorists; we return to the topic on p. 411.

The theoretical bent of this chapter is the theme of activity; i.e., the operationalization of the idea. This is not to say that such operationalizations are the only way in which one could think about the issue of appropriation. In particular, those who have studied the stability of beliefs and values, as well as those who have studied moral internalization, have explored their respective phenomena in terms of very alternative views of the human. One of these views, a highly prevalent one, is the memory model:

AN ALTERNATIVE PARADIGM: MEMORY FOR AN IDEA

If we depart from the psychology of the person who acts on the idea, thus who develops his own operationalization of the idea, it is then possible to turn to a qualitatively different kind of "neglecting of the source." In particular, the *memory* concept can capture the notion that someone who is exposed to a message (or moral, or creative idea), will, with the passage of time, tend to remember the *contents* better than the *source* of the contents.

This theme is nowhere more explicit than in the collected research on the *sleeper effect* (Greenwald, Pratkanis, Leippe, & Baumgardner, 1986; Gruder, Cook, Hennigan, Flay, Alessis, & Halamaj, 1978; Hovland, Lumsdaine, & Sheffield, 1949). The basic phenomenon, which has now been shown to be reproducible under very special circumstances, depends on the message recipients' gradually forgetting the source of a communication. Given that the forgetting curve for the incredible source is steeper than that for the text material, it

---

[5]In this context it is interesting to draw a comparison to Abelson's (1986) article, "Beliefs are like possessions." Abelson proposes that a variety of overt activities should induce the subjective "possession" of a belief; these include suffering for a belief, explaining a belief, defending a belief, and *attributing longevity to a belief* (p. 232). Abelson construes the longevity-projection as a type of experimental induction—as an independent variable that would increase subjective possession. The results of the two studies reported here would imply that there is an even tighter relationship between the projection of longevity and activity than Abelson had suspected: Ownership (or in this formulation—appropriation) is perhaps not only inducable by projected longevity, as Abelson suggests, but is also *reflected* in the person's sense of longevity, or primacy, regarding the idea.

becomes possible to predict that the adverse effects on persuasion of an incredible communicator will wain with the passage of time. In short, with the passage of time, the subject tends to dissociate the message from the negative source, and thus comes to believe the message.

Although the effect is obtainable only when the credibility-undermining manipulation occurs after exposure to the message (Gruder et al., 1978; Pratkanis, Greenwald, Leippe, & Baumgardner, 1985), one might nonetheless try to apply this memory model to selected appropriation phenomena. The idea would be that the passage of time is sufficient for subjects to dissociate the author from the content—quite independent of subjects' activity. To be sure, the subjects in the multitude of sleeper effect studies were invariably passive consumers of the message.

This suggestion is seconded by Hoffman (1977, p. 94), who uses a similar model to account for the internalization of moral ideas. Hoffman draws on a distinction by Tulving (1972), whereby "episodic" memory is the part of memory that deals with such contextual factors as the author or source of the moral idea, whereas "semantic" memory corresponds to the actual cognitive content of the moral principle. According to Hoffman's version of this distinction,

> The two types of memory are quite independent of each other. And what is especially important here is that semantic memory for an event is apt to be far more enduring than episodic memory. (p. 95)

And what is the fate of episodic memory, i.e., memory for the author, or source, of the moral principle?

> Subsequently, when the child is reminded of the ideas communicated in the inductions and perhaps feels empathy or guilt . . . he may not remember that he originally had these thoughts and feelings in response to parental discipline. (p. 95)

Continuing with a salience/memory model, Hoffman then notes that the likelihood of the child's continuing to think about the source will depend on the salience, or nonambiguity of the source. If the external sources are unclear, then the child "will experience these actions and thoughts as his own" (p. 96).

It is here that the critical difference between a memory model and the present appropriation notion can be seen. Operating on the basis of a memory model, one assumes that the contents that are to be recalled do not change; instead, all that changes is the person's memory for them. The present notion, whereby the person's *operationalization* of the idea is central, imparts an entirely different meaning to the individual's appropriated idea. It is proposed that one's own activity results in a product that is, for the actor, subjectively not identical with the original idea. As discussed earlier in this chapter, the person's exact operationalization is seldom given within the idea, thus the person's memory (i.e., that which has been appropriated) does not have the same referent as does the memory of the passive person. The active person recalls the operationalization, for example, concrete instances of "thou shall not steal." The more passive person, i.e., the person who has not operationalized the idea, recalls the idea as it was originally given—in abstract form.

Accordingly, when the concept of memory is brought to bear on the current topic, it should be applied within the context of the question, "Memory for what?" No matter whether we look at improvising activity (King and Janis), translating activity (see above), or any other active operationalization of the idea, the resultant *referent* of the idea is not the same for passive and active individuals. And the fact of this difference is said to underlie the primacy/causality and reliability effects—not a differential memory for an unchanging idea.

Even if there are conditions under which the Tulving (1972) reasoning, or sleeper-effect paradigm, leads to relatively quicker forgetting of the source, this effect in no way corresponds to the end effects of appropriation as described here. The literature that we have examined is quite clear on the point that the nonoperationalized idea, i.e., the idea that the person has *not* yet brought to an empirical-behavioral level, has little lasting impact on that person's conduct. Thus memory *for the original abstract idea,* as construed within research on audience persuasion or on person perception, is quite a different matter from the process of appropriation through operationalization. The latter brings the person away from the original idea and results in stability with respect to one's own operationalization, as well as primacy/causality with respect to one's own operationalization.

Action Mediating Memory for the Idea

One should not, however, say that the concept of *memory* plays no role in appropriation. Rather, we can ask what effects the person's own operationalizing has on memory for facets of the idea. One implication is already clear: As the person becomes progressively more active with regard to the original idea, and as the operationalization diverges progressively further from that of other individuals, the person will be less likely to think about or name other sources.

A second implication may be drawn from a recent line of thinking by Reiser, Black, and Abelson (1985). In the experimental paradigm, subjects were presented with 20 pairs of *experiences* and corresponding *specific actions*. For instance, "getting a hair cut" (the experience) was paired with "paying at the cash register" (concrete action). After the presentation of each pair, subjects were requested to press a button as soon as they had recalled an experience from their own past that matched the combination of the experience + concrete action pair.

When the experience (getting a hair cut) was presented on the video screen *prior* to the concrete action (paying), subjects' average reaction time was 7 sec. In contrast, they responded 2 sec more quickly when the concrete action preceded the presentation of the experience. In the language of Reiser et al., these results mean that concrete actions are central in the organization of autobiographical knowledge structures; once our own actions are salient, the broader experiences surrounding those actions are cognitively more accessible.

The attempt to make this memory work pertinent for the present formulation would ask the question, "What does speed of recall have to do with appropriation?" The answer is, "very little." But if we stretch the concept *experience,* then we could say that an ideal (moral, creative, or otherwise) plus its usual realm of application is an *experience*, and that one has greater cognitive access to it when attention is first steered toward relevant, specific actions. In turn, one could then assume that cognitive access to the idea brings forth a greater implementation of that idea in behavior. However, this reasoning is highly questionable. The person's behavior is not simply a cue that assists the calling up of an idea; rather, the behavior transforms the idea, such that what is then "called up" is the singular operationalization of the idea, not simply the idea as originally communicated.

There is a further difficulty in trying to reduce appropriation to availability-and-memory processes. If one's behavior stimulates the person's thinking about *experiences* associated with the idea, then behaving should also stimulate recall of the personal sources (authors) of the idea. This implication is clear in Abelson (1986), where he proposes that the ownership orientation can be strengthened by bringing the person to think of the origin of the belief. On the other hand, as spelled out earlier, the improvisatory character of the operationalization steers the person away from thinking about the source, thus activity should decrease one's mental access to the source, rather than increase it.

To sum up: A variety of memory/accessibility notions (Greenwald et al., 1986; Gruder et al., 1978; Hoffman, 1977; Hovland et al., 1949; Reiser et al., 1985; Tulving, 1972) can be brought to bear on the issue of whether the contents, or sources, are better recalled. A number of testable propositions result from these several treatments of source vs. contents. The important general point, however, is that we are dealing here with the appropriator's redefinition or transformation of the idea, thus the application of notions about memory is difficult, at best, since the contents of memory are transformed in the course of being operationalized.

Completely independent of memory processes, and also independent of the operationalization theme of this chapter, one can also view certain appropriation phenomena in terms of the person's pursuit of control over information. It looks like this:

A SECOND ALTERNATIVE PARADIGM:
APPROPRIATION AS SELF-BASED INFORMATION CONTROL

A very explicit case in point is formulated by Ross and Sicoly (1979), who suggest,

> One's sense of self-esteem may be enhanced by focusing on, or weighting more heavily, one's own inputs. . . . Similarly, a concern for personal efficacy or control (see deCharms, 1968; White, 1959) could lead individuals to dwell on their own contributions to a joint product. (p. 323)

To some extent Ross and Sicoly substantiate this thesis in a group problem-solving experiment (their Experiment 2); their subjects were more likely to take credit for group products if the products had been evaluated positively by the experimenter. In short, the basic idea is approximately, "self esteem needs lead directly to claiming more positive products as one's own doing."

The case described by Ross and Sicoly might be viewed as an aspect of a more general tendency to attribute responsibility for positive outcomes to one's own causality, and to transfer responsibility for negative happenings to others (see Osnabrügge, Stahlberg, & Frey, 1985; Snyder, Stephan, & Rosenfield, 1978). At the same time, it is not the case that Ross and Sicoly's subjects *disclaimed responsibility when the feedback was negative; however, the over*claiming for oneself was diminished.

On a still broader plane, one can argue that control motivation would lead to individuals' seeing more personal causality in their behaviors than reality would dictate (cf. deCharms, 1968; Langer, 1975; Wortman, 1976). We should then think that people would generally, quite aside from the activity-appropriation processes discussed here, have a propensity to overestimate the stability of their behaviors and thoughts (as illustrated in Bem & McConnell, 1970, and Goethals & Reckman, 1973) as well as a bent toward laying claim to primacy/causality in knowledge. The "I knew it all along effect" (Fischhoff, 1982) is a case in point. Quite aside from one's active involvement, there is a strong propensity to claim that one had knowledge that something would take place: "In hindsight, people consistently exaggerate what could have been anticipated in foresight" (p. 341).

A parallel undertaking could be imagined within the research area of *uniqueness* (Fromkin, 1970; Snyder & Fromkin, 1980). The idea, perhaps over-simplified, is that the person whose momentary manipulated uniqueness is low, on a certain dimension A, would show a heightened interest in being unique with respect to a certain set of information within Dimension B.

The phenomena of the person's "having known it all along," "having always held the attitude," or "being unique in holding the attitude" are clearly documentable; there is no question about their existence. However, the implications of the control area of research lead in directions different from those of the present area of inquiry. The crucial ingredient in the information-control line of thought is the person's need for control. This has been varied in several studies (cf. Berscheid, Graziano, Monson, & Dermer, 1976; Miller, Norman, & Wright, 1978; Pittman & Pittman, 1980) and it would not be surprising if, for example, the effects described by Fischhoff were even more obtainable among subjects whose acute desire for information control were heighted experimentally. Thus variation in control need is the research direction implied by this school, but not variation in the extent of operationalization of an idea.

What is the implication? A variation in control-need or control-orientation would lead to corresponding laying claim to ideas as one's own (as suggested in Ross & Sicoly, 1979). But there is also a definite contrast with the appropriation hypothesis of the present chapter: The appropriation idea assumes nothing more than a perceptual process, whereby the person's activity serves as the basis for tending to regard the idea as one's own. In short, the phenomena discussed under the heading *control* involve different variables from those dwelled upon here.

SOCIETY'S PERSPECTIVE: PLAGIARISM OR INTERNALIZATION? UNCIVILIZED OR CIVILIZED?

Thus far in this chapter the group has been viewed solely as a source, from which the person can appropriate (via operationalizing) the moral or creative content that the group has to offer. But there is much more to the group perspective, or more broadly cast, the societal perspective. Does the group do anything to further, or possibly to hinder, the individual's full appropriation of group-based content? Is the use of group-based ideas, and their appropriation, in any sense controlled by the group? These are particularly important questions in taking up the developmental perspective.

Developmental Psychology's View: Autonomy as an Ideal

The developmental psychology approach to the appropriation of ideas focuses on the consequences of the person's coming to *own* a moral concept. It is generally regarded as *better*, at least for society, when individuals have their own values or moralities. This proprietary orientation toward moral ideas is described by Piaget (1965) as the movement away from a heteronomous morality, toward an "autonomous" morality. According to Boyce and Jensen's (1978) characterization of the Piaget view, autonomy means being "subject to one's own law" (p. 93); ". . . the child no longer obeys the rules or commands given him by adults; he obeys himself" (p. 95).

That a "higher," more "mature" morality is associated with a sense of ownership or authorship is reflected even more poignantly in Kohlberg's (1980) characterization of his sixth stage of moral development:

> Stage 6, *universal ethical-principle orientation*. Right is defined by the decision of conscience in accord with self-chosen *ethical principles* appealing to logical comprehensiveness, universality, and consistency. p. 93)[6]

Neither Piaget nor Kohlberg is explicit on the cognitive transformation from heteronomous morality to autonomous morality. It is not clear how the child comes to choose, develop, or acquire his own moral principles, nor what "ownership" entails cognitively. Are they describing the child's taking-over of a parental morality, or is the suggestion that the arriving at one's own morality is a creative process, with somewhat unique content, without a clear source?

This issue is in part clarified by Deci and Ryan (1985), who describe internalization as:

> the process through which an individual acquires an attitude, belief, or behavioral regulation and progressively transforms it into a personal value, goal, or organization. It is the developmental process by which a child integrates the demands and values of the socializing environment. (p. 130)

Just as other developmental theorists, Deci and Ryan also emphasize the positive outcomes of an autonomous morality or value system, in noting that taking on values as one's own allows for more autonomy and more effective functioning (p. 130). However, Deci and Ryan are also not explicit on how the individual comes to be author, source, or sole representative of his values.

Of the developmental researchers, Hoffman (1977) is perhaps the most concrete in characterizing how a moral is transferred from having an outside origin to the status of being "one's own." As spelled out earlier, under the section on memory, Hoffman relies on a kind of sleeper effect—thus on the staying power of semantic memory and the forgetfulness of episodic memory—to account for the child's becoming author of his morality.

---

[6]Kohlberg's focus is not on the general psychological process of the individual's building in of societal values. Rather, Kohlberg's stages represent a series of value judgments made by the theorist, whereby the "highly developed morality" is recognized by its containing only certain classes of values. This point is made quite effectively by Schweder (1983):

> The dominant theme of Kohlberg's essays is that what is moral is not a matter of taste or opinion. Kohlberg abhors relativism. He shudders at the idea that the moral codes of man might be like the languages and foods of man; different but equal. (p. 105) . . . he holds out secular humanism, egalitarianism, and the Bill of Rights as rational ideals or objective endpoints for the evolution of moral ideas. (p. 104)

The development of a *creative style* may also be regarded as internalization, as spelled out in Gardner's (1973) *The Arts and Human Development*:

> The apprentice artist was required to perform gradually more difficult tasks and . . . through a combination of emulation and experimentation, he hit upon an appropriate technique. In the absence of such a milieu, artists have often created their own substitute. Thus Stravinsky imitated the styles of others, Mann first followed but later abandoned models . . . Some of the greatest composers . . . copied the music of other composers again and again . . . It extended their flexible command of musical resources. (p. 285)

Bandura (1977) also has something to say on the role of copying in the inception of new styles:

> Modeling probably contributes most to creative development in the inception of new styles. Once initiated, experiences with the new forms create further evolutionary changes . . . The progression of creative careers through distinct periods provides notable examples of this process. In his earliest works, Beethoven adopted the classical forms of Haydn and Mozart . . . Wagner fused Beethoven's symphonic mode with Weber's naturalistic enchantment . . . . (p. 48)

Thus to summarize the case for internalization of morals and internalization of creative style or potential, one can observe the following: The prevalent view is that certain kinds of exposure to existing values, or styles, can lead to the adopting of those styles as one's own. The *type* of exposure to those values and styles is, of course, the critical theoretical question. Some authors have stressed the individual's active dealing with those ideas (as Deci and Ryan, and Gardner), while others stress the learning or memory aspects of the exposure to ideas—as Hoffman. Those with stage models, psychologists such as Kohlberg (1980), discuss the possibility of arriving at one's own morality, but the process whereby this morality is drawn from existing social structures is nowhere specified. Further, it is also clear that developmental psychology sees the morally autonomous individual as a more responsible—i.e., a consistent, reliable, implementer of that idea.[7] Reliability in using an idea is associated with the person's possessing

---

[7]It should also be noted that the child's adherence to or claim to ownership of specific, internalizable societal norms is seldom, if ever, the focus of the measuring instruments in studies of moral internalization. Rather, the operational definitions of *internalization* are characteristically self-condemnation, confession, projecting guilt to a target-child, or resistance to the temptation to act contrary to moral norms or to expectations of authorities (Staub, 1979, p. 33). Thus the focus is more on what we may call the ''controllable child,'' rather than on the impact of specific, internalized norms on norm-specific thinking and norm-specific behavior. The child who acquiesces to societal pressures to be truthful, who confesses to wrong-doings, who takes the other's perspective, or who delays gratification when it is expected from an experimenter becomes the ''internalized'' individual. But wherein lies the autonomy? These dependent measures would appear to reflect the child's willingness to be controlled by authorities, rather than the readiness to act on one's norms, independent of the pressures of the immediate social milieu.

that idea, as formulated by Abelson (1986). But now the value judgment: Is the appropriation of an idea that was once represented by another source always esteemed by society?

Plagiarism—The Neglect of Concrete Others' Perspectives

"Lifting" an idea and representing it as one's own is, in common parlance, *plagiarism*. Since at least the time of the Roman laws, the official protection of the original source of an idea has been a cultural institution (Fuchs, 1983). The clearly instrumental, conscious variety of plagiarism, whereby a person simply attaches his name to another's product, is obviously not the same as what has been called internalization (above). The psychologically more interesting variety of plagiarism—"unconscious" or nonstrategic plagiarism (Schwenn, 1959)—is our topic here. When we focus on the individual instance of the person's acting on the idea, and the primacy/causality effects that surface in the research (Ross & Sicoly, 1979; Stephenson & Wicklund, 1983, Wicklund et al., See pp. 403–406), there is a clear sense in which the author, or original source of the idea, is disregarded by the individual. In considering the concrete acts of the person who is actively underway toward developing a creative style, there is an element of what one can call plagiarism involved when melodies, or themes, are simply imitated. Gardner (and many others) find the end result of this imitating and copying to be laudable; no one objects to the picture of the ripe and productive artist. But the issue here is what happens along the road to creative maturity.

At an early stage, the would-be artist no doubt copies with full consciousness of the original source. Then, as training and practice proceed, the person begins to (1) combine the sources together, and (2) insert material that has no clear source. It is, of course, at this point that the budding artist loses track of the specific sources. In fact, the moment that the products of at least two sources are combined, there would be a tendency to lay claim to the product as one's own. This tendency can only become greater as the combinations and innovations increase.

Society's reaction to the person's neglecting these original sources would, at the beginning, of course be negative. If it is clear to all that certain sources have been implemented in a combination product, the thinking behind plagiarism laws would hardly condone the person's springing himself loose from the original sources—in the sense of neglecting or not mentioning them. But once the operationalizations are sufficiently advanced, and the person develops into a reliable representative of the operationalizations, society no longer objects; at least, the psychology of creativity does not protest.

The development of one's own *value systems or moralities* would follow a course similar to that of the development of a creative repertoire, with one important difference: Because the moral principles are available to all, and do not qualify as creative products of individuals, the early stages of operationalizing moral principles and neglecting the source are not likely to be censured. This observation is reflected in the uninhibited laudatory reaction that the "morally autonomous" child receives from developmental psychology.

One can see elements of a contra-societal orientation on the part of the appropriating person. The course of developing one's own creative repertoire, system of morals, or values and attitudes, is accompanied by a neglect of the other's concrete perspective. Such a neglect, which is treated by society as egocentric thinking, immaturity, or even plagiarism, is of course an aspect that society would prefer not to see and which is censured. The end result of the appropriation process—the ripe, morally consistent, or creative person—is, on the other hand, a product that society welcomes whole-heartedly. These dual aspects, the seemingly necessary uncivilized appropriation process and the socially welcomed end result can be looked at in terms of psychological thinking about what makes for a civilized person. This is attempted in the next two sections.

From Uncivilized to Civilized: Self-awareness and the Role of the Group

A fair definition of *civilized* is "the person who is responsive to societal needs or demands." The ripeness or maturity of the civilized person is characteristically predicated on the *breadth* of the societal segment that is served by one's moral, creative, or otherwise capable actions. Following Kohlberg's (1980) model, the lower, immature levels of morality entail the person's prosocial orientation with respect to very concrete others; the person cannot be assumed to have a broader scale, highly cross-situational set of principles. Such individuals are ordered in the lower steps of Kohlberg's system and might generally be called heteronomous. These individuals would of course be regarded as civilized by those to whom they are obedient or congenial, but from the standpoint of psychological thinking, there appears to be a *qualitative* leap, from these heteronomous leanings to a condition of representing an *internalized* set of values or other ideas. Further, and in line with the thinking of Shibutani (1961), the person who has this internalized civilized potential is particularly likely to be controlled by that potential when self-aware (Duval & Wicklund, 1972; Wicklund, 1980). Thus the ideal, from the controlling-society's perspective, is the combination of the "ripe" or "internalized" individual who also happens to be self-aware, and who thereby acts on those internalized principles.

Among the civilized reactions that are especially likely given self-awareness, the literature shows that cheating decreases (Diener & Wallbom, 1976), unprovoked aggression is inhibited (Scheier, Fenigstein, & Buss, 1974), motivation to complete laboratory tasks increases (Liebling & Shaver, 1973; Wicklund & Duval, 1971), and consistency between values and actions increases markedly (Gibbons, 1983; Wucklund, 1982). Interestingly, behaving consistently with internalized ideas is not limited solely to standard moralities or norms. For instance, Hormuth (1982) found that self-focused individuals who describe themselves as creative are increasingly likely to behave in a creative manner. In short, and in accord with the Meadian (Mead 1934) argumentation of Shibutani (1961), self-directed attention brings the person to act on society's perspectives, whereby that perspective is already internalized, or owned. In this context we may note that the relationship between the possession of a value and subsequent behavior is often *zero* before self-awareness is induced (cf. Carver, 1975).

Self-awareness has a controlling function even when the control is not based on a strong, internalized cognitive repertoire. For example, conformity to concrete others is greater as self-awareness increases (Duval, 1976; Wicklund & Duval, 1971), just as the readiness to take a specific other's perspective is also greater (Hass, 1984; Stephenson & Wicklund, 1983). Thus self-focused attention would appear to serve a civilizing function, in the sense of (1) bringing forth greater attention to concrete others' perspectives, and (2) more attention to internalized values, given that they exist. What is, then, the totally *un*civilized state? This would be the complete absence of one's own criteria for action combined with an absence of self-directed attention.

It is clear from the study of creativity and morality that the "higher" sense of social control (i.e., via internalized values) is the target of education. Only then is the person said to be reliable for society as a whole, in the sense of functioning as the author of his own actions. But how does the person arrive at that state, of having appropriated the cognitive bases for civilized action?

The Uncivilized Treatment of Others' Perspectives: A Prerequisite for Appropriation

The literature shows that the self-aware person is responsive to others' perspectives and is also cautious, hesitant, and nonpersistent in acting:

1. In indicating how many of the group's 11 ideas were their own, the subjects of Stephenson and Wicklund (1983) became more modest (thus also more accurate) when they had first been exposed to a play-back of their own voices. Thus self-focus inhibited the appropriation of the group product.

2. A highly related point is the attunement of self-focused persons to the differences between themselves and the surrounding personal setting; this means, for instance, greater perspective-taking capacity (Hass, 1984; Stephenson & Wicklund, 1983); this also means a greater propensity toward altruism (Gibbons & Wicklund, 1982).

3. The cautiousness of the self-aware person is also greater, in that more

information items are weighed prior to a decision (Wicklund & Ickes, 1972); correspondingly, the self-aware person is less likely to persist in the face of a difficult challenge (Carver, Blaney, & Scheier, 1979), and there are also hints that the presumed uncertainty of the self-aware person is reflected in self-esteem ratings (Ickes, et al., 1973).

If we piece the above observations together, we arrive at the portrait of a person who would be hesitant in trying out or acting on a new idea, and who would not disregard the perspectives of others, who might be the sources of those ideas. At a minimum, then, it would appear as though appropriation necessitates a nonself-conscious individual, who acts freely on others' ideas, who does not reflect on the differences between perspectives. All of this can be labeled uncivilized behavior with respect to one's immediate group or social milieu. Moreover, if the absence of self-awareness behooves appropriation, this line of thought can be carried still a step further, in the direction of maximizing the kind of uncivilized behavior that should lead to appropriation:

The Deindividuated Group Setting.   In a pioneering study of the concept, Festinger, Pepitone, and Newcomb (1952) operationalized the existence of deindividuation through group members' inability to associate members' names with what was said during a group discussion. Picking up on this theme, Diener (1979) set up a group creativity-generating situation in which the members were to engage in activities that might "enhance their creativity for a later creativity test." In one group self-awareness was induced through various procedures that brought subjects' attention to themselves as individuals. In the other setting, designed to maximize deindividuation, a variety of devices was introduced to maximize the common group feeling, such as singing together and group physical activities.

In the subsequent reports of subjects in the deindividuated setting (and in contrast to the self-awareness-inducing setting), Diener found clear evidence of subjects' loss of personal identity feelings, sense of greater group unity, more liking for the group, and feeling oneself to be more similar to other group members. In addition, there was a lowered concern for what others might think and a general sense of disinhibition, not to mention a decided tendency to forget what others had said. Not only the group atmosphere characterized by Diener (1980), but also the atmosphere labeled "group think" (Janis, 1972; Janis & Mann, 1977) should be ideal for furthering the active orientation toward ideas and neglect of concrete others' perspectives.

At the same time, a contrast can be drawn with the "social loafing" model (Latané & Nida, 1980; see Paulus, 1983). The greater the size of the group, the more that the individual members' motivation is said to decline; thus such behaviors as clapping, cheering, or cognitive performance manifest an increasingly lackluster quality as the group size increases. One implication is that the intensity of internalization of group values, or ideas, would also decline as group size increases. That is, if group *size* (to be differentiated from extent of deindividuation) lowers members' activity levels, then operationalization-activity should likewise decrease (as suggested in a study by Harkins & Petty, 1982). Thus the degree of deindividuation, or other self-awareness-reducing properties of the group, would have to be balanced against the effects of number of members.

Concrete Perspective-Taking as an Inhibitor.   If society insists on civilized behavior from the beginning, thus lays great emphasis on the consideration of concrete others' perspectives (e.g., concrete others who represent the significant morals, values, or creative ideas), then the appropriation of such ideas to one's *own* repertoire will be retarded. It is interesting that the primary figure in developmental psychology whose theory is pertinent to this point, Hoffman (1977), regards concrete-perspective-taking as the *sine qua non* of civilized behavior, thus as an ideal index of the morally mature individual. In line with Hoffman's research directions, one would build an atmosphere around children that would make them, early on, highly responsive to the concrete perspectives of their parents, teachers, or other influence agents. Such a responsitivity would correspond to the effects of self-focused attention, as detailed earlier. However, if values or creative notions are to be appropriated, children would have to become active—to develop their own operationalizations of those ideas, and thereby neglect the perspective of the source. It is doubtful that appropriation can proceed via the passive memory process that Hoffman (1977) describes; rather, the active operationalizing of the ideas should be fundamental.

The Final Product of Appropriation: The Result of Group Influence?

By this point it should be clear that the appropriation hypothesis, as advanced here, does not partake of the characteristic persuasion or memory models, whereby exposure to an idea results in "learning" the idea (cf. Bandura, 1971). Appropriation, and thus being in the position to implement an idea independent of concrete group influence, is regarded as a process that (1) can be furthered by certain group *contexts* (see p. 417), but at the same time, (2) that will be inhibited to the extent that the person takes heed of individual member perspectives. The atmosphere that should be conducive is that of Diener, Janis, Ross and Sicoly, and Stephenson and Wicklund, whereby new ideas are available, where the absence of self-awareness allows others' perspectives to shrink into the background, and where the person can "try out" the various perspectives, perhaps in the brainstorming style of the Method 635 (Mehlhorn & Mehlhorn, 1979).

Accordingly, appropriation, thus the resulting civilized representation of ideas, can hardly be a direct product of group instruction (as in Bandura & Kupers' analysis, 1964), but rather, a product of the person's actively borrowing and finally "plagiarizing" the group's ideas as a basis for the personal operationalization. By exerting too much control at the early stages of this process, the group would perform a self-defeating function: The person would be responsive to concrete perspectives, thus obedient or congenial within the concrete context (as reflected in the usual dependent measures of "internalization"—see Footnote [7]), but of less use to the group and broader society in the long run.

ACKNOWLEDGMENTS

The author is grateful to Peter M. Gollwitzer, Thomas Reuter, Rudolf Schiffmann, Helmut Skowronek, and Daniel M. Wegner for their critical and encouraging comments on an earlier version of the manuscript. A special note of thanks is due to Paul B. Paulus, whose careful editing brought about numerous changes in the formulations.

REFERENCES

Abelson, R. P. (1986). Beliefs are like possessions. *Journal for the Theory of Social Behaviour, 16*, 223–250.

Allport, G. W., & Postman, L. J. (1947). *The psychology of rumor*. New York: Holt.

Aronson, E., & Carlsmith, J. M. (1963). Effect of severity of threat on the valuation of forbidden behavior. *Journal of Abnormal and Social Psychology, 66*, 584–588.

Bandura, A. (1971). *Social learning theory*. Morristown, NJ: General Learning Press.

Bandura, A. (1977). *Social learning theory*. Englewood Cliffs, NJ: Prentice-Hall.

Bandura, A., & Kupers, C. J. (1964). The transmission of patterns of self-reinforcement through modeling. *Journal of Abnormal and Social Psychology, 69*, 1–9.

Bem, D. J., & McConnell, H. K. (1970). Testing the self-perception explanation of dissonance phenomena: On the salience of premanipulation attitudes. *Journal of Personality and Social Psychology, 14*, 23–31.

Berscheid, E., Graziano, W., Monson, T., & Dermer, M. (1976). Outcome dependency: Attention, attribution, and attraction. *Journal of Personality and Social Psychology, 34*, 978–989.

Boyce, W. D., & Jensen, L. C. (1978). *Moral reasoning: A psychological-philosophical integration*. Lincoln: University of Nebraska Press.

Brehm, J. W., & Cohen, A. R. (1962). *Explorations in cognitive dissonance*. New York: Wiley.

Carver, C. S. (1975). Physical aggression as a function of objective self-awareness and attitudes toward punishment. *Journal of Experimental Social Psychology, 11*, 510–519.

Carver, C. S., Blaney, P. H., & Scheier, M. F. (1979). Reassertion and giving up: The interactive role of self-directed attention and outcome expectancy. *Journal of Personality and Social Psychology, 37*, 1859–1870.

Cohen, A. R. (1961). Cognitive tuning as a factor affecting impression formation. *Journal of Personality, 29*, 235–245.

deCharms, R. (1968). *Personal causation: The internal affective determinants of behavior*. New York: Academic Press.

Deci, E. L., & Ryan, R. M. (1985). *Intrinsic motivation and self-determination in human behavior*. New York: Plenum.

Diener, E. (1979). Deindividuation, self-awareness, and disinhibition. *Journal of Personality and Social Psychology, 37,* 1160–1171.

Diener, E. (1980). Deindividuation: The absence of self-awareness and self-regulation in group members. In P. B. Paulus (Ed.), *Psychology of group influence* (pp. 209–242). Hillsdale, NJ: Lawrence Erlbaum Associates.

Diener, E., & Wallbom, M. (1976). Effects of self-awareness on antinormative behavior. *Journal of Research in Personality, 10,* 107–111.

Duval, S. (1976). Conformity on a visual task as a function of personal novelty on attitudinal dimensions and being reminded of the object status of self. *Journal of Experimental Social Psychology, 12,* 87–98.

Duval, S., & Wicklund, R. A. (1972). *A theory of objective self-awareness.* New York: Academic Press.

Fazio, R. H. (1986). How do attitudes guide behavior? In R. M. Sorrentino & E. T. Higgins (Eds.), *Handbook of motivation & cognition: Foundations of social behavior* (pp. 204–243). New York: Guilford.

Fazio, R. H., & Zanna, M. P. (1978). On the predictive validity of attitudes: The roles of direct experience and confidence. *Journal of Personality, 46,* 228–243.

Festinger, L., & Carlsmith, J. M. (1959). Cognitive consequences of forced compliance. *Journal of Abnormal and Social Psychology, 58,* 203–210.

Festinger, L., Pepitone, A., & Newcomb, T. (1952). Some consequences of de-individuation in a group. *Journal of Abnormal and Social Psychology, 47,* 382–389.

Fischhoff, B. (1982). For those condemned to study the past: Heuristics and biases in hindsight. In D. Kahneman, P. Slovic, & A. Tversky (Eds.), *Judgment under uncertainty: Heuristics and biases* (pp. 335–351). New York: Cambridge University Press.

Freedman, J. L. (1965). Long-term behavioral effects of cognitive dissonance. *Journal of Experimental Social Psychology, 1,* 145–155.

Fromkin, H. L. (1970). Effects of experimentally aroused feelings of indistinctiveness upon valuation of scarce and novel experiences. *Journal of Personality and Social Psychology, 16,* 521–529.

Fuchs, E. (1983). *Urheberrechtsgedanke und -verletzung in der Geschichte des Plagiats unter besonderer Berücksichtigung der Musik.* Unpublished doctoral dissertation, Universität Tübingen.

Gardner, H. (1973). *The arts and human development: A psychological study of the artistic process.* New York: Wiley.

Gibbons, F. X. (1983). Self-attention and self-report: The "veridicality" hypothesis. *Journal of Personality, 51,* 517–542.

Gibbons, F. X., & Wicklund, R. A. (1982). Self-focused attention and helping behavior. *Journal of Personality and Social Psychology, 43,* 462–474.

Goethals, G. R., & Reckman, R. F. (1973). The perception of consistency in attitudes. *Journal of Experimental Social Psychology, 9,* 491–501.

Greenwald, A. G., Pratkanis, A. R., Leippe, M. R., & Baumgardner, M. H. (1986). Under what conditions does theory obstruct research progress? *Psychological Review, 93,* 216–229.

Gruder, C. L., Cook, T. D., Hennigan, K. M., Flay, B. R., Alessis, C., & Halamaj, J. (1978). Empirical tests of the absolute sleeper effect predicted from the discounting cue hypothesis. *Journal of Personality and Social Psychology, 36,* 1061–1074.

Harkins, S. G., & Petty, R. E. (1982). The effects of task difficulty and task uniqueness on social loafing. *Journal of Personality and Social Psychology, 43,* 1214–1229.

Hass, R. G. (1984). Perspective taking and self-awareness: Drawing an *E* on your forehead. *Journal of Personality and Social Psychology, 46,* 788–798.

Hoffman, M. L. (1977). Moral internalization: Current theory and research. In L. Berkowitz (Ed.), *Advances in experimental social psychology* (Vol. 10, pp. 85–133). New York: Academic Press.

Hormuth, S. E. (1982). Self-awareness and drive theory: Comparing internal responses and dominant responses. *European Journal of Social Psychology, 12,* 31–45.

Hovland, C. I., Lumsdaine, A. A., & Sheffield, F. D. (1949). *Experiments on mass communications.* New Jersey: Princeton University Press.

Ickes, W. J., Wicklund, R. A., & Ferris, C. B. (1973). Objective self-awareness and self-esteem. *Journal of Experimental Social Psychology, 9,* 202–219.

James, W. (1910). Psychology: *The briefer course.* New York: Holt.

Janis, I. L. (1972). *Victims of groupthink.* Boston: Houghton-Mifflin.

Janis, I. L., & Mann, L. (1977). *Decision making.* New York: Free Press.

Kahneman, D. (1973). *Attention and effort.* Englewood Cliffs, NJ: Prentice-Hall.

King, B. T., & Janis, I. L. (1956). Comparison of the effectiveness of improvised versus non-improvised role-playing in producing opinion changes. *Human Relations, 9,* 177–186.

Koffka, K. (1935). *Principles of Gestalt psychology.* New York: Harcourt, Brace & World.

Kohlberg, L. (1980). Stages of moral development as a basis for moral education. In B. Munsey (Ed.), *Moral development, moral education, and Kohlberg* (pp. 15–98). Birmingham, Alabama: Religious Education Press.

Krathwohl, D. R., Bloom, B. S., & Masia, B. B. (1975). *Taxonomie von Lernzielen im affektiven Bereich.* Weinheim, Federal Republic of Germany: Beltz-Verlag.

Langer, E. J. (1975). The illusion of control. *Journal of Personality and Social Psychology, 32,* 311–328.

Latané, B., & Nida, S. (1980). Social impact theory and group influence: A social engineering perspective. In P. B. Paulus (Ed.), *Psychology of group influence* (pp. 3–34). Hillsdale, NJ: Lawrence Erlbaum Associates.

Lewin, K. (1926). Untersuchungen zur Handlungs- und Affekt-Psychologie. II.: Vorsatz, Wille und Bedürfnis. *Psychologische Forschung, 7,* 330–385.

Liebling, B. A., & Shaver, P. (1973). Evaluation, self-awareness, and task performance. *Journal of Experimental Social Psychology, 9,* 297–306.

Mahler, W. (1933). Ersatzhandlungen verschiedenen Realitätsgrades. *Psychologische Forschung, 18,* 27–89.

Maier, N. R. F. (1931). Reasoning in humans. II. The solution of a problem and its appearance in consciousness. *The Journal of Comparative Psychology, 12,* 181–194.

Martin, J. E. (1982). Presentationalism: Toward a self-reflexive psychological theory. In W. B. Weimer & D. S. Palermo (Eds.), *Cognition and the symbolic processes* (Vol. 2, pp. 69–129). Hillsdale, NJ: Lawrence Erlbaum Associates.

McArthur, L., & Post, D. (1977). Figural emphasis and person perception. *Journal of Experimental Social Psychology, 13,* 520–535.

Mead, G. H. (1934). *Mind, self, and society.* Illinois: University of Chicago Press.

Mehlhorn, G., & Mehlhorn, H.-G. (1979). *Heureka: Methoden des Erfindens.* Berlin: Verlag Neues Leben.

Miller, D. T., Norman, S. A., & Wright, E. (1978). Distortion in person perception as a consequence of need for effective control. *Journal of Personality and Social Psychology, 36,* 598–607.

Osnabrügge, G., Stahlberg, D., & Frey, D. (1985). Die Theorie der kognizierten Kontrolle. In D. Frey & M. Irle (Eds.), *Theorien der Sozialpsychologie* (Vol. 3, pp. 127–172). Bern: Huber.

Paulus, P. B. (1983). Group influence on individual task performance. In P. B. Paulus (Ed.), *Basic group processes* (pp. 97–120). New York: Springer-Verlag.

Pepitone, A., McCauley, C., & Hammond, P. (1967). Change in attractiveness of forbidden toys as a function of severity of threat. *Journal of Experimental Social Psychology, 3,* 221–229.

Piaget, J. (1965). *The moral judgment of the child.* New York: Free Press.

Pittman, T. S., & Pittman, N. L. (1980). Deprivation of control and the attribution process. *Journal of Personality and Social Psychology, 39,* 377–389.

Pratkanis, A. R., Greenwald, A. G., Leippe, M. R., & Baumgardner, M. H. (1985). *In search of reliable persuasion effects: III. The sleeper effect is dead. Long live the sleeper effect.* Unpublished manuscript, Ohio State University, Columbus, Ohio.

Reiser, B. J., Black, J. B., & Abelson, R. P. (1985). Knowledge structures in the organization and retrieval of autobiographical memories. *Cognitive Psychology, 17,* 89–137.

Ross, M., & Sicoly, F. (1979). Egocentric biases in availability and attribution. *Journal of Personality and Social Psychology, 37,* 322–336.

Rotter, J. B. (1966). Generalized expectancies for internal versus external control of reinforcement. *Psychological Monographs, 80,* (1, Whole No. 609).

Scheier, M. F. (1976). Self-awareness, self-consciousness, and angry aggression. *Journal of Personality, 44,* 627–644.

Scheier, M. F., & Carver, C. S. (1977). Self-focused attention and the experience of emotion: Attraction, repulsion, elation, and depression. *Journal of Personality and Social Psychology, 35,* 625–636.

Scheier, M. F., Fenigstein, A., & Buss, A. H. (1974). Self-awareness and physical aggression. *Journal of Experimental Social Psychology, 10,* 264–273.

Schwenn, G. (1959). Das Plagiat in Titel und Text. Berlin: Verlag Franz Vahlen, *Internationale Gesellschaft für Urheberrecht,* e.V., *14,* 20–34.

Shibutani, T. (1961). *Society and personality: An interactionist approach to social psychology.* Englewood Cliffs, NJ: Prentice Hall.

Schweder, R. (1983). Review of Lawrence Kohlberg's essays in moral development, Vol. I. The philosophy of moral development. In J. A. Meacham (Ed.), *Contributions to human development* (pp. 104–109). Basel: S. Karger.

Snyder, C. R., & Fromkin, H. L. (1980). *Uniqueness: The human pursuit of difference.* New York: Plenum.

Snyder, M. L., Stephan, W. G., & Rosenfield, D. (1978). Attributional egotism. In J. H. Harvey, W. Ickes, & R. F. Kidd (Eds.), *New directions in attribution research* (Vol. 2). Hillsdale, NJ: Lawrence Erlbaum Associates.

Staub, E. (1979). *Positive social behavior and morality* (Vol. 2). New York: Academic Press.

Stephenson, B., & Wicklund, R. A. (1983). Self-directed attention and taking the other's perspective. *Journal of Experimental Social Psychology, 19,* 58–77.

Tulving, E. (1972). Episodic and semantic memory. In E. Tulving & W. Donaldson (Eds.), *Organization of memory* (pp. 381–403). New York: Academic Press.

Turner, E. A., & Wright, J. (1965). Effects of severity of threat and perceived availability on the attractiveness of objects. *Journal of Personality and Social Psychology, 2,* 128–132.

White, R. W. (1959). Motivation reconsidered: The concept of competence. *Psychological Review, 66,* 297–333.

Wicklund, R. A. (1980). Group contact and self-focused attention. In P. B. Paulus (Ed.), *Psychology of group influence* (pp. 189–208). Hillsdale, NJ: Lawrence Erlbaum Associates.

Wicklund, R. A. (1982). Self-focused attention and the validity of self-reports. In M. P. Zanna, E. T. Higgins, & C. P. Herman (Eds.), *Consistency in social behavior: The Ontario Symposium* (Vol. 2, pp. 149–172). Hillsdale, NJ: Lawrence Erlbaum Associates.

Wicklund, R. A., & Brehm, J. W. (1976). *Perspectives on cognitive dissonance.* Hillsdale, NJ: Lawrence Erlbaum Associates.

Wicklund, R. A., & Duval, S. (1971). Opinion change and performance facilitation as a result of objective self-awareness. *Journal of Experimental Social Psychology, 7,* 319–342.

Wicklund, R. A., & Ickes, W. J. (1972). The effect of objective self-awareness of predecisional exposure to information. *Journal of Experimental Social Psychology, 8,* 378–387.

Wicklund, R. A., Reuter, T., & Schiffmann, R. (1988). Acting on ideas: Appropriation to one's self. *Basic and Applied Social Psychology, 9,* 13–31.

Wortman, C. B. (1976). Causal attributions and personal control. In J. H. Harvey, W. J. Ickes, & R. F. Kidd (Eds.), *New directions in attribution research* (Vol. 1, pp. 23–52). Hillsdale, NJ: Lawrence Erlbaum Associates.

Zajonc, R. B. (1960). The process of cognitive tuning in communication. *Journal of Abnormal and Social Psychology, 61,* 159–167.

Zanna, M. P., & Fazio, R. H. (1982). The attitude-behavior relation: Moving toward a third generation of research. In M. P. Zanna, E. T. Higgins, & C. P. Herman (Eds.), *Consistency in social behavior: The Ontario Symposium* (Vol. 2, pp. 283–301). Hillsdale, NJ: Lawrence Erlbaum Associates.

Author Index

Subject Index